# Introduction to Languages and The Theory of Computation

### Third Edition

**John C. Martin**
*North Dakota State University*

Boston   Burr Ridge, IL   Dubuque, IA   Madison, WI   New York   San Francisco   St. Louis
Bangkok   Bogotá   Caracas   Kuala Lumpur   Lisbon   London   Madrid   Mexico City
Milan   Montreal   New Delhi   Santiago   Seoul   Singapore   Sydney   Taipei   Toronto

# McGraw-Hill Higher Education

A Division of The **McGraw-Hill** Companies

INTRODUCTION TO LANGUAGES AND THE THEORY OF COMPUTATION
THIRD EDITION

Published by McGraw-Hill, a business unit of The McGraw-Hill Companies, Inc., 1221 Avenue of the Americas, New York, NY 10020. Copyright © 2003, 1997, 1991 by The McGraw-Hill Companies, Inc. All rights reserved. No part of this publication may be reproduced or distributed in any form or by any means, or stored in a database or retrieval system, without the prior written consent of The McGraw-Hill Companies, Inc., including, but not limited to, in any network or other electronic storage or transmission, or broadcast for distance learning.

Some ancillaries, including electronic and print components, may not be available to customers outside the United States.

This book is printed on acid-free paper.

International 1 2 3 4 5 6 7 8 9 0 QPF/QPF 0 9 8 7 6 5 4 3 2
Domestic      2 3 4 5 6 7 8 9 0 QPF/QPF 0 9 8 7 6 5 4 3

ISBN 0-07-232200-4
ISBN 0-07-119854-7 (ISE)

Publisher: *Elizabeth A. Jones*
Developmental editor: *Melinda Dougharty*
Executive marketing manager: *John Wannemacher*
Lead project manager: *Peggy J. Selle*
Lead production supervisor: *Sandy Ludovissy*
Lead media project manager: *Audrey A. Reiter*
Designer: *K. Wayne Harms*
Cover/interior designer: *Rokusek Design*
Cover image: *Ryoichi Utsumi (IMA) Photonica*
Compositor: *Techsetters*
Typeface: *10/12 Times Roman*
Printer: *Quebecor World Fairfield, PA*

**Library of Congress Cataloging-in-Publication Data**

Martin, John C.
   Introduction to languages and the theory of computation / John Martin.—3rd ed.
      p. cm.
   Includes index.
   ISBN 0-07-232200-4—ISBN 0-07-119854-7
   1. Sequential machine theory. 2. Computable functions. I. Title.

QA267.5.S4 M29 2003
511.3—dc21

2002070865
CIP

INTERNATIONAL EDITION ISBN 0-07-119854-7
Copyright © 2003. Exclusive rights by The McGraw-Hill Companies, Inc., for manufacture and export. This book cannot be re-exported from the country to which it is sold by McGraw-Hill. The International Edition is not available in North America.

www.mhhe.com

TO PIPPA

# ABOUT THE AUTHOR

**John C. Martin** attended Rice University both as an undergraduate and as a graduate student, receiving a B.A. in mathematics in 1966 and a Ph.D. in 1971. He taught for two years at the University of Hawaii in Honolulu before joining the faculty of North Dakota State University, where he is an associate professor of computer science.

# CONTENTS

# PREFACE

This book is an introduction to the theory of computation. It emphasizes formal languages, models of computation, and computability, and it includes an introduction to computational complexity and *NP*-completeness.

Most students studying these topics have already had experience in the *practice* of computation. They have used a number of technologies related to computers; now they can begin to acquire an appreciation of computer science as a coherent discipline. The ideas are profound—and fun to think about—and the principles will not quickly become obsolete. Finally, students can gain proficiency with mathematical tools and formal methods, at the same time that they see how these techniques are applied to computing.

I believe that the best way to present theoretical topics such as the ones in this book is to take advantage of the clarity and precision of mathematical language—provided the presentation is accessible to readers who are still learning to use this language. The book attempts to introduce the necessary mathematical tools gently and gradually, in the context in which they are used, and to provide discussion and examples that make the language intelligible. The first two chapters present the topics from discrete mathematics that come up later, including a detailed discussion of mathematical induction. As a result, the text can be read by students without a strong background in discrete math, and it should also be appropriate for students whose skills in that area need to be consolidated and sharpened.

The organizational changes in the third edition are not as dramatic as those in the second. One chapter was broken up and distributed among the remaining fourteen, and sections of several chapters were reworked and rearranged. In addition to changes in organization, there were plenty of opportunities throughout to rewrite, to correct proofs and examples and make them easier to understand, to add examples, and to replace examples by others that illustrate principles better. Some exercises have been added, some others have been modified, and the exercises in each chapter have been grouped into ordinary ones and more challenging ones. In the Turing machine chapter, I have followed the advice of two reviewers in adopting a more standard and more intuitive definition of *halting*.

Whether or not Part I is covered in detail, I recommend covering Section 1.5, which introduces notation and terminology involving languages. It may also be desirable to review mathematical induction, particularly the sections on recursive definitions and structural induction and the examples having to do with formal languages. At North Dakota State, the text is used in a two-semester sequence required of undergraduate computer science majors, and there is more than enough material for both semesters. A one-semester course omitting most of Part I could cover regular and context-free languages, and the corresponding automata, and at least some of the theory of Turing machines and solvability. In addition, since most of Parts IV, V, and

VI are substantially independent of the first three parts, the text can also be used in a course on Turing machines, computability, and complexity.

I am grateful to the many people who have helped me with all three editions of this text. Particular thanks are due to Ting-Lu Huang, who pointed out an error in the proof of Theorem 4.2 in the second edition, and to Jonathan Goldstine, who provided several corrections to Chapters 7 and 8. I appreciate the thoughtful and detailed comments of Bruce Wieand, North Carolina State University; Edward Ashcroft, Arizona State University; Ding-Zhu Du, University of Minnesota; William D. Shoaff, Florida Institute of Technology; and Sharon Tuttle, Humboldt State University, who reviewed the second edition, and Ding-Zhu Du, University of Minnesota; Leonard M. Faltz, Arizona State University; and Nilfur Onder, Michigan Tech, who reviewed a preliminary version of this edition. Their help has resulted in a number of improvements, including the modification in Chapter 9 mentioned earlier. Melinda Dougharty at McGraw-Hill has been delightful to work with, and I also appreciate the support and professionalism of Betsy Jones and Peggy Selle. Finally, thanks once again to my wife Pippa for her help, both tangible and intangible.

John C. Martin

# INTRODUCTION

In order to study the theory of computation, let us try to say what a computation is. We might say that it consists of executing an *algorithm*: starting with some input and following a step-by-step procedure that will produce a result. Exactly what kinds of steps are allowed in an algorithm? One approach is to think about the steps allowed in high-level languages that are used to program computers (C, for example). Instead, however, we will think about the computers themselves. We will say that a step will be permitted in a computation if it is an operation the computer can make. In other words, a computation is simply a sequence of steps that can be performed by a computer! We will be able to talk precisely about algorithms and computations once we know precisely what kinds of computers we will study.

The computers will not be *actual* computers. In the first place, a theory based on the specifications of an actual piece of hardware would not be very useful, because it would have to be changed every time the hardware was changed or enhanced. Even more importantly, actual computers are much too complicated; the idealized computers we will study are simple. We will study several *abstract machines*, or models of computation, which will be defined mathematically. Some of them are as powerful in principle as real computers (or even more so, because they are not subject to physical constraints on memory), while the simpler ones are less powerful. These simpler machines are still worth studying, because they make it easier to introduce some of the mathematical formalisms we will use in our theory and because the computations they can carry out are performed by real-world counterparts in many real-world situations.

We can understand the "languages" part of the subject by considering the idea of a *decision problem*, a computational problem for which every specific instance can be answered "yes" or "no." A familiar numerical example is the problem: Given a positive integer $n$, is it prime? The number $n$ is encoded as a string of digits, and a computation that solves the problem starts with this input string. We can think about this as a *language recognition* problem: to take an arbitrary string of digits and determine whether it is one of the strings in the language of all strings representing primes. In the same way, solving any decision problem can be thought of as recognizing a certain language, the language of all strings representing instances of the problem for which the answer is "yes." Not all computational problems are decision problems, and the more powerful of our models of computation will allow us to handle more general kinds; however, even a more general problem can often be approached by considering a comparable decision problem. For example, if $f$ is a function, being able to answer the question: given $x$ and $y$, is $y = f(x)$? is tantamount to being able to compute $f(x)$ for an arbitrary $x$. The problem of language recognition will be a unifying theme in our discussion of abstract models of computation. Computing machines of different types can recognize languages of different complexity, and the various computation models will result in a corresponding hierarchy of language types.

The simplest type of abstract machine we consider is a *finite automaton*, or finite-state machine. The underlying principle is a very general one. Any system that is at each moment in one of a finite number of discrete states, and moves among these states in a predictable way in response to individual input signals, can be modeled by a finite automaton. The languages these machines can recognize are the *regular* languages, which can also be described as the ones obtained from one-element languages by repeated applications of certain basic operations. Regular languages include some that arise naturally as "pieces" of programming languages. The corresponding machines in software form have been applied to various problems in compiler design and text editing, among others.

The most obvious limitation of a finite automaton is that, except for being able to keep track of its current state, it has no memory. As you might expect, such a machine can recognize only simple languages. *Context-free* languages allow richer syntax than regular languages. They can be generated using context-free *grammars*, and they can be recognized by computing devices called *pushdown automata* (a pushdown automaton is a finite automaton with an auxiliary memory in the form of a stack). Context-free grammars were used originally to model properties of natural languages like English, which they can do only to a limited extent. They are important in computer science because they can describe much of the syntax of high-level programming languages and other related formal languages. The corresponding machines, pushdown automata, provide a natural way to approach the problem of *parsing* a statement in a high-level programming language: determining the syntax of the statement by reconstructing the sequence of rules by which it is derived in the context-free grammar.

Although the auxiliary memory makes a pushdown automaton a more powerful computing device than a finite automaton, the stack organization imposes constraints that keep the machine from being a general model of computation. A *Turing machine*, named for the English mathematician who invented it, is an even more powerful computer, and there is general agreement that such a machine is able to carry out any "step-by-step procedure" whatsoever. The languages that can be recognized by Turing machines are more general than context-free languages, and they can be produced by more general grammars. Moreover, since a Turing machine can print output strings as well as just answering yes or no, there is in principle nothing to stop such a machine from performing any computation that a full-fledged computer can, except that it is likely to do it more clumsily and less efficiently.

Nevertheless, there are limits to what a Turing machine can do; since we can describe this abstract model precisely, we can formulate specific computational problems that it cannot solve. At this point we no longer have the option of just coming up with a more powerful machine—there *are* no more powerful machines! The existence of these *unsolvable* problems means that the theory of computation is inevitably about the limitations of computers as well as their capabilities.

Finally, although a Turing machine is clumsy in the way it carries out computations, it is an effective yardstick for comparing the inherent complexity of one computational problem to that of another. Some problems that are solvable in principle are not really solvable in practice, because their solution would require impossible amounts of time and space. A simple criterion involving Turing machines is generally used to distinguish the tractable problems from the intractable ones. Although the criterion is simple, however, it is not always easy to decide which problems satisfy it. In the last chapter we discuss an interesting class of problems, those for which no one has found either a good algorithm or a convincing proof that none exists.

People have been able to compute for many thousands of years, but only very recently have people made machines that can, and *computation* as a pervasive part of our lives is an even more recent phenomenon. The theory of computation is slightly older than the electronic computer, because some of the pioneers in the field, Turing and others, were perceptive enough to anticipate the potential power of computers; their work provided the conceptual model on which the modern digital computer is based. The theory of computation has also drawn from other areas: mathematics, philosophy, linguistics, biology, and electrical engineering, to name a few. Remarkably, these elements fit together into a coherent, even elegant, theory, which has the additional advantage that it is useful and provides insight into many areas of computer science.

# 1

# Mathematical Notation and Techniques

This textbook starts by reviewing some of the most fundamental mathematical ideas: sets, functions, relations, and basic principles of logic. Later in the book we will study abstract "machines"; the components of an abstract machine are sets, and the way the machine works is described by a function from one set to another. In the last section of Chapter 1, we introduce languages, which are merely sets whose elements are strings of symbols. The notation introduced in this section will be useful later, as we study classes of languages and the corresponding types of abstract machines.

Reasoning about mathematical objects involves the idea of a proof, and this is the subject of Chapter 2. The emphasis is on one particular proof technique—the principle of mathematical induction—which will be particularly useful to us in this book. A closely related idea is that of an inductive, or recursive, definition. Definitions of this type will make it easy to define languages and to establish properties of the languages using mathematical induction. ■

# Basic Mathematical Objects

## 1.1 | SETS

A set is determined by its elements. An easy way to describe or specify a finite set is to list all its elements. For example,

$$A = \{11, 12, 21, 22\}$$

When we enumerate a set this way, the order in which we write the elements is irrelevant. The set $A$ could just as well be written $\{11, 21, 22, 12\}$. Writing an element more than once does not change the set: The sets $\{11, 21, 22, 11, 12, 21\}$ and $\{11, 21, 22, 12\}$ are the same.

Even if a set is infinite, it may be possible to start listing the elements in a way that makes it clear what they are. For example,

$$B = \{3, 5, 7, 9, \ldots\}$$

describes the set of odd integers greater than or equal to 3. However, although this way of describing a set is common, it is not always foolproof. Does $\{3, 5, 7, \ldots\}$ represent the same set, or does it represent the set of odd primes, or perhaps the set of integers bigger than 1 whose names contain the letter "e"?

A precise way of describing a set without listing the elements explicitly is to give a property that characterizes the elements. For example, we might write

$$B = \{x \mid x \text{ is an odd integer greater than 1}\}$$

or

$$A = \{x \mid x \text{ is a two-digit integer, each of whose digits is 1 or 2}\}$$

The notation "$\{x \mid$" at the beginning of both formulas is usually read "the set of all $x$ such that."

To say that $x$ is an element of the set $A$, we write

$$x \in A$$

Using this notation we might describe the set $C = \{3, 5, 7, 9, 11\}$ by writing

$$C = \{x \mid x \in B \text{ and } x \leq 11\}$$

A common way to shorten this slightly is to write

$$C = \{x \in B \mid x \leq 11\}$$

which we read "the set of $x$ in $B$ such that $x \leq 11$."

It is also customary to extend the notation in a different way. It would be reasonable to describe the set

$$D = \{x \mid \text{ there exist integers } i \text{ and } j, \text{ both } \geq 0, \text{ with } x = 3i + 7j\}$$

as "the set of numbers $3i + 7j$, where $i$ and $j$ are both nonnegative integers," and a concise way to write this is

$$D = \{3i + 7j \mid i, j \text{ are nonnegative integers}\}$$

Once we define $\mathcal{N}$ to be the set of nonnegative integers, or *natural numbers*, we can describe $D$ even more concisely by writing

$$D = \{3i + 7j \mid i, j \in \mathcal{N}\}$$

For two sets $A$ and $B$, we say that $A$ is a *subset* of $B$, and write $A \subseteq B$, if every element of $A$ is an element of $B$. Because a set is determined by its elements, two sets are equal if they have exactly the same elements, and this is the same as saying that each is a subset of the other. When we want to prove that $A = B$, we will need to show both statements: that $A \subseteq B$ and that $B \subseteq A$.

The *complement* of a set $A$ is the set $A'$ of everything that is not an element of $A$. This makes sense only in the context of some "universal set" $U$ containing all the elements we are discussing.

$$A' = \{x \in U \mid x \notin A\}$$

Here the symbol $\notin$ means "is not an element of." If $U$ is the set of integers, for example, then $\{1, 2\}'$ is the set of integers other than 1 or 2. The set $\{1, 2\}'$ would be different if $U$ were the set of all real numbers or some other universe.

Two other important operations involving sets are *union* and *intersection*. The union of $A$ and $B$ (sometimes referred to as "$A$ union $B$") is the set

$$A \cup B = \{x \mid x \in A \text{ or } x \in B\}$$

and the intersection of $A$ and $B$ is

$$A \cap B = \{x \mid x \in A \text{ and } x \in B\}$$

For example,

$$\{1, 2, 3, 4\} \cup \{2, 4, 6, 8\} = \{1, 2, 3, 4, 6, 8\}$$
$$\{1, 2, 3, 4\} \cap \{2, 4, 6, 8\} = \{2, 4\}$$

We can define another useful set operation, *set difference*, in terms of intersections and complements. The difference $A - B$ is the set of everything in $A$ but not in $B$. In other words,

$$A - B = \{x \mid x \in A \text{ and } x \notin B\}$$
$$= \{x \mid x \in A\} \cap \{x \mid x \notin B\}$$
$$= A \cap B'$$

For example,

$$\{1, 2, 3, 4\} - \{2, 4, 6, 8\} = \{1, 3\}$$

Note that the complement of any set $A$ is the same as $U - A$, where $U$ is the universe.

Introducing a special set $\emptyset$ called the *empty set*, or the set containing no elements, often makes it easier to write equations involving sets. For example, the formula $A \cap B = \emptyset$ expresses the fact that $A$ and $B$ are *disjoint*, or have no elements in common. If $C$ is a collection of subsets of a set, we say that the elements of $C$ are *pairwise disjoint* if for any two distinct elements $A$ and $B$ of $C$, $A \cap B = \emptyset$. (A note on terminology: "Distinct" just means "different." The phrase "three distinct elements" means three elements, no two of which are equal. We do not say "one distinct element.")

Once we have the union, intersection, difference, and complement operations, we can define sets using arbitrarily complicated formulas. It will be useful to have some basic rules for manipulating and simplifying such formulas. Here is a list of some standard set identities. In all these rules, $A$, $B$, and $C$ represent arbitrary sets. As before, $U$ represents the universe and $\emptyset$ is the empty set.

The *commutative* laws:

$$A \cup B = B \cup A \tag{1.1}$$
$$A \cap B = B \cap A \tag{1.2}$$

The *associative* laws:

$$A \cup (B \cup C) = (A \cup B) \cup C \tag{1.3}$$
$$A \cap (B \cap C) = (A \cap B) \cap C \tag{1.4}$$

The *distributive* laws:

$$A \cup (B \cap C) = (A \cup B) \cap (A \cup C) \tag{1.5}$$
$$A \cap (B \cup C) = (A \cap B) \cup (A \cap C) \tag{1.6}$$

The *idempotent* laws:

$$A \cup A = A \tag{1.7}$$
$$A \cap A = A \tag{1.8}$$

The *absorptive* laws:

$$A \cup (A \cap B) = A \tag{1.9}$$
$$A \cap (A \cup B) = A \tag{1.10}$$

The *De Morgan* laws:

$$(A \cup B)' = A' \cap B' \qquad \text{(1.11)}$$

$$(A \cap B)' = A' \cup B' \qquad \text{(1.12)}$$

Other laws involving complements:

$$(A')' = A \qquad \text{(1.13)}$$

$$A \cap A' = \emptyset \qquad \text{(1.14)}$$

$$A \cup A' = U \qquad \text{(1.15)}$$

Other laws involving the empty set:

$$A \cup \emptyset = A \qquad \text{(1.16)}$$

$$A \cap \emptyset = \emptyset \qquad \text{(1.17)}$$

Other laws involving the universal set:

$$A \cup U = U \qquad \text{(1.18)}$$

$$A \cap U = A \qquad \text{(1.19)}$$

To illustrate how identities of this type might be proved, let us give a proof of (1.12), the second De Morgan law. Since (1.12) asserts that two sets are equal, we will show that each of the two sets is a subset of the other.

> To show $(A \cap B)' \subseteq A' \cup B'$, we must show that every element of $(A \cap B)'$ is an element of $A' \cup B'$. Let $x$ be an arbitrary element of $(A \cap B)'$. Then by definition of complement, $x \notin A \cap B$. By definition of intersection, $x$ is not an element of both $A$ and $B$; therefore, either $x \notin A$ or $x \notin B$. Thus, $x \in A'$ or $x \in B'$, and so $x \in A' \cup B'$.
>
> To show $A' \cup B' \subseteq (A \cap B)'$, let $x$ be any element of $A' \cup B'$. Then $x \in A'$ or $x \in B'$. Therefore, either $x \notin A$ or $x \notin B$. Thus, $x$ is not an element of both $A$ and $B$, and so $x \notin A \cap B$. Therefore, $x \in (A \cap B)'$.

In order to visualize a set that is formed from primitive sets by using the set operations, it is often helpful to draw a *Venn diagram*. The idea is to draw a large region representing the universe and within that to draw schematic diagrams of the primitive sets, overlapping so as to show one region for each membership combination. (This may be difficult to do when there are more than three primitive sets; just as in our list of identities above, however, three is usually enough.) If we shade the primitive regions differently, the set we are interested in can be identified by the appropriate combination of shadings.

In the case of two sets $A$ and $B$, the basic Venn diagram is shown in Figure 1.1*a*. The four disjoint regions of the picture, corresponding to the sets $(A \cup B)'$, $A - B$, $B - A$, and $A \cap B$, are unshaded, shaded one way only, shaded the other way only, and shaded both ways, respectively. Figure 1.2 shows an unshaded Venn diagram for three sets. For practice, you might want to label each of the eight subregions, using a formula involving $A$, $B$, $C$, and appropriate set operations.

Venn diagrams can be used to confirm the truth of set identities. For example, Figure 1.1*b* illustrates the set $(A \cap B)'$, the left side of identity (1.12). It is obtained

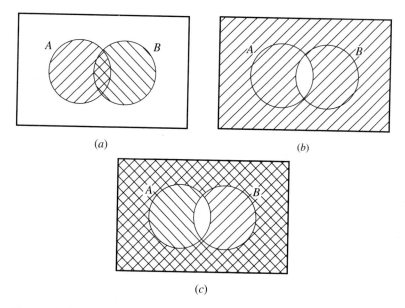

**Figure 1.1 |**
(a) A basic Venn diagram; (b), (c) The second De Morgan identity.

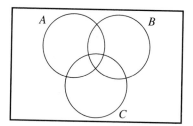

**Figure 1.2 |**
A three-set Venn diagram.

by shading all the regions that are not shaded twice in Figure 1.1a. On the other hand, Figure 1.1c shows the two sets $A'$ and $B'$, shaded in different ways. The union of these two sets (the right side of (1.12)) corresponds to the region in Figure 1.1c that is shaded at least once, and this is indeed the region shown in Figure 1.1b.

The *symmetric difference* $A \oplus B$ of the two sets $A$ and $B$ is defined by the formula

$$A \oplus B = (A - B) \cup (B - A)$$

and corresponds to the region in Figure 1.1a that is shaded exactly once. In Exercise 1.5, you are asked to use Venn diagrams to verify that the symmetric difference operation satisfies the associative law:

$$A \oplus (B \oplus C) = (A \oplus B) \oplus C$$

When Venn diagrams are used properly they can provide the basis for arguments that are both simple and convincing. (In Exercise 1.48 you are asked to show the associative property of symmetric difference without using Venn diagrams, and you will probably decide that the diagrams simplify the argument considerably.) Nevertheless, a proof based on pictures may be misleading, because the pictures may not show all the relevant properties of the sets involved. Because of the limitations of Venn diagrams in reasoning about sets, it is also important to be able to work with the identities directly. As an illustration of how these identities can be applied, let us simplify the expression $A \cup (B - A)$:

$$A \cup (B - A) = A \cup (B \cap A') \quad \text{(by definition of the } - \text{ operation)}$$
$$= (A \cup B) \cap (A \cup A') \quad \text{(by (1.5))}$$
$$= (A \cup B) \cap U \quad \text{(by (1.15))}$$
$$= A \cup B \quad \text{(by (1.19))}.$$

Rules (1.3) and (1.4), the associative laws for union and intersection, allow us in effect to apply these operations to more than two sets at once. According to (1.3), the two sets $A \cup (B \cup C)$ and $(A \cup B) \cup C$ are equal, so that we might as well write $A \cup B \cup C$ for either one. Furthermore, it is easy to see that this set can be described as follows:

$$A \cup B \cup C = \{x \mid x \in A \text{ or } x \in B \text{ or } x \in C\}$$
$$= \{x \mid x \text{ is an element of at least one of the sets } A, B, \text{ and } C\}$$

More generally, if $A_1, A_2, \ldots$ are sets, we can write

$$\bigcup_{i=1}^{n} A_i$$

to mean the set $\{x \mid x \in A_i \text{ for at least one } i \text{ with } 1 \leq i \leq n\}$; and

$$\bigcup_{i=1}^{\infty} A_i = \{x \mid x \in A_i \text{ for at least one } i \geq 1\}$$

Using (1.4), the associative law for intersection, we may write

$$\bigcap_{i=1}^{n} A_i = \{x \mid x \in A_i \text{ for every } i \text{ with } 1 \leq i \leq n\}$$

and so forth. Still more generally, if $P(i)$ is some condition involving $i$,

$$\bigcup_{P(i)} A_i$$

means the set $\{x \mid x \in A_i \text{ for at least one } i \text{ satisfying } P(i)\}$. In Chapter 4 we will encounter a set with the slightly intimidating formula

$$\bigcup_{p \in \delta^*(q,x)} \delta(p, a)$$

We do not need to know what the sets $\delta^*(q, x)$ and $\delta(p, a)$ are in order to understand that

$$\bigcup_{p \in \delta^*(q,x)} \delta(p, a) = \{x \mid x \in \delta(p, a) \text{ for at least one element } p \text{ of } \delta^*(q, x)\}$$

If $\delta^*(q, x)$ were $\{r, s, t\}$, for example, this formula would give us $\delta(r, a) \cup \delta(s, a) \cup \delta(t, a)$.

The elements of a set can be sets themselves. For any set $A$, the set of all subsets of $A$ is referred to as the *power set* of $A$, which we shall write $2^A$. The reason for this terminology and this notation is that if $A$ has $n$ elements, then $2^A$ has $2^n$ elements. To illustrate, suppose $A = \{1, 2, 3\}$. Then

$$2^A = \{\emptyset, \{1\}, \{2\}, \{3\}, \{1, 2\}, \{1, 3\}, \{2, 3\}, \{1, 2, 3\}\}$$

Notice that $\emptyset$ and $A$ are both elements: The empty set is a subset of every set, and every set is a subset of itself.

Here is one more important way to construct a set from given sets. For any two sets $A$ and $B$, we may consider a new set called the *Cartesian product* of $A$ and $B$, written $A \times B$ and read "$A$ cross $B$." It is the set of all *ordered pairs* $(a, b)$, where $a \in A$ and $b \in B$.

$$A \times B = \{(a, b) \mid a \in A \text{ and } b \in B\}$$

The word *ordered* means that the pair $(a, b)$ is different from the pair $(b, a)$, unless $a$ and $b$ happen to be the same. If $A$ has $n$ elements and $B$ has $m$ elements, then the set $A \times B$ has exactly $nm$ elements. For example,

$$\{a, b\} \times \{b, c, d\} = \{(a, b), (a, c), (a, d), (b, b), (b, c), (b, d)\}$$

More generally, the set of all "ordered $n$-tuples" $(a_1, a_2, \ldots, a_n)$, where $a_i \in A_i$ for each $i$, is denoted by $A_1 \times A_2 \times \cdots \times A_n$.

# 1.2 | Logic

## 1.2.1  Propositions and Logical Connectives

Even at this early stage we have already made use of logical statements and logical arguments (see the proof of identity (1.12) in Section 1.1). Before we go any further, we will briefly discuss logical propositions and some notation that will be useful in working with them.

A *proposition* is a declarative statement that is sufficiently objective, meaningful, and precise to have a *truth value* (one of the values *true* and *false*). The following statements satisfy these criteria and have truth values *true*, *false*, and *true*, respectively:

Fourteen is an even integer.

Winnipeg is the largest seaport in Canada.

$0 = 0$.

Consider the statements

$$x^2 < 4.$$
$$a^2 + b^2 = 3.$$

He has never held public office.

These look like precise, objective statements, but as they stand they cannot be said to have truth values. Essential information is missing: What are the values of $x$, $a$, and $b$, and who is "he"? Each of these propositions involves one or more *free variables*; for the proposition to have a truth value, each free variable must be assigned a specific value from an appropriate *domain*, or *universe*. In the first case, an appropriate domain for the free variable $x$ is a set of numbers. If the domain is chosen to be the set of natural numbers, for example, the values of $x$ that make the proposition true are those less than 2, and every other value of $x$ will make it false. If the domain is the set $\mathcal{R}$ of all real numbers, the proposition will be true for all choices of $x$ that are both greater than $-2$ and less than 2. The free variables in the second statement apparently also represent numbers. For the domain of natural numbers there are no values for $a$ and $b$ that would make the proposition true; for the domain of real numbers, $a = 1$ and $b = \sqrt{2}$ is one of many choices that would work. An appropriate domain for the third statement would be a set of people.

Just as we can combine numerical values by using algebraic operations like addition and subtraction, we can combine truth values, using *logical connectives*. A compound proposition is one formed from simpler propositions using a logical connective. When we add two numerical expressions, all we need to know in order to determine the numerical value of the answer is the numerical value of the two expressions. Similarly, when we combine logical expressions using a logical connective, all we need to know (in order to determine the truth value of the result) is the truth values of the original expressions. In other words, we can define a specific logical connective by saying, for each combination of truth values of the expressions being combined, what the truth value of the resulting expression is.

The three most common logical connectives are *conjunction*, *disjunction*, and *negation*, the symbols for which are $\wedge$, $\vee$, and $\neg$, respectively. These correspond to the English words *and*, *or*, and *not*. The conjunction $p \wedge q$ of $p$ and $q$ is read "$p$ and $q$," and the disjunction $p \vee q$ is read "$p$ or $q$." The negation $\neg p$ of $p$ is read "not $p$." These three connectives can be defined by the *truth tables* below.

| $p$ | $q$ | $p \wedge q$ | $p \vee q$ |
|-----|-----|--------------|------------|
| T | T | T | T |
| T | F | F | T |
| F | T | F | T |
| F | F | F | F |

| $p$ | $\neg p$ |
|-----|----------|
| T | F |
| F | T |

The entries in the truth tables are probably the ones you would expect, on the basis of the familiar meanings of the English words *and*, *or*, and *not*. For example, the proposition $p \wedge q$ is true if $p$ and $q$ are both true and false otherwise. The proposition $p \vee q$ is true if $p$ is true, or if $q$ is true, or if both $p$ and $q$ are true. (In everyday conversation "or" sometimes means *exclusive* or. Someone who says "Give me liberty or give me death!" probably expects only one of the two. However, exclusive or is a different logical connective, not the one we have defined.) Finally, the negation of a proposition is true precisely when the proposition is false.

Another important logical connective is the *conditional*. The proposition $p \rightarrow q$ is commonly read "if $p$, then $q$." Although this connective also comes up in everyday speech, it may not be obvious how it should be defined precisely. Consider someone giving directions, who says "If you cross a railroad track, you've gone too far." This statement should be true if you cross a railroad track and you have in fact gone too far. If you cross a railroad track and you have not gone too far, the statement should be false. The less obvious cases are the ones in which you do not cross a railroad track. Normally we do not consider the statement to be false in these cases; we assume that the speaker chooses not to commit himself, and we still give him credit for being a truthful person. Following this example, we define the truth table for the conditional as follows.

| $p$ | $q$ | $p \rightarrow q$ |
|-----|-----|-------------------|
| T | T | T |
| T | F | F |
| F | T | T |
| F | F | T |

If you are not convinced by the example that the last two entries of the truth table are the most reasonable choices, consider the proposition

$$x < 1 \rightarrow x < 2$$

where the domain associated with the free variable $x$ is the set of natural numbers. You would probably agree that this proposition ought to be true, no matter what value is substituted for $x$. However, by choosing $x$ appropriately we can obtain all three of the cases in which the truth-table value is true. If $x$ is chosen to be 0, then both $x < 1$ and $x < 2$ are true; if $x = 1$, the first is false and the second is true; and if $x > 1$, both are false. Therefore, if this compound proposition is to be true for every $x$, the truth table must be the one shown. The conditional proposition is taken to be true except in the single case where it must certainly be false.

One slightly confusing aspect of the conditional proposition is that when it is expressed in words, the word order is sometimes inverted. The statements "if $p$ then $q$" and "$q$ if $p$" mean the same thing: The crucial point is that the "if" comes just before $p$ in both cases. Perhaps even more confusing, however, is another common way of expressing the conditional. The proposition $p \rightarrow q$ is often read "$p$ *only if* $q$." It is important to understand that "if" and "only if" have different meanings. The two statements "$p$ if $q$" ($q \rightarrow p$) and "$p$ only if $q$" ($p \rightarrow q$) are both conditional statements, but with the order of $p$ and $q$ reversed. Each of these two statements is said to be the *converse* of the other.

The proposition $(p \rightarrow q) \wedge (q \rightarrow p)$ is abbreviated $p \leftrightarrow q$, and the connective $\leftrightarrow$ is called the *biconditional*. According to the previous paragraph, $p \leftrightarrow q$ might be read "$p$ only if $q$, and $p$ if $q$." It is usually shortened to "$p$ *if and only if* $q$." (It might seem more accurate to say "only if and if"; however, we will see shortly that it doesn't matter.) Another common way to read $p \leftrightarrow q$ is to say "if $p$ then $q$, and conversely."

With a compound proposition, composed of *propositional variables* (like $p$ and $q$) and logical connectives, we can determine the truth value of the entire proposition from the truth values of the propositional variables. This is a routine calculation based on the truth tables of the connectives. We can take care of all the cases at once by constructing the entire truth table for the compound proposition, considering one at a time the connectives from which it is built. We illustrate the way this might be done for the proposition $(p \vee q) \wedge \neg(p \rightarrow q)$.

| $p$ | $q$ | $p \vee q$ | $p \rightarrow q$ | $\neg(p \rightarrow q)$ | $(p \vee q) \wedge \neg(p \rightarrow q)$ |
|---|---|---|---|---|---|
| T | T | T | T | F | F |
| T | F | T | F | T | T |
| F | T | T | T | F | F |
| F | F | F | T | F | F |

The last column of the table, which is the desired result, is obtained by combining the third and fifth columns using the $\wedge$ operation. Another way of carrying out the same calculation is to include a column of the table for each operation in the expression and to fill in the columns in the order in which the operations might be carried out. The table below illustrates this approach.

| | | 1 | 4 | 3 | 2 |
|---|---|---|---|---|---|
| $p$ | $q$ | $(p \vee q)$ | $\wedge$ | $\neg$ | $(p \rightarrow q)$ |
| T | T | T | F | F | T |
| T | F | T | T | T | F |
| F | T | T | F | F | T |
| F | F | F | F | F | T |

The first two columns to be computed are those corresponding to the subexpressions $p \vee q$ and $p \rightarrow q$. Column 3 is obtained by negating column 2, and the final result in column 4 is obtained by combining columns 1 and 3 using the $\wedge$ operation.

A compound proposition is called a *tautology* if it is true in every case (that is, for every combination of truth values of the simpler propositions from which it is constructed). For example, $p \vee \neg p$ is a tautology, as you can see by constructing its two-row truth table. A *contradiction* is the opposite, a proposition that is false in every case. If $P$ is a tautology, $\neg P$ is a contradiction. Another example is $p \wedge \neg p$, where $p$ is any proposition. Although there are many different-looking formulas that turn out to be tautologies, logically (that is, with regard to their truth values) they are indistinguishable. The proposition *true* stands for any tautology: It is, by definition, always true. Similarly, *false* stands for any contradiction.

## 1.2.2 Logical Implication and Equivalence

Suppose now that $P$ and $Q$ are both compound propositions, built from propositional variables and logical connectives. Then in each case—that is, for each possible choice of the truth values of all these propositional variables—$P$ and $Q$ both have truth values. If $Q$ is true in each case in which $P$ is true, then we say $P$ *logically implies* $Q$, and we write $P \Rightarrow Q$. If $P$ and $Q$ have the same truth value in each case (in other words, if $P$ and $Q$ have exactly the same truth tables), we say $P$ and $Q$ are *logically equivalent*, written $P \Leftrightarrow Q$. Saying that $P \Leftrightarrow Q$ is the same as saying that $P \Rightarrow Q$ and $Q \Rightarrow P$. The significance of logical equivalence is that for any proposition appearing in a formula, we may substitute any other logically equivalent proposition, because the truth value of the overall expression remains unchanged.

The logical connective $\rightarrow$ and the relation $\Rightarrow$ of logical implication are similar ($P \rightarrow Q$ is read "if $P$ then $Q$," and $P \Rightarrow Q$ means that if $P$ is true, $Q$ must be true) but not the same. $P \rightarrow Q$ is a proposition just as $P$ and $Q$ are. It has a truth value, depending on the truth values of $P$ and $Q$. $P \Rightarrow Q$ is not a logical proposition in the same sense. It is a higher-level statement, if you like: a "meta-statement," or an assertion about the relationship between two propositions. If we know that $P \Rightarrow Q$, then there can be no case in which $P$ is true and $Q$ is not. In other words (because of the way we have defined the truth table for $\rightarrow$), the statement $P \rightarrow Q$ must always be true. Thus, the similarity between $\rightarrow$ and $\Rightarrow$ can be accounted for by saying that $P \Rightarrow Q$ means $P \rightarrow Q$ is a tautology. In exactly the same way, $P \Leftrightarrow Q$ means that $P \leftrightarrow Q$ is a tautology.

Logical implication and logical equivalence come up in proofs, which we shall discuss in a little more detail in Chapter 2. For now, let us note a number of fundamental logical equivalences that will be useful to us.

One approach would be simply to list the formulas we are interested in and establish each one by constructing its truth table. However, if we are careful we can obtain a number of them almost immediately from the set identities in Section 1.1. You may already have noticed a superficial resemblance between the logical connectives $\vee$ and $\wedge$ and the set operations $\cup$ and $\cap$, respectively. In fact, the similarity goes deeper than the shapes of the symbols, as we can see by considering a different approach to defining the set operations. We can define $A \cup B$, for example, by considering the four cases determined by an element's possible membership in $A$ and in $B$. In three of the four cases, the element is in $A \cup B$; the only case in which the element is not in $A \cup B$ is that in which the element is in neither $A$ nor $B$. This can be summarized by a "membership table" for the ∪ operation. Let T denote membership and F nonmembership.

| A | B | A ∪ B |
|---|---|-------|
| T | T | T |
| T | F | T |
| F | T | T |
| F | F | F |

Obviously, this duplicates the truth-table definition of ∨. Similarly, the membership table for ∩ corresponds to the truth table for ∧, and the membership table for the complement of a set corresponds to the truth table for negation.

To see how we can apply this observation, consider an example. We can establish the equality of the two sets $(A \cup B)'$ and $A' \cap B'$ by showing that they have the same membership table. The membership tables for these two sets, however, are obtained from those of $A$ and $B$ in exactly the same way that the truth tables for $\neg(a \vee b)$ and $\neg a \wedge \neg b$ are obtained from those of $a$ and $b$. The conclusion is that the truth tables for these two propositions are also identical, and the two propositions are logically equivalent.

What we obtain from this discussion is a list of logical equivalences corresponding to the set identities (1.1)–(1.19). The proposition corresponding to the empty set $\emptyset$ is the proposition *false*, and the one corresponding to the universe $U$ is *true*. (Recall the earlier discussion of the biconditional in which we mentioned that "only if and if" is really the same as "if and only if." We can now see the reason: According to the logical analogue of the commutative law for intersection in Equation (1.2), the two propositions $p \wedge q$ and $q \wedge p$ are logically equivalent.)

There are many other useful logical equivalences. We list just a few that involve the conditional connective:

$$(p \rightarrow q) \Leftrightarrow (\neg p \vee q)$$
$$(p \rightarrow q) \Leftrightarrow (\neg q \rightarrow \neg p)$$
$$\neg(p \rightarrow q) \Leftrightarrow (p \wedge \neg q)$$

The first of these formulas is a way of reducing a conditional proposition to one involving only the three original connectives. The second asserts that the conditional proposition $p \rightarrow q$ is logically equivalent to its *contrapositive*. This equivalence occurs in everyday speech: "If I drive, I don't drink" is equivalent to "If it is not true that I don't drink, then I don't drive," or, more simply, "If I drink, then I don't drive."

## 1.2.3 Logical Quantifiers and Quantified Statements

Let us return to propositions involving variables, which may be replaced by values from some domain or universe. Consider first a proposition with a *free* variable, say the proposition $x^2 < 4$ from Section 1.2.1, where the associated domain is the set of natural numbers. If we now modify this proposition by attaching the phrase "there exists an $x$ such that" at the beginning, then the proposition has been changed from a statement about $x$ to a statement about the domain. The status of the variable $x$ changes as well: It is no longer a free variable. If we tried to substitute a specific value from the universe for all occurrences of $x$ in the proposition, we would obtain a statement such as "there exists a 3 such that $3^2 < 4$," which is nonsense. We say that the statement "there exists an $x$ such that $x^2 < 4$" is a *quantified* statement. The phrase "there exists" is called the *existential quantifier*. The variable $x$ is said to be bound to the quantifier and is referred to as a *bound* variable. We write this statement in the compact form

$$\exists x(x^2 < 4)$$

The other quantifier is the *universal* quantifier, written $\forall$. The formula $\forall x(x^2 < 4)$ stands for the statement "for every $x$, $x^2 < 4$." If you are not familiar with this notation, the way to remember it is that $\forall$ is an upside-down A, for "all," and $\exists$ is a backwards E, for "exists."

If $P(x)$ is any proposition involving the free variable $x$ over some domain $U$, then by definition, the quantified statement $\exists x(P(x))$ is true if there is at least one value of $x$ in $U$ that makes the formula $P(x)$ true, and false otherwise. Similarly, $\forall x(P(x))$ is true precisely when $P(x)$ is true no matter what element of $U$ is substituted for $x$. If $P(x)$ is the formula $x^2 < 4$, then $\exists x(P(x))$ is true if the domain is the set of natural numbers, because $0^2 < 4$. It is false for the domain of positive even integers. The quantified statement $\forall x(P(x))$ is false for both of these domains.

The notation for quantified propositions occasionally varies. For example, the statement $\exists x(x^2 < 4)$ is sometimes written $\exists x : x^2 < 4$. We have chosen to use the parentheses in order to clarify the *scope* of the quantifier. In our example $\exists x(x^2 < 4)$, the scope of the quantifier is the statement $x^2 < 4$. If the quantified statement appears within a larger formula, then any $x$ outside this scope means something different. If you have studied a block-structured programming language such as Pascal or C, you may be reminded of the scope of a variable in a block of the program, and in fact the situations are very similar. If a block in a C program contains a declaration of an identifier $A$, then the scope of that declaration is limited to that block and its subblocks. To refer to $A$ outside the block is either an error or a reference to some other identifier declared outside the block.

Paying attention to the scope of quantifiers is particularly important in propositions with more than one quantifier. Consider, for example, the two propositions

$$\forall x(\exists y((x - y)^2 < 4))$$
$$\exists y(\forall x((x - y)^2 < 4))$$

where the domain is assumed to be the set of real numbers. Superficially these are similar. They both have the same quantifiers, associated with the same variables, and the inequalities are the same. However, the first statement is true and the second is not. They say different things, and we can see the difference by considering the scope of the universal quantifier in each one. In the first case, the entire clause $\exists y((x - y)^2 < 4)$ is within the scope of "$\forall x$," and so this clause is to be interpreted as a statement about the specific value $x$. In other words, we can interpret "$\exists y$" as "there exists a number $y$, which may depend on $x$." In this case the proposition is true, since $y$ could be chosen to be $x$, for example. In the second case, the existential quantifier is outside the scope of "$\forall x$," which means that for the statement to be true there would have to be a single number $y$ that satisfies the inequality no matter what $x$ is. This is not the case, because the inequality fails if $x = y + 2$.

Although we will not be using the $\exists$ and $\forall$ notation very often after this chapter, there are times when it is useful. One advantage of writing a quantified statement using this notation is that it forces you to specify, and therefore to understand, the scope of each quantifier.

## EXAMPLE 1.1    Alternative Notation for Quantified Statements

Consider quantified statements over some domain $U$, and assume that $A$ is a subset of $U$. Just as $\{x \in A \mid P(x)\}$ is sometimes written to mean "the set of elements $x$ in $A$ satisfying the property $P(x)$," people also write $\exists x \in A(P(x))$ to mean "there exists an $x$ in $A$ such that $P(x)$." Similarly, $\forall x \in A(P(x))$ means "for every $x$ in $A$, $P(x)$." It is interesting to rewrite both these statements in the original stricter notation. In the first case we want a statement of the form $\exists x(Q(x))$. Since we want our statement to say not only that there is an $x$ satisfying the property $P(x)$, but that there is such an $x$ that is also an element of $A$, we may take $Q(x)$ to be the statement $x \in A \land P(x)$. Our formula becomes

$$\exists x(x \in A \land P(x))$$

In the second case, the form of the statement is to be $\forall x(Q(x))$. If we tried the same choice for $Q(x)$, we would be saying not only that every $x$ satisfies $P(x)$, but also that every $x$ is an element of $A$. This is not what we want. The condition that $x$ be an element of $A$ is supposed to make the statement *weaker*, not stronger—we do not want to say that every $x$ satisfies $P(x)$, only that every $x$ in $A$ does. To say it another way, every $x$ satisfies $P(x)$ if it is also an element of $A$. A conditional statement is a reasonable choice for $Q(x)$, and our statement becomes

$$\forall x(x \in A \rightarrow P(x))$$

Sometimes the quantifier notation is relaxed even further, in order to write propositions like

$$\forall x > 0(P(x))$$

Just as in the previous formula, this could be rewritten in the form

$$\forall x(x > 0 \rightarrow P(x))$$

## EXAMPLE 1.2    A Quantified Statement Saying $p$ is Prime

Let us consider the statement "$p$ is prime," involving the free variable $p$ over the universe $\mathcal{N}$ of natural numbers. We will try to write this as a symbolic formula, using logical connectives and quantifiers, standard relational operators on integers ($>$, $=$, and so on), and the multiplication operation $*$. We take as our definition of a prime number a number greater than 1 whose only divisors are itself and 1. The first question is how to express the fact that one number is a divisor of another. The statement "$k$ is a divisor of $p$" means that $p$ is a multiple of $k$, or that there is an integer $m$ with $p = m * k$. Next, saying that the only divisors of $p$ are $p$ and 1 is the same as saying that every divisor of $p$ is either $p$ or 1. Adapting the second part of the previous example, we can restate this as "for every $k$, if $k$ is a divisor of $p$, then $k$ is either $p$ or 1." Putting all these pieces together, we obtain for "$p$ is prime" the proposition

$$(p > 1) \wedge \forall k (\exists m (p = m * k) \to (k = 1 \vee k = p))$$

Manipulating quantified statements often requires negating them. Let us consider how to express the negation of a quantified statement as a quantified statement—that is, to rewrite it so that the negation symbol does not appear before the quantifier. Saying "it is not the case that for every $x$, $P(x)$," or "not every $x$ satisfies $P$," is the same as saying that there is at least one $x$ that does not satisfy $P$. The conclusion is that $\neg \forall x (P(x))$ is the same as $\exists x (\neg P(x))$. Similarly, $\neg \exists x (P(x))$ is the same as $\forall x (\neg P(x))$. The rule is that to negate a quantified statement, we reverse the quantifier (change existential to universal, and vice versa) and take the negation sign inside the parentheses.

We can apply this rule one step at a time to statements containing several nested quantifiers. Let $s$ be the statement

$$\forall x (\exists y (\forall z (P(x, y, z))))$$

We negate $s$ as follows.

$$\begin{aligned}\neg s &= \neg(\forall x (\exists y (\forall z (P(x, y, z))))) \\ &= \exists x (\neg(\exists y (\forall z (P(x, y, z))))) \\ &= \exists x (\forall y (\neg(\forall z (P(x, y, z))))) \\ &= \exists x (\forall y (\exists z (\neg P(x, y, z))))\end{aligned}$$

## 1.3 | Functions

Functions, along with sets, are among the most basic objects in mathematics. The ones you are most familiar with are probably those that involve real numbers, with formulas like $x^2$ and $\log x$. The first of these formulas specifies for a real number $x$ another real number $x^2$. The second assigns a real number $\log x$ to a *positive* real number $x$ ($\log x$ makes sense only if $x > 0$). In general, a function assigns to each element of one set a single element of another set. The first set is called the *domain* of the function, the second set is the *codomain*, and if the function is $f$, the element of the codomain that is assigned to an element $x$ of the domain is denoted $f(x)$.

Natural choices for the domains of the functions with formulas $x^2$ and $\log x$ would probably be $\mathcal{R}$ (the set of real numbers) and $\{x \in \mathcal{R} \mid x > 0\}$, respectively; however, when we define a function $f$, we are free to choose the domain to be any set we want, as long as the rule or formula we have in mind gives us a meaningful value $f(x)$ for every $x$ in the set. The codomain of a function $f$ is specified in order to make it clear what kind of object $f(x)$ will be; however, it can also be chosen arbitrarily, provided that $f(x)$ belongs to the codomain for every $x$ in the domain. (This apparent arbitrariness can sometimes be confusing, and we discuss it a little more on page 19.)

We write

$$f : A \to B$$

to indicate that $f$ is a function with domain $A$ and codomain $B$. Although in simple examples we often stick to numerical functions (functions whose domain and codomain are both sets of numbers), the following examples include other kinds, and many of the functions we consider in this book will not deal with numbers directly at all.

Let $H$ be the set of human beings, alive and dead, and let $\mathcal{N} = \{0, 1, 2, \ldots\}$ be the set of *natural numbers*. Since $2^H$ is the set of all subsets of $H$, the set of all nonempty subsets is $2^H - \{\emptyset\}$.

1. $f_1 : \mathcal{N} \to \mathcal{N}$, defined by the formula $f_1(x) = x^2$
2. $f_2 : H \to H$, defined by the rule $f_2(x) = $ the mother of $x$
3. $f_3 : H \to \mathcal{N}$, defined by the rule $f_3(x) = $ the number of siblings of $x$
4. $f_4 : 2^H - \{\emptyset\} \to H$, defined by the rule $f_4(x) = $ the tallest person in the set $x$

In the last example, we are making the assumption that no two humans are exactly the same height, because otherwise there are sets $x$ for which the phrase "the tallest person in $x$" does not actually specify a function value.

### 1.3.1   One-to-one and Onto Functions

Suppose $f : A \to B$ and $S \subseteq A$. We write

$$f(S) = \{f(x) \mid x \in S\} = \{y \in B \mid y = f(x) \text{ for at least one } x \in S\}$$

In other words, $f(S)$ is the set of values that $f$ associates to elements of the subset $S$. This notation is potentially confusing, for now when we write $f(X)$, we might have in mind either a subset of $B$ (the one corresponding to the subset $X$ of $A$), or an element of $B$ (the one associated to the element $X$ of $A$). Generally, the context will make it clear which is intended.

The set $f(A)$, the set of all elements of the codomain that are associated to elements of $A$, is given a special name, the *range* of $f$. If $f : A \to B$, then it is true by the definition of a function from $A$ to $B$ that the range of $f$ is a subset of $B$ (that is, $f(A) \subseteq B$). It may not be the entire set $B$, since there may be elements of $B$ that are not assigned to any elements of $A$. If $f(A) = B$ (the range and codomain of $f$ are equal, or every element of the codomain is actually one of the values of the function), the function $f$ is said to be *onto*, or *surjective*, or a *surjection*.

The range of the function $f_1$ described previously is the set of all natural numbers that are perfect squares. Since not all natural numbers have this property, $f_1$ is not onto. Similarly, neither $f_2$ nor $f_3$ is onto. The range of $f_2$ is the set of all human females with at least one child, and the range of $f_3$, assuming that we do not count half-brothers or half-sisters as siblings, is probably $\{0, 1, \ldots, N\}$ for some $N$ less than 50. (This is not certain; it may be, for example, that one pair of parents had 41 children but no pair of parents ever had 40.) The function $f_4$ is onto. To see this, we must be able to find for each human being $y$ at least one nonempty set $S$ of humans so that $y$ is the tallest member of $S$. This is easy: The set $\{y\}$ is such a set.

Again assuming that $f : A \rightarrow B$, we say $f$ is *one-to-one*, or *injective*, or an *injection*, if no single element $y$ of $B$ can be $f(x)$ for more than one $x$ in $A$. In other words, $f$ is one-to-one if, whenever $f(x_1) = f(x_2)$, then $x_1 = x_2$. To say it yet another way, $f$ is one-to-one if, whenever $x_1$ and $x_2$ are different elements of $A$, then $f(x_1) \neq f(x_2)$. A *bijection* is a function that is both one-to-one and onto. If $f : A \rightarrow B$ is a bijection, we sometimes say that $A$ and $B$ are in one-to-one correspondence, or that there is a one-to-one correspondence between the two sets.

Of our four examples, only $f_1$ is one-to-one. The other three are not, because there are two people having the same mother, there are two people with the same number of siblings, and there are many nonempty sets of people with the same tallest element.

The terminology "one-to-one," although standard, is potentially confusing. It does not mean that to one element of $A$ there is assigned (only) one element of $B$. This property goes without saying; it is part of what $f : A \rightarrow B$ means. Nor does it mean that for one $y \in B$ there is one $x \in A$ with $f(x) = y$. If $f$ is not onto, then there is a $y$ for which there is no such $x$. "One-to-one" means the opposite of "many-to-one." One element of $B$ can be associated with only (at most) one element of $A$.

To a large extent, whether $f$ is one-to-one or onto depends on how we have specified the domain and codomain. Consider these examples. Here $\mathcal{R}$ denotes the set of all real numbers and $\mathcal{R}^+$ the set of all nonnegative real numbers.

1. $f : \mathcal{R} \rightarrow \mathcal{R}$, defined by $f(x) = x^2$, is neither one-to-one nor onto. It is not one-to-one, because $f(-1) = f(1)$. It is not onto, since $-1$ cannot be $f(x)$ for any $x$.
2. $f : \mathcal{R} \rightarrow \mathcal{R}^+$, defined by $f(x) = x^2$, is onto but not one-to-one.
3. $f : \mathcal{R}^+ \rightarrow \mathcal{R}$, defined by $f(x) = x^2$, is one-to-one but not onto.
4. $f : \mathcal{R}^+ \rightarrow \mathcal{R}^+$, defined by $f(x) = x^2$, is both one-to-one and onto.

In less formal discussions, you often come across phrases like "the function $f(x) = x^2$." Although such a phrase may be sufficient, depending on the context, these four examples should make it clear that in order to specify a function $f$ completely and discuss its properties, one must provide not only a rule by which the value $f(x)$ can be obtained from $x$, but also the domain and codomain of $f$.

On the other hand, we have already mentioned that the choice of domain and codomain can be somewhat arbitrary. These examples seem to confirm that, and we might want to consider a little more carefully whether this arbitrariness serves any purpose. When people say "the function $f(x) = x^2$" or "the function $f(x) = \log x$," they might be assumed to be using the convention that the domain is the largest set for which the formula makes sense (for $x^2$ the set $\mathcal{R}$ and for $\log x$ the set $\{x \in \mathcal{R} \mid x > 0\}$, assuming in both cases that only real numbers are involved). In the case of the codomain, it is not clear why we would choose $\mathcal{R}$ instead of $\mathcal{R}^+$ as the codomain of the function with formula $f(x) = x^2$, since it is true that $x^2 \geq 0$ for every real number $x$. In fact, it might seem that a good choice of codomain for any function $f$

with domain $A$ is simply the range $f(A)$, the set of all values obtained by applying the function to elements of the domain. (As we have already noticed, the range must always be a subset of the codomain, and if it is chosen as the codomain then $f$ is automatically onto.)

There are, however, valid reasons for allowing ourselves to specify the domain and codomain of a function as we wish. It might be appropriate because of the circumstances to limit the domain of the function: If $f(x)$ represents the weight of an object $x$ centimeters long, there is no reason to consider $x < 0$, even if the formula for $f(x)$ makes sense for these values. People do not always specify the codomain of a function $f$ with domain $A$ to be the set $f(A)$, because it may be difficult to say exactly what set this is. In examples involving real numbers, for example, it is tempting to write $f : \mathcal{R} \to \mathcal{R}$ at the outset—assuming that $f(x)$ is a real number for every real number $x$—and worry about exactly what subset of $\mathcal{R}$ the range is only if it is necessary. It may also be that the focus of the discussion is the two sets themselves, rather than the function. We might, for example, want to ask whether two specific sets $A$ and $B$ can be placed in one-to-one correspondence (in other words, whether there is a function with domain $A$ and codomain $B$ that is a bijection). In any case, even though it might occasionally seem unnecessary, we will try to specify both the domain and the codomain of any function we discuss.

### 1.3.2   Compositions and Inverses of Functions

Suppose we have functions $f : A \to B$ and $g : B \to C$. Then for any $x \in A$, $f(x)$ is in the domain of $g$, and it is therefore possible to talk about $g(f(x))$. More generally, if $f : A \to B, g : B_1 \to C$, and the range of $f$ is a subset of $B_1$, then $g(f(x))$ makes sense for each $x \in A$. The function $h : A \to C$ defined by $h(x) = g(f(x))$ is called the *composition* of $g$ and $f$ and is written $h = g \circ f$. For example, the function $h$ from $\mathcal{R}$ to $\mathcal{R}$ defined by $h(x) = \sin(x^2)$ is $g \circ f$, where $g(x) = \sin x$ and $f(x) = x^2$. The function $f \circ g$, on the other hand, is given by the formula $(\sin x)^2$. When you compute $g \circ f(x)$, take the formula for $g(x)$ and replace every occurrence of $x$ by the formula for $f(x)$.

You can verify by just tracing the definitions that if $f : A \to B, g : B \to C$, and $h : C \to D$, then the functions $h \circ (g \circ f)$ and $(h \circ g) \circ f$ from $A$ to $D$ are equal, and they are computed as follows. For $x \in A$, first take $f(x)$; then apply $g$ to that element of $B$ to obtain $g(f(x))$; then apply $h$ to that element of $C$ to obtain $h(g(f(x)))$. We summarize this property of composition by saying composition is associative; compare this to the set identities (1.3) and (1.4) in Section 1.1.

Let us show that if $f : A \to B$ and $g : B \to C$ are both one-to-one, then so is the composition $g \circ f$. To say that $g \circ f$ is one-to-one means that whenever $g \circ f(x_1) = g \circ f(x_2)$, then $x_1 = x_2$. But if $g(f(x_1)) = g(f(x_2))$, then since $g$ is one-to-one, $f(x_1) = f(x_2)$. Therefore, since $f$ is also one-to-one, $x_1 = x_2$.

Similarly, if $f : A \to B$ and $g : B \to C$ are both onto, $g \circ f$ is also onto. For any $z \in C$, there is an element $y \in B$ with $g(y) = z$, since $g$ is onto, and there is an element $x \in A$ with $f(x) = y$, since $f$ is onto. Therefore, for any $z \in C$, there is an $x \in A$ with $g(f(x)) = g \circ f(x) = z$.

It follows by combining these two observations that if $f$ and $g$ are both bijections, then the composition $g \circ f$ is also a bijection.

Suppose that $f : A \to B$ is a bijection (one-to-one and onto). Then for any $y \in B$, there is *at least* one $x \in A$ with $f(x) = y$, since $f$ is onto; and for any $y \in B$, there is *at most* one $x \in A$ with $f(x) = y$, since $f$ is one-to-one. Therefore, for any $y \in B$, it makes sense to speak of *the* element $x \in A$ for which $f(x) = y$, and we denote this $x$ by $f^{-1}(y)$. We now have a function $f^{-1}$ from $B$ to $A$: $f^{-1}(y)$ is the element $x \in A$ for which $f(x) = y$.

Note that we obtain the formula $f(f^{-1}(y)) = y$ immediately. For any $x \in A$, $f^{-1}(f(x))$ is defined to be the element $z \in A$ for which $f(z) = f(x)$. Since $x$ is also such an element, and since there can be only one, $z = x$. Thus we also have the formula $f^{-1}(f(x)) = x$. These two formulas summarize, and can be taken as the defining property of, the inverse function $f^{-1} : B \to A$:

$$\text{for every } x \in A, \ f^{-1}(f(x)) = x$$
$$\text{for every } y \in B, \ f(f^{-1}(y)) = y$$

Another slightly different use of the $f^{-1}$ notation makes sense for any function $f$, whether it is one-to-one or onto. If $f : A \to B$ and $S$ is any subset of $B$, we write

$$f^{-1}(S) = \{x \in A \mid f(x) \in S\}$$

so that $f^{-1}$ associates a *subset* of $A$ to each *subset* of $B$. The set $f^{-1}(B)$ is simply the domain $A$. Note also that if $f$ happens to be a bijection, so that $f^{-1}$ is a function from $B$ to $A$, then the set $f^{-1}(S)$ can be obtained as in the beginning of Section 1.3.1:

$$f^{-1}(S) = \{f^{-1}(y) \mid y \in S\}$$

This formula makes sense only if $f$ is a bijection, because only in that case does $f^{-1}$ associate an *element* $f^{-1}(y)$ of $A$ to each *element* $y$ of $B$.

## 1.3.3 Operations on a Set

We may view a function of two or more variables as one whose domain is (some subset of) a Cartesian product of two or more sets. For example, we might consider the function of the two variables $x$ and $y$ given by the formula

$$3x - xy$$

to be a function with domain $\mathcal{R} \times \mathcal{R}$ and codomain $\mathcal{R}$, since the formula makes sense, and yields a real number, for any ordered pair $(x, y)$ of real numbers.

We have seen several examples of this already in Section 1.1. If $U$ is a set, we may form the union of any two subsets $A$ and $B$ of $U$. The function $f$ given by the formula

$$f(A, B) = A \cup B$$

may be viewed as a function with domain $2^U \times 2^U$ (the set of ordered pairs of subsets of $U$) and codomain $2^U$.

For an even more familiar example, consider the operation of addition on the set $\mathcal{Z}$ of integers. For any two integers $x$ and $y$, $x + y$ is an integer. We may therefore view addition as being a function from $\mathcal{Z} \times \mathcal{Z}$ to $\mathcal{Z}$.

Union is a *binary* operation on the set $2^U$ of subsets of $U$. Addition is a binary operation on the set of integers. In general, a binary operation on a set $S$ is a function from $S \times S$ to $S$; in other words, it is a function that takes two elements of $S$ and produces an element of $S$. Other binary operations on $2^U$ are those of intersection and set difference. Other binary arithmetic operations on $\mathcal{Z}$ are multiplication and subtraction. In most of the familiar situations where a binary operation • on a set is involved, it is common to use the "infix" notation $x • y$ rather than the usual functional notation $•(x, y)$. For example, we write $A \cup B$ instead of $\cup(A, B)$, and $x + y$ instead of $+(x, y)$.

A *unary* operation on $S$ is simply a function from $S$ to $S$. For example, the complement operation is a unary operation on $2^U$, and negation is a unary operation on $\mathcal{Z}$.

If • is an arbitrary binary operation on a set $S$, and $T$ is a subset of $S$, we say that $T$ is *closed* under the operation • if $T • T \subseteq T$. In other words, $T$ is closed under • if the result of applying the operation to two elements of $T$ is, in fact, an element of $T$. Similarly, if $u$ is a unary operation on $S$, and $T \subseteq S$, $T$ is closed under $u$ if $u(T) \subseteq T$. For example, the set $\mathcal{N}$ is closed under the operation of addition (the sum of two natural numbers is a natural number), but not under the operation of subtraction (the difference of two natural numbers is not always a natural number). The set of finite subsets of $\mathcal{R}$ is closed under all the operations union, intersection, and set difference, since if $A$ and $B$ are finite sets of real numbers, all three of the sets $A \cup B$, $A \cap B$, and $A - B$ are finite sets of real numbers. The set of finite subsets of $\mathcal{R}$ is not closed under the complement operation, since the complement of a finite set of real numbers is not finite. The significance of a subset $T$ of $S$ being closed under • is that we can then think of • as an operation on $T$ itself; that is, if • is a binary operation, there is a function from $T \times T$ to $T$ whose value at each pair $(x, y) \in T \times T$ is the same as that of •. (It is tempting to say that the function *is* •, except that we identify two functions only if they have the same domains and codomains.)

Note that a few paragraphs back, division was not included among the binary arithmetic operations on $\mathcal{Z}$. There are two reasons for this. First, not every pair $(x, y)$ of integers is included in the domain of the (real) division operation, since division by 0 is not defined. Second, even if $y \neq 0$, the quotient $x/y$ may not be an integer; that is, the set of nonzero integers, thought of as a subset of $\mathcal{R}$, is not closed under the operation of division. One way around the second problem would be to use a different operation, such as integer division (in which the value is the integer quotient and the remainder is ignored). This leaves the problem of division by zero. One approach would be to say that integer division is a binary operation on the set of nonzero integers. Another approach, in which $0/x$ would still make sense whenever $x \neq 0$, would be to say that for any fixed nonzero $x$, the set of integers is closed under the unary operation of integer division by $x$.

Most of the time, we will be interested in unary or binary operations on a set. However, there are times when it will be useful to consider more general types. An *$n$-ary* operation on a set $S$ is a function from the $n$-fold Cartesian product $S \times S \times \cdots \times S$ to $S$. As we saw in the case of union and intersection, when we start with an associative binary operation $\bullet$, one for which $x \bullet (y \bullet z) = (x \bullet y) \bullet z$, there is a natural way to obtain for each $n \geq 2$ an $n$-ary operation. This is what we are doing, for example, when we consider the union of $n$ sets instead of two.

## 1.4 | Relations

A mathematical relation is a way of making more precise the intuitive idea of a relationship between objects. Since a function will turn out to be a special type of relation, we can start by giving a more precise definition of a function than the one in Section 1.3, and then generalize it.

In calculus, when you draw the graph of a function $f : \mathcal{R} \to \mathcal{R}$, you are specifying a set of points, or ordered pairs: all the ordered pairs $(x, y)$ for which $y = f(x)$. We might actualiy identify the function with its graph and say that the function *is* this set of pairs. Saying that a function is a set of ordered pairs makes it unnecessary to say that it is a "rule," or a "way of assigning," or any other such phrase. In general, we may define a function $f : A \to B$ to be a subset $f$ of $A \times B$ so that for each $a \in A$, there is exactly one element $b \in B$ for which $(a, b) \in f$. For each $a \in A$, this element $b$ is what we usually write as $f(a)$.

A function from $A$ to $B$ is a restricted type of correspondence between elements of the set $A$ and elements of the set $B$, restricted in that to every $a \in A$ there must correspond one and only one $b \in B$. A bijection from $A$ to $B$ is even more restricted; in the ordered-pair definition, for any $a \in A$ there must be one and only one $b \in B$ so that the pair $(a, b)$ belongs to the function, and for any $b \in B$ there is one and only one $a \in A$ so that $(a, b)$ belongs to the function. If we relax both these restrictions, then an element of $A$ can correspond to several elements of $B$, or possibly to none, and an element of $B$ can correspond to several elements of $A$, or possibly none. Although such a correspondence is no longer necessarily a function, either from $A$ to $B$ or from $B$ to $A$, it still makes sense to describe the correspondence by specifying a subset of $A \times B$. This is how we can define a relation from $A$ to $B$: It is simply a subset of $A \times B$. For an element $a \in A$, $a$ corresponds to, or is *related* to, an element $b \in B$ if the pair $(a, b)$ is in the subset. We will be interested primarily in the special case where $A$ and $B$ are the same set, and in that case we refer to the relation as a *relation on A*.

---

**Definition 1.1    A Relation on a Set**

A *relation* on a set $A$ is a subset of $A \times A$.

---

You are already familiar with many examples of relations on sets, even if you have not seen this formal definition before. When you write $a = b$, where $a$ and $b$ are elements of some set $A$, you are using the relation of equality. If we think of $=$ as a subset of $A \times A$, then we can write $(a, b) \in =$ instead of $a = b$. Of course, we are more accustomed to the notation $a = b$. For this reason, in the case of an arbitrary relation $R$ on a set $A$, we often write $a\,R\,b$ instead of $(a, b) \in R$. Both these notations mean that $a$ is related to $b$—or, if there is some doubt as to which relation is intended, related to $b$ via $R$.

The subset $=$ of $\mathcal{N} \times \mathcal{N}$, for example, is the set $\{(0, 0), (1, 1), (2, 2), \ldots\}$, containing all pairs $(i, i)$. The relation on $\mathcal{N}$ specified by the subset

$$\{(0, 1),$$
$$(0, 2), (1, 2),$$
$$(0, 3), (1, 3), (2, 3),$$
$$\ldots\}$$

of $\mathcal{N} \times \mathcal{N}$ is the relation $<$. Other familiar relations on $\mathcal{N}$ include $\leq$, $>$, $\geq$, and $\neq$. One that may not be quite as familiar is the "congruence mod $n$" relation. If $n$ is a fixed positive integer, we say $a$ is congruent to $b$ mod $n$, written $a \equiv_n b$, if $a - b$ is an integer multiple of $n$. In the interest of precision we write this symbolically: $a \equiv_n b$ means $\exists k(a - b = k * n)$. Note that the domain of the quantifier is the set of integers: The integer $k$ in this formula can be negative or 0. To illustrate, let $n = 3$. The subset $\equiv_3$ of $\mathcal{N} \times \mathcal{N}$ contains the ordered pairs $(0, 0)$, $(1, 1)$, $(1, 4)$, $(4, 1)$, $(7, 10)$, $(3, 6)$, $(8, 14)$, $(76, 4)$, and every other pair $(a, b)$ for which $a - b$ is divisible by 3.

So far, all our examples of relations are well-known ones that have commonly accepted names, such as $=$ and $\leq$. These are not the only ones, however. We are free to invent a relation on a set, either by specifying a condition that describes what it means for two elements to be related, or simply by listing the ordered pairs we want to be included. Consider the set $A = \{1, 2, 3, 4\}$. We might be interested in the relation $R_1$ on $A$ defined as follows: for any $a$ and $b$ in $A$, $a R_1 b$ if and only if $|a - b|$ is prime. The ordered pairs in $R_1$ are $(1, 3)$, $(3, 1)$, $(2, 4)$, $(4, 2)$, $(1, 4)$, and $(4, 1)$. We might also wish to consider the relation $R_2 = \{(1, 1), (1, 4), (3, 4), (4, 2)\}$. In this relation, 1 is related to both itself and 4, 3 is related to 4, 4 is related to 2, and there are no other relationships. Even if there is no simple way to say what it means for $a$ to be related to $b$, other than to say that $(a, b)$ is one of these four pairs, $R_2$ is a perfectly acceptable relation on $A$.

### 1.4.1  Equivalence Relations and Equivalence Classes

The type of relation we will be particularly interested in is characterized by three properties: *reflexivity*, *symmetry*, and *transitivity*.

---

**Definition 1.2    Properties of an Equivalence Relation**

Assume that $R$ is a relation on a set $A$; in other words, $R \subseteq A \times A$. As noted previously, we write $a R b$ instead of $(a, b) \in R$ to indicate that $a$ is related to $b$ via the relation $R$.

1. $R$ is *reflexive* if for every $a \in A$, $a R a$.
2. $R$ is *symmetric* if for every $a$ and $b$ in $A$, if $a R b$, then $b R a$.
3. $R$ is *transitive* if for every $a$, $b$, and $c$ in $A$, if $a R b$ and $b R c$, then $a R c$.
4. $R$ is an *equivalence relation* on $A$ if $R$ is reflexive, symmetric, and transitive.

It is useful to note one difference between the reflexive property and the other two properties in Definition 1.2. In order for the relation $R$ to be reflexive, every element of $A$ must be related to itself. In particular, there are a number of ordered pairs that *must* be in the relation: those of the form $(a, a)$. Another way to say this is that $A$ must contain as a subset the relation of equality on $A$. In the case of the other two properties, the definition says only that *if* certain elements are related, *then* certain others are related. If $R$ is symmetric, for example, two elements $a$ and $b$ need not be related; however, if one of the two pairs $(a, b)$ and $(b, a)$ is in the relation, then the other is also.

The definitions of reflexive, symmetric, and transitive all start out "For every. . . ." The negation of the quantified statement "For every. . ." is a quantified statement of the form "There exists. . . ." This means that to show a relation $R$ on a set is not reflexive, it is sufficient to show that there is at least one pair $(x, x)$ not in $R$. To show $R$ is not symmetric, all we have to do is find one pair $(a, b)$ so that $aRb$ and not $bRa$. And to show $R$ is not transitive, we just need to find one choice of $a$, $b$, and $c$ in the set so that $aRb$ and $bRc$ but not $aRc$. In the last case, $a$, $b$, and $c$ do not need to be all different. For example, if there are elements $a$ and $b$ of the set $A$ so that $aRb$, $bRa$, and not $aRa$, then $R$ is not transitive.

The relations $\leq$ and $\geq$ on the set $\mathcal{N}$ are reflexive (for every $a \in \mathcal{N}$, $a \leq a$ and $a \geq a$) but not symmetric; for example, the statement $1 \leq 3$ is true but $3 \leq 1$ is not. The $<$ relation and the $>$ relation are neither reflexive nor symmetric. The relation $\neq$ is neither reflexive nor transitive; for example, although $1 \neq 3$ and $3 \neq 1$, the statement $1 \neq 1$, which would be required by transitivity, fails.

The simplest example of an equivalence relation on any set is the equality relation. The three properties in Definition 1.2 are fundamental properties of equality: Any element is equal to itself; if $a$ is equal to $b$, then $b$ is equal to $a$; and if $a = b$ and $b = c$, then $a = c$. It seems reasonable to require that any relation we refer to as "equivalence" should also satisfy these properties, just because of the way we use the word informally. (In Section 1.2 we have also used the word in a more precise way, and in Exercise 1.33 you are asked to show that logical equivalence is in fact an equivalence relation.) An equivalence relation can be thought of as a generalization of the equality relation.

Let us show that for any fixed positive integer $n$, the congruence relation $\equiv_n$ on the set $\mathcal{N}$ is an equivalence relation. First, it is reflexive because for every $a \in \mathcal{N}$, $a - a = 0 * n$ and therefore $a - a$ is a multiple of $n$. Second, it is symmetric because for every $a$ and $b$, if $a \equiv_n b$, then for some $k$, $a - b = k * n$; it follows that $b - a = -k * n = (-k) * n$, and therefore $b \equiv_n a$. Finally, it is transitive. If $a \equiv_n b$ and $b \equiv_n c$, then for some integers $k$ and $m$, $a - b = kn$ and $b - c = mn$; therefore $a - c = (a - b) + (b - c) = (k + m)n$, and $a - c$ is a multiple of $n$.

An important general property of equivalence relations can be illustrated by this example. For the sake of concreteness, we fix a value of $n$, say 4. The set of elements of $\mathcal{N}$ equivalent to 0 is the set of natural numbers $i$ for which $i - 0$ is a multiple of 4: in other words, the set

$$\{0, 4, 8, 12, \ldots\}$$

The set of elements equivalent to 1 is

$$\{1, 5, 9, 13, \ldots\}$$

Similarly, the sets $\{x \mid x \equiv_4 2\}$ and $\{x \mid x \equiv_4 3\}$ are the sets

$$\{2, 6, 10, 14, \ldots\} \text{ and } \{3, 7, 11, 15, \ldots\}$$

respectively. Note that every natural number is in one of these four subsets, and that the four subsets are pairwise disjoint. These two properties are summarized by saying that the four subsets form a *partition* of $\mathcal{N}$: A partition of a set $A$ is a collection of pairwise disjoint subsets of $A$ whose union is $A$. The numbers equivalent to a particular integer, say 9, are the numbers in the same subset as 9: 1, 5, 9, 13, and so forth. The partition of $\mathcal{N}$ is another way of describing the relation. To say that two natural numbers are equivalent is simply to say that they are in the same subset. If we are told what the partition is, then effectively we know what the relation is.

Any partition of a set $A$ determines an equivalence relation on $A$ in exactly this way. If $\mathcal{C}$ is a partition of $A$ (that is, the sets in $\mathcal{C}$ are pairwise disjoint and $\bigcup_{S \in \mathcal{C}} S = A$), then we can define the relation $E$ on $A$ by saying

$aEb$ if and only if $a$ and $b$ belong to the same element of $\mathcal{C}$

We think of the elements of $A$ as being distributed into a number of *bins*, the bins being simply the elements of $\mathcal{C}$, the subsets that form the partition. Every element of $A$ is in exactly one bin. The relation $E$ is an equivalence relation, because the following are true:

**1.** Every element $a$ of $A$ is in the same bin as itself.

**2.** For any $a$ and $b$ of $A$, if $a$ and $b$ are in the same bin, so are $b$ and $a$.

**3.** For any $a$, $b$, and $c$ of $A$, if $a$ and $b$ are in the same bin, and $b$ and $c$ are also, then $a$ and $c$ are also.

The elements in the bin that contains $a$ are precisely the elements of $A$ (including $a$ itself) that are related to $a$ via this relation $E$.

Now we can turn this around and show that any equivalence relation on a set can be described in exactly this way. Suppose $R$ is an equivalence relation on $A$. For any element $a$ of $A$, we denote by $[a]_R$, or simply by $[a]$, the *equivalence class containing $a$*:

$$[a]_R = \{x \in A \mid xRa\}$$

Note that the "equivalence class containing $a$" really does contain $a$. Because $R$ is reflexive, $aRa$, which means that $a$ is one of the elements of $[a]$. Note also that since $R$ is symmetric, saying that $x \in [a]$ is really the same as saying that $a \in [x]$, or $aRx$. The reason is that if $x \in [a]$, then $xRa$, and then by the symmetry of $R$, $aRx$.

We have started with an equivalence relation on $A$, and we have obtained a collection of bins—namely, the equivalence classes. Now we check that they do actually form a partition of $A$. Of the two properties, the second is easier to check. Saying that the union of the equivalence classes is $A$ is the same as saying that every element of $A$ is in some equivalence class; however, as we have already noted, for any

$a \in A$, $a \in [a]$. The other condition is that any two distinct equivalence classes are disjoint; in other words, for any $a$ and $b$, if $[a] \neq [b]$, then $[a] \cap [b] = \emptyset$. Let us show the contrapositive statement, which amounts to the same thing: If $[a]$ and $[b]$ are not disjoint, then $[a] = [b]$. We start by showing that if $[a] \cap [b] \neq \emptyset$, then $[a] \subseteq [b]$. The same argument will show that $[b] \subseteq [a]$, and it will follow that $[a] = [b]$.

If $[a] \cap [b] \neq \emptyset$, then there is an $x$ that is an element of both $[a]$ and $[b]$. As we have noted above, if $x \in [a]$, then $aRx$. Let $y$ be any element of $[a]$. Then we have

$yRa$    (by definition of $[a]$)

$aRx$    (because $x \in [a]$ and therefore $a \in [x]$)

$xRb$    (by definition of $[b]$)

Using the transitivity of $R$ once, along with the first two statements, we may say that $yRx$; using it again with $yRx$ and $xRb$, we obtain $yRb$. What we have now shown is that any element of $[a]$ is an element of $[b]$, so that $[a] \subseteq [b]$.

We now have a partition of $A$ into bins, or equivalence classes. If $a$ and $b$ are elements satisfying $aRb$, then $a \in [b]$ and $b \in [b]$; in other words, if two elements are equivalent, they are in the same bin. On the other hand, if $a$ and $b$ are in the same bin, then since $b \in [b]$, we must have $a \in [b]$, so that $a$ and $b$ are related. The conclusion is that two elements are related if and only if they are in the same bin. Abstractly the equivalence relation $R$ on $A$ is no different from the relation $E$ described previously in terms of the partition.

This discussion can be summarized by the following theorem.

---

**Theorem 1.1**

For any partition $C$ of a set $A$, the relation $R$ on $A$ defined by

$xRy$ if and only if $x$ and $y$ belong to the same element of $C$

is an equivalence relation on $A$. Conversely, if $R$ is any equivalence relation on $A$, the set of equivalence classes is a partition of $A$, and two elements of $A$ are equivalent if and only if they are in the same equivalence class.

---

If $R$ is an equivalence relation on a set $A$, then according to the definition, figuring out what elements of $A$ are related to (equivalent to) $x$ means figuring out what the equivalence class containing $x$ is. Understanding the partition determined by the equivalence classes is another way of understanding the relation.

One other comment about the terminology is in order. We call $[a]$ the equivalence class containing $a$, but we must be careful to remember that it may contain other elements too. If it contains another element $b$, then we could refer to it just as accurately as the equivalence class containing $b$: the statement $b \in [a]$ is the same as the statement $bRa$, and as we have seen, this is also the same as $a \in [b]$.

To be a little more explicit, here are eight ways of saying the same thing:

$aRb$

$a$ and $b$ are in the same equivalence class

$$a \in [b]_R$$
$$b \in [a]_R$$
$$[a]_R = [b]_R$$
$$[a]_R \subseteq [b]_R$$
$$[b]_R \subseteq [a]_R$$
$$[a]_R \cap [b]_R \neq \emptyset$$

If we have a nonempty subset $S$ of $A$, then in order to show it is an equivalence class, we must show two things:

1. For any $x$ and $y$ in $S$, $x$ and $y$ are equivalent.
2. For any $x \in S$ and any $y \notin S$, $x$ and $y$ are not equivalent.

If we can do this, then for any $a \in S$, it follows from statement 1 that any element of $S$ is equivalent to $a$, so that $S \subseteq [a]$; and it follows from statement 2 that no element of $S'$ can be in $[a]$, so that $[a] \subseteq S$.

We have already calculated the equivalence class containing $i$ in the case of the equivalence relation $\equiv_4$ on the set $\mathcal{N}$. It is the set of all natural numbers that differ from $i$ by a multiple of 4. For any positive integer $n$, the equivalence classes for the equivalence relation $\equiv_n$ on $\mathcal{N}$ are

$$[0] = \{0, n, 2n, 3n, \ldots\}$$
$$[1] = \{1, n+1, 2n+1, \ldots\}$$
$$[2] = \{2, n+2, 2n+2, \ldots\}$$
$$\cdots$$
$$[n-1] = \{n-1, 2n-1, 3n-1, \ldots\}$$

These $n$ equivalence classes are distinct, because no two of the integers $0, 1, \ldots, n-1$ differ by a multiple of $n$, and they are the only ones, because among them they clearly account for all the nonnegative integers.

## 1.5 | Languages

By a *language* we mean simply a set of strings involving symbols from some alphabet. This definition will allow familiar languages like natural languages and high-level programming languages, and it will also allow random assortments of unrelated strings. It may be helpful before we go any further to consider how, or even whether, it makes sense to view a language like English as simply a set of strings. An English dictionary contains words: *dumpling, inquisition, notational, put,* etc. However, writing a sequence of English words is not the same as writing English. It makes somewhat more sense to say that English is a collection of legal sentences. We can say that the sentence "The cat is in the hat" is an element of the English language and that the string "dumpling dumpling put notational inquisition" is not. Taking sentences to be the basic units may seem arbitrary (why not paragraphs?), except that rules of English grammar usually deal specifically with constructing sentences. In the case of a high-level programming language, such as C or Pascal, the most reasonable way to think of the language as a set of strings is perhaps to take the strings to be complete programs in the language. (We normally ask a compiler to check the syntax of programs or subprograms, rather than individual statements.) Though we sometimes speak of "words" in a language, we should therefore keep in mind that if by a word we mean a string that is an element of the language, then a single word incorporates the rules of syntax or grammar that characterize the language.

When we discuss a language, we begin by specifying the alphabet, which contains all the legal symbols that can be used to form strings in the language. An alphabet is a finite set of symbols. In the case of common languages like English, we would want the alphabet to include the 26 letters, both uppercase and lowercase, as well as blanks and various punctuation symbols. In the case of programming languages, we would add the 10 numeric digits. Many examples in this book, however, involve a smaller alphabet, sometimes containing only two symbols and occasionally containing only one. Such alphabets make the examples easier to describe and can still accommodate most of the features we will be interested in.

A string over an alphabet $\Sigma$ is obtained by placing some of the elements of $\Sigma$ (possibly none) in order. The length of a string $x$ over $\Sigma$ is the number of symbols in the string, and we will denote this number by $|x|$. Some of the strings over the alphabet $\{a, b\}$ are $a, baa, aba$, and $aabba$, and we have $|a| = 1, |baa| = |aba| = 3$, and $|aabba| = 5$. Note that when we write $a$, we might be referring either to the symbol in the alphabet or to the string of length 1; for our purposes it will usually not be necessary to distinguish these. The *null string* (the string of length 0) is a string over $\Sigma$, no matter what alphabet $\Sigma$ is. We denote it by $\Lambda$. (To avoid confusion, we will never allow the letter $\Lambda$ to represent an element of $\Sigma$.)

For any alphabet $\Sigma$, the set of all strings over $\Sigma$ is denoted by $\Sigma^*$, and a language over $\Sigma$ is therefore a subset of $\Sigma^*$. For $\Sigma = \{a, b\}$, we have

$$\Sigma^* = \{a, b\}^* = \{\Lambda, a, b, aa, ab, ba, bb, aaa, aab, aba, abb, baa, \ldots\}$$

A few examples of languages over $\Sigma$ are

$$\{\Lambda, a, aa, aab\}$$
$$\{x \in \{a, b\}^* \mid |x| \le 8\}$$
$$\{x \in \{a, b\}^* \mid |x| \text{ is odd}\}$$
$$\{x \in \{a, b\}^* \mid n_a(x) \ge n_b(x)\}$$
$$\{x \in \{a, b\}^* \mid |x| \ge 2 \text{ and } x \text{ begins and ends with } b\}$$

In the fourth example, $n_a(x)$ and $n_b(x)$ represent the number of $a$'s and the number of $b$'s, respectively, in the string $x$.

Because languages are sets of strings, new languages can be constructed using set operations. For any two languages over an alphabet $\Sigma$, their union, intersection, and difference are also languages over $\Sigma$. When we speak of the complement of a language over $\Sigma$, we take the universal set to be the language $\Sigma^*$, so that $L' = \Sigma^* - L$. Note that any two languages can be considered to be languages over a common alphabet: if $L_1 \subseteq \Sigma_1^*$ and $L_2 \subseteq \Sigma_2^*$, then $L_1$ and $L_2$ are both subsets of $(\Sigma_1 \cup \Sigma_2)^*$. This creates the possibility of confusion, since now the complement of $L_1$ might be taken to be either $\Sigma_1^* - L_1$ or $(\Sigma_1 \cup \Sigma_2)^* - L_1$. However, it will usually be clear which alphabet is referred to.

The *concatenation* operation on strings will also allow us to construct new languages. If $x$ and $y$ are elements of $\Sigma^*$, the concatenation of $x$ and $y$ is the string $xy$ formed by writing the symbols of $x$ and the symbols of $y$ consecutively. If $x = abb$ and $y = ba$, $xy = abbba$ and $yx = baabb$. For any string $x$, $x\Lambda = \Lambda x = x$. Clearly, concatenation is associative: For any strings $x$, $y$, and $z$, $(xy)z = x(yz)$. This allows us to concatenate several strings without specifying the order in which the various concatenation operations are actually performed.

We say that a string $x$ is a *substring* of another string $y$ if there are strings $w$ and $z$, either or both of which may be null, so that $y = wxz$. The string *car* is a substring of each of the strings *descartes*, *vicar*, *carthage*, and *car*, but not of the string *charity*. A *prefix* of a string is an initial substring. For example, the prefixes of *abaa* are $\Lambda$ (which is a prefix of every string), *a*, *ab*, *aba*, and *abaa*. Similarly, a *suffix* is a final substring.

Now that we have the concatenation operation, we can apply it to languages as well as to strings. If $L_1, L_2 \subseteq \Sigma^*$,

$$L_1 L_2 = \{xy \mid x \in L_1 \text{ and } y \in L_2\}$$

For example,

$$\{hope, fear\}\{less, fully\} = \{hopeless, hopefully, fearless, fearfully\}$$

Just as concatenating a string $x$ with $\Lambda$ produces $x$, concatenating any language $L$ with $\{\Lambda\}$ produces $L$. In other words, $L\{\Lambda\} = \{\Lambda\}L = L$.

We use exponential notation to indicate the number of items being concatenated. These can be individual symbols, strings, or languages. Thus, if $\Sigma$ is an alphabet, $a \in \Sigma$, $x \in \Sigma^*$, and $L \subseteq \Sigma^*$,

$$a^k = aa \cdots a$$
$$x^k = xx \cdots x$$
$$\Sigma^k = \Sigma\Sigma \cdots \Sigma = \{x \in \Sigma^* \mid |x| = k\}$$
$$L^k = LL \cdots L$$

where in each case there are $k$ factors altogether. An important special case is the one in which $k = 0$:

$$a^0 = \Lambda \qquad x^0 = \Lambda$$
$$\Sigma^0 = \{\Lambda\} \qquad L^0 = \{\Lambda\}$$

These last four rules are analogous to formulas from algebra, and you can understand them the same way. For any real number $x$, $x^0$ is defined to be 1. One reason is that we want the formula $x^p x^q = x^{p+q}$ to hold for every $p$ and $q$, and in particular we want $x^0 x^q$ to be $x^q$. This means that $x^0$ should be the *unit of multiplication* (the real number $u$ for which $uy = y$ for every $y$), which is 1. The string that is the *unit of concatenation* is $\Lambda$ (because $\Lambda y = y$ for any string $y$), and the unit of concatenation for languages is $\{\Lambda\}$. Therefore, these are the appropriate choices for $x^0$ and $L^0$, respectively.

$L^k$ means the set of all strings that can be obtained by concatenating $k$ elements of $L$. Next we define the set of all strings that can be obtained by concatenating *any* number of elements of $L$:

$$L^* = \bigcup_{i=0}^{\infty} L^i$$

The operation $*$ in this formula is often called the Kleene star, after the mathematician S. C. Kleene. This use of the $*$ symbol is consistent with using $\Sigma^*$ to represent the set of strings over $\Sigma$, because strings are simply concatenations of zero or more symbols. Note that $\Lambda$ is always an element of $L^*$, no matter what $L$ is, since $L^0 = \{\Lambda\}$. Finally, we denote by $L^+$ the set of all strings obtainable by concatenating one or more elements of $L$:

$$L^+ = \bigcup_{i=1}^{\infty} L^i$$

You can check that $L^+ = L^*L = LL^*$. The two languages $L^*$ and $L^+$ may in fact be equal—see Exercise 1.38.

Strings, by definition, are finite (have only a finite number of symbols). Most interesting languages are infinite (contain an infinite number of strings). However, in order to work with these languages we must be able to specify or describe them in ways that are finite. At this point we may distinguish two possible approaches to this problem, which can be illustrated by examples:

$$L_1 = \{ab, bab\}^* \cup \{b\}\{bb\}^*$$
$$L_2 = \{x \in \{a, b\}^* \mid n_a(x) \geq n_b(x)\}$$

In the case of $L_1$, we describe the language by saying how an arbitrary string in the language can be constructed: either by concatenating an arbitrary number of strings, each of which is either $ab$ or $bab$, or by concatenating the string $b$ with an arbitrary number of copies of the string $bb$. We describe $L_2$, on the other hand, by specifying a property that characterizes the strings in the language. In other words, we say how to *recognize* a string in the language: Count the number of $a$'s and the number of $b$'s and compare the two. There is not always a clear line separating these approaches. The definition

$$L_3 = \{byb \mid y \in \{a, b\}^*\}$$

which is another way of describing the last language in our original group of five examples, could be interpreted as a method of generating strings in $L_3$ (start with an arbitrary string $y$ and add $b$ to each end) or as a method of recognizing elements of $L_3$ (check that the symbol on each end is $b$ and that the total length is at least 2). Even a definition that clearly belongs to the first category, like that of $L_1$, might immediately suggest a way of determining whether an arbitrary string belongs to $L_1$; and there might be obvious ways of generating all the strings in $L_2$, although the definition given is clearly of the second type.

We will be studying, on the one hand, more and more general ways of *generating* languages, beginning with ways similar to the ones used in the definition of $L_1$, and on the other hand, corresponding methods of greater and greater sophistication for *recognizing* strings in these languages. In the second approach, it will be useful to think of the algorithm for recognizing the language as being embodied in an *abstract machine*, and a precise description of the machine will effectively give us a precise way of specifying which strings are in the language. Initially these abstract machines will be fairly primitive, since it turns out that languages like $L_1$ can be recognized easily. A language like $L_2$ will require a more powerful type of abstract machine to recognize it, as well as a more general method of generating it. Before we are through, we will study machines equivalent in power to the most sophisticated computer.

## EXERCISES

**1.1.** Describe each of these infinite sets precisely, using a formula that does not involve "$\ldots$". If you wish, you can use $\mathcal{N}$, $\mathcal{R}$, $\mathcal{Z}$, and other sets discussed in the chapter.

    a.  $\{0, -1, 2, -3, 4, -5, \ldots\}$

    b.  $\{1/2, 1/4, 3/4, 1/8, 3/8, 5/8, 7/8, 1/16, 3/16, 5/16, 7/16, \ldots\}$

    c.  $\{10, 1100, 111000, 11110000, \ldots\}$ (a subset of $\{0, 1\}^*$)

    d.  $\{\{0\}, \{1\}, \{2\}, \ldots\}$

    e.  $\{\{0\}, \{0, 1\}, \{0, 1, 2\}, \{0, 1, 2, 3\}, \ldots\}$

    f.  $\{\{0\}, \{0, 1\}, \{0, 1, 2, 3\}, \{0, 1, 2, 3, 4, 5, 6, 7\}, \{0, 1, \ldots, 15\},$ $\{0, 1, 2, \ldots, 31\}, \ldots\}$

**1.2.** Label each of the eight regions in Figure 1.2, using $A$, $B$, $C$, and appropriate set operations.

**1.3.** Use Venn diagrams to verify each of the set identities (1.1)–(1.19).

**1.4.** Assume that $A$ and $B$ are sets. In each case, find a simpler expression representing the given set. The easiest way is probably to use Venn diagrams, but also practice manipulating the formulas using the set identities (1.1)–(1.19).

    a.  $A - (A - B)$

    b.  $A - (A \cap B)$

    c.  $(A \cup B) - A$

    d.  $(A - B) \cup (B - A) \cup (A \cap B)$

    e.  $(A' \cap B')'$

    f.  $(A' \cup B')'$

    g.  $A \cup (B \cap (A - (B - A)))$

    h.  $A' \cup (B - (A \cup (B' - A)))$

**1.5.** Show using Venn diagrams that the symmetric difference operation $\oplus$ satisfies the associative property $A \oplus (B \oplus C) = (A \oplus B) \oplus C$.

**1.6.** In each case, find a simpler statement (one not involving the symmetric difference operation) equivalent to the given one. Assume in each case that

$A$ and $B$ are subsets of $U$.

    a.  $A \oplus B = A$

    b.  $A \oplus B = A - B$

    c.  $A \oplus B = A \cup B$

    d.  $A \oplus B = A \cap B$

    e.  $A \oplus B = A'$

**1.7.**  In each case, find an expression for the indicated set, involving $A$, $B$, $C$, and the three operations $\cup$, $\cap$, and $'$.

    a.  $\{x \mid x \in A$ or $x \in B$ but not both$\}$

    b.  $\{x \mid x$ is an element of exactly one of the three sets $A$, $B$, and $C\}$

    c.  $\{x \mid x$ is an element of at most one of the three sets $A$, $B$, and $C\}$

    d.  $\{x \mid x$ is an element of exactly two of the three sets $A$, $B$, and $C\}$

    e.  $\{x \mid x$ is an element of at least one and at most two of the three sets $A$, $B$, and $C\}$

**1.8.**  For each integer $n$, denote by $C_n$ the set of all real numbers less than $n$, and for each positive number $n$ let $D_n$ be the set of all real numbers less than $1/n$. Express each of the following sets in a simpler form not involving unions or intersections. (For example, the answer to (a) is $C_{10}$.) Since $\infty$ is not a number, the expressions $C_\infty$ and $D_\infty$ do not make sense and should not appear in your answer.

    a.  $\bigcup_{n=1}^{10} C_n$

    b.  $\bigcup_{n=1}^{10} D_n$

    c.  $\bigcap_{n=1}^{10} C_n$

    d.  $\bigcap_{n=1}^{10} D_n$

    e.  $\bigcup_{n=1}^{\infty} C_n$

    f.  $\bigcup_{n=1}^{\infty} D_n$

    g.  $\bigcap_{n=1}^{\infty} C_n$

    h.  $\bigcap_{n=1}^{\infty} D_n$

    i.  $\bigcup_{n=-\infty}^{\infty} C_n$

    j.  $\bigcap_{n=-\infty}^{\infty} C_n$

**1.9.**  One might think that an empty set of real numbers and an empty set of sets are two different objects. Show that according to our definitions, there is only one set containing no elements.

**1.10.**  List the elements of $2^{2^{\{0,1\}}}$.

**1.11.**  Denote by $p$, $q$, and $r$ the statements $a = 1$, $b = 0$, and $c = 3$, respectively. Write each of the following statements symbolically, using $p$, $q$, $r$, $\wedge$, $\vee$, $\neg$, and $\rightarrow$.

    a.  Either $a = 1$ or $b \neq 0$.

    b.  $b = 0$ but neither $a = 1$ nor $c = 3$. (Note: in logic, unlike English, "but" and "and" are interchangeable.)

    c.  It is not the case that both $a \neq 1$ and $b = 0$.

    d.  If $a \neq 1$ then $c = 3$, but otherwise $c \neq 3$.

    e.  $b = 0$ only if either $a = 1$ or $c = 3$.

    f.  If it is not the case that either $a = 1$ or $b = 0$, then only if $c = 3$ is $a \neq 1$.

**1.12.**  Which of these statements are true?

    a.  If $1 + 1 = 2$, then $2 + 2 = 4$.

    b.  $1 + 1 = 3$ only if $2 + 2 = 6$.

    c.  $(1 = 2$ and $1 = 3)$ if and only if $1 = 3$.

    d.  If $1 + 1 = 3$ then $1 + 2 = 3$.

    e.  If $1 = 2$, then $2 = 3$ and $2 = 4$.

    f.  Only if $3 - 1 = 2$ is $1 - 2 = 0$.

**1.13.**  In each case, construct a truth table for the statement and use the result to find a simpler statement that is logically equivalent.

    a.  $(p \rightarrow q) \wedge (p \rightarrow \neg q)$

    b.  $p \vee (p \rightarrow q)$

    c.  $p \wedge (p \rightarrow q)$

    d.  $(p \rightarrow q) \wedge (\neg p \rightarrow q)$

    e.  $p \leftrightarrow (p \leftrightarrow q)$

    f.  $q \wedge (p \rightarrow q)$

**1.14.**  A principle of classical logic is *modus ponens*, which asserts that the proposition $(p \wedge (p \rightarrow q)) \rightarrow q$ is a tautology, or that $p \wedge (p \rightarrow q)$ logically implies $q$. Show that this result requires the truth table for the conditional statement $r \rightarrow s$ to be defined exactly as we defined it in the two cases where $r$ is false.

**1.15.**  Suppose $m_1$ and $m_2$ are integers representing months ($1 \leq m_i \leq 12$), and $d_1$ and $d_2$ are integers representing days ($d_i$ is at least 1 and no larger than the number of days in month $m_i$). For each $i$, the pair $(m_i, d_i)$ can be thought of as representing a date. We wish to write a logical proposition involving the four integers that says $(m_1, d_1)$ comes before $(m_2, d_2)$ in the calendar.

    a.  Find such a proposition that is a disjunction of two propositions.

    b.  Find such a proposition that is a conjunction of two propositions.

**1.16.**  Show that the statements $p \vee q \vee r \vee s$ and $(\neg p \wedge \neg q \wedge \neg r) \rightarrow s$ are equivalent.

**1.17.**  In each case, say whether the statement is a tautology, a contradiction, or neither.

    a.  $p \vee \neg(p \rightarrow p)$

    b.  $p \wedge \neg(p \rightarrow p)$

    c.  $p \rightarrow \neg p$

    d.  $(p \rightarrow \neg p) \vee (\neg p \rightarrow p)$

    e.  $(p \rightarrow \neg p) \wedge (\neg p \rightarrow p)$

**1.18.** Consider the statement "Everybody loves somebody sometime." In order to express this precisely, let $L(x, y, t)$ be a proposition involving the three free variables $x$, $y$, and $t$ that expresses the fact that $x$ loves $y$ at time $t$. (Here $x$ and $y$ are humans, and $t$ is a time.) Using this notation, express the original statement using quantifiers.

**1.19.** Let $F(x, t)$ be the proposition: You can fool person $x$ at time $t$. Using this notation, write a quantified statement to formalize Abraham Lincoln's statement: "You can fool all the people some of the time, and you can fool some of the people all the time, but you can not fool all the people all of the time." Give at least two different answers (not equivalent), representing different possible interpretations of the statement.

**1.20.** In each case below, say whether the given statement is true for the universe $(0, 1) = \{x \in \mathcal{R} \mid 0 < x < 1\}$, and say whether it is true for the universe $[0, 1] = \{x \in \mathcal{R} \mid 0 \le x \le 1\}$.

   a. $\forall x (\exists y (x > y))$

   b. $\forall x (\exists y (x \ge y))$

   c. $\exists y (\forall x (x > y))$

   d. $\exists y (\forall x (x \ge y))$

**1.21.** Suppose $A$ and $B$ are finite sets, $A$ has $n$ elements, and $f : A \to B$.

   a. If $f$ is one-to-one, what can you say about the number of elements of $B$?

   b. If $f$ is onto, what can you say about the number of elements of $B$?

**1.22.** In this problem, as usual, $\mathcal{R}$ denotes the set of real numbers, $\mathcal{R}^+$ the set of nonnegative real numbers, $\mathcal{N}$ the set of natural numbers (nonnegative integers), and $2^{\mathcal{R}}$ the set of subsets of $\mathcal{R}$. $[0, 1]$ denotes the set $\{x \in \mathcal{R} \mid 0 \le x \le 1\}$. In each case, say whether the indicated function is one-to-one, and say what its range is.

   a. $f_a : \mathcal{R}^+ \to \mathcal{R}^+$ defined by $f_a(x) = x + a$ (where $a$ is some fixed element of $\mathcal{R}^+$)

   b. $d : \mathcal{R}^+ \to \mathcal{R}^+$ defined by $d(x) = 2x$

   c. $t : \mathcal{N} \to \mathcal{N}$ defined by $t(x) = 2x$

   d. $g : \mathcal{R}^+ \to \mathcal{N}$ defined by $g(x) = \lfloor x \rfloor$ (the largest integer $\le x$)

   e. $p : \mathcal{R}^+ \to \mathcal{R}^+$ defined by $p(x) = x + \lfloor x \rfloor$

   f. $i : 2^{\mathcal{R}} \to 2^{\mathcal{R}}$ defined by $i(A) = A \cap [0, 1]$

   g. $u : 2^{\mathcal{R}} \to 2^{\mathcal{R}}$ defined by $u(A) = A \cup [0, 1]$

   h. $m : \mathcal{R}^+ \to \mathcal{R}^+$ defined by $m(x) = \min(x, 2)$

   i. $M : \mathcal{R}^+ \to \mathcal{R}^+$ defined by $M(x) = \max(x, 2)$

   j. $s : \mathcal{R}^+ \to \mathcal{R}^+$ defined by $s(x) = \min(x, 2) + \max(x, 2)$

**1.23.** Suppose $A$ and $B$ are sets, $f : A \to B$, and $g : B \to A$. If $f(g(y)) = y$ for every $y \in B$, then $f$ is a _____ function and $g$ is a _____ function. Give reasons for your answers.

**1.24.** Let $A = \{2, 3, 4, 6, 7, 12, 18\}$ and $B = \{7, 8, 9, 10\}$.

a. Define $f : A \to B$ as follows: $f(2) = 7$; $f(3) = 9$; $f(4) = 8$; $f(6) = f(7) = 10$; $f(12) = 9$; $f(18) = 7$. Find a function $g : B \to A$ so that for every $y \in B$, $f(g(y)) = y$. Is there more than one such $g$?

b. Define $g : B \to A$ as follows: $g(7) = 6$; $g(8) = 7$; $g(9) = 2$; $g(10) = 18$. Find a function $f : A \to B$ so that for every $y \in B$, $f(g(y)) = y$. Is there more than one such $f$?

**1.25.** Let $f_a, d, t, g, i$, and $u$ be the functions defined in Exercise 1.22. In each case, find a formula for the indicated function, and simplify it as much as possible.

a. $g \circ d$

b. $t \circ g$

c. $t \circ t$

d. $d \circ f_a$

e. $f_a \circ d$

f. $g \circ f_a$

g. $u \circ i$

h. $i \circ u$

**1.26.** In each case, show that $f$ is a bijection and find a formula for $f^{-1}$.

a. $f : \mathcal{R} \to \mathcal{R}$ defined by $f(x) = x$

b. $f : \mathcal{R}^+ \to \{x \in \mathcal{R} \mid 0 < x \le 1\}$ defined by $f(x) = 1/(1 + x)$

c. $f : \mathcal{R} \times \mathcal{R} \to \mathcal{R} \times \mathcal{R}$ defined by $f(x, y) = (x + y, x - y)$

**1.27.** Show that if $f : A \to B$ is a bijection, then $f^{-1}$ is also a bijection, and $(f^{-1})^{-1} = f$.

**1.28.** In each case, a relation on the set $\{1, 2, 3\}$ is given. Of the three properties, reflexivity, symmetry, and transitivity, determine which ones the relation has. Give reasons.

a. $R = \{(1, 3), (3, 1), (2, 2)\}$

b. $R = \{(1, 1), (2, 2), (3, 3), (1, 2)\}$

c. $R = \emptyset$

**1.29.** For each of the eight lines of the table below, construct a relation on $\{1, 2, 3\}$ that fits the description.

| reflexive | symmetric | transitive |
|-----------|-----------|------------|
| true | true | true |
| true | true | false |
| true | false | true |
| true | false | false |
| false | true | true |
| false | true | false |
| false | false | true |
| false | false | false |

**1.30.** Three relations are given on the set of all nonempty subsets of $\mathcal{N}$. In each case, say whether the relation is reflexive, whether it is symmetric, and whether it is transitive.

a. $R$ is defined by: $ARB$ if and only if $A \subseteq B$.

b. $R$ is defined by: $ARB$ if and only if $A \cap B \neq \emptyset$.

c. $R$ is defined by: $ARB$ if and only if $1 \in A \cap B$.

**1.31.** How would your answer to Exercise 1.30 change if in each case $R$ were the indicated relation on the set of *all* subsets of $\mathcal{N}$?

**1.32.** Let $R$ be a relation on a set $S$. Write three quantified statements (the domain being $S$ in each case), which say, respectively, that $R$ is not reflexive, $R$ is not symmetric, and $R$ is not transitive.

**1.33.** In each case, a set $A$ is specified, and a relation $R$ is defined on it. Show that $R$ is an equivalence relation.

a. $A = 2^S$, for some set $S$. An element $X$ of $A$ is related via $R$ to an element $Y$ if there is a bijection from $X$ to $Y$.

b. $A$ is an arbitrary set, and it is assumed that for some other set $B$, $f : A \to B$ is a function. For $x, y \in A$, $xRy$ if $f(x) = f(y)$.

c. Suppose $U$ is the set $\{1, 2, \ldots, 10\}$. $A$ is the set of all statements over the universe $U$—that is, statements involving at most one free variable, which can have as its value an element of $U$. (Included in $A$ are the statements *false* and *true*.) For two elements $r$ and $s$ of $A$, $rRs$ if $r \Leftrightarrow s$.

d. $A$ is the set $\mathcal{R}$, and for $x, y \in A$, $xRy$ if $x - y$ is an integer.

e. $A$ is the set of all infinite sequences $x = x_0 x_1 x_2 \cdots$ of 0's and 1's. For two such sequences $x$ and $y$, $xRy$ if there exists an integer $k$ so that $x_i = y_i$ for every $i \geq k$.

**1.34.** In Exercise 1.33a, if $S$ has exactly 10 elements, how many equivalence classes are there for the relation $R$? Describe them. What are the elements of the equivalence class containing $\{a, b\}$ (assuming $a$ and $b$ are two elements of $S$)?

**1.35.** In Exercise 1.33b, if $A$ and $B$ are both the set of real numbers, and $f$ is the function defined by $f(x) = x^2$, describe the equivalence classes.

**1.36.** In Exercise 1.33b, suppose $A$ has $n$ elements and $B$ has $m$ elements.

a. If $f$ is one-to-one (and not necessarily onto), how many equivalence classes are there?

b. If $f$ is onto (and not necessarily one-to-one), how many equivalence classes are there?

**1.37.** In Exercise 1.33c, how many equivalence classes are there? List some elements in the equivalence class containing the statement $(x = 3) \vee (x = 7)$. List some elements in the equivalence class containing the statement *true*, and some in the equivalence class containing *false*.

**1.38.** Let $L$ be a language. It is clear from the definitions that $L^+ \subseteq L^*$. Under what circumstances are they equal?

**1.39.** a.  Find a language $L$ over $\{a, b\}$ that is neither $\{\Lambda\}$ nor $\{a, b\}^*$ and satisfies $L = L^*$.

   b.  Find an infinite language $L$ over $\{a, b\}$ for which $L \neq L^*$.

**1.40.** In each case, give an example of languages $L_1$ and $L_2$ satisfying $L_1 L_2 = L_2 L_1$ as well as the additional conditions indicated.

   a.  Neither language is a subset of the other, and neither language is $\{\Lambda\}$.

   b.  $L_1$ is a proper nonempty subset of $L_2$ (*proper* means $L_1 \neq L_2$), and $L_1 \neq \{\Lambda\}$.

**1.41.** Let $L_1$ and $L_2$ be subsets of $\{0, 1\}^*$, and consider the two languages $L_1^* \cup L_2^*$ and $(L_1 \cup L_2)^*$.

   a.  Which of the two is always a subset of the other? Why? Give an example (i.e., say what $L_1$ and $L_2$ are) so that the opposite inclusion does not hold.

   b.  If $L_1^* \subseteq L_2^*$, then $(L_1 \cup L_2)^* = L_2^* = L_1^* \cup L_2^*$. Similarly if $L_2^* \subseteq L_1^*$. Give an example of languages $L_1$ and $L_2$ for which $L_1^* \not\subseteq L_2^*$, $L_2^* \not\subseteq L_1^*$, and $L_1^* \cup L_2^* = (L_1 \cup L_2)^*$.

**1.42.** Show that if $A$ and $B$ are languages over $\Sigma$ and $A \subseteq B$, then $A^* \subseteq B^*$.

**1.43.** Show that for any language $L$, $L^* = (L^*)^* = (L^+)^* = (L^*)^+$.

**1.44.** For a finite language $L$, denote by $|L|$ the number of elements of $L$. (For example, $|\{\Lambda, a, ababb\}| = 3$.) Is it always true that for finite languages $A$ and $B$, $|AB| = |A||B|$? Either prove the equality or find a counterexample.

**1.45.** List some elements of $\{a, ab\}^*$. Can you describe a simple way to recognize elements of this language? In other words, try to find a proposition $p(x)$ so that

   a.  $\{a, ab\}^*$ is precisely the set of strings $x$ satisfying $p(x)$; and

   b.  for any $x$, there is a simple procedure to test whether $x$ satisfies $p(x)$.

**1.46.** a.  Consider the language $L$ of all strings of $a$'s and $b$'s that do not end with $b$ and do not contain the substring $bb$. Find a finite language $S$ so that $L = S^*$.

   b.  Show that there is no language $S$ so that the language of all strings of $a$'s and $b$'s that do not contain the substring $bb$ is equal to $S^*$.

**1.47.** Let $L_1$, $L_2$, and $L_3$ be languages over some alphabet $\Sigma$. In each part below, two languages are given. Say what the relationship is between them. (Are they always equal? If not, is one always a subset of the other?) Give reasons for your answers, including counterexamples if appropriate.

   a.  $L_1(L_2 \cap L_3)$, $L_1 L_2 \cap L_1 L_3$

   b.  $L_1^* \cap L_2^*$, $(L_1 \cap L_2)^*$

   c.  $L_1^* L_2^*$, $(L_1 L_2)^*$

   d.  $L_1^*(L_2 L_1^*)^*$, $(L_1^* L_2)^* L_1^*$

# MORE CHALLENGING PROBLEMS

**1.48.** Show the associative property of symmetric difference (see Exercise 1.5) without using Venn diagrams.

**1.49.** Suppose that for a finite set $S$, $|S|$ denotes the number of elements of $S$, and let $A$, $B$, $C$, and $D$ be finite sets.

    a. Show that $|A \cup B| = |A| + |B| - |A \cap B|$.

    b. Show that $|A \cup B \cup C| = |A| + |B| + |C| - |A \cap B| - |A \cap C| - |B \cap C| + |A \cap B \cap C|$. (An element $x$ can be in none, one, two, or three of the sets $A$, $B$, and $C$. For each case, consider the contribution of $x$ to each of the terms on the right side of the formula.)

    c. Find a formula for $|A \cup B \cup C \cup D|$.

**1.50.**   a. How many elements are there in the following set?

$$\{\emptyset, \{\emptyset\}, \{\emptyset, \{\emptyset\}\}, \{\emptyset, \{\{\emptyset, \{\emptyset\}, \{\emptyset, \{\emptyset\}\}\}\}\}\}$$

    b. Describe precisely the algorithm you used to answer part (a).

**1.51.** Simplify the given set as much as possible in each case. Assume that all the numbers involved are real numbers.

    a.

$$\bigcap_{r>0}\{x \mid |x - a| < r\}$$

    b.

$$\bigcup_{r<1}\{x \mid |x - a| \leq r\}$$

**1.52.** Is it possible for two distinct, nonempty sets $A$ and $B$ to satisfy $A \times B \subseteq B \times A$? Give either an example of sets $A$ and $B$ for which this is true or a general reason why it is impossible.

**1.53.** Suppose that $A$ and $B$ are subsets of a universal set $U$.

    a. What is the relationship between $2^{A \cup B}$ and $2^A \cup 2^B$? (Under what circumstances are they equal? If they are not equal, is one necessarily a subset of the other, and if so, which one?) Give reasons for your answers.

    b. What is the relationship between $2^{A \cap B}$ and $2^A \cap 2^B$? Give reasons.

    c. What is the relationship between $2^{A \oplus B}$ and $2^A \oplus 2^B$? (The operator $\oplus$ is symmetric difference, as in Exercise 1.5.) Give reasons.

    d. What is the relationship between $2^{(A')}$ and $(2^A)'$? (Both are subsets of $2^U$.) Give reasons.

**1.54.** Find a statement logically equivalent to $p \leftrightarrow q$ that is in the form of a disjunction, and simplify it as much as possible. (One approach is to use the last paragraph of Section 1.2.2, from which it follows that $p \leftrightarrow q$ is equivalent to $(\neg p \vee q) \wedge (p \vee \neg q)$, and then to use distributive laws.)

**1.55.**  In each case, write a quantified statement, using the formal notation discussed in the chapter, that expresses the given statement. In both cases the set $A$ is assumed to be a subset of the domain, not necessarily the entire domain.

    a.  There is exactly one element $x$ in the set $A$ satisfying the condition $P$—that is, for which the proposition $P(x)$ holds.

    b.  There are at least two distinct elements in the set $A$ satisfying the condition $P$.

**1.56.**  Below are four pairs of statements. In all cases, the universe for the quantified statements is assumed to be the set $\mathcal{N}$. We say one statement logically implies the other if, for any choice of statements $p(x)$ and $q(x)$ for which the first is true, the second is also true. In each case, say whether the first statement logically implies the second, and whether the second logically implies the first. In each case where the answer is no, give an example of statements $p(x)$ and $q(x)$ to illustrate.

    a.

$$\forall x(p(x) \vee q(x))$$
$$\forall x(p(x)) \vee \forall x(q(x))$$

    b.

$$\forall x(p(x) \wedge q(x))$$
$$\forall x(p(x)) \wedge \forall x(q(x))$$

    c.

$$\exists x(p(x) \vee q(x))$$
$$\exists x(p(x)) \vee \exists x(q(x))$$

    d.

$$\exists x(p(x) \wedge q(x))$$
$$\exists x(p(x)) \wedge \exists x(q(x))$$

**1.57.**  Suppose $A$ and $B$ are sets and $f : A \to B$. Let $S$ and $T$ be subsets of $A$.

    a.  Is the set $f(S \cup T)$ a subset of $f(S) \cup f(T)$? If so, give a proof; if not, give a counterexample (i.e., specify sets $A$, $B$, $S$, and $T$ and a function $f$).

    b.  Is the set $f(S) \cup f(T)$ a subset of $f(S \cup T)$? Give either a proof or a counterexample.

    c.  Repeat part (a) with intersection instead of union.

    d.  Repeat part (b) with intersection instead of union.

    e.  In each of the first four parts where your answer is no, what extra assumption on the function $f$ would make the answer yes? Give reasons for your answer.

**1.58.** Suppose $n$ is a positive integer and $X = \{1, 2, \ldots, n\}$. Let $A = 2^X$; let $B$ be the set of all functions from $X$ to $\{0, 1\}$, and let $C = \{0, 1\}^n = \{0, 1\} \times \{0, 1\} \times \cdots \times \{0, 1\}$ (where there are $n$ factors).

    a. Describe an explicit bijection $f$ from $A$ to $B$. (In other words, define a function $f : A \to B$, by saying for each subset $S$ of $X$ what function from $X$ to $\{0, 1\}$ $f(S)$ is, and show that $f$ is a bijection.

    b. Describe an explicit bijection $g$ from $B$ to $C$. (In this case, you have to say, for each function $t : X \to \{0, 1\}$, what $n$-tuple $g(t)$ is, and then show $g$ is a bijection.)

    c. Describe an explicit bijection $h$ from $C$ to $A$. (Here you have to start with an $n$-tuple $N = (i_1, i_2, \ldots, i_n)$ and say what set $h(N)$ is, and then show $h$ is a bijection.)

**1.59.** Let $E$ be the set $\{1, 2, 3, \ldots\}$, $S$ the set of nonempty subsets of $E$, $T$ the set of nonempty proper subsets of $\mathcal{N}$, and $\mathcal{P}$ the set of partitions of $\mathcal{N}$ into two nonempty subsets.

    a. Suppose $f : T \to \mathcal{P}$ is defined by the formula $f(A) = \{A, \mathcal{N} - A\}$ (in other words, for a nonempty subset $A$ of $\mathcal{N}$, $f(A)$ is the partition of $\mathcal{N}$ consisting of the two subsets $A$ and $\mathcal{N} - A$). Is $f$ a bijection from $T$ to $\mathcal{P}$? Why or why not?

    b. Suppose $g : S \to \mathcal{P}$ be defined by $g(A) = \{A, \mathcal{N} - A\}$. Is $g$ a bijection from $S$ to $\mathcal{P}$? Why or why not?

**1.60.** Suppose $U$ is a set, $\circ$ is a binary operation on $U$, and $I_0$ is a subset of $U$.

    a. Let $S$ be the set of subsets of $U$ that contain $I_0$ as a subset and are closed under the operation $\circ$; let $T = \cap_{S \in S} S$. Show that $I_0 \subseteq T$ and that $T$ is closed under $\circ$.

    b. Show that the set $T$ defined in part (a) is the *smallest* subset of $U$ that contains $I_0$ and is closed under $\circ$, in the sense that for any other such set $T_1$, $T \subseteq T_1$.

**1.61.** Consider the following "proof" that any relation $R$ on a set A which is both symmetric and transitive must also be reflexive:

> Let $a$ be any element of $A$. Let $b$ be any element of $A$ for which $aRb$. Then since $R$ is symmetric, $bRa$. Now since $R$ is transitive, and since $aRb$ and $bRa$, it follows that $aRa$. Therefore, $R$ is reflexive.

Your answer to Exercise 1.29 shows that this proof cannot be correct. What is the first incorrect statement of the proof, and why is it incorrect?

**1.62.** Suppose $A$ is a set having $n$ elements.

    a. How many relations are there on $A$?

    b. How many reflexive relations are there on $A$?

    c. How many symmetric relations are there on $A$?

    d. How many relations are there on $A$ that are both reflexive and symmetric?

**1.63.**  Suppose $R$ is a relation on a nonempty set $A$.

   a.  Define $R^s = R \cup \{(x, y) \mid yRx\}$. Show that $R^s$ is symmetric and is the smallest symmetric relation on $A$ containing $R$ (i.e., for any symmetric relation $R_1$ with $R \subseteq R_1$, $R^s \subseteq R_1$).

   b.  Define $R^t$ to be the intersection of all transitive relations on $A$ containing $R$. Show that $R^t$ is transitive and is the smallest transitive relation on $A$ containing $R$.

   c.  Let $R^u = R \cup \{(x, y) \mid \exists z(xRz \text{ and } zRy)\}$. Is $R^u$ equal to the set $R^t$ in part (b)? Either prove that it is, or give an example in which it is not.

   The relations $R^s$ and $R^t$ are called the symmetric closure and transitive closure of $R$, respectively.

**1.64.**  Let $R$ be the equivalence relation in Exercise 1.33a. Assuming that $S$ is finite, find a function $f : 2^S \to \mathcal{N}$ so that for any $x, y \in 2^S$, $xRy$ if and only if $f(x) = f(y)$.

**1.65.**  Let $n$ be a positive integer. Find a function $f : \mathcal{N} \to \mathcal{N}$ so that for any $x, y \in \mathcal{N}$, $x \equiv_n y$ if and only if $f(x) = f(y)$.

**1.66.**  Let $A$ be any set, and let $R$ be any equivalence relation on $A$. Find a set $B$ and a function $f : A \to B$ so that for any $x, y \in A$, $xRy$ if and only if $f(x) = f(y)$.

**1.67.**  Suppose $R$ is an equivalence relation on a set $A$. A subset $S \subseteq A$ is *pairwise inequivalent* if no two distinct elements of $S$ are equivalent. $S$ is a *maximal pairwise inequivalent set* if $S$ is pairwise inequivalent and every element of $A$ is equivalent to some element of $S$. Show that a set $S$ is a maximal pairwise inequivalent set if and only if it contains exactly one element of each equivalence class.

**1.68.**  Suppose $R_1$ and $R_2$ are equivalence relations on a set $A$. As discussed in Section 1.4, the equivalence classes of $R_1$ and $R_2$ form partitions $P_1$ and $P_2$, respectively, of $A$. Show that $R_1 \subseteq R_2$ if and only if the partition $P_1$ is *finer* than $P_2$ (i.e., every subset in the partition $P_2$ is the union of one or more subsets in the partition $P_1$).

**1.69.**  Suppose $\Sigma$ is an alphabet. It is obviously possible for two distinct strings $x$ and $y$ over $\Sigma$ to satisfy the condition $xy = yx$, since this condition is always satisfied if $y = \Lambda$. Is it possible under the additional restriction that $x$ and $y$ are both nonnull? Either prove that this cannot happen, or describe precisely the circumstances under which it can.

**1.70.**  Show that there is no language $L$ so that $\{aa, bb\}^*\{ab, ba\}^* = L^*$.

**1.71.**  Consider the language $L = \{x \in \{0, 1\}^* \mid x = yy \text{ for some string } y\}$. We know that $L = L\{\Lambda\} = \{\Lambda\}L$ (because any language $L$ has this property). Is there any other way to express $L$ as the concatenation of two languages? Prove your answer.

# CHAPTER

# 2

# Mathematical Induction and Recursive Definitions

## 2.1 | PROOFS

A *proof* of a statement is essentially just a convincing argument that the statement is true. Ideally, however, a proof not only convinces but explains why the statement is true, and also how it relates to other statements and how it fits into the overall theory. A typical step in a proof is to derive some statement from (1) assumptions or hypotheses, (2) statements that have already been derived, and (3) other generally accepted facts, using general principles of logical reasoning. In a very careful, detailed proof, we might allow no "generally accepted facts" other than certain axioms that we specify initially, and we might restrict ourselves to certain specific rules of logical inference, by which each step must be justified. Being this careful, however, may not be feasible or worthwhile. We may take shortcuts ("It is obvious that ..." or "It is easy to show that ...") and concentrate on the main steps in the proof, assuming that a conscientious or curious reader could fill in the low-level details.

Usually what we are trying to prove involves a statement of the form $p \rightarrow q$. A *direct* proof assumes that the statement $p$ is true and uses this to show $q$ is true.

### The Product of Two Odd Integers Is Odd

**EXAMPLE 2.1**

*To prove:* For any integers $a$ and $b$, if $a$ and $b$ are odd, then $ab$ is odd.

### ■ Proof

We start by saying more precisely what our assumption means. An integer $n$ is odd if there exists an integer $x$ so that $n = 2x + 1$. Now let $a$ and $b$ be any odd integers. Then according to this definition, there is an integer $x$ so that $a = 2x + 1$, and there is an integer $y$ so that

$b = 2y + 1$. We wish to show that there is an integer $z$ so that $ab = 2z + 1$. Let us therefore calculate $ab$:

$$ab = (2x + 1)(2y + 1)$$
$$= 4xy + 2x + 2y + 1$$
$$= 2(2xy + x + y) + 1$$

Since we have shown that there is a $z$, namely, $2xy + x + y$, so that $ab = 2z + 1$, the proof is complete.

---

This is an example of a *constructive* proof. We proved the statement "There exists $z$ such that ..." by constructing a specific value for $z$ that works. A nonconstructive proof shows that such a $z$ must exist without providing any information about its value. Such a proof would not explain, it would only convince. Although in some situations this is the best we can do, people normally prefer a constructive proof if one is possible. In some cases, the method of construction is interesting in its own right. In these cases, the proof is even more valuable because it provides an algorithm as well as an explanation.

Since the statement we proved in Example 2.1 is the quantified statement "For any integers $a$ and $b$, . . . ," it is important to understand that it is *not* sufficient to give an example of $a$ and $b$ for which the statement is true. If we say "Let $a = 45$ and $b = 11$; then $a = 2(22) + 1$ and $b = 2(5) + 2$; therefore, $ab = (2 * 22 + 1)(2 * 5 + 1) = \ldots = 2 * 247 + 1$," we have proved nothing except that $45 * 11$ is odd. Finding a value of $x$ so that the statement $P(x)$ is true is a proof of the statement "There exists $x$ such that $P(x)$." Finding a value of $x$ for which $P(x)$ is false *disproves* the statement "For every $x$, $P(x)$" (or, if you prefer, proves the statement "It is not the case that for every $x$, $P(x)$"); this is called a *proof by counterexample*. To prove "For every $x$, $P(x)$," however, requires that we give an argument in which there are no restrictions on $x$. (Let us return briefly to the example with 45 and 11. It is not totally unreasonable to claim that the argument beginning "Let $a = 45$ and $b = 11$" is a proof of the quantified statement—after all, the algebraic steps involved are the same as the ones we presented in our official proof. The crucial point, however, is that there is nothing special about 45 and 11. Someone who offers this as a proof should at least point out that the same argument would work in general. For an argument this simple, such an observation may be convincing; even more convincing is an argument involving $a$ and $b$ like the one we gave originally.)

The alternative to a direct proof is an *indirect* proof, and the simplest form of indirect proof is a *proof by contrapositive*, using the logical equivalence of $p \to q$ and $\neg q \to \neg p$.

**EXAMPLE 2.2**    A Proof by Contrapositive

---

*To prove:* For any positive integers $i$, $j$, and $n$, if $i * j = n$, then either $i \leq \sqrt{n}$ or $j \leq \sqrt{n}$.

### ■ Proof

The statement we wish to prove is of the general form "For every $x$, if $p(x)$, then $q(x)$." For each $x$, the statement "If $p(x)$ then $q(x)$" is logically equivalent to "If not $q(x)$ then not $p(x)$," and therefore (by a general principle of logical reasoning) the statement we want to prove is equivalent to this: For any positive integers $i$, $j$, and $n$, if it is not the case that $i \leq \sqrt{n}$ or $j \leq \sqrt{n}$, then $i * j \neq n$.

If it is not true that $i \leq \sqrt{n}$ or $j \leq \sqrt{n}$, then $i > \sqrt{n}$ and $j > \sqrt{n}$. A generally accepted fact from mathematics is that if $a$ and $b$ are numbers with $a > b$, and $c$ is a number $> 0$, then $ac > bc$. Applying this to the inequality $i > \sqrt{n}$ with $c = j$, we obtain $i * j > \sqrt{n} * j$. Since $n > 0$, we know that $\sqrt{n} > 0$, and we may apply the same fact again to the inequality $j > \sqrt{n}$, this time letting $c = \sqrt{n}$, to obtain $j\sqrt{n} > \sqrt{n}\sqrt{n} = n$. We now have $i * j > j\sqrt{n} > n$, and it follows that $i * j \neq n$.

The second paragraph in this proof illustrates the fact that a complete proof, with no details left out, is usually not feasible. Even though the statement we are proving here is relatively simple, and our proof includes more detail than might normally be included, there is still a lot left out. Here are some of the details that were ignored:

1. $\neg(p \vee q)$ is logically equivalent to $\neg p \wedge \neg q$. Therefore, if it is not true that $i \leq \sqrt{n}$ or $j \leq \sqrt{n}$, then $i \not\leq \sqrt{n}$ and $j \not\leq \sqrt{n}$.
2. For any two real numbers $a$ and $b$, exactly one of the conditions $a < b$, $a > b$, and $a = b$ holds. (This is a generally accepted fact from mathematics.) Therefore, if $i \not\leq \sqrt{n}$, then $i > \sqrt{n}$, and similarly for $j$.
3. For any two real numbers $a$ and $b$, $a * b = b * a$. Therefore, $\sqrt{n} * j = j\sqrt{n}$.
4. The $>$ relation on the set of real numbers is transitive. Therefore, from the fact that $i * j > j\sqrt{n}$ and $j\sqrt{n} > n$ it follows that $i * j > n$.

Even if we include all these details, we have not stated explicitly the rules of inference we have used to arrive at the final conclusion, and we have used a number of facts about real numbers that could themselves be proved from more fundamental axioms. In presenting a proof, one usually tries to strike a balance: enough left out to avoid having the minor details obscure the main points and put the reader to sleep, and enough left in so that the reader will be convinced.

A variation of proof by contrapositive is *proof by contradiction*. In its most general form, proving a statement $p$ by contradiction means showing that if it is not true, some contradiction results. Formally, this means showing that the statement $\neg p \rightarrow false$ is true. It follows that the contrapositive statement $true \rightarrow p$ is true, and this statement is logically equivalent to $p$. If we wish to prove the statement $p \rightarrow q$ by contradiction, we assume that $p \rightarrow q$ is false. Because of the logical equivalence of $p \rightarrow q$ and $\neg p \vee q$, this means assuming that $\neg(\neg p \vee q)$, or $p \wedge \neg q$, is true. From this assumption we try to derive some statement that contradicts some statement we know to be true—possibly $p$, or possibly some other statement.

**EXAMPLE 2.3**     $\sqrt{2}$ Is Irrational

A real number $x$ is *rational* if there are two integers $m$ and $n$ so that $x = m/n$. We present one of the most famous examples of proof by contradiction: the proof, known to the ancient Greeks, that $\sqrt{2}$ is irrational.

■ **Proof**

Suppose for the sake of contradiction that $\sqrt{2}$ is rational. Then there are integers $m'$ and $n'$ with $\sqrt{2} = m'/n'$. By dividing both $m'$ and $n'$ by all the factors that are common to both, we obtain $\sqrt{2} = m/n$, for some integers $m$ and $n$ having no common factors. Since $m/n = \sqrt{2}$, $m = n\sqrt{2}$. Squaring both sides of this equation, we obtain $m^2 = 2n^2$, and therefore $m^2$ is even (divisible by 2). The result proved in Example 2.1 is that for any integers $a$ and $b$, if $a$ and $b$ are odd, then $ab$ is odd. Since a conditional statement is logically equivalent to its contrapositive, we may conclude that for any $a$ and $b$, if $ab$ is not odd, then either $a$ is not odd or $b$ is not odd. However, an integer is not odd if and only if it is even (Exercise 2.21), and so for any $a$ and $b$, if $ab$ is even, then $a$ or $b$ is even. If we apply this when $a = b = m$, we conclude that since $m^2$ is even, $m$ must be even. This means that for some $k$, $m = 2k$. Therefore, $(2k)^2 = 2n^2$. Simplifying this and canceling 2 from both sides, we obtain $2k^2 = n^2$. Therefore, $n^2$ is even. The same argument that we have already used shows that $n$ must be even, and so $n = 2j$ for some $j$. We have shown that $m$ and $n$ are both divisible by 2. This contradicts the previous statement that $m$ and $n$ have no common factor. The assumption that $\sqrt{2}$ is rational therefore leads to a contradiction, and the conclusion is that $\sqrt{2}$ is irrational.

**EXAMPLE 2.4**     Another Proof by Contradiction

*To prove:* For any sets $A$, $B$, and $C$, if $A \cap B = \emptyset$ and $C \subseteq B$, then $A \cap C = \emptyset$.

■ **Proof**

Again we try a proof by contradiction. Suppose that $A$, $B$, and $C$ are sets for which the conditional statement is false. Then $A \cap B = \emptyset$, $C \subseteq B$, and $A \cap C \neq \emptyset$. Therefore, there exists $x$ with $x \in A \cap C$, so that $x \in A$ and $x \in C$. Since $C \subseteq B$ and $x \in C$, it follows that $x \in B$. Therefore, $x \in A \cap B$, which contradicts the assumption that $A \cap B = \emptyset$. Since the assumption that the conditional statement is false leads to a contradiction, the statement is proved.

There is not always a clear line between a proof by contrapositive and one by contradiction. Any proof by contrapositive that $p \rightarrow q$ is true can easily be reformulated as a proof by contradiction. Instead of assuming that $\neg q$ is true and trying to show $\neg p$, assume that $p$ and $\neg q$ are true and derive $\neg p$; then the contradiction is that $p$ and $\neg p$ are both true. In the last example it seemed slightly easier to argue by contradiction, since we wanted to use the assumption that $C \subseteq B$. A proof by contrapositive would assume that $A \cap C \neq \emptyset$ and would try to show that

$$\neg((A \cap B = \emptyset) \wedge (C \subseteq B))$$

This approach seems a little more complicated, just because the formula we are trying to obtain is more complicated.

It is often convenient (or necessary) to use several different proof techniques within a single proof. Although the overall proof in the following example is not a proof by contradiction, this technique is used twice within the proof.

## There Must Be a Prime Between $n$ and $n!$ ■ EXAMPLE 2.5

For a positive integer $n$ the number $n!$ is defined to be the product $n * (n - 1) * \cdots * 2 * 1$ of all the positive integers less than or equal to $n$. *To prove:* For any integer $n > 2$, there is a prime $p$ satisfying $n < p < n!$.

### ■ Proof
Since $n > 2$, two distinct factors in $n!$ are $n$ and 2. Therefore, $n! \geq 2n = n + n > n + 1$, and thus $n! - 1 > n$. The number $n! - 1$ must have a factor $p$ that is a prime. (See Example 1.2 for the definition of a prime. The fact that every integer greater than 1 has a prime factor is a basic fact about positive integers, which we will prove in Example 2.11.) Since $p$ is a divisor of $n! - 1$, $p \leq n! - 1 < n!$. This gives us one of the inequalities we need. To show the other one, suppose for the sake of contradiction that $p \leq n$. Then since $p$ is one of the positive integers less than or equal to $n$, $p$ is a factor of $n!$. However, $p$ cannot be a factor of both $n!$ and $n! - 1$; if it were, it would be a factor of 1, their difference, and this is impossible. Therefore, the assumption that $p \leq n$ leads to a contradiction, and we may conclude that $n < p < n!$.

Another useful technique is to divide the proof into separate cases; this is illustrated by the next example.

## Strings of Length 4 Contain Substrings $yy$ ■ EXAMPLE 2.6

*To prove:* Every string $x$ in $\{0, 1\}^*$ of length 4 contains a nonnull substring of the form $yy$.

### ■ Proof
We can show the result by considering two separate cases. If $x$ contains two consecutive 0's or two consecutive 1's, then the statement is true for a string $y$ of length 1. In the other case, any symbol that follows a 0 must be a 1, and vice versa, so that $x$ must be either 0101 or 1010. The statement is therefore true for a string $y$ of length 2.

Even though the argument is simple, let us state more explicitly the logic on which it depends. We want to show that some proposition $P$ is true. The statement $P$ is logically equivalent to *true* $\rightarrow P$. If we denote by $p$ the statement that $x$ contains two consecutive 0's or two consecutive 1's, then $p \lor \neg p$ is true. This means *true* $\rightarrow P$ is logically equivalent to

$$(p \lor \neg p) \rightarrow P$$

which in turn is logically equivalent to

$$(p \rightarrow P) \land (\neg p \rightarrow P)$$

This last statement is what we actually prove, by showing that each of the two separate conditional statements is true.

In this proof, there was some choice as to which cases to consider. A less efficient approach would have been to divide our two cases into four subcases: (i) $x$ contains two consecutive 0's; (and so forth). An even more laborious proof would be to consider the 16 strings of length 4 individually, and to show that the result is true in each case. Any of these approaches is valid, as long as our cases cover all the possibilities and we can complete the proof in each case.

---

The examples in this section provide only a very brief introduction to proofs. Learning to read proofs takes a lot of practice, and creating your own is even harder. One thing that does help is to develop a critical attitude. Be skeptical. When you read a step in a proof, ask yourself, "Am I convinced by this?" When you have written a proof, read it over as if someone else had written it (it is best to read aloud if circumstances permit), and as you read each step ask yourself the same question.

## 2.2 | THE PRINCIPLE OF MATHEMATICAL INDUCTION

Very often, we wish to prove that some statement involving a natural number $n$ is true for every sufficiently large value of $n$. The statement might be a numerical equality:

$$\sum_{i=1}^{n} i = n(n+1)/2$$

The number of subsets of $\{1, 2, \ldots, n\}$ is $2^n$.

It might be an inequality:

$$n! > 2^n$$

It might be some other assertion about $n$, or about a set with $n$ elements, or a string of length $n$:

There exist positive integers $j$ and $k$ so that $n = 3j + 7k$.

Every language with exactly $n$ elements is regular.

If $x \in \{0, 1\}^*$, $|x| = n$, and $x = 0y1$, then $x$ contains the substring 01.

(The term *regular* is defined in Chapter 3.) In this section, we discuss a common approach to proving statements of this type.

In both the last two examples, it might seem as though the explicit mention of $n$ makes the statement slightly more awkward. It would be simpler to say, "Every finite language is regular," and this statement is true; it would also be correct to let the last statement begin, "For any $x$ and $y$ in $\{0, 1\}^*$, if $x = 0y1, \ldots$." However, in both cases the simpler statement is equivalent to the assertion that the original statement is true for every nonnegative value of $n$, and formulating the statement so that it involves $n$ will allow us to apply the proof technique we are about to discuss.

We begin with the first example above, expressed without the summation notation:

$$1 + 2 + \cdots + n = n(n+1)/2$$

This formula is supposed to hold for every $n \geq 1$; however, it makes sense to consider it for $n = 0$ as well if we interpret the left side in that case to be the empty sum, which by definition is 0. Let us therefore try to prove that the statement is true for every $n \geq 0$.

How do we start? Unless we have any better ideas, we might very well begin by writing out the formula for the first few values of $n$, to see if we can spot a pattern.

$$
\begin{aligned}
n = 0 : &\qquad 0 = 0(0+1)/2 \\
n = 1 : &\qquad 0 + 1 = 1(1+1)/2 \\
n = 2 : &\qquad 0 + 1 + 2 = 2(2+1)/2 \\
n = 3 : &\qquad 0 + 1 + 2 + 3 = 3(3+1)/2 \\
n = 4 : &\qquad 0 + 1 + 2 + 3 + 4 = 4(4+1)/2
\end{aligned}
$$

As we are verifying these formulas, we probably realize after a few lines that in checking a specific case, say $n = 4$, it is not necessary to do all the arithmetic on the left side: $0 + 1 + 2 + 3 + 4$. We can take the left side of the previous formula, which we have already calculated, and add 4. When we calculated $0 + 1 + 2 + 3$, we obtained $3(3+1)/2$. So our answer for $n = 4$ is

$$3(3+1)/2 + 4 = 4(3/2 + 1) = 4(3+2)/2 = 4(4+1)/2$$

which is the one we wanted. Now that we have done this step, we can take care of $n = 5$ the same way, by taking the sum we just obtained for $n = 4$ and adding 5:

$$4(4+1)/2 + 5 = 5(4/2 + 1) = 5(4+2)/2 = 5(5+1)/2$$

These two calculations are similar—in fact, this is the pattern we were looking for, and we can probably see at this point that it will continue. Are we ready to write our proof?

### ■ Example 2.7. Proof Number 1

To show

$$0 + 1 + 2 + \cdots + n = n(n+1)/2 \qquad \text{for every } n \geq 0$$

$$
\begin{aligned}
n = 0 : &\quad 0 = 0(0+1)/2 \\
n = 1 : &\quad 0 + 1 = 0(0+1)/2 + 1 \quad \text{(by using the result for } n = 0) \\
&\qquad\qquad = 1(0/2 + 1) \\
&\qquad\qquad = 1(0+2)/2 \\
&\qquad\qquad = 1(1+1)/2 \\
n = 2 : &\quad 0 + 1 + 2 = 1(1+1)/2 + 2 \quad \text{(by using the result for } n = 1) \\
&\qquad\qquad = 2(1/2 + 1) \\
&\qquad\qquad = 2(1+2)/2 \\
&\qquad\qquad = 2(2+1)/2
\end{aligned}
$$

$$n = 3: \quad 0 + 1 + 2 + 3 = 2(2 + 1)/2 + 3 \quad \text{(by using the result for } n = 2)$$
$$= 3(2/2 + 1)$$
$$= 3(2 + 2)/2$$
$$= 3(3 + 1)/2$$

Since this pattern continues indefinitely, the formula is true for every $n \geq 0$.

---

Now let us criticize this proof. The conclusion, "the formula is true for every $n \geq 0$," is supposed to follow from the fact that "this pattern continues indefinitely." The phrase "this pattern" refers to the calculation that we have done three times, to derive the formula for $n = 1$ from $n = 0$, for $n = 2$ from $n = 1$, and for $n = 3$ from $n = 2$. There are at least two clear deficiencies in the proof. One is that we have not said explicitly what "this pattern" is. The second, which is more serious, is that we have not made any attempt to justify the assertion that it continues indefinitely. In this example, the pattern is obvious enough that people might accept the assertion without much argument. However, it would be fair to say that the most important statement in the proof is the one for which no reasons are given!

Our second version of the proof tries to correct both these problems at once: to describe the pattern precisely by doing the calculation, not just for three particular values of $n$ but for an *arbitrary* value of $n$, and in the process, to demonstrate that the pattern does not depend on the value of $n$ and therefore *does* continue indefinitely.

### ■ Example 2.7. Proof Number 2

To show

$$0 + 1 + 2 + \cdots + n = n(n + 1)/2 \qquad \text{for every } n \geq 0$$

$$n = 0: \qquad\qquad 0 = 0(0 + 1)/2$$
$$n = 1: \qquad\quad 0 + 1 = 0(0 + 1)/2 + 1 \quad \text{(by using the result for } n = 0)$$
$$= 1(0/2 + 1)$$
$$= 1(0 + 2)/2$$
$$= 1(1 + 1)/2$$
$$n = 2: \qquad 0 + 1 + 2 = 1(1 + 1)/2 + 2 \quad \text{(by using the result for } n = 1)$$
$$= 2(1/2 + 1)$$
$$= 2(1 + 2)/2$$
$$= 2(2 + 1)/2$$
$$n = 3: \quad 0 + 1 + 2 + 3 = 2(2 + 1)/2 + 3 \quad \text{(by using the result for } n = 2)$$
$$= 3(2/2 + 1)$$
$$= 3(2 + 2)/2$$
$$= 3(3 + 1)/2$$

In general, for any value of $k \geq 0$, the formula for $n = k + 1$ can be derived from the one for $n = k$ as follows:

$$0 + 1 + 2 + \cdots + (k+1) = (0 + 1 + \cdots + k) + (k+1)$$
$$= k(k+1)/2 + (k+1) \quad \text{(from the result for } n = k)$$
$$= (k+1)(k/2 + 1)$$
$$= (k+1)(k+2)/2$$
$$= (k+1)((k+1) + 1)/2$$

Therefore, the formula holds for every $n \geq 0$.

We might now say that the proof has more than it needs. Presenting the calculations for three specific values of $n$ originally made it easier for the reader to spot the pattern; now, however, the pattern has been stated explicitly. To the extent that the argument for these three specific cases is taken to be part of the proof, it obscures the two *essential* parts of the proof: (1) checking the formula for the initial value of $n$, $n = 0$, and (2) showing in general that once we have obtained the formula for one value of $n$ ($n = k$), we can derive it for the next value ($n = k + 1$). These two facts together are what allow us to conclude that the formula holds for every $n \geq 0$. Neither by itself would be enough. (On one hand, the formula for $n = 0$, or even for the first million values of $n$, might be true just by accident. On the other hand, it would not help to know that we can always derive the formula for the case $n = k + 1$ from the one for the case $n = k$, if we could never get off the ground by showing that it *is* actually true for some starting value of $k$.)

The principle that we have used in this example can now be formulated in general.

### The Principle of Mathematical Induction

Suppose $P(n)$ is a statement involving an integer $n$. Then to prove that $P(n)$ is true for every $n \geq n_0$, it is sufficient to show these two things:

1. $P(n_0)$ is true.
2. For any $k \geq n_0$, if $P(k)$ is true, then $P(k + 1)$ is true.

A *proof by induction* is an application of this principle. The two parts of such a proof are called the *basis step* and the *induction* step. In the induction step, we *assume* that $k$ is a number $\geq n_0$ and that the statement $P(n)$ is true in the case $n = k$; we call this assumption the *induction hypothesis*. Let us return to our example one last time in order to illustrate the format of a proof by induction.

### ■ Example 2.7. Proof Number 3 (by induction)

Let $P(n)$ be the statement

$$1 + 2 + 3 + \cdots + n = n(n+1)/2$$

To show that $P(n)$ is true for every $n \geq 0$.

**Basis step.** We must show that $P(0)$ is true. $P(0)$ is the statement $0 = 0(0 + 1)/2$, and this is obviously true.

**Induction hypothesis.**

$$k \geq 0 \quad \text{and} \quad 1 + 2 + 3 + \cdots + k = k(k+1)/2$$

**Statement to be shown in induction step.**

$$1 + 2 + 3 + \cdots + (k+1) = (k+1)((k+1)+1)/2$$

**Proof of induction step.**

$$
\begin{aligned}
1 + 2 + 3 + \cdots + (k+1) &= (1 + 2 + \cdots + k) + (k+1) \\
&= k(k+1)/2 + (k+1) \quad \text{(by the induction hypothesis)} \\
&= (k+1)(k/2 + 1) \\
&= (k+1)(k+2)/2 \\
&= (k+1)((k+1)+1)/2
\end{aligned}
$$

Whether or not you follow this format exactly, it is advisable always to include in your proof explicit statements of the following:

- The general statement involving $n$ that is to be proved.
- The statement to which it reduces in the basis step (the general statement, but with $n_0$ substituted for $n$).
- The induction hypothesis (the general statement, with $k$ substituted for $n$, and preceded by "$k \geq n_0$, and").
- The statement to be shown in the induction step (with $k + 1$ substituted for $n$).
- The point during the induction step at which the induction hypothesis is used.

The advantage of formulating a general principle of induction is that it supplies a general framework for proofs of this type. If you read in a journal article the phrase "It can be shown by induction that . . . ," even if the details are missing, you can supply them. Although including these five items explicitly may seem laborious at first, the advantage is that it can help you to clarify for yourself exactly what you are trying to do in the proof. Very often, once you have gotten to this point, filling in the remaining details is a straightforward process.

| **EXAMPLE 2.8** | Strings of the Form $0y1$ Must Contain the Substring 01 |

Let us prove the following statement: For any $x \in \{0, 1\}^*$, if $x$ begins with 0 and ends with 1 (i.e., $x = 0y1$ for some string $y$), then $x$ must contain the substring 01.

You may wonder whether this statement requires an induction proof; let us begin with an argument that does not involve induction, at least explicitly. If $x = 0y1$ for some string $y \in \{0, 1\}^*$, then $x$ must contain at least one 1. The *first* 1 in $x$ cannot occur at the beginning, since $x$ starts with 0; therefore, the first 1 must be immediately preceded by a 0, which means that $x$ contains the substring 01. It would be hard to imagine a proof much simpler than this, and it seems convincing. It is interesting to observe, however, that this proof uses a fact about natural numbers (every nonempty subset has a smallest element) that is equivalent to the principle of mathematical induction. We will return to this statement later, when we have a slightly modified version of the induction principle. See Example 2.12 and the discussion before that example.

In any case, we are interested in illustrating the principle of induction at least as much as in the result itself. Let us try to construct an induction proof. Our initial problem is that mathematical induction is a way of proving statements of the form "For every $n \geq n_0, \ldots,$" and our statement is not of this form. This is easy to fix, and the solution was suggested at the beginning of this section. Consider the statement $P(n)$: If $|x| = n$ and $x = 0y1$ for some string $y \in \{0, 1\}^*$, then $x$ contains the substring 01. In other words, we are introducing an integer $n$ into our statement, specifically in order to use induction. If we can prove that $P(n)$ is true for every $n \geq 2$, it will follow that the original statement is true. (The integer we choose is the length of the string, and we could describe the method of proof as *induction on the length of the string*. There are other possible choices; see Exercise 2.6.)

In the basis step, we wish to prove the statement "If $|x| = 2$ and $x = 0y1$ for some string $y \in \{0, 1\}^*$, then $x$ contains the substring 01." This statement is true, because if $|x| = 2$ and $x = 0y1$, then $y$ must be the null string $\Lambda$, and we may conclude that $x = 01$. Our induction hypothesis will be the statement: $k \geq 2$, and if $|x| = k$ and $x = 0y1$ for some string $y \in \{0, 1\}^*$, then $x$ contains the substring 01. In the induction step, we must show: if $|x| = k + 1$ and $x = 0y1$ for some $y \in \{0, 1\}^*$, then $x$ contains the substring 01. (These three statements are obtained from the original statement $P(n)$ very simply: first, by substituting 0 for $n$; second, by substituting $k$ for $n$, and adding the phrase "$k \geq 2$, and" at the beginning; third, by substituting $k + 1$ for $n$. These three steps are always the same, and the basis step is often as easy to prove as it is here. Now the mechanical part is over, and we must actually think about how to continue the proof!)

We have a string $x$ of length $k + 1$, about which we want to prove something. We have an induction hypothesis that tells us something about certain strings of length $k$, the ones that begin with 0 and end with 1. In order to apply the induction hypothesis, we need a string of length $k$ to apply it to. We can get a string of length $k$ from $x$ by leaving out one symbol. Let us try deleting the initial 0. (See Exercise 2.5.) The remainder, $y1$, is certainly a string of length $k$, and we know that it ends in 1, but it may not begin with 0—and we can apply the induction hypothesis only to strings that do. However, if $y1$ does not begin with 0, it must begin with 1, and in this case $x$ starts with the substring 01! If $y1$ does begin with 0, then the induction hypothesis tells us that it must contain the substring 01, so that $x = 0y1$ must contain the substring too.

Now that we have figured out the crucial steps, we can afford to be a little more concise in our official proof. We are trying to prove that for every $n \geq 2$, $P(n)$ is true, where $P(n)$ is the statement: If $|x| = n$ and $x = 0y1$ for some string $y \in \{0, 1\}^*$, then $x$ contains the substring 01.

**Basis step.** We must show that the statement $P(2)$ is true. $P(2)$ says that if $|x| = 2$ and $x = 0y$ for some $y \in \{0, 1\}^*$, then $x$ contains the substring 01. $P(2)$ is true, because if $|x| = 2$ and $x = 0y1$ for some $y$, then $x = 01$.

**Induction hypothesis.** $k \geq 2$ and $P(k)$; in other words, if $|x| = k$ and $x = 0y1$ for some $y \in \{0, 1\}^*$, then $x$ contains the substring 01.

**Statement to be shown in induction step.** $P(k + 1)$; that is, if $|x| = k + 1$ and $x = 0y1$ for some $y \in \{0, 1\}^*$, then $x$ contains the substring 01.

**Proof of induction step.** Since $|x| = k + 1$ and $x = 0y1$, $|y1| = k$. If $y$ begins with 1, then $x$ begins with the substring 01. If $y$ begins with 0, then $y1$ begins with 0 and ends with 1; by the induction hypothesis, $y$ contains the substring 01, and therefore $x$ does also.

---

**EXAMPLE 2.9**    Verifying a Portion of a Program

The program fragment below is written in pseudocode. Lowercase letters represent constants, uppercase letters represent variables, and the constant $n$ is assumed to be nonnegative:

```
Y = 1;
for I = 1 to n
    Y = Y * x;
write(Y);
```

We would like to show that when this code is executed, the value printed out is $x^n$. We do this in a slightly roundabout way, by introducing a new integer $j$, the number of iterations of the loop that have been performed. Let $P(j)$ be the statement that the value of $Y$ after $j$ iterations is $x^j$. The result we want will follow from the fact that $P(j)$ is true for any $j \geq 0$, and the fact that "For $I = 1$ to $n$" results in $n$ iterations of the loop.

**Basis step.**  $P(0)$ is the statement that after 0 iterations of the loop, $Y$ has the value $x^0$. This is true because $Y$ receives the initial value 1 and after 0 iterations of the loop its value is unchanged.

**Inductive hypothesis.** $k \geq 0$, and after $k$ iterations of the loop the value of $Y$ is $x^k$.

**Statement to be proved in induction step.** After $k + 1$ iterations of the loop, the value of $Y$ is $x^{k+1}$.

**Proof of induction step.** The effect of the assignment statement $Y = Y * x$ is to replace the old value of $Y$ by that value times $x$; therefore, the value of $Y$ after any iteration is $x$ times the value before that iteration. Since $x * x^k = x^{k+1}$, the proof is complete.

---

Although the program fragment in this example is very simple, the example should suggest that the principle of mathematical induction can be a useful technique for verifying the correctness of programs. For another example, see Exercise 2.56.

You may occasionally find the principle of mathematical induction in a disguised form, which we could call the *minimal counterexample principle*. The last example in this section illustrates this.

---

**EXAMPLE 2.10**    A Proof Using the Minimal Counterexample Principle

*To show:* For every integer $n \geq 0$, $5^n - 2^n$ is divisible by 3.

Just as in an ordinary induction proof, we begin by checking that $P(n)$ is true for the starting value of $n$. This is true here, since $5^0 - 2^0 = 1 - 1 = 0$, and 0 is divisible by 3. Now if it is *not* true that $P(n)$ is true for every $n \geq 0$, then there are values of $n$ greater than or equal to 0 for which $P(n)$ is false, and therefore there must be a smallest such value, say $n = k$.

(See Example 2.12.) Since we have verified $P(0)$, $k$ must be at least 1. Therefore, $k - 1$ is at least 0, and since $k$ is the smallest value for which $P$ fails, $P(k - 1)$ is true. This means that $5^{k-1} - 2^{k-1}$ is a multiple of 3, say $3j$. Then, however,

$$5^k - 2^k = 5 * 5^{k-1} - 2 * 2^{k-1} = 3 * 5^{k-1} + 2 * (5^{k-1} - 2^{k-1}) = 3 * 5^{k-1} + 2 * 3j$$

This expression is divisible by 3. We have derived a contradiction, which allows us to conclude that our original assumption is false. Therefore, $P(n)$ is true for every $n \geq 0$.

---

You can probably see the similarity between this proof and one that uses the principle of mathematical induction. Although an induction proof has the advantage that it does not involve proof by contradiction, both approaches are equally valid.

Not every statement involving an integer $n$ is appropriate for mathematical induction. Using this technique on the statement

$$(2^n + 1)(2^n - 1) = 2^{2n} - 1$$

would be silly because the proof of the induction step would not require the induction hypothesis at all. The formula for $n = k + 1$, or for any other value, can be obtained immediately by expanding the left side of the formula and using laws of exponents. The proof would not be a *real* induction proof, and it would be misleading to classify it as one.

A general rule of thumb is that if you are tempted to use a phrase like "Repeat this process for each $n$," or "Since this pattern continues indefinitely" in a proof, there is a good chance that the proof can be made more precise by using mathematical induction. When you encounter one of these phrases while reading a proof, it is very likely a substitute for an induction argument. In this case, supplying the details of the induction may help you to understand the proof better.

## 2.3 | THE STRONG PRINCIPLE OF MATHEMATICAL INDUCTION

Sometimes, as in our first example, a proof by mathematical induction is called for, but the induction principle in Section 2.2 is not the most convenient tool.

### Integers Bigger Than 2 Have Prime Factorizations          **EXAMPLE 2.11**

---

Recall that a *prime* is a positive integer, 2 or bigger, that has no positive integer divisors except itself and 1. Part of the fundamental theorem of arithmetic is that every integer can be factored into primes. More precisely, let $P(n)$ be the statement that $n$ is either prime or the product of two or more primes; we will try to prove that $P(n)$ is true for every $n \geq 2$.

The basis step does not present any problems. $P(2)$ is true, since 2 is a prime. If we proceed as usual, then we take as the induction hypothesis the statement that $k \geq 2$ and $k$ is either prime or the product of two or more primes. We would like to show that $k + 1$ is either prime or the product of primes. If $k + 1$ happens to be prime, there is nothing left to prove. Otherwise, by the definition of prime, $k + 1$ has some positive integer divisor other than itself and 1. This means $k + 1 = r * s$ for some positive integers $r$ and $s$, neither of which is 1 or $k + 1$. It follows that $r$ and $s$ must both be greater than 1 and less than $k + 1$.

In order to finish the induction step, we would like to show that $r$ and $s$ are both either primes or products of primes; it would then follow, since $k + 1$ is the product of $r$ and $s$, that $k + 1$ is a product of two or more primes. Unfortunately, the only information our induction hypothesis gives us is that $k$ is a prime or a product of primes, and this tells us nothing about $r$ or $s$.

Consider, however, the following intuitive argument, in which we set about verifying the statement $P(n)$ one value of $n$ at a time:

2 is a prime.

3 is a prime.

$4 = 2 * 2$, which is a product of primes since $P(2)$ is known to be true.

5 is a prime.

$6 = 2 * 3$, which is a product of primes since $P(2)$ and $P(3)$ are known to be true.

7 is a prime.

$8 = 2 * 4$, which is a product of primes since $P(2)$ and $P(4)$ are known to be true.

$9 = 3 * 3$, which is a product of primes since $P(3)$ is known to be true.

$10 = 2 * 5$, which is a product of primes since $P(2)$ and $P(5)$ are known to be true.

11 is a prime.

$12 = 2 * 6$, which is a product of primes since $P(2)$ and $P(6)$ are known to be true.

. . .

This seems as convincing as the intuitive argument given at the start of Example 2.7. Furthermore, we can describe explicitly the pattern illustrated by the first 11 steps: For each $k \geq 2$, either $k + 1$ is prime or it is the product of two numbers $r$ and $s$ for which the proposition $P$ has already been shown to hold.

The difference between the pattern appearing here and the one we saw in Example 2.7 is this: At each step in the earlier example we were able to obtain the truth of $P(k + 1)$ by knowing that $P(k)$ was true, and here we need to know that $P$ holds, not only for $k$ but also for all the values up to $k$. The following modified version of the induction principle will allow our proof to proceed.

---

### The Strong Principle of Mathematical Induction

Suppose $P(n)$ is a statement involving an integer $n$. Then to prove that $P(n)$ is true for every $n \geq n_0$, it is sufficient to show these two things:

1. $P(n_0)$ is true.
2. For any $k \geq n_0$, if $P(n)$ is true for every $n$ satisfying $n_0 \leq n \leq k$, then $P(k + 1)$ is true.

To use this principle in a proof, we follow the same steps as before except for the way we state the induction hypothesis. The statement here is that $k$ is some integer $\geq n_0$ and that *all* the statements $P(n_0)$, $P(n_0 + 1), \ldots, P(k)$ are true. With this change, we can finish the proof we began earlier.

### ■ Example 2.11. Proof by induction.

*To show:* $P(n)$ is true for every $n \geq 2$, where $P(n)$ is the statement: $n$ is either a prime or a product of two or more primes.

> **Basis step.** $P(2)$ is the statement that 2 is either a prime or a product of two or more primes. This is true because 2 is a prime.
>
> **Induction hypothesis.** $k \geq 2$, and for every $n$ with $2 \leq n \leq k$, $n$ is either prime or a product of two or more primes.
>
> **Statement to be shown in induction step.** $k + 1$ is either prime or a product of two or more primes.
>
> **Proof of induction step.** We consider two cases. If $k + 1$ is prime, the statement $P(k + 1)$ is true. Otherwise, by definition of a prime, $k + 1 = r * s$, for some positive integers $r$ and $s$, neither of which is 1 or $k + 1$. It follows that $2 \leq r \leq k$ and $2 \leq s \leq k$. Therefore, by the induction hypothesis, both $r$ and $s$ are either prime or the product of two or more primes. Therefore, their product $k + 1$ is the product of two or more primes, and $P(k + 1)$ is true.

The strong principle of induction is also referred to as the principle of *complete* induction, or *course-of-values* induction. The first example suggests that it is as plausible intuitively as the ordinary induction principle, and in fact the two are equivalent. As to whether they are *true*, the answer may seem a little surprising. Neither can be proved using other standard properties of the natural numbers. (Neither can be disproved, either!) This means, in effect, that in order to use the induction principle, we must adopt it as an axiom. A well-known set of axioms for the natural numbers, the *Peano* axioms, includes one similar to the induction principle.

Twice in Section 2.2 we had occasion to use the *well-ordering* principle for the natural numbers, which says that every nonempty subset of $\mathcal{N}$ has a smallest element. As obvious as this statement probably seems, it is also impossible to prove without using induction or something comparable. In the next example, we show that it follows from the strong principle of induction. (It can be shown to be equivalent.)

## The Well-ordering Principle for the Natural Numbers  **EXAMPLE 2.12**

*To prove:* Every nonempty subset of $\mathcal{N}$, the set of natural numbers, has a smallest element. (What we are actually proving is that if the strong principle of mathematical induction is true, then every nonempty subset of $\mathcal{N}$ has a smallest element.)

First we need to find a way to express the result in the form "For every $n \geq n_0$, $P(n)$." Every nonempty subset $A$ of $\mathcal{N}$ contains a natural number, say $n$. If every subset of $\mathcal{N}$

containing $n$ has a smallest element, then $A$ does. With this in mind, we let $P(n)$ be the statement "Every subset of $\mathcal{N}$ containing $n$ has a smallest element." We prove that $P(n)$ is true for every $n \geq 0$. (See Exercise 2.7.)

> **Basis step.** $P(0)$ is the statement that every subset of $\mathcal{N}$ containing 0 has a smallest element. This is true because 0 is the smallest natural number and therefore the smallest element of the subset.
>
> **Induction hypothesis.** $k \geq 0$, and for every $n$ with $0 \leq n \leq k$, every subset of $\mathcal{N}$ containing $n$ has a smallest element. (Put more simply, $k \geq 0$ and every subset of $\mathcal{N}$ containing an integer less than or equal to $k$ has a smallest element.)
>
> **Statement to be shown in induction step.** Every subset of $\mathcal{N}$ containing $k + 1$ has a smallest element.
>
> **Proof of induction step.** Let $A$ be any subset of $\mathcal{N}$ containing $k + 1$. We consider two cases. If $A$ contains no natural number less than $k + 1$, then $k + 1$ is the smallest element of $A$. Otherwise, $A$ contains some natural number $n$ with $n \leq k$. In this case, by the induction hypothesis, $A$ contains a smallest element.

The strong principle of mathematical induction is more appropriate here, since when we come up with an $n$ to which we want to apply the induction hypothesis, all we know about $n$ is that $n \leq k$. We do *not* know that $n = k$. It may not be obvious at the beginning of an induction proof whether the strong induction principle is required or whether you can get by with the original version. You can avoid worrying about this by *always* using the strong version. It allows you to adopt a stronger induction hypothesis, and so if an induction proof is possible at all, it will certainly be possible with the strong version. In any case, you can put off the decision until you reach the point where you have to prove $P(k + 1)$. If you can do this with only the assumption that $P(k)$ is true, then the original principle of induction is sufficient. If you need information about earlier values of $n$ as well, the strong version is needed.

We will see more examples of how the strong principle of mathematical induction is applied once we have discussed recursive definitions and the close relationship between them and mathematical induction.

## 2.4 | RECURSIVE DEFINITIONS

### 2.4.1 Recursive Definitions of Functions with Domain $\mathcal{N}$

The chances are that in a programming course you have seen a translation into some high-level programming language of the following definition:

$$n! = \begin{cases} 1 & \text{if } n = 0 \\ n * (n - 1)! & \text{if } n > 0 \end{cases}$$

This is one of the simplest examples of a recursive, or inductive, definition. It defines the factorial function on the set of natural numbers, first by defining the value at 0, and then by defining the value at any larger natural number in terms of its value at the previous one. There is an obvious analogy here to the basis step and the induction step in a proof by mathematical induction. The intuitive reason this is a valid definition is the same as the intuitive reason the principle of induction should be true: If we think of defining $n!$ for all the values of $n$ in order, beginning with $n = 0$, then for any $k \geq 0$, eventually we will have defined the value of $k!$, and at that point the definition will tell us how to obtain $(k + 1)!$.

In this section, we will look at a number of examples of recursive definitions of functions and examine more closely the relationship between recursive definitions and proofs by induction. We begin with more examples of functions on the set of natural numbers.

The Fibonacci Function    **EXAMPLE 2.13**

The Fibonacci function $f$ is usually defined as follows:

$$f(0) = 1$$
$$f(1) = 1$$
$$\text{for every } n \geq 1, \ f(n+1) = f(n) + f(n-1)$$

To evaluate $f(4)$, for example, we can use the definition in either a top-down fashion:

$$f(4) = f(3) + f(2)$$
$$= (f(2) + f(1)) + f(2)$$
$$= ((f(1) + f(0)) + f(1)) + (f(1) + f(0))$$
$$= ((1 + 1) + 1) + (1 + 1)$$
$$= 5$$

or a bottom-up fashion:

$$f(0) = 1$$
$$f(1) = 1$$
$$f(2) = f(1) + f(0) = 1 + 1 = 2$$
$$f(3) = f(2) + f(1) = 2 + 1 = 3$$
$$f(4) = f(3) + f(2) = 3 + 2 = 5$$

It is possible to give a nonrecursive algebraic formula for the number $f(n)$; see Exercise 2.53. However, the recursive definition is the one that most people remember and prefer to use.

If the definition of the factorial function is reminiscent of the principle of mathematical induction, then the definition of the Fibonacci function suggests the strong principle of induction. This is because the definition of $f(n + 1)$ involves not only $f(n)$ but $f(n - 1)$. This observation is useful in proving facts about $f$. For example, let us prove that

$$\text{for every } n \geq 0, \ f(n) \leq (5/3)^n$$

**Basis step.** We must show that $f(0) \leq (5/3)^0$; this is true, since $f(0)$ and $(5/3)^0$ are both 1.

**Induction hypothesis.** $k \geq 0$, and for every $n$ with $0 \leq n \leq k$, $f(n) \leq (5/3)^n$.

**Statement to show in induction step.** $f(k+1) \leq (5/3)^{k+1}$.

**Proof of induction step.** Because of the way $f$ is defined, we consider two cases in order to make sure that our proof is valid for *every* value of $k \geq 0$. If $k = 0$, then $f(k+1) = f(1) = 1$, by definition, and in this case the inequality is clearly true. If $k > 0$, then we must use the recursive part of the definition, which is $f(k+1) = f(k) + f(k-1)$. Since both $k$ and $k-1$ are $\leq k$, we may apply the induction hypothesis to both terms, obtaining

$$
\begin{aligned}
f(k+1) &= f(k) + f(k-1) \\
&\leq (5/3)^k + (5/3)^{k-1} \\
&= (5/3)^{k-1}(5/3 + 1) \\
&= (5/3)^{k-1}(8/3) \\
&= (5/3)^{k-1}(24/9) \\
&< (5/3)^{k-1}(25/9) \ = \ (5/3)^{k+1}
\end{aligned}
$$

**EXAMPLE 2.14**    The Union of $n$ Sets

Suppose $A_1, A_2, \ldots$ are subsets of some universal set $U$. For each $n \geq 0$, we may define $\bigcup_{i=1}^{n} A_i$ as follows:

$$
\bigcup_{i=1}^{0} A_i = \emptyset
$$

$$
\text{for every } n \geq 0, \ \bigcup_{i=1}^{n+1} A_i = \left( \bigcup_{i=1}^{n} A_i \right) \cup A_{n+1}
$$

For each $n$, $\bigcup_{i=1}^{n} A_i$ is a set, in particular a subset of $U$; therefore, it makes sense to view the recursive definition as defining a function from the set of natural numbers to the set of subsets of $U$. What we have effectively done in this definition is to extend the binary operation of union so that it can be applied to $n$ operands. (We discussed this possibility for associative operations like union near the end of Section 1.1.) This procedure is familiar to you in other settings, although you may not have encountered a formal recursive definition like this one before. When you add $n$ numbers in an expression like $\sum_{i=1}^{n} a_i$, for example, you are extending the binary operation of addition to $n$ operands. The notational device used to do this is the summation sign: $\Sigma$ bears the same relation to the binary operation $+$ that $\bigcup$ does to the binary operation $\cup$. A recursive definition of $\Sigma$ would follow the one above in every detail:

$$
\sum_{i=1}^{0} a_i = 0
$$

$$
\text{for every } n \geq 0, \ \sum_{i=1}^{n+1} a_i = \left( \sum_{i=1}^{n} a_i \right) + a_{n+1}
$$

Similarly, we could define the intersection of $n$ sets, the product of $n$ numbers, the concatenation of $n$ strings, the concatenation of $n$ languages, and so forth. (The only difficulty we would have with the last two is that we have not introduced a notation for the concatenation operator—we have written the concatenation of $x$ and $y$ as simply $xy$.) We are also free to use one of these general definitions in a special case. For example, we might consider the concatenation of $n$ languages, all of which are the same language $L$:

$$L^0 = \{\Lambda\}$$
$$\text{for every } n \geq 0, \ L^{n+1} = L^n L$$

Of course, we already have nonrecursive definitions of many of these things. Our definition of $\bigcup_{i=1}^n A_i$ in Section 1.1 is

$$\bigcup_{i=1}^{n} A_i = \{x \mid x \in A_i \text{ for at least one } i \text{ with } 1 \leq i \leq n\}$$

The definition of $L^n$ in Section 1.5 is

$$L^n = LL \cdots L \ (n \text{ factors in all})$$

and we also described it as the set of all strings that can be obtained by concatenating $n$ elements of $L$. It may not be obvious that we have gained anything by introducing the recursive definition. The nonrecursive definition of the $n$-fold union is clear enough, and even with the ellipses $(\ldots)$ it is not difficult to determine which strings are included in $L^n$. However, the recursive definition has the same advantage over the ellipses that we discussed in the first proof in Example 2.7; rather than *suggesting* what the general step is in this $n$-fold concatenation, it comes right out and says it. After all, when you construct an element of $L^n$, you concatenate two strings, not $n$ strings at once. The recursive definition is more consistent with the *binary* nature of concatenation, and more explicit about how the concatenation is done: An $(n + 1)$-fold concatenation is obtained by concatenating an element of $L^k$ and an element of $L$. The recursive definition has a dynamic, or algorithmic, quality that the other one lacks. Finally, and probably most important, the recursive definition has a practical advantage. It gives us a natural way of constructing proofs using mathematical induction.

Suppose we want to prove the generalized De Morgan law:

$$\text{for every } n \geq 0, \ \left(\bigcup_{i=1}^{n} A_i\right)' = \bigcap_{i=1}^{n} A_i'$$

In the induction step, we must show something about

$$\left(\bigcup_{i=1}^{k+1} A_i\right)'$$

Using the recursive definition, we begin by replacing this with

$$\left(\left(\bigcup_{i=1}^{k} A_i\right) \cup A_{k+1}\right)'$$

at which point we can use the original De Morgan law to complete the proof, since we have expressed the $(k + 1)$-fold union as a *two*-fold union.

This example illustrates again the close relationship between the principle of mathematical induction and the idea of recursive definitions. Not only are the two ideas similar in principle, they are almost inseparable in practice. Recursive definitions are useful in constructing induction proofs, and induction is the natural proof technique to use on objects defined recursively.

The relationship is so close, in fact, that in induction proofs we might use recursive definitions without realizing it. In Example 2.7, we proved that

$$1 + 2 + \cdots + n = n(n + 1)/2$$

and the crucial observation in the induction step was that

$$(1 + 2 + \cdots + (k + 1)) = (1 + 2 + \cdots + k) + (k + 1)$$

This is exactly the formula we would have obtained from the recursive definition of the summation operator $\Sigma$ in Example 2.14. In other words, although we had not formally adopted this definition at the time, the property of summation that we needed for the induction argument was the one the definition provides.

### 2.4.2 Recursive Definitions of Sets

We can also define a single set recursively. Although such a definition may not involve an integer $n$ explicitly, the principle is similar. We specify certain objects that are in the set to start with, and we describe one or more general methods for obtaining new elements of the set from existing ones.

---

**EXAMPLE 2.15**    Recursive Definition of $L^*$

---

Suppose $L$ is a language over some alphabet $\Sigma$. We have previously defined $L^*$ as the union of the sets $L^n$ for $n \geq 0$. From our recursive definition of $L^n$ it follows that for any $n$, any $x \in L^n$, and any $y \in L$, the string $xy$ is an element of $L^{n+1}$ and therefore of $L^*$. Furthermore, every element of $L^*$ can be obtained this way except $\Lambda$, which comes from $L^0$. This suggests the following more direct recursive definition of $L^*$.

1. $\Lambda \in L^*$.
2. For any $x \in L^*$ and any $y \in L$, $xy \in L^*$.
3. No string is in $L^*$ unless it can be obtained by using rules 1 and 2.

To illustrate, let $L = \{a, ab\}$. According to rule 1, $\Lambda \in L^*$. One application of rule 2 adds the strings in $L^1 = L$, which are $\Lambda a = a$ and $\Lambda ab = ab$. Another application of rule 2 adds the strings in $L^2$, which are $\Lambda a$, $\Lambda ab$, $aa$, $aab$, $aba$, and $abab$. For any $k \geq 0$, a string obtained by concatenating $k$ elements of $L$ can be produced from the definition by using $k$ applications of rule 2.

An even simpler illustration is to let $L$ be $\Sigma$, which is itself a language over $\Sigma$. Then a string of length $k$ in $\Sigma^*$, which is a concatenation of $k$ symbols belonging to $\Sigma$, can be produced by $k$ applications of rule 2.

This way of defining $L^*$ recursively is not the only way. Here is another possibility.

1. $\Lambda \in L^*$.
2. For any $x \in L$, $x \in L^*$.

**3.** For any two elements $x$ and $y$ of $L^*$, $xy \in L^*$.
**4.** No string is in $L^*$ unless it can be obtained by using rules 1, 2, and 3.

In this approach, rules 1 and 2 are both necessary in the basis part of the definition, since rule 1 by itself would provide no strings other than $\Lambda$ to concatenate in the recursive part.

The first definition is a little closer to our original definition of $L^*$, and perhaps a little easier to work with, because there is a direct correspondence between the applications of rule 2 needed to generate an element of $L^*$ and the strings of $L$ that are being concatenated. The second definition allows more flexibility as to how to produce a string in the language. There is a sense, however, in which both definitions capture the idea of all possible concatenations of strings of $L$, and for this reason it may not be too difficult to convince yourself that both definitions really do work—that the set being defined is $L^*$ in each case. Exercise 2.63 asks you to consider the question in more detail.

### Palindromes    **EXAMPLE 2.16**

Let $\Sigma$ be any alphabet. The language *pal* of *palindromes* over $\Sigma$ can be defined as follows:

**1.** $\Lambda \in pal$.
**2.** For any $a \in \Sigma$, $a \in pal$.
**3.** For any $x \in pal$ and any $a \in \Sigma$, $axa \in pal$.
**4.** No string is in *pal* unless it can be obtained by using rules 1, 2, and 3.

The strings that can be obtained by using rules 1 and 2 exclusively are the elements of *pal* of even length, and those obtained by using rules 2 and 3 are of odd length. A simple nonrecursive definition of *pal* is that it is the set of strings that read the same backwards as forwards. (See Exercise 2.60.)

In Example 2.14, we mentioned the algorithmic, or constructive, nature of the recursive definition of $L^n$. In the case of a language such as *pal*, this aspect of the recursive definition can be useful both from the standpoint of generating elements of the language and from the standpoint of recognizing elements of the language. The definition says, on the one hand, that we can construct palindromes by starting with either $\Lambda$ or a single symbol, and continuing to concatenate a symbol onto both ends of the current string. On the other hand, it says that if we wish to test a string to see if it's a palindrome, we may first compare the leftmost and rightmost symbols, and if they are equal, reduce the problem to testing the remaining substring.

### Fully Parenthesized Algebraic Expressions    **EXAMPLE 2.17**

Let $\Sigma$ be the alphabet $\{i, (, ), +, -\}$. Below is a recursive definition of the language $AE$ of fully parenthesized algebraic expressions involving the binary operators $+$ and $-$ and the identifier $i$. The term *fully parenthesized* means exactly one pair of parentheses for every operator.

**1.** $i \in AE$.
**2.** For any $x, y \in AE$, both $(x + y)$ and $(x - y)$ are elements of $AE$.
**3.** No string is in $AE$ unless it can be obtained by using rules (1) and (2).

Some of the strings in $AE$ are $i$, $(i + i)$, $(i - i)$, $((i + i) - i)$, and $((i - (i - i)) + i)$.

| **EXAMPLE 2.18** | Finite Subsets of the Natural Numbers |

We define a set $\mathcal{F}$ of subsets of the natural numbers as follows:

1. $\emptyset \in \mathcal{F}$.
2. For any $n \in \mathcal{N}$, $\{n\} \in \mathcal{F}$.
3. For any $A$ and $B$ in $\mathcal{F}$, $A \cup B \in \mathcal{F}$.
4. Nothing is in $\mathcal{F}$ unless it can be obtained by using rules 1, 2, and 3.

We can obtain any two-element subset of $\mathcal{N}$ by starting with two one-element sets and using rule 3. Because we can then apply rule 3 to any two-element set $A$ and any one-element set $B$, we obtain all the three-element subsets of $\mathcal{N}$. It is easy to show using mathematical induction that for any natural number $n$, any $n$-element subset of $\mathcal{N}$ is an element of $\mathcal{F}$; we may conclude that $\mathcal{F}$ is the collection of all finite subsets of $\mathcal{N}$.

---

Let us consider the last statement in each of the recursive definitions in this section. In each case, the previous statements describe ways of producing new elements of the set being defined. The last statement is intended to remove any ambiguity: Unless an object can be shown using these previous rules to belong to the set, it does *not* belong to the set.

We might choose to be even a little more explicit. In Example 2.17, we might say, "No string is in $AE$ unless it can be obtained by *a finite number of applications of* rules 1 and 2." Here this extra precision hardly seems necessary, as long as it is understood that "string" means something of finite length; in Example 2.18 it is easier to see that it might be appropriate. One might ask whether there are any infinite sets in $\mathcal{F}$. We would hope that the answer is "no" because we have already agreed that the definition is a reasonable way to define the collection of *finite* subsets of $\mathcal{N}$. On the one hand, we could argue that the only way rule 3 could produce an infinite set would be for one of the sets $A$ or $B$ to be infinite already. On the other hand, think about using the definition to show that an infinite set $C$ is not in $\mathcal{F}$. This means showing that $C$ cannot be obtained by using rule 3. For an infinite set $C$ to be obtained this way, either $A$ or $B$ (both of which must be elements of $\mathcal{F}$) would have to be infinite—but how do we know that cannot happen? The definition is not really precise unless it makes it clear that rules 1 to 3 can be used only a finite number of times in obtaining an element of $\mathcal{F}$. Remember also that we think of a recursive definition as a constructive, or algorithmic, definition, and that in any actual construction we would be able to apply any of the rules in the definition only a finite number of times.

Let us describe even more carefully the steps that would be involved in "a finite number of applications" of rules 1 to 3 in Example 2.18. Take a finite subset $A$ of $\mathcal{N}$ that we might want to obtain from the definition of $\mathcal{F}$, say $A = \{2, 3, 7, 11, 14\}$. There are a number of ways we can use the definition to show that $A \in \mathcal{F}$. One obvious approach is to start with $\{2\}$ and use rule 3 four times, adding one more element each time, so that the four steps give us the subsets $\{2, 3\}$, $\{2, 3, 7\}$, $\{2, 3, 7, 11\}$, and $\{2, 3, 7, 11, 14\}$. Each time, the new subset is obtained by applying rule 3 to two sets, one a set we had obtained earlier by using rule 3, the other a one-element set (one of the elements of $\mathcal{F}$ specified explicitly by rule 2). Another approach would be to start with two one-element sets, say {2} and {7}, to add elements one at a time to each so as to obtain the sets {2, 3} and {7, 11, 14}, and then to use rule 3 once more to obtain their union. In both of these approaches, we can write a *sequence* of sets representing the preliminary steps we take to obtain the one we want. We might include in our sequence all the one-element sets we use, in addition to the two-, three-, or four-element subsets we obtain along the way. In the first case, therefore, the sequence might look like this:

| | | | |
|---|---|---|---|
| 1. {2} | 2. {3} | 3. {2, 3} | 4. {7} |
| 5. {2, 3, 7} | 6. {11} | 7. {2, 3, 7, 11} | 8. {14} |
| 9. {2, 3, 7, 11, 14} | | | |

and in the second case the sequence might be

| | | | |
|---|---|---|---|
| 1. {2} | 2. {3} | 3. {2, 3} | 4. {7} |
| 5. {11} | 6. {7, 11} | 7. {14} | 8. {7, 11, 14} |
| 9. {2, 3, 7, 11, 14} | | | |

In both cases, there is considerable flexibility as to the order of the terms. The significant feature of both sequences is that every term is either one of the specific sets mentioned in statements 1 and 2 of the definition, or it is obtained from two terms appearing earlier in the sequence by using statement 3.

A precise way of expressing statement 4 in the definition would therefore be to say:

No set $A$ is in $\mathcal{F}$ unless there is a positive integer $n$ and a sequence $A_1, A_2, \ldots, A_n$, so that $A_n = A$, and for every $i$ with $1 \le i \le n$, $A_i$ is either $\emptyset$, or a one-element set, or $A_j \cup A_k$ for some $j, k < i$.

A recursive definition of a set like $\mathcal{F}$ is not usually this explicit. Probably the most common approach is to say something like our original statement 4; a less formal approach would be to say "Nothing else is in $\mathcal{F}$," and sometimes the final statement is skipped altogether.

## An Induction Proof Involving a Language Defined Recursively   **EXAMPLE 2.19**

Suppose that the language $L$, a subset of $\{0, 1\}^*$, is defined recursively as follows.

1.   $\Lambda \in L$.
2.   For any $y \in L$, both $0y$ and $0y1$ are in $L$.
3.   No string is in $L$ unless it can be obtained from rules 1 and 2.

In order to determine what the strings in $L$ are, we might try to use the definition to generate the first few elements. We know $\Lambda \in L$. From rule 2 it follows that 0 and 01 are both in $L$. Using rule 2 again, we obtain 00, 001, and 0011; one more application produces 000, 0001, 00011, and 000111. After studying these strings, we may be able to guess that the strings in $L$ are all those of the form $0^i 1^j$, where $i \ge j \ge 0$. Let us prove that every string of this form is in $L$.

To simplify the notation, let $A = \{0^i 1^j \mid i \geq j \geq 0\}$. The statement $A \subseteq L$, as it stands, does not involve an integer. Just as we did in Example 2.8, however, we can introduce the length of a string as an integer on which to base an induction proof.

*To prove:* $A \subseteq L$; i.e., for every $n \geq 0$, every $x \in A$ satisfying $|x| = n$ is an element of $L$.

**Basis step.** We must show that every $x$ in $A$ with $|x| = 0$ is an element of $L$. This is true because if $|x| = 0$, then $x = \Lambda$, and statement 1 in the definition of $L$ tells us that $\Lambda \in L$.

**Induction hypothesis.** $k \geq 0$, and every $x$ in $A$ with $|x| = k$ is an element of $L$.

**Statement to show in induction step.** Every $x$ in $A$ with $|x| = k + 1$ is an element of $L$.

**Proof of induction step.** Suppose $x \in A$, and $|x| = k + 1$. Then $x = 0^i 1^j$, where $i \geq j \geq 0$, and $i + j = k + 1$. We are trying to show that $x \in L$. According to the definition, the only ways this can happen are for $x$ to be $\Lambda$, for $x$ to be $0y$ for some $y \in L$, and for $x$ to be $0y1$ for some $y \in L$. The first case is impossible, since $|x| = k + 1 > 0$. In either of the other cases, we can obtain the conclusion we want *if* we know that the string $y$ is in $L$. Presumably we will show this by using the induction hypothesis. However, at this point we have a slight problem. If $x = 0y1$, then the string $y$ to which we want to apply the induction hypothesis is not of length $k$, but of length $k - 1$. Fortunately, the solution to the problem is easy: Use the strong induction principle instead, which allows us to use the stronger induction hypothesis. The statement to be shown in the induction step remains the same.

**Induction hypothesis (revised).** $k \geq 0$, and every $x$ in $A$ with $|x| \leq k$ is an element of $L$.

**Proof of induction step (corrected version).** Suppose $x \in A$ and $|x| = k + 1$. Then $x = 0^i 1^j$, where $i \geq j \geq 0$ and $i + j = k + 1$. We consider two cases. If $i > j$, then we can write $x = 0y$ for some $y$ that still has at least as many 0's as 1's (i.e., for some $y \in A$). In this case, since $|y| = k$, it follows from the induction hypothesis that $y \in L$; therefore, since $x = 0y$, it follows from the first part of statement 2 in the definition of $L$ that $x$ is also an element of $L$. In the second case, when $i = j$, we know that there must be at least one 0 and one 1 in the string. Therefore, $x = 0y1$ for some $y$. Furthermore, $y \in A$, because $y = 0^{i-1} 1^{j-1}$ and $i = j$. Since $|y| \leq k$, it follows from the induction hypothesis that $y \in L$. Since $x = 0y1$, we can use the second part of statement 2 in the definition of $L$ to conclude that $x \in L$.

---

The two sets $L$ and $A$ are actually equal. We have now proved half of this statement. The other half, the statement $L \subseteq A$, can also be proved by induction on the length of the string (see Exercise 2.41). In the next section, however, we consider another approach to an induction proof, which is more naturally related to the recursive definition of $L$ and is probably easier.

# 2.5 | STRUCTURAL INDUCTION

We have already noticed the very close correspondence between recursive definitions of functions on the set $\mathcal{N}$ and proofs by mathematical induction of properties of those functions. The correspondence is exact, in the sense that when we want to prove something about $f(k+1)$ in the induction step of a proof, we can consult the definition of $f(k+1)$, the recursive part of the definition.

When we began to formulate recursive definitions of sets, there was usually no integer involved explicitly (see Examples 2.15–2.19), and it may have appeared that any correspondence between the recursive definition and induction proofs involving elements of the set would be less direct (even though there is a general similarity between the recursive definition and the induction principle). In this section, we consider the correspondence more carefully. We can start by identifying an integer that arises naturally from the recursive definition, which can be introduced for the purpose of an induction proof. However, when we look more closely at the proof, we will be able to dispense with the integer altogether, and what remains will be an induction proof based on the structure of the definition itself.

The example we use to illustrate this principle is essentially a continuation of Example 2.19.

Continuation of Example 2.19  **EXAMPLE 2.20**

We have the language $L$, defined recursively as follows:

1.  $\Lambda \in L$.
2.  For every $x \in L$, both $0x$ and $0x1$ are in $L$.

The third statement in the definition of $L$ says that every element of $L$ is obtained by starting with $\Lambda$ and applying statement 2 a finite number of times (zero or more).

We also have the language $A = \{0^i 1^j \mid i \geq j \geq 0\}$. In Example 2.19, we proved that $A \subseteq L$, using mathematical induction on the length of the string. Now we wish to prove the opposite inclusion $L \subseteq A$. As we have already pointed out, there is no reason why using the length of the string would not work in an induction proof in this direction too—a string in $L$ has a length, just as every other string does. However, for each element $x$ of $L$, there is another integer that is associated with $x$ not just because $x$ is a string, but specifically because $x$ is an element of $L$. This is the number of times rule 2 is used in order to obtain $x$ from the definition. We construct an induction proof, based on this number, that $L \subseteq A$.

*To prove:* For every $n \geq 0$, every $x \in L$ obtained by $n$ applications of rule 2 is an element of $L$.

> **Basis step.** We must show that if $x \in L$ and $x$ is obtained without using rule 2 at all, then $x \in A$. The only possibility for $x$ in this case is $\Lambda$, and $\Lambda \in A$ because $\Lambda = 0^0 1^0$.
>
> **Induction hypothesis.** $k \geq 0$, and every string in $L$ that can be obtained by $k$ applications of rule 2 is an element of $A$.
>
> **Statement to show in induction step.** Any string in $L$ that can be obtained by $k+1$ applications of rule 2 is in $A$.
>
> **Proof of induction step.** Let $x$ be an element of $L$ that is obtained by $k+1$ applications of rule 2. This means that either $x = 0y$ or $x = 0y1$, where in either case $y$ is a string in $L$ that can be obtained by using the rule $k$ times. By the induction hypothesis, $y \in A$, so that $y = 0^i 1^j$, with $i \geq j \geq 0$. Therefore, either $x = 0^{i+1} 1^j$ or $x = 0^{i+1} 1^{j+1}$, and in either case $x \in A$.

As simple as this proof is, we can make it even simpler. There is a sense in which the integers $k$ and $k+1$ are extraneous. In the induction step, we wish to show that the *new* element $x$ of $L$, the one obtained by applying rule 2 of the definition to some other element $y$ of $L$, is an element of $A$. It is true that $y$ is obtained by applying the rule $k$ times, and therefore $x$ is obtained by applying the rule $k+1$ times. The only fact we need in the induction step, however, is that $y \in A$ and for *any* element $y$ of $L$ that is in $A$, both $0y$ and $0y1$ are also elements of $A$. Once we verify this, $k$ and $k + 1$ are needed only to make the proof fit the framework of a standard induction proof.

Why not just leave them out? We still have a basis step, except that instead of thinking of $\Lambda$ as the string obtained from zero applications of rule 2, we just think of it as the string in rule 1, the basis part of the definition of $L$. In the recursive part of the definition, we apply one of two possible operations to an element $y$ of $L$. What we will need to know about the string $y$ in the induction step is that it is in $A$, and therefore it is appropriate to designate this as our induction hypothesis. The induction step is simply to show that for this string $y$, $0y$ and $0y1$ (the two strings obtained from $y$ by applying the operations in the definition) are both in $L$.

We can call this version of mathematical induction *structural induction*. Although there is an underlying integer involved, just as in an ordinary induction proof, it is usually unnecessary to mention it explicitly. Instead, the steps of the proof follow the structure of the recursive definition directly. Below is our modified proof for this example.

*To prove:* $L \subseteq A$.

**Basis step.** We must show that $\Lambda \in A$. This is true, because $\Lambda = 0^0 1^0$.

**Induction hypothesis.** The string $y \in L$ is an element of $A$.

**Statement to show in induction step.** Both $0y$ and $0y1$ are elements of $A$.

**Proof of induction step.** Since $y \in A$, $y = 0^i 1^j$, with $i \geq j \geq 0$. Therefore, $0y = 0^{i+1} 1^j$, and $0y1 = 0^{i+1} 1^{j+1}$, and both strings are in $A$.

In the induction step, instead of talking about an arbitrary string $x$ obtainable by $k + 1$ applications of rule 2, the proof is more explicit in anticipating *how* it is obtained: It will be either $0y$ or $0y1$, where in either case $y$ is a string obtainable by $k$ applications of rule 2. In the original proof, this property of $y$ is needed in order to be able to apply the induction hypothesis to $y$; in the structural induction proof, we anticipate the property of $y$ that follows from the induction hypothesis, and simply take the induction hypothesis to be that $y$ *does* satisfy this property.

Although we will not formulate an official Principle of Structural Induction, the preceding example and the ones to follow should make it clear how to use this technique. If we have a recursive definition of a set $L$, structural induction can be used to show that every element of $L$ has some property. In the previous example, the "property" is that of belonging to the set $A$, and any property we are interested in can be expressed this way if we wish (we can always replace the phrase "has the property" by the phrase "belongs to the set of objects having the property").

## Another Property of Fully Parenthesized Algebraic Expressions    **EXAMPLE 2.21**

Let us return to the language *AE* defined in Example 2.17. *AE*, a subset of $\Sigma^* = \{i, (, ), +, -\}^*$, is defined as follows:

**1.** $i \in AE$.
**2.** For any $x$ and $y$ in $AE$, $(x + y)$ and $(x - y)$ are in $AE$.
**3.** No other strings are in $AE$.

This time we try to show that every element of the set has the property of not containing the substring )(. As in the previous example, we could set up an induction proof based on the number of times rule 2 is used in obtaining a string from the definition. Notice that in this approach we would want the strong principle of induction: If $z$ is obtained by a total of $k + 1$ applications of rule 2, then either $z = (x + y)$ or $z = (x - y)$, where in either case both $x$ and $y$ are obtained by $k$ or *fewer* (not exactly $k$) applications of rule 2. However, in a proof by structural induction, since the integer $k$ is not present explicitly, these details are unnecessary. What we really need to know about $x$ and $y$ is that they both have the desired property, and the statement that they do is the appropriate induction hypothesis.

*To prove:* No string in *AE* contains the substring )(.

> **Basis step.** The string $i$ does not contain the substring )(. (This is obvious.)
>
> **Induction hypothesis.** $x$ and $y$ are strings that do not contain the substring )(.
>
> **Statement to show in induction step.** Neither $(x + y)$ nor $(x - y)$ contains the substring )(.
>
> **Proof of induction step.** In both the expressions $(x + y)$ and $(x - y)$, the symbol preceding $x$ is not ), the symbol following $x$ is not (, the symbol preceding $y$ is not ), and the symbol following $y$ is not (. Therefore, the only way )( could appear would be for it to occur in $x$ or $y$ separately.
>
> Note that for the sake of simplicity, we made the induction hypothesis weaker than we really needed to (that is, we proved slightly more than was necessary). In order to use structural induction, we must show that if $x$ and $y$ are any strings in *AE* not containing )(, then neither $(x + y)$ nor $(x - y)$ contains )(. In our induction step, we showed this not only for $x$ and $y$ in *AE*, but for *any* $x$ and $y$. This simplification is often, though not always, possible (see Exercise 2.69).

## The Language of Strings with More *a*'s than *b*'s    **EXAMPLE 2.22**

Suppose that the language $L \subseteq \{a, b\}^*$ is defined as follows:

**1.** $a \in L$.
**2.** For any $x \in L$, $ax \in L$.
**3.** For any $x$ and $y$ in $L$, all the strings $bxy$, $xby$, and $xyb$ are in $L$.
**4.** No other strings are in $L$.

Let us prove that every element of $L$ has more *a*'s than *b*'s. Again we may use the structural induction principle, and just as in the previous example, we can simplify the induction step by proving something even stronger than we need. We will show that

1. $a$ has more $a$'s than $b$'s.
2. For any $x$ having more $a$'s than $b$'s, $ax$ also does.
3. For any $x$ and $y$ having more $a$'s than $b$'s, each of the strings $bxy$, $xby$, and $xyb$ also does.

If we were using ordinary induction on the number of applications of steps 2 or 3 in the recursive definition of $L$, an appropriate induction hypothesis would be that any element of $L$ obtainable by $k$ or fewer applications has more $a$'s than $b$'s. Since we can anticipate that we will use this hypothesis either on a single string $x$ to which we will apply step 2 or on two strings $x$ and $y$ to which we will apply step 3, we formulate our induction hypothesis to take care of either case.

*To prove:* Every element of $L$ has more $a$'s than $b$'s.

> **Basis step.** The string $a$ has more $a$'s than $b$'s. (This is obvious.)
>
> **Induction hypothesis.** $x$ and $y$ are strings containing more $a$'s than $b$'s.
>
> **Statement to show in induction step.** Each of the strings $ax$, $bxy$, $xby$, and $xyb$ has more $a$'s than $b$'s.
>
> **Proof of induction step.** The string $ax$ clearly has more $a$'s than $b$'s, since $x$ does. Since both $x$ and $y$ have more $a$'s than $b$'s, $xy$ has at least two more $a$'s than $b$'s, and therefore any string formed by inserting one more $b$ still has at least one more $a$ than $b$'s.

In Exercise 2.64 you are asked to prove the converse, that every string in $\{a, b\}^*$ having more $a$'s than $b$'s is in the language $L$.

| **EXAMPLE 2.23** | The Transitive Closure of a Relation |

For any relation $R$ on a set $S$, the *transitive closure* of $R$ (see Exercise 1.63) is the relation $R^t$ on $S$ defined as follows:

1. $R \subseteq R^t$.
2. For any $x, y, z \in S$, if $(x, y) \in R^t$ and $(y, z) \in R^t$, then $(x, z) \in R^t$.
3. No other pairs are in $R^t$.

(It makes sense to summarize statements 1 to 3 by saying that $R^t$ is the *smallest transitive relation containing $R$*.) Let us show that if $R_1$ and $R_2$ are relations on $S$ with $R_1 \subseteq R_2$, then $R_1^t \subseteq R_2^t$.

Structural induction is appropriate here since the statement we want to show says that every pair in $R_1^t$ satisfies the property of membership in $R_2^t$.

The basis step is to show that every element of $R_1$ is an element of $R_2^t$. This is true because $R_1 \subseteq R_2 \subseteq R_2^t$; the first inclusion is our assumption, and the second is just statement 1 in the definition of $R_2^t$. The induction hypothesis is that $(x, y)$ and $(y, z)$ are elements of $R_1$ that are in $R_2^t$, and in the induction step we must show that $(x, z) \in R_2^t$. Once again the argument is simplified slightly by proving more than we need. For *any* pairs $(x, y)$ and $(y, z)$ in $R_2^t$, whether they are in $R_1$ or not, $(x, z) \in R_2^t$, because this is exactly what statement 2 in the definition of $R_2^t$ says.

---

A recursive definition of a set can also provide a useful way of defining a function on the set. The function definition can follow the structure of the definition, in much the same way that a proof using structural induction does. This idea is illustrated by the next example.

## Recursive Definitions of the Length and Reverse Functions   EXAMPLE 2.24

In Example 2.15 we saw a recursive definition of the set $\Sigma^*$, for an alphabet $\Sigma$:

1. $\Lambda \in \Sigma^*$.
2. For every $x \in \Sigma^*$, and every $a \in \Sigma$, $xa \in \Sigma^*$.
3. No other elements are in $\Sigma^*$.

Two useful functions on $\Sigma^*$ are the length function, for which we have already given a nonrecursive definition, and the reverse function $rev$, which assigns to each string the string obtained by reversing the order of the symbols. Let us give a recursive definition of each of these. The length function can be defined as follows:

1. $|\Lambda| = 0$.
2. For any $x \in \Sigma^*$ and any $a \in \Sigma$, $|xa| = |x| + 1$.

For the reverse function we will often use the notation $x^r$ to stand for $rev(x)$, the reverse of $x$. Here is one way of defining the function recursively.

1. $\Lambda^r = \Lambda$.
2. For any $x \in \Sigma^*$ and any $a \in \Sigma$, $(xa)^r = ax^r$.

To convince ourselves that these are both valid definitions of functions on $\Sigma^*$, we could construct a proof using structural induction to show that every element of $\Sigma^*$ satisfies the property of being assigned a unique value by the function.

Let us now show, using structural induction, a useful property of the length function: For every $x$ and $y$ in $\Sigma^*$,

$$|xy| = |x| + |y|$$

(The structural induction, like the recursive definition of the length function itself, follows the recursive definition of $\Sigma^*$ above.) The formula seems obvious, of course, from the way we normally think about the length function. The point is that we do not have to depend on our intuitive understanding of length; the recursive definition is a practical one to use in discussing properties of the function. For the proof we choose $y$ as the string on which to base the induction (see Exercise 2.34). That is, we interpret the statement as a statement about $y$—namely, that for every $x$, $|xy| = |x| + |y|$. The basis step of the structural induction is to show that this statement is true when $y = \Lambda$. It is, because for every $x$,

$$|x\Lambda| = |x| = |x| + 0 = |x| + |\Lambda|$$

The induction hypothesis is that $y$ is a string for which the statement holds, and in the induction step we consider $ya$, for an arbitrary $a \in \Sigma$. We want to show that for any $x$, $|x(ya)| = |x| + |ya|$:

$$|x(ya)| = |(xy)a| \quad \text{(because concatenation is associative)}$$
$$= |xy| + 1 \quad \text{(by the recursive definition of the length function)}$$
$$= (|x| + |y|) + 1 \quad \text{(by the induction hypothesis)}$$
$$= |x| + (|y| + 1) \quad \text{(because addition is associative)}$$
$$= |x| + |ya| \quad \text{(by the definition of the length function)}$$

In this case, structural induction is not much different from ordinary induction on the length of $y$, but a little simpler. The proof involves lengths of strings because we are proving a statement about lengths of strings; at least we did not have to introduce them gratuitously in order to provide a framework for an induction proof.

---

Finally, it is worth pointing out that the idea of structural induction is general enough to include the ordinary induction principle as a special case. When we prove that a statement $P(n)$ is true for every $n \geq n_0$, we are showing that every element of the set $S = \{n \mid n \geq n_0\}$ satisfies the property $P$. The set $S$ can be defined recursively as follows:

1.  $n_0 \in S$.
2.  For every $n \in S$, $n + 1 \in S$.
3.  No integer is in $S$ unless it can be obtained from rules 1 and 2.

If we compare the induction step in an ordinary induction proof to that in a proof by structural induction, we see that they are the same. In the first case, the induction hypothesis is the statement that $P(k)$ is true for some $k \geq n_0$, and the induction step is to show that $P(k + 1)$ is true. In the second case, we assume that some element $n$ of $S$ satisfies the property $P$, and show that the element obtained from $n$ by rule 2 (i.e., $n + 1$) also satisfies $P$.

## EXERCISES

**2.1.** Prove that the statements $(p \vee q) \rightarrow r$ and $(p \rightarrow r) \vee (q \rightarrow r)$ are logically equivalent. (See Example 2.6.)

**2.2.** For each of Examples 2.5 and 2.6, how would you classify the given proof: constructive, nonconstructive, or something in-between? Why?

**2.3.** Prove that if $a$ and $b$ are even integers, then $ab$ is even.

**2.4.** Prove that for any positive integers $i$, $j$, and $n$, if $i * j = n$, then either $i \geq \sqrt{n}$ or $j \geq \sqrt{n}$. (See Example 2.2. The statement in that example may be more obviously useful since it tells you that for an integer $n > 1$, if none of the integers $j$ in the range $2 \leq j \leq \sqrt{n}$ is a divisor of $n$, then $n$ is prime.)

**2.5.** In the induction step in Example 2.8, starting with $x = 0y1$, we used $y1$ as the string of length $k$ to which we applied the induction hypothesis. Redo the induction step, this time using $0y$ instead.

**2.6.** Prove the statement in Example 2.8 by using mathematical induction on the number of 0's in the string, rather than on the length of the string.

**2.7.** In Example 2.12, in order to show that every nonempty subset of $\mathcal{N}$ has a smallest element, we chose $P(n)$ to be the statement: Every subset of $\mathcal{N}$ containing $n$ has a smallest element. Consider this alternative choice for $P(n)$: Every subset of $\mathcal{N}$ containing at least $n$ elements has a smallest element. (We would want to try to prove that this statement $P(n)$ is true for every $n \geq 1$.) Why would this *not* be an appropriate choice?

In all the remaining exercises in this chapter, with the exception of 46 through 48, "prove" means "prove, using an appropriate version of mathematical induction."

**2.8.** Prove that for every $n \geq 0$,

$$\sum_{i=1}^{n} i^2 = \frac{n(n + 1)(2n + 1)}{6}$$

**2.9.** Suppose that $a_0, a_1, \ldots,$ is a sequence of real numbers. Prove that for any $n \geq 1$,

$$\sum_{i=1}^{n} (a_i - a_{i-1}) = a_n - a_0$$

**2.10.** Prove that for every $n \geq 1$,

$$7 + 13 + 19 + \cdots + (6n + 1) = n(3n + 4)$$

**2.11.** Prove that for every $n \geq 0$,

$$\sum_{i=1}^{n} \frac{1}{i(i + 1)} = \frac{n}{n + 1}$$

**2.12.** For natural numbers $n$ and $i$ satisfying $0 \leq i \leq n$, let $C(n, i)$ denote the number $n!/(i!(n - i)!)$.

    a. Show that if $0 < i < n$, then $C(n, i) = C(n - 1, i - 1) + C(n - 1, i)$. (You don't need mathematical induction for this.)

    b. Prove that for any $n \geq 0$,

$$\sum_{i=0}^{n} C(n, i) = 2^n$$

**2.13.** Suppose $r$ is a real number other than 1. Prove that for any $n \geq 0$,

$$\sum_{i=1}^{n} r^i = \frac{1 - r^{n+1}}{1 - r}$$

**2.14.** Prove that for any $n \geq 0$,

$$1 + \sum_{i=1}^{n} i * i! = (n + 1)!$$

**2.15.** Prove that for any $n \geq 4$, $n! > 2^n$.

**2.16.** Prove that if $a_0, a_1, \ldots$ is a sequence of real numbers so that $a_n \leq a_{n+1}$ for every $n \geq 0$, then for every $m, n \geq 0$, if $m \leq n$, then $a_m \leq a_n$.

**2.17.** Suppose $x$ is any real number greater than $-1$. Prove that for any $n \geq 0$, $(1 + x)^n \geq 1 + nx$. (Be sure you say in your proof exactly how you use the assumption that $x > -1$.)

**2.18.** A fact about infinite series is that the series $\sum_{i=1}^{\infty} 1/i$ diverges (i.e., is infinite). Prove the following statement, which implies the result: For every $n \geq 1$, there is an integer $k_n \geq 1$ so that $\sum_{i=1}^{k_n} 1/i > n$. (Hint: the sum $1/(k+1) + 1/(k+2) + \cdots + 1/(2k)$ is at least how big?)

**2.19.** Prove that for every $n \geq 1$,

$$\sum_{i=1}^{n} i * 2^i = (n - 1) * 2^{n+1} + 2$$

**2.20.** Prove that for every $n \geq 2$,

$$1 + \sum_{i=2}^{n} \frac{1}{\sqrt{i}} > \sqrt{n}$$

**2.21.** Prove that for every $n \geq 0$, $n$ is either even or odd, but not both. (By definition, an integer $n$ is even if there is an integer $i$ so that $n = 2 * i$, and $n$ is odd if there is an integer $i$ so that $n = 2 * i + 1$.)

**2.22.** Prove that for any language $L \subseteq \{0, 1\}^*$, if $L^2 \subseteq L$, then $L^+ \subseteq L$.

**2.23.** Suppose that $\Sigma$ is an alphabet, and that $f : \Sigma^* \to \Sigma^*$ has the property that $f(a) = a$ for every $a \in \Sigma$ and $f(xy) = f(x)f(y)$ for every $x, y \in \Sigma^*$. Prove that for every $x \in \Sigma^*$, $f(x) = x$.

**2.24.** Prove that for every $n \geq 0$, $n(n^2 + 5)$ is divisible by 6.

**2.25.** Suppose $a$ and $b$ are integers with $0 \leq a < b$. Prove that for every $n \geq 1$, $b^n - a^n$ is divisible by $b - a$.

**2.26.** Prove that every positive integer is the product of a power of 2 and an odd integer.

**2.27.** Suppose that $A_1, A_2, \ldots$ are sets. Prove that for every $n \geq 1$,

$$\left( \bigcap_{i=1}^{n} A_i \right)' = \bigcup_{i=1}^{n} A_i'$$

**2.28.** Prove that for every $n \geq 1$, the number of subsets of $\{1, 2, \ldots, n\}$ is $2^n$.

**2.29.** Prove that for every $n \geq 1$ and every $m \geq 1$, the number of functions from $\{1, 2, \ldots, n\}$ to $\{1, 2, \ldots, m\}$ is $m^n$.

**2.30.** In calculus, a basic formula involving derivatives is the product formula, which says that if $f$ and $g$ are functions that have derivatives, $\frac{d}{dx}(f * g) = f * \frac{dg}{dx} + \frac{df}{dx} * g$. Using this formula and the fact that $\frac{dx}{dx} = 1$, prove that for any $n \geq 1$, $\frac{d}{dx}(x^n) = nx^{n-1}$.

**2.31.** The numbers $a_n$, for $n \geq 0$, are defined recursively as follows:

$$a_0 = -2; \quad a_1 = -2; \quad \text{for } n \geq 2, \ a_n = 5a_{n-1} - 6a_{n-2}$$

Prove that for every $n \geq 0$, $a_n = 2 * 3^n - 4 * 2^n$.

**2.32.** The Fibonacci function was defined in Example 2.13 using the definition

$$f_0 = 0; \quad f_1 = 1; \quad \text{for } n \geq 2, \ f_n = f_{n-1} + f_{n-2}$$

a. Suppose $C$ is a positive real number satisfying $C > 8/13$. Prove that for every $n \geq 0$, $f_n < C(13/8)^n$.

b. Prove that for every $n \geq 0$, $\sum_{i=0}^{n} f_i^2 = f_n f_{n+1}$.

c. Prove that for every $n \geq 0$, $\sum_{i=0}^{n} f_i = f_{n+2} - 1$.

**2.33.** Suppose we define a real-valued function $f$ on the natural numbers as follows:

$$f(0) = 0; \quad \text{for } n > 0, \ f(n) = \sqrt{1 + f(n-1)}$$

a. Prove that for every $n \geq 0$, $f(n) < 2$.

b. Prove that $f$ is an increasing function; in other words, for every $n \geq 0$, $f(n+1) > f(n)$.

**2.34.** In Example 2.24, a proof was given using structural induction based on the string $y$ that for any strings $x$ and $y$, $|xy| = |x| + |y|$. Can you prove the result using structural induction based on $x$? Why or why not?

**2.35.** Prove that for any string $x$, $|x^r| = |x|$.

**2.36.** Prove that if $x$ is any string in $AE$ (see Example 2.17), then any prefix of $x$ contains at least as many left parentheses as right.

**2.37.** Suppose we modify the definition of $AE$ to remove the restriction that the expressions be fully parenthesized. We call the new language $GAE$. One way to define $GAE$ is as follows.

    (i) $i \in GAE$.

    (ii) For any $x$ and $y$ in $GAE$, both the strings $x + y$ and $x - y$ are in $GAE$.

    (iii) For any $x \in GAE$, the string $(x)$ is in $GAE$.

    (iv) No other strings are in $GAE$.

a. Prove that every string in $AE$ is in $GAE$.

b. Prove that every prefix of every string in $GAE$ has at least as many left parentheses as right.

c. Suppose that we define an integer-valued function $N$ on the language $GAE$ as follows. $N(i) = 0$; for any $x$ and $y$ in $GAE$, $N$ assigns to both the strings $x + y$ and $x - y$ the larger of the two numbers $N(x)$ and $N(y)$; for any $x \in GAE$, $N$ assigns the value $N(x) + 1$ to the string $(x)$.

Describe in words (nonrecursively) what the value $N(x)$ means for a string $x \in GAE$.

**2.38.** Consider the following modified version of the strong induction principle, in which the basis step seems to have been eliminated.

> To prove that the statement $P(n)$ is true for every $n \geq n_0$, it is sufficient to show that for any $k \geq n_0$, if $P(n)$ is true for every $n$ satisfying $n_0 \leq n < k$, then $P(k)$ is true.

Assuming that the strong principle of mathematical induction is correct, prove that this modified version is correct. (Note that the basis step has not really been eliminated, only disguised.)

**2.39.** In each part below, a recursive definition is given of a subset of $\{a, b\}^*$. Give a simple nonrecursive definition in each case. Assume that each definition includes an implicit last statement: "Nothing is in $L$ unless it can be obtained by the previous statements."

  a.  $a \in L$; for any $x \in L$, $xa$ and $xb$ are in $L$.
  b.  $a \in L$; for any $x \in L$, $bx$ and $xb$ are in $L$.
  c.  $a \in L$; for any $x \in L$, $ax$ and $xb$ are in $L$.
  d.  $a \in L$; for any $x \in L$, $xb$, $xa$, and $bx$ are in $L$.
  e.  $a \in L$; for any $x \in L$, $xb$, $ax$, and $bx$ are in $L$.
  f.  $a \in L$; for any $x \in L$, $xb$ and $xba$ are in $L$.

**2.40.** Give recursive definitions of each of the following sets.

  a.  The set $\mathcal{N}$ of all natural numbers.
  b.  The set $S$ of all integers (positive and negative) divisible by 7.
  c.  The set $T$ of positive integers divisible by 2 or 7.
  d.  The set $U$ of all strings in $\{0, 1\}^*$ containing the substring 00.
  e.  The set $V$ of all strings of the form $0^i 1^j$, where $j \leq i \leq 2j$.
  f.  The set $W$ of all strings of the form $0^i 1^j$, where $i \geq 2j$.

**2.41.** Let $L$ and $A$ be the languages defined in Example 2.19. Prove that $L \subseteq A$ by using induction on the length of the string.

**2.42.** Below are recursive definitions of languages $L_1$ and $L_2$, both subsets of $\{a, b\}^*$. Prove that each is precisely the language $L$ of all strings not containing the substring $aa$.

  a.  $\Lambda \in L_1$; $a \in L_1$;
      For any $x \in L_1$, $xb$ and $xba$ are in $L_1$;
      Nothing else is in $L_1$.
  b.  $\Lambda \in L_2$; $a \in L_2$;
      For any $x \in L_2$, $bx$ and $abx$ are in $L_2$;
      Nothing else is in $L_2$.

**2.43.** For each $n \geq 0$, we define the strings $a_n$ and $b_n$ in $\{0, 1\}^*$ as follows:

$$a_0 = 0; \quad b_0 = 1; \quad \text{for } n > 0, a_n = a_{n-1}b_{n-1}; b_n = b_{n-1}a_{n-1}$$

Prove that for every $n \geq 0$, the following statements are true.

a. The strings $a_n$ and $b_n$ are of the same length.

b. The strings $a_n$ and $b_n$ differ in every position.

c. The strings $a_{2n}$ and $b_{2n}$ are palindromes.

d. The string $a_n$ contains neither the substring 000 nor the substring 111.

**2.44.** The "pigeonhole principle" says that if $n + 1$ objects are distributed among $n$ pigeonholes, there must be at least one pigeonhole that ends up with more than one object. A more formal version of the statement is that if $f : A \rightarrow B$ and the sets $A$ and $B$ have $n + 1$ and $n$ elements, respectively, then $f$ cannot be one-to-one. Prove the second version of the statement.

**2.45.** The following argument cannot be correct, because the conclusion is false. Say exactly which statement in the argument is the first incorrect one, and why it is incorrect.)

> *To prove:* all circles have the same diameter. More precisely, for any $n \geq 1$, if $S$ is any set of $n$ circles, then all the elements of $S$ have the same diameter. The basis step is to show that all the circles in a set of 1 circle have the same diameter, and this is obvious. The induction hypothesis is that $k \geq 1$ and for any set $S$ of $k$ circles, all elements of $S$ have the same diameter. We wish to show that for this $k$, and any set $S$ of $k + 1$ circles, all the circles in $S$ have the same diameter. Let $S = \{C_1, C_2, \ldots, C_{k+1}\}$. Consider the subsets $T = \{C_1, C_2, \ldots, C_k\}$ and $R = \{C_1, C_2, \ldots, C_{k-1}, C_{k+1}\}$. $T$ is simply $S$ with the circle $C_{k+1}$ deleted, and $R$ is $S$ with the element $C_{k-1}$ deleted. Since both $T$ and $R$ are sets of $k$ circles, all the circles in $T$ have the same diameter, and all the circles in $R$ have the same diameter; these statements follow from the induction hypothesis. Now observe that $C_{k-1}$ is an element of both $T$ and $R$. If $d$ is the diameter of this circle, then any circle in $T$ has diameter $d$, and so does any circle in $R$. Therefore, all the circles in $S$ have this same diameter.

# MORE CHALLENGING PROBLEMS

**2.46.** Prove that if $p$ and $q$ are distinct primes, and the integer $n$ is divisible by both $p$ and $q$, then $n$ is divisible by $pq$. You may use the following generally accepted fact from mathematics: If $p$ is prime and $m$ and $n$ are positive integers so that $mn$ is divisible by $p$, then either $m$ is divisible by $p$ or $n$ is divisible by $p$.

**2.47.** Prove that if $p$ and $q$ are distinct primes, then $pq$ is the smallest integer that is divisible by both $p$ and $q$.

**2.48.** Prove that if $n$ is any positive integer that is not a perfect square, then $\sqrt{n}$ is not rational. (See Example 2.3. You may need the generally accepted fact mentioned in Exercise 2.46.)

**2.49.**  Prove that for every $n \geq 1$,

$$\sum_{i=1}^{n} \sqrt{i} > 2n\sqrt{n}/3$$

**2.50.**  Prove that every integer greater than 17 is a nonnegative integer combination of 4 and 7. In other words, for every $n > 17$, there exist integers $i_n$ and $j_n$, both $\geq 0$, so that $n = i_n * 4 + j_n * 7$.

**2.51.**  Prove that for every $n \geq 1$, the number of subsets of $\{1, 2, \ldots, n\}$ having an even number of elements is $2^{n-1}$.

**2.52.**  Prove that the ordinary principle of mathematical induction implies the strong principle of mathematical induction. In other words, show that if $P(n)$ is a statement involving $n$ that we wish to establish for every $n \geq N$, and

   **1.** The ordinary principle of mathematical induction is true;

   **2.** $P(N)$ is true;

   **3.** For every $k \geq N$, $(P(N) \wedge P(N+1) \wedge \ldots P(k)) \Rightarrow P(k+1)$

   then $P(n)$ is true for every $n \geq N$.

**2.53.**  Suppose that $f$ is the Fibonacci function (see Example 2.13).

   a.  Prove that for every $n \geq 0$, $f_n = c(a^n - b^n)$, where

$$c = \frac{1}{\sqrt{5}}, \quad a = \frac{1 + \sqrt{5}}{2}, \quad \text{and } b = \frac{1 - \sqrt{5}}{2}$$

   b.  Prove that for every $n \geq 0$, $f_{n+1}^2 = f_n f_{n+2} + (-1)^n$.

**2.54.**  Prove that every positive integer can be expressed uniquely as the sum of distinct powers of 2. (Another way to say this is that every positive integer has a unique binary representation. Note that there are really two things to show: first, that every positive integer can be expressed as the sum of distinct powers of 2; and second, that for every positive integer $n$, there cannot be two different sets of powers of 2, both of which sum to $n$.)

**2.55.**  Prove that for any $n \geq 1$, and any sequence $a_1, a_2, \ldots, a_n$ of positive real numbers, and any sequence $b_1, b_2, \ldots, b_n$ that is a permutation (rearrangement) of the $a_i$'s,

$$\frac{a_1}{b_1} + \frac{a_2}{b_2} + \cdots + \frac{a_n}{b_n} \geq n$$

and the two expressions are equal if and only if $b_i = a_i$ for every $i$.

**2.56.**  Consider the following loop, written in pseudocode:

```
while B do
    S;
```

The meaning of this is what you would expect. Test B; if it is true, execute S; test B again; if it is still true, execute S again; test B again; and so forth. In other words, continue executing S as long as the condition B remains true. A condition $P$ is called an *invariant* of the loop if whenever $P$ and B are both true and S is executed once, $P$ is still true.

a.  Prove that if $P$ is an invariant of the loop, and $P$ is true before the first iteration of the loop (i.e., when B is tested the first time), then *if* the loop eventually terminates (i.e., after some number of iterations, B is false), $P$ is still true.

b.  Suppose $x$ and $y$ are integer variables, and initially $x \geq 0$ and $y > 0$. Consider the following program fragment:

```
q = 0;
r = x;
while r >= y do
    q = q + 1;
    r = r - y;
```

(The loop condition B is $r \geq y$, and the loop body S is the pair of assignment statements.) By considering the condition $(r \geq 0) \wedge (x = q * y + r)$, prove that when this loop terminates, the values of $q$ and $r$ will be the integer quotient and remainder, respectively, when $x$ is divided by $y$; in other words, $x = q * y + r$ and $0 \leq r < y$.

**2.57.** Suppose $f$ is a function defined on the set of positive integers and satisfying these two conditions:

(i)  $f(1) = 1$

(ii)  for $n \geq 1$, $f(2n) = f(2n + 1) = 2f(n)$

Prove that for every positive integer $n$, $f(n)$ is the largest power of 2 less than or equal to $n$.

**2.58.** The total time $T(n)$ required to execute a particular recursive sorting algorithm on an array of $n$ elements is one second if $n = 1$, and otherwise no more than $Cn + 2T(n/2)$ for some constant $C$ independent of $n$. Prove that if $n$ is any power of 2, say $2^k$, then

$$T(n) \leq n * (Ck + 1) = n(C \log_2 n + 1)$$

**2.59.** The function *rev*: $\Sigma^* \to \Sigma^*$ was defined recursively in Example 2.24. Using the recursive definition, prove the following facts about *rev*. (Recall that $rev(x)$ is also written $x^r$.)

a.  For any strings $x$ and $y$ in $\Sigma^*$, $(xy)^r = y^r x^r$.

b.  For any string $x \in \Sigma^*$, $(x^r)^r = x$.

c.  For any string $x \in \Sigma^*$ and any $n \geq 0$, $(x^n)^r = (x^r)^n$.

**2.60.** On the one hand, we have a recursive definition of the set *pal*, given in Example 2.16. On the other hand, we have a recursive definition of $x^r$, the reverse of the string $x$, in Example 2.24. Using these definitions, prove that $pal = \{x \in \Sigma^* \mid x^r = x\}$.

**2.61.** Prove that the language $L$ defined by the recursive definition below is the set of all elements of $\{a, b\}^*$ not containing the substring *aab*.

$\Lambda \in L$;

For every $x \in L$, $xa$, $bx$, and $abx$ are in $L$;

Nothing else is in $L$.

**2.62.** In each part below, a recursive definition is given of a subset of $\{a, b\}^*$. Give a simple nonrecursive definition in each case. Assume that each definition includes an implicit last statement: "Nothing is in $L$ unless it can be obtained by the previous statements."

a. $\Lambda$, $a$, and $aa$ are in $L$; for any $x \in L$, $xb$, $xba$, and $xbaa$ are in $L$.

b. $\Lambda \in L$; for any $x \in L$, $ax$, $xb$, and $xba$ are in $L$.

**2.63.** Suppose $L \subseteq \{0, 1\}^*$. Two languages $L_1$ and $L_2$ are defined recursively below. (These two definitions were both given in Example 2.15 as possible definitions of $L^*$.)

Definition of $L_1$:

1. $\Lambda \in L_1$.
2. For any $x \in L_1$ and any $y \in L$, $xy \in L_1$.
3. No string is in $L_1$ unless it can be obtained by using rules 1 and 2.

Definition of $L_2$:

1. $\Lambda \in L_2$.
2. For any $x \in L$, $x \in L_2$.
3. For any two elements $x$ and $y$ of $L_2$, $xy \in L_2$.
4. No string is in $L_2$ unless it can be obtained by using rules 1, 2, and 3.

a. Prove that $L_1 \subseteq L_2$.

b. Prove that for any two strings $x$ and $y$ in $L_1$, $xy \in L_1$.

c. Prove that $L_2 \subseteq L_1$.

**2.64.** Let $L$ be the language defined in Example 2.22. Prove that $L$ contains every element of $\{a, b\}^*$ having more $a$'s than $b$'s.

**2.65.** $\Lambda \in L$; for every $x$ and $y$ in $L$, $axby$ and $bxay$ are both in $L$; nothing else is in $L$. Prove that $L$ is precisely the set of strings in $\{a, b\}^*$ with equal numbers of $a$'s and $b$'s.

**2.66.** Suppose $S$ and $T$ are both finite sets of strings, $\Lambda \notin T$, and we have a function $e : S \to T$. The function $e$ can be thought of as an *encoding* of the elements of $S$, using the elements of $T$ as code words. In this situation we can then encode $S^*$ by letting the code string for $x_1 x_2 \ldots x_n$ be $e^*(x_1 x_2 \ldots x_n) = e(x_1) e(x_2) \ldots e(x_n)$. The encoding $e$ has the *prefix property* if there do not exist elements $x_1$ and $x_2$ of $S$ so that $x_1 \neq x_2$ and $e(x_1)$ is a prefix of $e(x_2)$. (If $e$ has the prefix property, then in particular $e$ is one-to-one.) Prove that if $e$ has the prefix property, then every element of $T^*$ has at most one decoding—that is, the function $e^*$ is one-to-one.

**2.67.** (Adapted from the book by Paulos [1998]). A certain remote village contains a large number of husband-wife couples. Exactly $n$ of the husbands are unfaithful to their wives. Each wife is immediately aware of any *other* husband's infidelity and knows that the same is true of the other wives; however, she has no way of knowing whether her own husband has been unfaithful. (No wife ever informs on any other woman's husband.) The village also has a very strict code of morality; each wife follows the code rigidly and knows that the other wives do also. If any wife determines conclusively that her husband has been unfaithful, she must kill him on the same day she finds this out. At midnight each night, if anyone in the village has been killed that day, a public announcement is made, so that everyone then knows. Finally, all the wives in the village are expert reasoners, and each wife is aware that all the other wives are expert reasoners.

   One day, a guru, whose pronouncements all the wives trust absolutely, visits the village, convenes a meeting of all the wives, and announces to them that there is at least one unfaithful husband in the village. What happens as a result? Prove your answer. (Hint: if $n = 1$, the wife of the unfaithful husband already knows that no other husband is unfaithful. She concludes that her husband is unfaithful and kills him that day.)

**2.68.** Suppose $P(m, n)$ is a statement involving two natural numbers $m$ and $n$, and suppose we can show these two statements: i) $P(0, 0)$ is true; ii) For any natural numbers $i$ and $j$, if $P(i, j)$ is true, then $P(i, j + 1)$ and $P(i + 1, j)$ are true. Does it follow that $P(m, n)$ is true for all natural numbers $m$ and $n$? Give reasons for your answer.

**2.69.** Suppose $S$ is a set of integers defined as follows: $0 \in S$; for every $x \in S$, $x + 5 \in S$; no other elements are in $S$. In order to show using structural induction that every element of $S$ satisfies some property $P$, it is enough to show that 0 satisfies $P$, and if $x \in S$ and $x$ satisfies $P$, then $x + 5$ also satisfies $P$. Give an example of a property $P$ for which this is true but for which it is not true that $x + 5$ satisfies $P$ for every integer $x$ satisfying $P$. In other words, give an example in which the structural induction proof cannot be simplified as we did in Examples 2.21 and 2.23.

**2.70.** Suppose that $U$ is a *finite* set that is closed under some binary operation $\circ$, and $I$ is a subset of $U$. Suppose also that $S$ is defined as follows:

1. Every element of $I$ is an element of $S$.

2. For every $x$ and $y$ in $S$, $x \circ y \in S$.

3. Nothing else is in $S$.

Describe an algorithm that will determine, for some arbitrary element of $U$, whether or not it is in $S$. (In particular, for each element of $U$, no matter whether the answer is yes or no for that element, the algorithm must produce the answer after a finite number of steps.)

# 2

# Regular Languages and Finite Automata

Interesting languages are likely to be infinite but must be describable in some finite way. One method is to describe how the strings in the language can be *generated* from simpler strings, using string operations, or how the language itself can be generated from simpler languages using set operations. Another approach is to specify an algorithmic procedure for *recognizing* whether a given string is in the language.

The simplest languages we consider in this book are the *regular* languages, which are those that can be generated from one-element languages by applying certain standard operations a finite number of times. They are also precisely the ones that can be recognized by devices called *finite automata* (FA), simple computing machines with severely restricted memories. The second characterization provides some insight into what it means for a language not to be regular, and it gives us a simple model of computation we can generalize later, when we study more general languages.

In Part II, we consider these two as well as other characterizations of regular languages. We obtain algorithms for translating one description of a language into another description of a different type; we gain experience in using formal methods to describe languages and trying to answer questions about them, in a simple setting in which the models are relatively simple and the questions generally *have* answers; and we examine ways in which regular languages themselves are useful in real-world applications. ■

# 3

# Regular Languages and Finite Automata

## 3.1 | REGULAR LANGUAGES AND REGULAR EXPRESSIONS

Nonnull strings over an alphabet $\Sigma$ are created by concatenating simple strings, those of length 1. Since concatenation can also be thought of as an operation on languages, we may consider the languages obtained by concatenation from the simple languages of the form $\{a\}$, where $a \in \Sigma$. If concatenation is the only operation we allow, however, we can get only single strings or languages that contain single strings. Adding the set operation of union permits languages with several elements, and if we allow the Kleene * operation, which arises naturally from concatenation, we can produce infinite languages as well.

To the simple languages of the form $\{a\}$, we add two more: the empty language $\emptyset$ and the language $\{\Lambda\}$ whose only element is the null string.

A *regular* language over an alphabet $\Sigma$ is one that can be obtained from these basic languages using the operations of union, concatenation, and Kleene *. A regular language can therefore be described by an explicit formula. It is common to simplify the formula slightly, by leaving out the set brackets {} or replacing them with parentheses and by replacing $\cup$ by $+$; the result is called a *regular expression*.

Here are several examples of regular languages over the alphabet $\{0, 1\}$, along with the corresponding regular expressions.

| *Language* | *Corresponding Regular Expression* |
|---|---|
| **1.** $\{\Lambda\}$ | $\Lambda$ |
| **2.** $\{0\}$ | $0$ |
| **3.** $\{001\}$ (i.e., $\{0\}\{0\}\{1\}$) | $001$ |
| **4.** $\{0, 1\}$ (i.e., $\{0\} \cup \{1\}$) | $0 + 1$ |
| **5.** $\{0, 10\}$ (i.e., $\{0\} \cup \{10\}$) | $0 + 10$ |

| *Language* | *Corresponding Regular Expression* |
|---|---|
| **6.** $\{1, \Lambda\}\{001\}$ | $(1 + \Lambda)001$ |
| **7.** $\{110\}^*\{0, 1\}$ | $(110)^*(0 + 1)$ |
| **8.** $\{1\}^*\{10\}$ | $1^*10$ |
| **9.** $\{10, 111, 11010\}^*$ | $(10 + 111 + 11010)^*$ |
| **10.** $\{0, 10\}^*(\{11\}^* \cup \{001, \Lambda\})$ | $(0 + 10)^*((11)^* + 001 + \Lambda)$ |

We think of a regular expression as representing the "most typical string" in the corresponding language. For example, $1^*10$ stands for a string that consists of the substring 10 preceded by any number of 1's.

The phrase we used above, "obtained from these basic languages using the operations of union, concatenation, and Kleene $^*$," should suggest a recursive definition of the type we studied in Section 2.4.2. It will be helpful to complicate the definition a little so that it defines not only the regular languages but also the regular expressions corresponding to them.

---

**Definition 3.1    Regular Languages and Regular Expressions over $\Sigma$**

The set $R$ of regular languages over $\Sigma$, and the corresponding regular expressions, are defined as follows.

1. $\emptyset$ is an element of $R$, and the corresponding regular expression is $\emptyset$.
2. $\{\Lambda\}$ is an element of $R$, and the corresponding regular expression is $\Lambda$.
3. For each $a \in \Sigma$, $\{a\}$ is an element of $R$, and the corresponding regular expression is $a$.
4. If $L_1$ and $L_2$ are any elements of $R$, and $r_1$ and $r_2$ are the corresponding regular expressions,
   (a) $L_1 \cup L_2$ is an element of $R$, and the corresponding regular expression is $(r_1 + r_2)$;
   (b) $L_1 L_2$ is an element of $R$, and the corresponding regular expression is $(r_1 r_2)$;
   (c) $L_1^*$ is an element of $R$, and the corresponding regular expression is $(r_1^*)$.

Only those languages that can be obtained by using statements 1–4 are regular languages over $\Sigma$.

---

The empty language is included in the definition primarily for the sake of consistency. There will be a number of places where we will want to say things like "To every something-or-other, there corresponds a regular language," and without the language $\emptyset$ we would need to make exceptions for trivial special cases.

Our definition of regular expressions is really a little more restrictive in several respects than we need to be in practice. We use notation such as $L^2$ for languages, and it is reasonable to use similar shortcuts in the case of regular expressions. Thus we sometimes write $(r^2)$ to stand for the regular expression $(rr)$, $(r^+)$ to stand for the regular expression $((r^*)r)$, and so forth. You should also note that the regular expressions we get from the definition are *fully parenthesized*. We will usually relax this requirement, using the same rules that apply to algebraic expressions: The Kleene * operation has the highest precedence and + the lowest, with concatenation in between. This rule allows us to write $a + b^*c$, for example, instead of $(a + ((b^*)c))$. Just as with algebraic expressions, however, there are times when parentheses are necessary. The regular expression $(a + b)^*$ is a simple example, since the languages corresponding to $(a + b)^*$ and $a + b^*$ are not the same.

Let us agree to identify two regular expressions if they correspond to the same language. At the end of the last paragraph, for example, we could simply have said

$$(a + b)^* \neq a + b^*$$

instead of saying that the two expressions correspond to different languages. With this convention we can look at a few examples of rules for simplifying regular expressions over $\{0, 1\}$:

$$1^*(1 + \Lambda) = 1^*$$
$$1^*1^* = 1^*$$
$$0^* + 1^* = 1^* + 0^*$$
$$(0^*1^*)^* = (0 + 1)^*$$
$$(0 + 1)^*01(0 + 1)^* + 1^*0^* = (0 + 1)^*$$

(All five are actually special cases of more general rules. For example, for any two regular expressions $r$ and $s$, $(r^*s^*)^* = (r + s)^*$.) These rules are really statements about languages, which we could have considered in Chapter 1. The last one is probably the least obvious. It says that the language of all strings of 0's and 1's (the right side) can be expressed as the union of two languages, one containing all the strings having the substring 01, the other containing all the others. (Saying that all the 1's precede all the 0's is the same as saying that 01 is not a substring.)

Although there are times when it is helpful to simplify a regular expression as much as possible, we will not attempt a systematic discussion of the algebra of regular expressions. Instead, we consider a few more examples.

Strings of Even Length **EXAMPLE 3.1**

Let $L \subseteq \{0, 1\}^*$ be the language of all strings of even length. (Since 0 is even, $\Lambda \in L$.) Is $L$ regular? If it is, what is a regular expression corresponding to it?

Any string of even length can be obtained by concatenating zero or more strings of length 2. Conversely, any such concatenation has even length. It follows that

$$L = \{00, 01, 10, 11\}^*$$

so that one regular expression corresponding to $L$ is $(00 + 01 + 10 + 11)^*$. Another is $((0 + 1)(0 + 1))^*$.

| **EXAMPLE 3.2** | Strings with an Odd Number of 1's |

Let $L$ be the language of all strings of 0's and 1's containing an odd number of 1's. Any string in $L$ must contain at least one 1, and it must therefore start with a string of the form $0^i 10^j$. There is an even number (possibly zero) of additional 1's, each followed by zero or more 0's. This means that the rest of the string is the concatenation of zero or more pieces of the general form $10^m 10^n$. One regular expression describing $L$ is therefore

$$0^*10^*(10^*10^*)^*$$

A slightly different expression, which we might have obtained by stopping the initial substring immediately after the 1, is

$$0^*1(0^*10^*1)^*0^*$$

If we had begun by considering the *last* 1 in the string, rather than the first, we might have ended up with

$$(0^*10^*1)^*0^*10^*$$

A more complicated answer that is still correct is

$$0^*(10^*10^*)^*1(0^*10^*1)^*0^*$$

In this case the 1 that is emphasized is somewhere in the middle, with an even number of 1's on either side of it. There are still other ways we could describe a typical element of $L$, depending on which aspect of the structure we wanted to emphasize, and there is not necessarily one that is the simplest or the most natural. The important thing in all these examples is that the regular expression must be general enough to describe every string in the language. One that does not quite work, for example, is

$$(10^*10^*)^*10^*$$

since it does not allow for strings beginning with 0. We could correct this problem by inserting $0^*$ at the beginning, to obtain

$$0^*(10^*10^*)^*10^*$$

This is a way of showing the last 1 in the string explicitly, slightly different from the third regular expression in this example.

| **EXAMPLE 3.3** | Strings of Length 6 or Less |

Let $L$ be the set of all strings over $\{0, 1\}$ of length 6 or less. A simple but inelegant regular expression corresponding to $L$ is

$$\Lambda + 0 + 1 + 00 + 01 + 10 + 11 + 000 + \cdots + 111110 + 111111$$

A regular expression to describe the set of strings of length exactly 6 is

$$(0 + 1)(0 + 1)(0 + 1)(0 + 1)(0 + 1)(0 + 1)$$

or, in our extended notation, $(0 + 1)^6$. To reduce the length, however, we may simply allow some or all of the factors to be $\Lambda$. We may therefore describe $L$ by the regular expression

$$(0 + 1 + \Lambda)^6$$

## Strings Ending in 1 and Not Containing 00     EXAMPLE 3.4

This time we let $L$ be the language

$$L = \{x \in \{0, 1\}^* \mid x \text{ ends with 1 and does not contain the substring 00}\}$$

In order to find a regular expression for $L$, we try stating the defining property of strings in $L$ in other ways. Saying that a string does not contain the substring 00 is the same as saying that no 0 can be followed by 0, or in other words, every 0 either comes at the very end or is followed immediately by 1. Since strings in $L$ cannot have 0 at the end, every 0 must be followed by 1. This means that copies of the strings 01 and 1 can account for the entire string and therefore that every string in $L$ corresponds to the regular expression $(1 + 01)^*$. This regular expression is a little too general, however, since it allows the null string. The definition says that strings in $L$ must end with 1, and this is stronger than saying they cannot end with 0. We cannot fix the problem by adding a 1 at the end, to obtain $(1+01)^*1$ because now our expression is not general enough; it does not allow 01. Allowing this choice at the end, we obtain $(1 + 01)^*(1 + 01)$, or $(1 + 01)^+$.

## The Language of C Identifiers     EXAMPLE 3.5

For this example a little more notation will be useful. Let us temporarily use $l$ (for "letter") to denote the regular expression

$$a + b + \cdots + z + A + B + \cdots + Z$$

and $d$ (for "digit") to stand for

$$0 + 1 + 2 + \cdots + 9$$

An identifier in the C programming language is any string of length 1 or more that contains only letters, digits, and underscores (_) and begins with a letter or an underscore. Therefore, a regular expression for the language of all C identifiers is

$$(l + \_)(l + d + \_)^*$$

## Real Literals in Pascal     EXAMPLE 3.6

Suppose we keep the abbreviations $l$ and $d$ as in the previous example and introduce the additional abbreviations $s$ (for "sign") and $p$ (for "point"). The symbol $s$ is shorthand for $\Lambda + a + m$, where $a$ is "plus" and $m$ is "minus." Consider the regular expression

$$sd^+(pd^+ + pd^+Esd^+ + Esd^+)$$

(Here E is not an abbreviation, but one of the symbols in the alphabet.) A typical string corresponding to this regular expression has this form: first a sign (plus, minus, or neither); one or more digits; then *either* a decimal point and one or more digits, which may or may not be followed by an E, a sign, and one or more digits, *or* just the E, the sign, and one or more digits. (If nothing else, you should be convinced by now that one regular expression is often worth several lines of prose.) This is precisely the specification for a real "literal," or constant, in the Pascal programming language. If the constant is in exponential format, no decimal point is needed. If there is a decimal point, there must be at least one digit immediately preceding and following it.

---

## 3.2 | THE MEMORY REQUIRED TO RECOGNIZE A LANGUAGE

When we discuss the problem of *recognizing* a language (deciding whether an arbitrary input string is in the language), we will be following two conventions for the time being. First, we will restrict ourselves to a single pass through the input, from left to right. Although this restriction is somewhat arbitrary, it allows us to consider how much information must be "remembered" during the processing of the input, and this turns out to be a useful criterion for classifying languages. Second, rather than waiting until the end of the input string to reach a decision (and having to assume that the end of the string is marked explicitly), we make a tentative decision after each input symbol. This allows us to process a string the same way, whether it represents the entire input or a prefix of a longer string. The processing produces a sequence of tentative decisions, one for each prefix, and the final answer for the string is simply the last of these.

   The question we want to consider is how much information we need to remember at each step, in order to guarantee that our sequence of decisions will always be correct. The two extremes are that we remember everything (that is, exactly what substring we have read) and that we remember nothing. Remembering nothing might be enough! For example, if the language is empty, the algorithm that answers "no" at each step, regardless of the input, is the correct one; if the language is all of $\Sigma^*$, answering "yes" at each step is correct. In both these trivial cases, since the answer we return is always the same, we can continue to return the right answer without remembering what input symbols we have read, or remembering that we have read one substring rather than another.

   In any situation other than these two trivial ones, however, the answers in the sequence are not identical. There are two strings $x$ and $y$ for which the answers are different. This means that the information we remember at the point when we have received input string $x$ must be different from what we remember when we have received input string $y$, for otherwise we would have no way to distinguish the two strings. Therefore, in at least one of these two situations we must remember *something*.

---

**EXAMPLE 3.7**    Strings Ending with 0

Let $L$ be the language $\{0, 1\}^*\{0\}$ of all strings in $\{0, 1\}^*$ that end with 0. Then for any nonnull input string $x$, whether or not $x \in L$ depends only on the last symbol. Another way to say this is that there is no need to distinguish between one string ending with 0 and any other string ending with 0, or between one string ending with 1 and any other string ending with 1. Any two strings ending with the same symbol can be treated exactly the same way.

The only string not accounted for is $\Lambda$. However, there is no need to distinguish between $\Lambda$ and a string ending with 1: Neither is in the language, because neither ends with 0, and once we get one more symbol we will not remember enough to distinguish the resulting strings anyway, because they will both end with the same symbol. The conclusion is that there are only two cases (either the string ends with 0 or it does not), and at each step we must remember only which case we have currently.

## Strings with Next-to-Last Symbol 0    EXAMPLE 3.8

Let $L$ be the language of all strings in $\{0, 1\}^*$ with next-to-last symbol 0. Following the last example, we can say that the decision we make for a string depends on its next-to-last symbol and that we must remember at least that much information. Is that enough? For example, is it necessary to distinguish between the strings 01 and 00, both of which have next-to-last symbol 0?

Any algorithm that does not distinguish between these two strings, and treats them exactly the same, is also unable to distinguish the two strings obtained after one more input symbol. Now it is clear that such an algorithm cannot work: If the next input is 0, for example, the two resulting strings are 010 and 000, and only one of these is in the language. For the same reason, any correct algorithm must also distinguish between 11 and 10 because their last symbols are different.

We conclude that, for this language, it is apparently necessary to remember both the last two symbols. For strings of length at least 2, there are four separate cases. Just as in the previous example, we can see that the three input strings of length less than 2 do not require separate cases. Both the strings $\Lambda$ and 1 can be treated exactly like 11, because for either string at least two more input symbols will be required before the current string is in the language, and at that point, the string we had before those two symbols is irrelevant. The string 0 represents the same case as 10: Neither string is in the language, and once another input is received, both current strings will have the same last two symbols. The four cases we must distinguish are these:

a. The string is $\Lambda$ or 1 or ends with 11.
b. The string is 0 or ends with 10.
c. The string ends with 00.
d. The string ends with 01.

## Strings Ending with 11    EXAMPLE 3.9

This time, let $L = \{0, 1\}^*\{11\}$, the language of all strings in $\{0, 1\}^*$ ending with 11. We can easily formulate an algorithm for recognizing $L$ in which we remember only the last two symbols of the input string. This time, in fact, we can get by with even a little less.

First, it is *not* sufficient to remember only whether the current string ends with 11. For example, suppose the algorithm does not distinguish between a string ending in 01 and one ending in 00, on the grounds that neither ends in 11. Then if the next input is 1, the algorithm will not be able to distinguish between the two new strings, which end in 11 and 01, respectively.

This is not correct, since only one of these strings is in $L$. The algorithm must remember enough now to distinguish between 01 and 00, so that it will be able if necessary to distinguish between 011 and 001 one symbol later.

Two strings ending in 00 and 10, however, do not need to be distinguished. Neither string is in $L$, and no matter what the next symbol is, the two resulting strings will have the same last two symbols. For the same reason, the string 1 can be identified with any string ending in 01.

Finally, the two strings 0 and $\Lambda$ can be identified with all the other strings ending in 0: In all these cases, at least two more input symbols are required to produce an element of $L$, and at that point it will be unnecessary to remember anything but the last two symbols.

Any algorithm recognizing $L$ and following the rules we have adopted must distinguish the following three cases, and it is sufficient for the algorithm to remember which of these the current string represents:

a.   The string does not end in 1. (Either it is $\Lambda$ or it ends in 0.)
b.   The string is 1 or ends in 01.
c.   The string ends in 11.

---

**EXAMPLE 3.10**     Strings with an Even Number of 0's and an Odd Number of 1's

Consider the language of strings $x$ in $\{0, 1\}^*$ for which $n_0(x)$ is even and $n_1(x)$ is odd. One way to get by with remembering less than the entire current string would be to remember just the *numbers* of 0's and 1's we have read, ignoring the way the symbols are arranged. For example, it is not necessary to remember whether the current string is 011 or 101. However, remembering this much information would still require us to consider an infinite number of distinct cases, and an algorithm that remembers much less information can still work correctly. There is no need to distinguish between the strings 011 and 0001111, for example: The current answers are both "no," and the answers will continue to be the same, no matter what input symbols we get from now on. In the case of 011 and 001111, the current answers are also both "no"; however, these two strings must be distinguished, since if the next input is 1, the answer should be "no" in the first case but "yes" in the second.

The reason 011 and 0001111 can be treated the same is that both have an odd number of 0's and an even number of 1's. The reason 011 and 001111 must be distinguished is that one has an odd number of 0's, the other an even number. It is essential to remember the parity (i.e., even or odd) of both the number of 0's and the number of 1's, and this is also sufficient. Once again, we have four distinct cases, and the only information about an input string that we must remember is which of these cases it represents.

---

**EXAMPLE 3.11**     A Recognition Algorithm for the Language in Example 3.4

As in Example 3.4, let

$$L = \{x \in \{0, 1\}^* \mid x \text{ ends in 1 and does not contain the substring 00}\}$$

Suppose that in the course of processing an input string, we have seen the string $s$ so far. If $s$ already contains the substring 00, then that fact is all we need to remember; $s$ is not in $L$, and no matter what input we get from here on, the result will never be in $L$. Let us denote this case by the letter $N$.

Consider next two other cases, in both of which 00 has not yet occurred: case 0, in which the last symbol of $s$ is 0, and case 1, in which the last symbol is 1. In the first case, if the next input is 0 we have case $N$, and if the next input is 1 we have case 1. Starting in case 1, the inputs 0 and 1 take us to cases 0 and 1, respectively. These three cases account for all substrings except $\Lambda$. This string, however, must be distinguished from all the others. It would not be correct to say that the null string corresponds to case $N$, because unlike that case there are possible subsequent inputs that would give us a string in $L$. $\Lambda$ does not correspond to case 0, because if the next input is 0 the answers should be different in the two cases; and it does not correspond to case 1, because the *current* answers should already be different.

Once again we have managed to divide the set $\{0, 1\}^*$ into four types of strings so that in order to recognize strings in $L$ it is sufficient at each step to remember which of the four types we have so far.

---

We can summarize Examples 3.7–3.11 by the schematic diagrams in Figure 3.1. A diagram like this can be interpreted as a flowchart for an algorithm recognizing the language. In each diagram, the circles correspond to the distinct cases the algorithm is keeping track of, or the distinct types of strings in our classification. The two circles in Figure 3.1$a$ (corresponding to Example 3.7) represent strings that do not end with 0 and strings that do, respectively. In Figures 3.1$b$ and 3.1$c$, corresponding to Examples 3.8 and 3.9, the circles represent the cases involving the last two symbols that must be distinguished. In Figure 3.1$d$, the label used in each circle is a description of the parities of the number of 0's and the number of 1's, respectively, in the current string. We have already discussed the labeling scheme in Figure 3.1$e$.

In these diagrams, the short arrow not originating at one of the circles indicates the starting point of the algorithm, the case that includes the null string $\Lambda$. The double circles in each case designate cases in which the current string is actually an element of $L$. This is the way the flowchart indicates the answer the algorithm returns for each string.

The arrows originating at a circle tell us, for each possible next symbol, which case results. As we have already described, this information is all the algorithm needs to remember. In Figure 3.1$e$, for example, if at some point we are in case 0 (i.e., the current substring ends in 0 and does not contain 00) and the next symbol is 1, the arrow labeled 1 allows us to forget everything except the fact that the new substring ends with 1 and does not contain 00.

The last sentence of the preceding paragraph is misleading in one sense. Although in studying the algorithm it is helpful to think of case 1 as meaning "The substring we have received so far ends in 1 and does not contain 00," it is not necessary to think of it this way at all. We could give the four cases arbitrary, meaningless labels, and as long as we are able to keep track of which case we are currently in, we will be able to execute the algorithm correctly. The procedure is purely mechanical and requires no understanding of the significance of the cases. A computer program, or a machine, could do it.

This leads us to another possible interpretation of these diagrams, which is the one we will adopt. We think of Figure 3.1$e$, for example, as specifying an *abstract*

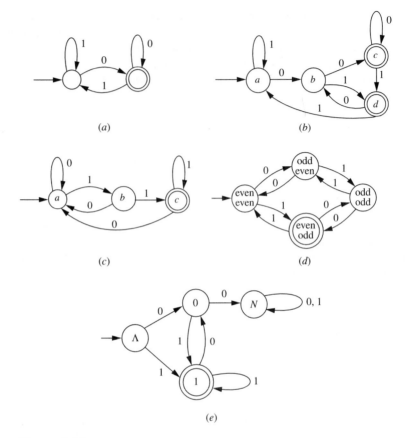

**Figure 3.1 |**
(a) Strings ending in 0; (b) Strings with next-to-last symbol 0; (c) Strings ending
with 11; (d) Strings with $n_0$ even and $n_1$ odd; (e) A recognition algorithm for the
language in Example 3.4.

*machine* that would work as follows: The machine is at any time in one of four
possible *states*, which we have arbitrarily labeled $\Lambda, 0, 1$, and $N$. When it is activated
initially, it is in state $\Lambda$. The machine receives successive *inputs* of 0 or 1, and as a
result of being in a certain state and receiving a certain input, it moves to the state
specified by the corresponding arrow. Finally, certain states are *accepting* states (state
1 is the only one in this example). A string of 0's and 1's is in $L$ if and only if the
state the machine is in as a result of processing that string is an accepting state.

It seems reasonable to refer to something of this sort as a "machine," since
one can visualize an actual piece of hardware that works according to these rough
specifications. The specifications do not say exactly how the hardware works—
exactly how the input is transmitted to the machine, for example, or whether a "yes"
answer corresponds to a flashing light or a beep. For that matter, the "machine"
might exist only in software form, so that the strings are input data to a program. The

phrase *abstract machine* means that it is a specification, in some minimal sense, of the capabilities the machine needs to have. The machine description does not say what physical status the "states" and "inputs" have. The abstraction at the heart of the machine is the *set* of states and the *function* that specifies, for each combination of state and input symbol, the state the machine goes to next. The crucial property is the *finiteness* of the set of states. This is significant because the size of the set puts an absolute limit on the amount of information the machine can (or needs to) remember. Although strings in the language can be arbitrarily long—and will be, unless the language is finite—remembering a fixed amount of information, independent of the size of the input, is sufficient. Being able to distinguish between these states (or between strings that lead to these states) is the only form of memory the machine has.

The more states a machine of this type has, the more complicated a language it will be able to recognize. However, the requirement that the set of states be finite is a significant constraint, and we will be able to find many languages (see Theorem 3.3 for an example) that cannot be recognized by this type of machine, or this type of algorithm. We will show in Chapter 4 that the languages that can be recognized this way are precisely the regular languages. The conclusion, which may not have been obvious from the discussion in Section 3.1, is that regular languages are fairly simple, at least in principle, and there are many languages that are not regular.

# 3.3 | FINITE AUTOMATA

In Section 3.2, we were introduced to a simple type of language-recognizing machine. Now we are ready for the official definition.

---

**Definition 3.2    Definition of a Finite Automaton**

A *finite automaton*, or *finite-state machine* (abbreviated FA) is a 5-tuple $(Q, \Sigma, q_0, A, \delta)$, where

   $Q$ is a finite set    (whose elements we will think of as *states*);
   $\Sigma$ is a finite alphabet of *input symbols*;
   $q_0 \in Q$    (the *initial* state);
   $A \subseteq Q$    (the set of *accepting* states);
   $\delta$ is a function from $Q \times \Sigma$ to $Q$    (the *transition* function).

For any element $q$ of $Q$ and any symbol $a \in \Sigma$, we interpret $\delta(q, a)$ as the state to which the FA moves, if it is in state $q$ and receives the input $a$.

---

If you have not run into definitions like this before, you might enjoy what the mathematician R. P. Boas had to say about them, in an article in *The American Mathematical Monthly* (88: 727–731, 1981) entitled "Can We Make Mathematics Intelligible?":

There is a test for identifying some of the future professional mathematicians at an early age. These are students who instantly comprehend a sentence beginning "Let $X$ be an ordered quintuple $(a, T, \pi, \sigma, \mathcal{B})$, where ..." They are even more promising if they add, "I never really understood it before."

Whether or not you "instantly comprehend" a definition of this type, you can appreciate the practical advantages. Specifying a finite automaton requires that we specify five things: two sets $Q$ and $\Sigma$, an element $q_0$ and a subset $A$ of $Q$, and a function from $Q \times \Sigma$ to $Q$. Defining a finite automaton to be a 5-tuple may seem strange at first, but it is simply efficient use of notation. It allows us to talk about the five things at once as though we are talking about one "object"; it will allow us to say

Let $M = (Q, \Sigma, q_0, A, \delta)$ be an FA

instead of

Let $M$ be an FA with state set $Q$, input alphabet $\Sigma$, initial state $q_0$, set of accepting states $A$, and transition function $\delta$.

**EXAMPLE 3.12**  ## Strings Ending with 10

Figure 3.2a gives a transition diagram for an FA with seven states recognizing $L = \{0, 1\}^*\{10\}$, the language of all strings in $\{0, 1\}^*$ ending in 11. Until it gets more than two inputs, the FA remembers exactly what it has received (there is a separate state for each possible input string of length 2 or less). After that, it cycles back and forth among four states, "remembering" the last two symbols it has received. Figure 3.2b describes this machine in tabular form, by giving the values of the transition function for each state-input pair.

We would expect from Example 3.9 that this FA is more complicated than it needs to be. In particular, the rows for the three states 1, 01, and 11 in the transition table are exactly the same. If $x$, $y$, and $z$ are strings causing the FA to be in the three states, then $x$, $y$, and $z$ do not need to be distinguished now, since none of the three states is an accepting state; and the three strings that will result one input symbol later *cannot* be distinguished. The conclusion is that the three states do not represent cases that need to be distinguished. We could merge them into one and call it state $B$.

The rows for the three states 0, 00, and 10 are also identical. These three states cannot all be merged into one, because 10 is an accepting state and the other two are not. The two nonaccepting states can, and we call the new state $A$.

At this point, the number of states has been reduced to 4, and we have the transition table

| | | Input | |
|---|---|---|---|
| | | **0** | **1** |
| | $\Lambda$ | $A$ | $B$ |
| **State** | $A$ | $A$ | $B$ |
| | $B$ | 10 | $B$ |
| | 10 | $A$ | $B$ |

We can go one step further, using the same reasoning as before. In this new FA, the rows for states $A$ and $\Lambda$ are the same, and neither $\Lambda$ nor $A$ is an accepting state. We can therefore

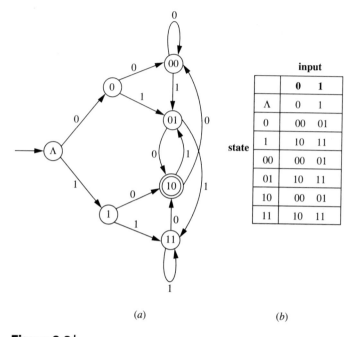

(a)                          (b)

**Figure 3.2 |**
A finite automaton recognizing {0, 1}*{10}. (a) Transition diagram;
(b) Transition table.

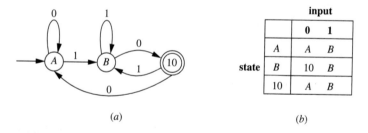

(a)                          (b)

**Figure 3.3 |**
A simplified finite automaton recognizing {0, 1}*{10}: (a) Transition
diagram; (b) Transition table.

include Λ in the state A as well. The three resulting states are A, B, and 10, and it is easy to see that the number cannot be reduced any more. The final result and the corresponding transition table are pictured in Figure 3.3.

We might describe state A as representing "no progress toward 11," meaning that the machine has received either no input at all, or an input string ending with 0 but not 10. B stands for "halfway there," or last symbol 1. As we observed after Example 3.11, however, these descriptions of the states are not needed to specify the abstract machine completely.

The analysis that led to the simplification of the FA in this example can be turned into a systematic procedure for minimizing the number of states in a given FA. See Section 5.2 for more details.

---

For an arbitrary FA $M = (Q, \Sigma, q_0, A, \delta)$, the expression $\delta(q, a)$ is a concise way of writing "the state to which the FA goes, if it is in state $q$ and receives input $a$." The next step is to extend the notation so that we can describe equally concisely "the state in which the FA ends up, if it begins in state $q$ and receives the string $x$ of input symbols." Let us write this as $\delta^*(q, x)$. The function $\delta^*$, then, is an extension of the transition function $\delta$ from the set $Q \times \Sigma$ to the larger set $Q \times \Sigma^*$. How do we define the function $\delta^*$ precisely? The idea behind the function is simple enough. If $x$ is the string $a_1 a_2 \ldots a_n$, we want to obtain $\delta^*(q, x)$ by first going to the state $q_1$ to which $M$ goes from state $q$ on input $a_1$; then going to the state $q_2$ to which $M$ goes from $q_1$ on input $a_2$; ...; and finally, going to the state $q_n$ to which $M$ goes from $q_{n-1}$ on input $a_n$. Unfortunately, so far this does not sound either particularly precise or particularly concise. Although we can replace many of the phrases by mathematical formulas (for example, "the state to which $M$ goes from state $q$ on input $a_1$" is simply $\delta(q, a_1)$), we still have the problem of the ellipses. At this point, we might be reminded of the discussion in Example 2.14.

The easiest way to define $\delta^*$ precisely is to give a recursive definition. For a particular state $q$, we are trying to define the expression $\delta^*(q, x)$ for each string $x$ in $\Sigma^*$. Using the recursive definition of $\Sigma^*$ (Example 2.15), we can proceed as follows: Define $\delta^*(q, \Lambda)$; then, assuming we know what $\delta^*(q, y)$ is, define $\delta^*(q, ya)$ for an element $a$ of $\Sigma$.

The "basis" part of the definition is not hard to figure out. We do not expect the state of the FA to change as a result of getting the input string $\Lambda$, and we define $\delta^*(q, \Lambda) = q$, for every $q \in Q$. Now, $\delta^*(q, ya)$ is to be the state that results when $M$ begins in state $q$ and receives first the input string $y$, then the single additional symbol $a$. The state $M$ is in after getting $y$ is $\delta^*(q, y)$; and from any state $p$, the state to which $M$ moves from $p$ on the single input symbol $a$ is $\delta(p, a)$. This means that the recursive part of the definition should define $\delta^*(q, ya)$ to be $\delta(\delta^*(q, y), a)$.

---

**Definition 3.3    The Extended Transition Function $\delta^*$**

Let $M = (Q, \Sigma, q_0, A, \delta)$ be an FA. We define the function

$$\delta^* : Q \times \Sigma^* \to Q$$

as follows:

1. For any $q \in Q$, $\delta^*(q, \Lambda) = q$
2. For any $q \in Q$, $y \in \Sigma^*$, and $a \in \Sigma$,

$$\delta^*(q, ya) = \delta(\delta^*(q, y), a)$$

---

It is important to understand that, in adopting the recursive definition of $\delta^*$, we have not abandoned the intuitive idea with which we first approached the definition.

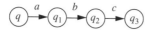

**Figure 3.4 |**

The point is that the recursive definition is the best way to capture this intuitive idea in a formal definition. Using this definition to calculate $\delta^*(q, x)$ amounts to just what you would expect, given what we wanted the function $\delta^*$ to represent: processing the symbols of $x$, one at a time, and seeing where the transition function $\delta$ takes us at each step. Suppose for example that $M$ contains the transitions shown in Figure 3.4.

Let us use Definition 3.3 to calculate $\delta^*(q, abc)$:

$$
\begin{aligned}
\delta^*(q, abc) &= \delta(\delta^*(q, ab), c) \\
&= \delta(\delta(\delta^*(q, a), b), c) \\
&= \delta(\delta(\delta^*(q, \Lambda a), b), c) \\
&= \delta(\delta(\delta(\delta^*(q, \Lambda), a), b), c) \\
&= \delta(\delta(\delta(q, a), b), c) \\
&= \delta(\delta(q_1, b), c) \\
&= \delta(q_2, c) \\
&= q_3
\end{aligned}
$$

Note that in the calculation above, it was necessary to calculate $\delta^*(q, a)$ by using the recursive part of the definition, since the basis part involves $\delta^*(q, \Lambda)$. Fortunately, $\delta^*(q, a)$ turned out to be $\delta(q, a)$; for strings of length 1 (i.e., elements of $\Sigma$), $\delta$ and $\delta^*$ can be used interchangeably. For a string $x$ with $|x| \neq 1$, however, writing $\delta(q, x)$ is incorrect, because the pair $(q, x)$ does not belong to the domain of $\delta$.

Other properties you would expect $\delta^*$ to satisfy can be derived from our definition. For example, a natural generalization of statement 2 of the definition is the formula

$$
\delta^*(q, xy) = \delta^*(\delta^*(q, x), y)
$$

which should be true for any $q \in Q$ and any two strings $x$ and $y$. The proof is by mathematical induction, and the details are left to you in Exercise 3.22.

Now we can state more concisely what it means for an FA to accept a string and what it means for an FA to accept a language.

---

**Definition 3.4    Acceptance by an FA**

Let $M = (Q, \Sigma, q_0, A, \delta)$ be an FA. A string $x \in \Sigma^*$ is *accepted* by $M$ if $\delta^*(q_0, x) \in A$. If a string is not accepted, we say it is *rejected* by $M$. The *language* accepted by $M$, or the language recognized by $M$, is the set

$$
L(M) = \{x \in \Sigma^* \mid x \text{ is accepted by } M\}
$$

If $L$ is any language over $\Sigma$, $L$ is accepted, or recognized, by $M$ if and only if $L = L(M)$.

**Figure 3.5 |**

Notice what the last statement in the definition does *not* say. It does not say that *L* is accepted by *M* if every string in *L* is accepted by *M*. If it did, we could use the FA in Figure 3.5 to accept any language, no matter how complex. The power of a machine does not lie in the number of strings it accepts, but in its ability to discriminate—to accept some and reject others. In order to accept a language *L*, an FA has to accept all the strings in *L* *and* reject all the strings in *L'*.

The terminology introduced in Definition 3.4 allows us to record officially the following fact, which we have mentioned already but will not prove until Chapter 4.

> **Theorem 3.1**
> A language *L* over the alphabet $\Sigma$ is regular if and only if there is an FA with input alphabet $\Sigma$ that accepts *L*.

This theorem says on the one hand that if *M* is any FA, there is a regular expression corresponding to the language $L(M)$; and on the other hand, that given a regular expression, there is an FA that accepts the corresponding language. The proofs in Chapter 4 will actually give us ways of constructing both these things. Until then, many examples are simple enough that we can get by without a formal algorithm.

**EXAMPLE 3.13** | Finding a Regular Expression Corresponding to an FA

Let us try to describe by a regular expression the language *L* accepted by the FA in Figure 3.6. The state labeled *A* is both the initial state and an accepting state; this tells us that $\Lambda \in L$. More generally, even-length strings of 0's (of which $\Lambda$ is one) are in *L*. These are the only strings *x* for which $\delta^*(A, x) = A$, because the only arrow to *A* from another state is the one from state 0, and the only arrow to that state is the one from *A*. These strings correspond to the regular expression $(00)^*$.

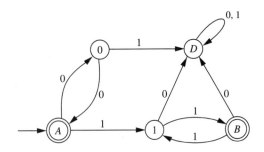

**Figure 3.6 |**
A finite automaton accepting {00}*{11}*.

The state labeled $D$ serves the same purpose in this example that $N$ did in Example 3.11. Once the FA reaches $D$, it stays in that state; a string $x$ for which $\delta^*(A, x) = D$ cannot be a prefix of any element of $L$.

The easiest way to reach the other accepting state $B$ from $A$ is with the string 11. Once the FA is in state $B$, any even-length string of 1's returns it to $B$, and these are the only strings that do this. Therefore, if $x$ is a string that causes the FA to go from $A$ to $B$ without revisiting $A$, $x$ must be of the form $11(11)^k$ for some $k \geq 0$. The most general type of string that causes the FA to reach state $B$ is a string of this type preceded by one of the form $(00)^j$, and a corresponding regular expression is $(00)^*11(11)^*$.

By combining the two cases (the strings $x$ for which $\delta^*(A, x) = A$ and those for which $\delta^*(A, x) = B$), we conclude that the language $L$ corresponds to the regular expression $(00)^* + (00)^*11(11)^*$, which can be simplified to

$$(00)^*(11)^*$$

## Another Example of a Regular Expression Corresponding to an FA   EXAMPLE 3.14

Next we consider the FA $M$ in Figure 3.7, with input alphabet $\{a, b\}$. One noteworthy feature of this FA is the fact that every arrow labeled $b$ takes the machine to state $B$. As a result, every string ending in $b$ causes $M$ to be in state $B$; in other words, for any string $x$, $\delta^*(A, xb) = B$. Therefore, $\delta^*(A, xbaaa) = \delta^*(\delta^*(A, xb), aaa) = \delta^*(B, aaa) = E$, which means that any string ending in $baaa$ is accepted by $M$. (The first of these equalities uses the formula in Exercise 3.22.)

On the other hand, we can see from the diagram that the only way to get to state $E$ is to reach $D$ first and then receive input $a$; the only way to reach $D$ is to reach $C$ and then receive $a$; the only way to reach $C$ is to reach $B$ and then receive $a$; and the only way to reach $B$ is to receive input $b$, although this could happen in any state. Therefore, it is also true that any

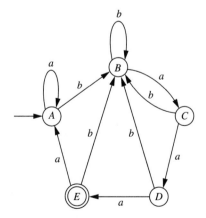

**Figure 3.7 |**
A finite automaton $M$ accepting $\{a, b\}^*\{baaa\}$.

string accepted by $M$ must end in *baaa*. The language $L(M)$ is the set of all strings ending in *baaa*, and a regular expression corresponding to $L(M)$ is $(a + b)^*baaa$.

This is a roundabout way of arriving at a regular expression. It depends on our noticing certain distinctive features of the FA, and it is not clear that the approach will be useful for other machines. An approach that might seem more direct is to start at state $A$ and try to build a regular expression as we move toward $E$. Since $\delta(A, a) = A$, we begin the regular expression with $a^*$. Since $\delta(A, b) = B$ and $\delta(B, b) = B$, we might write $a^*bb^*$ next. Now the symbol $a$ takes us to $C$, and we try $a^*bb^*a$. At this point it starts to get complicated, however, because we can now go back to $B$, loop some more with input $b$, then return to $C$—and we can repeat this any number of times. This might suggest $a^*bb^*a(bb^*a)^*$. As we get closer to $E$, there are more loops, and loops within loops, to take into account, and the formulas quickly become unwieldy. We might or might not be able to carry this to completion, and even if we can, the resulting formula will be complicated. We emphasize again that we do not yet have a systematic way to solve these problems, and there is no need to worry at this stage about complicated examples.

**EXAMPLE 3.15**     Strings Containing Either *ab* or *bba*

In this example we consider the language $L$ of all strings in $\{a, b\}^*$ that contain at least one of the two substrings $ab$ and $bba$ ($L$ corresponds to the regular expression $(a+b)^*(ab+bba)(a+b)^*$), and try to construct a finite automaton accepting $L$.

We start with two observations. These two strings themselves should be accepted by our FA; and if $x$ is any string that is accepted, then any other string obtained by adding symbols to the end of $x$ should also be accepted. Figure 3.8a shows a first attempt at an FA (obviously uncompleted) incorporating these features. (We might have started with two separate accepting states, but the transitions from both would have been the same, and one is enough.)

In order to continue, we need transitions labeled $a$ and $b$ from each of the states $p, r$, and $s$, and we may need additional states. It will help to think at this point about what each of the

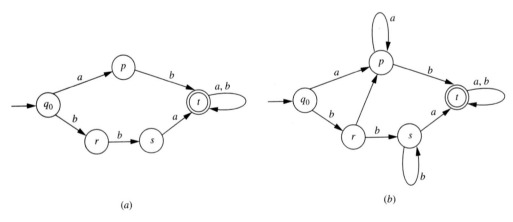

(a)     (b)

**Figure 3.8** |
Strings containing either *ab* or *bba*.

nonaccepting states is supposed to represent. First, being in a nonaccepting state means that we have not yet received one of the two desired strings. Being in the initial state $q_0$ should presumably mean that we have made no progress at all toward getting one of these two strings. It seems as though any input symbol at all represents some progress, however: An $a$ is at least potentially the first symbol in the substring $ab$, and $b$ might be the first symbol in $bba$. This suggests that once we have at least one input symbol, we should never need to return to the initial state.

It is not correct to say that $p$ is the state the FA should be in if the last input symbol received was an $a$, because there are arrows labeled $a$ that go to state $t$. It should be possible, however, to let $p$ represent the state in which the last input symbol was $a$ and we have not yet seen either $ab$ or $bba$. If we are already in this state and the next input symbol we receive is $a$, then nothing has really changed; in other words, $\delta(p, a)$ should be $p$.

We can describe the states $r$ and $s$ similarly. If the last input symbol was $b$, and it was not preceded by a $b$, and we have not yet arrived in the accepting state, we should be in state $r$. We should be in state $s$ if we have just received two consecutive $b$'s but have not yet reached the accepting state. What should $\delta(r, a)$ be? The $b$ that got us to state $r$ is no longer doing us any good, since it was not followed by $b$. In other words, it looked briefly as though we were making progress toward getting the string $bba$, but now it appears that we are not. We do not have to start over, however, because at least we have an $a$. We conclude that $\delta(r, a) = p$. We can also see that $\delta(s, b) = s$: If we are in state $s$ and get input $b$, we have not made any further progress toward getting $bba$, but neither have we lost any ground.

At this point, we have managed to define the missing transitions in Figure 3.8$a$ without adding any more states, and thus we have an FA that accepts the language $L$. The transition diagram is shown in Figure 3.8$b$.

## Another Example of an FA Corresponding to a Regular Expression     **EXAMPLE 3.16**

We consider another regular expression,

$$r = (11 + 110)^*0$$

and try to construct an FA accepting the corresponding language $L$. In the previous example, our preliminary guess at the structure of the FA turned out to provide all the states we needed. Here it will not be so straightforward. We will just proceed one symbol at a time, and for each new transition try to determine whether it can go to a state that is already present or whether it will require a new state.

The null string is not in $L$, which tells us that the initial state $q_0$ should not be an accepting state. The string 0, however, is in $L$, so that from $q_0$ the input symbol 0 must take us to an accepting state. The string 1 is not in $L$; furthermore, 1 must be distinguished from $\Lambda$, because the subsequent input string 110 should take us to an accepting state in one case and not in the other (i.e., $110 \in L$ and $1110 \notin L$.) At this point, we have determined that we need at least the states in Figure 3.9$a$.

The language $L$ contains 0 but no other strings beginning with 0. It also contains no strings beginning with 10. It is appropriate, therefore, to introduce a state $s$ that represents all the strings that fail for either reason to be a prefix of an element of $L$ (Figure 3.9$b$). Once our FA reaches the state $s$, which is not an accepting state, it never leaves this state.

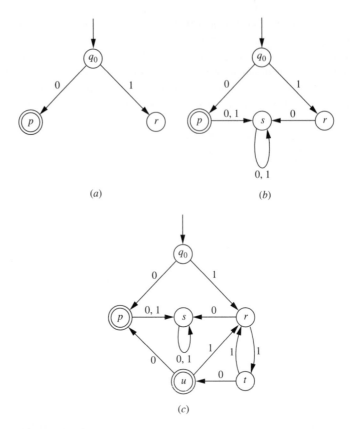

**Figure 3.9 |**
A finite automaton accepting $L_3$.

We must now consider the situation in which the FA is in state $r$ and receives the input 1. It should not stay in state $r$, because the strings 1 and 11 need to be distinguished (for example, $110 \in L$, but $1110 \notin L$). It should not return to the initial state, because $\Lambda$ and 11 need to be distinguished. Therefore, we need a new state $t$. From $t$, the input 0 must lead to an accepting state, since $110 \in L$. This accepting state cannot be $p$, because 110 is a prefix of a longer string in $L$ and 0 is not. Let $u$ be the new accepting state. If the FA receives a 0 in state $u$, then we have the same situation as an initial 0: The string 1100 is in $L$ but is not a prefix of any longer string in $L$. So we may let $\delta(u, 0) = p$. We have yet to define $\delta(t, 1)$ and $\delta(u, 1)$. States $t$ and $u$ can be thought of as "the end of one of the strings 11 and 110." (The reason $u$ is accepting is that 110 can also be viewed as 11 followed by 0.) In either case, if the next symbol is 1, we should think of it as the first symbol in *another* occurrence of one of these two strings. This means that it is appropriate to define $\delta(t, 1) = \delta(u, 1) = r$, and we arrive at the FA shown in Figure 3.9c.

The procedure we have followed here may seem hit-or-miss. We continued to add states as long as it was necessary, stopping only when all transitions from every state had been drawn and went to states that were already present. Theorem 3.1 is the reason we can be sure that the process *will* eventually stop. If we used the same approach for a language that was not regular, we would never be able to stop: No matter how many states we created, defining the transitions from those states would require yet more states. The step that is least obvious and most laborious in our procedure is determining whether a given transition needs to go to a new state, and if not, which existing state is the right one. The algorithm that we develop in Chapter 4 uses a different approach that avoids this difficulty.

# 3.4 | DISTINGUISHING ONE STRING FROM ANOTHER

Using a finite automaton to recognize a language $L$ depends on the fact that there are groups of strings so that strings within the same group do not need to be distinguished from each other by the machine. In other words, it is not necessary for the machine to remember exactly which string within the group it has read so far; remembering which group the string belongs to is enough. The number of distinct states the FA needs in order to recognize a language is related to the number of distinct strings that must be distinguished from each other. The following definition specifies precisely the circumstances under which an FA recognizing $L$ must distinguish between two strings $x$ and $y$, and the lemma that follows spells out explicitly how such an FA accomplishes this. (It says simply that the FA is in different states as a result of processing the two strings).

---

**Definition 3.5    Distinguishable Strings with Respect to $L$**

Let $L$ be a language in $\Sigma^*$, and $x$ any string in $\Sigma^*$. The set $L/x$ is defined as follows:

$$L/x = \{z \in \Sigma^* \mid xz \in L\}$$

Two strings $x$ and $y$ are said to be *distinguishable with respect to $L$* if $L/x \neq L/y$. Any string $z$ that is in one of the two sets but not the other (i.e., for which $xz \in L$ and $yz \notin L$, or vice versa) is said to distinguish $x$ and $y$ with respect to $L$. If $L/x = L/y$, $x$ and $y$ are indistinguishable with respect to $L$.

---

In order to show that two strings $x$ and $y$ are distinguishable with respect to a language $L$, it is sufficient to find one string $z$ so that either $xz \in L$ and $yz \notin L$, or $xz \notin L$ and $yz \in L$ (in other words, so that $z$ is in one of the two sets $L/x$ and $L/y$ but not the other). For example, if $L$ is the language in Example 3.9, the set of all strings in $\{0, 1\}^*$ that end in 10, we observed that 00 and 01 are distinguishable with respect to $L$, because we can choose $z$ to be the string 0; that is, $000 \notin L$ and

$010 \in L$. The two strings 0 and 00 are indistinguishable with respect to $L$, because the two sets $L/0$ and $L/00$ are equal; each is just the set $L$ itself. (The only way $0z$ or $00z$ can end in 10 is for $z$ to have this property.)

**Lemma 3.1**   Suppose $L \subseteq \Sigma^*$ and $M = (Q, \Sigma, q_0, A, \delta)$ is an FA recognizing $L$. If $x$ and $y$ are two strings in $\Sigma^*$ that are distinguishable with respect to $L$, then $\delta^*(q_0, x) \neq \delta^*(q_0, y)$.

***Proof***   The assumption that $x$ and $y$ are distinguishable with respect to $L$ means that there is a string $z$ in one of the two sets $L/x$ and $L/y$ but not the other. In other words, one of the two strings $xz$ and $yz$ is in $L$ and the other is not. Because we are also assuming that $M$ accepts $L$, it follows that one of the two states $\delta^*(q_0, xz)$ and $\delta^*(q_0, yz)$ is an accepting state and the other is not. In particular, therefore,

$$\delta^*(q_0, xz) \neq \delta^*(q_0, yz)$$

According to Exercise 3.22,

$$\delta^*(q_0, xz) = \delta^*(\delta^*(q_0, x), z)$$
$$\delta^*(q_0, yz) = \delta^*(\delta^*(q_0, y), z)$$

Because the left sides of these two equations are unequal, the right sides must be, and therefore $\delta^*(q_0, x) \neq \delta^*(q_0, y)$. ∎

**Theorem 3.2**

Suppose $L \subseteq \Sigma^*$ and, for some positive integer $n$, there are $n$ strings in $\Sigma^*$, any two of which are distinguishable with respect to $L$. Then every FA recognizing $L$ must have at least $n$ states.

***Proof***

Suppose $x_1, x_2, \ldots, x_n$ are $n$ strings, any two of which are distinguishable with respect to $L$. If $M = (Q, \Sigma, q_0, A, \delta)$ is any FA with fewer than $n$ states, then by the pigeonhole principle (Exercise 2.44), the states $\delta^*(q_0, x_1), \delta^*(q_0, x_2), \ldots, \delta^*(q_0, x_n)$ are not all distinct, and so for some $i \neq j$, $\delta^*(q_0, x_i) = \delta^*(q_0, x_j)$. Since $x_i$ and $x_j$ are distinguishable with respect to $L$, it follows from the lemma that $M$ cannot recognize $L$.

We interpret Theorem 3.2 as putting a lower bound on the memory requirements of any FA that is capable of recognizing $L$. To make this interpretation more concrete, we might think of the states as being numbered from 1 through $n$ and assume that there is a register in the machine that stores the number of the current state. The binary representation of the number $n$ has approximately $\log_2(n)$ binary digits, and thus the register needs to be able to hold approximately $\log_2(n)$ bits of information.

The Language $L_n$ EXAMPLE 3.17

Suppose $n \geq 1$, and let

$$L_n = \{x \in \{0, 1\}^* \mid |x| \geq n \text{ and the } n\text{th symbol from the right in } x \text{ is } 1\}$$

There is a straightforward way to construct an FA recognizing $L_n$, by creating a distinct state for every possible substring of length $n$ or less, just as we did in Example 3.12. In this way the FA will be able to remember the last $n$ symbols of the current input string. For each $i$, the number of strings of length exactly $i$ is $2^i$. If we add these numbers for the values of $i$ from 0 to $n$, we obtain $2^{n+1} - 1$ (Exercise 2.13); therefore, this is the total number of states. Figure 3.10 illustrates this FA in the case $n = 3$.

The eight states representing strings of length 3 are at the right. Not all the transitions from these states are shown, but the rule is simply

$$\delta(abc, d) = bcd$$

The accepting states are the four for which the third symbol from the end is 1.

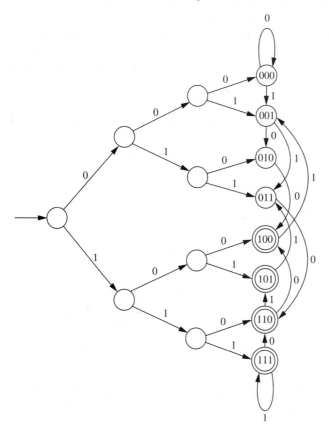

**Figure 3.10 |**
A finite automaton accepting $L_3$.

We might ask whether there is some simpler FA, perhaps using a completely different approach, that would cut the number of states to a number more manageable than $2^{n+1} - 1$. Although the number can be reduced just as in Example 3.12, we can see from Theorem 3.2 that any FA recognizing $L_n$ must have at least $2^n$ states. To do this, we show that any two strings of length $n$ (of which there are $2^n$ in all) are distinguishable with respect to $L_n$.

Let $x$ and $y$ be two distinct strings of length $n$. They must differ in the $i$th symbol (from the left), for some $i$ with $1 \leq i \leq n$. For the string $z$ that we will use to distinguish these two strings with respect to $L_n$, we can choose any string of length $i - 1$. Then $xz$ and $yz$ still differ in the $i$th symbol, and now the $i$th position is precisely the $n$th from the right. In other words, one of the strings $xz$ and $yz$ is in $L$ and the other is not, which implies that $L/x \neq L/y$. Therefore, $x$ and $y$ are distinguishable with respect to $L_n$.

---

Theorem 3.2 is potentially a way of showing that some languages cannot be accepted by any FA. According to the theorem, if there is a large set of strings, any two of which are distinguishable with respect to $L$, then any FA accepting $L$ must have a large number of states. What if there is a *really* large (i.e., infinite) set $S$ of strings with this property? Then no matter what $n$ is, we can choose a subset of $S$ with $n$ elements, which will be "pairwise distinguishable" (i.e., any two elements are distinguishable). Therefore, no matter what $n$ is, any FA accepting $L$ must have at least $n$ states. If this is true, the only way an FA can recognize $L$ at all is for it to have an infinite set of states, which is exactly what a *finite* automaton is not allowed to have. Such a language $L$ cannot be recognized by any abstract machine, or algorithm, of the type we have described, because no matter how much memory we provide, it will not be enough.

The following theorem provides our first example of such a language. In the proof, we show not only that there is an infinite "pairwise distinguishable" set of strings, but an even stronger statement, that the set $\Sigma^*$ itself has this property: *Any two strings are distinguishable with respect to the language.* This means that in attempting to recognize the language, following the conventions we have adopted, we cannot afford to forget anything. No matter what input string $x$ we have received so far, we must remember that it is $x$ and not some other string. The second conclusion of the theorem is a result of Theorem 3.1.

---

**Theorem 3.3**

The language *pal* of palindromes over the alphabet $\{0, 1\}$ cannot be accepted by any finite automaton, and it is therefore not regular.

*Proof*

As we described above, we will show that for any two distinct strings $x$ and $y$ in $\{0, 1\}^*$, $x$ and $y$ are distinguishable with respect to *pal*. To show this, we consider first the case when $|x| = |y|$, and we let $z = x^r$. Then $xz = xx^r$, which is in *pal*, and $yz$ is not. If $|x| \neq |y|$, we may as well assume that $|x| < |y|$, and we let $y = y_1 y_2$, where $|y_1| = |x|$. Again, we look for a string $z$ so that $xz \in pal$ and $yz \notin pal$. Any $z$ of the form

$z = ww^r x^r$ satisfies $xz \in pal$. In order to guarantee that $yz \notin pal$, we can choose $w$ to be any string different from $y_2$ but of the same length. Then

$$yz = y_1 y_2 z = y_1 y_2 ww^r x^r$$

Of the five substrings, the two on the ends both have length $|x|$, and all three of the others have length $|y_2|$. In order for $yz$ to be a palindrome, therefore, the fourth substring, $w^r$, must be the reverse of the second, $y_2$. This is impossible, however, since $w \neq y_2$. In either case, we have shown that $L/x \neq L/y$ (where $L = pal$).

In Chapter 5 we will consider other nonregular languages and find other methods for demonstrating that a language is nonregular. Definition 3.5 will also come up again in Chapter 5; the indistinguishability relation can be used in an elegant description of a "minimum-state" FA recognizing a given regular language.

# 3.5 | UNIONS, INTERSECTIONS, AND COMPLEMENTS

Suppose $L_1$ and $L_2$ are both regular languages over an alphabet $\Sigma$. There are FAs $M_1$ and $M_2$ accepting $L_1$ and $L_2$, respectively (Theorem 3.1); on the other hand, the languages $L_1 \cup L_2$, $L_1 L_2$, and $L_1^*$ are also regular (Definition 3.1) and can therefore be accepted by FAs. It makes sense to ask whether there are natural ways to obtain machines for these three languages from the two machines $M_1$ and $M_2$.

The language $L_1 \cup L_2$ is different in one important respect from the other two: Whether a string $x$ belongs to $L_1 \cup L_2$ depends only on whether $x \in L_1$ and whether $x \in L_2$. As a result, not only is there a simple solution to the problem in this case, but with only minor changes the same method also works for the two languages $L_1 \cap L_2$ and $L_1 - L_2$. We will wait until Chapter 4 to consider the two remaining languages $L_1 L_2$ and $L_1^*$.

If as we receive input symbols we execute two algorithms simultaneously, one to determine whether the current string $x$ is in $L_1$, the other to determine whether $x$ is in $L_2$, we will be able to say at each step whether $x$ is in $L_1 \cup L_2$. If $M_1 = (Q_1, \Sigma, q_1, A_1, \delta_1)$ and $M_2 = (Q_2, \Sigma, q_2, A_2, \delta_2)$ are FAs recognizing $L_1$ and $L_2$, respectively, a finite automaton $M$ should be able to recognize $L_1 \cup L_2$ if it can remember at each step both the information that $M_1$ remembers and the information $M_2$ remembers. Abstractly, this amounts to "remembering" the ordered pair $(p, q)$, where $p$ and $q$ are the current states of $M_1$ and $M_2$. Accordingly, we can construct $M$ by taking our set of states to be the set of all possible ordered pairs, $Q_1 \times Q_2$. The initial state will be the pair $(q_1, q_2)$ of initial states. If $M$ is in the state $(p, q)$ (which means that $p$ and $q$ are the current states of $M_1$ and $M_2$) and receives input symbol $a$, it should move to the state $(\delta_1(p, a), \delta_2(q, a))$, since the two components of this pair are the states to which the individual machines would move.

What we have done so far is independent of which of the three languages ($L_1 \cup L_2$, $L_1 \cap L_2$, and $L_1 - L_2$) we wish to accept. All that remains is to specify the set of accepting states so that the strings accepted are the ones we want. For the language $L_1 \cup L_2$, for example, $x$ should be accepted if it is in either $L_1$ or $L_2$; this means that the state $(p, q)$ should be an accepting state if either $p$ or $q$ is an accepting state of its respective FA. For the languages $L_1 \cap L_2$ and $L_1 - L_2$, the accepting states of the machine are defined similarly.

---

**Theorem 3.4**

Suppose $M_1 = (Q_1, \Sigma, q_1, A_1, \delta_1)$ and $M_2 = (Q_2, \Sigma, q_2, A_2, \delta_2)$ accept languages $L_1$ and $L_2$, respectively. Let $M$ be an FA defined by $M = (Q, \Sigma, q_0, A, \delta)$, where

$$Q = Q_1 \times Q_2$$
$$q_0 = (q_1, q_2)$$

and the transition function $\delta$ is defined by the formula

$$\delta((p, q), a) = (\delta_1(p, a), \delta_2(q, a))$$

(for any $p \in Q_1$, $q \in Q_2$, and $a \in \Sigma$). Then

1. If $A = \{(p, q) \mid p \in A_1 \text{ or } q \in A_2\}$, $M$ accepts the language $L_1 \cup L_2$;
2. If $A = \{(p, q) \mid p \in A_1 \text{ and } q \in A_2\}$, $M$ accepts the language $L_1 \cap L_2$;
3. If $A = \{(p, q) \mid p \in A_1 \text{ and } q \notin A_2\}$, $M$ accepts the language $L_1 - L_2$.

*Proof*

We have already sketched the main idea. Since acceptance by $M_1$ and $M_2$ is defined in terms of the functions $\delta_1^*$ and $\delta_2^*$, respectively, and acceptance by $M$ in terms of $\delta^*$, we need the formula

$$\delta^*((p, q), x) = (\delta_1^*(p, x), \delta_2^*(q, x))$$

which holds for any $x \in \Sigma^*$ and any $(p, q) \in Q$, and can be verified easily by using mathematical induction (Exercise 3.32). A string $x$ is accepted by $M$ if and only if $\delta^*((q_1, q_2), x) \in A$. By our formula, this is true if and only if

$$(\delta_1^*(q_1, x), \delta_2^*(q_2, x)) \in A$$

If the set $A$ is defined as in case 1, this is the same as saying that $\delta_1^*(q_1, x) \in A_1$ or $\delta_2^*(q_2, x) \in A_2$, or in other words, that $x \in L_1 \cup L_2$. Cases 2 and 3 are similar.

---

We may consider the special case in which $L_1$ is all of $\Sigma^*$. $L_1 - L_2$ is therefore $L_2'$, the complement of $L_2$. The construction in the theorem can be used, where $M_1$ is the trivial FA with only the state $q_1$, which is an accepting state. However, this description of $M$ is unnecessarily complicated. Except for the names of the states, it is the same as

$$M_2' = (Q_2, \Sigma, q_2, Q_2 - A_2, \delta_2)$$

which we obtain from $M_2$ by just reversing accepting and nonaccepting states.

It often happens, as in the following example, that the FA we need for one of these three languages is even simpler than the construction in Theorem 3.4 would seem to indicate.

An FA Accepting $L_1 - L_2$   **EXAMPLE 3.18**

Suppose $L_1$ and $L_2$ are the subsets

$$L_1 = \{x \mid 00 \text{ is not a substring of } x\}$$
$$L_2 = \{x \mid x \text{ ends with } 01\}$$

of $\{0, 1\}^*$. The languages $L_1$ and $L_2$ are recognized by the FAs in Figure 3.11a.

The construction in the theorem, for any of the three cases, produces an FA with nine states. In order to draw the transition diagram, we begin with the initial state $(A, P)$. Since $\delta_1(A, 0) = B$ and $\delta_2(P, 0) = Q$, we have $\delta((A, P), 0) = (B, Q)$. Similarly, $\delta((A, P), 1) = (A, P)$. Next we calculate $\delta((B, Q), 0)$ and $\delta((B, Q), 1)$. As we continue this process, as

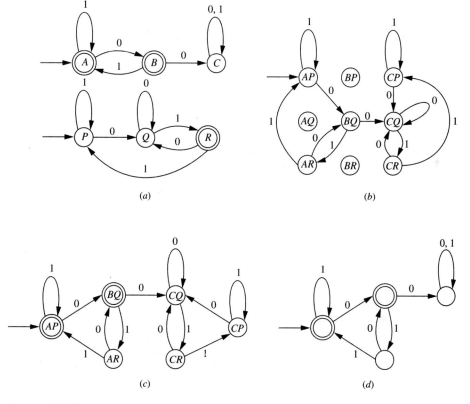

**Figure 3.11** |
Constructing a finite automaton to accept $L_1 - L_2$.

soon as a new state is introduced, we calculate the transitions from this state. After a few steps we obtain the partial diagram in Figure 3.11b. We now have six states; each of them can be reached from $(A, P)$ as a result of some input string, and every transition from one of these six goes to one of these six. We conclude that the other three states are not reachable from the initial state, and therefore that they can be left out of our FA (Exercise 3.29).

Suppose now that we want our FA to recognize the language $L_1 - L_2$. Then we designate as our accepting states those states $(X, Y)$ from among the six for which $X$ is either $A$ or $B$ and $Y$ is not $R$. These are $(A, P)$ and $(B, Q)$, and the resulting FA is shown in Figure 3.11c.

In fact, we can simplify this FA even further. None of the states $(C, P)$, $(C, Q)$, or $(C, R)$ is an accepting state, and once the machine enters one of these states, it remains in one of them. Therefore, we may replace all of them with a single state, obtaining the FA shown in Figure 3.11d.

## EXERCISES

**3.1.** In each case, find a string of minimum length in $\{0, 1\}^*$ *not* in the language corresponding to the given regular expression.

   a.  $1^*(01)^*0^*$

   b.  $(0^* + 1^*)(0^* + 1^*)(0^* + 1^*)$

   c.  $0^*(100^*)^*1^*$

   d.  $1^*(0 + 10)^*1^*$

**3.2.** Consider the two regular expressions

$$r = 0^* + 1^* \qquad s = 01^* + 10^* + 1^*0 + (0^*1)^*$$

   a.  Find a string corresponding to $r$ but not to $s$.

   b.  Find a string corresponding to $s$ but not to $r$.

   c.  Find a string corresponding to both $r$ and $s$.

   d.  Find a string in $\{0, 1\}^*$ corresponding to neither $r$ nor $s$.

**3.3.** Let $r$ and $s$ be arbitrary regular expressions over the alphabet $\Sigma$. In each case, find a simpler regular expression corresponding to the same language as the given one.

   a.  $(r + s + rs + sr)^*$

   b.  $(r(r + s)^*)^+$

   c.  $r(r^*r + r^*) + r^*$

   d.  $(r + \Lambda)^*$

   e.  $(r + s)^*rs(r + s)^* + s^*r^*$

**3.4.** Prove the formula

$$(111^*)^* = (11 + 111)^*$$

**3.5.** Prove the formula

$$(aa^*bb^*)^* = \Lambda + a(a + b)^*b$$

**3.6.** In the definition of regular languages, Definition 3.1, statement 2 can be omitted without changing the set of regular languages. Why?

**3.7.** The set of regular languages over $\Sigma$ is the smallest set that contains all the languages $\emptyset$, $\{\Lambda\}$, and $\{a\}$ (for every $a \in \Sigma$) and is closed under the operations of union, concatenation, and Kleene *. In each case below, describe the smallest set of languages that contains all these "basic" languages and is closed under the specified operations.

   a.  union

   b.  concatenation

   c.  Kleene *

   d.  union and concatenation

   e.  union and Kleene *

**3.8.** Find regular expressions corresponding to each of the languages defined recursively below.

   a.  $\Lambda \in L$;   if $x \in L$, then $001x$ and $x11$ are elements of $L$;   nothing is in $L$ unless it can be obtained from these two statements.

   b.  $0 \in L$;   if $x \in L$, then $001x$, $x001$, and $x11$ are elements of $L$; nothing is in $L$ unless it can be obtained from these two statements.

   c.  $\Lambda \in L$;   $0 \in L$; if $x \in L$, then $001x$ and $11x$ are in $L$;   nothing is in $L$ unless it can be obtained from these three statements.

**3.9.** Find a regular expression corresponding to each of the following subsets of $\{0, 1\}^*$.

   a.  The language of all strings containing exactly two 0's.

   b.  The language of all strings containing at least two 0's.

   c.  The language of all strings that do not end with 01.

   d.  The language of all strings that begin or end with 00 or 11.

   e.  The language of all strings not containing the substring 00.

   f.  The language of all strings in which the number of 0's is even.

   g.  The language of all strings containing no more than one occurrence of the string 00. (The string 000 should be viewed as containing two occurrences of 00.)

   h.  The language of all strings in which every 0 is followed immediately by 11.

   i.  The language of all strings containing both 11 and 010 as substrings.

**3.10.** Describe as simply as possible the language corresponding to each of the following regular expressions.

   a.  $0^*1(0^*10^*1)^*0^*$

b. $((0 + 1)^3)^*(\Lambda + 0 + 1)$

c. $(1 + 01)^*(0 + 01)^*$

d. $(0 + 1)^*(0^+1^+0^+ + 1^+0^+1^+)(0 + 1)^*$     (Give an answer of the form: all strings containing both the substring _____ and the substring _____.)

**3.11.** Show that if $L$ is a regular language, then the language $L^n$ is regular for every $n \geq 0$.

**3.12.** Show that every finite language is regular.

**3.13.** The function $rev : \Sigma^* \to \Sigma^*$ is defined in Example 2.24. For a language $L$, let $L^r$ denote the language $\{rev(x) \mid x \in L\} = \{x^r \mid x \in L\}$.

a. If $e$ is the regular expression $(001 + 11010)^*1010$, and $L_e$ is the corresponding language, give a regular expression corresponding to $L_e^r$.

b. Taking this example as a model, give a recursive definition of a function *rrev* from the set of regular expressions over $\Sigma$ to itself, so that for any regular expression $r$ over $\Sigma$, the language corresponding to *rrev*$(r)$ is the reverse of the language corresponding to $r$. Give a proof that your function has this property.

c. Show that if $L$ is a regular language, then $L^r$ is regular.

**3.14.** In the C programming language, all the following expressions represent valid numerical "literals":

| | | | | |
|---|---|---|---|---|
| 3 | 13. | .328 | 41.16 | +45.80 |
| +0 | -01 | -14.4 | 1e12 | +1.4e6 |
| -2.e+7 | 01E-06 | 0.2E-20 | -.4E-7 | 00e0 |

The letter e or E refers to an exponent, and if it appears, the number following it is an integer. Based on these examples, write a regular expression representing the language of numerical literals. You can use the same shorthand as in Example 3.4: $l$ for "letter," $d$ for "digit," $a$ for '+', $m$ for '−', and $p$ for "point." Assume that there are no limits on the number of consecutive digits in any part of the expression.

**3.15.** The *star height* of a regular expression $r$ over $\Sigma$, denoted by $sh(r)$, is defined as follows:

(i)   $sh(\emptyset) = 0$.

(ii)  $sh(\Lambda) = 0$.

(iii) $sh(a) = 0$ for every $a \in \Sigma$.

(iv)  $sh((rs)) = sh((r + s)) = \max(sh(r), sh(s))$.

(v)   $sh((r^*)) = sh(r) + 1$.

Find the star heights of the following regular expressions.

a. $(a(a + a^*aa) + aaa)^*$

b. $(((a + a^*aa)aa)^* + aaaaaa^*)^*$

**3.16.** For both the regular expressions in the previous exercise, find an equivalent regular expression of star height 1.

**3.17.** For each of the FAs pictured in Figure 3.12, describe, either in words or by writing a regular expression, the strings that cause the FA to be in each state.

**3.18.** Let $x$ be a string in $\{0, 1\}^*$ of length $n$. Describe an FA that accepts the string $x$ and no other strings. How many states are required?

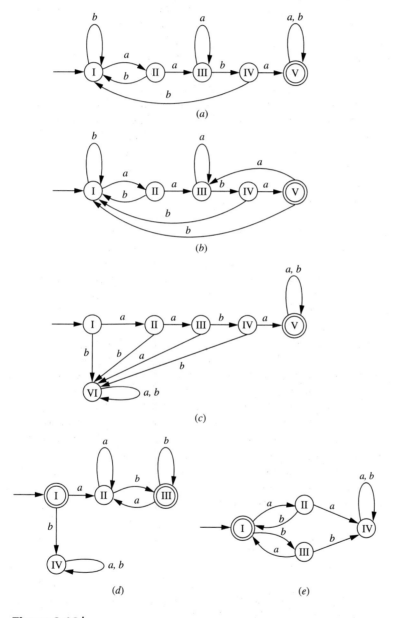

**Figure 3.12 |**

**3.19.** For each of the languages in Exercise 3.9, draw an FA recognizing the language.

**3.20.** For each of the following regular expressions, draw an FA recognizing the corresponding language.

    a.   $(0 + 1)^*0$

    b.   $(11 + 10)^*$

    c.   $(0 + 1)^*(1 + 00)(0 + 1)^*$

    d.   $(111 + 100)^*0$

    e.   $0 + 10^* + 01^*0$

    f.   $(0 + 1)^*(01 + 110)$

**3.21.** Draw an FA that recognizes the language of all strings of 0's and 1's of length at least 1 that, if they were interpreted as binary representations of integers, would represent integers evenly divisible by 3. Your FA should accept the string 0 but no other strings with leading 0's.

**3.22.** Suppose $M$ is the finite automaton $(Q, \Sigma, q_0, A, \delta)$.

    a.   Using mathematical induction or structural induction, show that for any $x$ and $y$ in $\Sigma^*$, and any $q \in Q$,

$$\delta^*(q, xy) = \delta^*(\delta^*(q, x), y)$$

       Two reasonable approaches are to base the induction on $x$ and to base it on $y$. One, however, works better than the other.

    b.   Show that if for some state $q$, $\delta(q, a) = q$ for every $a \in \Sigma$, then $\delta^*(q, x) = q$ for every $x \in \Sigma^*$.

    c.   Show that if for some state $q$ and some string $x$, $\delta^*(q, x) = q$, then for every $n \geq 0$, $\delta^*(q, x^n) = q$.

**3.23.** If $L$ is a language accepted by an FA $M$, then there is an FA accepting $L$ with more states than $M$ (and therefore there is no limit to the number of states an FA accepting $L$ can have). Explain briefly why this is true.

**3.24.** Show by an example that for some regular language $L$, any FA recognizing $L$ must have more than one accepting state. Characterize those regular languages for which this is true.

**3.25.** For the FA pictured in Figure 3.11$d$, show that there cannot be any other FA with fewer states accepting the same language.

**3.26.** Let $z$ be a fixed string of length $n$ over the alphabet $\{0, 1\}$. What is the smallest number of states an FA can have if it accepts the language $\{0, 1\}^*\{z\}$? Prove your answer.

**3.27.** Suppose $L$ is a subset of $\{0, 1\}^*$. Does an infinite set of distinguishable pairs with respect to $L$ imply an infinite set that is pairwise distinguishable with respect to $L$? In particular, if $x_0, x_1, \ldots$ is a sequence of distinct strings in $\{0, 1\}^*$ so that for any $n \geq 0$, $x_n$ and $x_{n+1}$ are distinguishable with respect to $L$, does it follow that $L$ is not regular? Either give a proof that it does follow, or provide an example of a regular language $L$ and a sequence of strings $x_0$, $x_1, \ldots$ with this property.

**3.28.** Let $L \subseteq \{0, 1\}^*$ be an infinite language, and for each $n \geq 0$, let $L_n = \{x \in L \mid |x| = n\}$. Denote by $s(n)$ the number of states an FA must have in order to accept $L_n$. What is the smallest that $s(n)$ can be if $L_n \neq \emptyset$? Give an example of an infinite language $L$ so that for every $n$ satisfying $L_n \neq \emptyset$, $s(n)$ is this minimum number.

**3.29.** Suppose $M = (Q, \Sigma, q_0, A, \delta)$ is an FA. If $p$ and $q$ are elements of $Q$, we say $q$ is *reachable* from $p$ if there is a string $x \in \Sigma^*$ so that $\delta^*(p, x) = q$. Let $M_1$ be the FA obtained from $M$ by deleting any states that are not reachable from $q_0$ (and any transitions to or from such states). Show that $M_1$ and $M$ recognize the same language. (Note: we might also try to simplify $M$ by eliminating the states from which no accepting state is reachable. The result might be a pair $(q, a) \in Q \times \Sigma$ for which no transition is defined, so that we do not have an FA. In Chapter 4 we will see that this simplification can still be useful.)

**3.30.** Let $M = (Q, \Sigma, q_0, A, \delta)$ be an FA. Let $M_1 = (Q, \Sigma, q_0, R, \delta)$, where $R$ is the set of states in $Q$ from which some element of $A$ is reachable (see Exercise 3.29). What is the relationship between the language recognized by $M_1$ and the language recognized by $M$? Prove your answer.

**3.31.** Suppose $M = (Q, \Sigma, q_0, A, \delta)$ is an FA, and suppose that there is some string $z$ so that for every $q \in Q$, $\delta^*(q, z) \in A$. What conclusion can you draw, and why?

**3.32.** (For this problem, refer to the proof of Theorem 3.4.) Show that for any $x \in \Sigma^*$ and any $(p, q) \in Q$, $\delta^*((p, q), x) = (\delta_1^*(p, x), \delta_2^*(q, x))$.

**3.33.** Let $M_1$, $M_2$, and $M_3$ be the FAs pictured in Figure 3.13, recognizing languages $L_1$, $L_2$, and $L_3$, respectively.

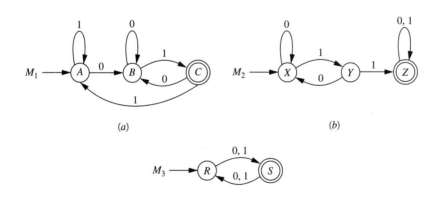

(a)

(b)

(a)

**Figure 3.13** |

Draw FAs recognizing the following languages.

a. $L_1 \cup L_2$

b. $L_1 \cap L_2$

c. $L_1 - L_2$

d. $L_1 \cap L_3$

e. $L_3 - L_2$

# MORE CHALLENGING PROBLEMS

**3.34.** Prove that for any two regular expressions $r$ and $s$ over $\Sigma$, $(r^*s^*)^* = (r + s)^*$.

**3.35.** Prove the formula

$$(00^*1)^*1 = 1 + 0(0 + 10)^*11$$

**3.36.** Find a regular expression corresponding to each of the following subsets of $\{0, 1\}^*$.

a. The language of all strings not containing the substring 000.

b. The language of all strings that do not contain the substring 110.

c. The language of all strings containing both 101 and 010 as substrings.

d. The language of all strings in which both the number of 0's and the number of 1's are even.

e. The language of all strings in which both the number of 0's and the number of 1's are odd.

**3.37.** Suppose $r$ is a regular expression over $\Sigma$. Show that if for each symbol in $r$ that is an element of $\Sigma$ another regular expression over $\Sigma$ is substituted, the result is a regular expression over $\Sigma$.

**3.38.** Let $c$ and $d$ be regular expressions over $\Sigma$.

a. Show that the formula $r = c + rd$, involving the variable $r$, is true if the regular expression $cd^*$ is substituted for $r$.

b. Show that if $\Lambda$ is not in the language corresponding to $d$, then any regular expression $r$ satisfying $r = c + rd$ corresponds to the same language as $cd^*$.

**3.39.** Describe precisely an algorithm that could be used to eliminate the symbol $\emptyset$ from any regular expression that does not correspond to the empty language.

**3.40.** Describe an algorithm that could be used to eliminate the symbol $\Lambda$ from any regular expression whose corresponding language does not contain the null string.

**3.41.** The *order* of a regular language $L$ is the smallest integer $k$ for which $L^k = L^{k+1}$, if there is one, and $\infty$ otherwise.

a. Show that the order of $L$ is finite if and only if there is an integer $k$ so that $L^k = L^*$, and that in this case the order of $L$ is the smallest $k$ so that $L^k = L^*$.

    b.  What is the order of the regular language $\{\Lambda\} \cup \{aa\}\{aaa\}^*$?

    c.  What is the order of the regular language $\{a\} \cup \{aa\}\{aaa\}^*$?

    d.  What is the order of the language corresponding to the regular expression $(\Lambda + b^*a)(b + ab^*ab^*a)^*$?

**3.42.** A *generalized regular expression* is defined the same way as an ordinary regular expression, except that two additional operations, intersection and complement, are allowed. So, for example, the generalized regular expression $abb\emptyset' \cap (\emptyset'aaa\emptyset')'$ represents the set of all strings in $\{a, b\}^*$ that start with $abb$ and don't contain the substring $aaa$.

    a.  Show that the subset $\{aba\}^*$ of $\{a, b\}^*$ can be described by a generalized regular expression with no occurrences of $^*$.

    b.  Can the subset $\{aa\}^*$ be described this way? Give reasons for your answer.

**3.43.** For each of the following regular expressions, draw an FA recognizing the corresponding language.

    a.  $(1 + 110)^*0$

    b.  $(1 + 10 + 110)^*0$

    c.  $1(01 + 10)^* + 0(11 + 10)^*$

    d.  $1(1 + 10)^* + 10(0 + 01)^*$

    e.  $(010 + 00)^*(10)^*$

**3.44.** Let $M = (Q, \Sigma, q_0, A, \delta)$ be an FA. Below are other conceivable methods of defining the extended transition function $\delta^*$ (see Definition 3.3). In each case, determine whether it is in fact a valid definition of a function on the set $Q \times \Sigma^*$, and why. *If* it is, show using mathematical induction that it defines the same function that Definition 3.3 does.

    a.  For any $q \in Q$, $\delta^*(q, \Lambda) = q$; for any $y \in \Sigma^*$, $a \in \Sigma$, and $q \in Q$, $\delta^*(q, ya) = \delta^*(\delta^*(q, y), a)$.

    b.  For any $q \in Q$, $\delta^*(q, \Lambda) = q$; for any $y \in \Sigma^*$, $a \in \Sigma$, and $q \in Q$, $\delta^*(q, ay) = \delta^*(\delta(q, a), y)$.

    c.  For any $q \in Q$, $\delta^*(q, \Lambda) = q$; for any $q \in Q$ and any $a \in \Sigma$, $\delta^*(q, a) = \delta(q, a)$; for any $q \in Q$, and any $x$ and $y$ in $\Sigma^*$, $\delta^*(q, xy) = \delta^*(\delta^*(q, x), y)$.

**3.45.** Let $L$ be the set of even-length strings over $\{0, 1\}$ whose first and second halves are identical; in other words, $L = \{ww \mid w \in \{0, 1\}^*\}$. Use the technique of Theorem 3.3 to show that $L$ is not regular: Show that for any two strings $x$ and $y$ in $\{0, 1\}^*$, $x$ and $y$ are distinguishable with respect to $L$.

**3.46.** Let $L$ be the language $\{0^n1^n \mid n \geq 0\}$.

    a.  Find two distinct strings $x$ and $y$ that are indistinguishable with respect to $L$.

    b.  Show that $L$ is not regular, by showing that there is an infinite set of strings, any two of which are distinguishable with respect to $L$.

**3.47.** As in Example 3.17, let

$$L_n = \{x \in \{0, 1\}^* \mid |x| \geq n \text{ and the } n\text{th symbol from the right in } x \text{ is } 1\}$$

It is shown in that example that any FA recognizing $L_n$ must have at least $2^n$ states. Draw an FA with four states that recognizes $L_2$. For any $n \geq 1$, describe how to construct an FA with $2^n$ states that recognizes $L_n$.

**3.48.** Let $n$ be a positive integer and $L = \{x \in \{0, 1\}^* \mid |x| = n \text{ and } n_0(x) = n_1(x)\}$. What is the minimum number of states in any FA that recognizes $L$? Give reasons for your answer.

**3.49.** Let $n$ be a positive integer and $L = \{x \in \{0, 1\}^* \mid |x| = n \text{ and } n_0(x) < n_1(x)\}$. What is the minimum number of states in any FA that recognizes $L$? Give reasons for your answer.

**3.50.** Let $n$ be a positive integer, and let $L$ be the set of all strings in *pal* of length $2n$. In other words,

$$L = \{xx^r \mid x \in \{0, 1\}^n\}$$

What is the minimum number of states in any FA that recognizes $L$? Give reasons for your answer.

**3.51.** Languages such as that in Example 3.9 are regular for what seems like a particularly simple reason: In order to test a string for membership, we need to examine only the last few symbols. More precisely, there is an integer $n$ and a set $S$ of strings of length $n$ so that for any string $x$ of length $n$ or greater, $x$ is in the language if and only if $x = yz$ for some $z \in S$. (In Example 3.9, we may take $n$ to be 2 and $S$ to be the set $\{11\}$.) Show that any language $L$ having this property is regular.

**3.52.** Show that every finite language has the property in the previous problem.

**3.53.** Give an example of an infinite regular language (a subset of $\{0, 1\}^*$) that does not have the property in Exercise 3.51, and prove that it does not.

**3.54.** (This exercise is due to Hermann Stamm-Wilbrandt.) Consider the language

$$L = \{x \in \{0, 1, 2\}^* \mid x \text{ does not contain the substring } 01\}$$

Show that for every $i \geq 0$, the number of strings of length $i$ in $L$ is $f(2i + 2)$, where $f$ is the Fibonacci function (see Example 2.13). Hint: draw an FA accepting $L$, with initial state $q_0$, and consider for each state $q$ in your FA and each integer $i$, the set $S(q, i)$ of all strings $x$ of length $i$ satisfying $\delta^*(q_0, x) = q$.

**3.55.** Consider the two FAs in Figure 3.14. If you examine them closely you can see that they are really identical, except that the states have different names: State $p$ corresponds to state $A$, $q$ corresponds to $B$, and $r$ corresponds to $C$. Let us describe this correspondence by the *relabeling function* $i$; that is, $i(p) = A$, $i(q) = B$, $i(r) = C$. What does it mean to say that under this correspondence, the two FAs are "really identical?" It means several things: First, the initial states correspond to each other; second, a state is an accepting state if and only if the corresponding state is; and finally, the

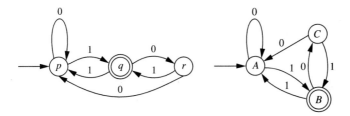

**Figure 3.14 |**

transitions among the states of the first FA are the same as those among the corresponding states of the other. For example, if $\delta_1$ and $\delta_2$ are the transition functions,

$$\delta_1(p, 0) = p \quad \text{and} \quad \delta_2(i(p), 0) = i(p)$$
$$\delta_1(p, 1) = q \quad \text{and} \quad \delta_2(i(p), 1) = i(q)$$

These formulas can be rewritten

$$\delta_2(i(p), 0) = i(\delta_1(p, 0)) \text{ and } \delta_2(i(p), 0) = i(\delta_1(p, 0))$$

and these and all the other relevant formulas can be summarized by the general formula

$$\delta_2(i(s), a) = i(\delta_1(s, a)) \text{ for every state } s \text{ and alphabet symbol } a$$

In general, if $M_1 = (Q_1, \Sigma, q_1, A_1, \delta_1)$ and $M_2 = (Q_2, \Sigma, q_2, A_2, \delta_2)$ are FAs and $i : Q_1 \to Q_2$ is a bijection (i.e., one-to-one and onto), we say that $i$ is an *isomorphism from $M_1$ to $M_2$* if these conditions are satisfied:

(i)   $i(q_1) = q_2$
(ii)  for any $q \in Q_1$, $i(q) \in A_2$ if and only if $q \in A_1$
(iii) for every $q \in Q_1$ and every $a \in \Sigma$, $i(\delta_1(q, a)) = \delta_2(i(q), a)$

and we say $M_1$ is *isomorphic to $M_2$* if there is an isomorphism from $M_1$ to $M_2$. This is simply a precise way of saying that $M_1$ and $M_2$ are "essentially the same."

a.  Show that the relation $\sim$ on the set of FAs over $\Sigma$, defined by $M_1 \sim M_2$ if $M_1$ is isomorphic to $M_2$, is an equivalence relation.

b.  Show that if $i$ is an isomorphism from $M_1$ to $M_2$ (notation as above), then for every $q \in Q_1$ and $x \in \Sigma^*$,

$$i(\delta_1^*(q, x)) = \delta_2^*(i(q), x)$$

c.  Show that two isomorphic FAs accept the same language.

d.  How many one-state FAs over the alphabet $\{0, 1\}$ are there, no two of which are isomorphic?

e.  How many pairwise nonisomorphic two-state FAs over {0, 1} are there, in which both states are reachable from the initial state and at least one state is accepting?

f.  How many distinct languages are accepted by the FAs in the previous part?

g.  Show that the FAs described by these two transition tables are isomorphic. The states are 1–6 in the first, A–F in the second; the initial states are 1 and A, respectively; the accepting states in the first FA are 5 and 6, and D and E in the second.

| $q$ | $\delta_1(q,0)$ | $\delta_1(q,1)$ | $q$ | $\delta_2(q,0)$ | $\delta_2(q,1)$ |
|-----|-----------------|-----------------|-----|-----------------|-----------------|
| 1   | 3               | 5               | A   | B               | E               |
| 2   | 4               | 2               | B   | A               | D               |
| 3   | 1               | 6               | C   | C               | B               |
| 4   | 4               | 3               | D   | B               | C               |
| 5   | 2               | 4               | E   | F               | C               |
| 6   | 3               | 4               | F   | C               | F               |

h.  Specify a reasonable algorithm for determining whether or not two given FAs are isomorphic.

# Nondeterminism and Kleene's Theorem

## 4.1 | NONDETERMINISTIC FINITE AUTOMATA

One of our goals in this chapter is to prove that a language is regular if and only if it can be accepted by a finite automaton (Theorem 3.1). However, examples like Example 3.16 suggest that finding a finite automaton (FA) corresponding to a given regular expression can be tedious and unintuitive if we rely only on the techniques we have developed so far, which involve deciding at each step how much information about the input string it is necessary to remember. An alternative approach is to consider a formal device called a nondeterministic finite automaton (NFA), similar to an FA but with the rules relaxed somewhat. Constructing one of these devices to correspond to a given regular expression is often much simpler. Furthermore, it will turn out that NFAs accept exactly the same languages as FAs, and that there is a straightforward procedure for converting an NFA to an equivalent FA. As a result, not only will it be easier in many examples to construct an FA by starting with an NFA, but introducing these more general devices will also help when we get to our proof.

A Simpler Approach to Accepting $\{11, 110\}^*\{0\}$ | **EXAMPLE 4.1**

Figure 4.1$a$ shows the FA constructed in Example 3.16, which recognizes the language $L$ corresponding to the regular expression $(11 + 110)^*0$. Now look at the diagram in Figure 4.1$b$. If we concentrate on the resemblance between this device and an FA, and ignore for the moment the ways in which it fails to satisfy the normal FA rules, we can see that it reflects much more clearly the structure of the regular expression.

For any string $x$ in $L$, a path through the diagram corresponding to $x$ can be described as follows. It starts at $q_0$, and for each occurrence of one of the strings 11 or 110 in the portion of $x$ corresponding to $(11 + 110)^*$, it takes the appropriate loop that returns to $q_0$; when the final 0 is encountered, the path moves to the accepting state $q_4$. In the other direction, we can also

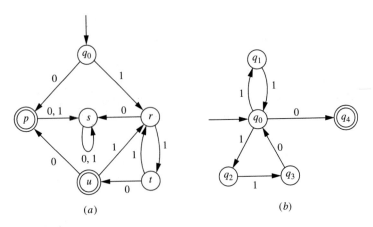

**Figure 4.1 |**
A simpler approach to accepting {11, 110}*{0}.

see that any path starting at $q_0$ and ending at $q_4$ corresponds to a string matching the regular expression.

Let us now consider the ways in which the diagram in Figure 4.1*b* differs from that of an FA, and the way in which it should be interpreted if we are to view it as a language-accepting device. There are two apparently different problems. From some states there are not transitions for both input symbols (from state $q_4$ there are no transitions at all); and from one state, $q_0$, there is more than one arrow corresponding to the same input.

The way to interpret the first of these features is easy. The absence of an $a$-transition from state $q$ means that from $q$ there is no input string beginning with $a$ that can result in the device's being in an accepting state. We could create a transition by introducing a "dead" state to which the device could go from $q$ on input $a$, having the property that once the device gets to that state it can never leave it. However, leaving this transition out makes the picture simpler, and because it would never be executed during any sequence of moves leading to an accepting state, leaving it out does not hurt anything except that it violates the rules.

The second violation of the rules for FAs seems to be more serious. The diagram indicates two transitions from $q_0$ on input 1. It does not specify an unambiguous action for that state-input combination, and therefore apparently no longer represents a recognition algorithm or a language-recognizing machine.

As we will see shortly, there is an FA that operates in such a way that it simulates the diagram correctly and accepts the right language. However, even as it stands, we can salvage much of the intuitive idea of a machine from the diagram, if we are willing to give the machine an element of *nondeterminism*. An ordinary finite automaton is deterministic: The moves it makes while processing an input string are completely determined by the input symbols and the state it starts in. To the extent that a device is nondeterministic, its behavior is unpredictable. There may be situations (i.e., state-input combinations) in which it has a choice of possible moves, and in these cases it selects a move in some unspecified way. One way to describe this is to say that it *guesses* a move.

For an ordinary (deterministic) FA $M$, saying what it means for a string to be accepted by $M$ is easy: $x$ is accepted if the sequence of moves determined by the input symbols of $x$ causes $M$ to end up in an accepting state. If $M$ is allowed to guess, we must think more carefully about what acceptance means. (Should we say that $x$ is accepted if *some* choice of moves corresponding to the string $x$ leads to an accepting state, or should we require that *every* choice does?) Returning to our example, it is helpful to think about the regular expression $(11 + 110)^*0$ corresponding to the language we are trying to accept, and the problem of trying to decide directly whether a string $x$ (for example, 11110110) matches this regular expression. As we read the input symbols of $x$, there are several ways we might try to match them to the regular expression. Some approaches will not work, such as matching the prefix 1111 with $(11 + 110)^*$. If there is at least one way that does work, we conclude that $x$ corresponds to the regular expression. (If we make a wrong guess during this matching process, we might fail to accept a string that is actually in the language; however, wrong guesses will never cause us to accept a string that is not in the language.)

This analogy suggests the appropriate way of making sense of Figure 4.1$b$. Instead of asking whether *the* path corresponding to a string leads to an accepting state (as with an ordinary FA), we ask whether *some* path corresponding to the string does. In following the diagram, when we are in state $q_0$ and we receive input symbol 1 we guess which arrow labeled 1 is the appropriate one to follow. Guessing wrong might result in a "no" answer for a string that is actually in the language. This does not invalidate the approach, because for a string in the language there will be at least one sequence of guesses that leads to acceptance, and for a string not in the language no sequence of guesses will cause the string to be accepted.

We are almost ready for a formal definition of the abstract device illustrated by Figure 4.1$b$. The only change we will need to make to the definition of an FA involves the transition function. As we saw in Example 4.1, for a particular combination of state and input symbol, there may be no states specified to which the device should go, or there may be several. All we have to do in order to accommodate both these cases is to let the value of the transition function be a *set* of states—possibly the empty set, possibly one with several elements. In other words, our transition function $\delta$ will still be defined on $Q \times \Sigma$ but will now have values in $2^Q$ (the set of subsets of $Q$). Our interpretation will be that $\delta(q, a)$ represents the set of states that the device can legally be in, as a result of being in state $q$ at the previous step and then processing input symbol $a$.

---

**Definition 4.1    A Nondeterministic Finite Automaton**

A nondeterministic finite automaton, abbreviated NFA, is a 5-tuple $M = (Q, \Sigma, q_0, A, \delta)$, where $Q$ and $\Sigma$ are nonempty finite sets, $q_0 \in Q$, $A \subseteq Q$, and

$$\delta : Q \times \Sigma \to 2^Q$$

$Q$ is the set of states, $\Sigma$ is the alphabet, $q_0$ is the initial state, and $A$ is the set of accepting states.

Just as in the case of FAs, it is useful to extend the transition function $\delta$ from $Q \times \Sigma$ to the larger set $Q \times \Sigma^*$. For an NFA $M$, $\delta^*$ should be defined so that $\delta^*(p, x)$ is the set of states $M$ can legally be in as a result of starting in state $p$ and processing the symbols in the string $x$. The recursive formula for FAs was

$$\delta^*(p, xa) = \delta(\delta^*(p, x), a)$$

where $p$ is any state, $x$ is any string in $\Sigma^*$, and $a$ is any single alphabet symbol. We will give a recursive definition here as well, but just as before, let us start gradually, with what may still seem like a more straightforward approach. As before, we want to say that the only state $M$ can get to from $p$ as a result of processing $\Lambda$ is $p$; the only difference now is that we must write $\delta^*(p, \Lambda) = \{p\}$, rather than $\delta^*(p, \Lambda) = p$.

If $x = a_1 a_2 \cdots a_n$, then saying $M$ can be in state $q$ after processing $x$ means that there are states $p_0, p_1, p_2, \ldots, p_n$ so that $p_0 = p$, $p_n = q$, and

$M$ can get from $p_0$ (or $p$) to $p_1$ by processing $a_1$;

$M$ can get from $p_1$ to $p_2$ by processing $a_2$;

. . .

$M$ can get from $p_{n-2}$ to $p_{n-1}$ by processing $a_{n-1}$;

$M$ can get from $p_{n-1}$ to $p_n$ (or $q$) by processing $a_n$.

A simpler way to say "$M$ can get from $p_{i-1}$ to $p_i$ by processing $a_i$" (or "$p_i$ is one of the states to which $M$ can get from $p_{i-1}$ by processing $a_i$") is

$$p_i \in \delta(p_{i-1}, a_i)$$

We may therefore define the function $\delta^*$ as follows.

---

**Definition 4.2a     Nonrecursive Definition of $\delta^*$ for an NFA**

For an NFA $M = (Q, \Sigma, q_0, A, \delta)$, and any $p \in Q$, $\delta^*(p, \Lambda) = \{p\}$. For any $p \in Q$ and any $x = a_1 a_2 \cdots a_n \in \Sigma^*$ (with $n \geq 1$), $\delta^*(p, x)$ is the set of all states $q$ for which there is a sequence of states $p = p_0, p_1, \ldots, p_{n-1}$, $p_n = q$ satisfying

$$p_i \in \delta(p_{i-1}, a_i) \text{ for each } i \text{ with } 1 \leq i \leq n$$

---

Although the sequence of statements above was intended specifically to say that $p_n \in \delta^*(p_0, a_1 a_2 \cdots a_n)$, there is nothing to stop us from looking at intermediate points along the way and observing that for each $i \geq 1$,

$$p_i \in \delta^*(p_0, a_1 a_2 \cdots a_i)$$

In order to obtain a recursive description of $\delta^*$, it is helpful in particular to consider $i = n - 1$ and to let $y$ denote the string $a_1 a_2 \cdots a_{n-1}$. Then we have

$$p_{n-1} \in \delta^*(p, y)$$
$$p_n \in \delta(p_{n-1}, a_n)$$

In other words, if $q \in \delta^*(p, ya_n)$, then there is a state $r$ (namely, $r = p_{n-1}$) in the set $\delta^*(p, y)$ so that $q \in \delta(r, a_n)$. It is also clear that this argument can be reversed: If $q \in \delta(r, a_n)$ for some $r \in \delta^*(p, y)$, then we may conclude from the definition that $q \in \delta^*(p, ya_n)$. The conclusion is the recursive formula we need:

$$\delta^*(p, ya_n) = \{q \mid q \in \delta(r, a_n) \text{ for some } r \in \delta^*(p, y)\}$$

or more concisely,

$$\delta^*(p, ya_n) = \bigcup_{r \in \delta^*(p, y)} \delta(r, a_n)$$

---

**Definition 4.2b    Recursive Definition of $\delta^*$ for an NFA**

Let $M = (Q, \Sigma, q_0, A, \delta)$ be an NFA. The function $\delta^* : Q \times \Sigma^* \to 2^Q$ is defined as follows.

1. For any $q \in Q$, $\delta^*(q, \Lambda) = \{q\}$.
2. For any $q \in Q$, $y \in \Sigma^*$, and $a \in \Sigma$,

$$\delta^*(q, ya) = \bigcup_{r \in \delta^*(q, y)} \delta(r, a)$$

---

We want the statement that a string $x$ is accepted by an NFA $M$ to mean that there is a sequence of moves $M$ can make, starting in its initial state and processing the symbols of $x$, that will lead to an accepting state. In other words, $M$ accepts $x$ if the set of states in which $M$ can end up as a result of processing $x$ contains at least one accepting state.

---

**Definition 4.3    Acceptance by an NFA**

Let $M = (Q, \Sigma, q_0, A, \delta)$ be an NFA. The string $x \in \Sigma^*$ is accepted by $M$ if $\delta^*(q_0, x) \cap A \neq \emptyset$. The language recognized, or accepted, by $M$ is the set $L(M)$ of all strings accepted by $M$. For any language $L \subseteq \Sigma^*$, $L$ is recognized by $M$ if $L = L(M)$.

---

Using the Recursive Definition of $\delta^*$ in an NFA        **EXAMPLE 4.2**

Let $M = (Q, \Sigma, q_0, A, \delta)$, where $Q = \{q_0, q_1, q_2, q_3\}$, $\Sigma = \{0, 1\}$, $A = \{q_3\}$, and $\delta$ is given by the following table.

| $q$ | $\delta(q, 0)$ | $\delta(q, 1)$ |
|-----|---------------|---------------|
| $q_0$ | $\{q_0\}$ | $\{q_0, q_1\}$ |
| $q_1$ | $\{q_2\}$ | $\{q_2\}$ |
| $q_2$ | $\{q_3\}$ | $\{q_3\}$ |
| $q_3$ | $\emptyset$ | $\emptyset$ |

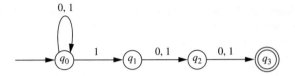

**Figure 4.2** |

Then $M$ can be represented by the transition diagram in Figure 4.2. Let us try to determine $L(M)$ by calculating $\delta^*(q_0, x)$ for a few strings $x$ of increasing length. First observe that from the nonrecursive definition of $\delta^*$ it is almost obvious that $\delta$ and $\delta^*$ agree for strings of length 1 (see also Exercise 4.3). We see from the table that $\delta^*(q_0, 0) = \{q_0\}$ and $\delta^*(q_0, 1) = \{q_0, q_1\}$;

$$\delta^*(q_0, 11) = \bigcup_{r \in \delta^*(q_0, 1)} \delta(r, 1) \quad \text{(by definition of } \delta^*)$$

$$= \bigcup_{r \in \{q_0, q_1\}} \delta(r, 1)$$

$$= \delta(q_0, 1) \cup \delta(q_1, 1)$$

$$= \{q_0, q_1\} \cup \{q_2\}$$

$$= \{q_0, q_1, q_2\}$$

$$\delta^*(q_0, 01) = \bigcup_{r \in \delta^*(q_0, 0)} \delta(r, 1)$$

$$= \bigcup_{r \in \{q_0\}} \delta(r, 1)$$

$$= \delta(q_0, 1)$$

$$= \{q_0, q_1\}$$

$$\delta^*(q_0, 111) = \bigcup_{r \in \delta^*(q_0, 11)} \delta(r, 1)$$

$$= \delta(q_0, 1) \cup \delta(q_1, 1) \cup \delta(q_2, 1)$$

$$= \{q_0, q_1, q_2, q_3\}$$

$$\delta^*(q_0, 011) = \bigcup_{r \in \delta^*(q_0, 01)} \delta(r, 1)$$

$$= \delta(q_0, 1) \cup \delta(q_1, 1)$$

$$= \{q_0, q_1, q_2\}$$

We observe that 111 is accepted by $M$ and 011 is not. You can see if you study the diagram in Figure 4.2 that $\delta^*(q_0, x)$ contains $q_1$ if and only if $x$ ends with 1; that for any $y$ with $|y| = 2$, $\delta^*(q_0, xy)$ contains $q_3$ if and only if $x$ ends with 1; and, therefore, that the language recognized by $M$ is

$$\{0, 1\}^* \{1\} \{0, 1\}^2$$

This is the language we called $L_3$ in Example 3.17, the set of strings with length at least 3 having a 1 in the third position from the end. By taking the diagram in Figure 4.2 as a model, you can easily construct for any $n \geq 1$ an NFA with $n + 1$ states that recognizes $L_n$. Since we showed in Example 3.17 that any ordinary FA accepting $L_n$ needs at least $2^n$ states, it is now clear that an NFA recognizing a language may have considerably fewer states than the simplest FA recognizing the language.

The formulas above may help to convince you that the recursive definition of $\delta^*$ is a workable tool for investigating the NFA, and in particular for testing a string for membership in the language $L(M)$. Another approach that provides an effective way of visualizing the behavior of the NFA as it processes a string is to draw a *computation tree* for that string. This is just a tree diagram tracing the choices the machine has at each step, and the paths through the states corresponding to the possible sequences of moves. Figure 4.3 shows the tree for the NFA above and the input string 101101.

Starting in $q_0$, $M$ can go to either $q_0$ or $q_1$ using the first symbol of the string. In either case, there is only one choice at the next step, with the symbol 0. This tree shows several types of paths: those that end prematurely (with fewer than six moves), because $M$ arrives in a state from which there is no move corresponding to the next input symbol; those that contain six

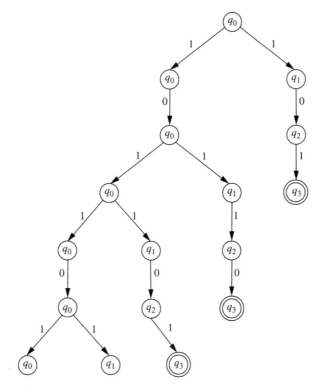

**Figure 4.3 |**
A computation tree for the NFA in Figure 4.2, as it processes 101101.

moves and end in a nonaccepting state; and one path of length 6 that ends in the accepting state and therefore shows the string to be accepted.

It is easy to read off from the diagram the sets $\delta^*(q_0, y)$ for prefixes $y$ of $x$. For example, $\delta^*(q_0, 101) = \{q_0, q_1, q_3\}$, because these three states are the ones that appear at that level of the tree. Deciding whether $x$ is accepted is simply a matter of checking whether any accepting states appear in the tree at level $|x|$ (assuming that the root of the tree, the initial state, is at level 0).

We now want to show that although it may be easier to construct an NFA accepting a given language than to construct an FA, nondeterministic finite automata as a group are no more powerful than FAs: Any language that can be accepted by an NFA can also be recognized by a (possibly more complicated) FA.

We have discussed the fact that a (deterministic) finite automaton can be interpreted as an algorithm for recognizing a language. Although an NFA might not represent an algorithm directly, there are certainly algorithms that can determine for any string $x$ whether or not there is a sequence of moves that corresponds to the symbols of $x$ and leads to an accepting state. Looking at the tree diagram in Figure 4.3, for example, suggests some sort of *tree traversal* algorithm, of which there are several standard ones. A *depth-first* traversal corresponds to checking the possible paths sequentially, following each path until it stops, and then seeing if it stops in an accepting state after the correct number of steps. A *breadth-first*, or level-by-level, traversal of the tree corresponds in some sense to testing the paths in parallel.

The question we are interested in, however, is not whether there is an algorithm for recognizing the language, but whether there is one that corresponds to a (deterministic) finite automaton. We will show that there is by looking carefully at the definition of an NFA, which contains a potential mechanism for eliminating the nondeterminism directly.

The definition of a finite automaton, either deterministic or nondeterministic, involves the idea of a *state*. The nondeterminism present in an NFA appears whenever there are state-input combinations for which there is not exactly one resulting state. In a sense, however, the nondeterminism in an NFA is only apparent, and arises from the notion of state that we start with. We will be able to transform the NFA into an FA by redefining *state* so that for each combination of state and input symbol, exactly one state results. The way to do this is already suggested by the definition of the transition function of an NFA. Corresponding to a particular state-input pair, we needed the function to have a single value, and the way we accomplished this was to make the value a set. All we have to do now is carry this idea a little further and consider a state in our FA to be a subset of $Q$, rather than a single element of $Q$. (There is a partial precedent for this in the proof of Theorem 3.4, where we considered states that were pairs of elements of $Q$.) Then corresponding to the "state" $S$ and the input symbol $a$ (i.e., to the set of all the pairs $(p, a)$ for which $p \in S$), there is exactly one "state" that results: the union of all the sets $\delta(p, a)$ for $p \in S$. All of a sudden, the nondeterminism has disappeared! Furthermore, the resulting machine simulates the original device in an obvious way, provided that we define the initial and final states correctly.

This technique is important enough to have acquired a name, the *subset construction*: States in the FA are subsets of the state set of the NFA.

---

**Theorem 4.1**

For any NFA $M = (Q, \Sigma, q_0, A, \delta)$ accepting a language $L \subseteq \Sigma^*$, there is an FA $M_1 = (Q_1, \Sigma, q_1, A_1, \delta_1)$ that also accepts $L$.

*Proof*

$M_1$ is defined as follows:

$$Q_1 = 2^Q \qquad q_1 = \{q_0\} \qquad \text{for } q \in Q_1 \text{ and } a \in \Sigma, \delta_1(q, a) = \bigcup_{r \in q} \delta(r, a)$$

$$A_1 = \{q \in Q_1 \mid q \cap A \neq \emptyset\}$$

The last definition is the right one because a string $x$ should be accepted by $M_1$ if, starting in $q_0$, the set of states in which $M$ might end up as a result of processing $x$ contains at least one element of $A$.

The fact that $M_1$ accepts the same language as $M$ follows from the fact that for any $x \in \Sigma^*$,

$$\delta_1^*(q_1, x) = \delta^*(q_0, x)$$

which we now prove using structural induction on $x$. Note that the functions $\delta_1^*$ and $\delta^*$ are defined in different ways: $\delta^*$ in Definition 4.2b, since $M$ is an NFA, and $\delta_1^*$ in Definition 3.3, since $M_1$ is an FA.

If $x = \Lambda$,

$$
\begin{aligned}
\delta_1^*(q_1, x) &= \delta_1^*(q_1, \Lambda) \\
&= q_1 \quad \text{(by definition of } \delta_1^*) \\
&= \{q_0\} \quad \text{(by definition of } q_1) \\
&= \delta^*(q_0, \Lambda) \quad \text{(by definition of } \delta^*) \\
&= \delta^*(q_0, x)
\end{aligned}
$$

The induction hypothesis is that $x$ is a string satisfying $\delta_1^*(q_1, x) = \delta^*(q_0, x)$, and we wish to prove that for any $a \in \Sigma$, $\delta_1^*(q_1, xa) = \delta^*(q_0, xa)$:

$$
\begin{aligned}
\delta_1^*(q_1, xa) &= \delta_1(\delta_1^*(q_1, x), a) \quad \text{(by definition of } \delta_1^*) \\
&= \delta_1(\delta^*(q_0, x), a) \quad \text{(by the induction hypothesis)} \\
&= \bigcup_{r \in \delta^*(q_0, x)} \delta(r, a) \quad \text{(by definition of } \delta_1) \\
&= \delta^*(q_0, xa) \quad \text{(by definition of } \delta^*)
\end{aligned}
$$

That $M$ and $M_1$ recognize the same language is now easy to see. A string $x$ is accepted by $M_1$ if $\delta_1^*(q_1, x) \in A_1$; we can now say that this is true if and only if $\delta^*(q_0, x) \in A_1$; and using the definition of $A_1$, we conclude that this is true if and only if $\delta^*(q_0, x) \cap A \neq \emptyset$. In other words, $x$ is accepted by $M_1$ if and only if $x$ is accepted by $M$.

---

It is important to realize that the proof of the theorem provides an algorithm (the subset construction) for removing the nondeterminism from an NFA. Let us illustrate the algorithm by returning to the NFA in Example 4.2.

**EXAMPLE 4.3**   ## Applying the Subset Construction to Convert an NFA to an FA

The table in Example 4.2 shows the transition function of the NFA shown in Figure 4.2. The subset construction could produce an FA with as many as 16 states, since $Q$ has 16 subsets. (In general, if $M$ has $n$ states, $M_1$ may have as many as $2^n$, the number of subsets of a set with $n$ elements.) However, we can get by with fewer if we follow the same approach as in Example 3.18 and use only those states that are reachable from the initial state. The transition function in our FA will be $\delta_1$, and we proceed to calculate some of its values. Each time a new state (i.e., a new subset) $S$ appears in our calculation, we must subsequently include the calculation of $\delta_1(S, 0)$ and $\delta_1(S, 1)$:

$$\delta_1(\{q_0\}, 0) = \{q_0\}$$
$$\delta_1(\{q_0\}, 1) = \{q_0, q_1\}$$
$$\delta_1(\{q_0, q_1\}, 0) = \delta(\{q_0\}, 0) \cup \delta(\{q_1\}, 0) = \{q_0\} \cup \{q_2\} = \{q_0, q_2\}$$
$$\delta_1(\{q_0, q_1\}, 1) = \delta(\{q_0\}, 1) \cup \delta(\{q_1\}, 1) = \{q_0, q_1\} \cup \{q_2\} = \{q_0, q_1, q_2\}$$
$$\delta_1(\{q_0, q_2\}, 0) = \delta(\{q_0\}, 0) \cup \delta(\{q_2\}, 0) = \{q_0\} \cup \{q_3\} = \{q_0, q_3\}$$
$$\delta_1(\{q_0, q_2\}, 1) = \{q_0, q_1\} \cup \{q_3\} = \{q_0, q_1, q_3\}$$

It turns out that in the course of the calculation, eight distinct states (i.e., sets) arise. We knew already from the discussion in Example 3.17 that at least this many would be necessary.

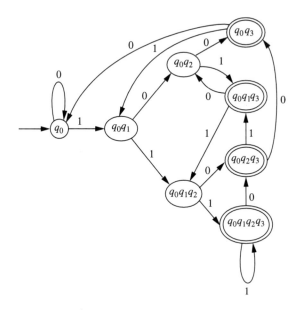

**Figure 4.4 |**
The subset construction applied to the NFA in Figure 4.2.

Therefore, although we should not expect this to happen in general, the calculation in this case produces the FA with the fewest possible states recognizing the desired language. It is shown in Figure 4.4.

### Another Example Illustrating the Subset Construction | EXAMPLE 4.4

We close this section by returning to the first NFA we looked at, the one shown in Figure 4.1$b$. In fact, the FA produced by our algorithm is the one in Figure 4.1$a$; let us see how we obtain it.

If we carry out the calculations analogous to those in the previous example, the distinct states of the FA that are necessary, in the order they appear, turn out to be $\{q_0\}$, $\{q_4\}$, $\{q_1, q_2\}$, $\emptyset$, $\{q_0, q_3\}$, and $\{q_0, q_4\}$. The resulting transition table follows:

| $q$ | $\delta_1(q, 0)$ | $\delta_1(q, 1)$ |
|---|---|---|
| $\{q_0\}$ | $\{q_4\}$ | $\{q_1, q_2\}$ |
| $\{q_4\}$ | $\emptyset$ | $\emptyset$ |
| $\{q_1, q_2\}$ | $\emptyset$ | $\{q_0, q_3\}$ |
| $\emptyset$ | $\emptyset$ | $\emptyset$ |
| $\{q_0, q_3\}$ | $\{q_0, q_4\}$ | $\{q_1, q_2\}$ |
| $\{q_0, q_4\}$ | $\{q_4\}$ | $\{q_1, q_2\}$ |

You can recognize this as the FA shown in Figure 4.1$a$ by substituting $p$ for $\{q_4\}$, $r$ for $\{q_1, q_2\}$, $s$ for $\emptyset$, $t$ for $\{q_0, q_3\}$, and $u$ for $\{q_0, q_4\}$. (Strictly speaking, you should also substitute $q_0$ for $\{q_0\}$.)

## 4.2 | NONDETERMINISTIC FINITE AUTOMATA WITH Λ-TRANSITIONS

One further modification of finite automata will be helpful in our upcoming proof that regular languages are the same as those accepted by FAs. We introduce the new devices by an example that suggests some of the ways they will be used in the proof.

### How a Device More General Than an NFA Can Be Useful | EXAMPLE 4.5

Figures 4.5$a$ and 4.5$b$ show simple NFAs $M_1$ and $M_2$ accepting the two languages $L_1 = \{0\}\{1\}^*$ and $L_2 = \{0\}^*\{1\}$, respectively, over the alphabet $\{0, 1\}$.

We consider two ways of combining these languages, using the operations of concatenation and union (two of the three operations involved in the definition of regular languages), and in each case we will try to incorporate the existing NFAs in a composite device $M$ accepting the language we are interested in. Ideally, the structure of $M_1$ and $M_2$ will be preserved more or less intact in the resulting machine, and the way we combine the two NFAs will depend only on the operation being used to combine the two languages.

First we try the language $L_1 L_2$ corresponding to the regular expression $01^*0^*1$. In this case, $M$ should in some sense start out the way $M_1$ does and finish up the way $M_2$ does. The

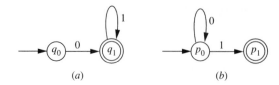

**Figure 4.5 |**

(a) An NFA accepting $\{0\}\{1\}^*$; (b) An NFA accepting $\{0\}^*\{1\}$.

question is just how to connect the two. The string 0 takes $M_1$ from $q_0$ to $q_1$; since 0 is not itself an element of $L_1 L_2$, we do not expect the state $q_1$ to be an accepting state in $M$. We might consider the possible ways to interpret an input symbol once we have reached the state $q_1$. At that point, a 0 (if it is part of a string that will be accepted) can only be part of the $0^*$ term from the second language. This might suggest connecting $q_1$ to $p_0$ by an arrow labeled 0; this cannot be the only connection, because a string in $L$ does not require a 0 at this point. The symbol 1 in state $q_1$ could be either part of the $1^*$ term from the first language, which suggests a connecting arrow from $q_1$ to $p_0$ labeled 1, or the 1 corresponding to the second language, which suggests an arrow from $q_1$ to $p_1$ labeled 1. These three connecting arrows turn out to be enough, and the resulting NFA is shown in Figure 4.6a.

We introduced a procedure in Chapter 3 to take care of the union of two languages provided we have an FA for each one, but it is not hard to see that the method is not always satisfactory if we have NFAs instead (Exercise 4.12). One possible NFA to handle $L_1 \cup L_2$ is shown in Figure 4.6b. This time it may not be obvious whether making $q_0$ the initial state, rather than $p_0$, is a natural choice or simply an arbitrary one. The label 1 on the connecting arrow from $q_0$ to $p_1$ is the 1 in the regular expression $0^*1$, and the 0 on the arrow from $q_0$ to $p_0$ is part of the $0^*$ in the same regular expression. The NFA accepts the language corresponding to the regular expression $01^* + 1 + 00^*1$, which can be simplified to $01^* + 0^*1$.

For both $L_1 L_2$ and $L_1 \cup L_2$, we have found relatively simple composite NFAs, and it is possible in both cases to see how the two original diagrams are incorporated into the result. However, in both cases the structure of the original diagrams has been obscured somewhat in the process of combining them, because the extra arrows used to connect the two depend on the regular expressions being combined, not just on the combining operation. We do not yet seem to have a general method that will work for two arbitrary NFAs.

One way to solve this problem, it turns out, is to combine the two NFAs so as to create a nondeterministic device with even a little more freedom in guessing. In the case of concatenation, for example, we will allow the new device to guess while in state $q_1$ that it will receive no more inputs that are to be matched with $1^*$. In making this guess it commits itself to proceeding to the second part of the regular expression $01^*0^*1$; it will be able to make this guess, however, without any reference to the actual structure of the second part—in particular, without receiving any input (or, what amounts to the same thing, receiving only the null string $\Lambda$ as input). The resulting diagram is shown in Figure 4.7a.

In the second case, we provide the NFA with an initial state that has nothing to do with either $M_1$ or $M_2$, and we allow it to guess before it has received any input whether it will be

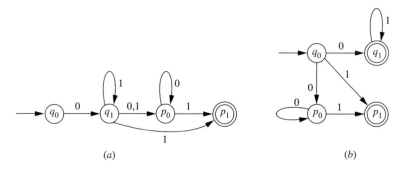

**Figure 4.6** |
(a) An NFA accepting $\{0\}\{1\}^*\{0\}^*\{1\}$; (b) An NFA accepting $\{0\}\{1\}^* \cup \{0\}^*\{1\}$.

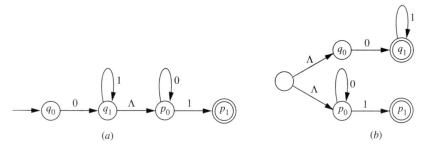

**Figure 4.7** |
(a) An NFA-$\Lambda$ accepting $\{0\}\{1\}^*\{0\}^*\{1\}$; (b) An NFA-$\Lambda$ accepting $\{0\}\{1\}^* \cup \{0\}^*\{1\}$.

looking for an input string in $L_1$ or one in $L_2$. Making this guess requires only $\Lambda$ as input and allows the machine to begin operating exactly like $M_1$ or $M_2$, whichever is appropriate. The result is shown in Figure 4.7b.

To summarize, the devices in Figure 4.7 are more general than NFAs in that they are allowed to make transitions, not only on input symbols from the alphabet, but also on null inputs.

---

**Definition 4.4    A Nondeterministic Finite Automaton with**
**                      $\Lambda$-Transitions**

A nondeterministic finite automaton with $\Lambda$-transitions (abbreviated NFA-$\Lambda$) is a 5-tuple $(Q, \Sigma, q_0, A, \delta)$, where $Q$ and $\Sigma$ are finite sets, $q_0 \in Q$, $A \subseteq Q$, and

$$\delta : Q \times (\Sigma \cup \{\Lambda\}) \to 2^Q$$

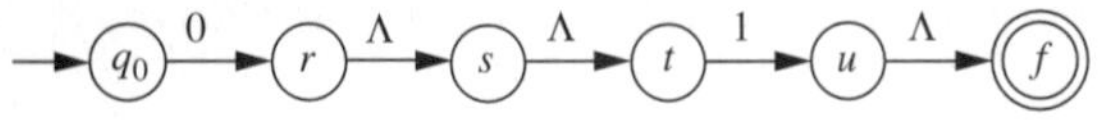

**Figure 4.8** |

As before, we need to define an extended function $\delta^*$ in order to give a precise definition of acceptance of a string by an NFA-$\Lambda$. The idea is still that $\delta^*(q, x)$ will be the set of all states in which the NFA-$\Lambda$ can legally end up as a result of starting in state $q$ and processing the symbols in $x$. However, there is now a further complication, since "processing the symbols in $x$" allows for the possibility of $\Lambda$-transitions interspersed among ordinary transitions. Figure 4.8 illustrates this. We want to say that the string 01 is accepted, since $0\Lambda\Lambda 1\Lambda = 01$ and the path corresponding to these five inputs leads from $q_0$ to an accepting state.

Again we start with a nonrecursive definition, which is a straightforward if not especially elegant adaptation of Definition 4.2a.

---

**Definition 4.5a     Nonrecursive Definition of $\delta^*$ for an NFA-$\Lambda$**

For an NFA-$\Lambda$ $M = (Q, \Sigma, q_0, A, \delta)$, states $p, q \in Q$, and a string $x = a_1 a_2 \cdots a_n \in \Sigma^*$, we will say $M$ moves from $p$ to $q$ by a sequence of transitions corresponding to $x$ if there exist an integer $m \geq n$, a sequence $b_1, b_2, \ldots, b_m \in \Sigma \cup \{\Lambda\}$ satisfying $b_1 b_2 \cdots b_m = x$, and a sequence of states $p = p_0, p_1, \ldots, p_m = q$ so that for each $i$ with $1 \leq i \leq m$, $p_i \in \delta(p_{i-1}, b_i)$.
    For $x \in \Sigma^*$ and $p \in Q$, $\delta^*(p, x)$ is the set of all states $q \in Q$ such that there is a sequence of transitions corresponding to $x$ by which $M$ moves from $p$ to $q$.

---

For example, in Figure 4.8 there is a sequence of transitions corresponding to 01 by which the device moves from $q_0$ to $f$; there is a sequence of transitions corresponding to the string $\Lambda$ by which it moves from $r$ to $t$; and there is also a sequence of transitions corresponding to $\Lambda$ by which it moves from any state to itself (namely, the empty sequence).

Coming up with a recursive definition of $\delta^*$ is not as easy this time. The recursive part of the definition will still involve defining $\delta^*$ for a string with one extra alphabet symbol $a$. However, if we denote by $S$ the set of states that the device may be in before the $a$ is processed, we obtain the new set by allowing all possible transitions from elements of $S$ on the input $a$, as well as all subsequent $\Lambda$-transitions. This suggests that we also want to modify the basis part of the definition, so that the set $\delta^*(q, \Lambda)$ contains not only $q$ but any other states that the NFA-$\Lambda$ can reach from $q$ by using $\Lambda$-transitions. Both these modifications can be described in terms of the $\Lambda$-*closure* of a set $S$ of states. This set, which we define recursively in Definition 4.6, is to be the set of all states that can be reached from elements of $S$ by using $\Lambda$-transitions.

---

**Definition 4.6    Λ-Closure of a Set of States**

Let $M = (Q, \Sigma, q_0, A, \delta)$ be an NFA-Λ, and let $S$ be any subset of $Q$. The Λ-closure of $S$ is the set $\Lambda(S)$ defined as follows.

1. Every element of $S$ is an element of $\Lambda(S)$;
2. For any $q \in \Lambda(S)$, every element of $\delta(q, \Lambda)$ is in $\Lambda(S)$;
3. No other elements of $Q$ are in $\Lambda(S)$.

---

We know in advance that the set $\Lambda(S)$ is finite. As a result, we can translate the recursive definition into an algorithm for calculating $\Lambda(S)$ (Exercise 2.70).

**Algorithm to Calculate $\Lambda(S)$**   Start with $T = S$. Make a sequence of passes, in each pass considering every $q \in T$ and adding to $T$ all elements of $\delta(q, \Lambda)$ that are not already elements of $T$. Stop after any pass in which $T$ does not change. The set $\Lambda(S)$ is the final value of $T$. ■

The Λ-closure of a set is the extra ingredient we need to define the function $\delta^*$ recursively. If $\delta^*(q, y)$ is the set of all the states that can be reached from $q$ using the symbols of $y$ as well as Λ-transitions, then

$$\bigcup_{r \in \delta^*(q,y)} \delta(r, a)$$

is the set of states we can reach in one more step by using the symbol $a$, and the Λ-closure of this set includes any additional states that we can reach with subsequent Λ-transitions.

---

**Definition 4.5b    Recursive Definition of $\delta^*$ for an NFA-Λ**

Let $M = (Q, \Sigma, q_0, A, \delta)$ be an NFA-Λ. The extended transition function $\delta^* : Q \times \Sigma^* \to 2^Q$ is defined as follows.

1. For any $q \in Q$, $\delta^*(q, \Lambda) = \Lambda(\{q\})$.
2. For any $q \in Q$, $y \in \Sigma^*$, and $a \in \Sigma$,

$$\delta^*(q, ya) = \Lambda \left( \bigcup_{r \in \delta^*(q,y)} \delta(r, a) \right)$$

A string $x$ is accepted by $M$ if $\delta^*(q_0, x) \cap A \neq \emptyset$. The language recognized by $M$ is the set $L(M)$ of all strings accepted by $M$.

---

**EXAMPLE 4.6**     Applying the Definitions of $\Lambda(S)$ and $\delta^*$

We consider the NFA-$\Lambda$ shown in Figure 4.9, first as an illustration of how to apply the algorithm for computing $\Lambda(S)$, and then to demonstrate that Definition 4.5b really does make it possible to calculate $\delta^*(q, x)$.

Suppose we consider $S = \{s\}$. After one iteration, $T$ is $\{s, w\}$, after two iterations it is $\{s, w, q_0\}$, after three iterations it is $\{s, w, q_0, p, t\}$, and in the next iteration it is unchanged. $\Lambda(\{s\})$ is therefore $\{s, w, q_0, p, t\}$.

Let us calculate $\delta^*(q_0, 010)$ using the recursive definition. This set is defined in terms of $\delta^*(q_0, 01)$, which is defined in terms of $\delta^*(q_0, 0)$, and so on. We therefore approach the calculation from the bottom up, calculating $\delta^*(q_0, \Lambda)$, then $\delta^*(q_0, 0)$, $\delta^*(q_0, 01)$, and finally $\delta^*(q_0, 010)$:

$$\delta^*(q_0, \Lambda) = \Lambda(\{q_0\})$$
$$= \{q_0, p, t\}$$

$$\delta^*(q_0, 0) = \Lambda \left( \bigcup_{\rho \in \delta^*(q_0, \Lambda)} \delta(\rho, 0) \right)$$

$$= \Lambda(\delta(q_0, 0) \cup \delta(p, 0) \cup \delta(t, 0))$$
$$= \Lambda(\emptyset \cup \{p\} \cup \{u\})$$
$$= \Lambda(\{p, u\})$$
$$= \{p, u\}$$

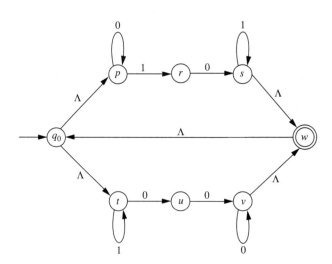

**Figure 4.9** |
The NFA-$\Lambda$ for Example 4.6.

$$\delta^*(q_0, 01) = \Lambda \left( \bigcup_{\rho \in \delta^*(q_0, 0)} \delta(\rho, 1) \right)$$

$$= \Lambda(\delta(p, 1) \cup \delta(u, 1))$$

$$= \Lambda(\{r\})$$

$$= \{r\}$$

$$\delta^*(q_0, 010) = \Lambda \left( \bigcup_{\rho \in \delta^*(q_0, 01)} \delta(\rho, 0) \right)$$

$$= \Lambda(\delta(r, 0))$$

$$= \Lambda(\{s\})$$

$$= \{s, w, q_0, p, t\}$$

(The last equality is the observation we made near the beginning of this example.) Because $\delta^*(q_0, 010)$ contains $w$, and because $w$ is an element of $A$, 010 is accepted.

Looking at the figure, you might argue along this line instead: The string $\Lambda 010 \Lambda$ is the same as 010; the picture shows the sequence

$$q_0 \xrightarrow{\Lambda} p \xrightarrow{0} p \xrightarrow{1} r \xrightarrow{0} s \xrightarrow{\Lambda} w$$

of transitions; therefore 010 is accepted. In an example as simple as this one, going through the detailed calculations is not necessary in order to decide whether a string is accepted. The point, however, is that with the recursive definitions of $\Lambda(S)$ and $\delta^*$, we can proceed on a solid algorithmic basis and be confident that the calculations (which are indeed feasible) will produce the correct answer.

In Section 4.1, we showed (Theorem 4.1) that NFAs are no more powerful than FAs with regard to the languages they can accept. In order to establish the same result for NFA-$\Lambda$s, it is sufficient to show that any NFA-$\Lambda$ can be replaced by an equivalent NFA; the notation we have developed now allows us to prove this.

**Theorem 4.2**

If $L \subseteq \Sigma^*$ is a language that is accepted by the NFA-$\Lambda$ $M = (Q, \Sigma, q_0, A, \delta)$, then there is an NFA $M_1 = (Q_1, \Sigma, q_1, A_1, \delta_1)$ that also accepts $L$.

**Proof**

In the proof of Theorem 4.1, we started with an NFA and removed all traces of nondeterminism by changing our notion of *state*. A $\Lambda$-transition is a type of nondeterminism; for example, if the transitions in $M$ include

$$p \xrightarrow{0} q \xrightarrow{\Lambda} r$$

then from state $p$, the input symbol 0 allows us to go to either $q$ or $r$. Since $M_1$ is still allowed to be nondeterministic, we can eliminate the $\Lambda$-transition without changing the states, by simply adding the transition from $p$ to $r$ on input 0.

This approach will work in general. We can use the same state set $Q$ and the same initial state in $M_1$. What we must do is to define the transition function $\delta_1$ so that if $M$ allows us to move from $p$ to $q$ using certain symbols together with $\Lambda$-transitions, then $M_1$ will allow us to move from $p$ to $q$ using those symbols without the $\Lambda$-transitions.

Essentially, we have the solution already, as a result of the definition of $\delta^*$ for the NFA-$\Lambda$ $M$ (Definition 4.5b). For a state $q$ and an input symbol $a$,

$$\delta^*(q, a) = \delta^*(q, \Lambda a)$$

$$= \Lambda \left( \bigcup_{r \in \delta^*(q, \Lambda)} \delta(r, a) \right)$$

$$= \Lambda \left( \bigcup_{r \in \Lambda(\{q\})} \delta(r, a) \right)$$

Remember what this means: $\bigcup_{r \in \Lambda(\{q\})} \delta(r, a)$ is the set of states that can be reached from $q$, using the input symbol $a$ but possibly also $\Lambda$-transitions beforehand. The $\Lambda$-closure of this set is the set of states that can be reached from $q$, using the input symbol $a$ but allowing $\Lambda$-transitions both before and after. This is exactly what we want $\delta_1(q, a)$ to be, in order to incorporate into our NFA transition function the nondeterminism that arises from the possibility of $\Lambda$-transitions.

Finally, there is a slight change that may be needed in specifying the accepting states of $M_1$. If the initial state $q_0$ of $M$ is not an accepting state, but it is possible to get from $q_0$ to an accepting state using only $\Lambda$-transitions, then $q_0$ must be made an accepting state in $M_1$—otherwise $\delta_1^*(q_0, \Lambda)$, which is $\{q_0\}$ because $M_1$ is an NFA, will not intersect $A$.

To summarize, we have decided that $M_1$ will be the NFA $(Q, \Sigma, q_0, A_1, \delta_1)$, where for any $q \in Q$ and $a \in \Sigma$,

$$\delta_1(q, a) = \delta^*(q, a)$$

and

$$A_1 = \begin{cases} A \cup \{q_0\} & \text{if } \Lambda(\{q_0\}) \cap A \neq \emptyset \text{ in } M \\ A & \text{otherwise} \end{cases}$$

The point of our definition of $\delta_1$ is that we want $\delta_1^*(q, x)$ to be the set of states that $M$ can reach from $q$, using the symbols of the string $x$ together with $\Lambda$-transitions. In other words, we want

$$\delta_1^*(q, x) = \delta^*(q, x)$$

This formula may not be correct when $x = \Lambda$ (because $M_1$ is an NFA, $\delta_1^*(q, \Lambda) = \{q\}$, whereas $\delta^*(q, \Lambda)$ may contain additional states), and that is the reason for our definition of $A_1$ above. We now show, however, that for any nonnull string the formula is true.

The proof is by structural induction on $x$. For the basis step we consider $x = a \in \Sigma$. In this case, $\delta^*(q, x) = \delta_1(q, a)$ by definition of $\delta_1$, and $\delta_1(q, a) = \delta_1^*(q, a)$ simply because $M_1$ is an NFA (see Example 4.2 and Exercise 4.3).

In the induction step, we assume that $|y| \geq 1$ and that $\delta_1^*(q, y) = \delta^*(q, y)$ for any $q \in Q$. We want to show that for $a \in \Sigma$, $\delta_1^*(q, ya) = \delta^*(q, ya)$. We have

$$\delta_1^*(q, ya) = \bigcup_{r \in \delta_1^*(q,y)} \delta_1(r, a) \quad \text{(by Definition 4.2b)}$$

$$= \bigcup_{r \in \delta^*(q,y)} \delta_1(r, a) \quad \text{(by the induction hypothesis)}$$

$$= \bigcup_{r \in \delta^*(q,y)} \delta^*(r, a) \quad \text{(by definition of } \delta_1)$$

$$= \bigcup_{r \in \delta^*(q,y)} \Lambda \left( \bigcup_{\rho \in \Lambda\{r\}} \delta(\rho, a) \right) \quad \text{(by Definition 4.5b)}$$

The $\Lambda$-closure operator has the property that the union of $\Lambda$-closures is the $\Lambda$-closure of the union (Exercise 4.40). We may therefore write the last set as

$$\Lambda \left( \bigcup_{r \in \delta^*(q,y)} \left( \bigcup_{\rho \in \Lambda\{r\}} \delta(\rho, a) \right) \right)$$

However, it follows from the definition of $\Lambda$-closure (and the fact that $\delta^*(q, y)$ is a $\Lambda$-closure) that for every $r \in \delta^*(q, y)$, $\Lambda\{r\} \subseteq \delta^*(q, y)$; therefore, the two separate unions are unnecessary, and the formula reduces to

$$\Lambda \left( \bigcup_{r \in \delta^*(q,y)} \delta(r, a) \right)$$

which is the definition of $\delta^*(q, ya)$. The induction is complete.

Now it is not hard to show that $M_1$ recognizes $L$, the language recognized by $M$. First we consider the case when $\Lambda(\{q_0\}) \cap A = \emptyset$ in $M$. Then the null string is accepted by neither $M$ nor $M_1$. For any other string $x$, we have shown that $\delta_1^*(q_0, x) = \delta^*(q_0, x)$, and we know that the accepting states of $M$ and $M_1$ are the same. Therefore, $x$ is accepted by $M_1$ if and only if it is accepted by $M$.

In the other case, when $\Lambda(\{q_0\}) \cap A \neq \emptyset$, we have defined $A_1$ to be $A \cup \{q_0\}$. This time $\Lambda$ is accepted by both $M$ and $M_1$. For any other $x$, again we have $\delta_1^*(q_0, x) = \delta^*(q_0, x)$. If this set contains a state in $A$, then both $M$ and $M_1$ accept $x$. If not, the only way $x$ could be accepted by one of the two machines but not the other would be for $\delta^*(q_0, x)$ to contain $q_0$. (It would then intersect $A_1$ but not $A$.) However, this cannot happen either. By definition, $\delta^*(q_0, x)$ is the $\Lambda$-closure of a set. If $\delta^*(q_0, x)$ contained $q_0$, it would have to contain every element of $\Lambda(\{q_0\})$, and therefore, since $\Lambda(\{q_0\}) \cap A \neq \emptyset$, it would have to contain an element of $A$.

In either case, we may conclude that $M$ and $M_1$ accept exactly the same strings, and the proof is complete.

We think of NFAs as generalizations of FAs, and of NFA-$\Lambda$s as generalizations of NFAs. It is technically not *quite* correct to say that every FA is an NFA, since the values of the transition function are states in one case and sets of states in the other; similarly, the domain of the transition function in an NFA is $Q \times \Sigma$, and in an NFA-$\Lambda$ it is $Q \times (\Sigma \cup \{\Lambda\})$. Practically speaking, we can ignore these technicalities. The following theorem formalizes this assertion and ties together the results of Theorems 4.1 and 4.2.

**Theorem 4.3**

For any alphabet $\Sigma$, and any language $L \subset \Sigma^*$, these three statements are equivalent:

1. $L$ can be recognized by an FA.
2. $L$ can be recognized by an NFA.
3. $L$ can be recognized by an NFA-$\Lambda$.

*Proof*

According to Theorems 4.1 and 4.2, statement 3 implies statement 2, and statement 2 implies statement 1. It is therefore sufficient to show that statement 1 implies statement 3.

Suppose that $L$ is accepted by the FA $M = (Q, \Sigma, q_0, A, \delta)$. We construct an NFA-$\Lambda$ $M_1 = (Q, \Sigma, q_0, A, \delta_1)$ accepting $L$ as follows. $\delta_1 : Q \times (\Sigma \cup \{\Lambda\}) \to 2^Q$ is defined by the formulas

$$\delta_1(q, \Lambda) = \emptyset \qquad\qquad \delta_1(q, a) = \{\delta(q, a)\}$$

(for any $q \in Q$ and any $a \in \Sigma$). The first formula just says that there are no $\Lambda$-transitions in $M_1$, and the second says that the transition functions $\delta$ and $\delta_1$ are identical (so that there is really no nondeterminism at all), except for the technical difference that the value is a state in one case and a set containing only that state in the other. It can be verified almost immediately that $M_1$ accepts $L$ (Exercise 4.21).

Just as in the case of Theorem 4.1, the proof of Theorem 4.2 provides us with an algorithm for eliminating $\Lambda$-transitions from an NFA-$\Lambda$. We illustrate the algorithm in two examples, in which we can also practice the algorithm for eliminating nondeterminism.

Converting an NFA-$\Lambda$ to an NFA        **EXAMPLE 4.7**

Let $M$ be the NFA-$\Lambda$ pictured in Figure 4.10$a$, which accepts the language $\{0\}^*\{01\}^*\{0\}^*$. We show in tabular form the values of the transition function, as well as the values $\delta^*(q, 0)$ and $\delta^*(q, 1)$ that give us the values of the transition function in the resulting NFA.

| $q$ | $\delta(q, \Lambda)$ | $\delta(q, 0)$ | $\delta(q, 1)$ | $\delta^*(q, 0)$ | $\delta^*(q, 1)$ |
|---|---|---|---|---|---|
| $A$ | $\{B\}$ | $\{A\}$ | $\emptyset$ | $\{A, B, C, D\}$ | $\emptyset$ |
| $B$ | $\{D\}$ | $\{C\}$ | $\emptyset$ | $\{C, D\}$ | $\emptyset$ |
| $C$ | $\emptyset$ | $\emptyset$ | $\{B\}$ | $\emptyset$ | $\{B, D\}$ |
| $D$ | $\emptyset$ | $\{D\}$ | $\emptyset$ | $\{D\}$ | $\emptyset$ |

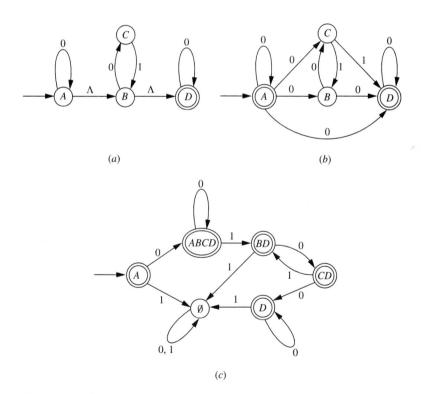

(a)                    (b)

(c)

**Figure 4.10** |
An NFA-$\Lambda$, an NFA, and an FA for $\{0\}^*\{01\}^*\{0\}^*$.

For example, $\delta^*(A, 0)$ is calculated using the formula

$$\delta^*(A, 0) = \Lambda\left(\bigcup_{r \in \Lambda(\{A\})} \delta(r, 0)\right)$$

In a more involved example we might feel more comfortable carrying out each step literally: calculating $\Lambda(\{A\})$, finding $\delta(r, 0)$ for each $r$ in this set, forming the union, and calculating the $\Lambda$-closure of the result. In this simple example, we can see that from $A$ with input 0, $M$ can stay in $A$, move to $B$ (using a 0 followed by a $\Lambda$-transition), move to $C$ (using a $\Lambda$-transition and then a 0), or move to $D$ (using the 0 either immediately preceded or immediately followed by two $\Lambda$-transitions). The other entries in the last two columns of the table can be obtained similarly. Since $M$ can move from the initial state to $D$ using only $\Lambda$-transitions, $A$ must be an accepting state in $M_1$, which is shown in Figure 4.10$b$.

Having the values $\delta_1(q, 0)$ and $\delta_1(q, 1)$ in tabular form is useful in arriving at an FA. For example (if we denote the transition function of the FA by $\delta_2$), in order to compute $\delta_2(\{C, D\}, 0)$ we simply form the union of the sets in the third and fourth rows of the $\delta^*(q, 0)$ column of the table; the result is $\{D\}$. It turns out in this example that the sets of states that came up as we filled in the table for the NFA were all we needed, and the resulting FA is shown in Figure 4.10$c$.

| EXAMPLE 4.8 | Another Example of Converting an NFA-$\Lambda$ to an NFA |

For our last example we consider the NFA-$\Lambda$ in Figure 4.11$a$, recognizing the language $\{0\}^*(\{01\}^*\{1\} \cup \{1\}^*\{0\})$. Again we show the transition function in tabular form, as well as the transition function for the resulting NFA.

| $q$ | $\delta(q, \Lambda)$ | $\delta(q, 0)$ | $\delta(q, 1)$ | $\delta^*(q, 0)$ | $\delta^*(q, 1)$ |
|-----|----------------------|----------------|----------------|------------------|------------------|
| $A$ | $\{B, D\}$ | $\{A\}$ | $\emptyset$ | $\{A, B, C, D, E\}$ | $\{D, E\}$ |
| $B$ | $\emptyset$ | $\{C\}$ | $\{E\}$ | $\{C\}$ | $\{E\}$ |
| $C$ | $\emptyset$ | $\emptyset$ | $\{B\}$ | $\emptyset$ | $\{B\}$ |
| $D$ | $\emptyset$ | $\{E\}$ | $\{D\}$ | $\{E\}$ | $\{D\}$ |
| $E$ | $\emptyset$ | $\emptyset$ | $\emptyset$ | $\emptyset$ | $\emptyset$ |

The NFA we end up with is shown in Figure 4.11$b$. Note that the initial state $A$ is not an accepting state, since in the original device an accepting state cannot be reached with only $\Lambda$-transitions.

Unlike the previous example, when we start to eliminate the nondeterminism from our NFA, new sets of states are introduced in addition to the ones shown. For example,

$$\delta_2(\{A, B, C, D, E\}, 1) = \{D, E\} \cup \{E\} \cup \{B\} \cup \{D\} \cup \emptyset = \{B, D, E\}$$

$$\delta_2(\{B, D, E\}, 0) = \{C\} \cup \{E\} \cup \emptyset = \{C, E\}$$

The calculations are straightforward, and the result is shown in Figure 4.11$c$.

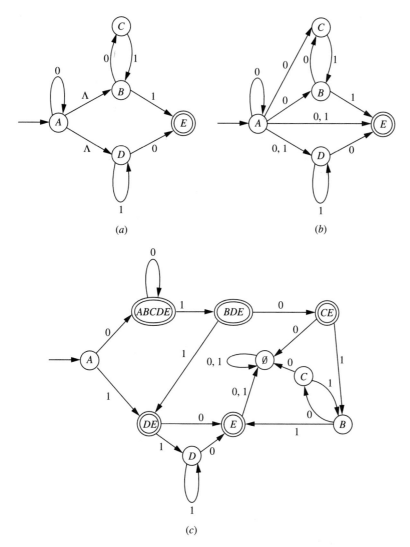

**Figure 4.11 |**
An NFA-$\Lambda$, an NFA, and an FA for $\{0\}^*\{01\}^*\{1\} \cup \{1\}^*\{0\}$.

## 4.3 | KLEENE'S THEOREM

Sections 4.1 and 4.2 of this chapter have provided the tools we need to prove Theorem 3.1. For convenience we have stated the two parts, the "if" and the "only if," as separate results.

**Theorem 4.4     Kleene's Theorem, Part 1**
Any regular language can be accepted by a finite automaton.

*Proof*
Because of Theorem 4.3, it is sufficient to show that every regular language can be accepted by an NFA-$\Lambda$. The set of regular languages over the alphabet $\Sigma$ is defined in Definition 3.1 to contain the basic languages $\emptyset$, $\{\Lambda\}$, and $\{a\}$ ($a \in \Sigma$), to be closed under the operations of union, concatenation, and Kleene $*$, and to be the smallest set of languages that has those two properties. This allows us to prove using structural induction that every regular language over $\Sigma$ can be accepted by an NFA-$\Lambda$. The basis step of the proof is to show that the three basic languages can be accepted by NFA-$\Lambda$s. The induction hypothesis is that $L_1$ and $L_2$ are languages that can be accepted by NFA-$\Lambda$s, and the induction step is to show that $L_1 \cup L_2$, $L_2 L_2$, and $L_1^*$ can also be. NFA-$\Lambda$s for the three basic languages are shown in Figure 4.12.

Now suppose that $L_1$ and $L_2$ are recognized by the NFA-$\Lambda$s $M_1$ and $M_2$, respectively, where for both $i = 1$ and $i = 2$,

$$M_i = (Q_i, \Sigma, q_i, A_i, \delta_i)$$

By renaming states if necessary, we may assume that $Q_1 \cap Q_2 = \emptyset$. We will construct NFA-$\Lambda$s $M_u$, $M_c$, and $M_k$, recognizing the languages $L_1 \cup L_2$, $L_1 L_2$, and $L_1^*$, respectively. Pictures will be helpful here also; schematic diagrams presenting the general idea in each case are shown in Figure 4.13. (You will observe that the first two cases have already been illustrated in Example 4.5.) In the three parts of the figure, both $M_1$ and $M_2$ are shown as having two accepting states.

**Construction of $M_u = (Q_u, \Sigma, q_u, A_u, \delta_u)$.** Let $q_u$ be a new state, not in either $Q_1$ or $Q_2$, and let

$$Q_u = Q_1 \cup Q_2 \cup \{q_u\} \qquad A_u = A_1 \cup A_2$$

Now we define $\delta_u$ so that $M_u$ can move from its initial state to either $q_1$ or $q_2$ by a $\Lambda$-transition, and then make exactly the same moves that the respective $M_i$ would. Formally, we define

$$\delta_u(q_u, \Lambda) = \{q_1, q_2\} \qquad \delta_u(q_u, a) = \emptyset \text{ for every } a \in \Sigma$$

and for each $q \in Q_1 \cup Q_2$ and $a \in \Sigma \cup \{\Lambda\}$,

$$\delta_u(q, a) = \begin{cases} \delta_1(q, a) & \text{if } q \in Q_1 \\ \delta_2(q, a) & \text{if } q \in Q_2 \end{cases}$$

For either value of $i$, if $x \in L_i$, then $M_u$ can process $x$ by moving to $q_i$ on a $\Lambda$-transition and then executing the moves that cause $M_i$ to accept $x$. On the other hand, if $x$ is accepted by $M_u$, there is a sequence of transitions corresponding to $x$, starting at $q_u$ and ending at an element of $A_1$ or $A_2$. The first of these transitions must be a $\Lambda$-transition from $q_u$ to either $q_1$ or $q_2$, since there are no other transitions from $q_u$. Thereafter, since $Q_1 \cap Q_2 = \emptyset$, either

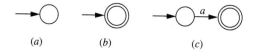

**Figure 4.12 |**
NFA-Λs for the three basic regular languages.

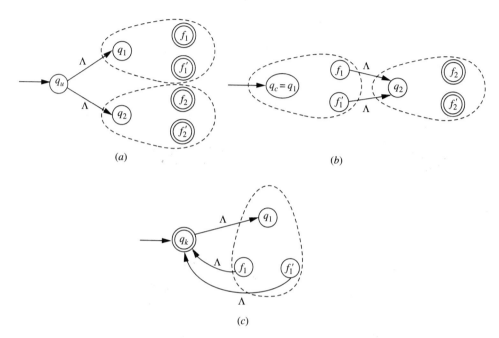

**Figure 4.13 |**
NFA-Λs for union, concatenation, and Kleene *.

all the transitions are between elements of $Q_1$ or all are between elements of $Q_2$. It follows that $x$ must be accepted by either $M_1$ or $M_2$.

**Construction of $M_c = (Q_c, \Sigma, q_c, A_c, \delta_c)$.** In this case we do not need any new states. Let $Q_c = Q_1 \cup Q_2$, $q_c = q_1$, and $A_c = A_2$. (In Figure 4.13b, we illustrate this by making $f_2$ and $f_2'$ accepting states in $M_c$, but not $f_1$ or $f_1'$.) The transitions will include all those of $M_1$ and $M_2$, as well as a Λ-transition from each state in $A_1$ to $q_2$. In other words, for any $q$ not in $A_1$, and $\alpha \in \Sigma \cup \{\Lambda\}$, $\delta_c(q, \alpha)$ is defined to be either $\delta_1(q, \alpha)$ or $\delta_2(q, \alpha)$, depending on whether $q$ is in $Q_1$ or $Q_2$. For $q \in A_1$,

$$\delta_c(q, a) = \delta_1(q, a) \text{ for every } a \in \Sigma, \text{ and } \delta_c(q, \Lambda) = \delta_1(q, \Lambda) \cup \{q_2\}$$

On an input string $x_1x_2$, where $x_i \in L_i$ for both values of $i$, $M_c$ can process $x_1$, arriving at a state in $A_1$; jump from this state to $q_2$ by a Λ-transition; and then process $x_2$ the way $M_2$ would, so that $x_1x_2$ is accepted. Conversely, if $x$ is accepted by $M_c$, there is a sequence of transitions corresponding to $x$ that begins at $q_1$ and ends at an element of $A_2$. One of them must therefore be from an element of $Q_1$ to an element of $Q_2$, and according to the definition of $\delta_c$ this can only be a $\Lambda$-transition from an element of $A_1$ to $q_2$. Because $Q_1 \cap Q_2 = \emptyset$, all the previous transitions are between elements of $Q_1$ and all the subsequent ones are between elements of $Q_2$. It follows that $x = x_1 \Lambda x_2 = x_1 x_2$, where $x_1$ is accepted by $M_1$ and $x_2$ is accepted by $M_2$; in other words, $x \in L_1 L_2$.

**Construction of $M_k = (Q_k, \Sigma, q_k, A_k, \delta_k)$.** Let $q_k$ be a new state not in $Q_1$, and let $Q_k = Q_1 \cup \{q_k\}$ and $A_k = \{q_k\}$. Once again all the transitions of $M_1$ will be allowed in $M_k$, but in addition there is a $\Lambda$-transition from $q_k$ to $q_1$, and there is a $\Lambda$-transition from each element of $A_1$ to $q_k$. More precisely,

$\delta_k(q_k, \Lambda) = \{q_1\}$ and $\delta_k(q_k, a) = \emptyset$ for $a \in \Sigma$.

For $q \in Q_1$ and $\alpha \in \Sigma \cup \{\Lambda\}$, $\delta_k(q, \alpha) = \delta_1(q, \alpha)$ unless $q \in A_1$ and $\alpha = \Lambda$.

For $q \in A_1$, $\delta_k(q, \Lambda) = \delta_1(q, \Lambda) \cup \{q_k\}$.

Suppose $x \in L_1^*$. If $x = \Lambda$, then clearly $x$ is accepted by $M_k$. Otherwise, for some $m \geq 1$, $x = x_1 x_2 \cdots x_m$, where $x_i \in L_1$ for each $i$. $M_k$ can move from $q_k$ to $q_1$ by a $\Lambda$-transition; for each $i$, $M_k$ moves from $q_1$ to an element $f_i$ of $A_1$ by a sequence of transitions corresponding to $x_i$; and for each $i$, $M_k$ then moves from $f_i$ back to $q_k$ by a $\Lambda$-transition. It follows that $(\Lambda x_1 \Lambda)(\Lambda x_2 \Lambda) \cdots (\Lambda x_m \Lambda) = x$ is accepted by $M_k$. On the other hand, if $x$ is accepted by $M_k$, there is a sequence of transitions corresponding to $x$ that begins and ends at $q_k$. Since the only transition from $q_k$ is a $\Lambda$-transition to $q_1$, and the only transitions to $q_k$ are $\Lambda$-transitions from elements of $A_1$, $x$ can be decomposed in the form

$$x = (\Lambda x_1 \Lambda)(\Lambda x_2 \Lambda) \cdots (\Lambda x_m \Lambda)$$

where, for each $i$, there is a sequence of transitions corresponding to $x_i$ from $q_1$ to an element of $A_1$. Therefore, $x \in L_1^*$.

Since we have constructed an NFA-$\Lambda$ recognizing $L$ in each of the three cases, the proof is complete.

The constructions in the proof of Theorem 4.4 provide an algorithm for constructing an NFA-$\Lambda$ corresponding to a given regular expression. The next example illustrates its application, as well as the fact that there may be simplifications possible along the way.

## Applying the Algorithm in the Proof of Theorem 4.4 EXAMPLE 4.9

Let $r$ be the regular expression $(00 + 1)^*(10)^*$. We illustrate first the literal application of the algorithm, ignoring possible shortcuts. The primitive (zero-operation) regular expressions appearing in $r$ are shown in Figure 4.14$a$. The NFA-$\Lambda$s corresponding to 00 and 10 are now constructed using concatenation and are shown in Figure 4.14$b$. Next, we form the NFA-$\Lambda$ corresponding to $(00 + 1)$, as in Figure 4.14$c$. Figures 4.14$d$ and 4.14$e$ illustrate the NFA-$\Lambda$s corresponding to $(00 + 1)^*$ and $(10)^*$, respectively. Finally, the resulting NFA-$\Lambda$ formed by concatenation is shown in Figure 4.14$f$.

It is probably clear in several places that there are states and $\Lambda$-transitions called for in the general construction that are not necessary in this example. The six parts of Figure 4.15

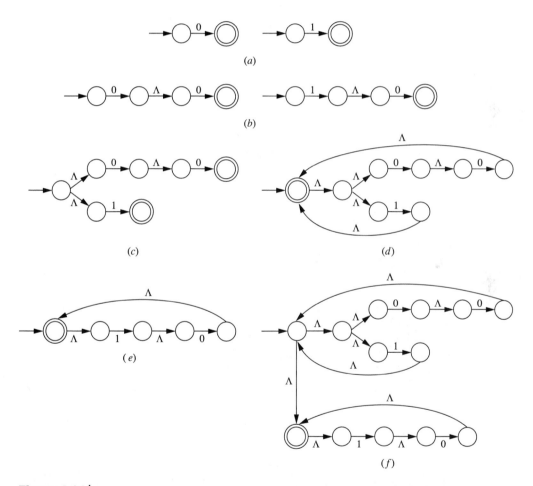

$(a)$

$(b)$

$(c)$ $(d)$

$(e)$ $(f)$

**Figure 4.14 |**
Constructing an NFA-$\Lambda$ for $(00 + 1)^*(10)^*$.

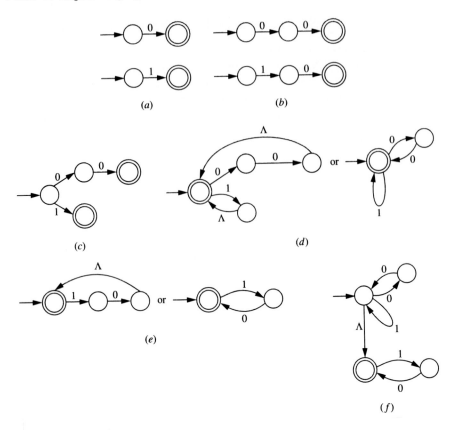

**Figure 4.15 |**
A simplified NFA-$\Lambda$ for $(00 + 1)^*(10)^*$.

parallel those of Figure 4.14 and incorporate some obvious simplifications. One must be a little careful with simplifications such as these, as Exercises 4.32 to 4.34 illustrate.

We know from Sections 4.1 and 4.2 of this chapter how to convert an NFA-$\Lambda$ obtained from Theorem 4.4 into an FA. Although we have not yet officially considered the question of simplifying a given FA as much as possible, we will see how to do this in Chapter 5.

If we have NFA-$\Lambda$s $M_1$ and $M_2$, the proof of Theorem 4.4 provides us with algorithms for constructing new NFA-$\Lambda$s to recognize the union, concatenation, and Kleene * of the corresponding languages. The first two of these algorithms were illustrated in Example 4.5. As a further example, we start with the FAs shown in Figures 4.16a and 4.16b (which were shown in Examples 3.12 and 3.13 to accept the languages $\{0, 1\}^*\{10\}$ and $\{00\}^*\{11\}^*$, respectively). We can apply the algorithms for union and Kleene *, making one simplification in the second step, to obtain the

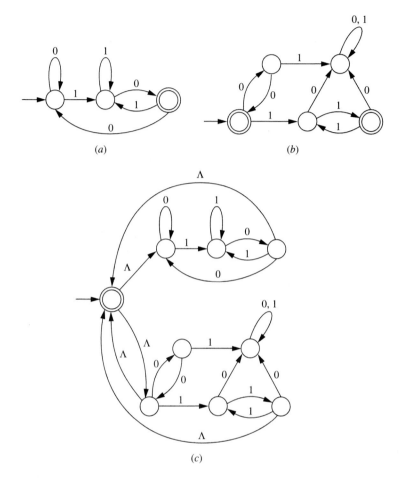

**Figure 4.16 |**
An NFA-$\Lambda$ for $((0 + 1)^*10 + (00)^*(11)^*)^*$.

NFA-$\Lambda$ in Figure 4.16*c* recognizing the language

$$(\{0, 1\}^*\{10\} \cup \{00\}^*\{11\}^*)^*$$

**Theorem 4.5    Kleene's Theorem, Part 2**
The language accepted by any finite automaton is regular.

*Proof*
Let $L \subseteq \Sigma^*$ be accepted by the FA $M = (Q, \Sigma, q_0, A, \delta)$. What this means is that $L = \{x \in \Sigma^* \mid \delta^*(q_0, x) \in A\}$. By considering the individual elements of $A$, we can express $L$ as the union of a finite number of sets of the form $\{x \in \Sigma^* \mid \delta^*(q_0, x) = q\}$; because finite unions of regular

sets are regular, it will be sufficient to show that for any two states $p$ and $q$, the set

$$L(p, q) = \{x \in \Sigma^* \mid \delta^*(p, x) = q\}$$

is regular.

In looking for ways to use mathematical induction, we have often formulated statements involving the length of a string. At first this approach does not seem promising, because we are trying to prove a property of a language, not a property of individual strings in the language. However, rather than looking at the number of transitions in a particular path from $p$ to $q$ (i.e., the length of a string in $L(p, q)$), we might look at the number of *distinct* states through which $M$ passes in moving from $p$ to $q$. It turns out to be more convenient to consider, for each $k$, a specific set of $k$ states, and to consider the set of strings that cause $M$ to go from $p$ to $q$ by going through only states in that set. If $k$ is large enough, this set of strings will be all of $L(p, q)$.

To simplify notation, let us relabel the states of $M$ using the integers 1 through $n$, where $n$ is the number of states. Let us also formalize the idea of a path *going through* a state $s$: for a string $x$ in $\Sigma^*$, we say $x$ represents a path from $p$ to $q$ going through $s$ if there are nonnull strings $y$ and $z$ so that

$$x = yz \qquad \delta^*(p, y) = s \qquad \delta^*(s, z) = q$$

Note that a path can go to a state, or from a state, without going through it. In particular, the path

$$p \xrightarrow{a} q \xrightarrow{b} r$$

goes through $q$, but not through $p$ or $r$. Now, for $j \geq 0$, we let $L(p, q, j)$ be the set of strings corresponding to paths from $p$ to $q$ that go through no state numbered higher than $j$. No string in $L(p, q)$ can go through a state numbered higher than $n$, because there *are* no states numbered higher than $n$. In other words,

$$L(p, q, n) = L(p, q)$$

The problem, therefore, is to show that $L(p, q, n)$ is regular, and this will obviously follow if we can show that $L(p, q, j)$ is regular for every $j$ with $0 \leq j \leq n$. (This is where the induction comes in.) In fact, there is no harm in asserting that $L(p, q, j)$ is regular for every $j \geq 0$; this is not really a stronger statement, since for any $j \geq n$, $L(p, q, j) = L(p, q, n)$, but this way it will look more like an ordinary induction proof.

For the basis step we need to show that $L(p, q, 0)$ is regular. Going through no state numbered higher than 0 means going through no state at all, which means that the string can contain no more than one symbol. Therefore,

$$L(p, q, 0) \subseteq \Sigma \cup \{\Lambda\}$$

and $L(p, q, 0)$ is regular because it is finite. (See the discussion after the proof for an explicit formula for $L(p, q, 0)$.)

The induction hypothesis is that $0 \leq k$ and that for every $p$ and $q$ satisfying $0 \leq p, q \leq n$, the language $L(p, q, k)$ is regular. We wish to show that for every $p$ and $q$ in the same range, $L(p, q, k + 1)$ is regular. As we have already observed, $L(p, q, k + 1) = L(p, q, k)$ if $k \geq n$, and we assume for the remainder of the proof that $k < n$.

A string $x$ is in $L(p, q, k+1)$ if it represents a path from $p$ to $q$ that goes through no state numbered higher than $k + 1$. There are two ways this can happen. First, the path can bypass the state $k + 1$ altogether, in which case it goes through no state higher than $k$, and $x \in L(p, q, k)$. Second, the path can go through $k + 1$ and nothing higher. In this case, it goes from $p$ to the first occurrence of $k + 1$, then loops from $k + 1$ back to itself zero or more times, then goes from the last occurrence of $k + 1$ to $q$. (See Figure 4.17.) This means that we can write $x$ as $yzw$, where $y$ corresponds to the path from $p$ to the first occurrence of $k + 1$, $z$ to all the loops from $k + 1$ back to itself, and $w$ to the path from $k + 1$ to $q$. The crucial observation here is that in each of the two parts $y$ and $w$, and in each of the individual loops making up $z$, the path does not go through any state higher than $k$; in other words,

$$y \in L(p, k + 1, k) \qquad w \in L(k + 1, q, k) \qquad z \in L(k + 1, k + 1, k)^*.$$

It follows that in either of the two cases,

$$x \in L(p, q, k) \ \cup \ L(p, k + 1, k)L(k + 1, k + 1, k)^*L(k + 1, q, k)$$

On the other hand, it is also clear that any string in this right-hand set is an element of $L(p, q, k + 1)$, since the corresponding path goes from $p$ to $q$ without going through any state higher than $k + 1$. Therefore,

$$L(p, q, k+1) = L(p, q, k) \cup L(p, k+1, k)L(k+1, k+1, k)^*L(k+1, q, k)$$

Each of the languages appearing in the right side of the formula is regular because of the induction hypothesis, and $L(p, q, k+1)$ is obtained from them by using the operations of union, concatenation, and Kleene *. Therefore, $L(p, q, k + 1)$ is regular.

**Figure 4.17** |

The only property of $L(p, q, 0)$ that is needed in the proof of Theorem 4.5 is that it is finite. It is simple enough, however, to find an explicit formula. This formula and the others used in the proof are given below and provide a summary of the steps in the algorithm provided by the proof for finding a regular expression corresponding to a given FA:

$$L(p, q, 0) = \begin{cases} \{a \in \Sigma \mid \delta(p, a) = q\} & \text{if } p \neq q \\ \{a \in \Sigma \mid \delta(p, a) = p\} \cup \{\Lambda\} & \text{if } p = q \end{cases}$$

$$L(p, q, k+1) = L(p, q, k) \cup L(p, k+1, k)L(k+1, k+1, k)^*L(k+1, q, k)$$

$$L(p, q) = L(p, q, n)$$

$$L = \bigcup_{q \in A} L(q_0, q)$$

**EXAMPLE 4.10**     Applying the Algorithm in the Proof of Theorem 4.5

Let $M = (Q, \Sigma, q_0, A, \delta)$ be the FA pictured in Figure 4.18. In carrying out the algorithm above for finding a regular expression corresponding to $M$, we construct tables showing regular expressions $r(p, q, j)$ corresponding to the languages $L(p, q, j)$ for $0 \leq j \leq 2$.

| $p$ | $r(p, 1, 0)$ | $r(p, 2, 0)$ | $r(p, 3, 0)$ |
|---|---|---|---|
| 1 | $a + \Lambda$ | $b$ | $\emptyset$ |
| 2 | $a$ | $\Lambda$ | $b$ |
| 3 | $a$ | $b$ | $\Lambda$ |

| $p$ | $r(p, 1, 1)$ | $r(p, 2, 1)$ | $r(p, 3, 1)$ |
|---|---|---|---|
| 1 | $a^*$ | $a^*b$ | $\emptyset$ |
| 2 | $a^+$ | $\Lambda + a^+b$ | $b$ |
| 3 | $a^+$ | $a^*b$ | $\Lambda$ |

| $p$ | $r(p, 1, 2)$ | $r(p, 2, 2)$ | $r(p, 3, 2)$ |
|---|---|---|---|
| 1 | $a^*(ba^+)^*$ | $a^*(ba^+)^*b$ | $a^*(ba^+)^*bb$ |
| 2 | $a^+(ba^+)^*$ | $(a^+b)^*$ | $(a^+b)^*b$ |
| 3 | $a^+ + a^*(ba^+)^+$ | $a^*b(a^+b)^*$ | $\Lambda + a^*b(a^+b)^*b$ |

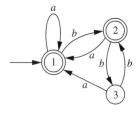

**Figure 4.18**

Although many of these table entries can be obtained by inspection, the formula can be used wherever necessary. In a number of cases, simplifications have been made in the expressions produced by the formula.

For example,

$$r(1, 3, 1) = r(1, 3, 0) + r(1, 1, 0)r(1, 1, 0)^*r(1, 3, 0)$$
$$= \emptyset$$

because $r(1, 3, 0) = \emptyset$, and the concatenation of any language with $\emptyset$ is $\emptyset$.

$$r(3, 2, 1) = r(3, 2, 0) + r(3, 1, 0)r(1, 1, 0)^*r(1, 2, 0)$$
$$= b + a(a + \Lambda)^*b$$
$$= \Lambda b + a^+b$$
$$= a^*b$$

$$r(1, 1, 2) = r(1, 1, 1) + r(1, 2, 1)r(2, 2, 1)^*r(2, 1, 1)$$
$$= a^* + a^*b(a^+b)^*a^+$$
$$= a^* + a^*(ba^+)^*ba^+$$
$$= a^* + a^*(ba^+)^+$$
$$= a^*(ba^+)^*$$

$$r(3, 2, 2) = r(3, 2, 1) + r(3, 2, 1)r(2, 2, 1)^*r(2, 2, 1)$$
$$= a^*b + a^*b(a^+b)^*(\Lambda + a^+b)$$
$$= a^*b + a^*b(a^+b)^*$$
$$= a^*b(a^+b)^*$$

The two accepting states are 1 and 2, and so the regular expression $r$ we are looking for is $r(1, 1, 3) + r(1, 2, 3)$. We use the formula for both, making a few simplifications along the way:

$$r(1, 1, 3) = r(1, 1, 2) + r(1, 3, 2)r(3, 3, 2)^*r(3, 1, 2)$$
$$= a^*(ba^+)^* + a^*(ba^+)^*bb(\Lambda + a^*b(a^+b)^*b)^*(a^+ + a^*(ba^+)^+)$$
$$= a^*(ba^+)^* + a^*(ba^+)^*bb(a^*(ba^+)^*bb)^*(a^+ + a^*(ba^+)^+)$$
$$= a^*(ba^+)^* + (a^*(ba^+)^*bb)^+(a^+ + a^*(ba^+)^+)$$

$$r(1, 2, 3) = r(1, 2, 2) + r(1, 3, 2)r(3, 3, 2)^*r(3, 2, 2)$$
$$= a^*(ba^+)^*b + a^*(ba^+)^*bb(a^*b(a^+b)^*b)^*a^*b(a^+b)^*$$
$$= a^*(ba^+)^*b + a^*(ba^+)^*bb(a^*(ba^+)^*bb)^*a^*b(a^+b)^*$$
$$= a^*(ba^+)^*b + (a^*(ba^+)^*bb)^+a^*(ba^+)^*b$$
$$= (a^*(ba^+)^*bb)^*a^*(ba^+)^*b$$
$$r = r(1, 1, 3) + r(1, 2, 3)$$

If you wish, you can almost certainly find ways to simplify this further.

## EXERCISES

**4.1.** In the NFA pictured in Figure 4.19, calculate each of the following.

    a. $\delta^*(1, bb)$

    b. $\delta^*(1, bab)$

    c. $\delta^*(1, aabb)$

    d. $\delta^*(1, aabbab)$

    e. $\delta^*(1, aba)$

**4.2.** An NFA with states 1–5 and input alphabet $\{a, b\}$ has the following transition table.

| $q$ | $\delta(q, a)$ | $\delta(q, b)$ |
|---|---|---|
| 1 | $\{1, 2\}$ | $\{1\}$ |
| 2 | $\{3\}$ | $\{3\}$ |
| 3 | $\{4\}$ | $\{4\}$ |
| 4 | $\{5\}$ | $\emptyset$ |
| 5 | $\emptyset$ | $\{5\}$ |

    a. Draw a transition diagram.

    b. Calculate $\delta^*(1, ab)$.

    c. Calculate $\delta^*(1, abaab)$.

**4.3.** Let $M = (Q, \Sigma, q_0, A, \delta)$ be an NFA. Show that for any $q \in Q$ and any $a \in \Sigma$, $\delta^*(q, a) = \delta(q, a)$.

**4.4.** Suppose $L \subseteq \Sigma^*$ is a regular language. If every FA accepting $L$ has at least $n$ states, then every NFA accepting $L$ has at least _____ states. (Fill in the blank, and explain your answer.)

**4.5.** In Definition 4.2b, $\delta^*$ is defined recursively in an NFA by first defining $\delta^*(q, \Lambda)$ and then defining $\delta^*(q, ya)$, where $y \in \Sigma^*$ and $a \in \Sigma$. Give an

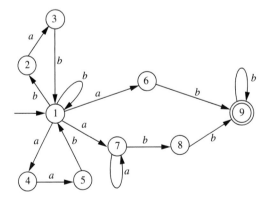

**Figure 4.19** |

acceptable recursive definition in which the recursive part of the definition defines $\delta^*(ay)$ instead.

**4.6.** Give an example of a regular language $L$ containing $\Lambda$ that cannot be accepted by any NFA having only one accepting state, and show that your answer is correct.

**4.7.** Can every regular language not containing $\Lambda$ be accepted by an NFA having only one accepting state? Prove your answer.

**4.8.** (Refer to Exercise 3.29). Let $M = (Q, \Sigma, q_0, A, \delta)$ be an FA.

    a.  Show that if every state other than $q_0$ from which no element of $A$ can be reached is deleted, then what remains is an NFA recognizing the same language.

    b.  Show that if all states not reachable from $q_0$ are deleted and all states other than $q_0$ from which no element of $A$ can be reached are deleted, what remains is an NFA recognizing the same language.

**4.9.** Let $M = (Q, \Sigma, q_0, A, \delta)$ be an NFA, let $m$ be the maximum size of any of the sets $\delta(q, a)$ for $q \in Q$ and $a \in \Sigma$, and let $x$ be a string of length $n$ over the input alphabet.

    a.  What is the maximum number of distinct paths that there might be in the computation tree corresponding to $x$?

    b.  In order to determine whether $x$ is accepted by $M$, it is sufficient to replace the complete computation tree by one that is perhaps smaller, obtained by "pruning" the original one so that no level of the tree contains more than $|Q|$ nodes (and no level contains more nodes than there are at that level of the original tree). Explain why this is possible, and how it might be done.

**4.10.** In each part of Figure 4.20 is pictured an NFA. Using the subset construction, draw an FA accepting the same language. Label the final picture so as to make it clear how it was obtained from the subset construction.

**4.11.** After the proof of Theorem 3.4, we observed that if $M = (Q, \Sigma, q_0, A, \delta)$ is an FA accepting $L$, then the FA $M' = (Q, \Sigma, q_0, Q - A, \delta)$ accepts $L'$. Does this still work if $M$ is an NFA? If so, prove it. If not, explain why, and find a counterexample.

**4.12.** As in the previous problem, we consider adapting Theorem 3.4 to the case of NFAs. For $i = 1$ and 2, let $M_i = (Q_i, \Sigma, q_i, A_i, \delta_i)$, and let $M = (Q_1 \times Q_2, \Sigma, (q_1, q_2), A, \delta)$, where $A$ is defined as in the theorem for each of the three cases and $\delta$ still needs to be defined. If $M_1$ and $M_2$ are FAs, the appropriate definition of $\delta$ is to use the formula $\delta(p, q) = (\delta_1(p), \delta_2(q))$. If $M_1$ and $M_2$ are NFAs, let us define $\delta((p, q), a) = \delta_1(p, a) \times \delta_2(q, a)$. (This says for example that if from state $p$ $M_1$ can reach either $p_1$ or $p_2$ on input $a$, and from state $r$ $M_2$ can reach either $r_1$ or $r_2$ on input $a$, then $M$ can reach any of the four states $(p_1, r_1), (p_1, r_2), (p_2, r_1), (p_2, r_2)$ from $(p, r)$ on input $a$.)

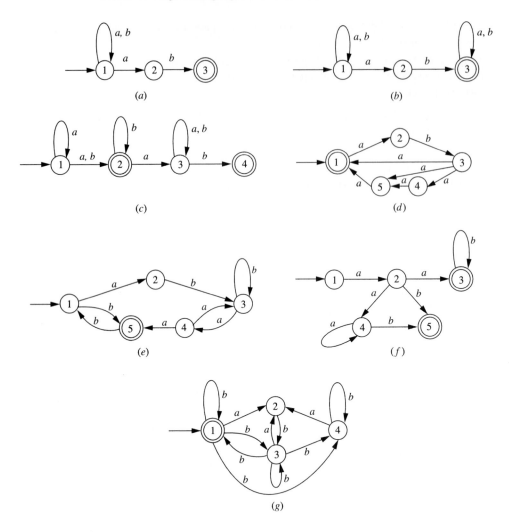

**Figure 4.20** |

Do the conclusions of the theorem still hold in this more general situation? Answer in each of the three cases (union, intersection, difference), and give reasons for your answer.

**4.13.** In Figure 4.21 is a transition diagram of an NFA-$\Lambda$. For each string below, say whether the NFA-$\Lambda$ accepts it:

  a.  *aba*

  b.  *abab*

  c.  *aaabbb*

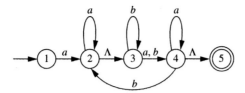

**Figure 4.21 |**

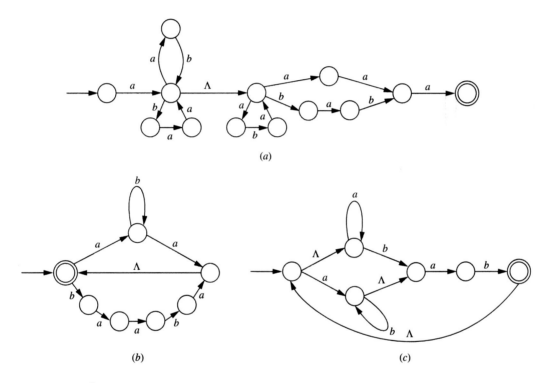

**Figure 4.22 |**

**4.14.** Find a regular expression corresponding to the language recognized by the NFA-Λ pictured in Figure 4.21. You should be able to do it without applying Kleene's theorem: First find a regular expression describing the most general way of reaching state 4 the first time, and then find a regular expression describing the most general way, starting in state 4, of moving to state 4 the next time.

**4.15.** For each of the NFA-Λs shown in Figure 4.22, find a regular expression corresponding to the language it recognizes.

**4.16.** A transition table is given for an NFA-$\Lambda$ with seven states.

| $q$ | $\delta(q, a)$ | $\delta(q, b)$ | $\delta(q, \Lambda)$ |
|---|---|---|---|
| 1 | $\emptyset$ | $\emptyset$ | $\{2\}$ |
| 2 | $\{3\}$ | $\emptyset$ | $\{5\}$ |
| 3 | $\emptyset$ | $\{4\}$ | $\emptyset$ |
| 4 | $\{4\}$ | $\emptyset$ | $\{1\}$ |
| 5 | $\emptyset$ | $\{6, 7\}$ | $\emptyset$ |
| 6 | $\{5\}$ | $\emptyset$ | $\emptyset$ |
| 7 | $\emptyset$ | $\emptyset$ | $\{1\}$ |

Find:

a. $\Lambda(\{2, 3\})$

b. $\Lambda(\{1\})$

c. $\Lambda(\{3, 4\})$

d. $\delta^*(1, ba)$

e. $\delta^*(1, ab)$

f. $\delta^*(1, ababa)$

**4.17.** A transition table is given for another NFA-$\Lambda$ with seven states.

| $q$ | $\delta(q, a)$ | $\delta(q, b)$ | $\delta(q, \Lambda)$ |
|---|---|---|---|
| 1 | $\{5\}$ | $\emptyset$ | $\{4\}$ |
| 2 | $\{1\}$ | $\emptyset$ | $\emptyset$ |
| 3 | $\emptyset$ | $\{2\}$ | $\emptyset$ |
| 4 | $\emptyset$ | $\{7\}$ | $\{3\}$ |
| 5 | $\emptyset$ | $\emptyset$ | $\{1\}$ |
| 6 | $\emptyset$ | $\{5\}$ | $\{4\}$ |
| 7 | $\{6\}$ | $\emptyset$ | $\emptyset$ |

Calculate $\delta^*(1, ba)$.

**4.18.** For each of these regular expressions over $\{0, 1\}$, draw an NFA-$\Lambda$ recognizing the corresponding language. (You should not need the construction in Kleene's theorem to do this.)

a. $(0 + 1)^*(011 + 01010)(0 + 1)^*$

b. $(0 + 1)(01)^*(011)^*$

c. $010^* + 0(01 + 10)^*11$

**4.19.** Suppose $M$ is an NFA-$\Lambda$ accepting $L \subseteq \Sigma^*$. Describe how to modify $M$ to obtain an NFA-$\Lambda$ recognizing $rev(L) = \{x^r \mid x \in L\}$.

**4.20.** In each part of Figure 4.23, two NFA-$\Lambda$s are illustrated. Decide whether the two accept the same language, and give reasons for your answer.

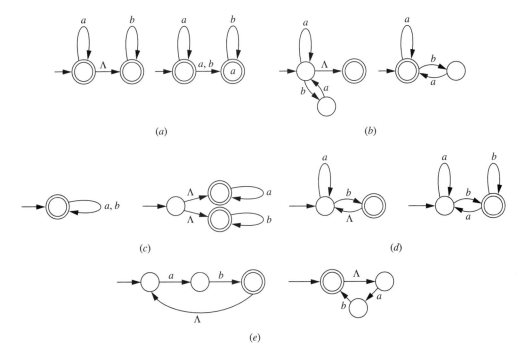

(a)

(b)

(c)

(d)

(e)

**Figure 4.23 |**

**4.21.** Let $M = (Q, \Sigma, q_0, A, \delta)$ be an FA, and let $M_1 = (Q, \Sigma, q_0, A, \delta_1)$ be the NFA-$\Lambda$ defined in the proof of Theorem 4.3, in which $\delta_1(q, \Lambda) = \emptyset$ and $\delta_1(q, a) = \{\delta(q, a)\}$, for every $q \in Q$ and $a \in \Sigma$. Give a careful proof that for every $q \in Q$ and $x \in \Sigma^*$, $\delta_1^*(q, x) = \{\delta^*(q, x)\}$. Recall that the two functions $\delta^*$ and $\delta_1^*$ are defined differently.

**4.22.** Let $M_1$ be the NFA-$\Lambda$ obtained from the FA $M$ as in the proof of Theorem 4.3. The transition function $\delta_1$ of $M_1$ is defined so that $\delta_1(q, \Lambda) = \emptyset$ for every state $q$. Would defining $\delta_1(q, \Lambda) = \{q\}$ also work? Give reasons for your answer.

**4.23.** Let $M = (Q, \Sigma, q_0, A, \delta)$ be an NFA-$\Lambda$. The proofs of Theorems 4.2 and 4.1 describe a two-step process for obtaining an FA $M_1 = (Q_1, \Sigma, q_1, A_1, \delta_1)$ that accepts the language $L(M)$. Do it in one step, by defining $Q_1, q_1, A_1$, and $\delta_1$ directly in terms of $M$.

**4.24.** Let $M = (Q, \Sigma, q_0, A, \delta)$ be an NFA-$\Lambda$. In the proof of Theorem 4.2, the NFA $M_1$ might have more accepting states than $M$: The initial state $q_0$ is made an accepting state if $\Lambda(\{q_0\}) \cap A \neq \emptyset$. Explain why it is not necessary to make *all* the states $q$ for which $\Lambda(\{q\}) \cap A \neq \emptyset$ accepting states in $M_1$.

**4.25.** Suppose $M = (Q, \Sigma, q_0, A, \delta)$ is an NFA-$\Lambda$ recognizing a language $L$. Let $M_1$ be the NFA-$\Lambda$ obtained from $M$ by adding $\Lambda$-transitions from each element of $A$ to $q_0$. Describe (in terms of $L$) the language $L(M_1)$.

**4.26.** Suppose $M = (Q, \Sigma, q_0, A, \delta)$ is an NFA-Λ recognizing a language $L$.

    a.  Describe how to construct an NFA-Λ $M_1$ with no transitions to its initial state so that $M_1$ also recognizes $L$.

    b.  Describe how to construct an NFA-Λ $M_2$ with exactly one accepting state and no transitions from that state so that $M_2$ also recognizes $L$.

**4.27.** Suppose $M$ is an NFA-Λ with exactly one accepting state $q_f$ that recognizes the language $L \subseteq \{0, 1\}^*$. In order to find NFA-Λs recognizing the languages $\{0\}^*L$ and $L\{0\}^*$, we might try adding 0-transitions from $q_0$ to itself and from $q_f$ to itself, respectively. Draw transition diagrams to show that neither technique always works.

**4.28.** In each part of Figure 4.24 is pictured an NFA-Λ. Use the algorithm illustrated in Example 4.7 to draw an NFA accepting the same language.

**4.29.** In each part of Figure 4.25 is pictured an NFA-Λ. Draw an FA accepting the same language.

**4.30.** Give an example (i.e., draw a transition diagram) to illustrate the fact that in the construction of $M_u$ in the proof of Theorem 4.4, the two sets $Q_1$ and $Q_2$ must be disjoint.

**4.31.** Give an example to illustrate the fact that in the construction of $M_c$ in the proof of Theorem 4.4, the two sets $Q_1$ and $Q_2$ must be disjoint.

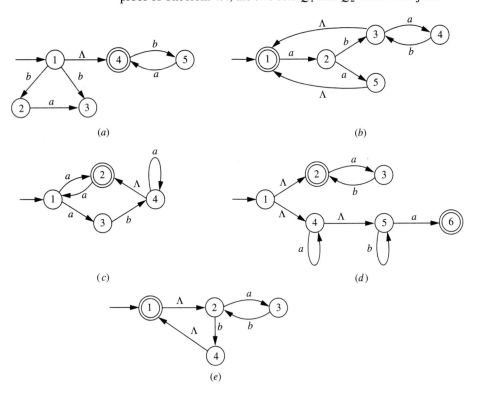

**Figure 4.24**

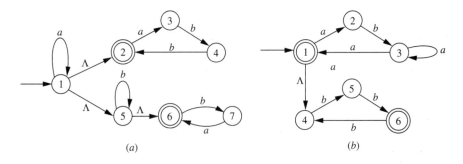

(a)

(b)

**Figure 4.25** ⎮

**4.32.** In the construction of $M_u$ in the proof of Theorem 4.4, consider this alternative to the construction described: Instead of a new state $q_u$ and $\Lambda$-transitions from it to $q_1$ and $q_2$, make $q_1$ the initial state of the new NFA-$\Lambda$, and create a $\Lambda$-transition from it to $q_2$. Either prove that this works in general, or give an example in which it fails.

**4.33.** In the construction of $M_c$ in the proof of Theorem 4.4, consider the simplified case in which $M_1$ has only one accepting state. Suppose that we eliminate the $\Lambda$-transition from the accepting state of $M_1$ to $q_2$, and merge these two states into one. Either show that this would always work in this case, or give an example in which it fails.

**4.34.** In the construction of $M_k$ in the proof of Theorem 4.4, suppose that instead of adding a new state $q_k$, with $\Lambda$-transitions from it to $q_1$ and to it from each accepting state of $Q_1$, we make $q_1$ both the initial state and the accepting state, and create $\Lambda$-transitions from each accepting state of $M_1$ to $q_k$. Either show that this works in general, or give an example in which it fails.

**4.35.** In each case below, find an NFA-$\Lambda$ recognizing the language corresponding to the regular expression, by applying literally the algorithm in the chapter. Do not attempt to simplify the answer.

    a. $((ab)^*b + ab^*)^*$

    b. $aa(ba)^* + b^*aba^*$

    c. $(ab + (aab)^*)(aa + a)$

**4.36.** In Figures 4.26a and 4.26b are pictured FAs $M_1$ and $M_2$, recognizing languages $L_1$ and $L_2$, respectively. Draw NFA-$\Lambda$s recognizing each of the following languages, using the constructions in this chapter:

    a. $L_1L_2$

    b. $L_1L_1L_2$

    c. $L_1 \cup L_2$

    d. $L_1^*$

    e. $L_2^* \cup L_1$

    f. $L_2L_1^*$

    g. $L_1L_2 \cup (L_2L_1)^*$

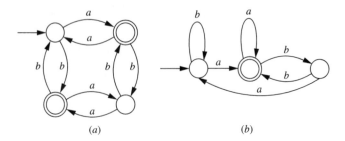

**Figure 4.26 |**

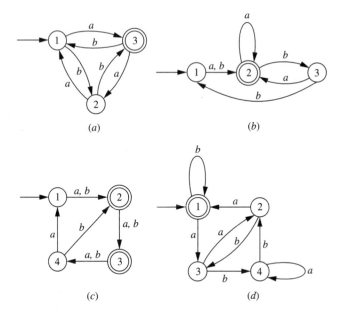

**Figure 4.27 |**

**4.37.** Draw NFAs accepting $L_1L_2$ and $L_2L_1$, where $L_1$ and $L_2$ are as in the preceding problem. Do this by connecting the two given diagrams directly, by arrows with appropriate labels.

**4.38.** Use the algorithm of Theorem 4.5 to find a regular expression corresponding to each of the FAs shown in Figure 4.27. In each case, if the FA has $n$ states, construct tables showing $L(p, q, j)$ for each $j$ with $0 \leq j \leq n - 1$.

# MORE CHALLENGING PROBLEMS

**4.39.** Which of the following, if any, would be a correct substitute for the second part of Definition 4.5b? Give reasons for your answer.

a. $\delta^*(q, ay) = \Lambda \left( \bigcup_{r \in \delta(q,a)} \delta^*(r, y) \right)$

b. $\delta^*(q, ay) = \bigcup_{r \in \delta(q,a)} \Lambda(\delta^*(r, y))$

c. $\delta^*(q, ay) = \bigcup_{r \in \Lambda(\delta(q,a))} \delta^*(r, y)$

d. $\delta^*(q, ay) = \bigcup_{r \in \Lambda(\delta(q,a))} \Lambda(\delta^*(r, y))$

**4.40.** Let $M = (Q, \Sigma, q_0, A, \delta)$ be an NFA-$\Lambda$. This exercise involves properties of the $\Lambda$-closure of a set $S$. Since $\Lambda(S)$ is defined recursively (Definition 4.6), structural induction can be used to show that every state in $\Lambda(S)$ satisfies some property—such as being a member of some other set.

   a. Show that if $S$ and $T$ are subsets of $Q$ for which $S \subseteq T$, then $\Lambda(S) \subseteq \Lambda(T)$.

   b. Show that for any $S \subseteq Q$, $\Lambda(\Lambda(S)) = \Lambda(S)$.

   c. Show that if $S, T \subseteq Q$, then $\Lambda(S \cup T) = \Lambda(S) \cup \Lambda(T)$.

   d. Show that if $S \subseteq Q$, then $\Lambda(S) = \bigcup_{p \in S} \Lambda(\{p\})$.

   e. Draw a transition diagram to illustrate the fact that $\Lambda(S \cap T)$ and $\Lambda(S) \cap \Lambda(T)$ are not always the same. Which is always a subset of the other?

   f. Draw a transition diagram illustrating the fact that $\Lambda(S')$ and $\Lambda(S)'$ are not always the same. Which is always a subset of the other? Under what circumstances are they equal?

**4.41.** Let $M = (Q, \Sigma, q_0, A, \delta)$ be an NFA-$\Lambda$. A set $S \subseteq Q$ is called $\Lambda$-*closed* if $\Lambda(S) = S$.

   a. Show that the union of two $\Lambda$-closed sets is $\Lambda$-closed.

   b. Show that the intersection of two $\Lambda$-closed sets is $\Lambda$-closed.

   c. Show that for any subset $S$ of $Q$, $\Lambda(S)$ is the smallest $\Lambda$-closed set of which $S$ is a subset.

**4.42.**   a. Let $M = (Q, \Sigma, q_0, A, \delta)$ be an NFA. Show that for every $q \in Q$ and every $x, y \in \Sigma^*$,

$$\delta^*(q, xy) = \bigcup_{r \in \delta^*(q,x)} \delta^*(r, y)$$

   b. Prove the same formula, this time assuming that $M$ is an NFA-$\Lambda$.

**4.43.** Suppose $M = (Q, \Sigma, q_0, A, \delta)$ is an NFA. We may consider a new NFA $M_1 = (Q, \Sigma, q_0, A, \delta_1)$ obtained by letting $\delta_1(q, a) = \delta(q, a)$ if $|\delta(q, a)| \leq 1$ and, for every pair $(q, a)$ for which $|\delta(q, a)| > 1$, choosing one state $p \in \delta(q, a)$ arbitrarily and letting $\delta_1(q, a) = \{p\}$. Although $M_1$ is not necessarily an FA, it could easily be converted to an FA, because it never has more than one choice of moves.

If $S$ is the set of all pairs $(q, a)$ for which $|\delta(q, a)| > 1$, and $c$ denotes some specific sequence of choices, one choice for each element of $S$, then we let $M_1^c$ denote the specific NFA that results. What is the relationship between $L(M)$ and the collection of languages $L(M_1^c)$ obtained by considering all possible sequences $c$ of choices? Be as precise as you can, and give reasons for your answer.

**4.44.** Let $M = (Q, \Sigma, q_0, A, \delta)$ be an NFA-$\Lambda$ recognizing a language $L$. Assume that there are no transitions to $q_0$, that $A$ has only one element, $q_f$, and that there are no transitions from $q_f$.

   a. Let $M_1$ be obtained from $M$ by adding $\Lambda$-transitions from $q_0$ to every state that is reachable from $q_0$ in $M$. (If $p$ and $q$ are states, $q$ is reachable from $p$ if there is a string $x \in \Sigma^*$ such that $q \in \delta^*(p, x)$.) Describe (in terms of $L$) the language accepted by $M_1$.

   b. Let $M_2$ be obtained from $M$ by adding $\Lambda$-transitions to $q_f$ from every state from which $q_f$ is reachable in $M$. Describe in terms of $L$ the language accepted by $M_2$.

   c. Let $M_3$ be obtained from $M$ by adding both the $\Lambda$-transitions in (a) and those in (b). Describe the language accepted by $M_3$.

   d. Let $M_4$ be obtained from $M$ by adding $\Lambda$-transitions from $p$ to $q$ whenever $q$ is reachable from $p$ in $M$. Describe the language accepted by $M_4$.

**4.45.** In Example 4.5, we started with NFAs $M_1$ and $M_2$ and incorporated them into a composite NFA $M$ accepting $L(M_1) \cup L(M_2)$ in such a way that no new states were required.

   a. Show by considering the languages $\{0\}^*$ and $\{1\}^*$ that this is not always possible. (Each of the two languages can obviously be accepted by a one-state NFA; show that their union cannot be accepted by a two-state NFA.)

   b. Describe a reasonably general set of circumstances in which this *is* possible. (Find a condition that might be satisfied by one or both of the NFAs that would make it possible.)

**4.46.** Suppose $\Sigma_1$ and $\Sigma_2$ are alphabets, and the function $f : \Sigma_1^* \to \Sigma_2^*$ is a *homomorphism*; i.e., $f(xy) = f(x)f(y)$ for every $x, y \in \Sigma_1^*$.

   a. Show that $f(\Lambda) = \Lambda$.

   b. Show that if $L \subseteq \Sigma_1^*$ is regular, then $f(L)$ is regular. ($f(L)$ is the set $\{y \in \Sigma_2^* \mid y = f(x) \text{ for some } x \in L\}$.)

   c. Show that if $L \subseteq \Sigma_2^*$ is regular, then $f^{-1}(L)$ is regular. ($f^{-1}(L)$ is the set $\{x \in \Sigma_1^* \mid f(x) \in L\}$.)

**4.47.** Suppose $M = (Q, \Sigma, q_0, A, \delta)$ is an NFA-$\Lambda$. For two (not necessarily distinct) states $p$ and $q$, we define the regular expression $e(p, q)$ as follows: $e(p, q) = l + r_1 + r_2 + \cdots + r_k$, where $l$ is either $\Lambda$ (if $\delta(p, \Lambda)$ contains $q$)

or $\emptyset$, and the $r_i$'s are all the elements $a$ of $\Sigma$ for which $\delta(p, a)$ contains $q$. It's possible for $e(p, q)$ to be $\emptyset$, if there are no transitions from $p$ to $q$; otherwise, $e(p, q)$ represents the "most general" transition from $p$ to $q$.

If we generalize this by allowing $e(p, q)$ to be an arbitrary regular expression over $\Sigma$, we get what is called an *expression graph*. If $p$ and $q$ are two states in an expression graph $G$, and $x \in \Sigma^*$, we say that $x$ allows $G$ to move from $p$ to $q$ if there are states $p_0, p_1, \ldots, p_m$, with $p_0 = p$ and $p_m = q$, so that $x$ corresponds to the regular expression $e(p_0, p_1)e(p_1, p_2) \cdots e(p_{n-1}, p_n)$. This allows us to say how $G$ accepts a string $x$ ($x$ allows $G$ to move from the initial state to an accepting state), and therefore to talk about the language accepted by $G$. It is easy to see that in the special case where $G$ is simply an NFA-$\Lambda$, the two definitions for the language accepted by $G$ coincide. (See Definition 4.5a.) It is also not hard to convince yourself, using Theorem 4.4, that for any expression graph $G$, the language accepted by $G$ can be accepted by an NFA-$\Lambda$.

We can use the idea of an expression graph to obtain an alternate proof of Theorem 4.5, as follows. Starting with an FA $M$ accepting $L$, we may easily convert it to an NFA-$\Lambda$ $M_1$ accepting $L$, so that $M_1$ has no transitions to its initial state $q_0$, exactly one accepting state $q_f$ (which is different from $q_0$), and no transitions from $q_f$. The remainder of the proof is to specify a reduction technique to reduce by one the number of states other than $q_0$ and $q_f$, obtaining an equivalent expression graph at each step, until $q_0$ and $q_f$ are the only states remaining. The regular expression $e(q_0, q_f)$ then describes the language accepted. If $p$ is the state to be eliminated, the reduction step involves redefining $e(q, r)$ for every pair of states $q$ and $r$ other than $p$.

Describe in more detail how this reduction can be done. Then apply this technique to the FAs in Figure 4.27 to obtain regular expressions corresponding to their languages.

# CHAPTER

# 5

# Regular and Nonregular Languages

## 5.1 I A CRITERION FOR REGULARITY

Kleene's theorem (Theorems 4.4 and 4.5) provides a useful characterization of regular languages: A language is regular (describable by a regular expression) if and only if it can be accepted by a finite automaton. In other words, a language can be *generated* in a simple way, from simple primitive languages, if and only if it can be *recognized* in a simple way, by a device with a finite number of states and no auxiliary memory. There is a construction algorithm associated with each half of the theorem, so that if we already have a regular expression, we can find an FA to accept the corresponding language, and if we already have an FA, we can find a regular expression to describe the language it accepts.

Suppose now that we have a language over the alphabet $\Sigma$ specified in some way that involves neither a regular expression nor an FA. How can we tell whether it is regular? (What inherent property of a language identifies it as being regular?) And, if we suspect that the language is regular, how can we find either a regular expression describing it or an FA accepting it?

We have a partial answer to the first question already. According to Theorem 3.2, if there are infinitely many strings that are "pairwise distinguishable" with respect to $L$, then $L$ cannot be regular. (To say it another way, if $L$ is regular, then every set that is pairwise distinguishable with respect to $L$ is finite.) It is useful to reformulate this condition slightly, using Definition 3.5. Recall that $L/x$ denotes the set $\{y \in \Sigma^* \mid xy \in L\}$. If we let $I_L$ be the indistinguishability relation on $\Sigma^*$, defined by

$$x I_L y \text{ if and only if } L/x = L/y$$

then $I_L$ is an equivalence relation on $\Sigma^*$ (Exercise 1.33b), and saying that two strings are distinguishable with respect to $L$ means that they are in different equivalence classes of $I_L$. The statement above can therefore be reformulated as follows: If $L$

is regular, then the set of equivalence classes for the relation $I_L$ is finite. In order to obtain a characterization of regularity using this approach, we need to show that the converse is also true, that if the set of equivalence classes is finite then $L$ is regular.

Once we do this, we will have an answer to the first question above (how can we tell whether $L$ is regular?), in terms of the equivalence classes of the relation $I_L$. Furthermore, it turns out that if our language $L$ is regular, identifying these equivalence classes will also give us an answer to the second question (how can we find an FA?), because there is a simple way to use the equivalence classes to construct an FA accepting $L$. This FA is *the* most natural one to accept $L$, in the sense that it has the fewest possible states; and an interesting by-product of the discussion will be a method for taking any FA known to accept $L$ and simplifying it as much as possible.

We wish to show that if the the set of equivalence classes of $I_L$ is finite, then there is a finite automaton accepting $L$. The discussion may be easier to understand, however, if we start with a language $L$ known to be regular, and with an FA $M = (Q, \Sigma, q_0, A, \delta)$ recognizing $L$. If $q \in Q$, then adapting the notation introduced in Section 4.3, we let

$$L_q = \{x \in \Sigma^* \mid \delta^*(q_0, x) = q\}$$

We remember from Chapter 1 that talking about equivalence relations on a set is essentially the same as talking about partitions of the set: An equivalence relation determines a partition (in which the subsets are the equivalence classes), and a partition determines an equivalence relation (in which being equivalent means belonging to the same subset). At this point, there are two natural partitions of $\Sigma^*$ that we might consider: the one determined by the equivalence relation $I_L$, and the one formed by all the sets $L_q$ for $q \in Q$. The relationship between them is given by Lemma 3.1. If $x$ and $y$ are in the same $L_q$ (in other words, if $\delta^*(q_0, x) = \delta^*(q_0, y)$), then $L/x = L/y$, so that $x$ and $y$ are in the same equivalence class of $I_L$. This means that each set $L_q$ must be a subset of a single equivalence class, and therefore that every equivalence class of $I_L$ is the union of one or more of the $L_q$'s (Exercise 1.68). In particular, there can be no fewer of the $L_q$'s than there are equivalence classes of $I_L$. If the two numbers are the same, then the two partitions are identical, each set $L_q$ is precisely one of the equivalence classes of $I_L$, and $M$ is an FA with the fewest possible states recognizing $L$.

These observations suggest how to turn things around and begin from the other end. If we have an FA accepting $L$, then under certain circumstances, the strings in one of the equivalence classes of $I_L$ are precisely those that correspond to one of the states of the FA. If we are not given an FA to start with, but we know the equivalence classes of $I_L$, then we might try to construct an FA with exactly this property: Rather than starting with a state $q$ and considering the corresponding set $L_q$ of strings, this time we have the set of strings and we hope to specify a state to which the set will correspond. However, the point is that we do not have to *find* a state like this, we can simply *define* one. A "state" is an abstraction anyway; why not go ahead and say that a state is a set of strings—specifically, one of the equivalence classes of $I_L$? If there are only a finite number of these equivalence classes, then we have at least the first ingredient of a finite automaton accepting $L$: a finite set of states.

Once we commit ourselves to this abstraction, filling in the remaining details is surprisingly easy. Because one of the strings that cause an FA to be in the initial state is $\Lambda$, we choose for our initial state the equivalence class containing $\Lambda$. Because we want the FA to accept $L$, we choose for our accepting states those equivalence classes containing elements of $L$. And because in the recognition algorithm we change the current string by concatenating one more input symbol, we compute the value of our transition function by taking a string in our present state (equivalence class) and concatenating it with the input symbol. The resulting string determines the new equivalence class.

Before making our definition official, we need to look a little more closely at this last step. "Taking a string in our present state and concatenating it with the input symbol" means that if we start with an equivalence class $q$ containing a string $x$, then $\delta(q, a)$ should be the equivalence class containing $xa$. Writing this symbolically, we should have

$$\delta([x], a) = [xa]$$

where for any string $z$, $[z]$ denotes the equivalence class containing $z$. As an assertion about a string $x$, this is a perfectly straightforward formula, which may be true or false, depending on how $\delta([x], a)$ is defined. If we want the formula to be the *definition* of $\delta([x], a)$, we must consider a potential problem. We are trying to define $\delta(q, a)$, where $q$ is an equivalence class (a set of strings). We have taken a string $x$ in the set $q$, which allows us to write $q = [x]$. However, there is nothing special about $x$; the set $q$ could just as easily be written as $[y]$ for any other string $y \in q$. If our definition is to make any sense, it must tell us what $\delta(q, a)$ is, whether we write $q = [x]$ or $q = [y]$. The formula gives us $[xa]$ in one case and $[ya]$ in the other; obviously, unless $[xa] = [ya]$, our definition is nonsense. Fortunately, the next lemma takes care of the potential problem.

**Lemma 5.1**  $I_L$ is *right invariant* with respect to concatenation. In other words, for any $x, y \in \Sigma^*$ and any $a \in \Sigma$, if $x \, I_L \, y$, then $xa \, I_L \, ya$. Equivalently, if $[x] = [y]$, then $[xa] = [ya]$.

***Proof***  Suppose $x \, I_L \, y$ and $a \in \Sigma$. Then $L/x = L/y$, so that for any $z' \in \Sigma^*$, $xz'$ and $yz'$ are either both in $L$ or both not in $L$. Therefore, for any $z \in \Sigma^*$, $xaz$ and $yaz$ are either both in $L$ or both not in $L$ (because we can apply the previous statement with $z' = az$), and we conclude that $xa I_L ya$.  ∎

---

**Theorem 5.1**

Let $L \subseteq \Sigma^*$, and let $Q_L$ be the set of equivalence classes of the relation $I_L$ on $\Sigma^*$. (Each element of $Q$, therefore, is a set of strings.) If $Q_L$ is a finite set, then $M_L = (Q_L, \Sigma, q_0, A_L, \delta)$ is a finite automaton accepting $L$, where $q_0 = [\Lambda]$, $A_L = \{q \in Q_L \mid q \cap L \neq \emptyset\}$, and $\delta : Q_L \times \Sigma \to Q_L$ is defined by the formula $\delta([x], a) = [xa]$. Furthermore, $M_L$ has the fewest states of any FA accepting $L$.

*Proof*

According to Lemma 5.1, the formula $\delta([x], a) = [xa]$ is a meaningful definition of a function $\delta$ from $Q_L \times \Sigma$ to $Q_L$, and thus the 5-tuple $M_L$ has all the ingredients of an FA. In order to verify that $M_L$ recognizes $L$, we need the formula

$$\delta^*([x], y) = [xy]$$

for $x, y \in \Sigma^*$. The proof is by structural induction on $y$. The basis step is to show that $\delta^*([x], \Lambda) = [x\Lambda]$ for every $x$. This is easy, since the left side is $[x]$ because of the definition of $\delta^*$ in an FA (Definition 3.3), and the right side is $[x]$ because $x\Lambda = x$.

For the induction step, suppose that for some $y$, $\delta^*([x], y) = [xy]$ for every string $x$, and consider $\delta^*([x], ya)$ for $a \in \Sigma$:

$$\delta^*([x], ya) = \delta(\delta^*([x], y), a) \quad \text{(by definition of } \delta^*\text{)}$$
$$= \delta([xy], a) \quad \text{(by the induction hypothesis)}$$
$$= [xya] \quad \text{(by the definition of } \delta\text{)}$$

From this formula it follows that $\delta^*(q_0, x) = \delta^*([\Lambda], x) = [x]$. Our definition of $A$ tells us, therefore, that $x$ is accepted by $M_L$ if and only if $[x] \cap L \neq \emptyset$. What we want is that $x$ is accepted if and only if $x \in L$. But in fact the two statements $[x] \cap L \neq \emptyset$ and $x \in L$ are the same. One direction is obvious: If $x \in L$, then $[x] \cap L \neq \emptyset$, since $x \in [x]$. In the other direction, if $[x]$ contains an element $y$ of $L$, then $x$ must be in $L$. Otherwise the string $\Lambda$ would distinguish $x$ and $y$ with respect to $L$, and $x$ and $y$ could not both be elements of $[x]$. Therefore, $M_L$ accepts $L$.

Finally, if there are $n$ equivalence classes of $I_L$, then we can get a set of $n$ strings that are pairwise distinguishable by just choosing one string from each equivalence class. (No two of these strings are equivalent, or any two are distinguishable.) Theorem 3.2 implies that any FA accepting $L$ must have at least $n$ states. Since $M_L$ has exactly $n$, it has the fewest possible.

**Corollary 5.1** $L$ is a regular language if and only if the set of equivalence classes of $I_L$ is finite.

*Proof* Theorem 5.1 tells us that if the set of equivalence classes is finite, there is an FA accepting $L$; and Theorem 3.2 says that if the set is infinite, there can be no such FA. ∎

Corollary 5.1 was proved by Myhill and Nerode, and it is often called the Myhill-Nerode theorem.

It is interesting to observe that to some extent, the construction of $M_L$ in Theorem 5.1 makes sense even when the language $L$ is not regular. $I_L$ is an equivalence relation for any language $L$, and we can consider the set $Q_L$ of equivalence classes. Neither

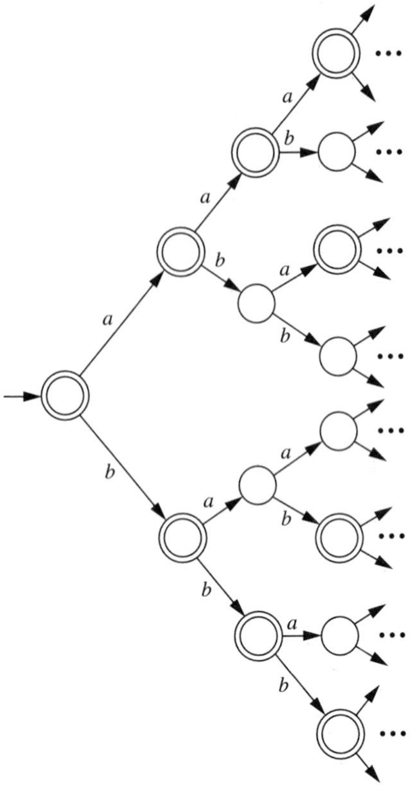

**Figure 5.1** |

the definition of $\delta : Q_L \times \Sigma \to Q_L$ nor the proof that $M_L$ accepts $L$ depends on the assumption that $Q_L$ is a finite set. It appears that even in the most general case, we have some sort of "device" that accepts $L$. If it is not a finite automaton, what is it?

Instead of inventing a name for something with an infinite number of states, let us draw a (partial) picture of it in a simple case we have studied. Let $L$ be the language *pal* of all palindromes over $\{a, b\}$. As we observed in the proof of Theorem 3.3, any two strings in $\{a, b\}^*$ are distinguishable with respect to $L$. Not only is the set $Q_L$ infinite, but there are as many equivalence classes as there are strings; each equivalence class contains exactly one string. Even in this most extreme case, there is no difficulty in visualizing $M_L$, as Figure 5.1 indicates.

The only problem, of course, is that there is no way to complete the picture, and no way to implement $M_L$ as a physical machine. As we have seen in other ways, the crucial aspect of an FA is precisely the finiteness of the set of states.

| **EXAMPLE 5.1** | Applying Theorem 5.1 to $\{0, 1\}^*\{10\}$ |

Consider the language discussed in Example 3.12,

$$L = \{x \in \{0, 1\}^* \mid x \text{ ends with } 10\}$$

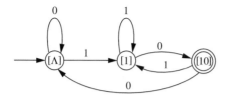

**Figure 5.2 |**
A minimum-state FA recognizing
$\{0, 1\}^*\{10\}$.

and consider the three strings $\Lambda$, 1, and 10. We can easily verify that any two of these strings are distinguishable with respect to $L$: The string $\Lambda$ distinguishes $\Lambda$ and 10, and also 1 and 10, while the string 0 distinguishes $\Lambda$ and 1. Therefore, the three equivalence classes $[\Lambda]$, $[1]$, and $[10]$ are distinct.

However, any string $y$ is equivalent to (indistinguishable from) one of these strings. If $y$ ends in 10, then $y$ is equivalent to 10; if $y$ ends in 1, $y$ is equivalent to 1; otherwise (if $y = \Lambda$, $y = 0$, or $y$ ends with 00), $y$ is equivalent to $\Lambda$. Therefore, these three equivalence classes are the only ones.

Let $M_L = (Q_L, \{0, 1\}, [\Lambda], \{[10]\}, \delta)$ be the FA we constructed in Theorem 5.1. Then

$$\delta([\Lambda], 0) = [\Lambda] \quad \text{and} \quad \delta([\Lambda], 1) = [1]$$

since $\Lambda 0$ is equivalent to $\Lambda$ and $\Lambda 1 = 1$. Similarly,

$$\delta([1], 0) = [10] \quad \text{and} \quad \delta([1], 1) = [1]$$

since 11 is equivalent to 1. Finally,

$$\delta([10], 0) = [\Lambda] \quad \text{and} \quad \delta([10], 1) = [1]$$

since 100 is equivalent to $\Lambda$ and 101 is equivalent to 1. It follows that the FA $M_L$ is the one shown in Figure 5.2. Not surprisingly, this is the same FA we came up with in Example 3.12, except for the names given to the states. (One reason it is not surprising is that the strings $\Lambda$, 1, and 10 were chosen to correspond to the three states in the previous FA!)

We used Theorem 3.2, which is the "only if" part of Theorem 5.1, to show that the language of palindromes over $\{0, 1\}$ is nonregular. We may use the same principle to exhibit a number of other nonregular languages.

## The Equivalence Classes of $I_L$ for $L = \{0^n 1^n \mid n > 0\}$     **EXAMPLE 5.2**

Let $L = \{0^n 1^n \mid n > 0\}$. The intuitive reason $L$ is not regular is that in trying to recognize elements of $L$, we must remember how many 0's we have seen, so that when we start seeing 1's we will be able to determine whether the number of 1's is exactly the same. In order to use Theorem 5.1 to show $L$ is not regular, we must show that there are infinitely many distinct equivalence classes of $I_L$. In this example, at least, let us do even more than that and describe the equivalence classes exactly.

Some strings are not prefixes of any elements of $L$ (examples include 1, 011, and 010), and it is not hard to see that the set of all such strings is an equivalence class (Exercise 5.4). The remaining strings are of three types: strings in $L$, strings of 0's ($0^i$, for some $i \geq 0$), and strings of the form $0^i 1^j$ with $0 < j < i$.

The set $L$ is itself an equivalence class of $I_L$. This is because for any string $x \in L$, $\Lambda$ is the only string that can follow $x$ so as to produce an element of $L$.

Saying as we did above that "we must remember how many 0's we have seen" suggests that two distinct strings of 0's should be in different equivalence classes. This is true: If $i \neq j$, the strings $0^i$ and $0^j$ are distinguished by the string $1^i$, because $0^i 1^i \in L$ and $0^j 1^i \notin L$. We now know that $[0^i] \neq [0^j]$. To see exactly what these sets are, we note that for *any* string $x$ other than $0^i$, the string $01^{i+1}$ distinguishes $0^i$ and $x$ (because $0^i 01^{i+1} \in L$ and $x01^{i+1} \notin L$). In other words, $0^i$ is equivalent only to itself, and $[0^i] = \{0^i\}$.

Finally, consider the string 000011, for example. There is exactly one string $z$ for which $000011z \in L$: the string $z = 11$. However, any other string $x$ having the property that $xz \in L$ if and only if $z = 11$ is equivalent to 000011, and these are the strings $0^{j+2}1^j$ for $j > 0$. No string other than one of these can be equivalent to 000011, and we may conclude that the equivalence class [000011] is the set $\{0^{j+2}1^j \mid j > 0\}$. Similarly, for each $k > 0$, the set $\{0^{j+k}1^j \mid j > 0\}$ is an equivalence class.

Let us summarize our conclusions. The set $L$ and the set of all nonprefixes of elements of $L$ are two of the equivalence classes; for each $i \geq 0$, the set with the single element $0^i$ is an equivalence class; and for each $k > 0$, the infinite set $\{0^{j+k}1^j \mid j > 0\}$ is an equivalence class. Since every string is in one of these equivalence classes, these are the only equivalence classes.

As we expected, we have shown in particular that there are infinitely many distinct equivalence classes, which allows us to conclude that $L$ is not regular.

---

**EXAMPLE 5.3**    Simple Algebraic Expressions

Let $L$ be the set of all legal algebraic expressions involving the identifier $a$, the operator $+$, and left and right parentheses. To show that the relation $I_L$ has infinitely many distinct equivalence classes, we can ignore much of the structure of $L$. The only fact we use is that the string

$$((\cdots(a)\cdots))$$

is in $L$ if and only if the numbers of left and right parentheses are the same. We may therefore consider the set $S = \{(^n \mid n \geq 0\}$, in the same way that we considered the strings $0^n$ in the previous example. For $0 \leq m < n$, the string $a)^m$ distinguishes $(^m$ and $(^n$, and so any two elements of $S$ are distinguishable with respect to $L$ (i.e., in different equivalence classes). We conclude from this that $L$ is not regular. Exercise 5.35 asks you to describe the equivalence classes of $I_L$ more precisely.

---

**EXAMPLE 5.4**    The Set of Strings of the Form *ww*

For yet another example where the set $S = \{0^n \mid n \geq 0\}$ can be used to prove a language nonregular, take $L$ to be the language

$$\{ww \mid w \in \{0, 1\}^*\}$$

of all even-length strings of 0's and 1's whose first and second halves are identical. This time, for a string $z$ that distinguishes $0^n$ and $0^m$ when $m \neq n$, we choose $z = 1^n 0^n 1^n$. The string $0^n z$ is in $L$, and the string $0^m z$ is not.

---

Exercise 5.20 asks you to get even a little more mileage out of the set $\{0^n \mid n \geq 0\}$ or some variation of it. We close this section with one more example.

---

## Another Nonregular Language from Theorem 5.1    EXAMPLE 5.5

Let $L = \{0, 011, 011000, 0110001111, \ldots\}$. A string in $L$ consists of groups of 0's alternated with groups of 1's. It begins with a single 0, and each subsequent group of identical symbols is one symbol longer than the previous group. Here we can show that the infinite set $L$ itself is pairwise distinguishable with respect to $L$, and therefore that $L$ is not regular. Let $x$ and $y$ be two distinct elements of $L$. Suppose $x$ and $y$ both end with groups of 0's, for example, $x$ with $0^j$ and $y$ with $0^k$. Then $x 1^{j+1} \in L$, but $y 1^{j+1} \notin L$. It is easy to see that similar arguments also work in the other three cases.

---

# 5.2 | MINIMAL FINITE AUTOMATA

Theorem 5.1 and Corollary 5.1 help us to understand a little better what makes a language $L$ regular. In a sense they provide an absolute answer to the question of how much information we need to remember at each step of the recognition algorithm: We can forget everything about the current string *except* which equivalence class of $I_L$ it belongs to. If there are infinitely many of these equivalence classes, then this is more information than any FA can remember, and $L$ cannot be regular. If the set of equivalence classes is finite, and if we can identify them, then we can use them to construct the simplest possible FA accepting $L$.

It is not clear in general just how these equivalence classes are to be identified or described precisely; in Example 5.1, where we did it by finding three pairwise distinguishable strings, we had a three-state FA recognizing $L$ to start with, so that we obtained little or no new information. In this section we will show that as long as we have *some* FA to start with, we can always find the simplest possible one. We will develop an algorithm for taking an arbitrary FA and modifying it if necessary so that the resulting machine has the fewest possible states (and the states correspond exactly to the equivalence classes of $I_L$).

Suppose we begin with the finite automaton $M = (Q, \Sigma, q_0, A, \delta)$. We consider again the two partitions of $\Sigma^*$ that we described in Section 5.1, one in which the subsets are the sets $L_q$ and one in which the subsets are the equivalence classes of $I_L$. If the two partitions are the same, then we already have the answer we want, and $M$ is already a minimum-state FA. If not, the fact that the first partition is finer than the second (one subset from the second partition might be the union of several from the first) tells us that we do not need to abandon our FA and start over, looking for one with fewer states; we just have to determine which sets $L_q$ we can combine to obtain an equivalence class.

Before we attack this problem, there is one obvious way in which we might be able to reduce the number of states in $M$ without affecting the $L_q$ partition at all. This is to eliminate the states $q$ for which $L_q = \emptyset$. For such a $q$, there are no strings $x$ satisfying $\delta^*(q_0, x) = q$; in other words, $q$ is unreachable from $q_0$. It is easy to formulate a recursive definition of the set of reachable states of $M$ and then use that to obtain an algorithm that finds all reachable states. If all the others are eliminated, the resulting FA still recognizes $L$ (Exercise 3.29). For the remainder of this discussion, therefore, we assume that all states of $M$ are reachable from $q_0$.

It may be helpful at this point to look again at Example 3.12. Figure 5.3*a* shows the original FA we drew for this language; Figure 5.3*b* shows the minimum-state FA we arrived at in Example 5.1; Figure 5.3*c* shows the partition corresponding to the original FA, with seven subsets; and Figure 5.3*d* shows the three equivalence classes of $I_L$, which are the sets $L_q$ for the minimum-state FA. We obtain the simpler FA from the first one by merging the three states 1, 2, and 4 into the state $A$, and by merging the states 3, 5, and 7 into $B$. State 6 becomes state $C$. Once we have done this, we can easily determine the new transitions. From any of the states 1, 2, and 4, the input symbol 0 takes us to one of those same states. Therefore, the transition from $A$ with input 0 must go to $A$. From 1, 2, or 4, the input 1 takes us to 3, 5, or 7. Therefore, the transition from $A$ with input 1 goes to $B$. The other cases are similar.

In general, starting with a finite automaton $M$, we may describe the problem in terms of identifying the *pairs* $(p, q)$ of states for which $L_p$ and $L_q$ are subsets of the same equivalence class. Let us write this condition as $p \equiv q$. What we will actually do is to solve the opposite problem: identify those pairs $(p, q)$ for which $p \not\equiv q$. The first step is to express the statement $p \equiv q$ in a slightly different way.

**Lemma 5.2**　Suppose $p, q \in Q$, and $x$ and $y$ are strings with $x \in L_p$ and $y \in L_q$ (in other words, $\delta^*(q_0, x) = p$ and $\delta^*(q_0, y) = q$). Then these three statements are all equivalent:

1. $p \equiv q$.
2. $L/x = L/y$ (i.e., $x I_L y$, or $x$ and $y$ are indistinguishable with respect to $L$).
3. For any $z \in \Sigma^*$, $\delta^*(p, z) \in A \Leftrightarrow \delta^*(q, z) \in A$ (i.e., $\delta^*(p, z)$ and $\delta^*(q, z)$ are either both in $A$ or both not in $A$).

*Proof*　To see that statements 2 and 3 are equivalent, we begin with the formulas

$$\delta^*(p, z) = \delta^*(\delta^*(q_0, x), z) = \delta^*(q_0, xz)$$
$$\delta^*(q, z) = \delta^*(\delta^*(q_0, y), z) = \delta^*(q_0, yz)$$

Saying that $L/x = L/y$ means that a string $z$ is in one set if and only if it is in the other, or that $xz \in L$ if and only if $yz \in L$; since $M$ accepts $L$, this is exactly the same as statement 3.

Now if statement 1 is true, then $L_p$ and $L_q$ are both subsets of the same equivalence class. This means that $x$ and $y$ are equivalent, which is statement 2. The converse is also true, because we know that if $L_p$ and $L_q$ are not both subsets of the

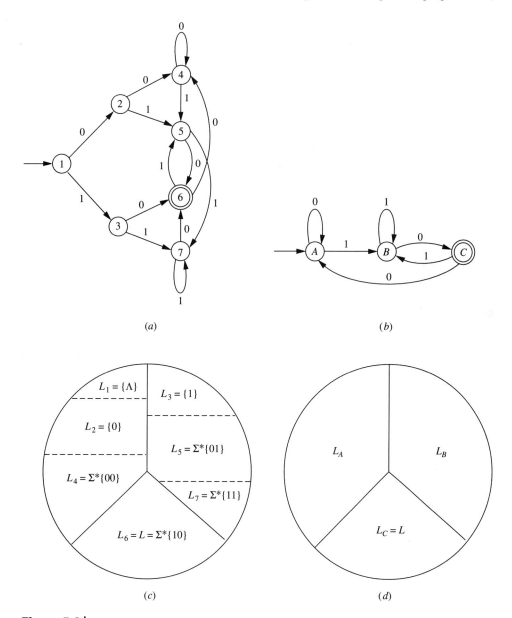

**Figure 5.3 |**
Two FAs for $\{0, 1\}^*\{10\}$ and the corresponding partitions of $\{0, 1\}^*$.

same equivalence class, then they are subsets of different equivalence classes, so that statement 2 does not hold. ∎

Let us now consider how it can happen that $p \not\equiv q$. According to the lemma, this means that for some $z$, exactly one of the two states $\delta^*(p, z)$ and $\delta^*(q, z)$ is in $A$.

The simplest way this can happen is with $z = \Lambda$, so that only one of the states $p$ and $q$ is in $A$. Once we have one pair $(p, q)$ with $p \not\equiv q$, we consider the situation where $r, s \in Q$, and for some $a \in \Sigma$, $\delta(r, a) = p$ and $\delta(s, a) = q$. We may write

$$\delta^*(r, az) = \delta^*(\delta^*(r, a), z) = \delta^*(\delta(r, a), z) = \delta^*(p, z)$$

and similarly, $\delta^*(s, az) = \delta^*(q, z)$. Since $p \not\equiv q$, then for some $z$, exactly one of the states $\delta^*(p, z)$ and $\delta^*(q, z)$ is in $A$; therefore, exactly one of $\delta^*(r, az)$ and $\delta^*(s, az)$ is in $A$, and $r \not\equiv s$.

These observations suggest the following recursive definition of a set $S$, which will turn out to be the set of all pairs $(p, q)$ with $p \not\equiv q$.

1.   For any $p$ and $q$ for which exactly one of $p$ and $q$ is in $A$, $(p, q)$ is in $S$.
2.   For any pair $(p, q) \in S$, if $(r, s)$ is a pair for which $\delta(r, a) = p$ and $\delta(s, a) = q$ for some $a \in \Sigma$, then $(r, s)$ is in $S$.
3.   No other pairs are in $S$.

It is not difficult to see from the comments preceding the recursive definition that for any pair $(p, q) \in S$, $p \not\equiv q$. On the other hand, it follows from Lemma 5.2 that we can show $S$ contains all such pairs by establishing the following statement: For any string $z \in \Sigma^*$, every pair of states $(p, q)$ for which only one of the states $\delta^*(p, z)$ and $\delta^*(q, z)$ is in $A$ is an element of $S$.

We do this by using structural induction on $z$. For the basis step, if only one of $\delta^*(p, \Lambda)$ and $\delta^*(q, \Lambda)$ is in $A$, then only one of the two states $p$ and $q$ is in $A$, and $(p, q) \in S$ because of statement 1 of the definition.

Now suppose that for some $z$, all pairs $(p, q)$ for which only one of $\delta^*(p, z)$ and $\delta^*(q, z)$ is in $A$ are in $S$. Consider the string $az$, where $a \in \Sigma$, and suppose that $(r, s)$ is a pair for which only one of $\delta^*(r, az)$ and $\delta^*(s, az)$ is in $A$. If we let $p = \delta(r, a)$ and $q = \delta(s, a)$, then we have

$$\delta^*(r, az) = \delta^*(\delta(r, a), z) = \delta^*(p, z)$$
$$\delta^*(s, az) = \delta^*(\delta(s, a), z) = \delta^*(q, z)$$

Our assumption on $r$ and $s$ is that only one of the states $\delta^*(r, az)$ and $\delta^*(s, az)$, and therefore only one of the states $\delta^*(p, z)$ and $\delta^*(q, z)$, is in $A$. Our induction hypothesis therefore implies that $(p, q) \in S$, and it then follows from statement 2 in the recursive definition that $(r, s) \in S$. (Note that in the recursive definition of $\Sigma^*$ implicit in this structural induction, the recursive step of the definition involves strings of the form $az$ rather than $za$.)

Now it is a simple matter to convert this recursive definition into an algorithm to identify all the pairs $(p, q)$ for which $p \not\equiv q$.

**Algorithm 5.1 (For Identifying the Pairs $(p, q)$ with $p \not\equiv q$)**   List all (unordered) pairs of states $(p, q)$ for which $p \not\equiv q$. Make a sequence of passes through these pairs. On the first pass, mark each pair of which exactly one element is in $A$. On each subsequent pass, mark any pair $(r, s)$ if there is an $a \in \Sigma$ for which $\delta(r, a) = p$,

$\delta(s, a) = q$, and $(p, q)$ is already marked. After a pass in which no new pairs are marked, stop. The marked pairs $(p, q)$ are precisely those for which $p \not\equiv q$. ∎

When the algorithm terminates, any pair $(p, q)$ that remains unmarked represents two states in our FA that can be merged into one, since the corresponding sets of strings are both subsets of the same equivalence class. In order to find the total number of equivalence classes, or the minimum number of states, we can make one final pass through the states of $M$; the first state of $M$ to be considered corresponds to one equivalence class; for each subsequent state $q$ of $M$, $q$ represents a new equivalence class only if the pair $(p, q)$ was marked by Algorithm 5.1 for every previous state $p$ of $M$. As we have seen in our example, once we have the states in the minimum-state FA, determining the transitions is straightforward. We return once more to Example 5.1 to illustrate the algorithm.

---

Minimizing the FA in Figure 5.3a          **EXAMPLE 5.6**

We apply Algorithm 5.1 to the FA in Figure 5.3a. Figure 5.4a shows all unordered pairs $(p, q)$ with $p \neq q$. The pairs marked 1 are those of which exactly one element is in $A$; they are marked on pass 1. The pairs marked 2 are those marked on the second pass. For example, $(2, 5)$ is one of these, since $\delta(2, 0) = 4$, $\delta(5, 0) = 6$, and the pair $(4, 6)$ was marked on pass 1.

A third pass produces no new marked pairs. Suppose for example that $(1, 2)$ is the first pair to be tested on the third pass. We calculate $\delta(1, 0) = 2$ and $\delta(2, 0) = 4$, and $(2, 4)$ is not marked. Similarly, $\delta(1, 1) = 3$ and $\delta(2, 1) = 5$, and $(3, 5)$ is not marked. It follows that $(1, 2)$ will not be marked on this pass.

If we now go through the seven states in numerical order, we see that there is an equivalence class containing state 1; state 2 is in the same class, since the pair $(1, 2)$ is unmarked; state 3 is in a new equivalence class, since $(1, 3)$ and $(2, 3)$ are both marked; state 4 is in the same class as 2, since $(2, 4)$ is unmarked; 5 is in the same class as 3; 6 is in a new class; and 7 is in the same class as 3. We conclude that the three equivalence classes of $I_L$ are $p_1 = L_1 \cup L_2 \cup L_4$, $p_2 = L_3 \cup L_5 \cup L_7$, and $p_3 = L_6$.

We found the transitions earlier. The resulting FA is shown in Figure 5.4b. Again, it is identical to the one obtained in Example 3.12 except for the names of the states.

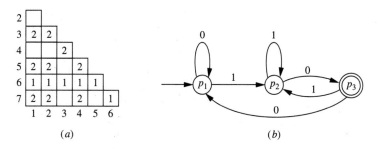

(a)                                              (b)

**Figure 5.4** |
Applying Algorithm 5.1 to the FA in Figure 5.3a.

# 5.3 | THE PUMPING LEMMA FOR REGULAR LANGUAGES

Every regular language can be accepted by a finite automaton, a recognizing device with a finite set of states and no auxiliary memory. We can use the finiteness of this set to derive another property shared by all regular languages. Showing that a language does not have this property will then be another way, in addition to using Corollary 5.1, of showing that the language is not regular. One reason this is useful is that the method we come up with can be adapted for use with more general languages, as we will see in Chapter 8.

Suppose $M = (Q, \Sigma, q_0, A, \delta)$ is an FA recognizing a language $L$. The property we are interested in has to do with paths through $M$ that contain "loops." An input string $x \in L$ requiring $M$ to enter some state twice corresponds to a path that starts at $q_0$, ends at some accepting state $q_f$, and contains a loop. (See Figure 5.5.) Any other path obtained from this one by changing the number of traversals of the loop will then also correspond to an element of $L$, different from $x$ in that it contains a different number of occurrences of the substring corresponding to the loop. This simple observation will lead to the property we want.

Suppose that the set $Q$ has $n$ elements. For any string $x$ in $L$ with length at least $n$, if we write $x = a_1 a_2 \cdots a_n y$, then the sequence of $n + 1$ states

$$q_0 = \delta^*(q_0, \Lambda)$$
$$q_1 = \delta^*(q_0, a_1)$$
$$q_2 = \delta^*(q_0, a_1 a_2)$$
$$\cdots$$
$$q_n = \delta^*(q_0, a_1 a_2 \cdots a_n)$$

must contain some state at least twice, by the pigeonhole principle (Exercise 2.44). This is where our loop comes from. Suppose $q_i = q_{i+p}$, where $0 \leq i < i + p \leq n$. Then

$$\delta^*(q_0, a_1 a_2 \cdots a_i) = q_i$$
$$\delta^*(q_i, a_{i+1} a_{i+2} \cdots a_{i+p}) = q_i$$
$$\delta^*(q_i, a_{i+p+1} a_{i+p+2} \cdots a_n y) = q_f \in A$$

To simplify the notation, let

$$u = a_1 a_2 \cdots a_i$$
$$v = a_{i+1} a_{i+2} \cdots a_{i+p}$$

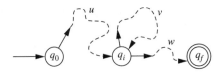

**Figure 5.5 |**

$$w = a_{i+p+1}a_{i+p+2}\cdots a_n y$$

(See Figure 5.5.) The string $u$ is interpreted to be $\Lambda$ if $i = 0$, and $w$ is interpreted to be $y$ if $i + p = n$.

Since $\delta^*(q_i, v) = q_i$, we have $\delta^*(q_i, v^m) = q_i$ for every $m \geq 0$, and it follows that $\delta^*(q_0, uv^m w) = q_f$ for every $m \geq 0$. Since $p > 0$ and $i + p \leq n$, we have proved the following result.

---

**Theorem 5.2**

Suppose $L$ is a regular language recognized by a finite automaton with $n$ states. For any $x \in L$ with $|x| \geq n$, $x$ may be written as $x = uvw$ for some strings $u$, $v$, and $w$ satisfying

$$|uv| \leq n$$
$$|v| > 0$$
$$\text{for any } m \geq 0, \ uv^m w \in L$$

---

This result is often referred to as the Pumping Lemma for Regular Languages, since we can think of it as saying that for an arbitrary string in $L$, provided it is sufficiently long, a portion of it can be "pumped up," introducing additional copies of the substring $v$, so as to obtain many more distinct elements of $L$.

The proof of the result was easy, but the result itself is complicated enough in its logical structure that applying it correctly requires some care. It may be helpful first to weaken it slightly by leaving out some information (where the integer $n$ comes from). Theorem 5.2a clarifies the essential feature and is sufficient for most applications.

---

**Theorem 5.2a    The Pumping Lemma for Regular Languages**

Suppose $L$ is a regular language. Then there is an integer $n$ so that for any $x \in L$ with $|x| \geq n$, there are strings $u$, $v$, and $w$ so that

| | |
|---|---|
| $x = uvw$ | (5.1) |
| $|uv| \leq n$ | (5.2) |
| $|v| > 0$ | (5.3) |
| for any $m \geq 0, \ uv^m w \in L$ | (5.4) |

---

In order to use the pumping lemma to show that a language $L$ is not regular, we must show that $L$ fails to have the property described in the lemma. We do this by assuming that the property is satisfied and deriving a contradiction.

The statement is of the form "There is an $n$ so that for any $x \in L$ with $|x| \geq n, \ldots$" We assume, therefore, that we have such an $n$, although we do not know what it is. We try to find a specific string $x$ with $|x| \geq n$ so that the statements involving $x$ in the theorem will lead to a contradiction. (The theorem says that under the assumption that $L$ is regular, *any* $x \in L$ with $|x| \geq n$ satisfies certain conditions; therefore, our specific $x$ satisfies these conditions; this leads to a contradiction; therefore, the assumption leads to a contradiction; therefore, $L$ is not regular.)

Remember, however, that we do not know what $n$ is. In effect, therefore, we must show that for *any* $n$, we can find an $x \in L$ with $|x| \geq n$ so that the statements about $x$ in the theorem lead to a contradiction. It may be that we have to choose $x$ carefully in order to obtain a contradiction. We are free to pick any $x$ we like, as long as $|x| \geq n$—but since we do not know what $n$ is, the choice of $x$ must involve $n$.

Once we have chosen $x$, we are *not* free to choose the strings $u$, $v$, and $w$ into which the theorem says $x$ can be decomposed. What we know is that there is *some* way to write $x$ as $uvw$ so that equations (5.2)–(5.4) are true. Because we must guarantee that a contradiction is produced, we must show once we have chosen $x$ that *any* choice of $u$, $v$, and $w$ satisfying equations (5.1)–(5.4) produces a contradiction. Let us use as our first illustration one of the languages that we already know is not regular.

## EXAMPLE 5.7  Application of the Pumping Lemma

Let $L = \{0^i 1^i \mid i \geq 0\}$. Suppose that $L$ is regular, and let $n$ be the integer in Theorem 5.2a. We can now choose any $x$ with $|x| \geq n$; a reasonable choice is $x = 0^n 1^n$. The theorem says that $x = uvw$ for some $u$, $v$, and $w$ satisfying equations (5.2)–(5.4). No matter what $u$, $v$, and $w$ are, the fact that (5.2) is true implies that $uv = 0^k$ for some $k$, and it follows from (5.3) that $v = 0^j$ for some $j > 0$. Equation (5.4) says that $uv^m w \in L$ for every $m \geq 0$. However, we can obtain a contradiction by considering $m = 2$. The string $uv^2 w$ contains $j$ extra 0's in the first part ($uv^2 w = 0^{n+j} 1^n$), and cannot be in $L$ because $j > 0$. This contradiction allows us to conclude that $L$ cannot be regular.

Let us look a little more closely at the way we chose $x$ in this example (which for this language just means the way we chose $|x|$). In the statement of the pumping lemma, the only condition $x$ needs to satisfy is $|x| \geq n$; with a little more effort, we can obtain a contradiction by starting with $x = 0^m 1^m$, for any $m \geq n/2$. However, now we can no longer assert that $uv = 0^k$. There are two other possibilities to consider. In each case, however, looking at $m = 2$ is enough to obtain a contradiction. If $v$ contains both 0's and 1's, then $v = 0^i 1^j$, so that $uv^2 w$ contains the substring 10 and is therefore not in $L$. If $v$ contains only 1's, then $v = 1^j$, and $uv^2 w = 0^n 1^{n+j}$, also not in $L$.

Again, the point is that when we use the pumping lemma to show $L$ is nonregular, we are free to choose $x$ any way we wish, as long as $|x| \geq n$ and as long as it will allow us to derive a contradiction. We try to choose $x$ so that getting the contradiction is as simple as possible. Once we have chosen $x$, we must be careful to show that a contradiction follows inevitably. Unless we can get a contradiction in every conceivable case, we have not accomplished anything.

Another feature of this example is that it allows us to prove more than we originally set out to. We started with the string $x = 0^n 1^n \in L$ and observed that for the strings $u$, $v$, and $w$, $uv^2 w$ fails to be an element, not only of $L$ but of the larger language $L_1 = \{x \in \{0, 1\}^* \mid n_0(x) = n_1(x)\}$. Therefore, our proof also allows us to conclude that $L_1$ is not regular.

However, with this larger language it is worth looking one more time at the initial choice of $x$, because specifying a length no longer determines the string, and not all strings of the same length are equally suitable. First we observe that choosing $x = 0^{n/2} 1^{n/2}$, which would have worked for the language $L$ (at least if $n$ is even), no longer works for $L_1$. The reason this string works for $L$ is that even if $v$ happens to contain both 0's and 1's, $uv^2w$ is not of the form $0^i 1^i$. (The contradiction is obtained, not by looking at the *numbers* of 0's and 1's, but by looking at the order of the symbols.) The reason it does not work for $L_1$ is that if $v$ contains *equal* numbers of 0's and 1's, then $uv^m w$ also has equal numbers of 0's and 1's, no matter what $m$ we use, and there is no contradiction.

If we had set out originally to show that $L_1$ was not regular, we might have chosen an $x$ in $L_1$ but not in $L$. An example of an inappropriate choice is the string $x = (01)^n$. Although this string is in $L_1$ and its length is at least $n$, look what happens when we try to produce a contradiction. If $x = uvw$, we have these possibilities:

1.  $v = (01)^j$ for some $j > 0$
2.  $v = 1(01)^j$ for some $j \geq 0$
3.  $v = 1(01)^j 0$ for some $j \geq 0$
4.  $v = (01)^j 0$ for some $j \geq 0$

Unfortunately, none of the conditions (5.2)–(5.4) gives us any information about $v$, except for some upper bounds on $j$. In cases 2 and 4 we can obtain a contradiction because the string $v$ that is being pumped has unequal numbers of 0's and 1's. In the other two cases, however, there is no contradiction, because $uv^m w$ has equal numbers of 0's and 1's for any $m$. We cannot guarantee that one of these cases does not occur, and therefore we are unable to finish the proof using this choice of $x$.

## Another Application of the Pumping Lemma    EXAMPLE 5.8

Consider the language

$$L = \{0^i x \mid i \geq 0, x \in \{0, 1\}^* \text{ and } |x| \leq i\}$$

Another description of $L$ is that it is the set of all strings of 0's and 1's so that at least the first half of $x$ consists of 0's. The proof that $L$ is not regular starts the same way as in the previous example. Assume that $L$ is regular, and let $n$ be the integer in Theorem 5.2a. We obviously should not try to start with a string $x$ of all 0's, because then no string obtained from $x$ by pumping could have any 1's, and there would be no chance of a contradiction. Suppose we try $x = 0^n 1^n$, just as in the previous example. Then if Equations (5.1)–(5.4) hold, it follows as before that $v = 0^j$ for some $j > 0$. In this example the term *pumping* is a little misleading. We cannot obtain a contradiction by looking at strings with additional copies of $v$, because initial 0's account for an even larger fraction of these strings than in $x$. However, Equation (5.4) also says that $uv^0 w \in L$. This does give us our contradiction, because $uv^0 w = uw = 0^{n-j} 1^n \notin L$. Therefore, $L$ is not regular.

## Application of the Pumping Lemma to *pal*    EXAMPLE 5.9

Let $L$ be *pal*, the languages of palindromes over $\{0, 1\}$. We know from Theorem 3.3 that $L$ is not regular, and now we can also use the pumping lemma to prove this. Suppose that $L$ is regular, and let $n$ be the integer in the statement of the pumping lemma. We must choose $x$ to be a palindrome of length at least $n$ that will produce a contradiction; let us try $x = 0^n 10^n$.

Then just as in the two previous examples, if Equations (5.1)–(5.4) are true, the string $v$ is a substring of the form $0^j$ (with $j > 0$) from the first part of $x$. We can obtain a contradiction using either $m = 0$ or $m > 1$. In the first case, $uv^m w = 0^{n-j}10^n$, and in the second case, if $m = 2$ for example, $uv^m w = 0^{n+j}10^n$. Neither of these is a palindrome, and it follows that $L$ cannot be regular.

It is often possible to get by with a weakened form of the pumping lemma. Here are two versions that leave out many of the conclusions of Theorem 5.2a but are still strong enough to show that certain languages are not regular.

---

**Theorem 5.3    Weak Form of Pumping Lemma**
Suppose $L$ is an infinite regular language. Then there are strings $u$, $v$, and $w$ so that $|v| > 0$ and $uv^m w \in L$ for every $m \geq 0$.

*Proof*
This follows immediately from Theorem 5.2a. No matter how big the integer $n$ in the statement of that theorem is, $L$ must contain a string at least that long, because $L$ has infinitely many elements.

---

Theorem 5.3 would be sufficient for Example 5.7, as you are asked to show in Exercise 5.21, but it is not enough to take care of Examples 5.8 or 5.9.

---

**Theorem 5.4    Even Weaker Form of Pumping Lemma**
Suppose $L$ is an infinite regular language. There are integers $p$ and $q$, with $q > 0$, so that for every $m \geq 0$, $L$ contains a string of length $p + mq$. In other words, the set of integers

$$lengths(L) = \{|x| \mid x \in L\}$$

contains the "arithmetic progression" of all integers $p + mq$ (where $m \geq 0$).

*Proof*
This follows from Theorem 5.3, by taking $p = |u| + |w|$ and $q = |v|$.

---

Theorem 5.4 would not be enough to show that the language in Example 5.7 is not regular. The next example shows a language for which it might be used.

---

**EXAMPLE 5.10**    An Application of Theorem 5.4

Let

$$L = \{0^n \mid n \text{ is prime}\} = \{0^2, 0^3, 0^5, 0^7, 0^{11}, \ldots\}$$

According to Theorem 5.4, in order to show that $L$ is not regular we just need to show that the set of primes cannot contain an infinite arithmetic progression of the form $\{p + mq \mid m \geq 0\}$; in other words, for any $p \geq 0$ and any $q > 0$, there is an integer $m$ so that $p + mq$ is not prime.

The phrase *not prime* means factorable into factors 2 or bigger. We could choose $m = p$, which would give

$$p + mq = p + pq = p(1 + q)$$

except that we are not certain that $p \geq 2$. Instead let $m = p + 2q + 2$. Then

$$\begin{aligned} p + mq &= p + (p + 2q + 2)q \\ &= (p + 2q) + (p + 2q)q \\ &= (p + 2q)(1 + q) \end{aligned}$$

and this is clearly not prime.

This example has a different flavor from the preceding ones and seems to have more to do with arithmetic, or number theory, than with languages. Yet it illustrates the fact, which will become even more obvious in the later parts of this book, that many statements about computation can be formulated as statements about languages. What we have found in this example is that a finite automaton is not a powerful enough device (it does not have enough memory) to solve the problem of determining, for an arbitrary integer, whether it is prime.

Corollary 5.1, in the first part of this chapter, gives a condition involving a language that is necessary *and* sufficient for the language to be regular. Theorem 5.2a gives a necessary condition. One might hope that it is also sufficient. This result (the converse of Theorem 5.2a) would imply that for any nonregular language $L$, the pumping lemma could be used to prove $L$ nonregular; constructing the proof would just be a matter of making the right choice for $x$. The next example shows that this is not correct: Showing that the conclusions of Theorem 5.2a hold (i.e., showing that there is no choice of $x$ that produces a contradiction) is not enough to show that the language is regular.

## The Pumping Lemma Cannot Show a Language Is Regular | **EXAMPLE 5.11**

Let

$$L = \{a^i b^j c^j \mid i \geq 1 \text{ and } j \geq 0\} \cup \{b^j c^k \mid j, k \geq 0\}$$

Let us show first that the conclusions of Theorem 5.2a hold. Take $n$ to be 1, and suppose that $x \in L$ and $|x| \geq n$. There are two cases to consider. If $x = a^i b^j c^j$, where $i > 0$, then define

$$u = \Lambda \qquad v = a \qquad w = a^{i-1} b^j c^j$$

Any string of the form $uv^m w$ is still of the form $a^l b^j c^j$ and is therefore an element of $L$ (whether or not $l$ is 0). If $x = b^i c^j$, then again let $u = \Lambda$ and let $v$ be the first symbol in $x$. It is still true that $uv^m w \in L$ for every $m \geq 0$.

However, $L$ is not regular, as you can show using Corollary 5.1. The details are almost identical to those in Example 5.7 and are left to Exercise 5.22.

## 5.4 | DECISION PROBLEMS

A finite automaton is a rudimentary computer. It receives input, and in response to that input produces the output "yes" or "no," in the sense that it does or does not end up in an accepting state. The computational problems that a finite automaton can solve are therefore limited to *decision* problems: problems that can be answered yes or no, like "Given a string $x$ of $a$'s and $b$'s, does $x$ contain an occurrence of the substring $baa$?" or "Given a regular expression $r$ and a string $x$, does $x$ belong to the language corresponding to $r$?" A decision problem of this type consists of a set of specific *instances*, or specific cases in which we want the answer. An instance of the first problem is a string $x$ of $a$'s and $b$'s, and the set of possible instances is the entire set $\{a, b\}^*$. An instance of the second is a pair $(r, x)$, where $r$ is a regular expression and $x$ is a string. In general, if the problem takes the form "Given $x$, is it true that ...?", then an instance is a particular value of $x$.

There are other possible formulations of a finite automaton, in which the machine operates essentially the same way but can produce more general outputs, perhaps in the form of strings over the input alphabet. What makes the finite automaton only a primitive model of computation is not that it is limited to solving decision problems, but that it can handle only *simple* decision problems. An FA cannot remember more than a fixed amount of information, and it is incapable of solving a decision problem if some instances of the problem would require the machine to remember more than this amount.

The generic decision problem that can be solved by a particular finite automaton is the *membership problem* for the corresponding regular language $L$: Given a string $x$, is $x$ an element of $L$? An instance of this problem is a string $x$. We might step up one level and formulate the *membership problem for regular languages:* Given a finite automaton $M$ and a string $x$, is $x$ accepted by $M$? (Or, equivalently, given a regular language specified by the finite automaton $M$, and a string $x$, is $x$ an element of the language?) Now an instance of the problem is a pair $(M, x)$, where $M$ is an FA and $x$ is a string. The problem has an easy solution—informally, it is simply to give the string $x$ to the FA $M$ as input and see what happens! If $M$ ends up in an accepting state as a result of processing $x$, the answer is yes; otherwise the answer is no. The reason this approach is acceptable as an algorithm is that $M$ behaves deterministically (that is, its specifications determine exactly what steps it will follow in processing $x$) and is guaranteed to produce an answer after $|x|$ steps.

In addition to the membership problem, we can formulate a number of other decision problems having to do with finite automata and regular languages, and some of them we already have decision algorithms to answer. Here is a list that is not by any means exhaustive. (The first problem on the list is one of the two mentioned above.)

1.  Given a regular expression $r$ and a string $x$, does $x$ belong to the language corresponding to $r$?

2.  Given a finite automaton $M$, is there a string that it accepts? (Alternatively, given an FA $M$, is $L(M) = \emptyset$?)

3.  Given an FA $M$, is $L(M)$ finite?

4. Given two finite automata $M_1$ and $M_2$, are there any strings that are accepted by both?

5. Given two FAs $M_1$ and $M_2$, do they accept the same language? In other words, is $L(M_1) = L(M_2)$?

6. Given two FAs $M_1$ and $M_2$, is $L(M_1)$ a subset of $L(M_2)$?

7. Given two regular expressions $r_1$ and $r_2$, do they correspond to the same language?

8. Given an FA $M$, is it a minimum-state FA accepting the language $L(M)$?

Problem 1 is a version of the membership problem for regular languages, except that we start with a regular expression rather than a finite automaton. Because we have an algorithm from Chapter 4 to take an arbitrary regular expression and produce an FA accepting the corresponding language, we can reduce problem 1 to the version of the membership problem previously mentioned.

Section 5.2 gives a decision algorithm for problem 8: Apply the minimization algorithm to $M$, and see if the number of states is reduced. Of the remaining problems, some are closely related to others. In fact, if we had an algorithm to solve problem 2, we could construct algorithms to solve problems 4 through 7. For problem 4, we could first use the algorithm presented in Section 3.5 to construct a finite automaton $M$ recognizing $L(M_1) \cap L(M_2)$, and then apply to $M$ the algorithm for problem 2. Problem 6 could be solved the same way, with $L(M_1) \cap L(M_2)$ replaced by $L(M_1) - L(M_2)$, because $L(M_1) \subseteq L(M_2)$ if and only if $L(M_1) - L(M_2) = \emptyset$. Problem 5 can be reduced to problem 6, since two sets are equal precisely when each is a subset of the other. Finally, a solution to problem 6 would give us one to problem 7, because of our algorithm for finding a finite automaton corresponding to a given regular expression.

Problems 2 and 3 remain. With regard to problem 2, one might ask how a finite automaton could fail to accept any strings. A trivial way is for it to have no accepting states. Even if $M$ does have accepting states, however, it fails to accept anything if none of its accepting states is reachable from the initial state. We can determine whether this is true by calculating $T_k$, the set of states that can be reached from $q_0$ by using strings of length $k$ or less, as follows:

$$T_k = \begin{cases} \{q_0\} & \text{if } k = 0 \\ T_{k-1} \cup \{\delta(q, a) \mid q \in T_{k-1} \text{ and } a \in \Sigma\} & \text{if } k > 0 \end{cases}$$

($T_k$ contains, in addition to the elements of $T_{k-1}$, the states that can be reached in one step from the elements of $T_{k-1}$.)

**Decision Algorithm for Problem 2 (Given an FA $M$, is $L(M) = \emptyset$?)** Compute the set $T_k$ for each $k \geq 0$, until either $T_k$ contains an accepting state or until $k > 0$ and $T_k = T_{k-1}$. In the first case $L(M) \neq \emptyset$, and in the second case $L(M) = \emptyset$. ∎

If $n$ is the number of states of $M$, then one of the two outcomes of the algorithm must occur by the time $T_n$ has been computed. This implies that the following algorithm would also work.

Begin testing all input strings, in nondecreasing order of length, for acceptance by $M$. If no strings of length $n$ or less are accepted, then $L(M) = \emptyset$.

Note, however, that this approach is likely to be much less efficient. For example, if we test the string 0101100 and later the string 01011000, all but the last step of the second test is duplicated effort.

The idea of testing individual strings in order to decide whether an FA accepts something is naturally tempting, but useless as an algorithm without some way to stop if the individual tests continue to fail. Only the fact that we can stop after testing strings of length $n$ makes the approach feasible. Theorem 5.2, the original form of the pumping lemma, is another way to see that this is possible. The pumping lemma implies that if $x$ is any string in $L$ of length at least $n$, then there is a shorter string in $L$ (the one obtained by deleting the middle portion $v$). Therefore, it is impossible for the shortest string in the language to have length $n$ or greater.

Perhaps surprisingly, the pumping lemma allows us to use a similar approach with problem 3. If the FA $M$ has $n$ states, and $x$ is any string in $L$ of length at least $n$, then there is a string $y$ in $L$ that is shorter than $x$ but not too much shorter: There exist $u$, $v$, and $w$ with $0 < |v| \le n$ so that $x = uvw \in L$ and $y = uw \in L$, so that the difference in length between $x$ and $y$ is at most $n$. Now consider strings in $L$ whose length is at least $n$. If there are any at all, then the pumping lemma implies that $L$ must be infinite (because there are infinitely many strings of the form $uv^i w$); in particular, if there is a string $x \in L$ with $n \le |x| < 2n$, then $L$ is infinite. On the other hand, if there are strings in $L$ of length at least $n$, it is impossible for the shortest such string $x$ to have length $2n$ or greater—because as we have seen, there would then have to be a shorter string $y \in L$ close enough in length to $x$ so that $|y| \ge n$. Therefore, if $L$ is infinite, there must be a string $x \in L$ with $n \le |x| < 2n$. We have therefore established that the following algorithm is a solution for problem 3.

**Decision Algorithm for Problem 3 (Given an FA $M$, is $L(M)$ finite?)**   Test input strings beginning with those of length $n$ (where $n$ is the number of states of $M$), in nondecreasing order of length. If there is a string $x$ with $n \le |x| < 2n$ that is accepted, then $L(M)$ is infinite; otherwise, $L(M)$ is finite.  ∎

There are at least two reasons for discussing, and trying to solve, decision problems like the ones in our list. One is the obvious fact that solutions may be useful. For a not entirely frivolous example, picture your hard-working instructor grading an exam question that asks for an FA recognizing a specific language. He or she knows a solution, but one student's paper shows a different FA. The instructor must then try to determine whether the two are equivalent, and this means answering an instance of problem 5. If the answer to a specific instance of the problem is the primary concern, then whether there is an efficient, or feasible, solution is at least as important as whether there is a solution in principle. The solution sketched above for problem 5 involves solving problem 2, and the second version of the decision algorithm given for problem 2 would not help much in the case of machines with a hundred states, even if a computer program and a fast computer were available.

Aside from the question of finding efficient algorithms, however, there is another reason for considering these decision problems, a reason that will assume greater significance later in the book. It is simply that not all decision problems can be solved.

An example of an easy-to-state problem that cannot be solved by any decision algorithm was formulated in the 1930s by the mathematician Alan Turing. He described a type of abstract machine, now called a Turing machine, more general than a finite automaton. These machines can recognize certain languages in the same way that FAs can recognize regular languages, and Turing's original unsolvable problem is simply the membership problem for this more general class of languages: Given a Turing machine $M$ and a string $x$, does $M$ accept $x$? (see Section 11.2). Turing machines are involved in this discussion in another way as well, because such a machine turns out to be a general model of computation. This is what allows us to formulate the idea of an algorithm precisely and to say exactly what "unsolvable" means.

Showing the existence of unsolvable problems—particularly ones that arise naturally and are easy to state—was a significant development in the theory of computation. The conclusion is that there are definite theoretical limits on what it is possible to compute. These limits have nothing to do with how smart we are, or how good at designing software; and they are not simply practical limits having to do with efficiency and the amount of time available, or physical considerations like the number of atoms available for constructing memory devices. Rather, they are fundamental limits inherent in the rules of logic and the nature of computation. We will be investigating these matters later in the book; for the moment, it is reassuring to find that many of the natural problems involving regular languages do have algorithmic solutions.

# 5.5 | REGULAR LANGUAGES AND COMPUTERS

Now that we have introduced the first class of languages we will be studying, we can ask what the relationship is between these simple languages and the familiar ones people use in computer science, programming languages such as C, Java, and Pascal. The answer is almost obvious: Programming languages are not regular. In the C language, for example, the string `main()` $\{^m\}^n$ is a valid program if and only if $m = n$, and this allows us to prove easily that the set of valid programs is not regular, using either Corollary 5.1 or the pumping lemma.

Although regular languages are not rich enough in structure to be programming languages themselves, however, we have seen in Examples 3.5 and 3.6 some of the ways they occur within programming languages. As a general rule, the *tokens* of a programming language, which include identifiers, literals, operators, reserved words, and punctuation, can be described by a regular expression. The first phase in compiling a program written in a high-level programming language is *lexical analysis*: identifying and classifying the tokens into which the individual characters are grouped. There are programs called lexical-analyzer generators. The input provided to such a program is a set of regular expressions specifying the structure of tokens, and the output produced by the program is a software version of an FA that can be incorporated as a token-recognizing module in a compiler. One of the most widely used of these is a program called lex, which is a tool provided in the Unix operating system. Although lex can be used in many situations that require the processing of structured input, it is used most often in conjunction with yacc, another Unix tool. The lexical analyzer produced by lex creates a string of tokens; and the *parser* produced by yacc, on the basis of grammar rules provided as input, is able to determine the syntactical structure of the token string. (yacc stands for *yet another compiler compiler.*) Regular expressions come up in Unix in other ways as well. The Unix text editor allows the user to specify a regular expression and searches for patterns in the text that match it. Other commands such as grep (global regular expression print) and egrep (extended global regular expression print) cause a specified file to be searched for lines containing strings that match a specified regular expression.

If regular languages cannot be programming languages, it would seem that finite automata are even less equipped to be computers. There are a number of obvious differences, some more significant than others, having to do with memory, output capabilities, programmability, and so on. We have seen several examples of languages, such as $\{0^n1^n \mid n \geq 0\}$, that no FA can recognize but for which a recognition program could be written by any programmer and run on just about any computer.

Well, yes and no; as obvious as this conclusion seems, it has to be qualified at least a little. Any physical computer is a finite device; it has, for some integer $n$, $n$ total bits of internal memory and disk space. (It may be connected to a larger network, but in that case we may think of the "computer" as the entire network and simply use a larger value of $n$.) We can describe the complete *state* of the machine by specifying the status of each bit of memory, each pixel on the screen, and so forth. The number of states is huge but still finite, and in this sense our computer is in fact an FA, where the inputs can be thought of as keystrokes, or perhaps bits in some external file being read. (In particular, the computer cannot *actually* recognize the language $\{0^j1^j\}$, because there is an integer $j$ so large that if the computer has read exactly $j$ 0's, it will not be able to remember this.)

As a way of understanding a computer, however, this observation is not helpful; there is hardly any practical difference between this finite number of possible states and infinity. Finite automata are simple machines, but having to think about a computer as an FA would complicate working with computers considerably. The situation is similar with regard to languages. One might argue that programming languages are effectively regular because the set of programs that one can physically write, or enter as input to a computer, is finite. However, though finite languages are simpler in some ways than infinite languages (in particular, they are always regular), restricting ourselves to finite languages would by no means simplify the discussion. Finite languages can be called *simple* because there is no need to consider any underlying structure—they are just sets of strings. However, with no underlying principle to impose some logical organization (some complexity!), a large set becomes unwieldy and complicated to deal with.

The advantage of a theoretical approach to computation is that we do not need to get bogged down in issues like memory size. Obviously there are many languages, including some regular ones, that no physical computer will ever be able to recognize; however, it still makes sense to distinguish between the logical problems that arise in recognizing some of these and the problems that arise in recognizing others. Finite automata and computers are different in principle, and what we are studying is what each is capable of in principle, not what a specific computer can do in practice. (Most people would probably agree that in principle, a computer *can* recognize the language $\{0^n 1^n \mid n \geq 0\}$.) As we progress further in the book, we will introduce abstract models that resemble a computer more closely. There will never be a perfect physical realization of any of them. Studying the conceptual model, however, is still the best way to understand both the potential and the limitations of the physical machines that approximate the model.

# EXERCISES

**5.1.** For which languages $L \subseteq \{0, 1\}^*$ is there only one equivalence class with respect to the relation $I_L$?

**5.2.** Let $x$ be an arbitrary string in $\{0, 1\}^*$, and let $L = \{x\}$. How many equivalence classes are there for the relation $I_L$? Describe them.

**5.3.** Find a language $L \subseteq \{0, 1\}^*$ for which every equivalence class of $I_L$ has exactly one element.

**5.4.** Show that for any language $L \subseteq \Sigma^*$, the set

$$S = \{x \in \Sigma^* \mid x \text{ is not a prefix of any element of } L\}$$

is one equivalence class of $I_L$, provided it is not empty.

**5.5.** Let $L \subseteq \Sigma^*$ be any language. Show that if $[\Lambda]$ (the equivalence class of $I_L$ containing $\Lambda$) is not $\{\Lambda\}$, then it is infinite.

**5.6.** Show that if $L \subseteq \Sigma^*$ is a language, $x \in \Sigma^*$, and $[x]$ (the equivalence class of $I_L$ containing $x$) is finite, then $x$ is a prefix of an element of $L$.

**5.7.** For a certain language $L \subseteq \{a, b\}^*$, $I_L$ has exactly four equivalence classes. They are $[\Lambda]$, $[a]$, $[ab]$, and $[b]$. It is also true that the three strings $a$, $aa$, and $abb$ are all equivalent, and that the two strings $b$ and $aba$ are equivalent. Finally, $ab \in L$, but $\Lambda$ and $a$ are not in $L$, and $b$ is not even a prefix of any element of $L$. Draw an FA accepting $L$.

**5.8.** Suppose there is a 3-state FA accepting $L \subseteq \{a, b\}^*$. Suppose $\Lambda \notin L$, $b \notin L$, and $ba \in L$. Suppose also that $a I_L b$, $\Lambda I_L bab$, $a I_L aaa$, and $b I_L bb$. Draw an FA accepting $L$.

**5.9.** Suppose there is a 3-state FA accepting $L \subseteq \{a, b\}^*$. Suppose $\Lambda \notin L$, $b \in L$, $ba \notin L$, and $baba \in L$, and that $\Lambda I_L a$ and $a I_L bb$. Draw an FA accepting $L$.

**5.10.** Find all possible languages $L \subseteq \{a, b\}^*$ for which $I_L$ has these three equivalence classes: the set of all strings ending in $b$, the set of all strings ending in $ba$, and the set of all strings ending in neither $b$ nor $ba$.

**5.11.** Find all possible languages $L \subseteq \{a, b\}^*$ for which $I_L$ has three equivalence classes, corresponding to the regular expressions $((a + b)a^*b)^*$, $((a + b)a^*b)^*aa^*$, and $((a + b)a^*b)^*ba^*$, respectively.

**5.12.** In Example 5.2, if the language is changed to $\{0^n 1^n \mid n \geq 0\}$ (i.e., $\Lambda$ is added to the original language), are there any changes in the partition of $\{0, 1\}^*$ corresponding to $I_L$? Explain.

**5.13.** Consider the language $L = \{x \in \{0, 1\}^* \mid n_0(x) = n_1(x)\}$ (where $n_0(x)$ and $n_1(x)$ are the number of 0's and the number of 1's, respectively, in $x$).

    a. Show that if $n_0(x) - n_1(x) = n_0(y) - n_1(y)$, then $x \, I_L \, y$.

    b. Show that if $n_0(x) - n_1(x) \neq n_0(y) - n_1(y)$, then $x$ and $y$ are distinguishable with respect to $x$.

    c. Describe all the equivalence classes of $I_L$.

**5.14.** Let $M = (Q, \Sigma, q_0, A, \delta)$ be an FA, and suppose that $Q_1$ is a subset of $Q$ such that $\delta(q, a) \in Q_1$ for every $q \in Q_1$ and every $a \in \Sigma$.

    a. Show that if $Q_1 \cap A = \emptyset$, then for any $p$ and $q$ in $Q_1$, $p \equiv q$.

    b. Show that if $Q_1 \subseteq A$, then for any $p$ and $q$ in $Q_1$, $p \equiv q$.

**5.15.** For a language $L$ over $\Sigma$, and two strings $x$ and $y$ in $\Sigma^*$ that are distinguishable with respect to $L$, let

$$d_{L,x,y} = \min\{|z| \mid z \text{ distinguishes } x \text{ and } y \text{ with respect to } L\}$$

    a. For the language $L = \{x \in \{0, 1\}^* \mid x \text{ ends in } 010\}$, find the maximum of the numbers $d_{L,x,y}$ over all possible pairs of distinguishable strings $x$ and $y$.

    b. If $L$ is the language of balanced strings of parentheses, if $|x| = m$ and $|y| = n$, find an upper bound involving $m$ and $n$ on the numbers $d_{L,x,y}$.

**5.16.** For each of the FAs pictured in Figure 5.6, use the minimization algorithm described in Algorithm 5.1 and illustrated in Example 5.6 to find a minimum-state FA recognizing the same language. (It's possible that the given FA may already be minimal.)

**5.17.** Find a minimum-state FA recognizing the language corresponding to each of these regular expressions.

    a. $(0^*10 + 1^*0)(01)^*$

    b. $(010)^*1 + (1^*0)^*$

**5.18.** Suppose that in applying Algorithm 5.1, we establish some fixed order in which to process the pairs, and we follow the same order on each pass.

    a. What is the maximum number of passes that might be required? Describe an FA, and an ordering of the pairs, that would require this number.

    b. Is there always a fixed order (depending on $M$) that would guarantee no pairs are marked after the second pass, so that the algorithm terminates after three passes?

**5.19.** For each of the NFA-$\Lambda$s pictured in Figure 5.7, find a minimum-state FA accepting the same language.

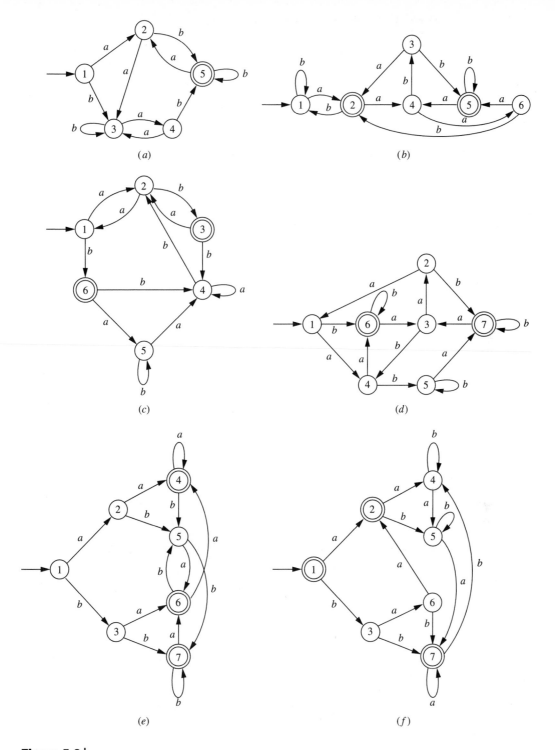

**Figure 5.6** |

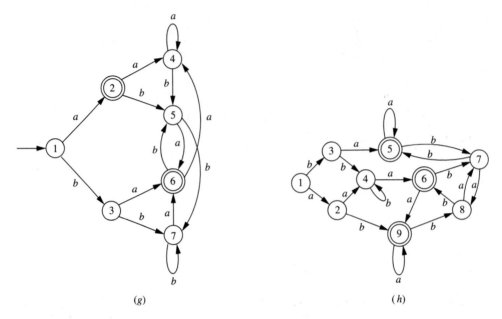

(g)                                                  (h)

**Figure 5.6 |**
Continued

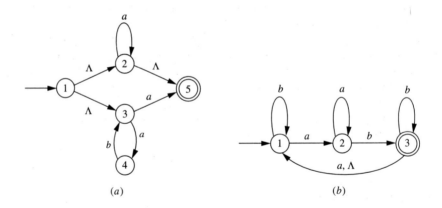

(a)                                                  (b)

**Figure 5.7 |**

**5.20.** In each of the following cases, prove that $L$ is nonregular by showing that any two elements of the infinite set $\{0^n \mid n \geq 0\}$ are distinguishable with respect to $L$.

 a.  $L = \{0^n 10^{2n} \mid n \geq 0\}$

 b.  $L = \{0^i 1^j 0^k \mid k > i + j\}$

 c.  $L = \{0^i 1^j \mid j = i \text{ or } j = 2i\}$

   d.   $L = \{0^i 1^j \mid j \text{ is a multiple of } i\}$

   e.   $L = \{x \in \{0, 1\}^* \mid n_0(x) < 2n_1(x)\}$

   f.   $L = \{x \in \{0, 1\}^* \mid \text{no prefix of } x \text{ has more 1's than 0's}\}$

**5.21.** Use Theorem 5.3 to show that $\{0^n 1^n \mid n \geq 0\}$ is not regular.

**5.22.** Use Corollary 5.1 to show that the language in Example 5.11 is not regular.

**5.23.** In each part of Exercise 5.20, use the pumping lemma for regular languages to show that the language is not regular.

**5.24.** Use the pumping lemma to show that each of these languages is not regular:

   a.   $L = \{ww \mid w \in \{0, 1\}^*\}$

   b.   $L = \{xy \mid x, y \in \{0, 1\}^* \text{ and } y \text{ is either } x \text{ or } x^r\}$

   c.   The language of algebraic expressions in Example 5.3.

**5.25.** Suppose $L$ is a language over $\{0, 1\}$, and there is a fixed integer $k$ so that for every $x \in \Sigma^*$, $xz \in L$ for some string $z$ with $|z| \leq k$. Does it follow that $L$ is regular? Why or why not?

**5.26.** For each statement below, decide whether it is true or false. If it is true, prove it. If not, give a counterexample. All parts refer to languages over the alphabet $\{0, 1\}$.

   a.   If $L_1 \subseteq L_2$ and $L_1$ is not regular, then $L_2$ is not regular.

   b.   If $L_1 \subseteq L_2$ and $L_2$ is not regular, then $L_1$ is not regular.

   c.   If $L_1$ and $L_2$ are nonregular, then $L_1 \cup L_2$ is nonregular.

   d.   If $L_1$ and $L_2$ are nonregular, then $L_1 \cap L_2$ is nonregular.

   e.   If $L$ is nonregular, then $L'$ is nonregular.

   f.   If $L_1$ is regular and $L_2$ is nonregular, then $L_1 \cup L_2$ is nonregular.

   g.   If $L_1$ is regular, $L_2$ is nonregular, and $L_1 \cap L_2$ is regular, then $L_1 \cup L_2$ is nonregular.

   h.   If $L_1$ is regular, $L_2$ is nonregular, and $L_1 \cap L_2$ is nonregular, then $L_1 \cup L_2$ is nonregular.

   i.   If $L_1, L_2, L_3, \ldots$ are all regular, then $\cup_{n=1}^{\infty} L_n$ is regular.

   j.   If $L_1, L_2, L_3, \ldots$ are all nonregular and $L_i \subseteq L_{i+1}$ for each $i$, then $\cup_{n=1}^{\infty} L_n$ is nonregular.

**5.27.** A number of languages over $\{0, 1\}$ are given in (a)–(h). In each case, decide whether the language is regular or not, and prove that your answer is correct.

   a.   The set of all strings $x$ beginning with a nonnull string of the form $ww$.

   b.   The set of all strings $x$ containing some nonnull substring of the form $ww$.

   c.   The set of odd-length strings over $\{0, 1\}$ with middle symbol 0.

   d.   The set of even-length strings over $\{0, 1\}$ with the two middle symbols equal.

   e.   The set of strings over $\{0, 1\}$ of the form $xyx$ for some $x$ with $|x| \geq 1$.

   f.   The set of nonpalindromes.

    g.  The set of strings beginning with a palindrome of length at least 3.

    h.  The set of strings in which the number of 0's is a perfect square.

**5.28.** Describe decision algorithms to answer each of these questions.

    a.  Given two FAs $M_1$ and $M_2$, are there any strings that are accepted by neither?

    b.  Given a regular expression $r$ and an FA $M$, are the corresponding languages the same?

    c.  Given an FA $M = (Q, \Sigma, q_0, A, \delta)$ and a state $q \in Q$, is there an $x$ with $|x| > 0$ so that $\delta^*(q, x) = q$?

    d.  Given an NFA-$\Lambda$ $M$ and a string $x$, does $M$ accept $x$?

    e.  Given two NFA-$\Lambda$s, do they accept the same language?

    f.  Given an NFA-$\Lambda$ $M$ and a string $x$, is there more than one sequence of transitions corresponding to $x$ that causes $M$ to accept $x$?

    g.  Given an FA $M$ accepting a language $L$, and given two strings $x$ and $y$, are $x$ and $y$ distinguishable with respect to $L$?

    h.  Given an FA $M$ accepting a language $L$, and a string $x$, is $x$ a prefix of an element of $L$?

    i.  Given an FA $M$ accepting a language $L$, and a string $x$, is $x$ a suffix of an element of $L$?

    j.  Given an FA $M$ accepting a language $L$, and a string $x$, is $x$ a substring of an element of $L$?

**5.29.** Find an example of a language $L \subseteq \{0, 1\}^*$ so that $L^*$ is not regular.

**5.30.** Find an example of a nonregular language $L \subseteq \{0, 1\}^*$ so that $L^*$ is regular.


## MORE CHALLENGING PROBLEMS

**5.31.** Let $L \subseteq \Sigma^*$ be a language, and let $L_1$ be the set of prefixes of elements of $L$. What is the relationship, if any, between the two partitions of $\Sigma^*$ corresponding to the equivalence relations $I_L$ and $I_{L_1}$, respectively? Explain.

**5.32.** a.  List all the subsets $A$ of $\{0, 1\}^*$ having the property that for some language $L \subseteq \{0, 1\}^*$ for which $I_L$ has exactly two equivalence classes, $A = [\Lambda]$.

    b.  For each set $A$ that is one of your answers to (a), how many distinct languages $L$ are there so that $I_L$ has two equivalence classes and $[\Lambda]$ is $A$?

**5.33.** Let $L = \{ww \mid w \in \{0, 1\}^*\}$. Describe all the equivalence classes of $I_L$.

**5.34.** Let $L$ be the language of "balanced" strings of parentheses—that is, all strings that are the strings of parentheses in legal algebraic expressions. For example, $\Lambda$, $()()$, and $((()()))$ are in $L$, $(()$ and $))(()$ are not. Describe all the equivalence classes of $I_L$.

**5.35.** a. Let $L$ be the language of all fully parenthesized algebraic expressions involving the operator $+$ and the identifier $i$. ($L$ can be defined recursively by saying $i \in L$, $(x + y) \in L$ for every $x$ and $y$ in $L$, and nothing else is in $L$.) Describe all the equivalence classes of $I_L$.

b. Answer the same question for the language $L$ in Example 5.3, defined by saying $a \in L$, $x + y \in L$ for every $x$ and $y$ in $L$, and $(x) \in L$ for every $x \in L$.

**5.36.** For an arbitrary string $x \in \{0, 1\}^*$, denote by $x^\sim$ the string obtained by replacing all 0's by 1's and vice versa. For example, $\Lambda^\sim = \Lambda$ and $(011)^\sim = 100$.

a. Define
$$L = \{xx^\sim \mid x \in \{0, 1\}^*\}$$
Determine the equivalence classes of $I_L$.

b. Define
$$L_1 = \{xy \mid x \in \{0, 1\}^* \text{ and } y \text{ is either } x \text{ or } x^\sim\}$$
Determine the equivalence classes of $I_{L_1}$.

**5.37.** Let $L = \{x \in \{0, 1\}^* \mid n_1(x) \text{ is a multiple of } n_0(x)\}$. Determine the equivalence classes of $I_L$.

**5.38.** Let $L$ be a language over $\Sigma$. We know that $I_L$ is a *right invariant* equivalence relation (i.e., for any $x$ and $y$ in $\Sigma^*$ and any $a \in \Sigma$, if $x \, I_L \, y$, then $xa \, I_L \, ya$). By the Myhill-Nerode theorem (Corollary 5.1), we know that if the set of equivalence classes of $I_L$ is finite, then $L$ is regular, and in this case $L$ is the union of some (zero or more) of these finitely many equivalence classes. Show that if $R$ is *any* right invariant equivalence relation such that the set of equivalence classes of $R$ is finite and $L$ is the union of some of the equivalence classes of $R$, then $L$ is regular.

**5.39.** If $P$ is a partition of $\{0, 1\}^*$ (i.e., a collection of pairwise disjoint subsets whose union is $\{0, 1\}^*$), then there is an equivalence relation $R$ on $\{0, 1\}^*$ whose equivalence classes are precisely the subsets in $P$. Let us say that $P$ is right invariant if the resulting equivalence relation is.

a. Show that for a subset $S$ of $\{0, 1\}^*$, $S$ is one of the subsets of some right invariant partition of $\{0, 1\}^*$ (not necessarily a finite partition) if and only if the following condition is satisfied: for any $x, y \in S$, and any $z \in \{0, 1\}^*$, $xz$ and $yz$ are either both in $S$ or both not in $S$.

b. To what simpler condition does this one reduce in the case where $S$ is a finite set?

c. Show that if a finite set $S$ satisfies this condition, then there is a finite right invariant partition having $S$ as one of its subsets.

d. For an arbitrary set $S$ satisfying the condition in part (a), there may be no finite right invariant partition having $S$ as one of its subsets. Characterize those sets $S$ for which there is.

**5.40.** For two languages $L_1$ and $L_2$ over $\Sigma$, we define the *quotient* of $L_1$ and $L_2$ to be the language

$$L_1/L_2 = \{x \mid \text{for some } y \in L_2, xy \in L_1\}$$

Show that if $L_1$ is regular and $L_2$ is any language, then $L_1/L_2$ is regular.

**5.41.** Suppose $L$ is a language over $\Sigma$, and $x_1, x_2, \ldots, x_n$ are strings that are pairwise distinguishable with respect to $L$; that is, for any $i \neq j$, $x_i$ and $x_j$ are distinguishable. How many distinct strings are necessary in order to distinguish between the $x_i$'s? In other words, what is the smallest number $k$ so that for some set $\{z_1, z_2, \ldots, z_k\}$, any two distinct $x_i$'s are distinguished, relative to $L$, by some $z_l$? Prove your answer. (Here is a way of thinking about the question that may make it easier. Think of the $x_i$'s as points on a piece of paper, and think of the $z_l$'s as cans of paint, each $z_l$ representing a different primary color. Saying that $z_l$ distinguishes $x_i$ and $x_j$ means that one of those two points is colored with that primary color and the other isn't. We allow a single point to have more than one primary color applied to it, and we assume that two distinct combinations of primary colors produce different resulting colors. Then the question is, how many different primary colors are needed in order to color the points so that no two points end up the same color?)

**5.42.** Suppose $M = (Q, \Sigma, q_0, A, \delta)$ is an FA accepting $L$. We know (Lemma 5.2) that if $p, q \in Q$ and $p \not\equiv q$, then there is a string $z$ so that exactly one of the two states $\delta^*(p, z)$ and $\delta^*(q, z)$ is in $A$. Find an integer $n$ (depending only on $M$) so that for any $p$ and $q$ with $p \not\equiv q$, there is such a $z$ with $|z| \leq n$.

**5.43.** Show that $L$ is regular if and only if there is an integer $n$ so that any two strings distinguishable with respect to $L$ can be distinguished by a string of length $\leq n$. (Use the two previous exercises.)

**5.44.** Suppose that $M_1 = (Q_1, \Sigma, q_1, A_1, \delta_1)$ and $M_2 = (Q_2, \Sigma, q_2, A_2, \delta_2)$ are both FAs accepting the language $L$, and both have as few states as possible. Show that $M_1$ and $M_2$ are isomorphic (see Exercise 3.55). Note that in both cases, the sets $L_q$ forming the partition of $\Sigma^*$ are precisely the equivalence classes of $I_L$. This tells you how to come up with a bijection from $Q_1$ to $Q_2$. What you must do next is to show that the other conditions of an isomorphism are satisfied.

**5.45.** Use the preceding exercise to describe another decision algorithm to answer the question "Given two FAs, do they accept the same language?"

**5.46.** Suppose $L$ and $L_1$ are both languages over $\Sigma$, and $M$ is an FA with alphabet $\Sigma$. Let us say that $M$ accepts $L$ *relative to* $L_1$ if $M$ accepts every string in the set $L \cap L_1$ and rejects every string in the set $L_1 - L$. Note that this is not in general the same as saying that $M$ accepts the language $L \cap L_1$.

Now suppose $L_1, L_2, \ldots$ are regular languages over $\Sigma$, $L_i \subseteq L_{i+1}$ for each $i$, and $\cup_{i=1}^{\infty} L_i = \Sigma^*$. For each $i$, let $n_i$ be the minimum number of states required to accept $L$ relative to $L_i$. If there is no FA accepting $L$ relative to $L_i$, we say $n_i$ is $\infty$.

    a.   Show that for each $i$, $n_i \leq n_{i+1}$.

    b.   Show that if the sequence $n_i$ is bounded (i.e., for some constant $C$, $n_i \leq C$ for every $i$), then $L$ is regular. (It follows in particular that if there is some fixed FA that accepts $L$ relative to $L_i$ for every $i$, then $L$ is regular.)

**5.47.**  Prove the following generalization of the pumping lemma, which can sometimes make it unnecessary to break the proof into cases. If $L$ is a regular language, then there is an integer $n$ so that for any $x \in L$, and any way of writing $x$ as $x = x_1 x_2 x_3$ with $|x_2| = n$, there are strings $u$, $v$, and $w$ so that

$$x_2 = uvw$$

$$|v| > 0$$

$$\text{for any } m \geq 0, \ x_1 uv^m wx_2 \in L$$

**5.48.**  Can you find a language $L \subseteq \{0, 1\}^*$ so that in order to prove $L$ nonregular, the pumping lemma is not sufficient but the statement in the preceding problem is?

**5.49.**  Describe decision algorithms to answer each of these questions.

    a.   Given a regular expression $r$, is there a simpler regular expression (i.e., one involving fewer operations) that is equivalent to $r$?

    b.   Given two FAs $M_1$ and $M_2$, is $L(M_1)$ a subset of $L(M_2)$?

    c.   Given two FAs $M_1$ and $M_2$, is every element of $L(M_1)$ a prefix of an element of $L(M_2)$?

    d.   Given two FAs $M_1 = (Q_1, \Sigma, q_1, A_1, \delta_1)$ and $M_2$, and two states $p, q \in Q_1$, is there a string $x \in L(M_2)$ so that $\delta_1^*(p, x) = q$?

**5.50.**  Below are a number of languages over $\{0, 1\}$. In each case, decide whether the language is regular or not, and prove that your answer is correct.

    a.   The set of all strings $x$ having some nonnull substring of the form $www$. (You may assume the following fact: There are arbitrarily long strings in $\{0, 1\}^*$ that do not contain any nonnull substring of the form $www$. In fact, such strings can be obtained using the construction in Exercise 2.43.)

    b.   The set of strings having the property that in every prefix, the number of 0's and the number of 1's differ by no more than 2.

    c.   The set of strings having the property that in some prefix, the number of 0's is 3 more than the number of 1's.

    d.   The set of strings in which the number of 0's and the number of 1's are both divisible by 5.

    e.   The set of strings $x$ for which there is an integer $k > 1$ (possibly depending on $x$) so that the number of 0's in $x$ and the number of 1's in $x$ are both divisible by $k$.

  f. (Assuming $L$ is a regular language), $Max(L) = \{x \in L \mid$ there is no nonnull string $y$ so that $xy \in L\}$.

  g. (Assuming $L$ is a regular language), $Min(L) = \{x \in L \mid$ no prefix of $x$ other than $x$ itself is in $L\}$.

**5.51.** A set $S$ of nonnegative integers is an *arithmetic progression* if for some integers $n$ and $p$,

$$S = \{n + ip \mid i \geq 0\}$$

Let $A$ be a subset of $\{0\}^*$, and let $S = \{|x| \mid x \in A\}$.

  a. Show that if $S$ is an arithmetic progression, then $A$ is regular.

  b. Show that if $A$ is regular, then $S$ is the union of a finite number of arithmetic progressions.

**5.52.** This exercise involves languages of the form

$$L = \{x \in \{a, b\}^* \mid n_a(x) = f(n_b(x))\}$$

for some function $f$ from the set of natural numbers to itself. Example 5.7 shows that if $f$ is the function defined by $f(n) = n$, then $L$ is nonregular. If $f$ is any constant function (e.g., $f(n) = 4$), $L$ is regular. One might ask whether $L$ can still be regular when $f$ is not restricted quite so severely.

  a. Show that if $L$ is regular, the function $f$ must be bounded—that is, there must be some integer $B$ so that $f(n) \leq B$ for every $n$. (Suggestion: suppose not, and apply the pumping lemma to strings of the form $a^{f(n)}b^n$.)

  b. Show that if $f(n) = n \bmod 2$, then $L$ is regular.

  c. $n \bmod 2$ is an *eventually periodic* function; that is, there are integers $n_0$ and $p$, with $p > 0$, so that for any $n \geq n_0$, $f(n) = f(n + p)$. Show that if $f$ is any eventually periodic function, $L$ is regular.

  d. Show that if $L$ is regular, then $f$ must be eventually periodic. (Suggestion: as in part (a), find a class of strings to which you can apply the pumping lemma.)

**5.53.** Find an example of a nonregular language $L \subseteq \{0, 1\}^*$ so that $L^2$ is regular.

**5.54.** Show that if $L$ is any language over a one-symbol alphabet, then $L^*$ is regular.

# 3

# Context-Free Languages and Pushdown Automata

**A** *context-free grammar* is a simple recursive method of specifying grammar rules by which strings in a language can be generated. All the regular languages can be generated this way, and there are also simple examples of context-free grammars generating nonregular languages. Grammar rules of this type permit syntax of more variety and sophistication than is possible with regular languages. To a large extent, they are capable of specifying the syntax of high-level programming languages and other formal languages.

A model of computation that corresponds to context-free languages, in the same way that finite automata correspond to regular languages, can be obtained by starting with the finite-state model and adding an auxiliary memory. Although the memory will be potentially infinite, it is sufficient to impose upon it a very simple organization, that of a *stack*. It is necessary, however, to retain the element of nondeterminism in these *pushdown automata*; otherwise, not every context-free language can be accepted this way. For any context-free grammar, there is a simple way to get a nondeterministic pushdown automaton accepting the language so that a sequence of moves by which a string is accepted simulates a derivation of the string in the grammar. For certain classes of grammars, this feature can be retained even when the nondeterminism is removed, so that the result is a parser for the grammar; we study this problem briefly.

The class of context-free languages is still not general enough to include all interesting or useful formal languages. Techniques similar to those in Chapter 5 can be used to exhibit simple non-context-free languages, and these techniques can also be used to find algorithms for certain decision problems associated with context-free languages. ■

# CHAPTER

# 6

# Context-Free Grammars

## 6.1 I EXAMPLES AND DEFINITIONS

Many of the languages we have considered, both regular and nonregular, can be described by recursive definitions. In our first example, involving a very simple regular language, a slight reformulation of the recursive definition leads us to the idea of a *context-free grammar*. These and other more general grammars that we will later study turn out to be powerful tools for describing and analyzing languages.

---

Using Grammar Rules to Describe a Language **EXAMPLE 6.1**

---

Let us consider the language $L = \{a, b\}^*$ of all strings over the alphabet $\{a, b\}$. In Example 2.15 we considered a recursive definition of $L$ equivalent to the following:

1. $\Lambda \in L$.
2. For any $S \in L$, $Sa \in L$.
3. For any $S \in L$, $Sb \in L$.
4. No other strings are in $L$.

We think of $S$ here as a *variable*, representing an arbitrary element of $L$ whose value is to be obtained by some combination of rules 1 to 3. Rule 1, which we write $S \to \Lambda$, indicates that one way of giving $S$ a value is to replace it by $\Lambda$. Rules 2 and 3 can be written $S \to Sa$ and $S \to Sb$. This means that $S$ can also be replaced by $Sa$ or $Sb$; in either case we must then obtain the final value by continuing to use the rules to give a value to the new $S$.

The symbol $\to$ is used for each of the rules by which a variable is replaced by a string. For two strings $\alpha$ and $\beta$, we will use the notation $\alpha \Rightarrow \beta$ to mean that $\beta$ can be obtained by applying one of these rules to a single variable in the string $\alpha$. Using this notation in our example, we can write

$$S \Rightarrow Sa \Rightarrow Sba \Rightarrow Sbba \Rightarrow \Lambda bba = bba$$

to describe the sequence of steps (the application of rules 2, 3, 3, and 1) used to obtain, or *derive*, the string *bba*. The derivation comes to an end at the point where we replace *S* by an actual string of alphabet symbols (in this case Λ); each step before that is roughly analogous to a recursive call, since we are replacing *S* by a string that still contains a variable.

We can simplify the notation even further by introducing the symbol | to mean "or" and writing the first three rules as

$$S \to \Lambda \mid Sa \mid Sb$$

(In our new notation, we dispense with writing rule 4, even though it is implicitly still in effect.) We note for future reference that in an expression such as *Sa* | *Sb*, the two alternatives are *Sa* and *Sb*, not *a* and *S*—in other words, the concatenation operation takes precedence over the | operation.

In Example 2.15 we also considered this alternative definition of *L*:

1. $\Lambda \in L$.
2. $a \in L$.
3. $b \in L$.
4. For every *x* and *y* in *L*, $xy \in L$.
5. No other strings are in *L*.

Using our new notation, we would summarize the "grammar rules" by writing

$$S \to \Lambda \mid a \mid b \mid SS$$

With this approach there is more than one way to obtain the string *bba*. Two derivations are shown below:

$$S \Rightarrow SS \Rightarrow bS \Rightarrow bSS \Rightarrow bbS \Rightarrow bba$$
$$S \Rightarrow SS \Rightarrow Sa \Rightarrow SSa \Rightarrow bSa \Rightarrow bba$$

The five steps in the first line correspond to rules 4, 3, 4, 3, and 2, and those in the second line to rules 4, 2, 4, 3, and 3.

---

In both cases in Example 6.1, the formulas obtained from the recursive definition can be interpreted as the grammar rules in a context-free grammar. Before we give the official definition of such a grammar, we consider two more examples. In Example 6.2, although the grammar is perhaps even simpler than that in Example 6.1, the corresponding language is one we know to be nonregular. Example 6.3 is perhaps more typical in that it includes a grammar containing more than one variable.

**EXAMPLE 6.2**   The Language $\{a^n b^n \mid n \geq 0\}$

The grammar rules

$$S \to aSb \mid \Lambda$$

are another way of describing the language *L* defined as follows:

1. $\Lambda \in L$.
2. For every $x \in L$, $axb \in L$.
3. Nothing else is in $L$.

The language $L$ is easily seen to be the nonregular language $\{a^n b^n \mid n \geq 0\}$. The grammar rules in the first part of Example 6.1, for the language $\{a, b\}^*$, allow $a$'s and $b$'s to be added independently of each other. Here, on the other hand, each time one symbol is added to one end of the string by an application of the grammar rule $S \rightarrow aSb$, the opposite symbol is added simultaneously to the other end. As we have seen, this constraint is not one that can be captured by any regular expression.

---

Palindromes     **EXAMPLE 6.3**

---

Let us consider both the language *pal* of palindromes over the alphabet $\{a, b\}$ and its complement $N$, the set of all nonpalindromes over $\{a, b\}$. From Example 2.16, we have the following recursive definition of *pal*:

1. $\Lambda, a, b \in pal$.
2. For any $S \in pal$, $aSa$ and $bSb$ are in *pal*.
3. No other strings are in *pal*.

We can therefore describe *pal* by the context-free grammar with the grammar rules

$$S \rightarrow \Lambda \mid a \mid b \mid aSa \mid bSb$$

The language $N$ also obeys rule 2: For any nonpalindrome $x$, both $axa$ and $bxb$ are nonpalindromes. However, a recursive definition of $N$ cannot be as simple as this definition of *pal*, because there is no finite set of strings that can serve as basis elements in the definition. There is no finite set $N_0$ so that every nonpalindrome can be obtained from an element of $N_0$ by applications of rule 2 (Exercise 6.42). Consider a specific nonpalindrome, say

*abbaaba*

If we start at the ends and work our way in, trying to match the symbols at the beginning with those at the end, the string looks like a palindrome for the first two steps. What makes it a nonpalindrome is the central portion *baa*, which starts with one symbol and ends with the opposite symbol; the string between those two can be anything. A string is a nonpalindrome if and only if it has a central portion of this type. These are the "basic" nonpalindromes, and we can therefore write the following definition of $N$:

1. For any $A \in \{a, b\}^*$, $aAb$ and $bAa$ are in $N$.
2. For any $S \in N$, $aSa$ and $bSb$ are in $N$.
3. No other strings are in $N$.

In order to obtain a context-free grammar describing $N$, we can now simply introduce a second variable $A$, representing an arbitrary element of $\{a, b\}^*$, and incorporate the grammar rules for this language from Example 6.1:

$$S \rightarrow aAb \mid bAa \mid aSa \mid bSb$$
$$A \rightarrow \Lambda \mid Aa \mid Ab$$

A derivation of the nonpalindrome *abbaaba*, for example, would look like

$$S \Rightarrow aSa \Rightarrow abSba \Rightarrow abbAaba \Rightarrow abbAaaba \Rightarrow abb\Lambda aaba = abbaaba$$

It is common, and often necessary, to include several variables in a context-free grammar describing a language $L$. There will still be one special variable that represents an arbitrary string in $L$, and it is customary to denote this one by $S$ (the *start* variable). The other variables can then be thought of as representing typical strings in certain auxiliary languages involved in the definition of $L$. (We can still interpret the grammar as a recursive definition of $L$, if we extend our notion of recursion slightly to include the idea of *mutual* recursion: rather than one object defined in terms of itself, several objects defined in terms of each other.)

Let us now give the general definition illustrated by these examples.

---

**Definition 6.1    Definition of a Context-Free Grammar**

A *context-free grammar* (CFG) is a 4-tuple $G = (V, \Sigma, S, P)$, where $V$ and $\Sigma$ are disjoint finite sets, $S$ is an element of $V$, and $P$ is a finite set of formulas of the form $A \to \alpha$, where $A \in V$ and $\alpha \in (V \cup \Sigma)^*$.

The elements of $V$ are called *variables*, or *nonterminal* symbols, and those of the alphabet $\Sigma$ are called *terminal* symbols, or *terminals*. $S$ is called the *start symbol*; and the elements of $P$ are called *grammar rules*, or *productions*.

---

Suppose $G = (V, \Sigma, S, P)$ is a CFG. As in the first three examples, we will reserve the symbol $\to$ for individual productions in $P$. We use the symbol $\Rightarrow$ for steps in a derivation such as those in Examples 6.1 and 6.3. Sometimes it is useful to indicate explicitly that the derivation is with respect to the CFG $G$, and in this case we write $\Rightarrow_G$.

$$\alpha \Rightarrow_G \beta$$

means that the string $\beta$ can be obtained from the string $\alpha$ by replacing some variable that appears on the left side of a production in $G$ by the corresponding right side, or that

$$\alpha = \alpha_1 A \alpha_2$$
$$\beta = \alpha_1 \gamma \alpha_2$$

and one of the productions in $G$ is $A \to \gamma$. (We can now understand better the term *context-free*. If at some point in a derivation we have obtained a string $\alpha$ containing the variable $A$, then we may continue by substituting $\gamma$ for $A$, no matter what the strings $\alpha_1$ and $\alpha_2$ are—that is, independent of the context.)

In this case, we will say that $\alpha$ derives $\beta$, or $\beta$ is derived from $\alpha$, in one step. More generally, we write

$$\alpha \Rightarrow_G^* \beta$$

(and shorten it to $\alpha \Rightarrow^* \beta$ if it is clear what grammar is involved) if $\alpha$ derives $\beta$ in zero or more steps; in other words, either $\alpha = \beta$, or there exist an integer $k \geq 1$ and strings $\alpha_0, \alpha_1, \ldots, \alpha_k$, with $\alpha_0 = \alpha$ and $\alpha_k = \beta$, so that $\alpha_i \Rightarrow_G \alpha_{i+1}$ for every $i$ with $0 \leq i \leq k - 1$.

---

**Definition 6.2    The Language Generated by a CFG**

Let $G = (V, \Sigma, S, P)$ be a CFG. The language generated by $G$ is

$$L(G) = \{x \in \Sigma^* \mid S \Rightarrow_G^* x\}$$

A language $L$ is a *context-free language* (CFL) if there is a CFG $G$ so that $L = L(G)$.

---

The Language of Algebraic Expressions          **EXAMPLE 6.4**

An important language in computer science is the language of legal algebraic expressions. For simplicity we restrict ourselves here to the simple expressions that can be formed from the four binary operators $+$, $-$, $*$, and $/$, left and right parentheses, and the single identifier $a$. Some of the features omitted, therefore, are unary operators, any binary operators other than these four, numerical literals such as 3.0 or $\sqrt{2}$, expressions involving functional notation, and more general identifiers. Many of these features could be handled simply enough; for example, the language of arbitrary identifiers can be "embedded" within this one by using a variable $A$ instead of the terminal symbol $a$ and introducing productions that allow any identifier to be derived from $A$. (See Examples 3.5 and 3.6.)

A recursive definition of our language is based on the observation that legal expressions can be formed by joining two legal expressions using one of the four operators or by enclosing a legal expression within parentheses, and that these two operations account for all legal expressions except the single identifier $a$. The most straightforward way of getting a context-free grammar, therefore, is probably to use the productions

$$S \rightarrow S + S \mid S - S \mid S * S \mid S/S \mid (S) \mid a$$

The string $a + (a * a)/a - a$ can be obtained from the derivation

$$S \Rightarrow S - S \Rightarrow S + S - S \Rightarrow a + S - S \Rightarrow a + S/S - S$$
$$\Rightarrow a + (S)/S - S \Rightarrow a + (S * S)/S - S \Rightarrow a + (a * S)/S - S$$
$$\Rightarrow a + (a * a)/S - S \Rightarrow a + (a * a)/a - S \Rightarrow a + (a * a)/a - a$$

It is easy to see that there are many other derivations as well. For example,

$$S \Rightarrow S/S \Rightarrow S + S/S \Rightarrow a + S/S \Rightarrow a + (S)/S$$
$$\Rightarrow a + (S * S)/S \Rightarrow a + (a * S)/S \Rightarrow a + (a * a)/S$$
$$\Rightarrow a + (a * a)/S - S \Rightarrow a + (a * a)/a - S \Rightarrow a + (a * a)/a - a$$

We would probably say that the first of these is more natural than the second. The first starts with the production

$$S \rightarrow S - S$$

and therefore indicates that we are interpreting the original expression as the difference of two other expressions. This seems correct because the expression would normally be evaluated as follows:

1. Evaluate $a * a$, and call its value $A$.
2. Evaluate $A/a$, and call its value $B$.
3. Evaluate $a + B$, and call its value $C$.
4. Evaluate $C - a$.

The expression "is" the difference of the subexpression with value $C$ and the subexpression $a$. The second derivation, by contrast, interprets the expression as a quotient. Although there is nothing in the grammar to rule out this derivation, it does not reflect our view of the correct structure of the expression.

One possible conclusion is that the context-free grammar we have given for the language may not be the most appropriate. It does not incorporate in any way the standard conventions, having to do with the precedence of operators and the left-to-right order of evaluation, that we use in evaluating the expression. (Precedence of operators dictates that in the expression $a + b * c$, the multiplication is performed before the addition; and the expression $a - b + c$ means $(a - b) + c$, not $a - (b + c)$.) Moreover, rather than having to choose between two derivations of a string, it is often desirable to select, if possible, a CFG in which a string can *have* only one derivation (except for trivial differences between the order in which two variables in some intermediate string are chosen for replacement). We will return to this question in Section 6.4, when we discuss *ambiguity* in a CFG.

**EXAMPLE 6.5**   The Syntax of Programming Languages

The language in the previous example and languages like those in Examples 3.5 and 3.6 are relatively simple ingredients of programming languages such as C and Pascal. To a large extent, context-free grammars can be used to describe the overall syntax of such languages.

In C, one might try to formulate grammar rules to specify what constitutes a legal statement. (As you might expect, a complete specification is very involved.) Two types of statements in C are *if* statements and *for* statements; if we represent an arbitrary statement by the variable ⟨statement⟩, the productions involving ⟨statement⟩ might look like

$$\langle statement \rangle \ \rightarrow \ \cdots \mid \langle \textit{if}\text{-statement} \rangle \mid \langle \textit{for}\text{-statement} \rangle \mid \cdots$$

The syntax of these two types of statements can be described by the rules

$$\langle \textit{if}\text{-statement} \rangle \ \rightarrow \ \text{if} \ ( \ \langle expression \rangle \ ) \ \langle statement \rangle$$

$$\langle \textit{for}\text{-statement} \rangle \ \rightarrow \ \text{for} \ ( \ \langle expression \rangle; \ \langle expression \rangle; \ \langle expression \rangle \ ) \ \langle statement \rangle$$

where ⟨expression⟩ is another variable, whose productions would also be difficult to describe completely.

Although in both cases the last term on the right side specifies a single statement, the logic of a program often requires more than one. It is therefore necessary to have our definition of ⟨statement⟩ allow a *compound* statement, which is simply a sequence of zero or more statements enclosed within {}. We could easily write a definition for ⟨compound-statement⟩ that would say this. A *syntax diagram* such as the one shown accomplishes the same thing.

A path through the diagram begins with {, ends with }, and can traverse the loop zero or more times.

### Grammar Rules for English   **EXAMPLE 6.6**

The advantage of using high-level programming languages like C and Pascal is that they allow us to write statements that look more like English. If we can use context-free grammars to capture many of the rules of programming languages, what about English itself, which has its own "grammar rules"?

English sentences that are sufficiently simple can be described by CFGs. A great many sentences could be taken care of by the productions

$$\langle \text{declarative sentence} \rangle \rightarrow \langle \text{subject phrase} \rangle \langle \text{verb phrase} \rangle \langle \text{object} \rangle \mid$$
$$\langle \text{subject phrase} \rangle \langle \text{verb phrase} \rangle$$

if we provided reasonable productions for each of the three variables on the right. Producing a wide variety of reasonable, idiomatic English sentences with context-free grammars, even context-free grammars of manageable size, is not hard; what *is* hard is doing this and at the same time disallowing gibberish. Even harder is disallowing sentences that seem to obey English syntax but that a native English speaker would probably never say, because they don't sound right.

Here is a simple example that might illustrate the point. Consider the productions

$$\langle \text{declarative sentence} \rangle \rightarrow \langle \text{subject} \rangle \langle \text{verb} \rangle \langle \text{object} \rangle$$
$$\langle \text{subject} \rangle \rightarrow \langle \text{proper noun} \rangle$$
$$\langle \text{proper noun} \rangle \rightarrow \text{John} \mid \text{Jane}$$
$$\langle \text{verb} \rangle \rightarrow \text{reminded}$$
$$\langle \text{object} \rangle \rightarrow \langle \text{proper noun} \rangle \mid \langle \text{reflexive pronoun} \rangle$$
$$\langle \text{reflexive pronoun} \rangle \rightarrow \text{himself} \mid \text{herself}$$

More than one sentence derivable from this grammar does not quite work: "John reminded herself" and "Jane reminded himself," for example. These could be eliminated in a straightforward way (at the cost of complicating the grammar) by introducing productions like

$$\langle \text{declarative sentence} \rangle \rightarrow \langle \text{masculine noun} \rangle \langle \text{verb} \rangle \langle \text{masculine reflexive pronoun} \rangle$$

A slightly more subtle problem is "Jane reminded Jane." Normally we do not say this, unless we have in mind two different people named Jane, but there is no obvious way to prohibit it without also prohibiting "Jane reminded John." (At least, there is no obvious way without essentially using a different production for every sentence we want to end up with. This trivial option is available here, since the language is finite.) To distinguish "Jane reminded John," which is a perfectly good English sentence, from "Jane reminded Jane" requires using *context*, and this is exactly what a context-free grammar does not allow.

## 6.2 | MORE EXAMPLES

In general, to show that a CFG generates a language, we must show two things: first, that every string in the language can be derived from the grammar, and second, that no other string can. In some of the examples in this section, at least one of these two statements is less obvious.

| **EXAMPLE 6.7** | A CFG for $\{x \mid n_0(x) = n_1(x)\}$ |

Consider the language

$$L = \{x \in \{0, 1\}^* \mid n_0(x) = n_1(x)\}$$

where $n_i(x)$ is the number of $i$'s in the string $x$.

As in Examples 6.1–6.3, we can begin by thinking about a recursive definition of $L$, and once we find one we can easily turn it into a context-free grammar.

Clearly, $\Lambda \in L$. Given a string $x$ in $L$, we get a longer string in $L$ by adding one 0 and one 1. (Conversely, any nonnull string in $L$ can be obtained this way.) One way to add the symbols is to add one at each end, producing either $0x1$ or $1x0$. This suggests the productions

$$S \to \Lambda \mid 0S1 \mid 1S0$$

Not every string in $L$ can be obtained from these productions, because some elements of $L$ begin and end with the same symbol; the strings 0110, 10001101, and 0010111100 are examples. If we look for ways of expressing each of these in terms of simpler elements of $L$, we might notice that each is the concatenation of two nonnull elements of $L$ (for example, the third string is the concatenation of 001011 and 1100). This observation suggests the production $S \to SS$.

It is reasonably clear that if $G$ is the CFG containing the productions we have so far,

$$S \to \Lambda \mid 0S1 \mid 1S0 \mid SS$$

then derivations in $G$ produce only strings in $L$. We will prove the converse, that $L \subseteq L(G)$.

It will be helpful to introduce the notation

$$d(x) = n_0(x) - n_1(x)$$

What we must show, therefore, is that for any string $x$ with $d(x) = 0$, $x \in L(G)$. The proof is by mathematical induction on $|x|$.

In the basis step of the proof, we must show that if $|x| = 0$ and $d(x) = 0$ (of course, the second hypothesis is redundant), then $x \in L(G)$. This is true because one of the productions in $G$ is $S \to \Lambda$.

Our induction hypothesis will be that $k \geq 0$ and that for any $y$ with $|y| \leq k$ and $d(y) = 0$, $y \in L(G)$. We must show that if $|x| = k + 1$ and $d(x) = 0$, then $x \in L(G)$.

If $x$ begins with 0 and ends with 1, then $x = 0y1$ for some string $y$ satisfying $d(y) = 0$. By the induction hypothesis, $y \in L(G)$. Therefore, since $S \Rightarrow_G^* y$, we can derive $x$ from $S$ by starting the derivation with the production $S \to 0S1$ and continuing to derive $y$ from the second $S$. The case when $x$ begins with 1 and ends with 0 is handled the same way, except that the production $S \to 1S0$ is used to begin the derivation.

The remaining case is the one in which $x$ begins and ends with the same symbol. Since $d(x) = 0$, $x$ has length at least 2; suppose for example that $x = 0y0$ for some string $y$. We would like to show that $x$ has a derivation in $G$. Such a derivation would have to start with the production $S \to SS$; in order to show that there is such a derivation, we would like to show that $x = wz$, where $w$ and $z$ are shorter strings that can both be derived from $S$. (It will then follow that we can start the derivation with $S \to SS$, then continue by deriving $w$ from the first $S$ and $z$ from the second.) Another way to express this condition is to say that $x$ has a prefix $w$ so that $0 < |w| < |x|$ and $d(w) = 0$.

Let us consider $d(w)$ for prefixes $w$ of $x$. The shortest nonnull prefix is 0, and $d(0) = 1$; the longest prefix shorter than $x$ is $0y$, and $d(0y) = -1$ (because the last symbol of $x$ is 0, and $d(x) = 0$). Furthermore, the $d$-value of a prefix changes by 1 each time an extra symbol is added. It follows that there must be a prefix $w$, longer than 0 and shorter than $0y$, with $d(w) = 0$. This is what we wanted to prove. The case when $x = 1y1$ is almost the same, and so the proof is concluded.

## Another CFG for $\{x \mid n_0(x) = n_1(x)\}$  |  **EXAMPLE 6.8**

Let us continue with the language $L = \{x \in \{0, 1\}^* \mid n_0(x) = n_1(x)\}$ of the last example; this time we construct a CFG with three variables, based on a different approach to a recursive definition of $L$.

One way to obtain an element of $L$ is to add both symbols to a string already in $L$. Another way, however, is to add a single symbol to a string that has one extra occurrence of the opposite symbol. Moreover, every element of $L$ can be obtained this way and in fact can be obtained by adding this extra symbol at the beginning. Let us introduce the variables $A$ and $B$, to represent strings with an extra 0 and an extra 1, respectively, and let us denote these two languages by $L_0$ and $L_1$:

$$L_0 = \{x \in \{0, 1\}^* \mid n_0(x) = n_1(x) + 1\} = \{x \in \{0, 1\}^* \mid d(x) = 1\}$$
$$L_1 = \{x \in \{0, 1\}^* \mid n_1(x) = n_0(x) + 1\} = \{x \in \{0, 1\}^* \mid d(x) = -1\}$$

where $d$ is the function in Example 6.7 defined by $d(x) = n_0(x) - n_1(x)$. Then it is easy to formulate the productions we need starting with $S$:

$$S \to 0B \mid 1A \mid \Lambda$$

It is also easy to find one production for each of the variables $A$ and $B$. If a string in $L_0$ begins with 0, or if a string in $L_1$ begins with 1, then the remainder is an element of $L$. Thus, it is appropriate to add the productions

$$A \to 0S \qquad B \to 1S$$

What remains are the strings in $L_0$ that start with 1 and the strings in $L_1$ that start with 0. In the first case, if $x = 1y$ and $x \in L_0$, then $y$ has two more 0's than 1's. If it were true that $y$ could be written as the concatenation of two strings, each with one extra 0, then we could complete the $A$-productions by adding $A \to 1AA$, and we could handle $B$ similarly.

In fact, the same technique we used in Example 6.7 will work here. If $d(x) = 1$ and $x = 1y$, then $\Lambda$ is a prefix of $y$ with $d(\Lambda) = 0$, and $y$ itself is a prefix of $y$ with $d(y) = 2$. Therefore, there is some intermediate prefix $w$ of $y$ with $d(w) = 1$, and $y = wz$ where $w, z \in L_0$.

This discussion should make it at least plausible that the context-free grammar with productions

$$S \rightarrow 0B \mid 1A \mid \Lambda$$
$$A \rightarrow 0S \mid 1AA$$
$$B \rightarrow 1S \mid 0BB$$

generates the language $L$. By taking the start variable to be $A$ or $B$, we could just as easily think of it as a CFG generating $L_0$ or $L_1$. It is possible without much difficulty to give an induction proof; see Exercise 6.50.

The following theorem provides three simple ways of obtaining new CFLs from languages that are known to be context-free.

---

**Theorem 6.1**
If $L_1$ and $L_2$ are context-free languages, then the languages $L_1 \cup L_2$, $L_1 L_2$, and $L_1^*$ are also CFLs.

*Proof*
The proof is constructive: Starting with CFGs

$$G_1 = (V_1, \Sigma, S_1, P_1) \quad \text{and} \quad G_2 = (V_2, \Sigma, S_2, P_2)$$

generating $L_1$ and $L_2$, respectively, we show how to construct a new CFG for each of the three cases.

   **A grammar $G_u = (V_u, \Sigma, S_u, P_u)$ generating $L_1 \cup L_2$.** First we rename the elements of $V_2$ if necessary so that $V_1 \cap V_2 = \emptyset$, and we define

$$V_u = V_1 \cup V_2 \cup \{S_u\}$$

where $S_u$ is a new symbol not in $V_1$ or $V_2$. Then we let

$$P_u = P_1 \cup P_2 \cup \{S_u \rightarrow S_1 \mid S_2\}$$

On the one hand, if $x$ is in either $L_1$ or $L_2$, then $S_u \Rightarrow^* x$ in the grammar $G_u$, because we can start a derivation with either $S_u \rightarrow S_1$ or $S_u \rightarrow S_2$ and continue with the derivation of $x$ in $G_1$ or $G_2$. Therefore,

$$L_1 \cup L_2 \subseteq L(G_u)$$

On the other hand, if $x$ is derivable from $S_u$ in $G_u$, the first step in any derivation must be

$$S_u \Rightarrow S_1 \quad \text{or} \quad S_u \Rightarrow S_2$$

In the first case, all subsequent productions used must be productions in $G_1$, because no variables in $V_2$ are involved, and thus $x \in L_1$; in the second case, $x \in L_2$. Therefore,

$$L(G_u) \subseteq L_1 \cup L_2$$

**A grammar $G_c = (V_c, \Sigma, S_c, P_c)$ generating $L_1 L_2$.** Again we relabel variables if necessary so that $V_1 \cap V_2 = \emptyset$, and define

$$V_c = V_1 \cup V_2 \cup \{S_c\}$$

This time we let

$$P_c = P_1 \cup P_2 \cup \{S_c \rightarrow S_1 S_2\}$$

If $x \in L_1 L_2$, then $x = x_1 x_2$, where $x_i \in L_i$ for each $i$. We may then derive $x$ in $G_c$ as follows:

$$S_c \Rightarrow S_1 S_2 \Rightarrow^* x_1 S_2 \Rightarrow^* x_1 x_2 = x$$

where the second step is the derivation of $x_1$ in $G_1$ and the third step is the derivation of $x_2$ in $G_2$. Conversely, if $x$ can be derived from $S_c$, then since the first step in the derivation must be $S_c \Rightarrow S_1 S_2$, $x$ must be derivable from $S_1 S_2$. Therefore, $x = x_1 x_2$, where for each $i$, $x_i$ can be derived from $S_i$ in $G_c$. Since $V_1 \cap V_2 = \emptyset$, being derivable from $S_i$ in $G_c$ means being derivable from $S_i$ in $G_i$, and so $x \in L_1 L_2$.

**A grammar $G^* = (V, \Sigma, S, P)$ generating $L_1^*$.** Let

$$V = V_1 \cup \{S\}$$

where $S \notin V_1$. The language $L_1^*$ contains strings of the form $x = x_1 x_2 \cdots x_k$, where each $x_i \in L_1$. Since each $x_i$ can be derived from $S_1$, then to derive $x$ from $S$ it is enough to be able to derive a string of $k$ $S_1$'s. We can accomplish this by including the productions

$$S \rightarrow S_1 S \mid \Lambda$$

in $P$. Therefore, let

$$P = P_1 \cup \{S \rightarrow S_1 S \mid \Lambda\}$$

The proof that $L_1^* \subseteq L(G^*)$ is straightforward. If $x \in L(G^*)$, on the other hand, then either $x = \Lambda$ or $x$ can be derived from some string of the form $S_1^k$ in $G^*$. In the second case, since the only productions in $G^*$ beginning with $S_1$ are those in $G_1$, we may conclude that

$$x \in L(G_1)^k \subseteq L(G_1)^*$$

Note that it really is necessary in the first two parts of the proof to make sure that $V_1 \cap V_2 = \emptyset$. Consider CFGs having productions

$$S_1 \rightarrow XA \qquad X \rightarrow c \qquad A \rightarrow a$$

and

$$S_2 \rightarrow XB \qquad X \rightarrow d \qquad B \rightarrow b$$

respectively. If we applied the construction in the first part of the proof without relabeling variables, the resulting grammar would allow the derivation

$$S \Rightarrow S_1 \Rightarrow XA \Rightarrow dA \Rightarrow da$$

even though $da$ is not derivable from either of the two original grammars.

**Corollary 6.1**   Every regular language is a CFL.

*Proof*
According to Definition 3.1, regular languages over $\Sigma$ are the languages obtained from $\emptyset$, $\{\Lambda\}$, and $\{a\}$ $(a \in \Sigma)$ by using the operations of union, concatenation, and Kleene *. Each of the primitive languages $\emptyset$, $\{\Lambda\}$, and $\{a\}$ is a context-free language. (In the first case we can use the trivial grammar with no productions, and in the other two cases one production is sufficient.) The corollary therefore follows from Theorem 6.1, using the principle of structural induction. ∎

**EXAMPLE 6.9**   A CFG Equivalent to a Regular Expression

Let $L$ be the language corresponding to the regular expression

$$(011 + 1)^*(01)^*$$

We can take a few obvious shortcuts in the algorithm provided by the proof of Theorem 6.1. The productions

$$A \rightarrow 011 \mid 1$$

generate the language $\{011, 1\}$. Following the third part of the theorem, we can use the productions

$$B \rightarrow AB \mid \Lambda$$
$$A \rightarrow 011 \mid 1$$

with $B$ as the start symbol to generate the language $\{011, 1\}^*$. Similarly, we can use

$$C \rightarrow DC \mid \Lambda$$
$$D \rightarrow 01$$

to derive $\{01\}^*$ from the start symbol $C$. Finally, we generate the concatenation of the two languages by adding the production $S \rightarrow BC$. The final grammar has start symbol $S$, auxiliary variables $A, B, C$, and $D$, and productions

$$S \rightarrow BC$$
$$B \rightarrow AB \mid \Lambda$$
$$A \rightarrow 011 \mid 1$$
$$C \rightarrow DC \mid \Lambda$$
$$D \rightarrow 01$$

Starting with any regular expression, we can obtain an equivalent CFG using the techniques illustrated in this example. In the next section we will see that any regular language $L$ can also be described by a CFG whose productions all have a very simple form, and that such a CFG can be obtained easily from an FA accepting $L$.

---

A CFG for $\{x \mid n_0(x) \neq n_1(x)\}$     **EXAMPLE 6.10**

Consider the language

$$L = \{x \in \{0, 1\}^* \mid n_0(x) \neq n_1(x)\}$$

Neither of the CFGs we found in Examples 6.7 and 6.8 for the complement of $L$ is especially helpful here. As we will see in Chapter 8, there is no general technique for finding a grammar generating the complement of a given CFL—which may in some cases not be a context-free language at all. However, we can express $L$ as the union of the languages $L_0$ and $L_1$, where

$$L_0 = \{x \in \{0, 1\}^* \mid n_0(x) > n_1(x)\}$$
$$L_1 = \{x \in \{0, 1\}^* \mid n_1(x) > n_0(x)\}$$

and thus we concentrate on finding a CFG $G_0$ generating the language $L_0$. Clearly $0 \in L_0$, and for any $x \in L_0$, both $x0$ and $0x$ are in $L_0$. This suggests the productions

$$S \rightarrow 0 \mid S0 \mid 0S$$

We also need to be able to add 1's to our strings. We cannot expect that adding a 1 to an element of $L_0$ will always produce an element of $L_0$; however, if we have two strings in $L_0$, concatenating them produces a string with at least two more 0's than 1's, and then adding a single 1 will still yield an element of $L_0$. We could add it at the left, at the right, or between the two. The corresponding productions are

$$S \rightarrow 1SS \mid SS1 \mid S1S$$

It is not hard to see that any string derived by using the productions

$$S \rightarrow 0 \mid S0 \mid 0S \mid 1SS \mid SS1 \mid S1S$$

is an element of $L_0$ (see Exercise 6.43). In the converse direction we can do even a little better: if $G_0$ is the grammar with productions

$$S \rightarrow 0 \mid 0S \mid 1SS \mid SS1 \mid S1S$$

every string in $L_0$ can be derived in $G_0$.

The proof is by induction on the length of the string. We consider the case that is probably hardest and leave the others to the exercises. As in previous examples, let $d(x) = n_0(x) - n_1(x)$. The basis step, for a string in $L_0$ of length 1, is straightforward. Suppose that $k \geq 1$ and that any $x$ for which $|x| \leq k$ and $d(x) > 0$ can be derived in $G_0$; and consider a string $x$ for which $|x| = k + 1$ and $d(x) > 0$.

We consider the case in which $x = 0y0$ for some string $y$. If $x$ contains only 0's, it can be derived from $S$ using the productions $S \rightarrow 0 \mid 0S$; we assume, therefore, that $x$ contains at least one 1. Our goal is to show that $x$ has the form

$$x = w1z \text{ for some } w \text{ and } z \text{ with } d(w) > 0 \text{ and } d(z) > 0$$

Once we have done this, the induction hypothesis will tell us that both $w$ and $z$ can be derived from $S$, so that we will be able to derive $x$ by starting with the production

$$S \to S1S$$

To show that $x$ has this form, suppose $x$ contains $n$ 1's, where $n \geq 1$. For each $i$ with $1 \leq i \leq n$, let $w_i$ be the prefix of $x$ up to but not including the $i$th 1, and $z_i$ the suffix of $x$ that follows this 1. In other words, for each $i$,

$$x = w_i 1 z_i$$

where the 1 is the $i$th 1 in $x$. If $d(w_n) > 0$, then we may let $w = w_n$ and $z = z_n$. The string $z_n$ is $0^j$ for some $j > 0$ because $x$ ends with 0, and we have the result we want. Otherwise, $d(w_n) \leq 0$. In this case we select the *first* $i$ with $d(w_i) \leq 0$, say $i = m$. Now since $x$ begins with 0, $d(w_1)$ must be $> 0$, which implies that $m \geq 2$. At this point, we can say that $d(w_{m-1}) > 0$ and $d(w_m) \leq 0$. Because $w_m$ has only one more 1 than $w_{m-1}$, $d(w_{m-1})$ can be no more than 1. Therefore, $d(w_{m-1}) = 1$. Since $x = w_{m-1}1z_{m-1}$, and $d(x) > 0$, it follows that $d(z_{m-1}) > 0$. This means that we get the result we want by letting $w = w_{m-1}$ and $z = z_{m-1}$. The proof in this case is complete.

For the other two cases, the one in which $x$ starts with 1 and the one in which $x$ ends with 1, see Exercise 6.44.

Now it is easy enough to obtain a context-free grammar $G$ generating $L$. We use $S$ as our start symbol, $A$ as the start symbol of the grammar we have just derived generating $L_0$, and $B$ as the start symbol for the corresponding grammar generating $L_1$. The grammar $G$ then has the productions

$$S \to A \mid B$$
$$A \to 0 \mid 0A \mid 1AA \mid AA1 \mid A1A$$
$$B \to 1 \mid 1B \mid 0BB \mid BB0 \mid B0B$$

**EXAMPLE 6.11**    Another Application of Theorem 6.1

Let $L = \{0^i 1^j 0^k \mid j > i + k\}$. We try expressing $L$ as the concatenation of CFLs, although what may seem at first like the obvious approach—writing $L$ as a concatenation $L_1 L_2 L_3$, where these three languages contain strings of 0's, strings of 1's, and strings of 0's, respectively—is doomed to failure. $L$ contains both $0^1 1^3 0^1$ and $0^1 1^4 0^2$, but if we allowed $L_1$ to contain $0^1$, $L_2$ to contain $1^3$, and $L_3$ to contain $0^2$, then $L_1 L_2 L_3$ would also contain $0^1 1^3 0^2$, and this string is not an element of $L$.

Observe that

$$0^i 1^{i+k} 0^k = 0^i 1^i\, 1^k 0^k$$

The only difference between this and a string $x$ in $L$ is that $x$ has at least one extra 1 in the middle:

$$x = 0^i 1^i\, 1^m\, 1^k 0^k \quad \text{(for some } m > 0)$$

A correct formula for $L$ is therefore $L = L_1 L_2 L_3$, where

$$L_1 = \{0^i 1^i \mid i \geq 0\}$$
$$L_2 = \{1^m \mid m > 0\}$$
$$L_3 = \{1^k 0^k \mid k \geq 0\}$$

The second part of Theorem 6.1, applied twice, reduces the problem to finding CFGs for these three languages.

$L_1$ is essentially the language in Example 6.2, $L_3$ is the same with the symbols 0 and 1 reversed, and $L_2$ can be generated by the productions

$$B \rightarrow 1B \mid 1$$

(The second production is $B \rightarrow 1$, not $B \rightarrow \Lambda$, since we want only nonnull strings.)

The final CFG $G = (V, \Sigma, S, P)$ incorporating these pieces is shown below.

$$V = \{S, A, B, C\} \qquad \Sigma = \{0, 1\}$$
$$P = \{\, S \rightarrow ABC$$
$$A \rightarrow 0A1 \mid \Lambda$$
$$B \rightarrow 1B \mid 1$$
$$C \rightarrow 1C0 \mid \Lambda\}$$

A derivation of $01^40^2 = (01)(1)(1^20^2)$, for example, is

$$S \Rightarrow ABC \Rightarrow 0A1BC \Rightarrow 0\Lambda 1BC \Rightarrow 011C$$
$$\Rightarrow 0111C0 \Rightarrow 01111C00 \Rightarrow 01111\Lambda 00 = 0111100$$

# 6.3 I REGULAR GRAMMARS

The proof of Theorem 6.1 provides an algorithm for constructing a CFG corresponding to a given regular expression. In this section, we consider another way of obtaining a CFG for a regular language $L$, this time starting with an FA accepting $L$. The resulting grammar is distinctive in two ways. First, the productions all have a very simple form, closely related to the moves of the FA; second, the construction is reversible, so that a CFG of this simple type can be used to generate a corresponding FA.

We can see how to proceed by looking at an example, the FA in Figure 6.1. It accepts the language $L = \{0, 1\}^*\{10\}$, the set of all strings over $\{0, 1\}$ that end in 10. One element of $L$ is $x = 110001010$. We trace its processing by the FA, as follows.

| Substring processed so far | State |
|---:|:---:|
| $\Lambda$ | $A$ |
| 1 | $B$ |
| 11 | $B$ |
| 110 | $C$ |
| 1100 | $A$ |
| 11000 | $A$ |
| 110001 | $B$ |
| 1100010 | $C$ |
| 11000101 | $B$ |
| 110001010 | $C$ |

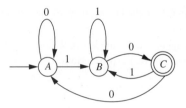

**Figure 6.1 |**

If we list the lines of this table consecutively, separated by $\Rightarrow$, we obtain

$$A \Rightarrow 1B \Rightarrow 11B \Rightarrow 110C \Rightarrow 1100A \Rightarrow 11000A \Rightarrow 110001B$$
$$\Rightarrow 1100010C \Rightarrow 11000101B \Rightarrow 110001010C$$

This looks like a derivation in a grammar. The grammar can be obtained by specifying the variables to be the states of the FA and starting with the productions

$$A \rightarrow 1B$$
$$B \rightarrow 1B$$
$$B \rightarrow 0C$$
$$C \rightarrow 0A$$
$$A \rightarrow 0A$$
$$C \rightarrow 1B$$

These include every production of the form

$$P \rightarrow aQ$$

where

$$P \overset{a}{\rightarrow} Q$$

is a transition in the FA. The start symbol is $A$, the initial state of the FA. To complete the derivation, we must remove the $C$ from the last string. We do this by adding the production $B \rightarrow 0$, so that the last step in the derivation is actually

$$11000101B \Rightarrow 110001010$$

Note that the production we have added is of the form

$$P \rightarrow a$$

where

$$P \overset{a}{\rightarrow} F$$

is a transition from $P$ to an accepting state $F$.

Any FA leads to a grammar in exactly this way. In our example it is easy to see that the language generated is exactly the one recognized by the FA. In general, we must qualify the statement slightly because the rules we have described for obtaining productions do not allow $\Lambda$-productions; however, it will still be true that the nonnull strings accepted by the FA are precisely those generated by the resulting grammar.

A significant feature of any derivation in such a grammar is that until the last step there is exactly one variable in the current string; we can think of it as the "state of the derivation," and in this sense the derivation simulates the processing of the string by the FA.

---

**Definition 6.3    Regular Grammars**

A grammar $G = (V, \Sigma, S, P)$ is *regular* if every production takes one of the two forms

$$B \rightarrow aC$$
$$B \rightarrow a$$

for variables $B$ and $C$ and terminals $a$.

---

**Theorem 6.2**

For any language $L \subseteq \Sigma^*$, $L$ is regular if and only if there is a regular grammar $G$ so that $L(G) = L - \{\Lambda\}$.

*Proof*

First, suppose that $L$ is regular, and let $M = (Q, \Sigma, q_0, A, \delta)$ be an FA accepting $L$. Define the grammar $G = (V, \Sigma, S, P)$ by letting $V = Q$, $S = q_0$, and

$$P = \{B \rightarrow aC \mid \delta(B, a) = C\} \cup \{B \rightarrow a \mid \delta(B, a) = F \text{ for some } F \in A\}$$

Suppose that $x = a_1 a_2 \cdots a_n$ is accepted by $M$, and $n \geq 1$. Then there is a sequence of transitions

$$\rightarrow q_0 \xrightarrow{a_1} q_1 \xrightarrow{a_2} q_2 \xrightarrow{a_3} \cdots \xrightarrow{a_{n-1}} q_{n-1} \xrightarrow{a_n} q_n$$

where $q_n \in A$. By definition of $G$, we have the corresponding derivation

$$S = q_0 \Rightarrow a_1 q_1 \Rightarrow a_1 a_2 q_2 \Rightarrow \cdots \Rightarrow a_1 a_2 \cdots a_{n-1} q_{n-1} \Rightarrow a_1 a_2 \cdots a_{n-1} a_n$$

Similarly, if $x$ is generated by $G$, it is clear that $x$ is accepted by $M$.

Conversely, suppose $G = (V, \Sigma, S, P)$ is a regular grammar generating $L$. To some extent we can reverse the construction above: We can define states corresponding to all the variables and create a transition

$$B \xrightarrow{a} C$$

for every production of the form $B \rightarrow aC$. Note that this is likely to introduce nondeterminism. We can handle the other type of production by adding one extra state $f$, which will be the only accepting state, and letting every production $B \rightarrow a$ correspond to a transition $B \xrightarrow{a} f$.

Our machine $M = (Q, \Sigma, q_0, A, \delta)$ is therefore an NFA. $Q$ is the set $V \cup \{f\}$, $q_0$ the start symbol $S$, and $A$ the set $\{f\}$. For any $q \in V$ and $a \in \Sigma$,

$$\delta(q, a) = \begin{cases} \{p \mid \text{the production } q \rightarrow ap \text{ is in } P\} & \text{if } q \rightarrow a \text{ is not in } P \\ \{p \mid q \rightarrow ap \text{ is in } P\} \cup \{f\} & \text{if } q \rightarrow a \text{ is in } P \end{cases}$$

There are no transitions out of $f$.

If $x = a_1 a_2 \cdots a_n \in L = L(G)$, then there is a derivation of the form

$$S \Rightarrow a_1 q_1 \Rightarrow a_1 a_2 q_2 \Rightarrow \cdots \Rightarrow a_1 a_2 \cdots a_{n-1} q_{n-1} \Rightarrow a_1 a_2 \cdots a_{n-1} a_n$$

and according to our definition of $M$, there is a corresponding sequence of transitions

$$q_0 \xrightarrow{a_1} q_1 \xrightarrow{a_2} \cdots \xrightarrow{a_{n-1}} q_{n-1} \xrightarrow{a_n} f$$

which implies that $x$ is accepted by $M$.

On the other hand, if $x = a_1 \cdots a_n$ is accepted by $M$, then $|x| \geq 1$ because $f$ is the only accepting state of $M$. The transitions causing $x$ to be accepted look like

$$q_0 \xrightarrow{a_1} q_1 \xrightarrow{a_2} \cdots \xrightarrow{a_{n-1}} q_{n-1} \xrightarrow{a_n} f$$

These transitions correspond to a derivation of $x$ in the grammar, and it follows that $x \in L(G)$.

Sometimes the term *regular* is applied to grammars that do not restrict the form of the reductions so severely. It can be shown (Exercise 6.12) that a language is regular if and only if it can be generated, except possibly for the null string, by a grammar in which all productions look like this:

$$B \rightarrow xC$$
$$B \rightarrow x$$

where $B$ and $C$ are variables and $x$ is a nonnull string of terminals. Grammars of this type are also called *linear*. The exercises discuss a few other variations as well.

## 6.4 | DERIVATION TREES AND AMBIGUITY

In a natural language such as English, understanding a sentence begins with understanding its grammatical structure, which means knowing how it is derived from the grammar rules for the language. Similarly, in a context-free grammar that specifies the syntax of a programming language or the rules for constructing an algebraic expression, interpreting a string correctly requires finding a correct derivation of the string in the grammar. A natural way of exhibiting the structure of a derivation is to draw a *derivation tree*, or *parse tree*. At the root of the tree is the variable with which the derivation begins. Interior nodes correspond to variables that appear in the derivation, and the children of the node corresponding to $A$ represent the symbols in a string $\alpha$ for which the production $A \rightarrow \alpha$ is used in the derivation. (In the case of a production $A \rightarrow \Lambda$, the node labeled $A$ has the single child $\Lambda$.)

In the simplest case, when the tree is the derivation tree for a string $x \in L(G)$ and there are no "$\Lambda$-productions" (of the form $A \rightarrow \Lambda$), the leaf nodes of the tree correspond precisely to the symbols of $x$. If there are $\Lambda$-productions, they show up in the tree, so that some of the leaf nodes correspond to $\Lambda$; of course, those nodes can be ignored as one scans the leaf nodes to see the string being derived, because $\Lambda$'s can be interspersed arbitrarily among the terminals without changing the string. In the most general case, we will also allow "derivations" that begin with some variable other than the start symbol of the grammar, and the string being derived may still contain some variables as well as terminal symbols.

In Example 6.4 we considered the CFG with productions

$$S \rightarrow S + S \mid S - S \mid S * S \mid S/S \mid (S) \mid a$$

The derivation

$$S \Rightarrow S - S \Rightarrow S * S - S \Rightarrow a * S - S \Rightarrow a * a - S \Rightarrow a * a - a$$

has the derivation tree show in Figure 6.2a. The derivation

$$S \Rightarrow S - S \Rightarrow S - S/S \Rightarrow \cdots \Rightarrow a - a/a$$

has the derivation tree shown in Figure 6.2b. In general, any derivation of a string in a CFL has a corresponding derivation tree (exactly one).

(There is a technical point here that is worth mentioning. With the two productions $S \rightarrow SS \mid a$, the sequence of steps $S \Rightarrow SS \Rightarrow SSS \Rightarrow^* aaa$ can be interpreted two ways, because in the second step it could be either the first $S$ or the second that is replaced by $SS$. The two interpretations correspond to two different derivation trees. For this reason, we say that specifying a derivation means giving not only the sequence of strings but also the position in each string at which the next substitution occurs. The steps $S \Rightarrow SS \Rightarrow SSS$ already represent two different derivations.)

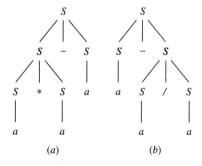

$(a)$ $\qquad$ $(b)$

**Figure 6.2 |**
Derivation trees for two algebraic
expressions.

**Figure 6.3 |**
Expression tree
corresponding to
Figure 6.1*a*.

Algebraic expressions such as the two shown in Figure 6.2 are often represented by *expression trees*—binary trees in which terminal nodes correspond to identifiers or constants and nonterminal nodes correspond to operators. The expression tree in Figure 6.3 conveys the same information as the derivation tree in Figure 6.2*a*, except that only the nodes representing terminal symbols are drawn.

One step in a derivation is the replacement of a variable (to be precise, a particular occurrence of a variable) by the string on the right side of a production. The derivation is the entire sequence of such steps, and in a *sequence* the order of the steps is significant. The derivations

$$S \Rightarrow S + S \Rightarrow a + S \Rightarrow a + a$$

and

$$S \Rightarrow S + S \Rightarrow S + a \Rightarrow a + a$$

are therefore different. However, they are different only in a trivial way: When the current string is $S + S$, the $S$ that is used in the next step is the leftmost $S$ in the first derivation and the rightmost in the second. A precise way to say that these derivations are not significantly different is to say that their derivation trees are the same. A derivation tree specifies completely which productions are used in the derivation, as well as where the right side of each production fits in the string being derived. It does not specify the "temporal" order in which the variables are used, and this order plays no role in using the derivation to interpret the string's structure. Two derivations that correspond to the same derivation tree are essentially the same.

Another way to compare two derivations is to normalize each of them, by requiring that each follow the same rule as to which variable to replace first whenever there is a choice, and to compare the normalized versions. A derivation is a *leftmost* derivation if the variable used in each step is always the leftmost variable of the ones in the current string. If the two derivations being compared are both leftmost and are still different, it seems reasonable to say that they are essentially, or significantly, different.

In fact, these two criteria for "essentially the same" are equivalent. On the one hand, leftmost derivations corresponding to different derivation trees are clearly different, because as we have already observed, any derivation corresponds to only one derivation tree. On the other hand, the derivation trees corresponding to two different leftmost derivations are also different, and we can see this as follows. Consider the first step at which the derivations differ; suppose that this step is

$$x A \beta \Rightarrow x \alpha_1 \beta$$

in one derivation and

$$x A \beta \Rightarrow x \alpha_2 \beta$$

in the other. Here $x$ is a string of terminals, since the derivations are leftmost; $A$ is a variable; and $\alpha_1 \neq \alpha_2$. The two derivation trees must both have a node labeled $A$, and the respective portions of the two trees to the left of this node must be identical, because the leftmost derivations have been the same up to this point. These two nodes have different sets of children, however, and the trees cannot be the same.

We conclude that a string of terminals has more than one derivation tree if and only if it has more than one leftmost derivation. Notice that in this discussion "leftmost" could just as easily be "rightmost"; the important thing is not what order is followed, only that some clearly defined order be followed consistently, so that the two normalized versions can be compared meaningfully.

As we have already noticed, a string can have two or more essentially different derivations in the same CFG.

---

**Definition 6.4    An Ambiguous CFG**

A context-free grammar $G$ is *ambiguous* if there is at least one string in $L(G)$ having two or more distinct derivation trees (or, equivalently, two or more distinct leftmost derivations).

---

It is not hard to see that the ambiguity defined here is closely related to the ambiguity we encounter every day in written and spoken language. The reporter who wrote the headline "Disabled Fly to See Carter," which appeared during the administration of the thirty-ninth U.S. President, probably had in mind a derivation such as

$$S \rightarrow \langle\text{collective noun}\rangle\langle\text{verb}\rangle \cdots$$

However, one that begins

$$S \rightarrow \langle\text{adjective}\rangle\langle\text{noun}\rangle \cdots$$

might suggest a more intriguing or at least less predictable story. Understanding a sentence or a newspaper headline requires picking the right grammatical derivation for it.

---

## Ambiguity in the CFG in Example 6.4    EXAMPLE 6.12

Let us return to the algebraic-expression CFG discussed in Example 6.4, with productions

$$S \rightarrow S + S \mid S - S \mid S * S \mid S/S \mid (S) \mid a$$

In that example we considered two essentially different derivations of the string

$$a + (a * a)/a - a$$

and in fact the two derivations were both leftmost, which therefore demonstrates the ambiguity of the grammar. This can also be demonstrated using only the productions $S \rightarrow S + S$ and $S \rightarrow a$; the string $a + a + a$ has leftmost derivations

$$S \Rightarrow S + S \Rightarrow a + S \Rightarrow a + S + S \Rightarrow a + a + S \Rightarrow a + a + a$$

and

$$S \Rightarrow S + S \Rightarrow S + S + S \Rightarrow a + S + S \Rightarrow a + a + S \Rightarrow a + a + a$$

The corresponding derivation trees are shown in Figures 6.4$a$ and 6.4$b$, respectively.

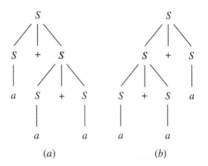

**Figure 6.4 |**
Two derivation trees for $a + a + a$.

Although the difference in the two interpretations of the string $a + a + a$ is not quite as dramatic as in Example 6.4 (the expression is viewed as the sum of two subexpressions in both cases), the principle is the same. The expression is interpreted as $a + (a + a)$ in one case, and $(a + a) + a$ in the other. The parentheses might be said to remove the ambiguity as to how the expression is to be interpreted. We will examine this property of parentheses more carefully in the next section, when we discuss an unambiguous CFG equivalent to this one.

It is easy to see by studying Example 6.12 that every CFG containing a production of the general form $A \rightarrow A\alpha A$ is ambiguous. However, there are more subtle ways in which ambiguity occurs, and characterizing the ambiguous context-free grammars in any nontrivial way turns out to be difficult or impossible (see Section 11.6).

**EXAMPLE 6.13** The "Dangling Else"

A standard example of ambiguity in programming languages is the "dangling else" phenomenon. Consider the productions

⟨statement⟩ → if (⟨expression⟩) ⟨statement⟩ |

if (⟨expression⟩) ⟨statement⟩ else ⟨statement⟩ |

⟨otherstatement⟩

describing the *if* statement of Example 6.5 as well as the related *if-else* statement, both part of the C language. Now consider the statement

```
if (expr1) if (expr2) f(); else g();
```

This can be derived in two ways from the grammar rules. In one, illustrated in Figure 6.5*a*, the *else* goes with the first *if*, and in the other, illustrated in Figure 6.5*b*, it goes with the second. A C compiler should interpret the statement the second way, but not as a result of the syntax rules given; this is additional information with which the compiler must be furnished.

Just as in Example 6.12, parentheses or their equivalent could be used to remove the ambiguity in the statement.

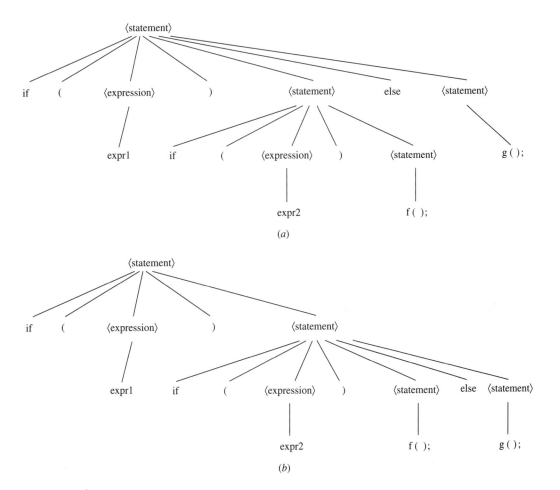

**Figure 6.5 |**
Two interpretations of a "dangling else."

```
if (expr1) {if (expr2) f();} else g();
```
forces the first interpretation, whereas
```
if (expr1) {if (expr2) f(); else g();}
```
forces the second. In some other languages, the appropriate version of "parentheses" is BEGIN …END.

It is possible, however, to find grammar rules equivalent to the given ones that incorporate the correct interpretation into the syntax. Consider the formulas

$$\langle statement \rangle \rightarrow \langle st1 \rangle \mid \langle st2 \rangle$$

$$\langle st1 \rangle \rightarrow \text{if } ((\langle expression \rangle)) \langle st1 \rangle \text{ else } \langle st1 \rangle \mid \langle otherstatement \rangle$$

$$\langle st2 \rangle \rightarrow \text{if } ((\langle expression \rangle)) \langle statement \rangle \mid$$

$$\text{if } ((\langle expression \rangle)) \langle st1 \rangle \text{ else } \langle st2 \rangle$$

These generate the same strings as the original rules and can be shown to be unambiguous. Although we will not present a proof of either fact, you can see the intuitive reason for the second. The variable ⟨ st1 ⟩ represents a statement in which every *if* is matched by a corresponding *else*, while any statement derived from ⟨ st2 ⟩ contains at least one unmatched *if*. The only variable appearing before *else* in these formulas is ⟨ st1 ⟩; since the *else* cannot match any of the *if*s in the statement derived from ⟨ st1 ⟩, it must match the *if* that appeared in the formula with the *else*.

It is interesting to compare both these sets of formulas with the corresponding ones in the official grammar for the Modula-2 programming language:

$$⟨statement⟩ → IF ⟨expression⟩ THEN ⟨statementsequence⟩ END \ |$$
$$IF ⟨expression⟩ THEN ⟨statementsequence⟩$$
$$ELSE ⟨statementsequence⟩ END \ |$$
$$⟨otherstatement⟩$$

These obviously resemble the rules for C in the first set above. However, the explicit END after each sequence of one or more statements allows the straightforward grammar rule to avoid the "dangling else" ambiguity. The Modula-2 statement corresponding most closely to the tree in Figure 6.5*a* is

```
IF A1 THEN IF A2 THEN S1 END ELSE S2 END
```

while Figure 6.5*b* corresponds to

```
IF A1 THEN IF A2 THEN S1 ELSE S2 END END
```

---

# 6.5 | AN UNAMBIGUOUS CFG FOR ALGEBRAIC EXPRESSIONS

Although it is possible to prove that some context-free languages are inherently ambiguous, in the sense that they can be produced only by ambiguous grammars, ambiguity is normally a property of the grammar rather than the language. If a CFG is ambiguous, it is often possible and usually desirable to find an equivalent unambiguous CFG. In this section, we will solve this problem in the case of the algebraic-expression grammar discussed in Example 6.4.

For the sake of simplicity we will use only the two operators + and ∗ in our discussion, so that $G$ has productions

$$S \ → \ S + S \ | \ S ∗ S \ | \ (S) \ | \ a$$

Once we obtain an unambiguous grammar equivalent to this one, it will be easy to reinstate the other operators.

Our final grammar will not have either $S → S + S$ or $S → S ∗ S$, because either production by itself is enough to produce ambiguity. We will also keep in mind the possibility, mentioned in Example 6.4, of incorporating into the grammar the standard rules of order and operator precedence: $*$ should have higher precedence than $+$, and $a + a + a$ should "mean" $(a + a) + a$, not $a + (a + a)$.

In trying to eliminate $S \to S + S$ and $S \to S * S$, it is helpful to remember Example 2.15, where we discussed possible recursive definitions of $L^*$. Two possible ways of obtaining new elements of $L^*$ are to concatenate two elements of $L^*$ and to concatenate an element of $L^*$ with an element of $L$; we observed that the second approach preserves the direct correspondence between one application of the recursive rule and one of the "primitive" strings being concatenated. Here this idea suggests that we replace $S \to S + S$ by either $S \to S + T$ or $S \to T + S$, where the variable $T$ stands for a *term*, an expression that cannot itself be expressed as a sum. If we remember that $a + a + a = (a + a) + a$, we would probably choose $S \to S + T$ as more appropriate; in other words, an expression consists of (all but the last term) plus the last term. Because an expression can also consist of a single term, we will also need the production $S \to T$. At this point, we have

$$S \to S + T \mid T$$

We may now apply the same principle to the set of terms. Terms can be products; however, rather than thinking of a term as a product of terms, we introduce *factors*, which are terms that cannot be expressed as products. The corresponding productions are

$$T \to T * F \mid F$$

So far we have a hierarchy of levels. Expressions, the most general objects, are sums of one or more terms, and terms are products of one or more factors. This hierarchy incorporates the precedence of multiplication over addition, and the productions we have chosen also incorporate the fact that both the $+$ and $*$ operations associate to the left.

It should now be easy to see where parenthesized expressions fit into the hierarchy. (Although we might say $(A)$ could be an expression or a term or a factor, we should permit ourselves only one way of deriving it, and we must decide which is most appropriate.) A parenthesized expression cannot be expressed directly as either a sum or a product, and it therefore seems most appropriate to consider it a factor. To say it another way, evaluation of a parenthetical expression should take precedence over any operators outside the parentheses; therefore, $(A)$ should be considered a factor, because in our hierarchy factors are evaluated first. What is inside the parentheses should be an *expression*, since it is not restricted at all.

The grammar that we end up with is $G1 = (V, \Sigma, S, P)$, where $V = \{S, T, F\}$ and $P$ contains the productions

$$S \to S + T \mid T$$
$$T \to T * F \mid F$$
$$F \to (S) \mid a$$

We must now prove two things: first, that $G1$ is indeed equivalent to the original grammar $G$, and second, that it is unambiguous. To avoid confusion, we relabel the start symbol in $G1$.

**Theorem 6.3**

Let $G$ be the context-free grammar with productions

$$S \rightarrow S + S \mid S * S \mid (S) \mid a$$

and let $G1$ be the context-free grammar with productions

$$S1 \rightarrow S1 + T \mid T$$
$$T \rightarrow T * F \mid F$$
$$F \rightarrow (S1) \mid a$$

Then $L(G) = L(G1)$.

*Proof*

**First, to show $L(G1) \subseteq L(G)$.** The proof is by induction on the length of a string in $L(G1)$. The basis step is to show that $a \in L(G)$, and this is clear.

In the induction step we assume that $k \geq 1$ and that every $y$ in $L(G1)$ satisfying $|y| \leq k$ is in $L(G)$. We must show that if $x \in L(G1)$ and $|x| = k + 1$, then $x \in L(G)$. Since $x \neq a$, any derivation of $x$ in $G1$ must begin in one of these three ways:

$$S1 \Rightarrow S1 + T$$
$$S1 \Rightarrow T \Rightarrow T * F$$
$$S1 \Rightarrow T \Rightarrow F \Rightarrow (S1)$$

We give a proof in the first case, and the other two are very similar. If $x$ has a derivation beginning $S1 \Rightarrow S1 + T$, then $x = y + z$, where $S1 \Rightarrow^*_{G1} y$ and $T \Rightarrow^*_{G1} z$. Since $S1 \Rightarrow^*_{G1} T$, it follows that $S1 \Rightarrow^*_{G1} z$. Therefore, since $|y|$ and $|z|$ must be $\leq k$, the induction hypothesis implies that $y$ and $z$ are both in $L(G)$. Since $G$ contains the production $S \rightarrow S + S$, the string $y + z$ is derivable from $S$ in $G$, and therefore $x \in L(G)$.

**Second, to show $L(G) \subseteq L(G1)$.** Again we use induction on $|x|$, and just as in the first part, the basis step is straightforward. We assume that $k \geq 1$ and that for every $y \in L(G$ with $|y| \leq k$, $y \in L(G1)$; we wish to show that if $x \in L(G)$ and $|x| = k + 1$, then $x \in L(G1)$.

The simplest case is that in which $x$ has a derivation in $G$ beginning $S \rightarrow (S)$. In this case $x = (y)$, for some $y$ in $L(G)$, and it follows from the inductive hypothesis that $y \in L(G1)$. Therefore, we can derive $x$ in $G1$, by starting the derivation $S1 \Rightarrow T \Rightarrow F \Rightarrow (S1)$ and then deriving $y$ from $S1$.

Suppose $x$ has a derivation in $G$ that begins $S \rightarrow S + S$. Then just as before, the induction hypothesis tells us that $x = y + z$, where $y$ and $z$ are both in $L(G1)$. Now, however, in order to conclude that $x \in L(G1)$, we need $z$ to be derivable from $T$; in other words, we would like $z$ to be a single term, the last of the terms whose sum is $x$. With this in mind, let

$$x = x_1 + x_2 + \cdots + x_n$$

where each $x_i \in L(G1)$ and $n$ is as large as possible. We have already determined that $n \geq 2$. Because of the way $n$ is defined, none of the $x_i$'s can have a derivation in $G1$ that begins $S1 \Rightarrow S1 + T$; therefore, every $x_i$ can be derived from $T$ in $G1$. Let

$$y = x_1 + x_2 + \cdots + x_{n-1} \qquad z = x_n$$

Then $y$ can be derived from $S1$, since $S1 \Rightarrow^*_{G1} T + T + \cdots + T \quad (n - 1$ terms), and $z$ can be derived from $T$. It follows that $x \in L(G1)$, since we can start with the production $S1 \rightarrow S1 + T$.

Finally, suppose that every derivation of $x$ in $G$ begins $S \Rightarrow S*S$. Then for some $y$ and $z$ in $L(G)$, $x = y*z$. This time we let

$$x = x_1 * x_2 * \cdots * x_n$$

where each $x_i \in L(G)$ and $n$ is as large as possible. (Note the difference between this statement and the one in the previous case.) Then by the inductive hypothesis, each $x_i \in L(G1)$. What we would like this time is for each $x_i$ to be derivable from $F$ in $G_1$. We can easily rule out the case where some $x_i$ has a derivation in $G1$ that begins $S1 \Rightarrow T \Rightarrow T * F$. If this were true, $x_i$ would be of the form $y_i * z_i$ for some $y_i, z_i \in L(G1)$; since we know $L(G1) \subseteq L(G)$, this would contradict the maximal property of the number $n$.

Suppose that some $x_i$ had a derivation in $G1$ beginning $S1 \Rightarrow S1 + T$. Then $x_i = y_i + z_i$ for some $y_i, z_i \in L(G1) \subseteq L(G)$. In this case,

$$x = x_1 * x_2 * \cdots * x_{i-1} * y_i + z_i * x_{i+1} * \cdots * x_n$$

This is impossible too. If we let $u$ and $v$ be the substrings before and after the $+$, respectively, we clearly have $u, v \in L(G)$, and therefore $x = u + v$. This means that we could derive $x$ in $G$ using a derivation that begins $S \Rightarrow S + S$, and we have assumed that this is not the case.

We may conclude that each $x_i$ is derivable from $F$ in $G1$. Then, as we did in the previous case, we let

$$y = x_1 * x_2 * \cdots * x_{n-1} \qquad z = x_n$$

The string $y$ is derivable from $T$ in $G1$, since $F * F * \cdots * F \quad (n - 1$ factors) is. Therefore, we may derive $x$ from $S1$ in $G1$ by starting the derivation $S1 \Rightarrow T \Rightarrow T * F$, and so $x \in L(G1)$.

In order to show that the grammar $G1$ is unambiguous, it will be helpful to concentrate on the parentheses in a string, temporarily ignoring the other terminal symbols. In a sense we want to convince ourselves that the grammar is unambiguous insofar as it generates strings of parentheses; this will then allow us to demonstrate the unambiguity of the entire grammar. In Exercise 5.34, we defined a string of parentheses to be *balanced* if it is the string of parentheses appearing in some legal algebraic expression. At this point, however, we must be a little more explicit.

### Definition 6.5    Balanced Strings of Parentheses

A string of left and right parentheses is *balanced* if it has equal numbers of left and right parentheses, and no prefix has more right than left. The *mate* of a left parenthesis in a balanced string is the first right parenthesis following it for which the string containing those two and everything in between is balanced. If $x$ is a string containing parentheses and other symbols, and the parentheses within $x$ form a balanced string, a symbol $\sigma$ in $x$ is *within parentheses* if $\sigma$ appears between some left parenthesis and its mate.

You should spend a minute convincing yourself that every left parenthesis in a balanced string has a mate (Exercise 6.30). The first observation we make is that the string of parentheses in any string obtained from $S1$ in the grammar $G1$ is balanced. Certainly it has equal numbers of left and right parentheses, since they are produced in pairs. Moreover, for every right parenthesis produced by a derivation in $G1$, a left parenthesis appearing before it is produced simultaneously, and so no prefix of the string can have more right parentheses than left.

Secondly, observe that in any derivation in $G1$, the parentheses between and including the pair produced by a single application of the production $F \rightarrow (S1)$ form a balanced string. This is because the parentheses within the string derived from $S1$ do, and because enclosing a balanced string of parentheses within parentheses yields a balanced string.

Now suppose that $x \in L(G1)$, and $(_0$ is any left parenthesis in $x$. The statement that there is only one leftmost derivation of $x$ in $G1$ will follow if we can show that $G1$ is unambiguous, and we will be able to do this very soon. For now, however, the discussion above allows us to say that even if there are several leftmost derivations of $x$, the right parenthesis produced at the same time as $(_0$ is the same for any of them—it is simply the mate of $(_0$. To see this, let us consider a fixed derivation of $x$. In this derivation, the step in which $(_0$ is produced also produces a right parenthesis, which we call $)_0$. As we have seen in the previous paragraph, the parentheses in $x$ beginning with $(_0$ and ending with $)_0$ form a balanced string. This implies that the mate of $(_0$ cannot appear after $)_0$, because of how "mate" is defined.

However, the mate of $(_0$ cannot appear before $)_0$ either. Suppose $\alpha$ is the string of parentheses starting just after $(_0$ and ending with the mate of $(_0$. The string $\alpha$ has an excess of right parentheses, because $(_0 \alpha$ is balanced. Let $\beta$ be the string of parentheses strictly between $(_0$ and $)_0$. Then $\beta$ is balanced. If the mate of $(_0$ appeared before $)_0$, $\alpha$ would be a prefix of $\beta$, and this is impossible. Therefore, the mate of $(_0$ coincides with $)_0$.

The point of this discussion is that when we say that something is *within parentheses*, we can be sure that the parentheses it is within are the two parentheses produced by the production $F \rightarrow (S1)$, no matter what derivation we have in mind. This is the ingredient we need for our theorem.

**Theorem 6.4**
The context-free grammar $G1$ with productions

$$S1 \rightarrow S1 + T \mid T$$
$$T \rightarrow T * F \mid F$$
$$F \rightarrow (S1) \mid a$$

is unambiguous.

*Proof*
We wish to show that every string $x$ in $L(G1)$ has only one leftmost derivation from $S1$. The proof will be by mathematical induction on $|x|$, and it will actually be easier to prove something apparently stronger: For any $x$ derivable from one of the variables $S1$, $T$, or $F$, $x$ has only one leftmost derivation from that variable.

For the basis step, we observe that $a$ can be derived from any of the three variables, and that in each case there is only one derivation.

In the induction step, we assume that $k \geq 1$ and that for every $y$ derivable from $S1$, $T$, or $F$ for which $|y| \leq k$, $y$ has only one leftmost derivation from that variable. We wish to show the same result for a string $x$ with $|x| = k+1$.

Consider first the case in which $x$ contains at least one $+$ not within parentheses. Since the only $+$'s in strings derivable from $T$ or $F$ are within parentheses, $x$ can be derived only from $S1$, and any derivation of $x$ must begin $S1 \Rightarrow S1 + T$, where this $+$ is the last $+$ in $x$ that is not within parentheses. Therefore, any leftmost derivation of $x$ from $S1$ has the form

$$S1 \; \Rightarrow \; S1 + T \; \Rightarrow^* \; y + T \; \Rightarrow^* \; y + z$$

where the last two steps represent leftmost derivations of $y$ from $S1$ and $z$ from $T$, respectively, and the $+$ is still the last one not within parentheses. The induction hypothesis tells us that $y$ has only one leftmost derivation from $S1$ and $z$ has only one from $T$. Therefore, $x$ has only one leftmost derivation from $S1$.

Next consider the case in which $x$ contains no $+$ outside parentheses but at least one $*$ outside parentheses. This time $x$ can be derived only from $S1$ or $T$; any derivation from $S1$ must begin $S1 \Rightarrow T \Rightarrow T * F$; and any derivation from $T$ must begin $T \Rightarrow T * F$. In either case, the $*$ must be the last one in $x$ that is not within parentheses. As in the first case, the subsequent steps of any leftmost derivation must be

$$T * F \; \Rightarrow^* \; y * F \; \Rightarrow^* \; y * z$$

consisting first of a leftmost derivation of $y$ from $T$ and then of a leftmost derivation of $z$ from $F$. Again the induction hypothesis tells us that there is only one possible way for these derivations to proceed, and so there is only one leftmost derivation of $x$ from $S1$ or $T$.

Finally, suppose $x$ contains no $+$'s or $*$'s outside parentheses. Then $x$ can be derived from any of the variables, but the only derivation from $S1$ begins $S1 \Rightarrow T \Rightarrow F \Rightarrow (S1)$, and the only derivation from $T$ or $F$ begins the same way with the first one or two steps omitted. Therefore, $x = (y)$, where $S1 \Rightarrow^* y$. By the induction hypothesis, $y$ has only one leftmost derivation from $S1$, and it follows that $x$ has only one from each of the three variables. This completes the proof.

## 6.6 | SIMPLIFIED FORMS AND NORMAL FORMS

Ambiguity is one undesirable property of a context-free grammar that we might wish to eliminate. In this section we discuss some slightly more straightforward ways of improving a grammar without changing the resulting language: first by eliminating certain types of productions that may be awkward to work with, and then by standardizing the productions so that they all have a certain "normal form."

We begin by trying to eliminate "$\Lambda$-productions," those of the form $A \to \Lambda$, and "unit productions," in which one variable is simply replaced by another. To illustrate how these improvements might be useful, suppose that a grammar contains neither type of production, and consider a derivation containing the step

$$\alpha \Rightarrow \beta$$

If there are no $\Lambda$-productions, then the string $\beta$ must be at least as long as $\alpha$; if there are no unit productions, $\alpha$ and $\beta$ can be of equal length only if this step consists of replacing a variable by a single terminal. To say it another way, if $l$ and $t$ represent the length of the current string and the number of terminals in the current string, respectively, then the quantity $l + t$ must increase at each step of the derivation. The value of $l + t$ is 1 for the string $S$ and $2k$ for a string $x$ of length $k$ in the language. We may conclude that a derivation of $x$ can have no more than $2k - 1$ steps. In particular, we now have an algorithm for determining whether a given string $x$ is in the language generated by the grammar: If $|x| = k$, try all possible sequences of $2k - 1$ productions, and see if any of them produces $x$. Although this is not usually a practical algorithm, at least it illustrates the fact that information about the form of productions can be used to derive conclusions about the resulting language.

In trying to eliminate $\Lambda$-productions from a grammar, we must begin with a qualification. We obviously cannot eliminate all productions of this form if the string $\Lambda$ itself is in the language. This obstacle is only minor, however: We will be able to show that for any context-free language $L$, $L - \{\Lambda\}$ can be generated by a CFG with no $\Lambda$-productions. A preliminary example will help us see how to proceed.

Eliminating $\Lambda$-productions from a CFG    **EXAMPLE 6.14**

Let $G$ be the context-free grammar with productions

$$S \rightarrow ABCBCDA$$
$$A \rightarrow CD$$
$$B \rightarrow Cb$$
$$C \rightarrow a \mid \Lambda$$
$$D \rightarrow bD \mid \Lambda$$

The first thing this example illustrates is probably obvious already: We cannot simply throw away the $\Lambda$-productions without adding anything. In this case, if $D \rightarrow \Lambda$ is eliminated then nothing can be derived, because the $\Lambda$-production is the only way to remove the variable $D$ from the current string.

Let us consider the production $S \rightarrow ABCBCDA$, which we write temporarily as

$$S \rightarrow ABC_1BC_2DA$$

The three variables $C_1$, $C_2$, and $D$ on the right side all begin $\Lambda$-productions, and each can also be used to derive a nonnull string. In a derivation we may replace none, any, or all of these three by $\Lambda$. Without $\Lambda$-productions, we will need to allow for all these options by adding productions of the form $S \rightarrow \alpha$, where $\alpha$ is a string obtained from $ABCBCDA$ by deleting some or all of $\{C_1, C_2, D\}$. In other words, we will need at least the productions

$$S \rightarrow ABBC_2DA \mid ABC_1BDA \mid ABC_1BC_2A \mid$$
$$ABBDA \mid ABBC_2A \mid ABC_1BA \mid$$
$$ABBA$$

in addition to the one we started with, in order to make sure of obtaining all the strings that can be obtained from the original grammar.

If we now consider the variable $A$, we see that these productions are still not enough. Although $A$ does not begin a $\Lambda$-production, the string $\Lambda$ can be derived from $A$ (as can other nonnull strings). Starting with the production $A \rightarrow CD$, we can leave out $C$ or $D$, using the same argument as before. We cannot leave out both, because we do not want the production $A \rightarrow \Lambda$ in our final grammar. If we add subscripts to the occurrences of $A$, as we did to those of $C$, so that the original production is

$$S \rightarrow A_1BC_1BC_2DA_2$$

we need to add productions in which the right side is obtained by leaving out some subset of $\{A_1, A_2, C_1, C_2, D\}$. There are 32 subsets, which means that from this original production we obtain 31 others that will be added to our grammar.

The same reasoning applies to each of the original productions. If we can identify in the production $X \rightarrow \alpha$ all the variables occurring in $\alpha$ from which $\Lambda$ can be derived, then we can add all the productions $X \rightarrow \alpha'$, where $\alpha'$ is obtained from $\alpha$ by deleting some of these occurrences. In general this procedure might produce new $\Lambda$-productions—if so, they are ignored—and it might produce productions of the form $X \rightarrow X$, which also contribute nothing to the grammar and can be omitted.

In this case our final context-free grammar has 40 productions, including the 32 $S$-productions already mentioned and the ones that follow:

$$A \rightarrow CD \mid C \mid D$$
$$B \rightarrow Cb \mid b$$
$$C \rightarrow a$$
$$D \rightarrow bD \mid b$$

The procedure outlined in Example 6.14 is the one that we will show works in general. In presenting it more systematically, we give first a recursive definition of a *nullable* variable (one from which $\Lambda$ can be derived), and then we give the algorithm suggested by this definition for identifying such variables.

---

**Definition 6.6  Nullable Variables**

A *nullable* variable in a CFG $G = (V, \Sigma, S, P)$ is defined as follows.

1. Any variable $A$ for which $P$ contains the production $A \rightarrow \Lambda$ is nullable.
2. If $P$ contains the production $A \rightarrow B_1 B_2 \ldots B_n$ and $B_1, B_2, \ldots, B_n$ are nullable variables, then $A$ is nullable.
3. No other variables in $V$ are nullable.

---

**Algorithm FindNull (Finding the nullable variables in a CFG $(V, \Sigma, S, P)$)**

$N_0 = \{A \in V \mid P \text{ contains the production } A \rightarrow \Lambda\};$
$i = 0;$
do
   $i = i + 1;$
   $N_i = N_{i-1} \cup \{A \mid P \text{ contains } A \rightarrow \alpha \text{ for some } \alpha \in N_{i-1}^*\}$
while $N_i \neq N_{i-1};$
$N_i$ is the set of nullable variables.  ∎

You can easily convince yourself that the variables defined in Definition 6.6 are the variables $A$ for which $A \Rightarrow^* \Lambda$. Obtaining the algorithm FindNull from the definition is straightforward, and a similar procedure can be used whenever we have such a recursive definition (see Exercise 2.70). When we apply the algorithm in Example 6.14, the set $N_0$ is $\{C, D\}$. The set $N_1$ also contains $A$, as a result of the production $A \rightarrow CD$. Since no other productions have right sides in $\{A, C, D\}^*$, these three are the only nullable variables in the grammar.

**Algorithm 6.1 (Finding an equivalent CFG with no $\Lambda$-productions)**   Given a CFG $G = (V, \Sigma, S, P)$, construct a CFG $G1 = (V, \Sigma, S, P1)$ with no $\Lambda$-productions as follows.

1. Initialize $P1$ to be $P$.

2. Find all nullable variables in $V$, using Algorithm FindNull.

3. For every production $A \to \alpha$ in $P$, add to $P1$ every production that can be obtained from this one by deleting from $\alpha$ one or more of the occurrences of nullable variables in $\alpha$.

4. Delete all $\Lambda$-productions from $P1$. Also delete any duplicates, as well as productions of the form $A \to A$. ∎

---

**Theorem 6.5**

Let $G = (V, \Sigma, S, P)$ be any context-free grammar, and let $G1$ be the grammar obtained from $G$ by Algorithm 6.1. Then $G1$ has no $\Lambda$-productions, and $L(G1) = L(G) - \{\Lambda\}$.

*Proof*

That $G1$ has no $\Lambda$-productions is obvious. We show a statement that is slightly stronger than that in the theorem: For any variable $A \in V$, and any nonnull $x \in \Sigma^*$,

$$A \Rightarrow_G^* x \text{ if and only if } A \Rightarrow_{G1}^* x$$

We use the notation $A \Rightarrow_G^k x$ to mean that there is a $k$-step derivation of $x$ from $A$ in $G$.

We show first that for any $n \geq 1$, if $A \Rightarrow_G^n x$, then $A \Rightarrow_{G1}^* x$. The proof is by mathematical induction on $n$. For the basis step, suppose $A \Rightarrow_G^1 x$. Then $A \to x$ is a production in $P$. Since $x \neq \Lambda$, this production is also in $P1$, and so $A \Rightarrow_{G1}^* x$.

In the induction step we assume that $k \geq 1$ and that any string other than $\Lambda$ derivable from $A$ in $k$ or fewer steps in $G$ is derivable from $A$ in $G1$. We wish to show that if $x \neq \Lambda$ and $A \Rightarrow_G^{k+1} x$, then $A \Rightarrow_{G1}^* x$. Suppose that the first step in a $(k + 1)$-step derivation of $x$ in $G$ is $A \to X_1 X_2 \cdots X_n$, where each $X_i$ is either a variable or a terminal. Then $x = x_1 x_2 \cdots x_n$, where each $x_i$ is either equal to $X_i$ or derivable from $X_i$ in $k$ or fewer steps in $G$. Any $X_i$ for which the corresponding $x_i$ is $\Lambda$ is a nullable variable in $G$. If we delete these $X_i$'s from the string $X_1 X_2 \cdots X_n$, there are still some left, since $x \neq \Lambda$, and the resulting production is an element of $P1$. Furthermore, the induction hypothesis tells us that for each $X_i$ remaining in the right side of this production, $X_i \Rightarrow_{G1}^* x_i$. Therefore, $A \Rightarrow_{G1}^* x$.

Now we show the converse, that for any $n \geq 1$, if $A \Rightarrow_{G1}^n x$, then $A \Rightarrow_G^* x$; again the proof is by induction on $n$. If $A \Rightarrow_{G1}^1 x$, then $A \to x$ is a production in $P1$. This means that $A \to \alpha$ is a production in $P$, where $x$ is obtained from $\alpha$ by deleting zero or more nullable variables. It follows that $A \Rightarrow_G^* x$, because we can begin a derivation with the production $A \to \alpha$ and proceed by deriving $\Lambda$ from each of the nullable variables that was deleted to obtain $x$.

Suppose that $k \geq 1$ and that any string other than $\Lambda$ derivable from $A$ in $k$ or fewer steps in $G1$ is derivable from $A$ in $G$. We wish to show the same result for a string $x$ for which $A \Rightarrow_{G1}^{k+1} x$. Again, let the first step of a $(k+1)$-step derivation of $x$ in $G1$ be $A \rightarrow X_1 X_2 \cdots X_n$, where each $X_i$ is either a variable or a terminal. We may write $x = x_1 x_2 \cdots x_n$, where each $x_i$ is either equal to $X_i$ or derivable from $X_i$ in $k$ or fewer steps in $G_1$. By the induction hypothesis, $X_i \Rightarrow_G^* x_i$ for each $i$. By definition of $G1$, there is a production $A \rightarrow \alpha$ in $P$ so that $X_1 X_2 \cdots X_n$ can be obtained from $\alpha$ by deleting certain nullable variables. Since $A \Rightarrow_G^* X_1 X_2 \cdots X_n$, we can derive $x$ from $A$ in $G$ by first deriving $X_1 X_2 \cdots X_n$ and then deriving each $x_i$ from the corresponding $X_i$.

Eliminating $\Lambda$-productions from a grammar is likely to increase the number of productions substantially. We might ask whether any other undesirable properties are introduced. One partial answer is that if the context-free grammar $G$ is unambiguous, then the grammar $G1$ produced by Algorithm 6.1 is also (Exercise 6.64).

The next method of modifying a context-free grammar, eliminating unit productions, is similar enough in principle to what we have just done that we omit many of the details or leave them to the exercises. Just as it was necessary before to consider all nullable variables as well as those that actually begin $\Lambda$-productions, here it is necessary to consider all the pairs of variables $A$, $B$ for which $A \Rightarrow^* B$ as well as the pairs for which there is actually a production $A \rightarrow B$. In order to guarantee that eliminating unit productions does not also eliminate strings in the language, we make sure that whenever $B \rightarrow \alpha$ is a nonunit production and $A \Rightarrow^* B$, we add the production $A \rightarrow \alpha$.

In order to simplify the process of finding all such pairs $A$, $B$, we make the simplifying assumption that we have already used Algorithm 6.1 if necessary so that the grammar has no $\Lambda$-productions. It follows in this case that one variable can be derived from another only by a sequence of unit productions. For any variable $A$, we may therefore formulate the following recursive definition of the set of "$A$-derivable" variables (essentially, variables $B$ other than $A$ for which $A \Rightarrow^* B$), and the definition can easily be adapted to obtain an algorithm.

1.  If $A \rightarrow B$ is a production, $B$ is $A$-derivable.
2.  If $C$ is $A$-derivable, $C \rightarrow B$ is a production, and $B \neq A$, then $B$ is $A$-derivable.
3.  No other variables are $A$-derivable.

(Note that according to our definition, a variable $A$ is $A$-derivable only if $A \rightarrow A$ is actually a production.)

**Algorithm 6.2 (Finding an equivalent CFG with no unit productions)**   Given a context-free grammar $G = (V, \Sigma, S, P)$ with no $\Lambda$-productions, construct a grammar $G1 = (V, \Sigma, S, P1)$ having no unit productions as follows.

1.  Initialize $P1$ to be $P$.
2.  For each $A \in V$, find the set of $A$-derivable variables.

**3.** For every pair $(A, B)$ such that $B$ is $A$-derivable, and every nonunit production $B \to \alpha$, add the production $A \to \alpha$ to $P1$ if it is not already present in $P1$.

**4.** Delete all unit productions from $P1$.

---

**Theorem 6.6**

Let $G$ be any CFG without $\Lambda$-productions, and let $G1$ be the CFG obtained from $G$ by Algorithm 6.2. Then $G1$ contains no unit productions, and $L(G1) = L(G)$.

---

The proof is omitted (Exercise 6.62). It is worth pointing out, again without proof, that if the grammar $G$ is unambiguous, then the grammar $G1$ obtained from the algorithm is also.

Eliminating Unit Productions    **EXAMPLE 6.15**

Let $G$ be the algebraic-expression grammar obtained in the previous section, with productions

$$S \to S + T \mid T$$
$$T \to T * F \mid F$$
$$F \to (S) \mid a$$

The $S$-derivable variables are $T$ and $F$, and $F$ is $T$-derivable. In step 3 of Algorithm 6.2, the productions $S \to T * F \mid (S) \mid a$ and $T \to (S) \mid a$ are added to $P1$. When unit productions are deleted, we are left with

$$S \to S + T \mid T * F \mid (S) \mid a$$
$$T \to T * F \mid (S) \mid a$$
$$F \to (S) \mid a$$

---

In addition to eliminating specific types of productions, such as $\Lambda$-productions and unit productions, it may also be useful to impose restrictions upon the form of the remaining productions. Several types of "normal forms" have been introduced; we shall present one of them, the Chomsky normal form.

---

**Definition 6.7    Chomsky Normal Form**

A context-free grammar is in *Chomsky normal form* (CNF) if every production is of one of these two types:

$$A \to BC$$
$$A \to a$$

where $A$, $B$, and $C$ are variables and $a$ is a terminal symbol.

Transforming a grammar $G = (V, \Sigma, S, P)$ into Chomsky normal form may be done in three steps. The first is to apply Algorithms 6.1 and 6.2 to obtain a CFG $G1 = (V, \Sigma, S, P1)$ having neither $\Lambda$-productions nor unit productions so that $L(G1) = L(G)-\{\Lambda\}$. The second step is to obtain a grammar $G2 = (V2, \Sigma, S, P2)$, generating the same language as $G1$, so that every production in $P2$ is either of the form

$$A \to B_1 B_2 \cdots B_k$$

where $k \geq 2$ and each $B_i$ is a variable in $V2$, or of the form

$$A \to a$$

for some $a \in \Sigma$.

The construction of $G2$ is very simple. Since $P1$ contains no $\Lambda$-productions or unit productions, every production in $P1$ that is not already of the form $A \to a$ looks like $A \to \alpha$ for some string $\alpha$ of length at least 2. For every terminal $a$ appearing in such a string $\alpha$, we introduce a new variable $X_a$ and a new production $X_a \to a$, and replace $a$ by $X_a$ in all the productions where it appears (except those of the form $A \to a$).

For example, if there were two productions $A \to aAb$ and $B \to ab$, they would be replaced by $A \to X_a A X_b$ and $B \to X_a X_b$, and the productions $X_a \to a$ and $X_b \to b$ would be added. The only $X_a$-production is $X_a \to a$, and so it is reasonably clear that $G2$ is equivalent to $G1$.

The grammar $G2$ obtained this way now resembles a grammar in CNF, in the sense that the right side of every production is either a single terminal or a string of two or more variables. The last step is to replace each production having more than two variables on the right by an equivalent set of productions, each one having exactly two variables on the right. This process is described best by an example; the production

$$A \to BCDBCE$$

would be replaced by

$$A \to BY_1$$
$$Y_1 \to CY_2$$
$$Y_2 \to DY_3$$
$$Y_3 \to BY_4$$
$$Y_4 \to CE$$

The new variables $Y_1, Y_2, Y_3, Y_4$ are specific to this production and would be used nowhere else. Although this may seem wasteful, in terms of the number of variables, at least there is no doubt that the combined effect of this set of five productions is precisely equivalent to the original production. Adding these new variables and productions therefore does not change the language generated.

If we are willing to let these informal arguments suffice, we have obtained the following result.

> **Theorem 6.7**
>
> For any context-free grammar $G = (V, \Sigma, S, P)$, there is a CFG $G' = (V', \Sigma, S, P')$ in Chomsky normal form so that $L(G') = L(G) - \{\Lambda\}$.

## Converting a CFG to Chomsky Normal Form    EXAMPLE 6.16

Let $G$ be the grammar with productions

$$S \to AACD$$
$$A \to aAb \mid \Lambda$$
$$C \to aC \mid a$$
$$D \to aDa \mid bDb \mid \Lambda$$

Let us go through each step of the conversion to CNF.

1. **Eliminating $\Lambda$-productions.** The nullable variables are $A$ and $D$, and Algorithm 6.1 produces the grammar with productions

$$S \to AACD \mid ACD \mid AAC \mid CD \mid AC \mid C$$
$$A \to aAb \mid ab$$
$$C \to aC \mid a$$
$$D \to aDa \mid bDb \mid aa \mid bb$$

2. **Eliminating unit productions.** Here we may simply add the productions

$$S \to aC \mid a$$

and delete $S \to C$.

3. **Restricting the right sides of productions to single terminals or strings of two or more variables.** This step yields the productions

$$S \to AACD \mid ACD \mid AAC \mid CD \mid AC \mid X_aC \mid a$$
$$A \to X_aAX_b \mid X_aX_b$$
$$C \to X_aC \mid a$$
$$D \to X_aDX_a \mid X_bDX_b \mid X_aX_a \mid X_bX_b$$
$$X_a \to a$$
$$X_b \to b$$

4. **The final step to CNF.** There are six productions whose right sides are too long. Applying our algorithm produces the grammar with productions

$$
\begin{array}{lll}
S \to AT_1 & T_1 \to AT_2 & T_2 \to CD \\
S \to AU_1 & U_1 \to CD & \\
S \to AV_1 & V_1 \to AC &
\end{array}
$$

$$S \rightarrow CD \mid AC \mid X_aC \mid a$$
$$A \rightarrow X_aW_1 \qquad W_1 \rightarrow AX_b$$
$$A \rightarrow X_aX_b$$
$$C \rightarrow X_aC \mid a$$
$$D \rightarrow X_aY_1 \qquad Y_1 \rightarrow DX_a$$
$$D \rightarrow X_bZ_1 \qquad Z_1 \rightarrow DX_b$$
$$D \rightarrow X_aX_b \mid X_bX_b$$
$$X_a \rightarrow a \qquad X_b \rightarrow b$$

# EXERCISES

**6.1.** In each case, say what language is generated by the context-free grammar with the indicated productions.

a.
$$S \rightarrow aSa \mid bSb \mid \Lambda$$

b.
$$S \rightarrow aSa \mid bSb \mid a \mid b$$

c.
$$S \rightarrow aSb \mid bSa \mid \Lambda$$

d.
$$S \rightarrow aSa \mid bSb \mid aAb \mid bAa$$
$$A \rightarrow aAa \mid bAb \mid a \mid b \mid \Lambda$$

(See Example 6.3.)

e.
$$S \rightarrow aS \mid bS \mid a$$

f.
$$S \rightarrow SS \mid bS \mid a$$

g.
$$S \rightarrow SaS \mid b$$

h.
$$S \rightarrow aT \mid bT \mid \Lambda$$
$$T \rightarrow aS \mid bS$$

**6.2.** Find a context-free grammar corresponding to the "syntax diagram" in Figure 6.6.

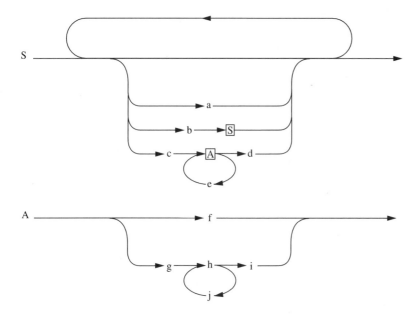

**Figure 6.6 |**

**6.3.** A context-free grammar is sometimes specified in the form of BNF rules; the letters are an abbreviation for Backus-Naur Form. In these rules, the symbol ::= corresponds to the usual →, and $\{X\}$ means zero or more occurrences of $X$. Find a context-free grammar corresponding to the BNF rules shown below. Uppercase letters denote variables, lowercase denote terminals.

$$P ::= p\ I;\ |\ p\ I\ (F\ \{;\ F\})$$
$$F ::= G\ |\ v\ G\ |\ f\ G\ |\ p\ I\ \{,\ I\}$$
$$G ::= I\ \{,\ I\}:\ I$$
$$I ::= L\ \{L_1\}$$
$$L_1 ::= L\ |\ D$$
$$L ::= a\ |\ b$$
$$D ::= 0\ |\ 1$$

**6.4.** In each case, find a CFG generating the given language.
   a.  The set of odd-length strings in $\{a, b\}^*$ with middle symbol $a$.
   b.  The set of even-length strings in $\{a, b\}^*$ with the two middle symbols equal.
   c.  The set of odd-length strings in $\{a, b\}^*$ whose first, middle, and last symbols are all the same.

**6.5.** In each case, the productions in a CFG are given. Prove that neither one generates the language $L = \{x \in \{0, 1\}^* \mid n_0(x) = n_1(x)\}$.

a.

$$S \rightarrow S01S \mid S10S \mid \Lambda$$

b.

$$S \rightarrow 0S1 \mid 1S0 \mid 01S \mid 10S \mid S01 \mid S10 \mid \Lambda$$

**6.6.** Consider the CFG with productions

$$S \rightarrow aSbScS \mid aScSbS \mid bSaScS \mid bScSaS \mid cSaSbS \mid cSbSaS \mid \Lambda$$

Does this generate the language $\{x \in \{a, b, c\}^* \mid n_a(x) = n_b(x) = n_c(x)\}$?
Prove your answer.

**6.7.** Find a context-free grammar generating the language of all regular expressions over an alphabet $\Sigma$:

a. If the definition of regular expression is interpreted strictly with regard to parentheses.

b. If the definition is interpreted so as to allow regular expressions that are not "fully parenthesized."

Be careful to distinguish between $\Lambda$-productions and productions whose right side is the symbol $\Lambda$ appearing in a regular expression; use $\lambda$ in the second case.

**6.8.** This problem gives proposed alternative constructions for the CFGs $G_u$, $G_c$, and $G^*$ in Theorem 6.1. In each case, either prove that the construction works, or give an example of grammars for which it doesn't and say why it doesn't.

a. (For $G_u$) $V_u = V_1 \cup V_2$;   $S_u = S_1$;   $P_u = P_1 \cup P_2 \cup \{S_1 \rightarrow S_2\}$

b. (For $G_c$) $V_c = V_1 \cup V_2$;   $S_c = S_1$;   $P_c = P_1 \cup P_2 \cup \{S_1 \rightarrow S_1S_1\}$

c. (For $G^*$) $V = V_1$;   $S = S_1$;   $P = P_1 \cup \{S_1 \rightarrow S_1S_1 \mid \Lambda\}$

**6.9.** Find context-free grammars generating each of these languages.

a. $\{a^i b^j c^k \mid i = j + k\}$

b. $\{a^i b^j c^k \mid j = i + k\}$

c. $\{a^i b^j c^k \mid j = i \text{ or } j = k\}$

d. $\{a^i b^j c^k \mid i = j \text{ or } i = k\}$

e. $\{a^i b^j c^k \mid i < j \text{ or } i > k\}$

f. $\{a^i b^j \mid i \leq 2j\}$

g. $\{a^i b^j \mid i < 2j\}$

h. $\{a^i b^j \mid i \leq j \leq 2i\}$

**6.10.** Describe the language generated by each of these grammars.

a. The regular grammar with productions

$$S \rightarrow aA \mid bC \mid b$$
$$A \rightarrow aS \mid bB$$
$$B \rightarrow aC \mid bA \mid a$$
$$C \rightarrow aB \mid bS$$

b. The grammar with productions

$$S \rightarrow bS \mid aA \mid \Lambda$$
$$A \rightarrow aA \mid bB \mid b$$
$$B \rightarrow bS$$

**6.11.** Show that for a language $L \subseteq \Sigma^*$ such that $\Lambda \notin L$, the following statements are equivalent.

a. $L$ is regular.

b. $L$ can be generated by a grammar in which all productions are either of the form $A \rightarrow xB$ or of the form $A \rightarrow x$ (where $A$ and $B$ are variables and $x \in \Sigma^+$).

c. $L$ can be generated by a grammar in which all productions are either of the form $A \rightarrow Bx$ or of the form $A \rightarrow x$ (where $A$ and $B$ are variables and $x \in \Sigma^+$).

**6.12.** Show that for any language $L \subseteq \Sigma^*$, the following statements are equivalent.

a. $L$ is regular.

b. $L$ can be generated by a grammar in which all productions are either of the form $A \rightarrow xB$ or of the form $A \rightarrow x$ (where $A$ and $B$ are variables and $x \in \Sigma^*$).

c. $L$ can be generated by a grammar in which all productions are either of the form $A \rightarrow Bx$ or of the form $A \rightarrow x$ (where $A$ and $B$ are variables and $x \in \Sigma^*$).

**6.13.** Given the FA shown in Figure 6.7, accepting the language $L$, find a regular grammar generating $L - \{\Lambda\}$.

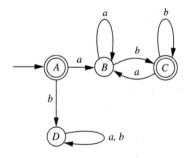

**Figure 6.7** |

**6.14.** Draw an NFA accepting the language generated by the grammar with productions

$$S \rightarrow abA \mid bB \mid aba$$
$$A \rightarrow b \mid aB \mid bA$$
$$B \rightarrow aB \mid aA$$

**6.15.** Show that if the procedure described in the proof of Theorem 6.2 is applied to an NFA instead of an FA, the result is still a regular grammar generating the language accepted by the NFA.

**6.16.** Consider the following statement. For any language $L \subseteq \Sigma^*$, $L$ is regular if and only if $L$ can be generated by some grammar in which every production takes one of the four forms $B \to a$, $B \to Ca$, $B \to aC$, or $B \to \Lambda$, where $B$ and $C$ are variables and $a \in \Sigma$. For both the "if" and the "only if" parts, give either a proof or a counterexample.

**6.17.** A context-free grammar is said to be *self-embedding* if there is some variable $A$ and two nonnull strings of terminals $\alpha$ and $\beta$ so that $A \Rightarrow^* \alpha A \beta$. Show that a language $L$ is regular if and only if it can be generated by a grammar that is not self-embedding.

**6.18.** Each of the following grammars, though not regular, generates a regular language. In each case, find a regular grammar generating the language.

a. $S \to SSS \mid a \mid ab$

b. $S \to AabB \qquad A \to aA \mid bA \mid \Lambda \qquad B \to Bab \mid Bb \mid ab \mid b$

c. $S \to AAS \mid ab \mid aab \qquad A \to ab \mid ba \mid \Lambda$

d. $S \to AB \qquad A \to aAa \mid bAb \mid a \mid b \qquad B \to aB \mid bB \mid \Lambda$

e. $S \to AA \mid B \qquad A \to AAA \mid Ab \mid bA \mid a \qquad B \to bB \mid b$

**6.19.** Refer to Example 6.4.

a. Draw the derivation tree corresponding to each of the two given derivations of $a + (a * a)/a - a$.

b. Write the rightmost derivation corresponding to each of the trees in (a).

c. How many distinct leftmost derivations of this string are there?

d. How many derivation trees are there for the string $a + a + a + a + a$?

e. How many derivation trees are there for the string $(a + (a + a)) + (a + a)$?

**6.20.** Give an example of a CFG and a string of variables and/or terminals derivable from the start symbol for which there is neither a leftmost derivation nor a rightmost derivation.

**6.21.** Consider the C statements
```
x = 1; if (a > 2) if (a > 4) x = 2; else x = 3;
```
a. What is the resulting value of x if $a = 3$? If $a = 1$?

b. Same question as in (a), but this time assume that the statement is interpreted as in Figure 6.5a.

**6.22.** Show that the CFG with productions

$$S \to a \mid Sa \mid bSS \mid SSb \mid SbS$$

is ambiguous.

**6.23.** Consider the context-free grammar with productions

$$S \to AB \qquad A \to aA \mid \Lambda \qquad B \to ab \mid bB \mid \Lambda$$

Any derivation of a string in this grammar must begin with the production $S \rightarrow AB$. Clearly, any string derivable from $A$ has only one derivation from $A$, and likewise for $B$. Therefore, the grammar is unambiguous. True or false? Why? (Compare with the proof of Theorem 6.4.)

**6.24.** In each part of Exercise 6.1, decide whether the grammar is ambiguous or not, and prove your answer.

**6.25.** For each of the CFGs in Examples 6.3, 6.9, and 6.11, determine whether or not the grammar is ambiguous, and prove your answer.

**6.26.** In each case, show that the grammar is ambiguous, and find an equivalent unambiguous grammar.

    a. $S \rightarrow SS \mid a \mid b$

    b. $S \rightarrow ABA \qquad A \rightarrow aA \mid \Lambda \qquad B \rightarrow bB \mid \Lambda$

    c. $S \rightarrow A \mid B \qquad A \rightarrow aAb \mid ab \qquad B \rightarrow abB \mid \Lambda$

    d. $S \rightarrow aSb \mid aaSb \mid \Lambda$

    e. $S \rightarrow aSb \mid abS \mid \Lambda$

**6.27.** Find an unambiguous context-free grammar equivalent to the grammar with productions

$$S \rightarrow aaaaS \mid aaaaaaaS \mid \Lambda$$

(See Exercise 2.50.)

**6.28.** The proof of Theorem 6.1 shows how to find a regular grammar generating $L$, given a finite automaton accepting $L$.

    a.  Under what circumstances is the grammar obtained this way unambiguous?

    b.  Describe how the grammar can be modified if necessary in order to make it unambiguous.

**6.29.** Describe an algorithm for starting with a regular grammar and finding an equivalent unambiguous grammar.

**6.30.** Show that every left parenthesis in a balanced string has a mate.

**6.31.** Show that if $a$ is a left parenthesis in a balanced string, and $b$ is its mate, then $a$ is the last left parentheses for which the string consisting of $a$ and $b$ and everything in between is balanced.

**6.32.** Find an unambiguous context-free grammar for the language of all algebraic expressions involving parentheses, the identifier $a$, and the four binary operators $+$, $-$, $*$, and $/$.

**6.33.** Show that the nullable variables defined by Definition 6.6 are precisely those variables $A$ for which $A \Rightarrow^* \Lambda$.

**6.34.** In each case, find a context-free grammar with no $\Lambda$-productions that generates the same language, except possibly for $\Lambda$, as the given CFG.

    a.

$$S \rightarrow AB \mid \Lambda \qquad A \rightarrow aASb \mid a \qquad B \rightarrow bS$$

b.

$$S \to AB \mid ABC$$
$$A \to BA \mid BC \mid \Lambda \mid a$$
$$B \to AC \mid CB \mid \Lambda \mid b$$
$$C \to BC \mid AB \mid A \mid c$$

**6.35.** In each case, given the context-free grammar $G$, find a CFG $G'$ with no $\Lambda$-productions and no unit productions that generates the language $L(G) - \{\Lambda\}$.

a.  $G$ has productions

$$S \to ABA \qquad A \to aA \mid \Lambda \qquad B \to bB \mid \Lambda$$

b.  $G$ has productions

$$S \to aSa \mid bSb \mid \Lambda \qquad A \to aBb \mid bBa \qquad B \to aB \mid bB \mid \Lambda$$

c.  $G$ has productions

$$S \to A \mid B \mid C \qquad A \to aAa \mid B \qquad B \to bB \mid bb$$
$$C \to aCaa \mid D \qquad D \to baD \mid abD \mid aa$$

**6.36.** A variable $A$ in a context-free grammar $G = (V, \Sigma, S, P)$ is *live* if $A \Rightarrow^* x$ for some $x \in \Sigma^*$. Give a recursive definition, and a corresponding algorithm, for finding all live variables in $G$.

**6.37.** A variable $A$ in a context-free grammar $G = (V, \Sigma, S, P)$ is *reachable* if $S \Rightarrow^* \alpha A \beta$ for some $\alpha, \beta \in (\Sigma \cup V)^*$. Give a recursive definition, and a corresponding algorithm, for finding all reachable variables in $G$.

**6.38.** A variable $A$ is a context-free grammar $G = (V, \Sigma, S, P)$ is *useful* if for some string $x \in \Sigma^*$, there is a derivation of $x$ that takes the form

$$S \Rightarrow^* \alpha A \beta \Rightarrow^* x$$

A variable that is not useful is *useless*. Clearly if a variable is either not live or not reachable (Exercises 6.36–6.37), then it is useless.

a.  Give an example in which a variable is both live and reachable but still useless.

b.  Let $G$ be a CFG. Suppose $G1$ is obtained by eliminating all dead variables from $G$ and eliminating all productions in which dead variables appear. Suppose $G2$ is then obtained from $G1$ by eliminating all variables unreachable in $G1$, as well as productions in which such variables appear. Show that $G2$ contains no useless variables, and $L(G2) = L(G)$.

c.  Show that if the two steps are done in the opposite order, the resulting grammar may still have useless variables.

d.  In each case, given the context-free grammar $G$, find an equivalent CFG with no useless variables.

i. $G$ has productions

$$S \rightarrow ABC \mid BaB \qquad A \rightarrow aA \mid BaC \mid aaa$$
$$B \rightarrow bBb \mid a \qquad C \rightarrow CA \mid AC$$

ii. $G$ has productions

$$S \rightarrow AB \mid AC \qquad A \rightarrow aAb \mid bAa \mid a \qquad B \rightarrow bbA \mid aaB \mid AB$$
$$C \rightarrow abCa \mid aDb \qquad D \rightarrow bD \mid aC$$

**6.39.** In each case, given the context-free grammar $G$, find a CFG $G'$ in Chomsky normal form generating $L(G) - \{\Lambda\}$.

a. $G$ has productions $S \rightarrow SS \mid (S) \mid \Lambda$

b. $G$ has productions $S \rightarrow S(S) \mid \Lambda$

c. $G$ is the CFG in Exercise 6.35c

d. $G$ has productions

$$S \rightarrow AaA \mid CA \mid BaB \qquad A \rightarrow aaBa \mid CDA \mid aa \mid DC$$
$$B \rightarrow bB \mid bAB \mid bb \mid aS \qquad C \rightarrow Ca \mid bC \mid D \qquad D \rightarrow bD \mid \Lambda$$

**6.40.** If $G$ is a context-free grammar in Chomsky normal form and $x \in L(G)$ with $|x| = k$, how many steps are there in a derivation of $x$ in $G$?

# MORE CHALLENGING PROBLEMS

**6.41.** Describe the language generated by the CFG with productions

$$S \rightarrow aS \mid aSbS \mid \Lambda$$

One way to understand this language is to replace $a$ and $b$ by left and right parentheses, respectively. However, the language can also be characterized by giving a property that every prefix of a string in the language must have.

**6.42.** Show that the language of all nonpalindromes over $\{a, b\}$ (see Example 6.3) cannot be generated by any CFG in which $S \rightarrow aSa \mid bSb$ are the only productions with variables on the right side.

**6.43.** Show using mathematical induction that every string produced by the context-free grammar with productions

$$S \rightarrow 0 \mid S0 \mid 0S \mid 1SS \mid SS1 \mid S1S$$

has more 0's than 1's.

**6.44.** Complete the proof in Example 6.10 that every string in $\{0, 1\}^*$ with more 0's than 1's can be generated by the CFG with productions $S \rightarrow 0 \mid 0S \mid 1SS \mid SS1 \mid S1S$. (Take care of the two remaining cases.)

**6.45.** Let $L$ be the language generated by the CFG with productions

$$S \rightarrow aSb \mid ab \mid SS$$

Show using mathematical induction that no string in $L$ begins with $abb$.

**6.46.** Describe the language generated by the CFG with productions

$$S \to ST \mid \Lambda \qquad T \to aS \mid bT \mid b$$

Prove that your answer is correct.

**6.47.** Show that the context-free grammar with productions

$$S \to bS \mid aT \mid \Lambda$$
$$T \to aT \mid bU \mid \Lambda$$
$$U \to aT \mid \Lambda$$

generates the language of all strings over the alphabet $\{a, b\}$ that do not contain the substring $abb$. One approach is to use mathematical induction to prove two three-part statements. In both cases, each part starts with "For every $n \geq 0$, if $x$ is any string of length $n$,". In the first statement, the three parts end as follows: (i) if $S \Rightarrow^* x$, then $x$ does not contain the substring $abb$; (ii) if $T \Rightarrow^* x$, then $x$ does not contain the substring $bb$; (iii) if $U \Rightarrow^* x$, then $x$ does not start with $b$ and does not contain the substring $bb$. In the second statement, the three parts end with the converses of (i), (ii), and (iii). The reason for using two three-part statements, rather than six separate statements, is that in proving each of the two, the induction hypothesis will say something about all three types of strings: those derivable from $S$, those derivable from $T$, and those derivable from $U$.

**6.48.** What language over $\{0, 1\}$ does the CFG with productions

$$S \to 00S \mid 11S \mid S00 \mid S11 \mid 01S01 \mid 01S10 \mid 10S10 \mid 10S01 \mid \Lambda$$

generate? Prove your answer.

**6.49.** Complete the proof of Theorem 6.3, by taking care of the two remaining cases in the first part of the proof.

**6.50.** Show using mathematical induction that the CFG with productions

$$S \to 0B \mid 1A \mid \Lambda$$
$$A \to 0S \mid 1AA$$
$$B \to 1S \mid 0BB$$

generates the language $L = \{x \in \{0, 1\}^* \mid n_0(x) = n_1(x)\}$ (See Example 6.8) It would be appropriate to formulate two three-part statements, as in Exercise 6.47, this time involving the variables $S$, $A$, and $B$ and the languages $L$, $L_0$, and $L_1$.

**6.51.** Prove that the CFG with productions $S \to 0S1S \mid 1S0S \mid \Lambda$ generates the language $L = \{x \in \{0, 1\}^* \mid n_0(x) = n_1(x)\}$.

**6.52.**  a.  Describe the language generated by the CFG $G$ with productions

$$S \to SS \mid (S) \mid \Lambda$$

  b.  Show that the CFG $G_1$ with productions

$$S_1 \to (S_1)S_1 \mid \Lambda$$

generates the same language. (One inclusion is easy. For the other one, it may be helpful to prove the following statements for a string $x \in L(G)$ with $|x| > 0$. First, if there is no derivation of $x$ beginning with the production $S \to (S)$, then there are strings $y$ and $z$, both in $L(G)$ and both shorter than $x$, for which $x = yz$. Second, if there are such strings $y$ and $z$, and if there are no other such strings $y'$ and $z'$ with $y'$ shorter than $y$, then there is a derivation of $y$ in $G$ that starts with the production $S \to (S)$.)

**6.53.** Show that the CFG with productions

$$S \to aSaSbS \mid aSbSaS \mid bSaSaS \mid \Lambda$$

generates the language $\{x \in \{a, b\}^* \mid n_a(x) = 2n_b(x)\}$.

**6.54.** Does the CFG with productions

$$S \to aSaSb \mid aSbSa \mid bSaSaS \mid \Lambda$$

generate the language of the previous problem? Prove your answer.

**6.55.** Show that the following CFG generates the language $\{x \in \{a, b\}^* \mid n_a(x) = 2n_b(x)\}$.

$$S \to SS \mid bTT \mid TbT \mid TTb \mid \Lambda \qquad T \to aS \mid SaS \mid Sa \mid a$$

**6.56.** For alphabets $\Sigma_1$ and $\Sigma_2$, a *homomorphism* from $\Sigma_1^*$ to $\Sigma_2^*$ is defined in Exercise 4.46. Show that if $f : \Sigma_1^* \to \Sigma_2^*$ is a homomorphism and $L \subseteq \Sigma_1^*$ is a context-free language, then $f(L) \subseteq \Sigma_2^*$ is also a CFG.

**6.57.** Show that the CFG with productions

$$S \to S(S) \mid \Lambda$$

is unambiguous.

**6.58.** Find context-free grammars generating each of these languages.
   a. $\{a^i b^j c^k \mid i \neq j + k\}$
   b. $\{a^i b^j c^k \mid j \neq i + k\}$

**6.59.** Find context-free grammars generating each of these languages, and prove that your answers are correct.
   a. $\{a^i b^j \mid i \leq j \leq 3i/2\}$
   b. $\{a^i b^j \mid i/2 \leq j \leq 3i/2\}$

**6.60.** Let $G$ be the context-free grammar with productions

$$S \to aS \mid aSbS \mid c$$

and let $G_1$ be the one with productions

$$S_1 \to T \mid U \qquad T \to aTbT \mid c \qquad U \to aS_1 \mid aTbU$$

($G_1$ is a simplified version of the second grammar in Example 6.13.)
   a. Show that $G$ is ambiguous.
   b. Show that $G$ and $G_1$ generate the same language.
   c. Show that $G_1$ is unambiguous.

**6.61.** Let $x$ be a string of left and right parentheses. A *complete pairing* of $x$ is a partition of the parentheses of $x$ into pairs such that (i) each pair consists of one left parenthesis and one right parenthesis appearing somewhere after it; and (ii) the parentheses *between* those in a pair are themselves the union of pairs. Two parentheses in a pair are said to be *mates* with respect to that pairing.

    a.  Show that there is at most one complete pairing of a string of parentheses.

    b.  Show that a string of parentheses has a complete pairing if and only if it is a balanced string, according to Definition 6.5, and in this case the two definitions of mates coincide.

**6.62.** Give a proof of Theorem 6.6. Suggestion: in order to show that $L(G) \subseteq L(G1)$, show that for every $n \geq 1$, and every string of variables and/or terminals that can be derived from $S$ in $G$ by an $n$-step leftmost derivation in which the last step is not a unit production can be derived from $S$ in $G1$.

**6.63.** Show that if a context-free grammar is unambiguous, then the grammar obtained from it by Algorithm 6.1 is also.

**6.64.** Show that if a context-free grammar with no $\Lambda$-productions is unambiguous, then the one obtained from it by Algorithm 6.2 is also.

# 7

# Pushdown Automata

## 7.1 | INTRODUCTION BY WAY OF AN EXAMPLE

In this chapter we investigate how to extend our finite-state model of computation so that we can recognize context-free languages. In our first example, we consider one of the simplest nonregular context-free languages. Although the abstract machine we describe is not obviously related to a CFG generating the language, we will see later that a machine of the same general type can be used with any CFL, and that one can be constructed very simply from a grammar.

An Abstract Machine to Accept Simple Palindromes  **EXAMPLE 7.1**

Let $G$ be the context-free grammar having productions

$$S \to aSa \mid bSb \mid c$$

$G$ generates the language

$$L = \{xcx^r \mid x \in \{a, b\}^*\}$$

The strings in $L$ are odd-length palindromes over $\{a, b\}$ (Example 6.3), except that the middle symbol is $c$. (We will consider ordinary palindromes shortly. For now, the "marker" in the middle makes it easier to recognize the string.)

It is not hard to design an algorithm for recognizing strings in $L$, using a single left-to-right pass. We will save the symbols in the first half of the string as we read them, so that once we encounter the $c$ we can begin matching incoming symbols with symbols already read. In order for this to work, we must retrieve the symbols we have saved using the rule "last in, first out" (often abbreviated LIFO): The symbol used to match the next incoming symbol is the one most recently read, or saved. The data structure incorporating the LIFO rule is a *stack*, which is usually implemented as a list in which one end is designated as the *top*. Items are always added ("pushed onto the stack") and deleted ("popped off the stack") at this end, and at any time, the only element of the stack that is immediately accessible is the one on top.

In trying to incorporate this algorithm in an abstract machine, it would be reasonable to say that the current "state" of the machine is determined in part by the current contents of the stack. However, this approach would require an infinite set of "states," because the stack needs to be able to hold arbitrarily long strings. It is convenient instead to continue using a finite set of states—although the machine is not a "finite-state machine" in the same way that an FA is, because the current state is not enough to specify the machine's status—and to think of the stack as a simple form of auxiliary memory. This means that a move of our machine will depend not only on the current state and input, but also on the symbol currently on top of the stack. Carrying out the move may change the stack as well as the state.

In this simple example, the set $Q$ of states will contain only three elements, $q_0$, $q_1$, and $q_2$. The state $q_0$, the initial state, is sufficient for processing the first half of the string. In this state, each input symbol is pushed onto the stack, regardless of what is currently on top. The machine stays in $q_0$ as long as it has not yet received the symbol $c$; when that happens, the machine moves to state $q_1$, leaving the stack unchanged. State $q_1$ is for processing the second half of the input string. Once the machine enters this state, the only string that can be accepted is the one whose second half (after the $c$) is the reverse of the string already read. In this state each input symbol is compared to the symbol currently on top of the stack. If they agree, that symbol is popped off the stack and both are discarded; otherwise, the machine will crash and the string will not be accepted. This phase of the processing ends when the stack is empty, provided the machine has not crashed. An empty stack means that every symbol in the first half of the string has been successfully matched with an identical input symbol in the second half, and at that point the machine enters the accepting state $q_2$.

Now we consider how to describe precisely the abstract machine whose operations we have sketched. Each move of the machine will be determined by three things:

1.  The current state
2.  The next input
3.  The symbol on top of the stack

and will consist of two parts:

1.  Changing states (or staying in the same state)
2.  Replacing the top stack symbol by a string of zero or more symbols

Describing moves this way allows us to consider the two basic stack moves as special cases: Popping the top symbol off the stack means replacing it by $\Lambda$, and pushing $Y$ onto the stack means replacing the top symbol $X$ by $YX$ (assuming that the left end of the string corresponds to the top). We could enforce the stack rules more strictly by requiring that a single move contain only one stack operation, either a push or a pop. However, replacing the stack symbol $X$ by the string $\alpha$ can be accomplished by a sequence of basic moves (a pop, followed by a sequence of zero or more pushes), and allowing the more general move helps to keep the number of distinct moves as small as possible.

In the case of a finite automaton, our transition function took the form

$$\delta : Q \times \Sigma \to Q$$

Here, if we allow the possibility that the stack alphabet $\Gamma$ (the set of symbols that can appear on the stack) is different from the input alphabet $\Sigma$, it looks as though we want

$$\delta : Q \times \Sigma \times \Gamma \rightarrow Q \times \Gamma^*$$

For a state $q$, an input $a$, and a stack symbol $X$,

$$\delta(q, a, X) = (p, \alpha)$$

means that in state $q$, with $X$ on top of the stack, we read the symbol $a$, move to state $p$, and replace $X$ on the stack by the string $\alpha$.

This approach raises a few questions. First, how do we describe a move if the stack is empty ($\delta(q, a, ?)$)? We avoid this problem by saying that initially there is a special *start symbol* $Z_0$ on the stack, and the machine is not allowed to move when the stack is empty. Provided that $Z_0$ is never removed from the stack and that no additional copies of $Z_0$ are pushed onto the stack, saying that $Z_0$ is on top means that the stack is effectively empty.

Second, how do we describe a move when the input is exhausted ($\delta(q, ?, X)$)? (Remember that in our example we want to move to $q_2$ if the stack is empty when all the input has been read.) The solution we adopt here is to allow moves that use only $\Lambda$ as input, corresponding to $\Lambda$-transitions in an NFA-$\Lambda$. This suggests that what we really want is

$$\delta : Q \times (\Sigma \cup \{\Lambda\}) \times \Gamma \rightarrow Q \times \Gamma^*$$

Of course, once we have moves of the form $\delta(q, \Lambda, X)$, we can make them before all the input has been read; if the next input symbol is not read in a move, it is still there to be read subsequently.

We have already said that there may be situations when the machine will crash—that is, when no move is specified. In the case of a finite automaton, when this happened we decided to make $\delta(q, a)$ a *subset* of $Q$, rather than an element, so that it could have the value $\emptyset$. At the same time we allowed for the possibility that $\delta(q, a)$ might contain more than one element, so that the FA became nondeterministic. Here we do the same thing, except that since $Q \times \Gamma^*$ is an infinite set we should say explicitly that $\delta(q, a, X)$ and $\delta(q, \Lambda, X)$ will always be finite. In our current example the nondeterminism is not necessary, but in many cases it is. Thus we are left with

$$\delta : Q \times (\Sigma \cup \{\Lambda\}) \times \Gamma \rightarrow \text{the set of finite subsets of } Q \times \Gamma^*$$

Now we can give a precise description of our simple-palindrome recognizer. $Q$ will be the set $\{q_0, q_1, q_2\}$, $q_0$ is the initial state, and $q_2$ is the only accepting state. The input alphabet $\Sigma$ is $\{a, b, c\}$, and the stack alphabet $\Gamma$ is $\{a, b, Z_0\}$. The transition function $\delta$ is given by Table 7.1. Remember that when we specify a string to be placed on the stack, the top of the stack corresponds to the left end of the string. This convention may seem odd at first, since if we were to push the symbols on one at a time we would have to do it right-to-left, or in reverse order. The point is that when we get around to processing the symbols on the stack, the order in which we encounter them is the same as the order in which they occurred in the string.

Moves 1 through 6 push the input symbols $a$ and $b$ onto the stack, moves 7 through 9 change state without affecting the stack, moves 10 and 11 match an input symbol with a stack symbol and discard both, and the last move is to accept provided there is nothing except $Z_0$ on the stack.

**Table 7.1** | Transition table for Example 7.1

| Move number | State | Input | Stack symbol | Move(s) |
|:-----------:|:-----:|:-----:|:------------:|:-------:|
| 1 | $q_0$ | $a$ | $Z_0$ | $(q_0, aZ_0)$ |
| 2 | $q_0$ | $b$ | $Z_0$ | $(q_0, bZ_0)$ |
| 3 | $q_0$ | $a$ | $a$ | $(q_0, aa)$ |
| 4 | $q_0$ | $b$ | $a$ | $(q_0, ba)$ |
| 5 | $q_0$ | $a$ | $b$ | $(q_0, ab)$ |
| 6 | $q_0$ | $b$ | $b$ | $(q_0, bb)$ |
| 7 | $q_0$ | $c$ | $Z_0$ | $(q_1, Z_0)$ |
| 8 | $q_0$ | $c$ | $a$ | $(q_1, a)$ |
| 9 | $q_0$ | $c$ | $b$ | $(q_1, b)$ |
| 10 | $q_1$ | $a$ | $a$ | $(q_1, \Lambda)$ |
| 11 | $q_1$ | $b$ | $b$ | $(q_1, \Lambda)$ |
| 12 | $q_1$ | $\Lambda$ | $Z_0$ | $(q_2, Z_0)$ |
| | (all other combinations) | | | none |

Let us trace the moves of the machine for three input strings: $abcba$, $ab$, and $acaa$.

| Move number | Resulting state | Unread input | Stack |
|:-----------:|:---------------:|:------------:|:-----:|
| (initially) | $q_0$ | $abcba$ | $Z_0$ |
| 1 | $q_0$ | $bcba$ | $aZ_0$ |
| 4 | $q_0$ | $cba$ | $baZ_0$ |
| 9 | $q_1$ | $ba$ | $baZ_0$ |
| 11 | $q_1$ | $a$ | $aZ_0$ |
| 10 | $q_1$ | $-$ | $Z_0$ |
| 12 | $q_2$ | $-$ | $Z_0$ |
| (accept) | | | |
| (initially) | $q_0$ | $ab$ | $Z_0$ |
| 1 | $q_0$ | $b$ | $aZ_0$ |
| 4 | $q_0$ | $-$ | $baZ_0$ |
| (crash) | | | |
| (initially) | $q_0$ | $acaa$ | $Z_0$ |
| 1 | $q_0$ | $caa$ | $aZ_0$ |
| 8 | $q_1$ | $aa$ | $aZ_0$ |
| 10 | $q_1$ | $a$ | $Z_0$ |
| 12 | $q_2$ | $a$ | $Z_0$ |

Note the last move on input string $acaa$. Although there is no move $\delta(q_1, a, Z_0)$, the machine can take the $\Lambda$-transition $\delta(q_1, \Lambda, Z_0)$ before running out of choices. We could say that the portion of the string read so far (i.e., $aca$) is accepted, since the machine is in an accepting state at this point; however, the entire input string is not accepted, because not all of it has been read.

Figure 7.1 shows a diagram corresponding to Example 7.1, modeled after (but more complicated than) a transition diagram for an FA. Each transition is labeled with an input (either an alphabet symbol or $\Lambda$), a stack symbol $X$, a slash ( / ), and a string $\alpha$ of stack symbols. The interpretation is that the transition may occur on the specified input and involves

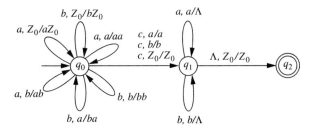

**Figure 7.1** |
Transition diagram for the pushdown automaton (PDA) in
Example 7.1.

replacing $X$ on the stack by $\alpha$. Even with the extra information required for labeling an arrow, a diagram of this type does not capture completely the PDA's behavior in the same way that a transition diagram for an FA does. With an FA, you can start at any point with just the diagram and the input symbols and trace the action of the machine by following the arrows. In Figure 7.1, however, you cannot follow the arrows without keeping track of the stack contents— possibly the entire contents—as you go. The number of possible combinations of state and stack contents is infinite, and it is therefore not possible to draw a "finite-state diagram" in the same sense as for an FA. In most cases we will describe pushdown automata in this chapter by transition tables similar to the one in Table 7.1, although it will occasionally also be useful to show a transition diagram.

## 7.2 | THE DEFINITION OF A PUSHDOWN AUTOMATON

Below is a precise definition of the type of abstract machine illustrated in Example 7.1. Remember that what is being defined is in general nondeterministic.

---

**Definition 7.1    Definition of a PDA**

A *pushdown automaton* (PDA) is a 7-tuple $M = (Q, \Sigma, \Gamma, q_0, Z_0, A, \delta)$, where

$Q$ is a finite set of states.
$\Sigma$ and $\Gamma$ are finite sets (the input and stack alphabets, respectively).
$q_0$, the initial state, is an element of $Q$.
$Z_0$, the initial stack symbol, is an element of $\Gamma$.
$A$, the set of accepting states, is a subset of $Q$.
$\delta : Q \times (\Sigma \cup \{\Lambda\}) \times \Gamma \rightarrow$ the set of finite subsets of $Q \times \Gamma^*$.

The function $\delta$ is called the transition function of $M$.

The stack alphabet $\Gamma$ and the initial stack symbol $Z_0$ are what make it necessary to have a 7-tuple rather than a 5-tuple. Otherwise, the components of the tuple are the same as in the case of an FA, except that the transition function $\delta$ is more complicated.

We can trace the operation of a finite automaton by keeping track of the current state at each step. In order to trace the operation of a PDA $M$, we must also keep track of the stack contents. If we are interested in what the machine does with a specific input string, it is also helpful to monitor the portion of the string yet to be read. A *configuration* of the PDA $M = (Q, \Sigma, \Gamma, q_0, Z_0, A, \delta)$ is a triple

$$(q, x, \alpha)$$

where $q \in Q, x \in \Sigma^*$, and $\alpha \in \Gamma^*$. Saying that $(q, x, \alpha)$ is the current configuration of $M$ means that $q$ is the current state, $x$ is the string of remaining unread input, and $\alpha$ is the current stack contents, where as usual it is the left end of $\alpha$ that corresponds to the top of the stack.

We write

$$(p, x, \alpha) \vdash_M (q, y, \beta)$$

to mean that one of the possible moves in the first configuration takes $M$ to the second. This can happen in two ways, depending on whether the move consumes an input symbol or is a $\Lambda$-transition. In the first case, $x = ay$ for some $a \in \Sigma$, and in the second case $x = y$; we can summarize both cases by saying $x = ay$ for some $a \in \Sigma \cup \{\Lambda\}$. In both cases, the string $\beta$ of stack symbols is obtained from $\alpha$ by replacing the first symbol $X$ by a string $\xi$ (in other words, $\alpha = X\gamma$ for some $X \in \Gamma$ and some $\gamma \in \Gamma^*$, and $\beta = \xi\gamma$ for some $\xi \in \Gamma^*$), and

$$(q, \xi) \in \delta(p, a, X)$$

More generally, we write

$$(p, x, \alpha) \vdash_M^* (q, y, \beta)$$

if there is a sequence of zero or more moves that takes $M$ from the first configuration to the second. As usual, if there is no possibility of confusion, we shorten $\vdash_M$ to $\vdash$ and $\vdash_M^*$ to $\vdash^*$. Using the new notation, we may define acceptance of a string by a PDA.

---

**Definition 7.2    Acceptance by a PDA**

If $M = (Q, \Sigma, \Gamma, q_0, Z_0, A, \delta)$ is a PDA and $x \in \Sigma^*$, $x$ is *accepted* by $M$ if

$$(q_0, x, Z_0) \vdash_M^* (q, \Lambda, \alpha)$$

for some $\alpha \in \Gamma^*$ and some $q \in A$. (The stack may or may not be empty when $x$ is accepted, because $\alpha$ may or may not be $\Lambda$.) A language $L \subseteq \Sigma^*$ is said to be accepted by $M$ if $L$ is precisely the set of strings accepted by $M$; in this case, we write $L = L(M)$.

---

Note that whether or not a string is accepted depends only on the current state when the string has been processed, not on the stack contents. We use the phrase *accepting configuration* to denote any configuration in which the state is an accepting state. This type of acceptance is sometimes called *acceptance by final state*. It will be convenient in Section 7.5 to look briefly at another type, acceptance by *empty stack*. In this approach, a string is said to be accepted if it allows the PDA to reach a configuration in which the stack is empty, regardless of whether the state is an accepting state. It is not hard to see (Section 7.5 and Exercises 7.41 and 7.42) that the two types of acceptance are equivalent, in the sense that if a language is accepted by some PDA using one mode of acceptance, there is another PDA using the other mode that also accepts the language.

It is worth emphasizing that when we say a string $x$ is accepted by a PDA, we mean that *there is* a sequence of moves that cause the machine to reach an accepting configuration as a result of reading the symbols of $x$. Since a PDA can be nondeterministic, there may be many other possible sequences of moves that do not lead to an accepting configuration. Each time there is a choice of moves, we may view the PDA as making a guess as to which one to make. Acceptance means that if the PDA guesses right at each step, it can reach an accepting configuration. In our next example, we will see a little more clearly what it means to guess right at each step.

## A PDA Accepting the Language of Palindromes **EXAMPLE 7.2**

This example involves the language *pal* of palindromes over $\{a, b\}$ (both even-length and odd-length), without the marker in the middle that provides the signal for the PDA to switch from the "pushing-input-onto-stack" state to the "comparing-input-symbol-to-stack-symbol" state. The general strategy for constructing a PDA to recognize this language sounds the same as in Example 7.1: Remember the symbols seen so far, by saving them on the stack, until we are ready to begin matching them with symbols in the second half of the string. This switch from one type of move to the other should happen when we reach the middle of the string, just as in Example 7.1. However, without a symbol marking the middle explicitly, the PDA has no way of knowing that the middle has arrived; it can only guess. Fortunately, there is no penalty for guessing wrong, as long as the guess does not allow a nonpalindrome to be accepted.

We think of the machine as making a sequence of "not yet" guesses as it reads input symbols and pushes them onto the stack. This phase can stop (with a "yes" guess) in two possible ways: The PDA may guess that the next input symbol is the one in the very middle of the string (and that the string is of odd length) and can therefore be discarded since it need not be matched by anything; or it may guess that the input string read so far is the first half of the (even-length) string and that any subsequent input symbols should therefore be used to match stack symbols. In effect, if the string read so far is $x$, the first "yes" guess that might be made is that another input symbol $s$ should be read and that the input string will be $xsx^r$. The second possible guess, which can be made without reading another symbol, is that the input string will be $xx^r$. In either case, from this point on the PDA is committed. It makes no more guesses, attempts to process the remaining symbols as if they belong to the second half, and can accept no string other than the one it has guessed the input string to be.

This approach cannot cause a nonpalindrome to be accepted, because each time the PDA makes a "yes" guess, it is then unable to accept any string not of the form $xsx^r$ or $xx^r$. On the other hand, the approach allows every palindrome to be accepted: Every palindrome looks like either $xsx^r$ or $xx^r$, and in either case, there is a permissible sequence of choices that involves making the correct "yes" guess at just the right time to cause the string to be accepted. It is still possible, of course, that for an input string $z$ that is a palindrome the PDA guesses "yes" at the wrong time or makes the wrong type of "yes" guess; it might end up accepting some palindrome other than $z$, or simply stop in a nonaccepting state. This does not mean that the PDA is incorrect, but only that the PDA did not choose the particular sequence of moves that *would* have led to acceptance of $z$.

The transition table for our PDA is shown in Table 7.2. The sets $Q$, $\Gamma$, and $A$ are the same as in Example 7.1, and there are noticeable similarities between the two transition tables. The moves in the first six lines of Table 7.1 show up as *possible* moves in the corresponding lines of Table 7.2, and the last three lines of the two tables (which represent the processing of the second half of the string) are identical.

The fact that the first six lines of Table 7.2 show two possible moves tells us that there is genuine nondeterminism. The two choices in each of these lines are to guess "not yet," as in Table 7.1, and to guess that the input symbol is the middle symbol of the (odd-length) string. The input symbol is read in both cases; the first choice causes it to be pushed onto the stack, and the second choice causes it to be discarded.

However, there is also nondeterminism of a less obvious sort. Suppose for example that the PDA is in state $q_0$, the top stack symbol is $a$, and the next input symbol is $a$, as in line 3. In addition to the two moves shown in line 3, there is a third choice shown in line 8: not to read the input symbol at all, but to execute a $\Lambda$-transition to state $q_1$. This represents the other "yes" guess, the guess that as a result of reading the most recent symbol (now on top of the stack), we have reached the middle of the (even-length) string. This choice is made without even looking at the next input symbol. (Another approach would have been to read the $a$, use it to match the $a$ on the stack, and move to $q_1$, all on the same move; however, the moves shown in the table preserve the distinction between the state $q_0$ in which all the guessing occurs and the state $q_1$ in which all the comparison-making occurs.)

Note that the $\Lambda$-transition in line 8 is not in itself the source of nondeterminism. The move in line 12, for example, is the only possible move from state $q_1$ if $Z_0$ is the top stack

**Table 7.2** | Transition table for Example 7.2

| Move number | State | Input | Stack symbol | Move(s) |
|:-----------:|:-----:|:-----:|:------------:|:-------:|
| 1 | $q_0$ | $a$ | $Z_0$ | $(q_0, aZ_0), (q_1, Z_0)$ |
| 2 | $q_0$ | $b$ | $Z_0$ | $(q_0, bZ_0), (q_1, Z_0)$ |
| 3 | $q_0$ | $a$ | $a$ | $(q_0, aa), (q_1, a)$ |
| 4 | $q_0$ | $b$ | $a$ | $(q_0, ba), (q_1, a)$ |
| 5 | $q_0$ | $a$ | $b$ | $(q_0, ab), (q_1, b)$ |
| 6 | $q_0$ | $b$ | $b$ | $(q_0, bb), (q_1, b)$ |
| 7 | $q_0$ | $\Lambda$ | $Z_0$ | $(q_1, Z_0)$ |
| 8 | $q_0$ | $\Lambda$ | $a$ | $(q_1, a)$ |
| 9 | $q_0$ | $\Lambda$ | $b$ | $(q_1, b)$ |
| 10 | $q_1$ | $a$ | $a$ | $(q_1, \Lambda)$ |
| 11 | $q_1$ | $b$ | $b$ | $(q_1, \Lambda)$ |
| 12 | $q_1$ | $\Lambda$ | $Z_0$ | $(q_2, Z_0)$ |
| | (all other combinations) | | | none |

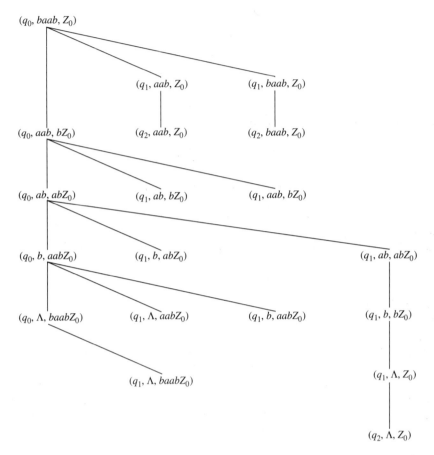

**Figure 7.2 |**
Computation tree for the PDA in Table 7.2, with input *baab*.

symbol. Line 8 represents nondeterminism because if the PDA is in state $q_0$ and $a$ is the top stack symbol, there is a choice between a move that reads an input symbol and one that does not. We will return to this point in Section 7.3.

Just as in Section 4.1, we can draw a computation tree for a PDA such as this one, showing the configuration at each step and the possible choices of moves at each step. Figure 7.2 shows such a tree for the string *baab*, which is a palindrome.

Each time there is a choice, the possible moves are shown left-to-right in the order they appear in Table 7.2. In particular, in each configuration along the left edge of Figure 7.2 except the last one, the PDA is in state $q_0$ and there is at least one unread input symbol. At each of these points, the PDA can choose from three possible moves. Continuing down the left edge of the figure represents a "not yet" guess that reads an input and pushes it onto the stack. The other two possibilities are the two moves to state $q_1$, one that reads an input symbol and one that does not.

The sequence of moves that leads to acceptance is

$$(q_0, baab, Z_0) \vdash (q_0, aab, bZ_0)$$
$$\vdash (q_0, ab, abZ_0)$$
$$\vdash (q_1, ab, abZ_0)$$
$$\vdash (q_1, b, bZ_0)$$
$$\vdash (q_1, \Lambda, Z_0)$$
$$\vdash (q_2, \Lambda, Z_0) \quad \text{(accept)}$$

This sequence of moves is the one in which the "yes" guess of the right type is made at exactly the right time. Paths that deviate from the vertical path too soon terminate before the PDA has finished reading the input; the machine either crashes or enters the accepting state $q_2$ prematurely (so that the string accepted is a palindrome of length 0 or 1, not the one we have in mind). Paths that follow the vertical path too long cause the PDA either to crash or to run out of input symbols before getting a chance to empty the stack.

## 7.3 | DETERMINISTIC PUSHDOWN AUTOMATA

The PDA in Example 7.1 never has a choice of more than one move, and it is appropriate to call it a deterministic PDA. The one in Example 7.2 illustrates both types of nondeterminism: that in which there are two or more moves involving the same combination of state, stack symbol, and input, and that in which, for some combination of state and stack symbol, the machine has a choice of reading an input symbol or making a $\Lambda$-transition.

---

**Definition 7.3    Definition of a deterministic PDA**

Let $M = (Q, \Sigma, \Gamma, q_0, Z_0, A, \delta)$ be a pushdown automaton. $M$ is *deterministic* if there is no configuration for which $M$ has a choice of more than one move. In other words, $M$ is deterministic if it satisfies both the following conditions.

1. For any $q \in Q$, $a \in \Sigma \cup \{\Lambda\}$, and $X \in \Gamma$, the set $\delta(q, a, X)$ has at most one element.
2. For any $q \in Q$ and $X \in \Gamma$, if $\delta(q, \Lambda, X) \neq \emptyset$, then $\delta(q, a, X) = \emptyset$ for every $a \in \Sigma$.

A language $L$ is a *deterministic context-free language* (DCFL) if there is a deterministic PDA (DPDA) accepting $L$.

---

Note that our definition does not require the transition function to be defined for every combination of state, input, and stack symbol; in a deterministic PDA, it is still possible for one of the sets $\delta(q, a, X)$ to be empty. In this sense, our notion of determinism is a little less strict than in Chapter 4, where we called a finite automaton nondeterministic if there was a pair $(q, a)$ for which $\delta(q, a)$ did not have exactly one element.

The last statement in the definition anticipates to some extent the results of the next two sections, which show that the languages that can be accepted by PDAs are precisely the context-free languages. The last statement also suggests another way in which CFLs are more complicated than regular languages. We did not define a "deterministic regular language" in Chapter 4, although we considered both NFAs and deterministic FAs. The reason is that for any NFA there is an FA recognizing the same language; any regular language can be accepted by a deterministic FA. Not every context-free language, however, can be accepted by a deterministic PDA. It probably seemed obvious in Example 7.2 that the standard approach to accepting the language of palindromes cannot work without nondeterminism; we will be able to show in Theorem 7.1 that no other PDA can do any better, and that the language of palindromes is not a DCFL.

---

## A DPDA Accepting Balanced Strings of Brackets    **EXAMPLE 7.3**

---

Consider the language $L$ of all balanced strings involving two types of brackets: { } and [ ]. $L$ is the language generated by the context-free grammar with productions

$$S \rightarrow SS \mid [S] \mid \{S\} \mid \Lambda$$

(It is also possible to describe this type of "balanced" string using the approach of Definition 6.5; see Exercise 7.20.)

Our PDA will have two states: the initial state $q_0$, which is also the accepting state (note that $\Lambda$ is one element of $L$), and another state $q_1$. Left brackets of either type are saved on the stack, and one is discarded whenever it is on top of the stack and a right bracket of the same type is encountered in the input. The feature of strings in $L$ that makes this approach correct, and therefore makes a stack the appropriate data structure, is that when a right bracket in a balanced string is encountered, the left bracket it matches is the *last* left bracket of the same type that has appeared previously and has not already been matched. The signal that the string read so far is balanced is that the stack has no brackets on it (i.e., $Z_0$ is the top symbol), and if this happens in state $q_1$ the PDA will return to the accepting state $q_0$ via a $\Lambda$-transition, leaving the stack unchanged. From this point, if there is more input, the machine proceeds as if from the beginning.

Table 7.3 shows a transition table for such a deterministic PDA. To make it easier to read, the parentheses with which we normally enclose a pair specifying a single move have been omitted.

The input string {[ ]}[ ], for example, results in the following sequence of moves.

$$(q_0, \{[]\}[], Z_0) \vdash (q_1, []\}[], \{Z_0)$$
$$\vdash (q_1, ]\}[], [\{Z_0)$$
$$\vdash (q_1, \}[], \{Z_0)$$
$$\vdash (q_1, [], Z_0)$$

**Table 7.3** | Transition table for Example 7.3

| Move number | State | Input | Stack symbol | Move |
|:---:|:---:|:---:|:---:|:---:|
| 1 | $q_0$ | { | $Z_0$ | $q_1, \{Z_0$ |
| 2 | $q_0$ | [ | $Z_0$ | $q_1, [Z_0$ |
| 3 | $q_1$ | { | { | $q_1, \{\{$ |
| 4 | $q_1$ | [ | { | $q_1, [\{$ |
| 5 | $q_1$ | { | [ | $q_1, \{[$ |
| 6 | $q_1$ | [ | [ | $q_1, [[$ |
| 7 | $q_1$ | } | { | $q_1, \Lambda$ |
| 8 | $q_1$ | ] | [ | $q_1, \Lambda$ |
| 9 | $q_1$ | $\Lambda$ | $Z_0$ | $q_0, Z_0$ |
| | (all other combinations) | | | none |

$$\vdash (q_0, [], Z_0)$$

$$\vdash (q_1, ], [Z_0)$$

$$\vdash (q_1, \Lambda, Z_0)$$

$$\vdash (q_0, \Lambda, Z_0) \quad \text{(accept)}$$

You may very well have seen stacks used in the way we are using them here, with languages closely related to the set of balanced strings of parentheses. If you have written or studied a computer program that reads an algebraic expression and processes it (to "process" an expression could mean to evaluate it, to convert it to postfix notation, to build an expression tree to store it, or simply to check that it obeys the syntax rules), the program almost certainly involved at least one stack. If the program did not use recursion, the stack was explicit—storing values of subexpressions, perhaps, or parentheses and operators; if the algorithm was recursive, there was a stack behind the scenes, since stacks are the data structures involved whenever recursive algorithms are implemented.

**EXAMPLE 7.4**

## A DPDA to Accept Strings with More *a*'s Than *b*'s

For our last example of a DPDA, we consider

$$L = \{x \in \{a, b\}^* \mid n_a(x) > n_b(x)\}$$

The approach we use is similar in some ways to that in the previous example. There we saved left brackets on the stack so that they could eventually be matched by right brackets. Now we save excess symbols of either type, so that they can eventually be matched by symbols of the opposite type. The other obvious difference is that since the null string is not in $L$, the initial state is not accepting. With those differences in mind, it is easy to understand the DPDA described in Table 7.4. The only two states are the initial state $q_0$ and the accepting state $q_1$.

At any point when the stack contains only $Z_0$, the string read so far has equal numbers of *a*'s and *b*'s. It is almost correct to say that the machine is in the accepting state $q_1$ precisely when there is at least one *a* on the stack. This is not quite correct, because input *b* in state $q_1$ requires removing *a* from the stack and returning to $q_0$, at least temporarily; this guarantees that if the *a* just removed from the stack was the *only* one on the stack, the input string read so far (which has equal numbers of *a*'s and *b*'s) is not accepted. The $\Lambda$-transition is the way the PDA returns to the accepting state once it determines that there are additional *a*'s remaining on the stack.

**Table 7.4 |** Transition table for a DPDA to accept $L$

| Move number | State | Input | Stack symbol | Move |
|---|---|---|---|---|
| 1 | $q_0$ | $a$ | $Z_0$ | $(q_1, aZ_0)$ |
| 2 | $q_0$ | $b$ | $Z_0$ | $(q_0, bZ_0)$ |
| 3 | $q_0$ | $a$ | $b$ | $(q_0, \Lambda)$ |
| 4 | $q_0$ | $b$ | $b$ | $(q_0, bb)$ |
| 5 | $q_1$ | $a$ | $a$ | $(q_1, aa)$ |
| 6 | $q_1$ | $b$ | $a$ | $(q_0, \Lambda)$ |
| 7 | $q_0$ | $\Lambda$ | $a$ | $(q_1, a)$ |
| | (all other combinations) | | | none |

**Table 7.5 |** A DPDA with no $\Lambda$-transitions accepting $L$

| Move number | State | Input | Stack symbol | Move |
|---|---|---|---|---|
| 1 | $q_0$ | $a$ | $Z_0$ | $(q_1, Z_0)$ |
| 2 | $q_0$ | $b$ | $Z_0$ | $(q_0, bZ_0)$ |
| 3 | $q_0$ | $a$ | $b$ | $(q_0, \Lambda)$ |
| 4 | $q_0$ | $b$ | $b$ | $(q_0, bb)$ |
| 5 | $q_1$ | $a$ | $Z_0$ | $(q_1, aZ_0)$ |
| 6 | $q_1$ | $b$ | $Z_0$ | $(q_0, Z_0)$ |
| 7 | $q_1$ | $a$ | $a$ | $(q_1, aa)$ |
| 8 | $q_1$ | $b$ | $a$ | $(q_1, \Lambda)$ |
| | (all other combinations) | | | none |

If we can provide a way for the PDA to determine in advance whether an $a$ on the stack is the only one, then we can eliminate the need to leave the accepting state when $a$ is popped from the stack, and thereby eliminate $\Lambda$-transitions altogether. There are at least three natural ways we might manage this. One is to say that we will push $a$'s onto the stack only when we have an excess of at least two, so that in state $q_1$, top stack symbol $Z_0$ means one extra $a$, and top stack symbol $a$ means more than one. Another is to use a different stack symbol, say $A$, for the first extra $a$. A third is simply to introduce a new state specifically for the case in which there is exactly one extra $a$. The DPDA shown in Table 7.5 takes the first approach. As before, $q_1$ is the accepting state. There is no move specified from $q_1$ with stack symbol $b$ or from $q_0$ with stack symbol $a$, because neither of these situations will ever occur.

This PDA may be slightly easier to understand with the transition diagram shown in Figure 7.3.

We illustrate the operation of this machine on the input string *abbabaa*:

$$(q_0, abbabaa, Z_0) \vdash (q_1, bbabaa, Z_0)$$
$$\vdash (q_0, babaa, Z_0)$$
$$\vdash (q_0, abaa, bZ_0)$$
$$\vdash (q_0, baa, Z_0)$$
$$\vdash (q_0, aa, bZ_0)$$
$$\vdash (q_0, a, Z_0)$$
$$\vdash (q_1, \Lambda, Z_0) \quad \text{(accept)}$$

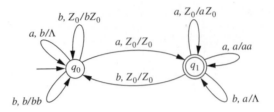

**Figure 7.3 |**
The DPDA in Table 7.5.

We conclude this section by showing the result we promised at the beginning: Not every language that can be accepted by a PDA can be accepted by a deterministic PDA.

**Theorem 7.1**
The language $pal = \{x \in \{a, b\}^* \mid x = x^r\}$ cannot be accepted by any DPDA.

*Proof*
Suppose for the sake of contradiction that $M = (Q, \{a, b\}, \Gamma, q_0, Z_0, A, \delta)$ is a DPDA accepting *pal*. We can easily modify $M$ if necessary (see Exercise 7.12) so that every move is either one of the form

$$\delta(p, s, X) = (q, \Lambda)$$

or one of the form

$$\delta(p, s, X) = (q, \alpha X)$$

where $s \in \{a, b, \Lambda\}$ and $\alpha \in \Gamma^*$. The effect of the modification is that $M$ can still remove a symbol from the stack or place another symbol on the stack, but it cannot do both in the same move.

We observe next that for any string $x$, $M$ must eventually read every symbol of $x$. The string $xx^r$, for example, is a palindrome, and $M$ must read it completely in order to accept it. However, because $M$ is deterministic, the moves it makes while processing $x$ in the course of accepting $xx^r$ are exactly the moves it must make on input $x$, whether or not $x$ is followed by anything else.

After $M$ has processed a string $x$, its stack is a certain height, depending on how much $M$ needs to remember about $x$. We may consider how much shorter the stack can ever get as a result of reading subsequent input symbols. For each $x$, let $y_x$ be a string for which this resulting stack height is as small as possible. (It cannot be 0, because $M$ must still be able to process longer strings with prefix $xy_x$.) In other words,

$$(q_0, xy_x, Z_0) \vdash^* (q_x, \Lambda, \alpha_x)$$

for some state $q_x$ and some string $\alpha_x \in \Gamma^*$ with $|\alpha_x| > 0$; and for any string $y$, any state $p$, and any string $\beta \in \Gamma^*$,

$$\text{if } (q_0, xy, Z_0) \vdash^* (p, \Lambda, \beta) \text{ then } |\beta| \geq |\alpha_x|$$

Because of our initial assumption about the moves of $M$, any move that involves removing a stack symbol decreases the stack height. Therefore, once $M$ reaches the configuration $(q_x, \Lambda, \alpha_x)$, as a result of processing the string $xy_x$, no symbols of the string $\alpha_x$ will ever be removed from the stack subsequently.

Let $A_x$ be the first symbol of the string $\alpha_x$. The set $S$ of all strings of the form $xy_x$ is infinite (because we may consider $x$ of any length), and the set of all ordered pairs $(q_x, A_x)$ is finite (because the entire set $Q \times \Gamma$ is finite). Therefore, there must be an infinite subset $T$ of $S$ so that for all the elements $xy_x$ of $T$, the pairs $(q_x, A_x)$ are equal. In particular, we can choose two different strings $u_1 = xy_x$ and $u_2 = wy_w$ so that

$$(q_0, u_1, Z_0) \vdash^* (q, \Lambda, A\beta_1)$$

and

$$(q_0, u_2, Z_0) \vdash^* (q, \Lambda, A\beta_2)$$

for some $q \in Q$, some $A \in \Gamma$, and some strings $\beta_1, \beta_2 \in \Gamma^*$. If we now look at longer strings of the form $u_1z$ and $u_2z$, we have

$$(q_0, u_1z, Z_0) \vdash^* (q, z, A\beta_1)$$

and

$$(q_0, u_2z, Z_0) \vdash^* (q, z, A\beta_2)$$

and the symbol $A$ is never removed from the stack as a result of processing the string $z$. The reason this is useful is that although the stack contents may not be the same in the two cases, the machine can never notice the difference. The ultimate result of processing the string $u_1z$ must be exactly the same as that of processing $u_2z$: Either both strings are accepted or neither is. Now, however, we have the contradiction we are looking for. On the one hand, $M$ treats $u_1z$ and $u_2z$ the same way; on the other hand, as we showed in the proof of Theorem 3.3, the two strings $u_1$ and $u_2$ are distinguishable with respect to *pal*, so that for some $z$, one of the strings $u_1z$, $u_2z$ is in *pal* and the other is not. This is impossible if $M$ accepts *pal*.

See Exercise 7.17 for some other examples of CFLs that are not DCFLs, and see Section 8.2 for some other methods of showing that languages are not DCFLs.

# 7.4 | A PDA CORRESPONDING TO A GIVEN CONTEXT-FREE GRAMMAR

Up to this point, the pushdown automata we have constructed have been based on simple symmetry properties of the strings in the languages being recognized, rather than on any features of context-free grammars generating the languages. As a result, it may not be obvious that *every* context-free language can be recognized by a PDA. However, that is what we will prove in this section.

Starting with a context-free grammar $G$, we want to build a PDA that can test an arbitrary string and determine whether it can be derived from $G$. The basic strategy is to *simulate* a derivation of the string in the given grammar. This will require guessing the steps of the derivation, and our PDA will be nondeterministic. (As we will see in Section 7.6, there are certain types of grammars for which we will be able to modify the PDA, keeping its essential features but eliminating the nondeterminism. The approach will be particularly useful in these cases, because for a string $x$ in the language, following the moves of the machine on input $x$ will not only allow us to confirm $x$'s membership in the language, but also reveal a derivation of $x$ in the grammar. Because of languages like *pal*, however, finding such a deterministic PDA is too much to expect in general.) As the simulation progresses, the machine will test the input string to make sure that it is still consistent with the derivation-in-progress. If the input string does in fact have a derivation from the grammar, and if the PDA's guesses are the ones that correctly simulate this derivation, the tests will confirm this and allow the machine to reach an accepting state.

There are at least two natural ways a PDA can simulate a derivation in the grammar. A step in the simulation corresponds to constructing a portion of the derivation tree, and the two approaches are called *top-down* and *bottom-up* because of the order in which these portions are constructed.

We will begin with the **top-down** approach. The PDA starts by pushing the start symbol $S$ (at the top of the derivation tree) onto the stack, and each subsequent step in the simulated derivation is carried out by replacing a variable on the stack (at a certain node in the tree) by the right side of a production beginning with that variable (in other words, adding the children of that node to the tree.) The stack holds the current string in the derivation, except that as terminal symbols appear at the left of the string they are matched with symbols in the input and discarded.

The two types of moves made by the PDA, after $S$ is placed on the stack, are

1.  Replace a variable $A$ on top of the stack by the right side $\alpha$ of some production $A \rightarrow \alpha$. This is where the guessing comes in.

2.  Pop a terminal symbol from the stack, provided it matches the next input symbol. Both symbols are then discarded.

At each step, the string of input symbols already read (which have been successfully matched with terminal symbols produced at the beginning of the string by the derivation), followed by the contents of the stack, exclusive of $Z_0$, constitutes the current string in the derivation. When a variable appears on top of the stack, it is because terminal symbols preceding it in the current string have already been matched, and thus it is the leftmost variable in the current string. Therefore, the derivation being simulated is a *leftmost* derivation. If at some point there is no longer any part of the current string remaining on the stack, the attempted derivation must have been successful at producing the input string read so far, and the PDA can accept.

We are now ready to give a more precise description of this top-down PDA and to prove that the strings it accepts are precisely those generated by the grammar.

**Definition 7.4     Top-down PDA corresponding to a CFG**

Let $G = (V, \Sigma, S, P)$ be a context-free grammar. We define $M = (Q, \Sigma, \Gamma, q_0, Z_0, A, \delta)$ as follows:

$$Q = \{q_0, q_1, q_2\} \quad A = \{q_2\} \quad \Gamma = V \cup \Sigma \cup \{Z_0\} \quad (\text{where } Z_0 \notin V \cup \Sigma)$$

The initial move of $M$ is to place $S$ on the stack and move to $q_1$: $\delta(q_0, \Lambda, Z_0) = \{(q_1, SZ_0)\}$. The only move to the accepting state $q_2$ is from $q_1$, when the stack is empty except for $Z_0$: $\delta(q_1, \Lambda, Z_0) = \{(q_2, Z_0)\}$. Otherwise, the only moves of $M$ are as follows:

1. For every $A \in V$, $\delta(q_1, \Lambda, A) = \{(q_1, \alpha) \mid A \to \alpha \text{ is a production in } G\}$
2. For every $a \in \Sigma$, $\delta(q_1, a, a) = \{(q_1, \Lambda)\}$

**Theorem 7.2**

Let $G = (V, \Sigma, S, P)$ be a context-free grammar. Then the top-down PDA $M$ described in Definition 7.4 accepts $L(G)$.

*Proof*
**First, to show $L(G) \subseteq L(M)$.** If $x$ is any string in $L(G)$, then the *last* step in a leftmost derivation of $x$ looks like

$$yAz \Rightarrow yy' = x$$

where $y$, $z$, and $y'$ are strings of terminals, and a typical intermediate step looks like

$$yA\alpha \Rightarrow yy'\beta$$

where again $y$ and $y'$ are strings of terminals for which $yy'$ is a prefix of $x$, and the string $\beta$ begins with a variable. We may take the second case as the representative one, if we say that $\beta$ either is $\Lambda$ or begins with a variable.

What we would like to show in this situation is that some sequence of moves of our PDA has the effect of reading the string $yy'$ of terminals, matching it with terminals from the stack, leaving the string $\beta$ (or actually $\beta Z_0$) on the stack, and leaving the PDA in state $q_1$. It will follow, from the special case in which $\beta = \Lambda$, that with the input string $x$ the PDA can reach the configuration $(q_1, \Lambda, Z_0)$; therefore, because of the move to $q_2$ described in the definition, the PDA accepts $x$.

A precise statement that says this and is suitable for proof by induction is the following:

For any $n \geq 1$, if $x \in L(G)$ and the $n$th step in a leftmost derivation of $x$ is $yA\alpha \Rightarrow yy'\beta$, where $x = yy'z$, $yy'$ is a string of terminals, and $\beta$ either is $\Lambda$ or begins with a variable, then

$$(q_0, x, Z_0) = (q_0, yy'z, Z_0) \vdash^* (q_1, z, \beta Z_0) \tag{7.1}$$

For the basis step of the proof, let $n = 1$. The first step in a derivation of $x$ is to use a production of the form $S \to y'\beta$, so that the string $y$ in (7.1) is null. Using the initial move in the definition of $M$ and a move of type (1), we have

$$(q_0, x, Z_0) = (q_0, y'z, Z_0) \vdash (q_1, y'z, SZ_0) \vdash (q_1, y'z, y'\beta Z_0)$$

However, using as many moves of type (2) as there are symbols in $y'$, the PDA is able to get from the last configuration shown to $(q_1, z, \beta)$, and we may conclude that

$$(q_0, x, Z_0) \vdash^* (q_1, z, \beta Z_0)$$

Now suppose that $k \geq 1$ and that our statement is true for every $n \leq k$. We wish to show that if the $(k + 1)$th step in a leftmost derivation of $x$ is $yA\alpha \Rightarrow yy'\beta$, then (7.1) is true. Let us look at the $k$th step in the leftmost derivation of $x$. It is of the form

$$wBy \Rightarrow ww'\beta' = ww'A\alpha$$

where $ww' = y$. This means that $x = ww'(y'z)$, and the induction hypothesis implies that

$$(q_0, x, Z_0) \vdash^* (q_1, y'z, A\alpha Z_0)$$

If the production used in the $(k + 1)$th step is $A \to \alpha'$, so that $\alpha'\alpha = y'\beta$, then using a move of type (1) we get

$$(q_1, y'z, A\alpha Z_0) \vdash (q_1, y'z, \alpha'\alpha Z_0) = (q_1, y'z, y'\beta Z_0)$$

Now, just as in the basis step, we may reach the configuration $(q_1, z, \beta Z_0)$ by using moves of type (2); this completes the proof that $L(G) \subseteq L(M)$.

**Next, to show $L(M) \subseteq L(G)$.** Roughly speaking, this means we need to show the converse of the previous statement; in other words, the configuration $(q_1, z, \beta Z_0)$ can occur only if some leftmost derivation in the grammar produces the string $y\beta$, where $x = yz$. To be precise, we show the following.

> For any $n \geq 1$, if there is a sequence of $n$ moves that leads from the configuration $(q_0, x, Z_0)$ to the configuration $(q_1, z, \beta Z_0)$, then for some $y \in \Sigma^*$, $x = yz$ and $S \Rightarrow_G^* y\beta$.

The basis step is easy because the only single move producing a configuration of the right form is the initial move of $M$; in this case $z = x$ and $\beta = S$, so that $y$ can be chosen to be $\Lambda$.

Suppose $k \geq 1$ and our statement is true for any $n \geq k$. Suppose also that some sequence of $k + 1$ moves produces the configuration $(q_1, z, \beta Z_0)$. We must show that $x = yz$ for some $y$ and that $S \Rightarrow^* y\beta$.

There are two possibilities for the $(k + 1)$th move in this sequence. One is that the next-to-last configuration is $(q_1, az, a\beta Z_0)$ and the last move is of type (1). In this case the induction hypothesis implies that for some $y' \in \Sigma^*$, $x = y'az$ and $S \Rightarrow^* y'a\beta$. We get the conclusion immediately by letting $y = y'a$.

The other possibility is that the next-to-last configuration is $(q_1, z, A\gamma Z_0)$ for some variable $A$ for which there is a production $A \to \alpha$ with $\alpha\gamma = \beta$. In this case, the induction hypothesis tells us that $x = yz$ for some $y \in \Sigma^*$ and $S \Rightarrow^* yA\gamma$. But then

$$S \Rightarrow^* yA\gamma \Rightarrow y\alpha\gamma = y\beta$$

This completes the induction proof.

Now, if $x$ is any string in $L(M)$,

$$(q_0, x, Z_0) \vdash^* (q_1, \Lambda, Z_0) \vdash (q_2, \Lambda, Z_0)$$

because $M$ can enter $q_2$ only via a $\Lambda$-transition with $Z_0$ on top of the stack. Letting $y = x$ and $z = \beta = \Lambda$ in the statement we proved by induction, we may conclude that $S \Rightarrow_G^* x$ and therefore that $x \in L(G)$.

## A Top-down PDA for the Strings with More $a$'s than $b$'s    EXAMPLE 7.5

Consider the language

$$L = \{x \in \{a, b\}^* \mid n_a(x) > n_b(x)\}$$

for which we constructed a DPDA in Example 7.4. From Example 6.10, we know that one context-free grammar for $L$ is the one with productions

$$S \to a \mid aS \mid bSS \mid SSb \mid SbS$$

Following the construction in the proof of Theorem 7.2, we obtain the PDA $M = (Q, \Sigma, \Gamma, q_0, Z_0, A, \delta)$, where $Q = \{q_0, q_1, q_2\}$, $\Sigma = \{a, b\}$, $\Gamma = \{S, a, b, Z_0\}$, $A = \{q_2\}$, and the transition function $\delta$ is defined by this table.

| State | Input | Stack symbol | Move(s) |
|-------|-------|--------------|---------|
| $q_0$ | $\Lambda$ | $Z_0$ | $(q_1, SZ_0)$ |
| $q_1$ | $\Lambda$ | $S$ | $(q_1, a), (q_1, aS), (q_1, bSS), (q_1, SSb), (q_1, SbS)$ |
| $q_1$ | $a$ | $a$ | $(q_1, \Lambda)$ |
| $q_1$ | $b$ | $b$ | $(q_1, \Lambda)$ |
| $q_1$ | $\Lambda$ | $Z_0$ | $(q_2, Z_0)$ |
| (all other combinations) | | | none |

We consider the string $x = abbaaa \in L$ and compare the moves made by $M$ in accepting $x$ with a leftmost derivation of $x$ in the grammar. Each move in which a variable is replaced on the stack by a string corresponds to a step in a leftmost derivation of $x$, and that step is shown to the right of the move. Observe that at each step, the stack contains (in addition to $Z_0$) the portion of the current string in the derivation that remains after removing the initial string of terminals read so far.

$$(q_0, abbaaa, Z_0)$$

| | | |
|---|---|---|
| $\vdash (q_1, abbaaa, SZ_0)$ | $S$ | |
| $\vdash (q_1, abbaaa, SbSZ_0)$ | $\Rightarrow SbS$ | |
| $\vdash (q_1, abbaaa, abSZ_0)$ | $\Rightarrow abS$ | |
| $\vdash (q_1, bbaaa, bSZ_0)$ | | |
| $\vdash (q_1, baaa, SZ_0)$ | | |
| $\vdash (q_1, baaa, bSSZ_0)$ | $\Rightarrow abbSS$ | |
| $\vdash (q_1, aaa, SSZ_0)$ | | |
| $\vdash (q_1, aaa, aSZ_0)$ | $\Rightarrow abbaS$ | |
| $\vdash (q_1, aa, SZ_0)$ | | |
| $\vdash (q_1, aa, aSZ_0)$ | $\Rightarrow abbaaS$ | |
| $\vdash (q_1, a, SZ_0)$ | | |
| $\vdash (q_1, a, aZ_0)$ | $\Rightarrow abbaaa$ | |
| $\vdash (q_1, \Lambda, Z_0)$ | | |
| $\vdash (q_2, \Lambda, Z_0)$ | | |

You may wish to trace the other possible sequences of moves by which $x$ can be accepted, corresponding to other possible leftmost derivations of $x$ in this CFG.

---

The opposite approach to top-down is **bottom-up**. In this approach, there are opposite counterparts to both types of moves in the top-down PDA. Instead of replacing a variable $A$ on the stack by the right side $\alpha$ of a production $A \rightarrow \alpha$ (which effectively extends the tree downward), the PDA removes $\alpha$ from the stack and replaces it by (or "reduces it to") $A$, so that the tree is extended upward. In both approaches, the contents of the stack represents a portion of the current string in the derivation being simulated; instead of removing a terminal symbol from the beginning of this portion (which appeared on the stack as a result of applying a production), the PDA "shifts" a terminal symbol from the input to the end of this portion, in order to prepare for a reduction.

Note that because shifting input symbols onto the stack reverses their order, the string $\alpha$ that is to be reduced to $A$ will appear on the stack in reverse; thus the PDA begins the reduction with the *last* symbol of $\alpha$ on top of the stack.

Note also that while the top-down approach requires only one move to apply a production $A \rightarrow \alpha$, the corresponding reduction in the bottom-up approach requires a sequence of moves, one for each symbol in the string $\alpha$. We are interested primarily in the sequence as a whole, and with the natural correspondence between a production in the grammar and the sequence of moves that accomplishes the reduction.

The process terminates when the start symbol $S$, left on the stack by the last reduction, is popped off the stack and $Z_0$ is the only thing left. The entire process simulates a derivation, in reverse order, of the input string. At each step, the current string in the derivation is formed by the contents of the stack (in reverse), followed by the string of unread input; because after each reduction the variable on top of the stack is the rightmost one in the current string, the derivation being simulated in reverse is a *rightmost* derivation.

## A Bottom-up PDA for Simple Algebraic Expressions

**EXAMPLE 7.6**

Let us illustrate this approach using the grammar $G$, a simplified version of the one in Section 6.4, with productions

$$(1) \quad S \rightarrow S + T$$
$$(2) \quad S \rightarrow T$$
$$(3) \quad T \rightarrow T * a$$
$$(4) \quad T \rightarrow a$$

The reason for numbering the productions will be seen presently. Suppose the input string is $a + a * a\$$, which has the rightmost derivation

$$\begin{aligned}
S &\Rightarrow S + T \\
&\Rightarrow S + T * a \\
&\Rightarrow S + a * a \\
&\Rightarrow T + a * a \\
&\Rightarrow a + a * a
\end{aligned}$$

The corresponding steps or groups of steps executed by the bottom-up PDA as the string $a + a * a$ is processed are shown in Table 7.6. Remember that at each point, the reverse of the string on the stack (omitting $Z_0$), followed by the string of unread input, constitutes the current string in the derivation, and the reductions occur in the opposite order from the corresponding steps in the derivation. For example, since the last step in the derivation is to replace $T$ by $a$, the first reduction replaces $a$ on the stack by $T$.

In Table 7.7 we show the details of the nondeterministic bottom-up PDA that carries out these moves. The shift moves allow the next input to be shifted onto the stack, regardless of the current stack symbol. The sequence of moves in a reduction can begin when the top stack symbol is the last symbol of $\alpha$, for some string $\alpha$ in a production $A \rightarrow \alpha$. If $|\alpha| > 1$, the moves in the sequence proceed on the assumption that the symbols below the top one are in fact the previous symbols of $\alpha$; they remove these symbols, from back to front, and place $A$

**Table 7.6** | Processing of $a + a * a$ by the bottom-up PDA corresponding to $G$

| Move | Production | Stack | Unread input |
|------|------------|-------|--------------|
| — | | $Z_0$ | $a + a * a$ |
| shift | | $a Z_0$ | $+ a * a$ |
| reduce | $T \rightarrow a$ | $T Z_0$ | $+ a * a$ |
| reduce | $S \rightarrow T$ | $S Z_0$ | $+ a * a$ |
| shift | | $+ S Z_0$ | $a * a$ |
| shift | | $a + S Z_0$ | $* a$ |
| reduce | $T \rightarrow a$ | $T + S Z_0$ | $* a$ |
| shift | | $* T + S Z_0$ | $a$ |
| shift | | $a * T + S Z_0$ | — |
| reduce | $T \rightarrow T * a$ | $T + S Z_0$ | — |
| reduce | $S \rightarrow S + T$ | $S Z_0$ | — |
| (pop $S$) | | $Z_0$ | — |
| (accept) | | | |

**Table 7.7** | The nondeterministic bottom-up PDA for $G$

| State | Input | Stack symbol | Move(s) |
|---|---|---|---|
| **Shift moves ($\sigma$ and $X$ are arbitrary)** | | | |
| $q$ | $\sigma$ | $X$ | $(q, \sigma X)$ |
| **Moves to reduce $S + T$ to $S$** | | | |
| $q$ | $\Lambda$ | $T$ | $(q_{1,1}, \Lambda)$ |
| $q_{1,1}$ | $\Lambda$ | $+$ | $(q_{1,2}, \Lambda)$ |
| $q_{1,2}$ | $\Lambda$ | $S$ | $(q, S)$ |
| **Moves to reduce $T$ to $S$** | | | |
| $q$ | $\Lambda$ | $T$ | $(q, S)$ |
| **Moves to reduce $T * a$ to $T$** | | | |
| $q$ | $\Lambda$ | $a$ | $(q_{3,1}, \Lambda)$ |
| $q_{3,1}$ | $\Lambda$ | $*$ | $(q_{3,2}, \Lambda)$ |
| $q_{3,2}$ | $\Lambda$ | $T$ | $(q, T)$ |
| **Moves to reduce $a$ to $T$** | | | |
| $q$ | $\Lambda$ | $a$ | $(q, T)$ |
| **Moves to accept** | | | |
| $q$ | $\Lambda$ | $S$ | $(q_1, \Lambda)$ |
| $q_1$ | $\Lambda$ | $Z_0$ | $(q_2, \Lambda)$ |
| (all other combinations) | | | none |

on the stack. Once such a sequence is started, a set of states unique to this sequence is what allows the PDA to remember how to complete the sequence. Suppose for example that we want to reduce the string $T * a$ to $T$. If we begin in some state $q$, with $a$ on top of the stack, the first step will be to remove $a$ and enter a state that we might call $q_{3,1}$. (Here is where we use the numbering of the productions: The notation is supposed to suggest that the PDA has completed one step of the reduction associated with production 3.) Starting in state $q_{3,1}$, the machine expects to see $*$ on the stack. If it does, it removes it and enters state $q_{3,2}$, from which the only possible move is to remove $T$ from the stack, replace it by $T$, and return to $q$. Of course, all the moves of this sequence are $\Lambda$-transitions, affecting only the stack.

Apart from the special states used for reductions, the PDA stays in the state $q$ during almost all the processing. When $S$ is on top of the stack, it pops $S$ and moves to $q_1$, from which it enters the accepting state $q_2$ if at that point the stack is empty except for $Z_0$. The input alphabet is $\{a, +, *\}$ and the stack alphabet is $\{a, +, *, S, T, Z_0\}$.

Note that in the shift moves, a number of combinations of input and stack symbol could be omitted. For example, when a string in the language is processed, the symbol $+$ will never occur simultaneously as both the input symbol and stack symbol. It does no harm to include these, however, since no string giving rise to these combinations will be reduced to $S$.

It can be shown without difficulty that this nondeterministic PDA accepts the language generated by $G$. Moreover, for any CFG, a nondeterministic PDA can be constructed along the same lines that accepts the corresponding language.

# 7.5 | A CONTEXT-FREE GRAMMAR CORRESPONDING TO A GIVEN PDA

It will be useful in this section to keep in mind the nondeterministic top-down PDA constructed in the previous section to simulate leftmost derivations in a given context-free grammar. If at some point in a derivation the current string is $x\alpha$, where $x$ is a string of terminals, then at some point in the simulation, the input string read so far is $x$ and the stack contains the string $\alpha$. The stack alphabet of the PDA is $\Sigma \cup V$. The moves are defined so that variables are removed from the stack and replaced by the right sides of productions, and terminals on the stack are used to match input symbols. In this construction the states are almost incidental; after the initial move, the PDA stays in the same state until it is ready to accept.

Now we consider the opposite problem, constructing a context-free grammar that generates the language accepted by a given PDA. The argument is reasonably complicated, but it will be simplified somewhat if we can assume that the PDA accepts the language *by empty stack* (see Section 7.2). Our first job, therefore, is to convince ourselves that this assumption can be made without loss of generality. We state the result in Theorem 7.3 below and give a brief sketch of the proof, leaving the details to the exercises.

---

**Theorem 7.3**

Suppose $M = (Q, \Sigma, \Gamma, q_0, Z_0, A, \delta)$ is a pushdown automaton accepting the language $L \subseteq \Sigma^*$. Then there is another PDA $M_1 = (Q_1, \Sigma, \Gamma_1, q_1, Z_1, A_1, \delta_1)$ accepting $L$ by empty stack. In other words, for any string $x$, $x \in L$ if and only if $(q_1, x, Z_1) \vdash^*_{M_1} (q, \Lambda, \Lambda)$ for some state $q \in Q_1$.

***Sketch of proof***    At the point when our original PDA $M$ accepts a string, its stack may not be empty. We would like to construct $M_1$ so that as the two machines $M$ and $M_1$ process the same input string, $M_1$'s stack will be empty precisely when $M$ enters an accepting state. If we simply make $M_1$ a replica of $M$, but with the ability to empty its stack automatically, without reading any more input, whenever $M$ enters an accepting state, then we will have part of what we want: Any time $M$ enters an accepting state, the string read so far will be accepted by $M_1$ by empty stack. The reason this is not quite sufficient is that $M$ might crash (in a nonaccepting state) with an empty stack; in this case, since $M_1$ copies $M$ exactly, its stack will be empty too, and it will therefore accept by empty stack a string that $M$ does not accept. To avoid this, we let $M_1$ start by placing on its stack a special symbol *under* the start symbol of $M$. This special symbol will allow $M_1$ to avoid emptying its stack until it is appropriate to do so.

The way we allow $M_1$ to empty its stack automatically when $M$ enters an accepting state is to provide it with a $\Lambda$-transition from this state to a special "stack-emptying" state, from which there are other $\Lambda$-transitions that just keep popping symbols off the stack until it is empty.

Now we may return to the problem we are trying to solve. We have a PDA $M$ that accepts a language $L$ by empty stack (let us represent this fact by writing $L = L_e(M)$), and we would like to construct a CFG generating $L$. It will be helpful to try to preserve as much as possible the correspondence in Theorem 7.2 between the operation of the PDA and the leftmost derivation being simulated. The current string in the derivation will consist of two parts, the string of input symbols read by the PDA so far and a remaining portion corresponding to the current stack contents. In fact, we will define our CFG so that this remaining portion consists entirely of variables, so as to highlight the correspondence between it and the stack contents: In order to produce a string of terminals, we must eventually eliminate all the variables from the current string, and in order for the input string to be accepted by the PDA (by empty stack), all the symbols on the stack must eventually be popped off.

We consider first a very simple approach, which is *too* simple to work in general. Take the variables in the grammar to be all possible stack symbols in the PDA, renamed if necessary so that no input symbols are included; take the start symbol to be $Z_0$; ignore the states of the PDA completely; and for each PDA move that reads $a$ (either $\Lambda$ or an element of $\Sigma$) and replaces $A$ on the stack by $B_1 B_2 \cdots B_m$, introduce the production

$$A \to a B_1 B_2 \cdots B_m$$

This approach will give us the correspondence outlined above between the current stack contents and the string of variables remaining in the current string being derived. Moreover, it will allow the grammar to generate all strings accepted by the PDA. The reason it is too simple is that by ignoring the states of the PDA we may be allowing other strings to be derived as well. To see an example, we consider Example 7.1. This PDA accepts the language $\{x c x^r \mid x \in \{a, b\}^*\}$. The acceptance is by final state, rather than by empty stack, but we can fix this, and eliminate the state $q_2$ as well, by changing move 12 to

$$\delta(q_1, \Lambda, Z_0) = \{(q_1, \Lambda)\}$$

instead of $\{(q_2, Z_0)\}$. We use $A$ and $B$ as stack symbols instead of $a$ and $b$. The moves of the PDA include these:

$$\delta(q_0, a, Z_0) = \{(q_0, A Z_0)\}$$
$$\delta(q_0, c, A) = \{(q_1, A)\}$$
$$\delta(q_1, a, A) = \{(q_1, \Lambda)\}$$
$$\delta(q_1, \Lambda, Z_0) = \{(q_1, \Lambda)\}$$

Using the rule we have tentatively adopted, we obtain the corresponding productions

$$Z_0 \to a A Z_0$$
$$A \to c A$$
$$A \to a$$
$$Z_0 \to \Lambda$$

The string *aca* has the leftmost derivation

$$Z_0 \Rightarrow aAZ_0 \Rightarrow acAZ_0 \Rightarrow acaZ_0 \Rightarrow aca$$

corresponding to the sequence of moves

$$(q_0, aca, Z_0) \vdash (q_0, ca, AZ_0) \vdash (q_1, a, AZ_0) \vdash (q_1, \Lambda, Z_0) \vdash (q_1, \Lambda, \Lambda)$$

If we run the PDA on the input string *aa* instead, the initial move is

$$(q_0, aa, Z_0) \vdash (q_0, a, AZ_0)$$

and at this point the machine crashes, because it is only in state $q_1$ that it is allowed to read *a* and replace *A* on the stack by $\Lambda$. However, our grammar also allows the derivation

$$Z_0 \Rightarrow aAZ_0 \Rightarrow aaZ_0 \Rightarrow aa$$

In order to eliminate this problem, we must modify our grammar so as to incorporate the states of the PDA. Rather than using the stack symbols themselves as variables, we try things of the form

$$[p, A, q]$$

where *p* and *q* are states. For the variable $[p, A, q]$ to be replaced by *a* (either $\Lambda$ or a terminal symbol), it must be the case that there is a PDA move that reads *a*, pops *A* from the stack, and takes the machine from state *p* to state *q*. More general productions involving the variable $[p, A, q]$ are to be thought of as representing any *sequence* of moves that takes the PDA from state *p* to state *q* and has the ultimate effect of removing *A* from the stack.

If the variable $[p, A, q]$ appears in the current string of a derivation, our goal is to replace it by $\Lambda$ or a terminal symbol. This will be possible if there is a move that takes the PDA from *p* to *q* and pops *A* from the stack. Suppose instead, however, that there is a move from *p* to some state $p_1$, that reads *a* and replaces *A* on the stack by $B_1 B_2 \cdots B_m$. It is appropriate to introduce *a* into our current string at this point, since we want the initial string of terminals to correspond to the input read so far. But it is now also appropriate to think of our original goal as being modified, as a result of all the new symbols that have been introduced on the stack. The most direct way to eliminate these new symbols $B_1, \ldots, B_m$ is as follows: to start in $p_1$ and make a sequence of moves—ending up in some state $p_2$, say—that result in $B_1$ being removed from the stack; then to make some more moves that remove $B_2$ and in the process move from $p_2$ to some other state $p_3$; ...; to move from $p_{m-1}$ to some $p_m$ and remove $B_{m-1}$; and finally, to move from $p_m$ to *q* and remove $B_m$. The actual moves of the PDA may not accomplish these steps directly, but this is what we want their ultimate effect to be. Because it does not matter what the states $p_2, p_3, \ldots, p_m$ are, we will allow any string of the form

$$a[p_1, B, p_2][p_2, B_2, p_3] \cdots [p_m, B_m, q]$$

to replace $[p, A, q]$ in the current string. In other words, we will introduce the productions

$$[p, A, q] \rightarrow a[p_1, B, p_2][p_2, B_2, p_3] \cdots [p_m, B_m, q]$$

for all possible sequences of states $p_2, \ldots, p_m$. Some such sequences will be dead ends, in the sense that there will be no sequence of moves following this sequence of states and having this ultimate effect. But no harm is done by introducing these productions, because for any derivation in which one of these dead-end sequences appears, there will be at least one variable that cannot be eliminated from the string, and so the derivation will not produce a string of terminals. If we denote by $S$ the start symbol of the grammar, the productions that we need to begin are those of the form

$$S \rightarrow [q_0, Z_0, q]$$

where $q_0$ is the initial state. When we accept strings by empty stack the final state is irrelevant, and thus we include a production of this type for every possible state $q$.

We now present the proof that the CFG we have described generates the language accepted by $M$.

---

**Theorem 7.4**
Let $M = (Q, \Sigma, \Gamma, q_0, Z_0, A, \delta)$ be a pushdown automaton accepting a language $L$ by empty stack; that is, $L = L_e(M)$. Then there is a context-free grammar $G$ with $L(G) = L$.

*Proof*
We define $G = (V, \Sigma, S, P)$ as follows:

$$V = \{S\} \cup \{[p, A, q] \mid A \in \Gamma, \; p, q \in Q\}$$

The set $P$ contains the following productions and only these:

1. For every $q \in Q$, the production $S \rightarrow [q_0, Z_0, q]$ is in $P$.
2. For every $q, q_1 \in Q$, $a \in \Sigma \cup \{\Lambda\}$, and $A \in \Gamma$, if $\delta(q, a, A)$ contains $(q_1, \Lambda)$, then the production $[q, A, q_1] \rightarrow a$ is in $P$.
3. For every $q, q_1 \in Q$, $a \in \Sigma \cup \{\Lambda\}$, $A \in \Gamma$, and $m \geq 1$, if $\delta(q, a, A)$ contains $(q_1, B_1 B_2 \cdots B_m)$ for some $B_1, \ldots, B_m \in \Gamma$, then for every choice of $q_2, \ldots, q_{m+1} \in Q$, the production

$$[q, A, q_{m+1}] \rightarrow a[q_1, B_1, q_2][q_2, B_2, q_3] \ldots [q_m, B_m, q_{m+1}]$$

is in $P$.

The main idea of the proof is to characterize the strings of terminals that can be derived from a variable $[q, A, q']$; specifically, to show that for any $q, q' \in Q$, $A \in \Gamma$, and $x \in \Sigma^*$,

$$(1) \quad [q, A, q'] \Rightarrow_G^* x \text{ if and only if } (q, x, A) \vdash_M^* (q', \Lambda, \Lambda)$$

From this result, the theorem will follow. On the one hand, if $x \in L_e(M)$, then $(q_0, x, Z_0) \vdash_M^* (q, \Lambda, \Lambda)$ for some $q \in Q$; then (1) implies that $[q_0, Z_0, q] \Rightarrow_G^* x$; therefore, $x \in L(G)$, because we can start a derivation with a production of type 1. On the other hand, if $x \in L(G)$, then the first step in any derivation of $x$ must be $S \Rightarrow [q_0, Z_0, q]$, for some $q \in Q$, which means that $[q_0, Z_0, q] \Rightarrow_G^* x$. It then follows from (1) that $x \in L_e(M)$.

Both parts of (1) are proved using mathematical induction. Let us introduce the notations $\Rightarrow^n$ and $\vdash^n$ (where $n$ is a nonnegative integer) to refer to $n$-step derivations in the grammar and sequences of $n$ moves of the PDA, respectively.

First we show that for every $n \geq 1$,

(2)   If $[q, A, q'] \Rightarrow_G^n x$, then $(q, x, A) \vdash_M^* (q', \Lambda, \Lambda)$

For the basis step of the proof, suppose that $[q, A, q'] \Rightarrow_G^1 x$. The only production that can allow this one-step derivation is one of type 2, and this can happen only if $x$ is either $\Lambda$ or an element of $\Sigma$ and $\delta(q, x, A)$ contains $(q', \Lambda)$. In this case, it is obviously true that $(q, x, A) \vdash (q', \Lambda, \Lambda)$.

For the induction step, suppose that $k \geq 1$ and that whenever $[q, A, q']$ $\Rightarrow_G^n x$ for some $n \leq k$, $(q, x, A) \vdash^* (q', \Lambda, \Lambda)$. Now suppose that $[q, A, q'] \Rightarrow^{k+1} x$. We wish to show that $(q, x, A) \vdash^* (q', \Lambda, \Lambda)$. Since $k \geq 1$, the first step of the derivation of $x$ must be

$$[q, A, q'] \Rightarrow a[q_1, B_1, q_2][q_2, B_2, q_3] \cdots [q_m, B_m, q']$$

for some $m \geq 1$, some $a \in \Sigma \cup \{\Lambda\}$, some sequence $B_1, B_2, \ldots, B_m \in \Gamma$, and some sequence $q_1, q_2, \ldots, q_m \in Q$, so that $\delta(q, a, A)$ contains $(q_1, B_1 \cdots B_m)$. The remaining part of the derivation takes each of the variables $[q_i, B_i, q_{i+1}]$ to some string $x_i$, and the variable $[q_m, B_m, q']$ to a string $x_m$. The strings $x_1, \ldots, x_m$ satisfy the formula $ax_1 \cdots x_m = x$, and each $x_i$ is derived from its respective variable in $k$ or fewer steps. The induction hypothesis, therefore, implies that for each $i$ with $1 \leq i \leq m - 1$,

$$(q_i, x_i, B_i) \vdash^* (q_{i+1}, \Lambda, \Lambda)$$

and that

$$(q_m, x_m, B_m) \vdash^* (q', \Lambda, \Lambda)$$

Suppose $M$ is in the configuration $(q, x, A) = (q, ax_1x_2 \cdots x_m, A)$. Because $\delta(q, a, A)$ contains $(q_1, B_1 \cdots B_m)$, $M$ can go in one step to the configuration

$$(q_1, x_1x_2 \cdots x_m, B_1B_2 \cdots B_m)$$

$M$ can then go in a sequence of steps to

$$(q_2, x_2 \cdots x_m, B_2 \cdots B_m)$$

then to $(q_3, x_3 \cdots x_m, B_3 \cdots B_m)$, and ultimately to $(q', \Lambda, \Lambda)$. Thus the result (2) follows.

To complete the proof of (1), we show that for every $n \geq 1$,

(3)   If $(q, x, A) \vdash^n (q', \Lambda, \Lambda)$, then $[q, A, q'] \Rightarrow^* x$

In the case $n = 1$, a string $x$ satisfying the hypothesis in (3) must be of length 0 or 1, and $\delta(q, x, A)$ must contain $(q', \Lambda)$. In this case, we may derive $x$ from $[q, A, q']$ using a production of type 2.

For the induction step, we suppose that $k \geq 1$ and that for any $n \leq k$, and any combination of $q, q' \in Q$, $x \in \Sigma^*$, and $A \in \Gamma$, if $(q, x, A) \vdash^n (q', \Lambda, \Lambda)$, then $[q, A, q'] \Rightarrow^* x$. Next we suppose that $(q, x, A) \vdash^{k+1} (q', \Lambda, \Lambda)$, and we wish to show that $[q, A, q'] \Rightarrow^* x$. We know that for some $a \in \Sigma \cup \{\Lambda\}$ and some $y \in \Sigma^*$, $x = ay$ and the first of the $k + 1$ moves is

$$(q, x, A) = (q, ay, A) \vdash (q_1, y, B_1 B_2 \cdots B_m)$$

Here $m \geq 1$, since $k \geq 1$, and the $B_i$'s are elements of $\Gamma$. In other words, $\delta(q, a, A)$ contains $(q_1, B_1 \cdots B_m)$. The $k$ subsequent moves end in the configuration $(q', \Lambda, \Lambda)$; therefore, for each $i$ with $1 \leq i \leq m$ there must be intermediate points at which the stack contains precisely the string $B_i B_{i+1} \cdots B_m$. For each such $i$, let $q_i$ be the state $M$ is in the first time the stack contains $B_i \cdots B_m$, and let $x_i$ be the portion of the input string that is consumed in going from $q_i$ to $q_{i+1}$ (or, if $i = m$, in going from $q_m$ to the configuration $(q', \Lambda, \Lambda)$). Then it must be the case that

$$(q_i, x_i, B_i) \vdash^* (q_{i+1}, \Lambda, \Lambda)$$

for each $i$ with $1 \leq i \leq m - 1$, and

$$(q_m, x_m, B_m) \vdash^* (q', \Lambda, \Lambda)$$

where each of the indicated sequences of moves has $k$ or fewer. Therefore, by the induction hypothesis,

$$[q_i, B_i, q_{i+1}] \Rightarrow_G^* x_i$$

for each $i$ with $1 \leq i \leq m - 1$, and

$$[q_m, B_m, q'] \Rightarrow^* x_m$$

Since $\delta(q, a, A)$ contains $(q_1, B_1 \cdots B_m)$, we know that

$$[q, A, q'] \Rightarrow a[q_1, B_1, q_2][q_2, B_2, q_3] \cdots [q_m, B_m, q']$$

(this is a production of type 3), and we may conclude that

$$[q, A, q'] \Rightarrow^* a x_1 x_2 \cdots x_m = x$$

This completes the induction and the proof of the theorem.

**EXAMPLE 7.7** Obtaining a CFG from a PDA Accepting Simple Palindromes

We return once more to the language $L = \{xcx^r \mid x \in \{a, b\}^*\}$ of Example 7.1, which we used to introduce the construction in Theorem 7.4. In that discussion we used the PDA whose transition table is shown below. (It is modified from the one in Example 7.1, both in using uppercase letters for stack symbols and in accepting by empty stack.)

| Move number | State | Input | Stack symbol | Move(s) |
|:---:|:---:|:---:|:---:|:---:|
| 1 | $q_0$ | $a$ | $Z_0$ | $(q_0, AZ_0)$ |
| 2 | $q_0$ | $b$ | $Z_0$ | $(q_0, BZ_0)$ |
| 3 | $q_0$ | $a$ | $A$ | $(q_0, AA)$ |
| 4 | $q_0$ | $b$ | $A$ | $(q_0, BA)$ |
| 5 | $q_0$ | $a$ | $B$ | $(q_0, AB)$ |
| 6 | $q_0$ | $b$ | $B$ | $(q_0, BB)$ |
| 7 | $q_0$ | $c$ | $Z_0$ | $(q_1, Z_0)$ |
| 8 | $q_0$ | $c$ | $A$ | $(q_1, A)$ |
| 9 | $q_0$ | $c$ | $B$ | $(q_1, B)$ |
| 10 | $q_1$ | $a$ | $A$ | $(q_1, \Lambda)$ |
| 11 | $q_1$ | $b$ | $B$ | $(q_1, \Lambda)$ |
| 12 | $q_1$ | $\Lambda$ | $Z_0$ | $(q_1, \Lambda)$ |
| (all other combinations) | | | | none |

In the grammar $G = (V, \Sigma, S, P)$ obtained from the construction in Theorem 7.4, $V$ contains $S$ as well as every object of the form $[p, X, q]$, where $X$ is a stack symbol and $p$ and $q$ can each be either $q_0$ or $q_1$. Productions of the following types are contained in $P$:

$$
\begin{aligned}
(0) \quad & S && \to [q_0, Z_0, q] \\
(1) \quad & [q_0, Z_0, q] && \to a[q_0, A, p][p, Z_0, q] \\
(2) \quad & [q_0, Z_0, q] && \to b[q_0, B, p][p, Z_0, q] \\
(3) \quad & [q_0, A, q] && \to a[q_0, A, p][p, A, q] \\
(4) \quad & [q_0, A, q] && \to b[q_0, B, p][p, A, q] \\
(5) \quad & [q_0, B, q] && \to a[q_0, A, p][p, B, q] \\
(6) \quad & [q_0, B, q] && \to b[q_0, B, p][p, B, q] \\
(7) \quad & [q_0, Z_0, q] && \to c[q_1, Z_0, q] \\
(8) \quad & [q_0, A, q] && \to c[q_1, A, q] \\
(9) \quad & [q_0, B, q] && \to c[q_1, B, q] \\
(10) \quad & [q_1, A, q_1] && \to a \\
(11) \quad & [q_1, B, q_1] && \to b \\
(12) \quad & [q_1, Z_0, q_1] && \to \Lambda
\end{aligned}
$$

Allowing all combinations of $p$ and $q$ gives 35 productions in all.

Consider the string $bacab$. The PDA accepts it by the sequence of moves

$$
\begin{aligned}
(q_0, bacab, Z_0) & \vdash (q_0, acab, BZ_0) \\
& \vdash (q_0, cab, ABZ_0) \\
& \vdash (q_1, ab, ABZ_0) \\
& \vdash (q_1, b, BZ_0) \\
& \vdash (q_1, \Lambda, Z_0) \\
& \vdash (q_1, \Lambda, \Lambda)
\end{aligned}
$$

The corresponding leftmost derivation in the grammar is

$$
\begin{aligned}
S & \Rightarrow [q_0, Z_0, q_1] \\
& \Rightarrow b[q_0, B, q_1][q_1, Z_0, q_1]
\end{aligned}
$$

$$\Rightarrow ba[q_0, A, q_1][q_1, B, q_1][q_1, Z_0, q_1]$$

$$\Rightarrow bac[q_1, A, q_1][q_1, B, q_1][q_1, Z_0, q_1]$$

$$\Rightarrow baca[q_1, B, q_1][q_1, Z_0, q_1]$$

$$\Rightarrow bacab[q_1, Z_0, q_1]$$

$$\Rightarrow bacab$$

From the sequence of PDA moves, it may look as though there are several choices of leftmost derivations. For example, we might start with the production $S \rightarrow [q_0, Z_0, q_0]$. Remember, however, that $[q_0, Z_0, q]$ represents a sequence of moves from $q_0$ to $q$ that has the ultimate effect of removing $Z_0$ from the stack. Since the PDA ends up in state $q_1$, it is clear that $q$ should be $q_1$. Similarly, it may seem as if the second step could be

$$[q_0, Z_0, q_1] \Rightarrow b[q_0, B, q_0][q_0, Z_0, q_1]$$

However, the sequence of PDA moves that starts in $q_0$ and eliminates $B$ from the stack ends with the PDA in state $q_1$, not $q_0$. In fact, because every move to state $q_0$ adds to the stack, the variable $[q_0, B, q_0]$ in this grammar is useless: No string of terminals can be derived from it.

# 7.6 | PARSING

Suppose that $G$ is a context-free grammar over an alphabet $\Sigma$. To *parse* a string $x \in \Sigma^*$ (to find a derivation of $x$ in the grammar $G$, or to determine that there is none) is often useful. Parsing a statement in a programming language, for example, is necessary in order to classify it according to syntax; parsing an algebraic expression is essentially what allows us to evaluate the expression. The problem of finding efficient parsing algorithms has led to a great deal of research, and there are many specialized techniques that depend on specific properties of the grammar.

In this section we return to the two natural ways presented in Section 7.4 of obtaining a PDA to accept the language $L(G)$. In both cases, the PDA not only accepts a string in $L(G)$ but does it by simulating a derivation of $x$ (in one case a leftmost derivation, in the other case rightmost). Although the official output of a PDA is just a yes-or-no answer, it is easy enough to enhance the machine slightly by allowing it to record its moves, so that any sequence of moves leading to acceptance causes a derivation to be displayed. However, neither construction by itself can be said to produce a parsing algorithm, because both PDAs are inherently nondeterministic. In each case, the simulation proceeds by *guessing* the next step in the derivation; if the guess is correct, its correctness will be confirmed eventually by the PDA.

One approach to obtaining a parsing algorithm would be to consider all possible sequences of guesses the PDA might make, in order to see whether one of them leads to acceptance. Exercise 7.47 asks you to use a backtracking strategy for doing this with a simple CFG. However, it is possible with both types of nondeterministic PDAs to confront the nondeterminism more directly: rather than making an arbitrary choice and then trying to confirm that it was the right one, trying instead to use all the information available in order to select the choice that will be correct. In the remainder of this section, we concentrate on two simple classes of grammars, for which the next input symbol and the top stack symbol in the corresponding PDA provide enough information at each step to determine the next move in the simulated derivation. In more general grammars, the approach at least provides a starting point for the development of an efficient parser.

### 7.6.1 Top-down parsing

A Top-down Parser for Balanced Strings of Parentheses     **EXAMPLE 7.8**

We consider the language of balanced strings of parentheses. For convenience, we modify it slightly by adding a special endmarker $ to the end of each string. The new language will be denoted $L$. If we use [ ] as our parentheses, the context-free grammar with productions

$$S \to T\$$$
$$T \to [T]T \mid \Lambda$$

is an unambiguous CFG generating $L$. In the top-down PDA obtained from this grammar, the only nondeterminism arises when the variable $T$ is on the top of the stack, and we have a choice of two moves using input $\Lambda$. If the next input symbol is [, then the correct move (or, conceivably, sequence of moves) must produce a [ on top of the stack to match it. Replacing $T$ by $[T]T$ will obviously do this; replacing $T$ by $\Lambda$ would have a chance of being correct only if the symbol below $T$ were either [ or $T$, and it is not hard to see that this never occurs. It appears, therefore, that if $T$ is on top of the stack, $T$ should be replaced by $[T]T$ if the next input symbol is [ and by $\Lambda$ if the next input is ] or $. The nondeterminism can be eliminated by *lookahead*—using the next input symbol as well as the stack symbol to determine the move.

In the case when $T$ is on the stack and the next input symbol is either ] or $, popping $T$ from the stack will lead to acceptance only if the symbol beneath it matches the input; thus the PDA needs to remember the input symbol long enough to match it with the new stack symbol. We can accomplish this by introducing the two states $q_]$ and $q_\$$ to which the PDA can move on the respective input symbol when $T$ is on top of the stack. In either of these states, the only correct move is to pop the corresponding symbol from the stack and return to $q_1$. For the sake of consistency, we also use a state $q_[$ for the case when $T$ is on top of the stack and the next input is [. Although in this case $T$ is replaced on the stack by the longer string $[T]T$, the move from $q_]$ is also to pop the [ from the stack and return to $q_1$. The alternative, which would be slightly more efficient, would be to replace these two moves by a single one that leaves the PDA in $q_1$ and replaces $T$ on the stack by $T]T$.

The transition table for the original nondeterministic PDA is shown in Table 7.8, and Table 7.9 describes the deterministic PDA obtained by incorporating lookahead.

The sequence of moves by which the PDA accepts the string [ ]$, and the corresponding steps in the leftmost derivation of this string, are shown below.

$$(q_0, [\,]\$, Z_0)$$
$$\vdash (q_1, [\,]\$, SZ_0) \qquad S$$
$$\vdash (q_1, [\,]\$, T\$Z_0) \qquad \Rightarrow T\$$$
$$\vdash (q_[, \,]\$, [T]T\$Z_0) \qquad \Rightarrow [T]T\$$$
$$\vdash (q_1, \,]\$, T]T\$Z_0)$$

**Table 7.8** | A nondeterministic top-down PDA for balanced strings of parentheses

| Move number | State | Input | Stack symbol | Move |
|---|---|---|---|---|
| 1 | $q_0$ | $\Lambda$ | $Z_0$ | $(q_1, SZ_0)$ |
| 2 | $q_1$ | $\Lambda$ | $S$ | $(q_1, T\$)$ |
| 3 | $q_1$ | $\Lambda$ | $T$ | $(q_1, [T]T), (q_1, \Lambda)$ |
| 4 | $q_1$ | $[$ | $[$ | $(q_1, \Lambda)$ |
| 5 | $q_1$ | $]$ | $]$ | $(q_1, \Lambda)$ |
| 6 | $q_1$ | $\$$ | $\$$ | $(q_1, \Lambda)$ |
| 7 | $q_1$ | $\Lambda$ | $Z_0$ | $(q_2, Z_0)$ |
| (all other combinations) | | | | none |

**Table 7.9** | Using lookahead to eliminate the nondeterminism from Table 7.8

| | | | | |
|---|---|---|---|---|
| 1 | $q_0$ | $\Lambda$ | $Z_0$ | $(q_1, SZ_0)$ |
| 2 | $q_1$ | $\Lambda$ | $S$ | $(q_1, T\$)$ |
| 3 | $q_1$ | $[$ | $T$ | $(q_[, [T]T)$ |
| 4 | $q_[$ | $\Lambda$ | $[$ | $(q_1, \Lambda)$ |
| 5 | $q_1$ | $]$ | $T$ | $(q_1, \Lambda)$ |
| 6 | $q_1$ | $\Lambda$ | $]$ | $(q_1, \Lambda)$ |
| 7 | $q_1$ | $\$$ | $T$ | $(q_\$, \Lambda)$ |
| 8 | $q_\$$ | $\Lambda$ | $\$$ | $(q_1, \Lambda)$ |
| 9 | $q_1$ | $[$ | $[$ | $(q_1, \Lambda)$ |
| 10 | $q_1$ | $]$ | $]$ | $(q_1, \Lambda)$ |
| 11 | $q_1$ | $\$$ | $\$$ | $(q_1, \Lambda)$ |
| 12 | $q_1$ | $\Lambda$ | $Z_0$ | $(q_2, Z_0)$ |
| (all other combinations) | | | | none |

$$\vdash (q_1, \$, ]T\$Z_0) \quad \Rightarrow []T\$$$
$$\vdash (q_1, \$, T\$Z_0)$$
$$\vdash (q_\$, \Lambda, \$Z_0) \quad \Rightarrow []\$$$
$$\vdash (q_1, \Lambda, Z_0)$$
$$\vdash (q_2, \Lambda, Z_0)$$

You can probably see that moves 9, 10, and 11 in the deterministic PDA, which were retained from the nondeterministic machine, will never actually be used. We include them because in a more general example moves of this type may still be necessary. Although we do not give a proof that the deterministic PDA accepts the language, you can convince yourself by tracing the moves for a few longer input strings.

In the top-down PDA obtained from a context-free grammar as in Definition 7.4, looking ahead to the next input may not be enough to determine the next move. Sometimes, however, straightforward modifications of the grammar are enough to establish this property, as the next two examples indicate.

Eliminating Left Recursion in a CFG $\quad$ **EXAMPLE 7.9**

Another unambiguous CFG for the language of Example 7.8 is the one with productions

$$S \to T\$$$

$$T \to T[T] \mid \Lambda$$

The standard top-down PDA produced from this grammar is exactly the same as the one in Example 7.8, except for the string replacing $T$ on the stack in the first move of line 3. We can see the potential problem by considering the input string [ ][ ][ ]$, which has the leftmost derivation

$$S \Rightarrow T\$ \Rightarrow T[T]\$ \Rightarrow T[T][T]\$ \Rightarrow T[T][T][T]\$ \Rightarrow \cdots \Rightarrow [\,][\,][\,]\$$$

The correct sequence of moves for this input string therefore begins

$$(q_0, [\,][\,][\,]\$, Z_0) \vdash (q_1, [\,][\,][\,]\$, SZ_0)$$

$$\vdash (q_1, [\,][\,][\,]\$, T\$Z_0)$$

$$\vdash (q_1, [\,][\,][\,]\$, T[T]\$Z_0)$$

$$\vdash (q_1, [\,][\,][\,]\$, T[T][T]\$Z_0)$$

$$\vdash (q_1, [\,][\,][\,]\$, T[T][T][T]\$Z_0)$$

In each of the last four configurations shown, the next input is [ and the top stack symbol is $T$, but the correct sequences of moves beginning at these four points are all different. Since the remaining input is exactly the same in all these configurations, looking ahead to the next input, or even farther ahead, will not help; there is no way to choose the next move on the basis of the input.

The problem arises because of the production $T \to T[T]$, which illustrates the phenomenon of *left recursion*. Because the right side begins with $T$, the PDA must make a certain number of identical moves before it does anything else, and looking ahead in the input provides no help in deciding how many. In this case we can eliminate the left recursion by modifying the grammar. Suppose in general that a grammar has the $T$-productions

$$T \to T\alpha \mid \beta$$

where the string $\beta$ does not begin with $T$. These allow all the strings $\beta\alpha^n$, for $n \geq 0$, to be obtained from $T$. If these two productions are replaced by

$$T \to \beta U \qquad U \to \alpha U \mid \Lambda$$

the language is unchanged and the left recursion has been eliminated. In our example, with $\alpha = [T]$ and $\beta = \Lambda$, we replace

$$T \to T[T] \mid \Lambda$$

by

$$T \to U \qquad U \to [T]U \mid \Lambda$$

and the resulting grammar allows us to construct a deterministic PDA much as in Example 7.8.

**EXAMPLE 7.10** Factoring in a CFG

Consider the context-free grammar with productions

$$S \to T\$$$

$$T \to [T] \mid [\,]T \mid [T]T \mid [\,]$$

This is the unambiguous grammar obtained from the one in Example 7.8 by removing $\Lambda$-productions from the CFG with productions $T \to [T]T \mid \Lambda$; the language is unchanged except that it no longer contains the string \$.

Although there is no left recursion in the CFG, we can tell immediately that knowing the next input symbol will not be enough to choose the nondeterministic PDA's next move when $T$ is on top of the stack. The problem here is that the right sides of all four $T$-productions begin with the same symbol. An appropriate remedy is to "factor" the right sides, as follows:

$$T \to [U \qquad U \to T] \mid ]T \mid T]T \mid ]$$

More factoring is necessary because of the $U$-productions; in the ones whose right side begins with $T$, we can factor out $T]$. We obtain the productions

$$S \to T\$ \qquad T \to [U$$

$$U \to T]W \mid ]W \qquad W \to T \mid \Lambda$$

We can simplify the grammar slightly by eliminating the variable $T$, and we obtain

$$S \to [U\$ \qquad U \to [U]W \mid ]W \qquad W \to [U \mid \Lambda$$

The DPDA we obtain by incorporating lookahead is shown in Table 7.10.

**Table 7.10** | A deterministic top-down PDA for Example 7.10

| Move number | State | Input | Stack symbol | Move |
|:---:|:---:|:---:|:---:|:---:|
| 1 | $q_0$ | $\Lambda$ | $Z_0$ | $(q_1, SZ_0)$ |
| 2 | $q_1$ | $\Lambda$ | $S$ | $(q_1, [U\$)$ |
| 3 | $q_1$ | $[$ | $U$ | $(q_[, [U]W)$ |
| 4 | $q_[$ | $\Lambda$ | $[$ | $(q_1, \Lambda)$ |
| 5 | $q_1$ | $]$ | $U$ | $(q_1, ]W)$ |
| 6 | $q_1$ | $\Lambda$ | $]$ | $(q_1, \Lambda)$ |
| 7 | $q_1$ | $[$ | $W$ | $(q_[, [U)$ |
| 8 | $q_1$ | $]$ | $W$ | $(q_1, \Lambda)$ |
| 9 | $q_1$ | $\$$ | $W$ | $(q_\$, \Lambda)$ |
| 10 | $q_\$$ | $\Lambda$ | $\$$ | $(q_1, \Lambda)$ |
| 11 | $q_1$ | $[$ | $[$ | $(q_1, \Lambda)$ |
| 12 | $q_1$ | $]$ | $]$ | $(q_1, \Lambda)$ |
| 13 | $q_1$ | $\$$ | $\$$ | $(q_1, \Lambda)$ |
| 14 | $q_1$ | $\Lambda$ | $Z_0$ | $(q_2, Z_0)$ |
| | (all other combinations) | | | none |

In Examples 7.9 and 7.10, we were able by a combination of factoring and eliminating left recursion to transform the CFG into what is called an LL(1) grammar, meaning that the nondeterministic top-down PDA produced from the grammar can be turned into a deterministic top-down parser by looking ahead to the next symbol. A grammar is LL($k$) if looking ahead $k$ symbols in the input is always enough to choose the next move of the PDA. Such a grammar allows the construction of a deterministic top-down parser, and there are systematic methods for determining whether a CFG is LL($k$) and for carrying out this construction (see the references).

For an LL(1) context-free grammar, a deterministic PDA is one way of formulating the algorithm that decides the next step in the derivation of a string by looking at the next input symbol. The method of *recursive descent* is another way. The name refers to a collection of mutually recursive procedures corresponding to the variables in the grammar.

## A Recursive-descent Parser for the LL(1) Grammar in Example 7.10    **EXAMPLE 7.11**

The context-free grammar is the one with productions

$$S \rightarrow [U\$$$

$$U \rightarrow ]W \mid [U]W$$

$$W \rightarrow [U \mid \Lambda$$

We give a C++ version of a recursive-descent parser. The term *recognizer* is really more accurate than *parser*, though it would not be difficult to add output statements to the program that would allow one to reconstruct a derivation of the string being recognized.

The program involves functions s, u, and w, corresponding to the three variables. Calls on these three functions correspond to substitutions for the respective variables during a derivation—or to replacement of those variables on the stack in a PDA implementation. There is a global variable curr_ch, whose value is assigned before any of the three functions is called. If the current character is one of those that the function expects, it is *matched*, and the input function is called to read and echo the next character. Otherwise, an error-handling function is called and told what the character should have been; in this case, the program terminates with an appropriate error message.

Note that the program's correctness depends on the grammar's being LL(1), since each of the functions can select the correct action on the basis of the current input symbol.

```
#include <iostream.h>
#include <stdlib.h>

char curr_ch;           // the current symbol

void s(), u(), w();     // recognize S, U, W, respectively
void match(char);       // compares curr_ch to the argument; aborts with
                        // error message if no match, otherwise returns.
void get_ch();          // reads the next symbol into curr_ch, with echo.
void error(char*);      // reports an error and aborts.  String argument.
void error(char);       //                              Character argument.
```

```
void main()
{  get_ch();  s();
   cout << endl << "Parsing complete.   "
        << "The above string is in the language." << endl;
}

void s()                                    // recognizes [U$
{  match('[');  u();  match('$');  }

void u()                                    // recognizes ]W  |  [U]W
{  switch (curr_ch)
   {  case ']': match(']');  w();  break;   // production ]W
      case '[':                             // production [U]W
              match('[');  u();  match(']');  w(); break;
      default : error("[ or ]");
   }
}

void w()                                        // recognizes [U  |   <Lambda>
{  if (curr_ch == '[')     { match('[');  u(); }   }

void get_ch()                     // read and echo next nonblank symbol
{  if (cin >> curr_ch)  cout << curr_ch;
   if (cin.eof() && curr_ch != '$')
   {  cout << " (End of Data)";  error("[ or ]");  }
}

void match(char this_ch)
{  if (curr_ch == this_ch)  get_ch();  else error(this_ch);  }

void error(char* some_chars)
{  cout << "\n  ERROR : Expecting one of " << some_chars << ".\n";
   exit(0);
}

void error(char a_char)
{  cout << "\n  ERROR : Expecting " << a_char << ".\n";
   exit(0);
}
```

Here is a sample of the output produced, for the strings [] [[] [[]]]$, $, []], and [[], respectively.

```
[] [[] [[]]]$
Parsing complete.  The above string is in the language.
```

```
$
  ERROR : Expecting [.
[]]
  ERROR : Expecting $.
[[] (End of Data)
  ERROR : Expecting one of [ or ].
```

The program is less complete than it might be, in several respects. In the case of a string not in the language, it reads and prints out only the symbols up to the first illegal one—that is, up to the point where the DPDA would crash. In addition, it does not read past the $; if the input string were [] $], for example, the program would merely report that [] $ is in the language. Finally, the error messages may seem slightly questionable. The second error, for example, is detected in the function s, after the return from the call on u. The production is $S \rightarrow [U\$$; the function "expects" to see $ at this point, although not every symbol other than $ would have triggered the error message. The symbol [ would be valid here and would have resulted in a different sequence of function calls, so that the program would not have performed the same test at this point in s.

## 7.6.2 Bottom-up parsing

Example 7.12 illustrates one of the simplest ways of obtaining a deterministic bottom-up parser from a nondeterministic bottom-up PDA.

A Deterministic Bottom-up Parser for a CFG  **EXAMPLE 7.12**

We consider the context-free grammar $G$ with productions

$$
\begin{array}{rll}
(0) & S & \rightarrow & S_1\$ \\
(1) & S_1 & \rightarrow & S_1 + T \\
(2) & S_1 & \rightarrow & T \\
(3) & T & \rightarrow & T * a \\
(4) & T & \rightarrow & a
\end{array}
$$

The last four are essentially those in Example 7.6; the endmarker $ introduced in production (0) will be useful here, as it was in the discussion of top-down parsing.

Table 7.11 shows the nondeterministic PDA in Example 7.6 with the additional reduction corresponding to grammar rule (0).

The other slight difference from the PDA in Example 7.6 is that because the start symbol $S$ occurs only in production (0) in the grammar, the PDA can move to the accepting state as soon as it sees $S$ on the stack.

Nondeterminism is present in two ways. First, there may be a choice as to whether to shift an input symbol onto the stack or to try to reduce a string on top of the stack. For example, if $T$ is the top stack symbol, the first choice is correct if it is the $T$ in the right side of $T * a$, and the second is correct if it is the $T$ in one of the $S_1$-productions. Second, there may be some

**Table 7.11** | A nondeterministic bottom-up
parser for $G$

| State | Input | Stack symbol | Move(s) |
|-------|-------|--------------|---------|
| **Shift moves ($\sigma$ and $X$ are arbitrary)** | | | |
| $q$ | $\sigma$ | $X$ | $(q, \sigma X)$ |
| **Moves to reduce $S_1\$$ to $S$** | | | |
| $q$ | $\Lambda$ | $\$$ | $(q_{0,1}, \Lambda)$ |
| $q_{0,1}$ | $\Lambda$ | $S_1$ | $(q, S)$ |
| **Moves to reduce $S_1 + T$ to $S_1$** | | | |
| $q$ | $\Lambda$ | $T$ | $(q_{1,1}, \Lambda)$ |
| $q_{1,1}$ | $\Lambda$ | $+$ | $(q_{1,2}, \Lambda)$ |
| $q_{1,2}$ | $\Lambda$ | $S_1$ | $(q, S_1)$ |
| **Moves to reduce $T$ to $S_1$** | | | |
| $q$ | $\Lambda$ | $T$ | $(q, S_1)$ |
| **Moves to reduce $T * a$ to $T$** | | | |
| $q$ | $\Lambda$ | $a$ | $(q_{3,1}, \Lambda)$ |
| $q_{3,1}$ | $\Lambda$ | $*$ | $(q_{3,2}, \Lambda)$ |
| $q_{3,2}$ | $\Lambda$ | $T$ | $(q, T)$ |
| **Moves to reduce $a$ to $T$** | | | |
| $q$ | $\Lambda$ | $a$ | $(q, T)$ |
| **Move to accept** | | | |
| $q$ | $\Lambda$ | $S$ | $(q_1, T)$ |
| (all other combinations) | | | none |

doubt as to which reduction is the correct one; for example, there are two productions whose right sides end with $a$. Answering the second question is easy. When we pop $a$ off the stack, if we find $*$ below it, we should attempt to reduce $T * a$ to $T$, and otherwise, we should reduce $a$ to $T$. Either way, the correct reduction is the one that reduces the longest possible string.

Returning to the first question, suppose the top stack symbol is $T$, and consider the possibilities for the next input. If it is $+$, we should soon have the string $S_1 + T$, in reverse order, on top of the stack, and so the correct move at this point is a reduction of either $T$ or $S_1 + T$ (depending on what is below $T$ on the stack) to $S_1$. If the next input is $*$, the reduction will be that of $T * a$ to $a$, and since we have $T$ already, we should shift. Finally, if it is $\$$, we should reduce either $T$ or $S_1 + T$ to $S_1$ to allow the reduction of $S_1\$$. In any case, we can make the decision on the basis of the next input symbol. What is true for this example is that there are certain combinations of top stack symbol and input symbol for which a reduction is always appropriate, and a shift is correct for all the other combinations. The set of pairs for which a reduction is correct is an example of a *precedence relation*. (It is a relation from $\Gamma$ to $\Sigma$, in the sense of Section 1.4.) There a number of types of *precedence grammars*, for which precedence relations can be used to obtain a deterministic shift-reduce parser. Our example, in which the decision to reduce can be made by examining the top stack symbol and the next input, and in which a reduction always reduces the longest possible string, is an example of a *weak precedence grammar*.

A deterministic PDA that acts as a shift-reduce parser for our grammar is shown in Table 7.12. In order to compare it to the nondeterministic PDA, we make a few observations. The stack symbols can be divided into three groups: (1) those whose appearance on top of the stack requires a shift regardless of the next input (these are $Z_0$, $S_1$, $+$, and $*$); (2) those that require a reduction or lead to acceptance ($a$, $\$$, and $S$); and (3) one, $T$, for which the correct choice can be made only by consulting the next input. In the DPDA, shifts in which the top stack symbol is of the second type have been omitted, since they do not lead to acceptance of any string and their presence would introduce nondeterminism. Shifts in which the top stack symbol is of the first or third type are shown, labeled "shift moves." If the top stack symbol is of the second type, the moves in the reduction are all $\Lambda$-transitions. If the PDA reads a symbol and decides to reduce, the input symbol will eventually be shifted onto the stack, once the reduction has been completed (the machine must remember the input symbol during the reduction); the eventual shift is shown, not under "shift moves," but farther down in the table, as part of the sequence of reducing moves.

**Table 7.12** | A deterministic bottom-up parser for $G$

| Move number | State | Input | Stack symbol | Move |
|---|---|---|---|---|
| | | **Shift moves** | | |
| 1 | $q$ | $\sigma$ | $X$ | $(q, \sigma X)$ |
| | ($\sigma$ is arbitrary; $X$ is either $Z_0$, $S_1$, $+$, or $*$.) | | | |
| 2 | $q$ | $\sigma$ | $T$ | $(q, \sigma T)$ |
| | ($\sigma$ is any input symbol other than $+$ or $\$$.) | | | |
| | | **Moves to reduce $S_1\$$ to $\$$** | | |
| 3 | $q$ | $\Lambda$ | $\$$ | $(q_\$, \Lambda)$ |
| 4 | $q_\$$ | $\Lambda$ | $S_1$ | $(q, S)$ |
| | **Moves to reduce either $a$ or $T * a$ to $T$** | | | |
| 5 | $q$ | $\Lambda$ | $a$ | $(q_{a,1}, \Lambda)$ |
| 6 | $q_{a,1}$ | $\Lambda$ | $*$ | $(q_{a,2}, \Lambda)$ |
| 7 | $q_{a,2}$ | $\Lambda$ | $T$ | $(q, T)$ |
| 8 | $q_{a,1}$ | $\Lambda$ | $X$ | $(q, TX)$ |
| | ($X$ is any stack symbol other than $*$.) | | | |
| | **Moves to reduce $S_1 + T$ or $T$ to $S_1$ and shift an input symbol** | | | |
| 9 | $q$ | $\sigma$ | $T$ | $(q_{T,\sigma}, \Lambda)$ |
| 10 | $q_{T,\sigma}$ | $\Lambda$ | $+$ | $(q'_{T,\sigma}, \Lambda)$ |
| 11 | $q'_{T,\sigma}$ | $\Lambda$ | $S_1$ | $(q, \sigma S_1)$ |
| 12 | $q_{T,\sigma}$ | $\Lambda$ | $X$ | $(q, \sigma S_1 X)$ |
| | ($\sigma$ is either $+$ or $\$$; $X$ is any stack symbol other than $+$.) | | | |
| | | **Move to accept** | | |
| 13 | $q$ | $\Lambda$ | $S$ | $(q_1, \Lambda)$ |
| | (all other combinations) | | | none |

We trace the moves of this PDA on the input string $a + a * a\$$.

$$
\begin{aligned}
(q, a + a * a\$, Z_0) &\vdash (q, +a * a\$, a Z_0) && \text{(move 1)} \\
&\vdash (q_{a,1}, +a * a\$, Z_0) && \text{(move 5)} \\
&\vdash (q, +a * a\$, T Z_0) && \text{(move 8)} \\
&\vdash (q_{T,+}, a * a\$, Z_0) && \text{(move 9)} \\
&\vdash (q, a * a\$, +S_1 Z_0) && \text{(move 12)} \\
&\vdash (q, *a\$, a + S_1 Z_0) && \text{(move 1)} \\
&\vdash (q_{a,1}, *a\$, +S_1 Z_0) && \text{(move 5)} \\
&\vdash (q, *a\$, T + S_1 Z_0) && \text{(move 8)} \\
&\vdash (q, a\$, *T + S_1, Z_0) && \text{(move 2)} \\
&\vdash (q, \$, a * T + S_1 Z_0) && \text{(move 1)} \\
&\vdash (q_{a,1}, \$, *T + S_1 Z_0) && \text{(move 5)} \\
&\vdash (q_{a,2}, \$, T + S_1 Z_0) && \text{(move 6)} \\
&\vdash (q, \$, T + S_1 Z_0) && \text{(move 7)} \\
&\vdash (q_{T,\$}, \Lambda, + S_1 Z_0) && \text{(move 9)} \\
&\vdash (q'_{T,\$}, \Lambda, S_1 Z_0) && \text{(move 10)} \\
&\vdash (q, \Lambda, \$S_1 Z_0) && \text{(move 11)} \\
&\vdash (q_\$, \Lambda, S_1 Z_0) && \text{(move 3)} \\
&\vdash (q, \Lambda, S Z_0) && \text{(move 4)} \\
&\vdash (q_1, \Lambda, Z_0) && \text{(move 13)} \\
&\quad \text{(accept)}
\end{aligned}
$$

# EXERCISES

**7.1.** For the PDA in Example 7.1, trace the sequence of moves made for each of the input strings *bbcbb* and *baca*.

**7.2.** For the PDA in Example 7.2, draw the computation tree showing all possible sequences of moves for the two input strings *aba* and *aabab*.

**7.3.** For a string $x \in \{a, b\}^*$ with $|x| = n$, how many possible complete sequences of moves can the PDA in Example 7.2 make, starting with input string $x$? (By a "complete" sequence of moves, we mean a sequence of moves starting in the initial configuration $(q_0, x, Z_0)$ and terminating in a configuration from which no move is possible.)

**7.4.** Modify the PDA described in Example 7.2 to accept each of the following subsets of $\{a, b\}^*$.

   a. The language of even-length palindromes.

   b. The language of odd-length palindromes.

**7.5.** Give transition tables for PDAs recognizing each of the following languages.

   a. The language of all nonpalindromes over $\{a, b\}$.

   b. $\{a^n x \mid n \geq 0,\ x \in \{a, b\}^* \text{ and } |x| \leq n\}$.

   c. $\{a^i b^j c^k \mid i, j, k \geq 0 \text{ and } j = i \text{ or } j = k\}$.

   d. $\{x \in \{a, b, c\}^* \mid n_a(x) < n_b(x) \text{ or } n_a(x) < n_c(x)\}$.

**7.6.** In both cases below, a transition table is given for a PDA with initial state $q_0$ and accepting state $q_2$. Describe in each case the language that is accepted.

| Move number | State | Input | Stack symbol | Move(s) |
|---|---|---|---|---|
| 1 | $q_0$ | $a$ | $Z_0$ | $(q_1, aZ_0)$ |
| 2 | $q_0$ | $b$ | $Z_0$ | $(q_1, bZ_0)$ |
| 3 | $q_1$ | $a$ | $a$ | $(q_1, a), (q_2, a)$ |
| 4 | $q_1$ | $b$ | $a$ | $(q_1, a)$ |
| 5 | $q_1$ | $a$ | $b$ | $(q_1, b)$ |
| 6 | $q_1$ | $b$ | $b$ | $(q_1, b), (q_2, b)$ |
| (all other combinations) | | | | none |

| Move number | State | Input | Stack symbol | Move(s) |
|---|---|---|---|---|
| 1 | $q_0$ | $a$ | $Z_0$ | $(q_0, XZ_0)$ |
| 2 | $q_0$ | $b$ | $Z_0$ | $(q_0, XZ_0)$ |
| 3 | $q_0$ | $a$ | $X$ | $(q_0, XX)$ |
| 4 | $q_0$ | $b$ | $X$ | $(q_0, XX)$ |
| 5 | $q_0$ | $c$ | $X$ | $(q_1, X)$ |
| 6 | $q_0$ | $c$ | $Z_0$ | $(q_1, Z_0)$ |
| 7 | $q_1$ | $a$ | $X$ | $(q_1, \Lambda)$ |
| 8 | $q_1$ | $b$ | $X$ | $(q_1, \Lambda)$ |
| 9 | $q_1$ | $\Lambda$ | $Z_0$ | $(q_2, Z_0)$ |
| (all other combinations) | | | | none |

**7.7.** Give a transition table for a PDA accepting the language in Example 7.1 and having only two states, the nonaccepting state $q_0$ and the accepting state $q_2$. (Use additional stack symbols.)

**7.8.** Show that every regular language can be accepted by a deterministic PDA $M$ with only two states in which there are no $\Lambda$-transitions and no symbols are ever removed from the stack.

**7.9.** Show that if $L$ is accepted by a PDA in which no symbols are ever removed from the stack, then $L$ is regular.

**7.10.** Suppose $L \subseteq \Sigma^*$ is accepted by a PDA $M$, and for some fixed $k$, and every $x \in \Sigma^*$, no sequence of moves made by $M$ on input $x$ causes the stack to have more than $k$ elements. Show that $L$ is regular.

**7.11.** Show that if $L$ is accepted by a PDA, then $L$ is accepted by a PDA that never crashes (i.e., for which the stack never empties and no configuration is reached from which there is no move defined).

**7.12.** Show that if $L$ is accepted by a PDA, then $L$ is accepted by a PDA in which every move either pops something from the stack (i.e., removes a stack symbol without putting anything else on the stack); or pushes a single symbol onto the stack on top of the symbol that was previously on top; or leaves the stack unchanged.

**7.13.** Give transition tables for deterministic PDAs recognizing each of the following languages.

  a. $\{x \in \{a, b\}^* \mid n_a(x) = n_b(x)\}$

  b. $\{x \in \{a, b\}^* \mid n_a(x) \neq n_b(x)\}$

  c. $\{x \in \{a, b\}^* \mid n_a(x) < 2n_b(x)\}$

  d. $\{a^n b^{n+m} a^m \mid n, m \geq 0\}$

**7.14.** Suppose $M_1$ and $M_2$ are PDAs accepting $L_1$ and $L_2$, respectively. Describe a procedure for constructing a PDA accepting each of the following languages. Note that in each case, nondeterminism will be necessary. Be sure to say precisely how the stack of the new machine works; no relationship is assumed between the stack alphabets of $M_1$ and $M_2$.

  a. $L_1 \cup L_2$

  b. $L_1 L_2$

  c. $L_1^*$

**7.15.** Show that if there are strings $x$ and $y$ in the language $L$ so that $x$ is a prefix of $y$ and $x \neq y$, then no DPDA can accept $L$ by empty stack.

**7.16.** Show that if there is a DPDA accepting $L$, and $ is not one of the symbols in the input alphabet, then there is a DPDA accepting the language $L\{\$\}$ by empty stack.

**7.17.** Show that none of the following languages can be accepted by a DPDA. (Determine exactly what property of the language *pal* is used in the proof of Theorem 7.1, and show that these languages also have that property.)

  a. The set of even-length palindromes over $\{a, b\}$

  b. The set of odd-length palindromes over $\{a, b\}$

  c. $\{xx^\sim \mid x \in \{0, 1\}^*\}$ (where $x^\sim$ means the string obtained from $x$ by changing 0's to 1's and 1's to 0's)

  d. $\{xy \mid x \in \{0, 1\}^*$ and $y$ is either $x$ or $x^\sim\}$

**7.18.** A *counter automaton* is a PDA with just two stack symbols, $A$ and $Z_0$, for which the string on the stack is always of the form $A^n Z_0$ for some $n \geq 0$. (In other words, the only possible change in the stack contents is a change in the number of $A$'s on the stack.) For some context-free languages, such as $\{0^i 1^i \mid i \geq 0\}$, the obvious PDA to accept the language is in fact a counter automaton. Construct a counter automaton to accept the given language in each case below.

  a. $\{x \in \{0, 1\}^* \mid n_0(x) = n_1(x)\}$

  b. $\{x \in \{0, 1\}^* \mid n_0(x) < 2n_1(x)\}$

**7.19.** Suppose that $M = (Q, \Sigma, \Gamma, q_0, Z_0, A, \delta)$ is a deterministic PDA accepting a language $L$. If $x$ is a string in $L$, then by definition there is a sequence of moves of $M$ with input $x$ in which all the symbols of $x$ are read. It is conceivable, however, that for some strings $y \notin L$, no sequence of moves causes $M$ to read all of $y$. This could happen in two ways: $M$ could either crash by not being able to move, or it could enter a loop in which there were infinitely many repeated $\Lambda$-transitions. Find an example of a DCFL $L \subseteq \{a, b\}^*$, a string $y \notin L$, and a DPDA $M$ accepting $L$ for which $M$ crashes on $y$ by not being able to move. (Say what $L$ is and what $y$ is, and give a transition table for $M$.) Note that once you have such an $M$, it can easily be modified so that $y$ causes it to enter an infinite loop of $\Lambda$-transitions.

**7.20.** Give a definition of "balanced string" involving two types of brackets (such as in Example 7.3) corresponding to Definition 6.5.

**7.21.** In each case below, you are given a CFG and a string $x$ that it generates. For the top-down PDA that is constructed from the grammar as in Definition 7.4, trace a sequence of moves by which $x$ is accepted, showing at each step the state, the unread input, and the stack contents. Show at the same time the corresponding leftmost derivation of $x$ in the grammar. See Example 7.5 for a guide.

a. The grammar has productions

$$S \rightarrow S + T \mid T \quad T \rightarrow T * F \mid F \quad F \rightarrow (S) \mid a$$

and $x = (a + a * a) * a$.

b. The grammar has productions $S \rightarrow S + S \mid S * S \mid (S) \mid a$, and $x = (a * a + a)$.

c. The grammar has productions $S \rightarrow (S)S \mid \Lambda$, and $x = ()(()())$.

**7.22.** Let $M$ be the PDA in Example 7.2, except that move number 12 is changed to $(q_2, \Lambda)$, so that $M$ does in fact accept by empty stack. Let $x = ababa$. Find a sequence of moves of $M$ by which $x$ is accepted, and give the corresponding leftmost derivation in the CFG obtained from $M$ as in Theorem 7.4.

**7.23.** Under what circumstances is the "nondeterministic" top-down PDA described in Definition 7.4 actually deterministic? (For what kind of language could this happen?)

**7.24.** In each case below, you are given a CFG and a string $x$ that it generates. For the nondeterministic bottom-up PDA that is constructed from the grammar as in Example 7.6, trace a sequence of moves by which $x$ is accepted, showing at each step the state, the stack contents, and the unread input. Show at the same time the corresponding rightmost derivation of $x$ (in reverse order) in the grammar. See Example 7.6 for a guide.

a. The grammar has productions $S \rightarrow S[S] \mid \Lambda$, and $x = [][[]]$.

b. The grammar has productions $S \rightarrow [S]S \mid \Lambda$, and $x = [][[]]$.

**7.25.** If the PDA in Theorem 7.4 is deterministic, what does this tell you about the grammar that is obtained? Can the resulting grammar have this property without the original PDA being deterministic?

**7.26.** Find the other useless variables in the CFG obtained in Example 7.7.

**7.27.** In each case, the grammar with the given productions satisfies the LL(1) property. For each one, give a transition table for the deterministic PDA obtained as in Example 7.8.

a. $S \rightarrow S_1\$ \quad S_1 \rightarrow AS_1 \mid \Lambda \quad A \rightarrow aA \mid b$
b. $S \rightarrow S_1\$ \quad S_1 \rightarrow aA \quad A \rightarrow aA \mid bA \mid \Lambda$
c. $S \rightarrow S_1\$ \quad S_1 \rightarrow aAB \mid bBA \quad A \rightarrow bS_1 \mid a \quad B \rightarrow aS_1 \mid b$

**7.28.** In each case, the grammar with the given productions does not satisfy the LL(1) property. Find an equivalent LL(1) grammar by factoring and eliminating left recursion.

a. $S \rightarrow S_1\$ \quad S_1 \rightarrow aaS_1b \mid ab \mid bb$
b. $S \rightarrow S_1\$ \quad S_1 \rightarrow S_1A \mid \Lambda \quad A \rightarrow Aa \mid b$
c. $S \rightarrow S_1\$ \quad S_1 \rightarrow S_1T \mid ab \quad T \rightarrow aTbb \mid ab$
d. $S \rightarrow S_1\$ \quad S_1 \rightarrow aAb \mid aAA \mid aB \mid bbA$

$$A \rightarrow aAb \mid ab \quad B \rightarrow bBa \mid ba$$

**7.29.** Show that for the CFG in part (c) of the previous exercise, if the last production were $T \rightarrow a$ instead of $T \rightarrow ab$, the grammar obtained by factoring and eliminating left recursion would not be LL(1). (Find a string that doesn't work, and identify the point at which looking ahead one symbol in the input isn't enough to decide what move the PDA should make.)

**7.30.** Consider the CFG with productions

$$S \rightarrow S_1\$ \quad S_1 \rightarrow S_1 + T \mid T \quad T \rightarrow T * F \mid F \quad F \rightarrow (S_1) \mid a$$

a. Write the CFG obtained from this one by eliminating left recursion.
b. Give a transition table for a DPDA that acts as a top-down parser for this language.

**7.31.** Suppose that in a grammar having a variable $T$, the $T$-productions are

$$T \rightarrow T\alpha_i \quad (1 \le i \le m) \qquad T \rightarrow \beta_i \quad (1 \le i \le n)$$

where none of the strings $\beta_i$ begins with $T$. Find a set of productions with which these can be replaced, so that the resulting grammar will be equivalent to the original and will have no left recursion involving $T$.

**7.32.** Let $G$ be the CFG with productions

$$S \rightarrow S_1\$ \quad S_1 \rightarrow (S_1 + S_1) \mid (S_1 * S_1) \mid a$$

so that $L(G)$ is the language of all fully parenthesized algebraic expressions involving the operators $+$ and $*$ and the identifier $a$. Give a transition table for a deterministic bottom-up parser obtained from this grammar as in Example 7.12.

**7.33.** Let $G$ have productions

$$S \rightarrow S_1\$ \quad S_1 \rightarrow S_1[S_1] \mid S_1[] \mid [S_1] \mid []$$

and let $G_1$ have productions

$$S \rightarrow S_1\$ \quad S_1 \rightarrow [S_1]S_1 \mid [S_1] \mid []S_1 \mid []$$

a. Give a transition table for a deterministic bottom-up parser obtained from $G$.
b. Show that $G_1$ is not a weak precedence grammar.

**7.34.** In the nondeterministic bottom-up parser given for the grammar in Example 7.12, the implicit assumption in the transition table was that the start symbol $S$ did not appear on the right side of any production. Why is there no loss of generality in making this assumption in general?

**7.35.** In the standard nondeterministic bottom-up parsing PDA for a grammar, obtained as in Example 7.12, consider a configuration in which the right side of a production is currently on top of the stack in reverse, and this string does not appear in the right side of any other production. Why is it always correct to reduce at this point?

**7.36.** a. Say exactly what the precedence relation is for the grammar in Example 7.12. In other words, for which pairs $(X, \sigma)$, where $X$ is a stack symbol and $\sigma$ an input symbol, is it correct to reduce when $X$ is on top of the stack and $\sigma$ is the next input?

b. Answer the same question for the larger grammar (also a weak precedence grammar) with productions

$$S \rightarrow S_1\$ \quad S_1 \rightarrow S_1 + T \mid S_1 - T \mid T$$
$$T \rightarrow T * F \mid T/F \mid F \quad F \rightarrow (S_1) \mid a$$

# MORE CHALLENGING PROBLEMS

**7.37.** Give transition tables for PDAs recognizing each of the following languages.
a. $\{a^i b^j \mid i \le j \le 2i\}$
b. $\{x \in \{a, b\}^* \mid n_a(x) < n_b(x) < 2n_a(x)\}$

**7.38.** Suppose $L \subseteq \Sigma^*$ is accepted by a PDA $M$, and for some fixed $k$, and every $x \in \Sigma^*$, at least one choice of moves allows $M$ to process $x$ completely so that the stack never contains more than $k$ elements. Does it follow that $L$ is regular? Prove your answer.

**7.39.** Suppose $L \subseteq \Sigma^*$ is accepted by a PDA $M$, and for some fixed $k$, and every $x \in L$, at least one choice of moves allows $M$ to accept $x$ in such a way that the stack never contains more than $k$ elements. Does it follow that $L$ is regular? Prove your answer.

**7.40.** Show that if $L$ is accepted by a DPDA, then there is a DPDA accepting the language $\{x\#y \mid x \in L \text{ and } xy \in L\}$. (The symbol $\#$ is assumed not to occur in any of the strings of $L$.)

**7.41.** Complete the proof of Theorem 7.3. Give a precise definition of the PDA $M_1$, and a proof that it accepts the same language as the original PDA $M$.

**7.42.** Prove the converse of Theorem 7.3: If there is a PDA $M = (Q, \Sigma, \Gamma, q_0, Z_0, A, \delta)$ accepting $L$ by empty stack (that is, $x \in L$ if and only if $(q_0, x, Z_0) \vdash_M^* (q, \Lambda, \Lambda)$ for some state $q$), then there is a PDA $M_1$ accepting $L$ by final state (i.e., the ordinary way).

**7.43.** Show that in the previous exercise, if $M$ is a deterministic PDA, then $M_1$ can also be taken to be deterministic.

**7.44.** Show that if $L$ is accepted by a PDA, then $L$ is accepted by a PDA having at most two states and no $\Lambda$-transitions.

**7.45.** Show that if $L$ is accepted by a PDA, then $L$ is accepted by a PDA in which there are at most two stack symbols in addition to $Z_0$.

**7.46.** Show that if $M$ is a DPDA accepting a language $L \subseteq \Sigma^*$, then there is a DPDA $M_1$ accepting $L$ for which neither of the phenomena in Exercise 7.19 occurs—that is, for every $x \in \Sigma^*$, $(q_0, x, Z_0) \vdash_{M_1}^* (q, \Lambda, \gamma)$ for some state $q$ and some string $\gamma$ of stack symbols.

**7.47.** Starting with the top-down nondeterministic PDA constructed as in Definition 7.4, one might try to produce a deterministic parsing algorithm by using a backtracking approach: specifying an order in which to try all the moves possible in a given configuration, and trying sequences of moves in order, backtracking whenever the machine crashes.

    a.  Describe such a backtracking algorithm in more detail for the grammar in Example 7.8, and trace the algorithm on several strings, including strings derivable from the grammar and strings that are not.

    b.  What possible problems may arise with such an approach for a general grammar?

# 8

# Context-Free and Non-Context-Free Languages

## 8.1 | THE PUMPING LEMMA FOR CONTEXT-FREE LANGUAGES

Neither the definition of context-free languages in terms of grammars nor the pushdown-automaton characterization in Chapter 7 makes it immediately obvious that there are formal languages that are not context-free. However, our brief look at natural languages (Example 6.6) has suggested some of the limitations of CFGs. In the first section of this chapter we formulate a principle, similar to the pumping lemma for regular languages (Theorem 5.2a), which will allow us to identify a number of non-context-free languages.

The earlier pumping lemma used the fact that a sufficiently long input string causes a finite automaton to visit some state more than once. Any such string can be written $x = uvw$, where $v$ is a substring that causes the FA to start in a state and return to that state; the result is that all the strings of the form $uv^i w$ are also accepted by the FA. Although we will get the comparable result for CFLs by using grammars instead of automata, the way it arises is similar. Suppose a derivation in a context-free grammar $G$ involves a variable $A$ more than once, in this way:

$$S \Rightarrow^* vAz \Rightarrow^* vwAyz \Rightarrow^* vwxyz$$

where $v, w, x, y, z \in \Sigma^*$. Within this derivation, both the strings $x$ and $wAy$ are derived from $A$. We may write

$$S \Rightarrow^* vAz \Rightarrow^* vwAyz \Rightarrow^* vw^2Ay^2z \Rightarrow^* vw^3Ay^3z \Rightarrow^* \cdots$$

and since $x$ can be derived from each of these $A$'s, we may conclude that all the strings $vxz, vwxyz, vw^2xy^2z, \ldots$ are in $L(G)$.

In order to obtain our pumping lemma, we must show that this duplication of variables occurs in the derivation of every sufficiently long string in $L(G)$. It will also be helpful to impose some restrictions on the strings $v$, $w$, $x$, $y$, and $z$, just as we did on the strings $u$, $v$, and $w$ in the simpler case.

The discussion will be a little easier if we can assume that the tree representing a derivation is a *binary* tree, which means simply that no node has more than two children. We can guarantee this by putting our grammar into Chomsky normal form (Section 6.6). The resulting loss of the null string will not matter, because the result we want involves only long strings.

Let us say that a *path* in a nonempty binary tree consists either of a single node or of a node, one of its descendants, and all the nodes in between. We will say that the *length* of a path is the number of nodes it contains, and the *height* of a binary tree is the length of the longest path. In any derivation whose tree has a sufficiently long path, some variable must reoccur. Lemma 8.1 shows that any binary tree will have a long path if the number of leaf nodes is sufficiently large. (In the case we are interested in, the binary tree is a derivation tree, and because there are no $\Lambda$-productions the number of leaf nodes is simply the length of the string being derived.)

**Lemma 8.1**  For any $h \geq 1$, a binary tree having more than $2^{h-1}$ leaf nodes must have height greater than $h$.

**Proof**  We prove, by induction on $h$, the contrapositive statement: If the height is no more than $h$, the number of leaf nodes is no greater than $2^{h-1}$. For the basis step, we observe that a binary tree with height $\leq 1$ has no more than one node and therefore no more than one leaf node.

In the induction step, suppose that $k \geq 1$ and that any binary tree of height $\leq k$ has no more than $2^{k-1}$ leaf nodes. Now let $T$ be a binary tree with height $\leq k + 1$. If $T$ has no more than one node, the result is clear. Otherwise, the left and right subtrees of $T$ both have height $\leq k$, and so by the induction hypothesis each has $2^{k-1}$ or fewer leaf nodes. The number of leaf nodes in $T$ is the sum of the numbers in the two subtrees and is therefore no greater than $2^{k-1} + 2^{k-1} = 2^k$. ■

**Theorem 8.1**

Let $G = (V, \Sigma, S, P)$ be a context-free grammar in Chomsky normal form, with a total of $p$ variables. Any string $u$ in $L(G)$ with $|u| \geq 2^{p+1}$ can be written as $u = vwxyz$, for some strings $v$, $w$, $x$, $y$, and $z$ satisfying

$$|wy| > 0$$
$$|wxy| \leq 2^{p+1}$$
$$\text{for any } m \geq 0, \; vw^m xy^m z \in L(G)$$

**Proof**

Lemma 8.1 shows that any derivation tree for $u$ must have height at least $p + 2$. (It has more than $2^p$ leaf nodes, and therefore its height is $> p + 1$.) Let us consider a path of maximum length and look at the bottom portion, consisting of a leaf node and the $p + 1$ nodes above it. Each of these $p + 1$ nodes corresponds to a variable, and since there are only $p$ distinct variables, some variable $A$ must appear twice in this portion of the path. Let $x$ be the portion of $u$ derived from the $A$ closest to the leaf, and let $t = wxy$ be the portion of $u$ derived from the other $A$. If $v$ and $z$ represent the beginning and ending portions of $u$, we have $u = vwxyz$. An illustration of what this might look like is provided in Figure 8.1.

The $A$ closest to the root in this portion of the path is the root of a binary derivation tree for $wxy$. Since we began with a path of maximum length, this tree has height $\leq p + 2$, and so by the lemma $|wxy| \leq 2^{p+1}$. The node containing this $A$ has two children, both corresponding to variables. If we let $B$ denote the one that is not an ancestor of the other $A$, then since $x$ is derived from that other $A$, the string of terminals derived from $B$ does not overlap $x$. It follows that either $w$ or $y$ is nonnull, and therefore $|wy| > 0$.

Finally,

$$S \Rightarrow^* vAz \Rightarrow^* vwAyz \Rightarrow^* vwxyz$$

(the first $A$ is the one in the higher node, the second the one in the lower), and so the third conclusion of the theorem follows from our preliminary discussion.

Just as in the case of the earlier pumping lemma, it is helpful to restate the result so as to emphasize the essential features.

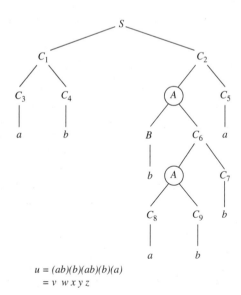

$$u = (ab)(b)(ab)(b)(a)$$
$$= v\ w\ x\ y\ z$$

**Figure 8.1** |

---

**Theorem 8.1a     The Pumping Lemma for Context-Free Languages**

Let $L$ be a CFL. Then there is an integer $n$ so that for any $u \in L$ satisfying $|u| \geq n$, there are strings $v, w, x, y$, and $z$ satisfying

$$u = vwxyz \tag{8.1}$$

$$|wy| > 0 \tag{8.2}$$

$$|wxy| \leq n \tag{8.3}$$

$$\text{For any } m \geq 0, \quad vw^m xy^m z \in L \tag{8.4}$$

*Proof*

We can find a context-free grammar in Chomsky normal form that generates $L - \{\Lambda\}$. If we let $p$ be the number of variables in this grammar and $n = 2^{p+1}$, the result is an immediate consequence of Theorem 8.1.

---

Using the pumping lemma for context-free languages requires the same sorts of precautions as in the case of the earlier pumping lemma for regular languages. In order to show that $L$ is not context-free, we assume it is and try to derive a contradiction. Theorem 8.1a says only that there exists an integer $n$, nothing about its value; because we can apply the theorem only to strings $u$ with length $\geq n$, the $u$ we choose must be defined in terms of $n$. Once we have chosen $u$, the theorem tells us only that there exist strings $v, w, x, y$, and $z$ satisfying the four properties; the only way to guarantee a contradiction is to show that *every* choice of $v, w, x, y, z$ satisfying the properties leads to a contradiction.

According to Chapter 7, a finite-state machine with an auxiliary memory in the form of a stack is enough to accept a CFL. An example of a language for which a single stack is sufficient is the language of strings of the form $(^i)^i$ (see Example 7.3), which could just as easily have been called $a^i b^i$. The $a$'s are saved on the stack so that the number of $a$'s can be compared to the number of $b$'s that follow. By the time all the $b$'s have been matched with $a$'s, the stack is empty, which means that the machine has forgotten how many there were. This approach, therefore, would not allow us to recognize strings of the form $a^i b^i c^i$. Rather than trying to show directly that no other approach using a single stack can work, we choose this language for our first proof using the pumping lemma.

---

**EXAMPLE 8.1**     The Pumping Lemma Applied to $\{a^i b^i c^i\}$

Let

$$L = \{a^i b^i c^i \mid i \geq 1\}$$

Suppose for the sake of contradiction that $L$ is context-free, and let $n$ be the integer in Theorem 8.1a. An obvious choice for $u$ with $|u| \geq n$ is $u = a^n b^n c^n$. Suppose $v, w, x, y$, and $z$ are any strings satisfying conditions (8.1)–(8.4). Since $|wxy| \leq n$, the string $wxy$ can contain at most two distinct types of symbol ($a$'s, $b$'s, and $c$'s), and since $|wy| > 0$, $w$ and $y$ together contain at least one. The string $vw^2 xy^2 z$ contains additional occurrences of the symbols in $w$ and $y$;

therefore, it cannot contain equal numbers of all three symbols. On the other hand, according to (8.4), $vw^2xy^2z \in L$. This is a contradiction, and our assumption that $L$ is a CFL cannot be correct.

Note that to get the contradiction, we started with $u \in L$ and showed that $vw^2xy^2z$ fails to be an element, not only of $L$ but also of the bigger language

$$L_1 = \{u \in \{a, b, c\}^* \mid n_a(u) = n_b(u) = n_c(u)\}$$

Therefore, our proof is also a proof that $L_1$ is not a context-free language.

---

## The Pumping Lemma Applied to $\{ss \mid s \in \{a, b\}^*\}$     **EXAMPLE 8.2**

Let

$$L = \{ss \mid s \in \{a, b\}^*\}$$

This language is similar in one obvious respect to the language of even-length palindromes, which is a context-free language: In both cases, in order to recognize a string in the language, a machine needs to remember the first half so as to be able to compare it to the second. For palindromes, the last-in, first-out principle by which a stack operates is obviously appropriate. In the case of $L$, however, when we encounter the first symbol in the second half of the string (even assuming that we know when we encounter it), the symbol we need to compare it to is the *first* in, not the last—in other words, it is buried at the bottom of the stack. Here again, arguing that the obvious approach involving a PDA fails does not prove that a PDA cannot be made to work. Instead, we apply the pumping lemma.

Suppose $L$ is a CFL, and let $n$ be the integer in Theorem 8.1a. This time the choice of $u$ is not as obvious; we try $u = a^n b^n a^n b^n$. Suppose that $v$, $w$, $x$, $y$, and $z$ are any strings satisfying (8.1)–(8.4). We must derive a contradiction from these facts, without making any other assumptions about the five strings.

As in Example 8.1, condition (8.2) tells us that $wxy$ can overlap at most two of the four contiguous groups of symbols. We consider several cases.

First, suppose $w$ or $y$ contains at least one $a$ from the first group of $a$'s. Since $|wxy| \leq n$, neither $w$ nor $y$ can contain any symbols from the second half of $u$. Consider $m = 0$ in condition (8.4). Omitting $w$ and $y$ causes at least one initial $a$ to be omitted, and does not affect the second half. In other words,

$$vw^0xy^0z = a^i b^j a^n b^n$$

where $i < n$ and $1 \leq j \leq n$. The midpoint of this string is somewhere within the substring $a^n$, and therefore it is impossible for it to be of the form $ss$.

Next, suppose $wxy$ contains no $a$'s from the first group but that $w$ or $y$ contains at least one $b$ from the first group of $b$'s. Again we consider $m = 0$; this time we can say

$$vw^0xy^0z = a^n b^i a^j b^n$$

where $i < n$ and $1 \leq j \leq n$. The midpoint is somewhere in the substring $b^i a^j$, and as before, the string cannot be in $L$.

We can get by with two more cases: case 3, in which $wxy$ contains no symbols from the first half of $u$ but at least one $a$, and case 4, in which $w$ or $y$ contains at least one $b$ from the second group of $b$'s. The arguments in these cases are similar to those in cases 2 and 1, respectively. We leave the details to you.

Just as in Example 8.1, there are other languages for which essentially the same proof works. Two examples in this case are $\{a^i b^i a^i b^i \mid i \geq 0\}$ and $\{a^i b^j a^i b^j \mid i, j \geq 0\}$. A similar proof shows that $\{scs \mid s \in \{a, b\}^*\}$ also fails to be context-free. Although the marker in the middle may appear to remove the need for nondeterminism, the basic problem that prevents a PDA from recognizing this language is still present.

---

In proofs of this type, there are several potential trouble-spots. It may not be obvious what string $u$ to choose. In Example 8.2, although $a^n b^n a^n b^n$ is not the only choice that works, there are many that do not (Exercise 8.2).

Once $u$ is chosen, deciding on cases to consider can be a problem. A straightforward way in Example 8.2 might have been to consider seven cases:

1. $wy$ contains only $a$'s from the first group;
2. $wy$ contains $a$'s from the first group and $b$'s from the first group;
3. $wy$ contains only $b$'s from the first group;

   ...

7. $wy$ contains only $b$'s from the last group.

There is nothing wrong with this, except that all other things being equal, four cases is better than seven. If you find yourself saying "Cases 6, 8, and 10 are handled exactly like cases 1, 3, and 5," perhaps you should try to reduce the number of cases. (Try to rephrase the proof in Example 8.2 so that there are only two cases.) The important thing in any case is to make sure your cases cover all the possibilities and that you do actually obtain a contradiction in each case.

Finally, for a specific case, you must choose the value of $m$ to use in order to obtain a contradiction. In the first case in Example 8.2, it was not essential to choose $m = 0$, but the string $vw^0 xy^0 z$ is probably easier to describe exactly than the string $vw^2 xy^2 z$. In some situations, choosing $m = 0$ will not work but choosing $m > 1$ will, and in some other situations the opposite is true.

## **EXAMPLE 8.3**   A Third Application of the Pumping Lemma

Let

$$L = \{x \in \{a, b, c\}^* \mid n_a(x) < n_b(x) \text{ and } n_a(x) < n_c(x)\}$$

The intuitive reason that no PDA can recognize $L$ is similar to the reason in Example 8.1; a stack allows the machine to compare the number of $a$'s to either the number of $b$'s or the number of $c$'s, but not both. Suppose $L$ is a CFL, and let $n$ be the integer in Theorem 8.1a. Let $u = a^n b^{n+1} c^{n+1}$. If (8.1)–(8.4) hold for strings $v$, $w$, $x$, $y$, and $z$, the string $wxy$ can contain at most two distinct symbols. This time, two cases are sufficient.

If $w$ or $y$ contains at least one $a$, then $wy$ cannot contain any $c$'s. Therefore, $vw^2 xy^2 z$ contains at least as many $a$'s as $c$'s and cannot be in $L$. If neither $w$ nor $y$ contains an $a$, then $vw^0xy^0z$ still contains $n$ $a$'s; since $wy$ contains one of the other two symbols, $vw^0xy^0z$ contains fewer occurrences of that symbol than $u$ does and therefore is not in $L$. We have obtained a contradiction and may conclude that $L$ is not context-free.

The language $\{a^ib^jc^k \mid i < j \text{ and } i < k\}$ can be shown to be non-context-free by exactly the same argument.

---

## The Set of Legal C Programs Is Not a CFL    **EXAMPLE 8.4**

The feature of the C programming language that we considered in Section 5.5, which prevents the language from being regular, can be taken care of by context-free grammars. In Chapter 6 we saw other examples of the way in which CFGs can describe much of the syntax of such high-level languages. CFGs cannot do this completely, however: There are some rules in these languages that depend on context, and Theorem 8.1a allows us to show that the set $L$ of all legal C programs is not a context-free language. (Very little knowledge of C is required for this example.)

A basic rule in C is that a variable must be declared before it is used. Checking that this rule is obeyed is essentially the same as determining whether a certain string has the form $xcx$, where $x$ is the identifier and $c$ is the string appearing between the declaration of $x$ and its use. As we observed in Example 8.2, the language $\{xcx \mid x \in \{a, b\}^*\}$ is not a CFL. Although we are now using a larger alphabet, and $c$ is no longer a single symbol, the basic problem is the same, provided identifiers are allowed to be arbitrarily long. Let us try to use the pumping lemma to show that $L$ is not a CFL.

Assume that $L$ is a CFL, and let $n$ be the integer in Theorem 8.1a. We want to choose a string $u$ in $L$ whose length is at least $n$, containing both a declaration of a variable and a separate, subsequent reference to the variable. The following will (barely) qualify:

```
main(){int aa...a;aa...a;}
```

where both identifiers have $n$ $a$'s. However, for a technical reason that will be mentioned in a minute, we complicate the program by including two subsequent references to the variable instead of one:

```
main(){int aa...a;aa...a;aa...a;}
```

Here it is assumed that all three identifiers are $a^n$. There is one blank in the program, after `int`, and it is necessary as a separator. About all that can be said for this program is that it will make it past the compiler, possibly with a warning. It declares an integer variable; then, twice, it evaluates the expression consisting of that identifier (the value is probably garbage, since the program has not initialized the variable), and does nothing with the value.

According to the pumping lemma, $u = vwxyz$, where (8.2)–(8.4) are satisfied. In particular, $vw^0xy^0z$ is supposed to be a valid C program. However, this is impossible. If $wy$ contains the blank or any of the symbols before it, then $vxz$ still contains at least most of the first occurrence of the identifier, and without `main(){int` and the blank, it cannot be syntactically correct. We are left with the case in which $wxy$ is a substring of "$a^n$; $a^n$; $a^n$;". If $wy$ contains either the final semicolon or bracket, the string $vxz$ is also illegal. If it contains one of the two intermediate semicolons, and possibly portions of one or both of the identifiers on either side, then $vxz$ has two identifiers, which are now not the same. Finally, if $wy$ contains only a portion of one of the identifiers and nothing else, then $vxz$ still has a variable declaration and two subsequent expressions consisting of an identifier, but the three identifiers are not all the same. In either of these last two situations, the declaration-before-use principle is violated. We conclude that $vxz$ is not a legal C program, and therefore that $L$ is not a context-free language.

   (The argument would almost work with the shorter program having only two occurrences of the identifier, but not quite. The case in which it fails is the case in which $wy$ contains the first semicolon and nothing else. Deleting it still leaves a valid program, consisting simply of a declaration of a variable with a longer name. Adding multiple copies is also legal because they are interpreted as harmless "empty" statements.)

   There are other examples of syntax rules whose violation cannot be detected by a PDA. We noted in Example 8.2 that $\{a^n b^m a^n b^m\}$ is not a context-free language, and we can imagine a situation in which being able to recognize a string of this type is essentially what is required. Suppose that two functions $f$ and $g$ are defined, having $n$ and $m$ formal parameters, respectively, and then calls on $f$ and $g$ are made. Then the numbers of parameters in the calls must agree with the numbers in the respective definitions.

   In the remainder of this section, we discuss a generalization of the pumping lemma, a slightly weakened form of what is known as Ogden's lemma. Although the pumping lemma provides some information about the strings $w$ and $y$ that are pumped, in the form of (8.2) and (8.3), it says very little about the location of these substrings in the string $u$. Ogden's lemma makes it possible to designate certain positions of $u$ as "distinguished" and to guarantee that the pumped portions include at least some of these distinguished positions. As a result, it is sometimes more convenient than the pumping lemma, and occasionally it can be used when the pumping lemma fails.

---

**Theorem 8.2    Ogden's Lemma**
Suppose $L$ is a context-free language. Then there is an integer $n$ so that if $u$ is any string in $L$ of length $n$ or greater, and any $n$ or more positions of $u$ are designated as "distinguished," then there are strings $v$, $w$, $x$, $y$, and $z$ satisfying

$$u = vwxyz \tag{8.5}$$

$$\text{the string } wy \text{ contains at least one distinguished position} \tag{8.6}$$

$$\text{the string } wxy \text{ contains no more than } n \text{ distinguished positions} \tag{8.7}$$

$$\text{the string } x \text{ contains at least one distinguished position} \tag{8.8}$$

$$\text{for every } m \geq 0, \ vw^m xy^m z \in L \tag{8.9}$$

*Proof*
Just as in the proof of the pumping lemma, let $n = 2^{p+1}$, where $p$ is the number of variables in a Chomsky normal form grammar generating $L - \{\Lambda\}$. Suppose $u$ is a string in $L$ in which $n$ or more positions are marked as distinguished. In order to obtain the strings $v$, $w$, $x$, $y$, and $z$, we start as

before, by selecting a path in a derivation tree for $u$ on which some variable $A$ occurs twice. Once we identify the two nodes corresponding to $A$, if we define the five strings exactly as before, it will follow that (8.5) and (8.9) hold. Only the other three properties depend on the particular way we choose the path, and so this is what we need to describe.

Beginning at the top, the path contains the root node, corresponding to $S$. For each interior node $N$ in the path, we extend the path downward one more step by selecting the child of $N$ having the larger number of distinguished positions among its descendants (breaking ties arbitrarily). Now we say that an interior node on this path is a *branch point* if both its children have at least one distinguished descendant. As we follow the path down the tree, starting at a branch point, the number of distinguished descendants of the current node decreases at the first step and remains constant thereafter until the next branch point is reached. It follows from the way the path is chosen that every branch point below the top one has at least half as many distinguished descendants as the branch point above it in the path. Using this result, we obtain the following lemma (corresponding to Lemma 8.1 in its contrapositive form), for which we interrupt our proof briefly.

**Lemma 8.2** If the binary tree consisting of a node on the path and its descendants has $h$ or fewer branch points, its leaf nodes include no more than $2^h$ distinguished nodes.

***Proof*** The proof is by induction and is virtually identical to that of Lemma 8.1, except that the number of branch points is used instead of the height, and the number of distinguished leaf nodes is used instead of the total number of leaf nodes. The reason the statement involves $2^h$ rather than $2^{h-1}$ is that the bottom-most branch point has two distinguished descendants rather than one. ∎

*Conclusion of proof of Theorem 8.2*
Since there are $n$ distinguished leaf nodes in the tree, and $n > 2^p$, Lemma 8.2 implies that there must be more than $p$ branch points in our path. Consider the $p+1$ branch points farthest down in the path, and the subtree whose root is the topmost such node. Since there are only $p$ variables in the grammar, at least two of these branch points are labeled with the same variable $A$. We now define the five strings $v$, $w$, $x$, $y$, and $z$ in terms of these two nodes exactly as in the proof of the pumping lemma. Property (8.6) follows from the definition of branch point, and (8.7) is an immediate consequence of Lemma 8.2. Property (8.8) is clearly true because the bottom $A$ is a branch point. As we observed above, the other two properties follow as in the proof of the pumping lemma.

Note that the ordinary pumping lemma is identical to the special case of Theorem 8.2 in which *all* the positions of $u$ are distinguished.

| **EXAMPLE 8.5** | ## Using Ogden's Lemma on $\{\, a^i b^i c^j \mid j \neq i \,\}$ |
|---|---|

Let $L = \{a^i b^i c^j \mid i, j \geq 0 \text{ and } j \neq i\}$. Suppose $L$ is a context-free language, and let $n$ be the integer in the statement of Theorem 8.2. One choice for the string $u$ is

$$u = a^n b^n c^{n+n!}$$

(The reason for this choice will be clear shortly.) Let us also designate the first $n$ positions of $u$ as the distinguished positions, and let us suppose that $v$, $w$, $x$, $y$, and $z$ satisfy (8.5)–(8.9).

First, we can see that if either $w$ or $y$ contains two distinct symbols, then we can obtain a contradiction by considering the string $vw^2xy^2z$, which will no longer have the form $a^*b^*c^*$. Second, we know that because $wy$ contains at least one distinguished position, $w$ or $y$ consists of $a$'s. It follows from these two observations that unless $w$ consists of $a$'s and $y$ consists of the same number of $b$'s, looking at $vw^2xy^2z$ will give us a contradiction, because this string has different numbers of $a$'s and $b$'s. Suppose now that $w = a^j$ and $y = b^j$. Let $k = n!/j$, which is still an integer, and let $m = k + 1$. Then the number of $a$'s in $vw^mxy^mz$ is

$$n + (m - 1) * j = n + k * j = n + n!$$

which is the same as the number of $c$'s. We have our contradiction, and therefore $L$ cannot be context-free.

With just the pumping lemma here, we would be in trouble: There would be no way to rule out the possibility that $w$ and $y$ contained only $c$'s, and therefore no way to guarantee a contradiction.

| **EXAMPLE 8.6** | ## Using Ogden's Lemma when the Pumping Lemma Fails |
|---|---|

Let $L = \{a^p b^q c^r d^s \mid p = 0 \text{ or } q = r = s\}$. It seems clear that $L$ should not be a CFL, because $\{a^q b^q c^q\}$ is not. The first thing we show in this example, however, is that $L$ satisfies the properties of the pumping lemma; therefore, the pumping lemma will not help us to show that $L$ is not context-free.

Suppose $n$ is any positive integer, and $u$ is any string in $L$ with $|u| \geq n$, say $u = a^p b^q c^r d^s$. We must show the existence of strings $v$, $w$, $x$, $y$, and $z$ satisfying (8.1)–(8.4). We consider two cases. If $p = 0$, then there are no restrictions on the numbers of $b$'s, $c$'s, or $d$'s, and the choices $w = b$, $v = x = y = \Lambda$ work. If $p > 0$, then we know that $q = r = s$, and the choices $w = a$, $v = x = y = \Lambda$ work.

Now we can use Theorem 8.2 to show that $L$ is indeed not a CFL. Suppose $L$ is a CFL, let $n$ be the integer in the theorem, let $u = ab^n c^n d^n$, and designate all but the first position of $u$ as distinguished. Suppose that $v$, $w$, $x$, $y$, and $z$ satisfy (8.5)–(8.9). Then the string $wy$ must contain one of the symbols $b$, $c$, or $d$ and cannot contain all three. Therefore, $vw^2xy^2z$ has one $a$ and does not have equal numbers of $b$'s, $c$'s, and $d$'s, which means that it cannot be in $L$.

## 8.2 | INTERSECTIONS AND COMPLEMENTS OF CONTEXT-FREE LANGUAGES

According to Theorem 6.1, the set of context-free languages is closed under the operations of union, concatenation, and Kleene *. For regular languages, we can add the intersection and complement operations to the list. We can now show, however, that for context-free languages this is not possible.

---

**Theorem 8.3**
There are CFLs $L_1$ and $L_2$ so that $L_1 \cap L_2$ is not a CFL, and there is a CFL $L$ so that $L'$ is not a CFL.

*Proof*
In Example 8.3 we observed that

$$L = \{a^i b^j c^k \mid i < j \text{ and } i < k\}$$

is not context-free. However, although no PDA can test both conditions $i < j$ and $i < k$ simultaneously, it is easy enough to build two PDAs that test the conditions separately. In other words, although the intersection $L$ of the two languages

$$L_1 = \{a^i b^j c^k \mid i < j\}$$

and

$$L_2 = \{a^i b^j c^k \mid i < k\}$$

is not a CFL, both languages themselves are. Another way to verify that $L_1$ is a CFL is to check that it is generated by the grammar with productions

$$S \rightarrow ABC \quad A \rightarrow aAb \mid \Lambda \quad B \rightarrow bB \mid b \quad C \rightarrow cC \mid \Lambda$$

Similarly, $L_2$ is generated by the CFG with productions

$$S \rightarrow AC \quad A \rightarrow aAc \mid B \quad B \rightarrow bB \mid \Lambda \quad C \rightarrow cC \mid c$$

The second statement in the theorem follows from the first and the formula

$$L_1 \cap L_2 = (L_1' \cup L_2')'$$

If complements of CFLs were always CFLs, then for any CFLs $L_1$ and $L_2$, the languages $L_1'$ and $L_2'$ would be CFLs, so would their union, and so would its complement. We know now that this is not the case.

---

## A CFL Whose Complement Is Not a CFL    **EXAMPLE 8.7**

The second part of the proof of Theorem 8.3 is a proof by contradiction and appears to be a nonconstructive proof. If we examine it more closely, however, we can use it to find an example. Let $L_1$ and $L_2$ be the languages defined in the first part of the proof. Then the language $L_1 \cap L_2 = (L_1' \cup L_2')'$ is not a CFL. Therefore, because the union of CFLs is a CFL, at least one of the three languages $L_1$, $L_2$, $L_1' \cup L_2'$ is a CFL whose complement is not a CFL. Let us try to determine which.

There are two ways a string can fail to be in $L_1$. It can fail to be an element of $R$, the language $\{a\}^*\{b\}^*\{c\}^*$, or it can be a string $a^i b^j c^k$ for which $i \geq j$. In other words,

$$L_1' = R' \cup \{a^i b^j c^k \mid i \geq j\}$$

The language $R'$ is regular because $R$ is, and therefore $R'$ is context-free. The second language involved in the intersection can be expressed as the concatenation

$$\{a^i b^j c^k \mid i \geq j\} = \{a^m \mid m \geq 0\} \{a^j b^j \mid j \geq 0\} \{c^k \mid k \geq 0\}$$

each factor of which is a CFL. Therefore, $L'_1$ is a CFL. A similar argument shows that $L'_2$ is also a CFL. We conclude that $L'_1 \cup L'_2$, or

$$R' \cup \{a^i b^j c^k \mid i \geq j \text{ or } i \geq k\}$$

is a CFL whose complement is not a CFL. (In fact, the second part alone is also an example; see Exercise 8.8.)

---

At this point it might be interesting to go back to Theorem 3.4, in which the intersection of two regular languages was shown to be regular, and see what goes wrong when we try to use the same construction for CFLs. We began with FAs $M_1$ and $M_2$ recognizing the two languages, and we constructed a composite machine $M$ whose states were pairs $(p, q)$ of states in $M_1$ and $M_2$, respectively. This allows $M$ to keep track of both machines at once, or to simulate running the two machines in parallel. A string is accepted by $M$ if it is accepted simultaneously by $M_1$ and $M_2$.

Suppose we have CFLs $L_1$ and $L_2$, and PDAs $M_1 = (Q_1, \Sigma, \Gamma_1, q_1, Z_1, A_1, \delta_1)$ and $M_2 = (Q_2, \Sigma, \Gamma_2, q_2, Z_2, A_2, \delta_2)$ accepting them. We can define states of a new machine $M$ in the same way, by letting $Q = Q_1 \times Q_2$. We might also construct the stack alphabet of $M$ by letting $\Gamma = \Gamma_1 \times \Gamma_2$, because this would let us use the top stack symbol of $M$ to determine those of $M_1$ and $M_2$. When we try to define the moves of $M$, however, things become complicated, even aside from the question of nondeterminism. In the simple case where $\delta_1(p, a, X) = \{(p', X')\}$ and $\delta_2(q, a, Y) = \{(q', Y')\}$, where $X, X' \in \Gamma_1$ and $Y, Y' \in \Gamma_2$, it is reasonable to let

$$\delta((p, q), a, (X, Y)) = \{((p', q'), (X', Y'))\}$$

However, what if $\delta_1(p, a, X) = \{(p', X'X)\}$ and $\delta_2(q, a, Y) = \{(q', \Lambda)\}$? Or, what if $\delta_1(p, a, X) = \{(p', X)\}$ and $\delta_2(q, a, Y) = \{(q', YYY)\}$? There is no obvious way to have $M$ keep track of both the states of $M_1$ and $M_2$ and the stacks of $M_1$ and $M_2$ and still operate like a PDA. Theorem 8.3 confirms that such a machine is indeed impossible in general.

We can salvage some positive results from this discussion. If $M_1$ is a PDA and $M_2$ is a PDA with *no* stack (in particular, a deterministic one—i.e., an FA) there is no obstacle to carrying out this construction. The stack on our new machine is simply the one associated with $M_1$. The result is the following theorem.

**Theorem 8.4**
If $L_1$ is a context-free language and $L_2$ is a regular language, then $L_1 \cap L_2$ is a context-free language.

*Proof*
Let $M_1 = (Q_1, \Sigma, \Gamma, q_1, Z_0, A_1, \delta_1)$ be a PDA accepting the language $L_1$, and let $M_2 = (Q_2, \Sigma, q_2, A_2, \delta_2)$ be an FA recognizing $L_2$. We define a

PDA $M = (Q, \Sigma, \Gamma, q_0, Z_0, A, \delta)$ as follows:

$$Q = Q_1 \times Q_2 \qquad q_0 = (q_1, q_2) \qquad A = A_1 \times A_2$$

For $p \in Q_1, q \in Q_2$, and $Z \in \Gamma$,

(1)  $\delta((p, q), a, Z)$

$$= \{((p', q'), \alpha) \mid (p', \alpha) \in \delta_1(p, a, Z) \text{ and } \delta_2(q, a) = q'\}$$

for every $a \in \Sigma$; and

(2)  $\delta((p, q), \Lambda, Z) = \{((p', q), \alpha) \mid (p', \alpha) \in \delta_1(p, \Lambda, Z)\}$

We can see that (1) and (2) allow $M$ to keep track of the states of $M_1$ and $M_2$. Note that because an FA is deterministic, the only way in which $M$ has a choice of moves is in the first component of the state; similarly, in the case of a $\Lambda$-transition of $M_1$, the second component of $M$'s state, the one corresponding to $M_2$, is unchanged. The contents of the stack at any time are just what they would be in the machine $M_1$.

We want to show that these two statements are equivalent: On the one hand, the input string $y$ allows $M_1$ to reach state $p$ with stack contents $\alpha$, and causes $M_2$ to reach state $q$; on the other hand, by processing $y$, $M$ can get to state $(p, q)$ with stack contents $\alpha$. More precisely, for any $n \geq 0$ and any $p \in Q_1, q \in Q_2, y, z \in \Sigma^*$, and $\alpha \in \Gamma^*$,

$$(q_1, yz, Z_1) \vdash_{M_1}^n (p, z, \alpha) \quad \text{and} \quad \delta_2^*(q_2, y) = q$$

if and only if

$$((q_1, q_2), yz, Z_1) \vdash_M^n ((p, q), z, \alpha)$$

where the notation $\vdash^n$ refers to a sequence of $n$ moves. The "only if" direction shows that $L(M_1) \cap L(M_2) \subseteq L(M)$, and the converse shows the opposite inclusion.

The two parts of the proof are both by induction on $n$ and are very similar. We show the "only if" part and leave the other to you. For the basis step, suppose that

$$(q_1, yz, Z_1) \vdash_{M_1}^0 (p, z, \alpha) \quad \text{and} \quad \delta_2^*(q_2, y) = q$$

This means that $y = \Lambda$, $p = q_1$, $\alpha = Z_1$, and $q = q_2$. In this case, it is clear that

$$((q_1, q_2), yz, Z_1) \vdash_M^0 ((p, q), z, \alpha) = ((q_1, q_2), yz, Z_1)$$

Now suppose that $k \geq 0$ and that the statement is true for $n = k$, and assume that

$$(q_1, yz, Z_1) \vdash_{M_1}^{k+1} (p, z, \alpha) \quad \text{and} \quad \delta_2^*(q_2, y) = q$$

We want to show that

$$((q_1, q_2), yz, Z_1) \vdash_M^{k+1} ((p, q), z, \alpha)$$

Consider the last move in the sequence of $k + 1$ moves of $M_1$. If it is a $\Lambda$-transition, then

$$(q_1, yz, Z_1) \vdash^k_{M_1} (p', z, \beta) \vdash_{M_1} (p, z, \alpha)$$

for some $p' \in Q_1$ and some $\beta \in \Gamma^*$. In this case the inductive hypothesis implies that

$$((q_1, q_2), yz, Z_1) \vdash^k_M ((p', q), z, \beta)$$

and from (2) we have

$$((p', q), z, \beta) \vdash_M ((p, q), z, \alpha)$$

which implies the result. Otherwise, $y = y'a$ for some $a \in \Sigma$, and

$$(q_1, y'az, Z_1) \vdash^k_{M_1} (p', az, \beta) \vdash_{M_1} (p, z, \alpha)$$

Let $q' = \delta^*_2(q_2, y')$. Then the induction hypothesis implies that

$$((q_1, q_2), y'az, Z_1) \vdash^k_M ((p', q'), az, \beta)$$

and from (1) we have

$$((p', q'), az, \beta) \vdash_M ((p, q), z, \alpha)$$

Again the result follows.

It is also worthwhile, in the light of Theorems 8.3 and 8.4, to re-examine the proof that the complement of a regular language is regular. If the finite automaton $M = (Q, \Sigma, q_0, A, \delta)$ recognizes the language $L$, then the finite automaton $M' = (Q, \Sigma, q_0, Q - A, \delta)$ recognizes $\Sigma^* - L$. We are free to apply the same construction to the pushdown automaton $M = (Q, \Sigma, \Gamma, q_0, Z_0, A, \delta)$ and to consider the PDA $M' = (Q, \Sigma, \Gamma, q_0, Z_0, Q - A, \delta)$. Theorem 8.3 says that even if $M$ accepts the context-free language $L$, $M'$ does not necessarily accept $\Sigma^* - L$. Why not?

The problem is nondeterminism. It may happen that for some $x \in \Sigma^*$,

$$(q_0, x, Z_0) \vdash^*_M (p, \Lambda, \alpha)$$

for some state $p \in A$, and

$$(q_0, x, Z_0) \vdash^*_M (q, \Lambda, \beta)$$

for some other state $q \notin A$. This means that the string $x$ is accepted by $M$ as well as by $M'$, since $q$ is an accepting state in $M'$. In the case of finite automata, nondeterminism can be eliminated: Every NFA-$\Lambda$ is equivalent to some FA. The corresponding result about PDAs is false (Theorem 7.1), and the set of CFLs is not closed under the complement operation.

We would expect that if $M$ is a *deterministic* PDA (DPDA) recognizing $L$, then the machine $M'$ constructed as above would recognize $\Sigma^* - L$. Unfortunately, this is still not quite correct. One reason is that there might be input strings that cause $M$ to enter an infinite sequence of $\Lambda$-transitions and are never processed to completion. Any such string would be accepted neither by $M$ nor by $M'$. However, the result in Exercise 7.46 shows that this difficulty can be resolved and that a DPDA can be constructed that recognizes $\Sigma^* - L$. It follows that the complement of a deterministic context-free language (DCFL) is a DCFL, and in particular that any context-free language whose complement is not a CFL (Theorem 8.3 and Example 8.7) cannot be a DCFL.

# 8.3 | DECISION PROBLEMS INVOLVING CONTEXT-FREE LANGUAGES

At the end of Chapter 5, we considered a number of decision problems involving regular languages, beginning with the membership problem: Given an FA $M$ and a string $x$, does $M$ accept $x$? We may formulate the same sorts of questions for context-free languages. For some of the questions, essentially the same algorithms work; for others, the inherent nondeterminism of PDAs requires us to find new algorithms; and for some, *no* algorithm is possible, although proving this requires a more sophisticated model of computation than we now have.

The basic membership problem for regular languages has a simple solution: To decide whether an FA $M$ accepts a string $x$, run $M$ with input $x$ and see what happens. In the case of PDAs, a solution cannot be this simple, because nondeterminism cannot always be eliminated. If we think of a PDA $M$ as making a move once a second, and choosing arbitrarily whenever it has a choice, then "what happens" may be different from one time to the next. A sequence of moves that ends up with the input $x$ being rejected does not mean there is no other sequence leading to acceptance. From the specifications for a PDA, we can very likely formulate some backtracking algorithm that will be guaranteed to answer the question. Simpler to describe (though probably inefficient to carry out) is the following approach, which depends on the fact that a CFG without $\Lambda$-productions or unit productions requires at most $2n - 1$ steps for the derivation of a string of length $n$.

**Decision algorithm for the membership problem. (Given a pushdown automaton $M$ and a string $x$, does $M$ accept $x$?)**    Use the construction in the proof of Theorem 7.4 to find a CFG $G$ generating the language recognized by $M$. If $x = \Lambda$, use Algorithm FindNull in Section 6.5 to determine whether the start symbol of $G$ is nullable. Otherwise, eliminate $\Lambda$-productions and unit productions from $G$, using Algorithms 6.1 and 6.2. Examine all derivations with one step, all those with two steps, and so on, until either a derivation of $x$ has been found or all derivations of length $2|x| - 1$ have been examined. If no derivation of $x$ has been found, $M$ does not accept $x$.

Note that since Theorems 7.2 and 7.4 let us go from a CFG to a PDA and vice versa, we can formulate any of these decision problems in terms of either a CFG or a PDA. We consider the decision problems corresponding to problems 2 and 3 in Chapter 5, but stated in terms of CFGs:

1. Given a CFG $G$, does it generate any strings? (Is $L(G) = \emptyset$?)
2. Given a CFG $G$, is $L(G)$ finite?

Theorem 8.1 provides us with a way of answering both questions. We transform $G$ into Chomsky normal form. Let $G'$ be the resulting grammar, $p$ the number of variables in $G'$, and $n = 2^{p+1}$. If $G'$ generates any strings, it must generate one of length less than $n$. Otherwise, apply the pumping lemma to a string $u$ of minimal length $(\geq n)$ generated by $G'$; then $u = vwxyz$, for some strings $v$, $w$, $x$, $y$, and $z$ with $|wy| > 0$ and $vxz \in L(G')$—and this contradicts the minimality of $u$. Similarly, if $L(G')$ is infinite, there must be a string $u \in L(G')$ with $n \leq |u| < 2n$; the proof is virtually identical to that of the corresponding result in Chapter 5. We therefore obtain the two decision algorithms that follow.

**Decision algorithms for problems 1 and 2.  (Given a CFG $G$, is $L(G) = \emptyset$?  Is $L(G)$ finite?)**   First, test whether $\Lambda$ can be generated from $G$, using the algorithm for the membership problem. If it can, then $L(G) \neq \emptyset$. In any case, let $G'$ be a Chomsky-normal-form grammar generating $L(G) - \{\Lambda\}$, and let $n = 2^{p+1}$, where $p$ is the number of variables in $G'$. For increasing values of $i$ beginning with 1, test strings of length $i$ for membership in $L(G)$. If for no $i < n$ is there a string of length $i$ in $L(G')$, and $\Lambda \notin L(G)$, then $L(G') = L(G) = \emptyset$. If for no $i$ with $n \leq i < 2n$ is there a string of length $i$ in $L(G)$, then $L(G)$ is finite; if there is a string $x \in L(G)$ with $n \leq |x| < 2n$, then $L(G)$ is infinite.

These algorithms are easy to describe, but obviously not so easy to carry out. Fortunately, for problems such as the membership problem for which it is important to find practical solutions, there are considerably more efficient algorithms [two well-known ones are those by Cocke-Younger-Kasami, described in the paper by Younger (*Information and Control* 10(2): 189–208, 1967) and Earley (*Communications of the ACM* 13(2): 94–102, 1970)]. If we go any farther down the list of decision problems in Chapter 5, formulated for CFGs or PDAs instead of regular expressions or FAs, we encounter problems for which there is no possible decision algorithm, even an extremely inefficient one. To take an example, given two CFGs, are there any strings generated by both? The algorithm given in Chapter 5 to solve the corresponding problem for FAs depends on the fact that the set of regular languages is closed under the operations of intersection and complement. Because the set of CFLs is not closed under these operations, we know at least that the earlier approach does not give us an algorithm; we will see in Chapter 11 that the problem is actually "unsolvable."

## EXERCISES

**8.1.**  In each case, show using the pumping lemma that the given language is not a CFL.

a.  $L = \{a^i b^j c^k \mid i < j < k\}$

b.  $L = \{x \in \{a, b\}^* \mid n_b(x) = n_a(x)^2\}$

c.  $L = \{a^n b^{2n} a^n \mid n \geq 0\}$

d.  $L = \{x \in \{a, b, c\}^* \mid n_a(x) = \max\{n_b(x), n_c(x)\}\}$

e.  $L = \{a^n b^m a^n b^{n+m} \mid m, n \geq 0\}$

**8.2.**  In the pumping-lemma proof in Example 8.2, give some examples of choices of strings $u \in L$ with $|u| \geq n$ that would not work.

**8.3.** In the proof given in Example 8.2 using the pumping lemma, the contradiction was obtained in each case by considering the string $vw^0xy^0z$. Would it have been possible instead to use $vw^2xy^2z$ in each case?

**8.4.** In Example 8.4, is it possible with Ogden's lemma rather than the pumping lemma to use the string $u$ mentioned first, with only two occurrences of the identifier?

**8.5.** Decide in each case whether the given language is a CFL, and prove your answer.

   a.  $L = \{a^n b^m a^m b^n \mid m, n \geq 0\}$

   b.  $L = \{xayb \mid x, y \in \{a, b\}^* \text{ and } |x| = |y|\}$

   c.  $L = \{xcx \mid x \in \{a, b\}^*\}$

   d.  $L = \{xyx \mid x, y \in \{a, b\}^* \text{ and } |x| \geq 1\}$

   e.  $L = \{x \in \{a, b\}^* \mid n_a(x) < n_b(x) < 2n_a(x)\}$

   f.  $L = \{x \in \{a, b\}^* \mid n_a(x) = 10n_b(x)\}$

   g.  $L =$ the set of non-balanced strings of parentheses

**8.6.** State and prove theorems that generalize Theorems 5.3 and 5.4 to context-free languages. Then give an example to illustrate each of the following possibilities.

   a.  Theorem 8.1a can be used to show that the language is a CFL, but the generalization of Theorem 5.3 cannot.

   b.  The generalization of Theorem 5.3 can be used to show the language is not a CFL, but the generalization of Theorem 5.4 cannot.

   c.  The generalization of Theorem 5.4 can be used to show the language is not a CFL.

**8.7.** Show that if $L$ is a DCFL and $R$ is regular, then $L \cap R$ is a DCFL.

**8.8.** In each case, show that the given language is a CFL but that its complement is not. (It follows in particular that the given language is not a DCFL.)

   a.  $\{a^i b^j c^k \mid i \geq j \text{ or } i \geq k\}$

   b.  $\{a^i b^j c^k \mid i \neq j \text{ or } i \neq k\}$

   c.  $\{x \in \{a, b\}^* \mid x \text{ is not } ww \text{ for any } w\}$

**8.9.** Use Ogden's lemma to show that the languages below are not CFLs.

   a.  $\{a^i b^{i+k} a^k \mid k \neq i\}$

   b.  $\{a^i b^i a^j b^j \mid j \neq i\}$

   c.  $\{a^i b^j a^i \mid j \neq i\}$

**8.10.** a.  Show that if $L$ is a CFL and $F$ is finite, $L - F$ is a CFL.

     b.  Show that if $L$ is not a CFL and $F$ is finite, then $L - F$ is not a CFL.

     c.  Show that if $L$ is not a CFL and $F$ is finite, then $L \cup F$ is not a CFL.

**8.11.** For each part of the previous exercise, say whether the statement is true if "finite" is replaced by "regular," and give reasons.

**8.12.** For each part of Exercise 8.10, say whether the statement is true if "CFL" is replaced by "DCFL," and give reasons.

**8.13.** Give an example of a DPDA $M$ accepting a language $L$ for which the language accepted by the machine obtained from $M$ by reversing accepting and nonaccepting states is not $L'$.

# MORE CHALLENGING PROBLEMS

**8.14.** If $L$ is a CFL, does it follow that $rev(L) = \{x^r \mid x \in L\}$ is a CFL? Give either a proof or a counterexample.

**8.15.** Decide in each case whether the given language is a CFL, and prove your answer.

   a. $L = \{x \in \{a, b\}^* \mid n_a(x)$ is a multiple of $n_b(x)\}$

   b. Given a CFG $L$, the set of all prefixes of elements of $L$

   c. Given a CFG $L$, the set of all suffixes of elements of $L$

   d. Given a CFG $L$, the set of all substrings of elements of $L$

   e. $\{x \in \{a, b\}^* \mid |x|$ is even and the first half of $x$ has more $a$'s than the second$\}$

   f. $\{x \in \{a, b, c\}^* \mid n_a(x), n_b(x),$ and $n_c(x)$ have a common factor greater than $1\}$

**8.16.** Prove the following variation of Theorem 8.1a. If $L$ is a CFL, then there is an integer $n$ so that for any $u \in L$ with $|u| \geq n$, and any choice of $u_1, u_2,$ and $u_3$ satisfying $u = u_1 u_2 u_3$ and $|u_2| \geq n$, there are strings $v, w, x, y,$ and $z$ satisfying the following conditions:

   (1) $u = vwxyz$

   (2) $wy \neq \Lambda$

   (3) Either $w$ or $y$ is a nonempty substring of $u_2$

   (4) For every $m \geq 0$, $vw^i xy^i z \in L$

   Hint: Suppose # is a symbol not appearing in strings in $L$, and let $L_1$ be the set of all strings that can be formed by inserting two occurrences of # into an element of $L$. Show that $L_1$ is a CFL, and apply Ogden's Lemma to $L_1$.

   This result is taken from Floyd and Beigel (1994).

**8.17.** Show that the result in the previous problem can be used in each part of Exercise 8.9.

**8.18.** Show that the result in Exercise 16 can be used in both Examples 8.5 and 8.6 to show that the language is not context-free.

**8.19.** The class of DCFLs is closed under the operation of complement, as discussed in Section 8.2. Under which of the following other operations is this class of languages closed? Give reasons for your answers.

   a. Union

   b. Intersection

   c. Concatenation

   d. Kleene *

   e. Difference

**8.20.** Use Exercise 7.40 and Exercise 8.7 to show that the following languages are not DCFLs. This technique is used in Floyd and Beigel (1994), where the language in Exercise 7.40 is referred to as Double-Duty($L$).

   a. *pal*, the language of palindromes over $\{0, 1\}$ (Hint: Consider the regular language corresponding to $0^*1^*0^*\#1^*0^*$.)

   b. $\{x \in \{a, b\}^* \mid n_b(x) = n_a(x) \text{ or } n_b(x) = 2n_a(x)\}$

   c. $\{x \in \{a, b\}^* \mid n_b(x) < n_a(x) \text{ or } n_b(x) > 2n_a(x)\}$

**8.21.** (Refer to Exercise 7.40) Consider the following argument to show that if $L \subseteq \Sigma^*$ is a CFL, then so is $\{x\#y \mid x \in L \text{ and } xy \in L\}$. (# is assumed to be a symbol not in $\Sigma$.)

   Let $M$ be a PDA accepting $L$, with state set $Q$. We construct a new PDA $M_1$ whose state set contains two states $q$ and $q'$ for every state $q \in Q$. $M_1$ copies $M$ up to the point where the input symbol # is encountered, but using the primed states rather than the original ones. Once this symbol is seen, if the current state is $q'$ for some $q \in A$ (i.e., if $M$ would have accepted the current string), then the machine switches over to the original states for the rest of the processing. Therefore, it enters an accepting state subsequently if and only if both the substring preceding the # and the entire string read so far, except for the #, would be accepted by $M$.

   Explain why this argument is not correct.

**8.22.** Show that the result at the beginning of the previous exercise is false. (Find a CFL $L$ so that $\{x\#y \mid x \in L \text{ and } xy \in L\}$ is not a CFL.)

**8.23.** Show that if $L \subseteq \{a\}^*$ is a CFL, then $L$ is regular.

**8.24.** Consider the language $L = \{x \in \{a, b\}^* \mid n_a(x) = f(n_b(x))\}$. Exercise 5.52 is to show that $L$ is regular if and only if $f$ is ultimately periodic; in other words, $L$ is regular if and only if there is a positive integer $p$ so that for each $r$ with $0 \leq r < p$, $f$ is eventually constant on the set $S_{p,r} = \{jp + r \mid j \geq 0\}$. Show that $L$ is a CFL if and only if there is a positive integer $p$ so that for each $r$ with $0 \leq r < p$, $f$ is eventually linear on the set $S_{p,r}$. "Eventually linear" on $S_{p,r}$ means that there are integers $N$, $c$, and $d$ so that for every $j \geq N$, $f(jp + r) = cj + d$. (Suggestion: for the "if" direction, show how to construct a PDA accepting $L$; for the converse, use the pumping lemma.)

**8.25.** Let

$$f(n) = \begin{cases} 4n + 7 & \text{if } n \text{ is even} \\ 4n + 13 & \text{if } n \text{ is odd} \end{cases}$$

   a. Show that the language $\{x \in \{a, b\}^* \mid n_b(x) = f(n_a(x))\}$ is a DCFL.

   b. Show that if $4n + 13$ is changed to $5n + 13$, $L$ is not a DCFL.

# Turing Machines and
# Their Languages

The abstract machines in Parts II and III can be viewed as embodying certain types of algorithms: those in which no more than a fixed amount of information can be remembered, and those in which information developed during the course of the algorithm can be retrieved only in accordance with a last-in-first-out rule. In this part, we describe an abstract machine called a Turing machine that is widely accepted as a general model of computation. Although the basic operations of such a machine are comparable in their simplicity to those of our earlier machines, the new machines can carry out a wide variety of computations. Besides accepting languages, they can compute functions and, according to the Church-Turing thesis, carry out any conceivable algorithmic procedure. In particular, the model can accommodate the idea of a stored-program computer, so that we can have a single "universal" machine execute any algorithm by giving it an input string that includes an encoding of the algorithm.

We discuss a few slightly different formulations of Turing machines, which enhance the efficiency and convenience of the basic model but do not enlarge the set of languages it can recognize or the set of functions it can compute. Then, after formalizing the distinction between *accepting* a language and *recognizing* a language (a distinction that is necessary because of the possibility that a Turing machine may loop forever on some inputs and never actually return an answer), we look more closely at the languages that Turing machines can accept. We consider other ways to characterize these languages, including grammars more general than context-free grammars. Finally, we confront the fact that there are many languages too complex to be accepted by any Turing machine (and therefore, by the Church-Turing thesis, too complex to be accepted by any algorithmic procedure). ∎

# 9

# Turing Machines

## 9.1 | DEFINITIONS AND EXAMPLES

The two models of computation we have studied so far involve severe restrictions on either the amount of memory (an FA can remember only its current state) or the way the memory is accessed (a PDA can access only the top stack symbol). Machines implementing these models turn out to be significantly less powerful, at least in principle, than the real computers we are familiar with.

In this chapter we study an abstract machine introduced by the English mathematician Alan Turing (*Proceedings of the London Mathematical Society* 2:230–265, 1936) and for that reason now called a *Turing machine*. Although it may still seem substantially different from a modern electronic computer (which did not exist when Turing formulated the model), the differences have more to do with efficiency, and *how* the computations are carried out, than with the types of computations possible. The work of Turing and his contemporaries provided much of the theoretical foundation for the modern computer.

Turing began by considering a *human* computer (that is, a human who is solving some problem algorithmically using a pencil and paper). He decided that without any loss of generality, the computer could be assumed to operate under these three rules: First, the only things written on the paper are symbols from some fixed finite set; second, each step taken by the computer depends only on the symbol he is currently examining and on his "state of mind" at the time; and third, although his state of mind might change as a result of symbols he has seen or computations he has made, only a finite number of distinct states of mind are possible.

Turing then set out to build an abstract machine that obeys these rules and can duplicate what he took to be the primitive steps carried out by a human computer during a computation:

1. Examining an individual symbol on the paper;
2. Erasing a symbol or replacing it by another;
3. Transferring attention from one part of the paper to another.

Some of these elements should seem familiar. A Turing machine will have a finite alphabet of symbols (actually two alphabets, an input alphabet and a possibly larger alphabet for use during the computation) and a finite set of states, corresponding to the possible "states of mind" of the human computer. Instead of a sheet of paper, Turing specified a linear "tape," which has a left end and is potentially infinite to the right. The tape is marked off into squares, each of which can hold one symbol from the alphabet; if a square has no symbol on it, we say that it contains the *blank* symbol. For convenience, we may think of the squares as being numbered, left-to-right, starting with 0, although this numbering is not part of the official model and it is not necessary to refer to the numbers in describing the operation of the machine. We think of the reading and writing as being done by a *tape head*, which at any time is centered on one square of the tape. In our version of a Turing machine—which is similar although not identical to the one proposed by Turing—a single move is determined by the current state and the current tape symbol, and consists of three parts:

1. Replacing the symbol in the current square by another, possibly different symbol;

2. Moving the tape head one square to the right or left (except that if it is already centered on the leftmost square, it cannot be moved to the left), or leaving it where it is;

3. Moving from the current state to another, possibly different state.

The tape serves as the input device (the input is simply the string, assumed to be finite, of nonblank symbols on the tape originally), the memory available for use during the computation, and the output device (the output is the string of symbols left on the tape at the end of the computation). The most significant difference between the Turing machine and the simpler machines we have studied is that in a Turing machine, processing a string is no longer restricted to a single left-to-right pass through the input. The tape head can move in both directions and erase or modify any symbol it encounters. The machine can examine part of the input, modify it, take time out to execute some computations in a different area of the tape, return to re-examine the input, repeat any of these actions, and perhaps stop the processing before it has looked at all the input.

For similar reasons, we can dispense with one duty previously performed by certain states—that of indicating provisional acceptance of the string read so far. In particular, we can get by with two *final*, or *halting*, states, beyond which the computation need not continue: a state $h_a$ that indicates acceptance and another $h_r$ that indicates rejection. If the machine is intended simply to accept or reject the input string, then it can move to the appropriate halt state once it has enough information to make a decision. If it is supposed to carry out some other computation, the accepting state indicates that the computation has terminated normally; the state $h_r$ can be used to indicate a "crash," arising from some abnormal situation in which the machine cannot carry out its mission as expected. In any case, the computation stops if the Turing maching reaches either of the two halt states. However—and this will turn out to be very important—it is also possible for the computation *not* to stop, and for the Turing machine to continue making moves forever.

> **Definition 9.1    Turing Machines**
>
> A *Turing machine* (TM) is a 5-tuple $T = (Q, \Sigma, \Gamma, q_0, \delta)$, where
>
> $Q$   is a finite set of states, assumed not to contain $h_a$ or $h_r$, the two *halting* states (the same symbols will be used for the halt states of every TM);
>
> $\Sigma$ and $\Gamma$ are finite sets, the *input* and *tape* alphabets, respectively, with $\Sigma \subseteq \Gamma$; $\Gamma$ is assumed not to contain $\Delta$, the *blank* symbol;
>
> $q_0$, the initial state, is an element of $Q$;
>
> $\delta : Q \times (\Gamma \cup \{\Delta\}) \rightarrow (Q \cup \{h_a, h_r\}) \times (\Gamma \cup \{\Delta\}) \times \{R,L,S\}$ is a partial function (that is, possibly undefined at certain points).

For elements $q \in Q, r \in Q \cup \{h_a, h_r\}$, $X, Y \in \Gamma \cup \{\Delta\}$, and $D \in \{R,L,S\}$, we interpret the formula

$$\delta(q, X) = (r, Y, D)$$

to mean that when $T$ is in state $q$ and the symbol on the current tape square is $X$, the machine replaces $X$ by $Y$ on that square, changes to state $r$, and either moves the tape head one square right, moves it one square left (if the tape head is not already on the leftmost square), or leaves it stationary, depending on whether $D$ is R, L, or S, respectively. When $r$ is either $h_a$ or $h_r$ in the formula, we say that $T$ *halts*. Once it has halted, it cannot move further, since $\delta$ is not defined at any pair $(h_a, X)$ or $(h_r, X)$.

Finally, we permit the machine to crash by entering the reject state in case it tries to move the tape head off the left end of the tape. This is a way for the machine to halt that is not reflected by the transition function $\delta$. If the tape head is currently on the leftmost square, the current state and tape symbol are $q$ and $a$, respectively, and $\delta(q, a) = (r, b, L)$, we will say that the machine leaves the tape head where it is, replaces the $a$ by $b$, and enters the state $h_r$ instead of $r$.

This terminology and these definitions are not completely standard. In our approach, a TM accepts a string by eventually entering the state $h_a$ after it starts with that input. Sometimes acceptance is defined to mean *halting* (in any halt state), and the only other way the computation is allowed to terminate is by crashing because there is no move possible. In either approach, what is significant is that an observer can see that the TM has stopped its processing and why it has stopped.

Normally a TM begins with an input string $x \in \Sigma^*$ near the beginning of its tape and all other tape squares blank. We do not always insist on this, for reasons to be explained in Section 9.3; however, we do always assume that when a TM begins its operation, there are at most a finite number of nonblank symbols on the tape. It follows that at any stage of a TM's computation, this will still be true. To describe the status of a TM at some point, we must specify the current state, the complete contents of the tape (through the rightmost nonblank symbol), and the current position of the tape head. With this in mind, we represent a *configuration* of the TM by a pair

$$(q, x\underline{a}y)$$

where $q \in Q$, $x$ and $y$ are strings over $\Gamma \cup \{\Delta\}$ (either or both possibly null), $a$ is a symbol in $\Gamma \cup \{\Delta\}$, and the underlined symbol represents the tape head position.

The notation is interpreted to mean that the string $xay$ appears on the tape, beginning in square 0, that the tape head is on the square containing $a$, and that all squares to the right of $y$ are blank. For a nonnull string $w$, writing $(q, x\underline{w})$ or $(q, x\underline{w}y)$ will mean that the tape head is positioned at the first symbol of $w$. If $(q, x\underline{a}y)$ represents a configuration, then $y$ may conceivably end in one or more blanks, and we would also say that $(q, x\underline{a}y\Delta)$ represents the same configuration; usually, however, when we write $(q, x\underline{a}y)$ the string $y$ will either be null or have a nonblank last symbol.

Just as in the case of PDAs, we can trace a sequence of moves by showing the configuration at each step. We write

$$(q, x\underline{a}y) \vdash_T (r, z\underline{b}w)$$

to mean that $T$ passes from the configuration on the left to that on the right in one move, and

$$(q, x\underline{a}y) \vdash_T^* (r, z\underline{b}w)$$

to mean that $T$ passes from the first configuration to the second in zero or more moves. For example, if $T$ is currently in the configuration $(q, aab\underline{a}\Delta a)$ and $\delta(q, a) = (r, \Delta, L)$, we would write

$$(q, aab\underline{a}\Delta a) \vdash_T (r, aa\underline{b}\Delta\Delta a)$$

The notations $\vdash_T$ and $\vdash_T^*$ are usually shortened to $\vdash$ and $\vdash^*$, respectively, as long as there is no ambiguity.

Input is provided to a TM by having the input string on the tape initially, beginning in square 1, and positioning the tape head on square 0, which is blank. The *initial configuration corresponding to input x* is therefore the configuration

$$(q_0, \underline{\Delta}x)$$

Now we can say how a TM accepts a string.

---

**Definition 9.2    Acceptance by a TM**

If $T = (Q, \Sigma, \Gamma, q_0, \delta)$ is a Turing machine, and $x \in \Sigma^*$, $x$ is accepted by $T$ if, starting in the initial configuration corresponding to input $x$, $T$ eventually reaches an accepting configuration. In other words, $x$ is accepted if there exist $y, z \in (\Gamma \cup \{\Delta\})^*$ and $a \in \Gamma \cup \{\Delta\}$ so that

$$(q_0, \underline{\Delta}x) \vdash_T^* (h_a, y\underline{a}z)$$

The *language accepted by T* is the set $L(T)$ of input strings accepted by $T$.

---

When a Turing machine processes an input string $x$, there are three possibilities. The machine can accept the string, by entering the state $h_a$; it can explicitly reject $x$, by entering the state $h_r$; or it can enter an *infinite loop*, so that it never halts but continues moving forever. In either of the first two cases, an observer sees the outcome and can tell whether or not the string is accepted. In the third case, however, although the string will not be accepted, the observer will never find this out—there *is* no outcome, and he is left in suspense. As undesirable as this may seem, we will find that it is sometimes inevitable. In the examples in this chapter, we can construct the machine so that this problem does not arise, and every input string is either accepted or explicitly rejected.

In most simple examples, it will be helpful once again to draw transition diagrams, similar to but more complicated than those for FAs. The move

$$\delta(q, X) = (r, Y, D)$$

(where $D$ is R, L, or S) will be represented as in Figure 9.1.

Our first example should make it clear, if it is not already, that Turing machines are at least as powerful as finite automata.

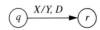

**Figure 9.1 |**
A single Turing machine move.

---

A TM Accepting {a, b}*{aba} {a, b}*    EXAMPLE 9.1

Consider the language

$$L = \{a, b\}^*\{aba\}\{a, b\}^* = \{x \in \{a, b\}^* \mid x \text{ contains the substring } aba\}$$

$L$ is a regular language, and we can draw an FA recognizing $L$ as in Figure 9.2a. It is not surprising that constructing a Turing machine to accept $L$ is also easy, and that in fact we can do it so that the transition diagrams look much alike. The TM is illustrated in Figure 9.2b. Its input and tape alphabets are both $\{a, b\}$. The initial state does not really correspond to a state in the FA, because the TM does not see any input until it moves the tape head past the initial blank.

Figure 9.2b shows explicitly the transitions to the reject state $h_r$ at each point where a blank (the one to the right of the input) is encountered before an occurrence of $aba$ has been found. Figure 9.2c shows a simplified diagram, even more similar to the transition diagram for the FA, in which these transitions are omitted. It is often convenient to simplify a diagram

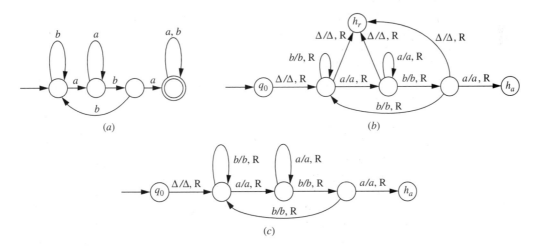

**Figure 9.2 |**
An FA and a TM to accept $\{a, b\}^*\{aba\}\{a, b\}^*$.

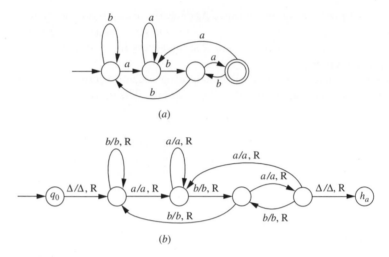

**Figure 9.3 |**
An FA and a TM to accept $\{a, b\}^*\{aba\}$.

this way; whenever we do, the diagram is to be interpreted as moving to the state $h_r$ for each combination of state and tape symbol for which no move is shown explicitly. What a TM does with the tape head on a final move of this type is essentially arbitrary, since the computation is now over; we may as well assume in general that the tape head moves to the right, as in Figure 9.2*b*. (We will talk later about combining two or more TMs, so that a second one picks up where the first one stops. In this case, what the first machine does on its last move is not arbitrary; however, we will allow such a composite TM to carry out a two-phase computation only if the first phase halts normally in the accept state $h_a$.)

Because this language is regular, the TM in Figure 9.2*a* or Figure 9.2*b* is able to process input strings the way a finite automaton is forced to, moving the tape head to the right at each step and never changing any tape symbols. Any regular language can be accepted by a TM that mimics an FA this way. As we would expect, this type of processing will not be sufficient to recognize a nonregular language.

Note also that as soon as the TM discovers *aba* on the tape, it enters the state $h_a$ and thereby accepts the entire input string, even though it may not have read all of it. Of course, some TMs must read all the input, even if the languages they accept are regular. For

$$L_1 = \{x \in \{a, b\}^* \mid x \text{ ends with } aba\}$$

for example, an FA and a TM are shown in Figure 9.3. Since the TM moves the tape head to the right on each move, it cannot accept without reading the blank to the right of the last input symbol. As in Figure 9.2*c*, the transitions to the reject state are not shown explicitly.

## EXAMPLE 9.2    A TM Accepting *pal*

To see a little more of the power of Turing machines, let us construct a TM to accept the language *pal* of palindromes over $\{a, b\}$. Later in this chapter we will introduce the possibility of nondeterminism in a TM, which would allow us to build a machine simulating the PDA in Example 7.2 directly. However, the flexibility of TMs allows us to select any algorithm, without restricting ourselves to a specific data structure such as a stack. We can easily formulate a deterministic approach by thinking of how a long string might be checked by hand. You might position your two forefingers at the the two ends. As your eyes jump repeatedly back and forth comparing the two end symbols, your fingers, which are the markers that tell your eyes how far to go, gradually move toward the center. In order to translate this into a TM algorithm, we can use blank squares for the markers at each end. Moving the markers toward the center corresponds to erasing (i.e., changing to blanks) the symbols that have just been tested. The tape head moves repeatedly back and forth, comparing the symbol at one end of the remaining nonblank string to the symbol at the other end. The transition diagram is shown in Figure 9.4. Again the tape alphabet is $\{a, b\}$, the same as the input alphabet. The machine takes the top path each time it finds an $a$ at the beginning and attempts to find a matching $a$ at the end.

If it encounters a $b$ in state $q_3$, so that it is unable to match the $a$ at the beginning, it enters the reject state $h_r$. (As in Figure 9.2c, this transition is not shown.) Similarly, it rejects from state $q_6$ if it is unable to match a $b$ at the beginning.

We trace the moves made by the machine for three different input strings: a nonpalindrome, an even-length palindrome, and an odd-length palindrome.

$$
\begin{aligned}
(q_0, \underline{\Delta}abaa) \quad &\vdash \ (q_1, \Delta\underline{a}baa) \quad \vdash \ (q_2, \Delta\Delta\underline{b}aa) \quad \vdash^* \ (q_2, \Delta\Delta baa\underline{\Delta}) \\
&\vdash \ (q_3, \Delta\Delta ba\underline{a}) \quad \vdash \ (q_4, \Delta\Delta\underline{b}a) \quad \vdash^* \ (q_4, \Delta\underline{\Delta}ba) \\
&\vdash \ (q_1, \Delta\Delta\underline{b}a) \quad \vdash \ (q_5, \Delta\Delta\Delta\underline{a}) \quad \vdash \ (q_5, \Delta\Delta\Delta a\underline{\Delta}) \\
&\vdash \ (q_6, \Delta\Delta\Delta\underline{a}) \quad \vdash \ (h_r, \Delta\Delta\Delta a\underline{\Delta}) \quad \text{(reject)}
\end{aligned}
$$

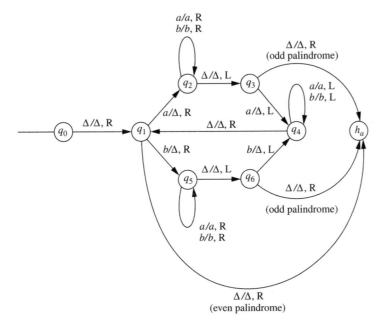

**Figure 9.4 |**

A TM to accept palindromes over $\{a, b\}$.

$$(q_0, \Delta \underline{a}a) \;\vdash\; (q_1, \Delta \underline{a}a) \;\vdash\; (q_2, \Delta \Delta \underline{a}) \;\vdash\; (q_2, \Delta \Delta a \underline{\Delta})$$
$$\vdash (q_3, \Delta \Delta \underline{a}) \quad\vdash\; (q_4, \Delta \underline{\Delta}) \quad\vdash\; (q_1, \Delta \Delta \underline{\Delta})$$
$$\vdash (h_a, \Delta \Delta \Delta \underline{\Delta}) \quad (\text{accept})$$

$$(q_0, \Delta \underline{a}ba) \;\vdash\; (q_1, \Delta \underline{a}ba) \;\vdash\; (q_2, \Delta \Delta \underline{b}a) \;\vdash^*\; (q_2, \Delta \Delta ba \underline{\Delta})$$
$$\vdash (q_3, \Delta \Delta b\underline{a}) \quad\vdash\; (q_4, \Delta \Delta \underline{b}) \quad\vdash\; (q_4, \Delta \underline{\Delta}b)$$
$$\vdash (q_1, \Delta \Delta \underline{b}) \quad\vdash\; (q_5, \Delta \Delta \Delta \underline{\Delta}) \;\vdash\; (q_6, \Delta \Delta \underline{\Delta})$$
$$\vdash (h_a, \Delta \Delta \Delta \underline{\Delta}) \quad (\text{accept})$$

<hr/>

**EXAMPLE 9.3**  A TM Accepting $\{ss \mid s \in \{a, b\}^*\}$

<hr/>

For our third example of a Turing machine as a language acceptor, we consider a language that we know from Example 8.2 not to be context-free. Let

$$L = \{ss \mid s \in \{a, b\}^*\}$$

The idea behind the TM will be to separate the processing into two parts: first, finding the middle of the string, and making it easier for the TM to distinguish the symbols in the second half from those in the first half; second, comparing the two halves. We accomplish the first task by working our way in from both ends simultaneously, changing symbols to their uppercase versions as we go. This means that our tape alphabet will include $A$ and $B$ in addition to the input symbols $a$ and $b$. Once we arrive at the middle—which will happen only if the string is of even length—we may change the symbols in the first half back to their original form. The second part of the processing is to start at the beginning again and, for each lowercase symbol in the first half, compare it to the corresponding uppercase symbol in the second. We keep track of our progress by changing lowercase symbols to uppercase and erasing the matching uppercase symbols.

There are two ways that an input string can be rejected. If its length is odd, the TM will discover this in the first phase. If the string has even length but a symbol in the first half fails to match the corresponding symbol in the second half, the TM will reject the string during the second phase.

The TM suggested by this discussion is shown in Figure 9.5. Again we trace it for three strings: two that illustrate both ways the TM can reject the input, and one that is in the language.

$$(q_0, \Delta \underline{a}ba) \;\vdash\; (q_1, \Delta \underline{a}ba) \;\vdash\; (q_2, \Delta A\underline{b}a) \;\vdash^*\; (q_2, \Delta Aba\underline{\Delta})$$
$$\vdash (q_3, \Delta A b\underline{a}) \quad\vdash\; (q_4, \Delta A\underline{b}A) \quad\vdash\; (q_4, \Delta \underline{A}bA)$$
$$\vdash (q_1, \Delta A\underline{b}a) \quad\vdash\; (q_2, \Delta AB\underline{A}) \quad\vdash\; (q_3, \Delta A\underline{B}A)$$
$$\vdash (h_r, \Delta AB\underline{A}) \quad (\text{reject})$$

$$(q_0, \Delta \underline{a}baa) \;\vdash\; (q_1, \Delta \underline{a}baa) \;\vdash\; (q_2, \Delta A\underline{b}aa) \;\vdash^*\; (q_2, \Delta Abaa\underline{\Delta})$$
$$\vdash (q_3, \Delta Aba\underline{a}) \quad\vdash\; (q_4, \Delta Ab\underline{a}A) \;\vdash^*\; (q_4, \Delta \underline{A}baA)$$
$$\vdash (q_1, \Delta A\underline{b}aA) \quad\vdash\; (q_2, \Delta AB\underline{a}A) \;\vdash\; (q_2, \Delta ABa\underline{A})$$
$$\vdash (q_3, \Delta AB\underline{a}A) \quad\vdash\; (q_4, \Delta A\underline{B}AA) \;\vdash\; (q_1, \Delta AB\underline{A}A)$$
$$\vdash (q_5, \Delta A\underline{B}AA) \quad\vdash\; (q_5, \Delta \underline{A}bAA) \;\vdash\; (q_5, \Delta \underline{a}bAA)$$
$$(\text{first phase completed})$$

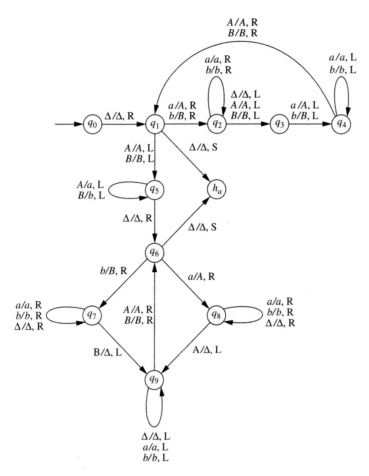

**Figure 9.5 |**
A Turing machine to accept $\{ss \mid s \in \{a, b\}^*\}$.

$\vdash (q_6, \Delta a\underline{b}AA) \quad \vdash (q_8, \Delta A\underline{b}AA) \quad \vdash (q_8, \Delta Ab\underline{A}A)$
$\vdash (q_9, \Delta A\underline{b}\Delta A) \quad \vdash (q_9, \Delta \underline{A}b\Delta A) \quad \vdash (q_6, \Delta A\underline{b}\Delta A)$
$\vdash (q_7, \Delta AB\underline{\Delta}A) \quad \vdash (q_7, \Delta AB\Delta\underline{A}) \quad \vdash (h_r, \Delta AB\Delta A\underline{\Delta}) \quad \text{(reject)}$

$(q_0, \underline{\Delta}abab) \quad \vdash^* \quad \cdots$

(same as previous case, up to 3rd-from-last move)
$\vdash (q_6, \Delta A\underline{b}\Delta B) \quad \vdash (q_7, \Delta AB\underline{\Delta}B) \quad \vdash (q_7, \Delta AB\Delta\underline{B})$
$\vdash (q_9, \Delta AB\underline{\Delta}) \quad \vdash (q_9, \Delta A\underline{B}) \quad \vdash (q_6, \Delta AB\underline{\Delta})$
$\vdash (h_a, \Delta AB\underline{\Delta}) \quad \text{(accept)}$

## 9.2 | COMPUTING A PARTIAL FUNCTION WITH A TURING MACHINE

Any computer program whose purpose is to produce a specified output string for every legal input string can be thought of as computing a function from one set of strings to another. Similarly, a Turing machine $T$ with input alphabet $\Sigma$ can compute a function $f$ whose domain is a subset of $\Sigma^*$. The idea is that for any string $x$ in the domain of $f$, whenever $T$ starts in the initial configuration corresponding to input $x$, $T$ will eventually halt with the output string $f(x)$ on the tape.

TMs in Section 9.1, which were used as language acceptors, did their jobs simply by halting in the accepting state or failing to do so, depending on whether the input string was in the language being accepted. The contents of the tape at the end of the computation were not important. In the case of a TM computing a function $f$, the emphasis is on the output produced for an input string in the domain of $f$. We might say that for an input string not in the domain, the result of the computation is irrelevant. However, we would like the TM to compute precisely the function $f$, not some other function with a larger domain. Therefore, we will also specify that for an input string $x$ not in the domain of $f$, the TM should not accept the input $x$. It follows that in the process of computing the function, the TM also incidentally accepts a language: the domain of the function.

It will be helpful in subsequent chapters to shift emphasis just slightly, and to talk about *partial* functions on $\Sigma^*$, rather than functions on subsets of $\Sigma^*$. This is largely a matter of convenience, and there is no real difference except in some of the terminology. A partial function $f$ on $\Sigma^*$ may be undefined at certain points (the points not in the domain of $f$); if it happens that $f$ is defined everywhere on $\Sigma^*$, we often emphasize the fact by referring to $f$ as a *total* function. In order for a Turing machine to compute $f$, it is appropriate for the values of $f$ to be strings over the tape alphabet of the machine.

A TM can handle a function of several variables as well. If the input is to represent the $k$-tuple $(x_1, x_2, \ldots, x_k) \in (\Sigma^*)^k$, the only change required is to relax slightly the rule for the input to a TM, and to allow the initial tape to contain all $k$ strings, separated by blanks.

---

**Definition 9.3     A TM Computing a Function**

Let $T = (Q, \Sigma, \Gamma, q_0, \delta)$ be a Turing machine, and let $f$ be a partial function on $\Sigma^*$ with values in $\Gamma^*$. We say that $T$ computes $f$ if for every $x \in \Sigma^*$ at which $f$ is defined,

$$(q_0, \underline{\Delta}x) \vdash_T^* (h_a, \underline{\Delta}f(x))$$

and no other $x \in \Sigma^*$ is accepted by $T$.

If $f$ is a partial function on $(\Sigma^*)^k$ with values in $\Gamma^*$, $T$ computes $f$ if for every $k$-tuple $(x_1, x_2, \ldots, x_k)$ at which $f$ is defined,

$$(q_0, \underline{\Delta}x_1 \Delta x_2 \Delta \cdots \Delta x_k) \vdash_T^* (h_a, \underline{\Delta}f(x_1, x_2, \ldots, x_k))$$

and no other input that is a $k$-tuple of strings is accepted by $T$. For two alphabets $\Sigma_1$ and $\Sigma_2$, and a positive integer $k$, a partial function $f : (\Sigma_1^*)^k \to \Sigma_2^*$ is *Turing-computable*, or simply *computable*, if there is a Turing machine computing $f$.

It is still not quite correct to say that a TM computes only one function. One reason is that two functions can look exactly alike except for having officially different codomains (see Section 1.3). Another reason is that a TM might be viewed as computing either a function of one variable or a function of more than one. For example, if $T$ computes the function $f : (\Sigma^*)^2 \to \Gamma^*$, then $T$ also computes $f_1 : \Sigma^* \to \Gamma^*$ defined by $f_1(x) = f(x, \Lambda)$. We can say, however, that for any specified $k$, and any $C \subseteq \Gamma^*$, a given TM computes at most one function of $k$ variables having codomain $C$.

Numerical functions of numerical arguments can also be computed by Turing machines, once we choose a way of representing the numbers by strings. We will restrict ourselves to natural numbers (nonnegative integers), and we generally use the "unary" representation, in which the integer $n$ is represented by the string $1^n = 11 \ldots 1$.

---

**Definition 9.4   Computing a Numerical Function**

Let $T = (Q, \{1\}, \Gamma, q_0, \delta)$ be a Turing machine. If $f$ is a partial function from $\mathcal{N}$, the set of natural numbers, to itself, $T$ computes $f$ if for every $n$ at which $f$ is defined,

$$(q_0, \underline{\Delta}1^n) \vdash_T^* (h_a, \underline{\Delta}1^{f(n)})$$

and for every other natural number $n$, $T$ fails to accept the input $1^n$. Similarly, if $f$ is a partial function from $\mathcal{N}^k$ to $\mathcal{N}$, $T$ computes $f$ if for every $k$-tuple $(n_1, n_2, \ldots, n_k)$ at which $f$ is defined,

$$(q_0, \underline{\Delta}1^{n_1} \Delta 1^{n_2} \Delta \cdots \Delta 1^{n_k}) \vdash_T^* (h_a, \underline{\Delta}1^{f(n_1, n_2, \ldots, n_k)})$$

and $T$ fails to accept if the input is any $k$-tuple at which $f$ is not defined.

---

Reversing a String     **EXAMPLE 9.4**

We consider the reverse function

$$rev : \{a, b\}^* \to \{a, b\}^*$$

The TM we construct in Figure 9.6 to compute the function will reverse the input string "in place" by moving from the ends toward the middle, at each step swapping a symbol in the first half with the matching one in the second half. In order to keep track of the progress made so far, symbols will also be changed to uppercase. A pass that starts in state $q_1$ with a lowercase symbol on the left changes it to the corresponding uppercase symbol and remembers it (by going to state $q_2$ in the case of an $a$ and $q_4$ in the case of a $b$) as it moves the tape head to the right. When the TM arrives at $q_3$ or $q_5$, if there is a lowercase symbol on the right corresponding to the one on

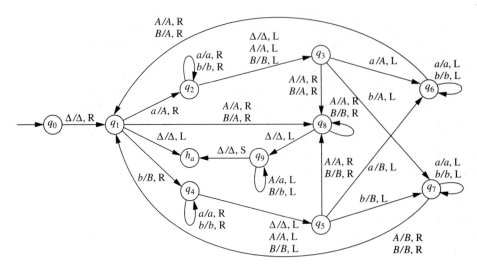

**Figure 9.6 |**
Reversing a string.

the left, the TM sees it, remembers it (by going to either $q_6$ or $q_7$), and changes it to the symbol it remembers from the left. The tape head is moved back to the left, and the first uppercase symbol that is encountered is changed to the (uppercase) symbol that had been on the right. For even-length strings, the last swap will return the TM to $q_1$, and at that point the absence of any more lowercase symbols sends the machine to $q_8$ and the final phase of processing. In the case of an odd-length string, the last pass will not be completed normally, because the machine will discover at either $q_3$ or $q_5$ that there is no lowercase symbol to swap with the one on the left (which therefore turns out to have been the middle symbol of the string). When the swaps have been completed, all that remains is to move the tape head to the end of the string and make one final pass back to the left, changing all the uppercase symbols back to lowercase.

We trace the TM in Figure 9.6 for the odd-length string $abb$ and the even-length string $baba$.

| $(q_0, \Delta abb)$ | $\vdash (q_1, \Delta \underline{a}bb)$ | $\vdash (q_2, \Delta A\underline{b}b)$ | $\vdash (q_2, \Delta Ab\underline{b})$ |
|---|---|---|---|
| | $\vdash (q_2, \Delta Abb\underline{\Delta})$ | $\vdash (q_3, \Delta Ab\underline{b})$ | $\vdash (q_7, \Delta A\underline{b}A)$ |
| | $\vdash (q_7, \Delta \underline{A}bA)$ | $\vdash (q_1, \Delta B\underline{b}A)$ | $\vdash (q_4, \Delta BB\underline{A})$ |
| | $\vdash (q_5, \Delta B\underline{B}A)$ | $\vdash (q_8, \Delta BB\underline{A})$ | $\vdash (q_8, \Delta BBA\underline{\Delta})$ |
| | $\vdash (q_9, \Delta BB\underline{A})$ | $\vdash (q_9, \Delta B\underline{B}a)$ | $\vdash (q_9, \Delta \underline{B}ba)$ |
| | $\vdash (q_9, \underline{\Delta}bba)$ | $\vdash (h_a, \underline{\Delta}bba)$ | |
| | | | |
| $(q_0, \Delta baba)$ | $\vdash (q_1, \Delta \underline{b}aba)$ | $\vdash (q_4, \Delta B\underline{a}ba)$ | $\vdash (q_4, \Delta Ba\underline{b}a)$ |
| | $\vdash (q_4, \Delta Bab\underline{a})$ | $\vdash (q_4, \Delta Baba\underline{\Delta})$ | $\vdash (q_5, \Delta Bab\underline{a})$ |
| | $\vdash (q_6, \Delta Ba\underline{b}B)$ | $\vdash (q_6, \Delta B\underline{a}bB)$ | $\vdash (q_6, \Delta \underline{B}abB)$ |
| | $\vdash (q_1, \Delta A\underline{a}bB)$ | $\vdash (q_2, \Delta AA\underline{b}B)$ | $\vdash (q_2, \Delta AAb\underline{B})$ |
| | $\vdash (q_3, \Delta AA\underline{b}B)$ | $\vdash (q_7, \Delta A\underline{A}AB)$ | $\vdash (q_1, \Delta AB\underline{A}B)$ |
| | $\vdash (q_8, \Delta ABA\underline{B})$ | $\vdash (q_8, \Delta ABAB\underline{\Delta})$ | $\vdash (q_9, \Delta ABA\underline{B})$ |
| | $\vdash^* (q_9, \underline{\Delta}abab)$ | $\vdash (h_a, \underline{\Delta}abab)$ | |

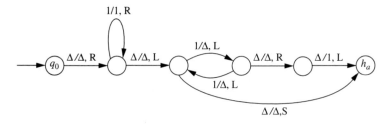

**Figure 9.7 |**
A Turing machine to compute $n$ mod 2.

<table>
<tr><td align="right">$n$ mod 2</td><td>**EXAMPLE 9.5**</td></tr>
</table>

The numerical function that assigns to each natural number $n$ the remainder when $n$ is divided by 2 can be computed by moving to the end of the input string, making a pass from right to left in which the 1's are counted and simultaneously erased, and either leaving a single 1 (if the original number was odd) or leaving nothing. The TM that performs this computation is shown in Figure 9.7.

<table>
<tr><td align="right">The Characteristic Function of a Set</td><td>**EXAMPLE 9.6**</td></tr>
</table>

For any language $L \subseteq \Sigma^*$, the *characteristic function* of $L$ is the function $\chi_L : \Sigma^* \to \{0, 1\}$ defined by the formula

$$\chi_L(x) = \begin{cases} 1 & \text{if } x \in L \\ 0 & \text{otherwise} \end{cases}$$

Computing the function $\chi_L$ is therefore similar in one respect to accepting the language $L$ (see Section 9.1); instead of distinguishing between strings in $L$ and strings not in $L$ by accepting or not accepting, the TM accepts every input, and distinguishes between the two types of strings by ending up in the configuration $(h_a, \underline{\Delta}1)$ in one case and the configuration $(h_a, \underline{\Delta}0)$ in the other.

If we have a TM $T$ computing $\chi_L$, we can easily obtain one that accepts $L$. All we have to do is modify $T$ so that when it leaves output 0, it enters the state $h_r$ instead of $h_a$. Sometimes it is possible to go the other way; a simple example is the language $L$ of palindromes over $\{a, b\}$ (Example 9.2). A TM accepting $L$ is shown in Figure 9.4, and a TM computing $\chi_L$ is shown in Figure 9.8.

It is obtained from the previous one by identifying the places in the transition diagram where the TM might reject, and modifying the TM so that instead of entering the state $h_r$ in those situations, it continues in a way that ends up in state $h_a$ with output 0. For any language $L$ accepted by a TM $T$ that halts on every input string, another TM can be constructed from $T$ that computes $\chi_L$, although the construction may be more complicated than in this example. A TM of either type effectively allows an observer to decide whether a given input string is in $L$; a "no" answer is produced in one case by the input being rejected and in the other case by output 0.

As we saw in Section 9.1, however, a TM can accept a language $L$ and still leave the question of whether $x \in L$ unanswered for some strings $x$, by looping forever on those inputs.

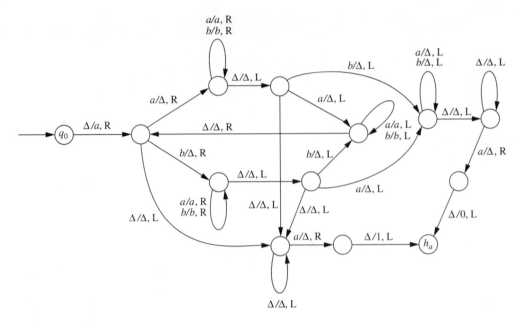

**Figure 9.8** |

Computing $\chi_L$ for the set of palindromes.

(If we could somehow *see* that the TM was in an infinite loop, we would have the answer; but if we were depending on the TM to tell us, we would wait forever.) In this case, a TM computing the function $\chi_L$ would be better, because it would guarantee an answer for every input. Unfortunately, it is no longer clear that such a machine can be obtained from $T$. We will return to this question in Chapter 10.

## 9.3 | COMBINING TURING MACHINES

One of the purposes of this chapter is to suggest the power and generality of Turing machines. As you can tell from the examples so far, much of the work that goes on during a TM computation consists of routine, repetitive tasks such as moving the tape head from one side of a string to the other or erasing a portion of the tape. If we were required to describe every TM monolithically, showing all the low-level details, we would quickly reach a practical limit on the complexity of the problems we could solve. The natural way to construct a complicated TM (or any other complicated algorithm or piece of software) is to build it from simpler, reusable components.

In the simplest case, we can construct a composite Turing machine by executing first one TM and then another. If $T_1$ and $T_2$ are TMs, with disjoint sets of nonhalting states and transition functions $\delta_1$ and $\delta_2$, respectively, we write $T_1 T_2$ to denote this composite TM. The set of states is the union of the two sets. $T_1 T_2$ begins in the initial state of $T_1$ and executes the moves of $T_1$ (using the function $\delta_1$) up to the point where $T_1$ would halt; for any move that would cause $T_1$ to halt in the accepting state, $T_1T_2$ executes the same move except that it moves instead to the initial state of $T_2$. At this point the tape head is positioned at the square on which $T_1$ halted. From this point on, the moves of $T_1T_2$ are the moves of $T_2$ (using the function $\delta_2$). If either $T_1$ or $T_2$ would reject during this process, $T_1T_2$ does also, and $T_1T_2$ accepts precisely if and when $T_2$ accepts.

In order to use this composite machine in a larger context, in a manner similar to a transition diagram but without showing the states explicitly, we might also write

$$T_1 \to T_2$$

We can also make the composition conditional, depending on the current tape symbol when $T_1$ halts. We might write

$$T_1 \overset{a}{\to} T_2$$

to stand for the composite machine $T_1 T' T_2$, where $T'$ is described by the diagram in Figure 9.9. This composite machine can be described informally as follows: It executes the TM $T_1$ (rejecting if $T_1$ rejects, and looping if $T_1$ loops); if and when $T_1$ accepts, it executes $T_2$ if the current tape symbol is $a$ and rejects otherwise.

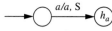

**Figure 9.9 |**

It is easier to understand at this point why we said in Section 9.1 that a TM is not always assumed to start with the tape head on the leftmost square of the tape. When a TM built to carry out some specific task is used as a component of a larger TM, it is likely to be called in the middle of a computation, when the tape head is at the spot on the tape where that task needs to be performed. It may be that the TM's only purpose is to change in some other specific way the tape contents and/or head position so as to create a beginning configuration appropriate for the component that follows.

Some TMs that would only halt in the rejecting state when viewed as self-contained machines (e.g., the TM that executes the algorithm "move the tape head one square to the left") can be used successfully in combination with others. On the other hand, if a TM halts normally when run independently, then it will halt normally when it is used as a component of a larger machine, provided that the tape has been prepared properly before its use. For example, a TM $T$ expecting to find an input string $z$ needs to begin in a configuration of the form $(q, y\underline{\Delta}z)$. As long as $T$ halts normally when processing input $z$ in the ordinary way, the processing of $z$ in this way does not depend on $y$. (The reason is that if $T$ halts normally when started in the configuration $(q, \underline{\Delta}z)$, then in particular $T$ will never attempt to move its tape head to the left of the blank; therefore, starting in the configuration $(q, y\underline{\Delta}z)$, $T$ will never actually see any of the symbols of $y$.) The correct execution of $T$ does, however, depend on the tape being blank to the right of $z$, unless more is known about the space required for the computation involving $z$.

In order to be able to describe composite TMs without having to describe every primitive operation as a separate TM, it is sometimes useful to use a mixed notation in which some but not all of the states of a TM are shown. For example, the diagram in Figure 9.10a, which is an abbreviated version of the one in Figure 9.10b, has a fairly obvious meaning. If the current tape symbol is $a$, execute the TM $T$; if it is $b$, halt in

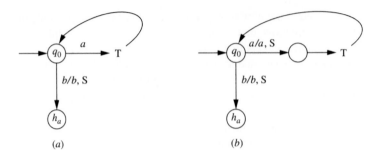

**Figure 9.10 |**

the accepting state; and if it is anything else, reject. In the first case, assuming $T$ halts normally, repeat the execution of $T$ until $T$ halts normally scanning some symbol other than $a$; if at that point the tape symbol is $b$, halt normally, otherwise reject. (The machine might also reject during one of the iterations of $T$; and it might loop forever, either because one of the iterations of $T$ does or because $T$ halts normally with current tape symbol $a$ every time.)

Although giving a completely precise definition of an arbitrary combination of TMs would be complicated, it is usually clear in specific examples what is involved. There is one possible source of confusion, however, in the notation we are adopting. Consider a TM $T$ of the form $T_1 \xrightarrow{a} T_2$. If $T_1$ halts normally scanning some symbol not specified explicitly (i.e., other than $a$), $T$ rejects. However, if $T_2$ halts normally, $T$ does also—even though *no* tape symbols are specified explicitly. We could avoid this seeming inconsistency by saying that if $T_1$ halts normally scanning a symbol other than $a$, $T$ halts normally, except that $T$ would then not be equivalent to the composition $T_1 T' T_2$ described above, and this seems undesirable. In our notation, if at the end of one sub-TM's operation at least one way is specified for the composite TM to continue, then any option that allows accepting at that point must be shown explicitly, as in Figures 9.11$a$ and 9.11$b$. (The second figure is a shortened form of the first.)

Some basic TM building blocks, such as moving the head a specified number of positions in one direction or the other, writing a specific symbol in the current square, and searching to one direction or the other for a specified symbol, are straightforward and do not need to be spelled out. We consider a few slightly more involved operations.

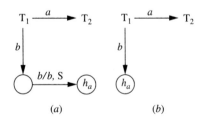

**Figure 9.11 |**

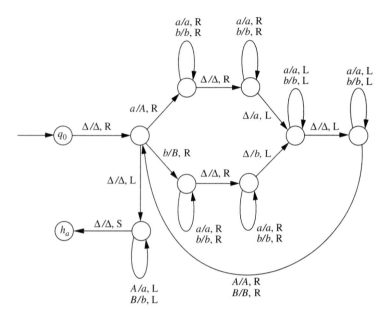

**Figure 9.12 |**
A Turing machine to copy strings.

## Copying a String   **EXAMPLE 9.7**

Let us construct a TM that creates a copy of its input string, to the right of the input but with a blank separating the copy from the original. We must be careful to specify the final position of the tape head as well; let us say that if the initial configuration is $(q_0, \underline{\Delta}x)$, where $x$ is a string of nonblank symbols, then the final configuration should be $(h_a, \underline{\Delta}x\Delta x)$. The TM will examine the first symbol, copy it in the right place, examine the second, copy it, and so on. It will keep track of its progress by changing the symbols it has copied to uppercase. We assume for simplicity that the input alphabet is $\{a, b\}$; all that is needed in a more general situation is a modified ("uppercase") version of each symbol in the input alphabet. When the copying is complete, the uppercase symbols will be changed back to the original. The TM is shown in Figure 9.12.

## Deleting a Symbol   **EXAMPLE 9.8**

It is often useful to delete a symbol from a string. A Turing machine does this by changing the tape contents from $y\underline{a}z$ to $y\underline{z}$, where $y \in (\Sigma \cup \{\Delta\})^*$, $a \in \Sigma \cup \{\Delta\}$, and $z \in \Sigma^*$. (Remember that $y\underline{z}$ means that the tape head is positioned on the first symbol of $z$, or on a blank if $z$ is null.) Again we assume that the input alphabet is $\{a, b\}$. The TM starts by replacing the symbol to be deleted by a blank, so that it can be located easily later. It moves to the right end of the string $z$ and makes a single pass from right to left, moving symbols one square to the left as it goes, until it hits the blank. The transition diagram is shown in Figure 9.13. The states labeled $q_a$ and $q_b$ are what allow the machine to remember a symbol between the time it erases it and the time it writes it in the next square to the left. Of course, before it writes each symbol, it reads the symbol being written over, which determines the state it should go to next.

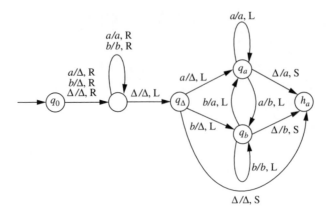

**Figure 9.13 |**
A Turing machine to delete a symbol.

---

*Inserting* a symbol $a$, or changing the tape contents from $y\underline{z}$ to $y\underline{az}$, would be done virtually the same way, except that the single pass would go from left to right, and the move that starts it off would write $a$ instead of $\Delta$. You are asked to complete this machine in Exercise 9.13.

---

The *Delete* machine transforms $y\underline{az}$ to $y\underline{z}$. What if it is called when the tape contents are not $y\underline{az}$, but $y\underline{az}\Delta w$, where $w$ is some arbitrary string of symbols? At first it might seem that the TM ought to be designed so as to finish with $y\underline{z}\Delta w$ on the tape. A closer look, however, shows that this is unreasonable. Unless we know something about the computations that have gone on before, or unless the rightmost nonblank symbol has been marked somehow so that we can recognize it, we have no way of finding it. The instructions "move the tape head to the square containing the rightmost nonblank symbol" cannot ordinarily be executed by a TM (Exercise 9.12). In general, a Turing machine is designed according to specifications, which say that if it starts in a certain configuration it should halt normally in some other specified configuration. The specifications may say nothing about what the result should be if the TM starts in some different configuration. The machine may satisfy its specifications and yet behave unpredictably, perhaps halting in $h_r$ or looping forever, in these abnormal situations.

---

**EXAMPLE 9.9**     Another Way of Accepting *pal*

Suppose that *Copy* is the TM in Figure 9.12 and *Reverse* is the one in Figure 9.6. Let *Equal* be a TM that works as follows: When started with tape $\underline{\Delta}x\Delta y$, where $x, y \in \{a, b\}^*$, *Equal* accepts if and only if $x = y$. Then the composite TM shown in Figure 9.14 accepts the language of palindromes over $\{a, b\}$ by comparing the input string to its reverse and accepting if and only if the two are equal.

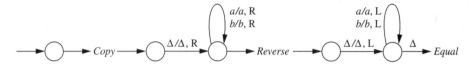

**Figure 9.14 |**
Another way of accepting *pal*.

---

# 9.4 | VARIATIONS OF TURING MACHINES: MULTITAPE TMs

The version of Turing machines introduced in Section 9.1 is not the only possible one. There are a number of variations in which slightly different conventions are followed with regard to starting configuration, permissible moves, protocols followed to accept strings, and so forth. In addition, the basic TM model can be enhanced in several natural ways. In this section we mention a few of the variations and investigate one enhanced version, the multitape TM, in some detail.

A more user-friendly TM, such as one with additional tapes, can make it easier to describe the implementation of an algorithm: The discussion can highlight the individual data items stored on the various tapes, without getting bogged down in the bookkeeping techniques that would be necessary if all the data were stored on and retrieved from a single tape. Thus it will often be useful to have these enhanced versions available in subsequent discussions. However, it will turn out that in spite of the extra convenience, there is no change in the ultimate computing power. Seeing the details needed to show this may help you to appreciate the power of a Turing machine. Finally, the discussion in this section will provide a useful example of how one type of computing machine can simulate another.

In order to compare two classes of abstract machines with regard to *computing power*, we must start by saying what we mean by this term. At this point, we are not considering speed, efficiency, or convenience; we are concerned only with whether the two types of machines can solve the same problems and get the same answers. A Turing machine of any type gives an "answer," first by accepting or failing to accept, and second by producing a particular output when it halts in the accepting state. This means that if we want to show that machines of type B are at least as powerful as those of type A, we need to show that for any machine $T_A$ of type A, there is a machine $T_B$ of type B that accepts exactly the same input strings as $T_A$ and produces exactly the same output as $T_A$ whenever it halts in the accepting state.

First we mention briefly a few minor variations on the basic model, each of them slightly *more* restrictive. One possibility is to require that in each move the tape head move either to the right or to the left. In this version, the values of the transition function $\delta$ are elements of $(Q \cup \{h_a, h_r\}) \times (\Gamma \cup \{\Delta\}) \times \{L,R\}$ instead of $(Q \cup \{h_a, h_r\}) \times (\Gamma \cup \{\Delta\}) \times \{L,R,S\}$. A second possibility is to say that a move can include writing a tape symbol or moving the tape head but not both. In this case $\delta$ would take values in $(Q \cup \{h_a, h_r\}) \times (\Gamma \cup \{\Delta\} \cup \{L,R\})$, where L and R are assumed not to be elements of $\Gamma$. In both cases it is easy to see that the restrictions do not reduce the power of the machine. You are referred to the exercises for the details.

One identifiable difference between a Turing machine and a typical human computer is that a TM has a one-dimensional tape with a left end, rather than sheets of paper that might be laid out in both directions. One way to try to increase the power of the machine, therefore, might be to remove one or both of these restrictions: to make the "tape" two-dimensional, or to remove the left end and make the tape potentially infinite in both directions. In either case we would start by specifying the rules under which the machine would operate, and the conventions that would be followed with regard to input and output. Again the conclusion is that the power of the machine is not significantly changed by either addition, and again we leave the details to the exercises.

Rather than modifying the tape, we might instead add extra tapes. We could decide in that case whether to have a single tape head, which would be positioned at the same square on all the tapes, or a head on each tape that could move independently of the others. We choose the second option. An $n$-tape Turing machine will be specifiable as before by a 5-tuple $T = (Q, \Sigma, \Gamma, q_0, \delta)$. It will make a move on the basis of its current state and the $n$-tuple of tape symbols currently being examined; since the tape heads move independently, we describe the transition function as a partial function

$$\delta : Q \times (\Gamma \cup \{\Delta\})^n \to (Q \cup \{h_a, h_r\}) \times (\Gamma \cup \{\Delta\})^n \times \{R,L,S\}^n$$

The notion of configuration generalizes in a straightforward way: A configuration of an $n$-tape TM is specified by an $(n + 1)$-tuple of the form

$$(q, x_1\underline{a_1}y_1, x_2\underline{a_2}y_2, \ldots, x_n\underline{a_n}y_n)$$

with the same restrictions as before on the strings $x_i$ and $y_i$.

We take the initial configuration corresponding to input string $x$ to be

$$(q_0, \underline{\Delta}x, \underline{\Delta}, \ldots, \underline{\Delta})$$

In other words, the first tape is the one used for the input. We will also say that the output of an $n$-tape TM is the final contents of tape 1. Tapes 2 through $n$ are used for auxiliary working space, and when the TM halts their contents are ignored. In particular, such a TM computes a function $f$ if, whenever it begins with an input string $x$ in (or representing an element in) the domain of $f$, it halts in some configuration $(h_a, \underline{\Delta}f(x), \ldots)$, where the contents of tapes 2 through $n$ are arbitrary, and otherwise it fails to accept.

It is obvious that for any $n \geq 2$, $n$-tape TMs are at least as powerful as ordinary 1-tape TMs. To simulate an ordinary TM, a TM with $n$ tapes simply acts as if tape 1 were its only one and leaves the others blank. We now show the converse.

---

**Theorem 9.1**

Let $n \geq 2$ and let $T_1 = (Q_1, \Sigma, \Gamma_1, q_1, \delta_1)$ be an $n$-tape Turing machine. Then there is a one-tape TM $T_2 = (Q_2, \Sigma, \Gamma_2, q_2, \delta_2)$, with $\Gamma_1 \subseteq \Gamma_2$, satisfying the following two conditions.

1. $L(T_2) = L(T_1)$; that is, for any $x \in \Sigma^*$, $T_2$ accepts input $x$ if and only if $T_1$ accepts input $x$.

2. For any $x \in \Sigma^*$, if

$$(q_1, \underline{\Delta}x, \underline{\Delta}, \ldots, \underline{\Delta}) \vdash_{T_1}^* (h_a, y\underline{a}z, y_2\underline{a_2}z_2, \ldots, y_n\underline{a_n}z_n)$$

(for some $a, a_i \in \Gamma_1 \cup \{\Delta\}$ and $y, z, y_i, z_i \in (\Gamma_1 \cup \{\Delta\})^*$), then

$$(q_2, \underline{\Delta}x) \vdash_{T_2}^* (h_a, y\underline{a}z)$$

In other words, if $T_1$ accepts input $x$, then $T_2$ accepts input $x$ and produces the same output as $T_1$.

### Proof

We give the proof for $n = 2$. It will be easy to see how to extend it to the general case.

We construct a one-tape TM that is capable of *simulating* the original two-tape machine, in an almost literal sense. It will act like, even *look* like, a machine with two tapes as it carries out its moves. The way to get a single tape to "look like" two tapes is to use a more complicated tape alphabet, so that what is on a single square makes it look like two squares, each with its own symbol. By adding even more symbols to the alphabet, we can take care of another technical problem with the simulation, how to keep track of the locations of the individual tape heads.

The tape alphabet $\Gamma_2$ includes the following kinds of symbols:

1. Ordinary symbols in $\Gamma = \Gamma_1 \cup \{\Delta\}$. These are necessary because input and output symbols of $T_2$ are of this form.

2. Elements of $\Gamma \times \Gamma$. A symbol $(X, Y)$ of this type in square $i$ is thought of as representing $X$ in square $i$ of the first tape and $Y$ in square $i$ of the second. We think of the tape as having two "tracks," corresponding to the two tapes of $T_1$. The two tracks do not exist initially but will be created gradually as $T_2$ moves its tape head farther and farther to the right.

3. Elements of $(\Gamma \times \Gamma') \cup (\Gamma' \times \Gamma) \cup (\Gamma' \times \Gamma')$, where $\Gamma'$ contains the same symbols as $\Gamma$, marked with ' to distinguish them from those of $\Gamma$. At any time during the simulation, there is one primed symbol on each track to designate the location of the tape head on the corresponding tape of $T_1$. A pair in which both symbols are primed represents the situation in which the tape head locations in $T_1$ are the same on both tapes.

4. An extra symbol, #, which is inserted initially into the leftmost square, making it easy to find the beginning of the tape whenever we want.

The next step of $T_2$, after inserting the symbol #, is to change the blank that is now in square 1 to the symbol $(\Delta', \Delta')$, signifying that the "head" on each track is now on square 1, and then move the actual head back to square 0. From now on, the two tracks will extend as far as $T_2$ has ever moved its tape head to the right; whenever it advances one square farther, it converts from the old single symbol to the new double symbol.

At this point the actual simulation starts. $T_1$ makes moves of the form

$$\delta(p, a_1, a_2) = (q, b_1, b_2, D_1, D_2)$$

where $a_1$ and $a_2$ are the symbols in the current squares of the respective tapes. Because $T_2$ has only one tape head, it must determine which move it is to make at the next step by locating the primed symbols on the two tracks of its tape; it then carries out the move by making the appropriate changes to both its tracks, including the creation of new primed symbols to reflect any changes in the positions of the tape heads of $T_1$.

It is obviously possible for $T_2$ to use its states to "remember" the current state $p$ of $T_1$. With this in mind, we can describe more precisely the steps $T_2$ might follow in simulating a single move of $T_1$, starting in the leftmost square of its tape.

1. Move the head to the right until a pair of the form $(a_1', c)$ is found ($c$ may or may not be a primed symbol), and remember $a_1$. Move back to the # at the beginning.
2. Locate the "head" on the second track the same way, by finding the pair of the form $(d, a_2')$ ($d$ may or may not be a primed symbol).
3. If the move of $T_1$ that has now been determined is $(q, b_1, b_2, D_1, D_2)$ as above, remember the state $q$, change the pair $(d, a_2')$ to $(d, b_2)$, and move the tape head in direction $D_2$.
4. If the current square contains #, reject, since $T_1$ would have crashed by trying to move the tape head off tape 2. If not, and if the new square does not contain a pair of symbols (because $D_2 = R$ and $T_2$ has not previously examined positions this far to the right), convert the symbol $a$ there to the pair $(a, \Delta')$; if the new square does contain a pair, say $(a, b)$, convert it to $(a, b')$. Move the tape head back to the beginning.
5. Locate the pair $(a_1', c)$ again, as in step 1. Change it to $(b_1, c)$ and move the tape head in direction $D_1$.
6. As in step 4, either reject, or change the single symbol $a$ to the pair $(a', \Delta)$, or change the pair $(a, b)$ to the pair $(a', b)$. Return to the beginning of the tape.

The diagram below illustrates one iteration in a simple case.

| # | $\Delta$ | $0'$ | $\Delta$ | $0$ | | $1$ | $\Delta$ |
|---|---|---|---|---|---|---|---|
| | $0$ | $1$ | $0$ | $1'$ | | | |

| # | $\Delta$ | $0'$ | $\Delta$ | $0$ | $1$ | | $\Delta$ |
|---|---|---|---|---|---|---|---|
| | $0$ | $1$ | $0$ | $0$ | $\Delta'$ | | |

$\cdots$

| # | $\Delta'$ | $\Delta$ | $\Delta$ | $0$ | $1$ | | $\Delta$ |
|---|---|---|---|---|---|---|---|
| | $0$ | $1$ | $0$ | $0$ | $\Delta'$ | | |

The symbols $a_1$ and $a_2$ are 0 and 1, $b_1$ and $b_2$ are $\Delta$ and 0, and $D_1$ and $D_2$ are L and R, respectively, so that the move being simulated is

$$\delta(p, 0, 1) = (q, \Delta, 0, L, R)$$

The second line represents the situation after step 4: The single symbol 1 has been changed to a pair of symbols, and the second one is primed to designate the resulting head position on the second tape. The third line shows the configuration after step 6.

As long as the halt state $h_a$ has not been reached, iterating these six steps allows $T_2$ to simulate the moves of $T_1$ correctly. If and when the new state is $h_a$, $T_2$ must carry out the following additional steps in order to finish up in the correct configuration.

7. Make a pass through the tape, converting each pair $(a, b)$ to the single symbol $a$. (One of these symbols $a$ will be a primed symbol.)
8. Delete the #, so that the remaining symbols begin in square 0.
9. Move the tape head to the primed symbol, change it to the corresponding unprimed symbol, and halt in state $h_a$ with the head in that position.

**Corollary 9.1.** Any language that is accepted by an $n$-tape TM can be accepted by an ordinary TM, and any function that is computed by an $n$-tape TM can be computed by an ordinary TM.

**Proof** The proof is immediate from Theorem 9.1.

# 9.5 | NONDETERMINISTIC TURING MACHINES

Nondeterminism plays different roles in the two simpler models of computation we studied earlier. It is convenient but not essential in the case of FAs, whereas the language *pal* is an example of a context-free language that cannot be accepted by any deterministic PDA. Turing machines have enough computing power that once again nondeterminism fails to add any more. Any language that can be accepted by a nondeterministic TM can be accepted by an ordinary one. The argument we present to show this involves a simulation more complex than that in the previous section. Nevertheless, the idea of the proof is straightforward, and the fact that the details get complicated can be taken as evidence that TMs capable of implementing complex algorithms can be constructed from the same kinds of routine operations we have used previously.

A *nondeterministic Turing machine* (NTM) $T = (Q, \Sigma, \Gamma, q_0, \delta)$ is defined exactly the same way as an ordinary TM, except that values of the transition function $\delta$ are subsets, rather than single elements, of the set $(Q \cup \{h_a, h_r\}) \times (\Gamma \cup \{\Delta\}) \times \{R, L, S\}$. We do not need to say that $\delta$ is a *partial* function, because now $\delta(q, a)$ is allowed to take the value $\emptyset$.

The notation for a TM configuration is also unchanged. To say that

$$(p, x\underline{a}y) \vdash_T (q, w\underline{b}z)$$

now means that beginning in the first configuration, there is at least one move that will produce the second. Similarly,

$$(p, x\underline{a}y) \vdash_T^* (q, w\underline{b}z)$$

means that there is at least one sequence of zero or more moves that takes $T$ from the first configuration to the second. With this definition, we may still say that a string $x \in \Sigma^*$ is accepted by $T$ if for some $a \in \Gamma \cup \{\Delta\}$ and some $y, z \in (\Gamma \cup \{\Delta\})^*$,

$$(q_0, \underline{\Delta}x) \vdash_T^* (h_a, y\underline{a}z)$$

The idea of *output* will not be as useful in the nondeterministic case, because for a given NTM there could conceivably be an infinite set of possible outputs. NTMs that produce output, such as those in Exercise 9.29, will be used primarily as components of larger machines. When we compare NTMs to ordinary TMs, we will restrict ourselves to machines used as language acceptors.

Because every TM can be interpreted as a nondeterministic TM, it is obvious that a language accepted by a TM can be accepted by an NTM. The converse is what we need to show.

---

**Theorem 9.2**
Let $T_1 = (Q_1, \Sigma, \Gamma_1, q_1, \delta_1)$ be an NTM. Then there is an ordinary (deterministic) TM $T_2 = (Q_2, \Sigma, \Gamma_2, q_2, \delta_2)$ with $L(T_2) = L(T_1)$.

*Proof*
The TM $T_2$ we are looking for will have the property that for any $x \in \Sigma^*$, $T_2$ accepts input $x$ if and only if there is *some* sequence of moves of $T_1$ on input $x$ that would cause it to accept. The strategy for constructing $T_2$ is simply to let it try *every* sequence of moves of $T_1$, one sequence at a time, accepting if and only if it finds a sequence that would cause $T_1$ to halt in the accepting state.

Although there may be many configurations in which $T_1$ has a choice of moves, there is some fixed upper bound on the number of choices it might ever have. We assume for the sake of simplicity that this maximum number is 2. The proof we present in this case will generalize easily. There is no harm in assuming further that whenever there are any moves at all, there are exactly two, which we label 0 and 1. (The order is arbitrary, and it is possible that both are actually the same move.)

For any input string $x$, we can use a *computation tree* such as the one in Figure 9.15 to represent the sequences of moves $T_1$ might make on input $x$. Nodes in the tree represent configurations of $T_1$. The root is the initial configuration corresponding to input $x$, and the children of any node $N$ correspond to the configurations $T_1$ might reach in one step from the configuration $N$. The convention we have adopted implies that every interior node has exactly two children, and a leaf node represents a halting configuration.

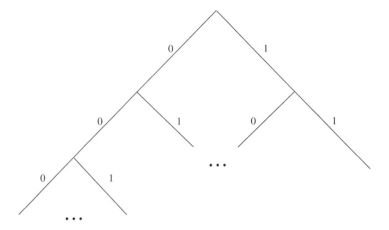

**Figure 9.15** |
The computation tree for a nondeterministic TM

We can therefore think of $T_2$'s job as searching the tree for accepting configurations. Because the tree might be infinite, a *breadth-first* approach is appropriate: $T_2$ will try all possible single moves, then all possible sequences of two moves, then all possible sequences of three moves, and so on. The machine we actually construct will be inefficient in that every sequence of $n + 1$ moves will involve repeating a sequence of $n$ moves tried previously. Even if the tree is finite (which means that for some $n$, every possible sequence of $n$ moves $T_1$ can make on input $x$ leads to a halt), $T_2$ will still loop forever if $T_1$ never accepts: It will attempt to try longer and longer sequences of moves, and the effect will be that it ends up repeating the same sequences of moves, in the same order, over and over. However, if $x \in L(T_1)$, then for some $n$ there is a sequence of $n$ moves that causes $T_1$ to accept input $x$, and $T_2$ will eventually get around to trying that sequence.

We will take advantage of Theorem 9.1 by giving $T_2$ three tapes. The first is used only to save the original input string, and its contents are never changed. The second is used to keep track of the sequence of moves of $T_1$ that $T_2$ is currently attempting to execute. The third is the "working tape," corresponding to $T_1$'s tape, where $T_2$ actually carries out the steps specified by the current string on tape 2. Every time $T_2$ begins trying a new sequence, the third tape is erased and the input from tape 1 re-copied onto it.

A particular sequence of moves will be represented by a string of binary digits. The string 001, for example, represents the following sequence: first, the move representing the first (i.e., 0th) of the two choices from the initial configuration $C_0$, which takes $T_1$ to some configuration $C_1$; next, the first possible move from the configuration $C_1$, which leads to some configuration $C_2$; next, the second possible move from $C_2$. Because moves

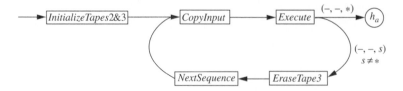

**Figure 9.16 |**
Simulating a nondeterministic TM by a three-tape TM.

0 and 1 may be the same, there may be several strings of digits that describe the same sequences of moves. There may also be strings of digits that do not correspond to sequences of moves, because the first few moves cause $T_1$ to halt. When $T_2$ encounters a digit that does not correspond to an executable move, it will abandon the string.

We will use the *canonical* ordering of $\{0, 1\}^*$, in which the strings are arranged in the order

$$\Lambda, 0, 1, 00, 01, 10, 11, 000, 001, \ldots, 111, 0000, \ldots$$

(For two strings of different lengths, the shorter one comes first, and the order of two strings of the same length is numerical.) Given a string $\alpha$ representing a sequence of moves, $T_2$ generates the next string in this ordering by interpreting $\alpha$ as a binary representation and adding 1—unless $\alpha = 1^k$, in which case the next string is $0^{k+1}$.

It is now easy to describe the general structure of $T_2$. It is composed of five smaller TMs called *InitializeTapes2&3*, *CopyInput*, *Execute*, *Erase-Tape3*, and *NextSequence*, combined as in Figure 9.16.

*InitializeTapes2&3* writes the symbol 0 in square 1 of tape 2, to represent the sequence of moves to be tried first, and places the symbol # in square 0 of tape 3. This marker allows $T_2$ to detect, and recover from, an attempt by $T_1$ to move its head off the tape. *CopyInput* copies the original input string $x$ from tape 1 onto tape 3, so that tape 3 has contents $\#\underline{\Delta}x$. *Execute* (which we will discuss in more detail shortly) is the TM that actually simulates the action of $T_1$ on this input, by executing the sequence of moves currently specified on tape 2. Its crucial feature is that it finishes with a symbol $s$ in the current square of tape 3, and $s = *$ if and only if the sequence of moves causes $T_1$ to accept. In this case $T_2$ accepts, and otherwise it continues with the *EraseTape3* component. *EraseTape3* restores tape 3 to the configuration $\#\underline{\Delta}$. It is able to complete this operation because the length of the string on tape 2 limits how far to the right the rightmost nonblank symbol on tape 3 can be. Finally, *NextSequence* is the component already mentioned, which updates the string of digits on tape 2 using the operation similar to adding 1 in binary. Figure 9.17 shows a one-tape TM that executes this transformation on an input string of 0's and 1's; *NextSequence* is the three-tape TM that carries out this transformation on the second tape only, ignoring tapes 1 and 3.

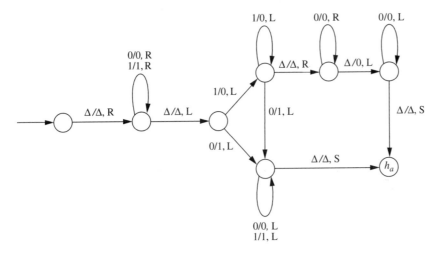

**Figure 9.17 |**
The one-tape version of *NextSequence*.

The problem of constructing $T_2$ has now been reduced to that of constructing the component *Execute*, which must simulate the sequence of moves of $T_1$ specified by the string of digits on tape 2. To describe this component in complete detail would be very tedious. Instead of trying to do this, we consider what a typical small portion of the transition diagram for $T_1$ might look like (Figure 9.18a), and give the corresponding portion of the diagram for *Execute* (Figure 9.18b). The states of *Execute* include all those of $T_1$, and others as well. We continue to assume that the maximum number of choices at any point in $T_1$'s operation is 2. We simplify things still further by assuming that $\Gamma_1 = \{a\}$, so that $a$ and $\Delta$ are the only symbols on $T_1$'s tape. Finally, since tape 1 is ignored by *Execute*, we have presented the portion of this machine in Figure 9.18b as a two-tape machine.

Suppose that Figure 9.18a shows all the transitions from state $p$. Thus, if the current tape symbol is $a$, there are two moves. The move that accepts is arbitrarily designated move 0 and the other move 1. If the current symbol is $\Delta$, $T_1$ rejects. The nonhalting move with tape symbol $a$ may also cause it to reject when it attempts to move the tape head left. Because *Execute* should not reject, we need to specify six moves from state $p$, one for each combination of the three possible symbols on tape 2 (0, 1, and $\Delta$) and the two on tape 3. (The symbol # also occurs on tape 3, but it will not occur as the current symbol in state $p$.)

The move made by *Execute* that simulates the accepting move of $T_1$ leaves the symbol * in the current position on tape 3 and causes *Execute* to accept. This is the first of the transitions shown from $p$ to $h$ in Figure 9.18b. Note that it ignores the instruction to move the head on tape 3 to the right, on

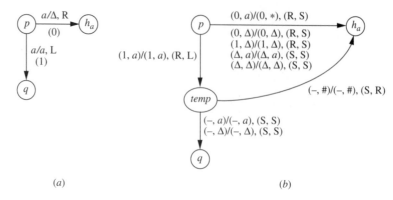

**Figure 9.18 |**
A typical small portion of *Execute*.

the assumption that once $T_1$ halts the current position on the tape is irrelevant. The next two transitions from $p$ to $h$ correspond to the moves that cause $T_1$ to reject. The last two are for the situation in which the symbol on tape 2 is $\Delta$, indicating that the current sequence of moves has been simulated completely.

The other move from state $p$ in *Execute* is the move corresponding to choice 1. This occurs when the current digit on tape 2 is 1 and the symbol on tape 3 is $a$. The reason this move does not go directly to state $q$ is that *Execute* must first test to see if the move is possible for $T_1$. It does this by moving the head on tape 3 to the left and entering a "temporary" state; from this state, any symbol on tape 3 other than # indicates that $T_1$ made the move safely, and *Execute* can then go to state $q$ as $T_1$ would have in the first place. The symbol # indicates a crash by $T_1$, and *Execute* halts normally after returning the tape head to the square to the right of #.

Although this small example does not illustrate every situation that can occur, it should help to convince you that the complete transition diagram for $T_1$ can eventually be transformed into a corresponding diagram for *Execute*. The conclusion is that it is indeed possible for $T_2$ to simulate every possible finite sequence of moves of $T_1$.

**EXAMPLE 9.10** A Simple Example of Nondeterminism

Consider the TM *Double* that works as follows. Using the *Copy* TM from Example 9.7, modified for a one-symbol input alphabet, it makes a copy of the numerical input. It then deletes the blank separating the original input from the copy and returns the tape head to square 0. Just as the name suggests, it doubles the value of the input.

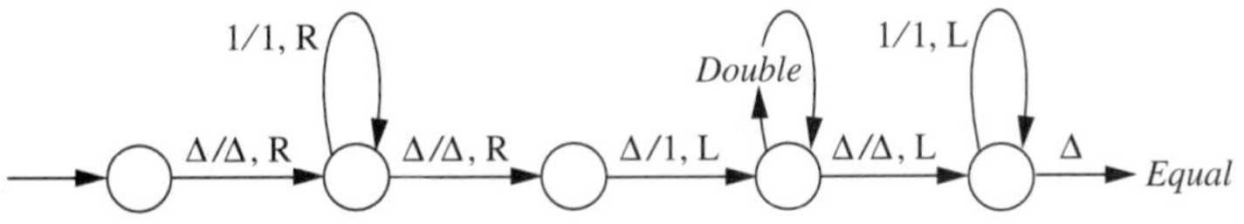

**Figure 9.19 |**
An NTM to accept strings of length $2^i$.

Now look at the nondeterministic TM $T$ in Figure 9.19. $T$ moves past the input string, places a single 1 on the tape, separated from the input by a blank, and after positioning the tape head on the blank, executes *Double* zero or more times before returning the tape head to square 0. Finally, it executes the TM *Equal*, which works as follows: Starting with tape contents $\Delta x \Delta y$, where $x$ and $y$ are strings of 1's, *Equal* accepts if and only if $x = y$ (see Example 9.9).

The nondeterminism in $T$ lies in the indeterminate number of times *Double* is executed. When *Equal* is finally executed, the string following the input on the tape represents some arbitrary power of 2. If the original input string happens to represent a power of 2, say $2^i$, then there is a sequence of choices $T$ can make that will cause the input to be accepted—namely, the sequence in which *Double* is executed exactly $i$ times. On the other hand, if the input string is not a power of 2, it will fail to be accepted, because in the last step it is compared to a string that *must* be a power of 2. Our conclusion is that $T$ accepts the language $\{1^{2^i} \mid i \geq 0\}$.

We do not need nondeterminism in order to accept this language. (Nondeterminism is never necessary, by Theorem 9.2.) It merely simplifies the description. One deterministic way to test whether an integer is a power of 2 is to test the integer first to see if it is 1 and, if not, perform a sequence of divisions by 2. If at any step before reaching 1 we get a nonzero remainder, we answer no. If we finally obtain the quotient 1 without any of the divisions producing a remainder, we answer yes. We would normally say, however, that *multiplying* by 2 is easier than *dividing* by 2. An easier approach, therefore, might be to start with 1 and perform a sequence of multiplications by 2. We could compare the result of each of these to the original input, accepting if we eventually obtained a number equal to it, and either rejecting if we eventually obtained a number larger than the input, or simply letting the iterations continue forever.

The nondeterministic solution $T$ in Figure 9.19 is closer to the second approach, except that instead of comparing the input to each of the numbers $2^i$, it guesses a value of $i$ and tests that value only. Removing the nondeterminism means replacing the guess by an iteration in which all the values are tested; a deterministic TM that did this would simply be a more efficient version of the TM constructed in the proof of Theorem 9.2, which tests all possible sequences of moves of $T$.

# 9.6 | UNIVERSAL TURING MACHINES

In our discussions so far, a Turing machine is created to execute a specific algorithm. If we have a Turing machine for computing one function, then computing a different function or doing some other calculation requires a different machine. Originally, electronic computers were limited in a similar way, and changing the calculation to be performed meant rewiring the machine.

A 1936 paper by Turing, however, anticipated the *stored-program* computers you are familiar with. Although a modern computer is still "hard-wired," it is completely flexible in that the task it performs is to execute the instructions stored in its memory, and these can represent any conceivable algorithm. Turing describes a "universal computing machine" that works as follows. It is a TM $T_u$ whose input consists essentially of a program and a data set for the program to process. The program takes the form of a string specifying some other (special-purpose) TM $T_1$, and the data set is a second string $z$ interpreted as input to $T_1$. $T_u$ then simulates the processing of $z$ by $T_1$. In this section we will describe one such universal Turing machine $T_u$.

The first step is to formulate a notational system in which we can encode both an arbitrary TM $T_1$ and an input string $z$ over an arbitrary alphabet as strings $e(T_1)$ and $e(z)$ over some fixed alphabet. The crucial aspect of the encoding is that it must not destroy any information; given the strings $e(T_1)$ and $e(z)$, we must be able to reconstruct the Turing machine $T_1$ and the string $z$. We will use the alphabet $\{0, 1\}$, although we must remember that the TM we are encoding may have a much larger alphabet. We start by assigning positive integers to each state, each tape symbol, and each of the three "directions" S, L, and R in the TM $T_1$ we want to encode.

At this point, a slight technical problem arises. We want the encoding function $e$ to be one-to-one, so that a string of 0's and 1's encodes at most one TM. Consider two TMs $T_1$ and $T_2$ that are identical except that the tape symbols of $T_1$ are $a$ and $b$ and those of $T_2$ are $a$ and $c$. If we really want to call these two TMs different, then in order to guarantee that their encodings are different, we must make sure that the integers assigned to $b$ and $c$ are different. To accommodate *any* TM and still ensure that the encoding is one-to-one, we must somehow fix it so that no symbol in any TM's alphabet receives the same number as any other symbol in any other TM's alphabet. The easiest way to handle this problem is to fix once and for all the set of symbols that can be used by TMs, and to number these symbols at the outset. This is the reason for the following

**Convention.**  We assume from this point on that there are two fixed infinite sets $\mathcal{Q} = \{q_1, q_2, \ldots\}$ and $\mathcal{S} = \{a_1, a_2, \ldots\}$ so that for any Turing machine $T = (Q, \Sigma, \Gamma, q_0, \delta)$, we have $Q \subseteq \mathcal{Q}$ and $\Gamma \subseteq \mathcal{S}$.  ∎

It should be clear that this assumption about states is not a restriction at all, because the names assigned to the states of a TM are irrelevant. Furthermore, as long as $\mathcal{S}$ contains all the letters, digits, and other symbols we might want in our input alphabets, the other assumption is equally harmless (no more restrictive, for example, than limiting the character set on a computer to 256 characters). Once we have a subscript attached to every possible state and tape symbol, we can represent a state or a symbol by a string of 0's of the appropriate length; 1's are used as separators.

---

**Definition 9.5   The Encoding Function e**

First we associate to each tape symbol (including $\Delta$), to each state (including $h_a$ and $h_r$), and to each of the three directions, a string of 0's. Let

$$s(\Delta) = 0$$
$$s(a_i) = 0^{i+1} \quad \text{(for each } a_i \in \mathcal{S})$$
$$s(h_a) = 0$$
$$s(h_r) = 00$$
$$s(q_i) = 0^{i+2} \quad \text{(for each } q_i \in \mathcal{Q})$$
$$s(S) = 0$$
$$s(L) = 00$$
$$s(R) = 000$$

Each move $m$ of a TM, described by the formula

$$\delta(p, a) = (q, b, D)$$

is encoded by the string

$$e(m) = s(p)1s(a)1s(q)1s(b)1s(D)1$$

and for any TM $T$, with initial state $q$, $T$ is encoded by the string

$$e(T) = s(q)1e(m_1)1e(m_2)1 \cdots e(m_k)1$$

where $m_1, m_2, \cdots, m_k$ are the distinct moves of $T$, arranged in some arbitrary order. Finally, any string $z = z_1 z_2 \cdots z_k$, where each $z_i \in \mathcal{S}$, is encoded by

$$e(z) = 1s(z_1)1s(z_2)1 \cdots s(z_k)1$$

---

The 1 at the beginning of the string $e(z)$ is included so that in a composite string of the form $e(T)e(z)$, there will be no doubt as to where $e(T)$ stops. Notice that one consequence is that the encoding $s(a)$ of a single symbol $a \in \mathcal{S}$ is different from the encoding $e(a)$ of the one-character string $a$.

Because the moves of a TM $T$ can appear in the string $e(T)$ in any order, there will in general be many correct encodings of $T$. However, any string of 0's and 1's can be the encoding of at most one TM.

## The Encoding of a Simple TM     **EXAMPLE 9.11**

Consider the TM illustrated in Figure 9.20, which transforms an input string of $a$'s and $b$'s by changing the leftmost $a$, if there is one, to $b$. Let us assume for simplicity that the tape symbols $a$ and $b$ are assigned the numbers 1 and 2, so that $s(a) = 00$ and $s(b) = 000$, and that the states $q_0$, $p$, and $r$ are given the numbers 1, 2, and 3, respectively. If we take the six moves in the order they appear, left-to-right, the first move $\delta(q_0, \Delta) = (p, \Delta, R)$ is encoded by the string

$$0^3 10^1 10^4 10^1 10^3 1 = 00010100001010001$$

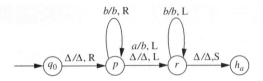

**Figure 9.20 |**

and the entire TM by the string

0001 000101000010100011 00001000100001000100011 000010010000010000010011
000010100000101010011 00000100010000010001011 000001010101011

Remember that the first part of the string, in this case 0001, is to identify the initial state of the TM. The individual moves in the remainder of the string are separated by spaces for readability.

The input to the universal TM $T_u$ will consist of a string of the form $e(T)e(z)$, where $T$ is a TM and $z$ is a string over $T$'s input alphabet. In Example 9.11, if the input string to $T$ were $baa$, the corresponding input string to $T_u$ would consist of the string $e(T)$ given in the example, followed by 10001001001. On any input string of the form $e(T)e(z)$, we want $T_u$ to accept if and only if $T$ accepts input $z$, and in this case we want the output from $T_u$ to be the encoded form of the output produced by $T$ on input $z$.

Now we are ready to construct $T_u$. It will be convenient to give it three tapes. According to our convention for multitape TMs, the first tape will be both the input and output tape. It will initially contain the input string $e(T)e(z)$. The second tape will be the working tape during the simulation of $T$, and the third tape will contain the encoded form of the state $T$ is currently in.

The first step of $T_u$ is to move the string $e(z)$ (except for the initial 1) from the end of tape 1 to tape 2, beginning in square 3. Since $T$ begins with its leftmost square blank, $T_u$ will write 01 (because $0 = s(\Delta)$) in squares 1 and 2 of tape 2; square 0 is left blank, and the tape head is positioned on square 1. The next step for $T_u$ is to copy the encoded form of $T$'s initial state from the beginning of tape 1 onto tape 3, beginning in square 1, and to delete it from tape 1.

After these initial steps, $T_u$ is ready to begin simulating the action of $T$ (encoded on tape 1) on the input string (encoded on tape 2). As the simulation starts, the three tape heads are all in square 1. The next move of $T$ at any point is determined by $T$'s state (encoded on tape 3) and the current symbol on $T$'s tape, whose encoding starts in the current position on tape 2. In order to simulate this move, $T_u$ must search tape 1 for the 5-tuple whose first two parts match this state-input combination. Abstractly this is a straightforward pattern-matching operation, and a TM that carries it out is shown in Figure 9.21. Since the search operation never changes any tape symbols, we have simplified the labeling slightly, by writing as

$$(a, b, c), (D_1, D_2, D_3)$$

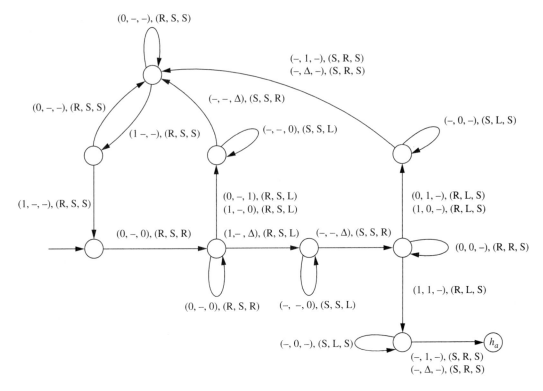

**Figure 9.21 |**
Finding the right move on tape 1.

what would normally be written as

$$(a, b, c)/(a, b, c), (D_1, D_2, D_3)$$

Once the appropriate 5-tuple is found, the last three parts tell $T_u$ how to simulate the move. To illustrate, suppose that before the search, $T_u$'s three tapes look like this:

$\Delta\underline{0}001010000101000110000100100000010001001100001\ldots$

$\Delta0100\underline{1}0010001\Delta\ldots$

$\Delta\underline{0}000\Delta\ldots$

The corresponding tape of $T$ would be

$$\Delta a\underline{a}b\Delta\ldots$$

assuming that the symbols numbered 1 and 2 are $a$ and $b$, respectively, and $T$ would be in state 2 (the one with encoding 0000). After the search of tape 1, the tapes look like this:

$\Delta0001010000101000110000100\underline{1}000001000100110001\ldots$

$\Delta0100\underline{1}0010001\Delta\ldots$

$\Delta\underline{0}000\Delta\ldots$

The 5-tuple on tape 1 specifies that $T$'s current symbol should be changed to $b$, the head should be moved left, and the state should be changed to state 3. These operations can be carried out by $T_u$ in a fairly straightforward way, and we omit the details. The final result is

$$\Delta \underline{0}0010100001010001100001001000001000100110001\ldots$$
$$\Delta 01\underline{0}0100010001\Delta\ldots$$
$$\Delta \underline{0}0000\Delta\ldots$$

and $T_u$ is now ready to simulate the next move.

There are several ways this process might stop. $T$ might halt abnormally, either because there is no move specified or because the move calls for it to move its tape head off the tape. In the first case, the search operation pictured in Figure 9.21 also halts abnormally (although the move to $h_r$ is not shown explicitly), because after the last 5-tuple on tape 1 has been tried unsuccessfully, the second of the 1's at the end takes the machine back to the initial state, and there is no move from that state with 1 on tape 1. We can easily arrange for $T_u$ to reject in the second case as well. Finally, $T$ may accept. $T_u$ detects this when it processes a 5-tuple on tape 1 whose third part is a single 0. In this case, after $T_u$ has changed tape 2 appropriately, it erases tape 1, copies tape 2 onto tape 1, and accepts.

## 9.7 | MODELS OF COMPUTATION AND THE CHURCH-TURING THESIS

A Turing machine is a model of computation more general than either a finite automaton or a pushdown automaton, and in this chapter we have seen examples of computations that are feasible on a TM but not on the simpler machines. A TM is not the only possible way of extending a PDA, and we might examine some other approaches briefly.

Our first example of a non-CFL (Example 8.1) was the language $L = \{a^n b^n c^n \mid n \geq 1\}$. The pumping lemma for CFLs tells us that a finite automaton with a single stack is not sufficient to recognize strings of this form. One stack is sufficient to accept $\{a^n b^n \mid n \geq 1\}$; it is not hard to see that *two* stacks are sufficient for $L$. Of course, if $\{a^n b^n c^n d^n \mid n \geq 1\}$ turned out to require three stacks, and $\{a^n b^n c^n d^n e^n \mid n \geq 1\}$ four, then this observation would not be useful. The interesting thing is that two are enough to handle all these languages (Exercise 9.49).

In Example 8.2, we considered $L = \{ss \mid s \in \{a, b\}^*\}$. If we ignore the apparent need for nondeterminism by changing the language to $\{scs \mid s \in \{a, b\}^*\}$, then we might consider trying to accept this language using a finite automaton with a *queue* instead of a stack. We could load the first half of the string on the queue, and the "first in, first out" operation of the queue would allow us to compare the first and second halves from left to right.

Although it is not at all obvious from these two simple examples, both approaches lead to families of abstract machines with the same computing power as Turing machines. With appropriate conventions regarding input and output, both these models can be considered as general models of computation and have been studied from this point of view. They are investigated in more detail in Exercises 9.49–9.53.

Still, a Turing machine seems like a more natural approach to a general-purpose computer, perhaps because of Turing's attempt to incorporate into TM moves the primitive steps carried out by a human computer. Even a few examples, such as the TM accepting $\{ss \mid s \in \{a, b\}^*\}$ in Example 9.3 or the one computing the reverse function in Example 9.4, are enough to suggest that TMs have the basic features required to carry out algorithms of arbitrary complexity. The point is not that recognizing strings of the form $ss$ is a particularly complex calculation, but that even algorithms of much greater logical complexity depend ultimately on the same sorts of routine manipulations that appear in these two examples. Designing algorithms to solve problems can of course be difficult; implementing an algorithm on a TM is primarily a matter of organizing the data storage areas, and choosing bookkeeping mechanisms for keeping track of the progress of the algorithm. A simple model of computation such as an FA puts severe restrictions on the *type* of algorithm that can be executed. A TM allows one to design an algorithm without reference to the machine and to have confidence that the result can be implemented.

To say that the Turing machine is a general model of computation is simply to say that any algorithmic procedure that can be carried out at all (by a human, a team of humans, or a computer) can be carried out by a TM. This statement was first formulated by Alonzo Church, a logician, in the 1930s (*American Journal of Mathematics* 58:345–363, 1936), and it is usually referred to as *Church's thesis*, or the *Church-Turing thesis*. It is not a mathematically precise statement because we do not have a precise definition of the term *algorithmic procedure*, and therefore it is not something we can prove. Since the invention of the TM, however, enough evidence has accumulated to cause the Church-Turing thesis to be generally accepted. Here is an informal summary of some of the evidence.

1. The nature of the model makes it seem likely that all the steps that are crucial to human computation can be carried out by a TM. Of course, there are differences in the details of how they are carried out. A human normally works with a two-dimensional sheet of paper, not a one-dimensional tape, and a human is perhaps not restricted to transferring his or her attention to the location immediately adjacent to the current one. However, although working within the constraints imposed by a TM might make certain steps in a computation awkward, it does not appear to limit the types of computation that are possible. For example, if the two-dimensional aspect of the paper really plays a significant role in a computation, the TM tape can be organized so as to simulate two dimensions. This may mean that two locations contiguous on a sheet of paper are not contiguous on the tape; the only consequence is that the TM may require more moves to do what a human could do in one.

2. Various enhancements of the TM model have been suggested in order to make the operation more like that of a human computer, or more convenient, or more efficient. These include the enhancements mentioned in this chapter, such as doubly infinite tapes, multiple tapes, and nondeterminism. In each case, it is possible to show that the computing power of the machine is unchanged.

3. Other theoretical models of computation have been proposed. These include machines such as those mentioned earlier in this section, machines that are

closer to modern computers in their operation, and various notational systems (simple programming-type languages, grammars, and others) that can be used to describe computations. Again, in every case, the model has been shown to be equivalent to the Turing machine.

4.  Since the introduction of the TM, no one has suggested any type of computation that ought to be included in the category of "algorithmic procedure" and *cannot* be implemented on a TM.

As we observed earlier, the Church-Turing thesis is not a statement for which a precise proof is possible, because of the imprecision in the term "algorithmic procedure." Once we adopt the thesis, however, we are effectively giving a precise meaning to the term: An algorithm is a procedure that can be executed on a TM. The advantage of having such a definition is that it provides a starting point for a discussion of problems that can be solved algorithmically and problems (if any) that cannot. This discussion begins in Chapter 10 and continues in Chapter 11.

Another way in which the Church-Turing thesis will be used in the rest of the book is that when we want to describe a solution to a problem, we will often be satisfied with a verbal description of the algorithm; translating it into a detailed TM implementation may be tedious but is generally straightforward.

## EXERCISES

**9.1.**  Trace the TM in Figure 9.5 (the one accepting the language $\{ss \mid s \in \{a, b\}^*\}$) on the string *aaba*. Show the configuration at each step.

**9.2.**  Below is a transition table for a TM.

| $q$ | $\sigma$ | $\delta(q, \sigma)$ | $q$ | $\sigma$ | $\delta(q, \sigma)$ | $q$ | $\sigma$ | $\delta(q, \sigma)$ |
|---|---|---|---|---|---|---|---|---|
| $q_0$ | $\Delta$ | $(q_1, \Delta, R)$ | $q_2$ | $\Delta$ | $(h_a, \Delta, R)$ | $q_6$ | $a$ | $(q_6, a, R)$ |
| $q_1$ | $a$ | $(q_1, a, R)$ | $q_3$ | $\Delta$ | $(q_4, a, R)$ | $q_6$ | $b$ | $(q_6, b, R)$ |
| $q_1$ | $b$ | $(q_1, b, R)$ | $q_4$ | $a$ | $(q_4, a, R)$ | $q_6$ | $\Delta$ | $(q_7, b, L)$ |
| $q_1$ | $\Delta$ | $(q_2, \Delta, L)$ | $q_4$ | $b$ | $(q_4, b, R)$ | $q_7$ | $a$ | $(q_7, a, L)$ |
| $q_2$ | $a$ | $(q_3, \Delta, R)$ | $q_4$ | $\Delta$ | $(q_7, a, L)$ | $q_7$ | $b$ | $(q_7, b, L)$ |
| $q_2$ | $b$ | $(q_5, \Delta, R)$ | $q_5$ | $\Delta$ | $(q_6, b, R)$ | $q_7$ | $\Delta$ | $(q_2, \Delta, L)$ |

a.  What is the final configuration if the input is *ab*?

b.  What is the final configuration if the input is *baa*?

c.  Describe what the TM does for an arbitrary input string in $\{a, b\}^*$.

**9.3.**  Let $T = (Q, \Sigma, \Gamma, q_0, \delta)$ be a TM, and let $s$ and $t$ be the sizes of the sets $Q$ and $\Gamma$, respectively. How many distinct configurations of $T$ could there possibly be in which all tape squares past square $n$ are blank and $T$'s tape head is on or to the left of square $n$? (The tape squares are numbered beginning with 0.)

**9.4.**  The TM shown in Figure 9.2*b* (obtained from the FA in Figure 9.2*a*) accepts a string as soon as it finds the substring *aba*. Draw another TM accepting the same language that is more similar to the FA in that it accepts a string only after it has read all the symbols of the string.

**9.5.** Figures 9.2 and 9.3 show two examples of converting an FA to a TM accepting the same language. Describe precisely how this can be done for an arbitrary FA.

**9.6.** Draw a transition diagram for a Turing machine accepting each of the following languages.

   a. $\{a^i b^j \mid i < j\}$
   b. $\{a^n b^n c^n \mid n \geq 0\}$
   c. $\{x \in \{a, b, c\}^* \mid n_a(x) = n_b(x) = n_c(x)\}$
   d. The language of balanced strings of parentheses
   e. The language of all nonpalindromes over $\{a, b\}$
   f. $\{www \mid w \in \{a, b\}^*\}$

**9.7.** Describe the language (a subset of $\{1\}^*$) accepted by the TM in Figure 9.22.

**9.8.** We do not define $\Lambda$-transitions for a TM. Why not? What features of a TM make it unnecessary or inappropriate to talk about $\Lambda$-transitions?

**9.9.** Suppose $T_1$ and $T_2$ are TMs accepting languages $L_1$ and $L_2$ (both subsets of $\Sigma^*$), respectively. If we were following as closely as possible the method used in the case of finite automata to accept the language $L_1 L_2$, we might form the composite TM $T_1 T_2$. (See the construction of $M_c$ in the proof of Theorem 4.4.) Explain why this approach, or any obvious modification of it, will not work.

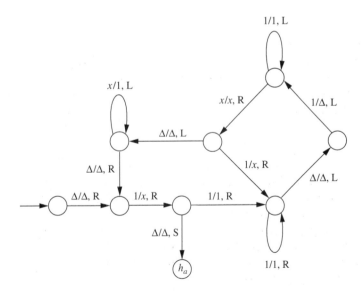

**Figure 9.22**

**9.10.** Given TMs $T_1 = (Q_1, \Sigma_1, \Gamma_1, q_1, \delta_1)$ and $T_2 = (Q_2, \Sigma_2, \Gamma_2, q_2, \delta_2)$, with $\Gamma_1 \subseteq \Sigma_2$, give a precise definition of the TM $T_1 T_2 = (Q, \Sigma, \Gamma, q_0, \delta)$. Say precisely what $Q$, $\Sigma$, $\Gamma$, $q_0$, and $\delta$ are.

**9.11.** Suppose $T$ is a TM accepting a language $L$. Describe how you would modify $T$ to obtain another TM accepting $L$ that never halts in the reject state $h_r$.

**9.12.** Suppose $T$ is a TM that accepts every input. We would like to construct a TM $R_T$ so that for every input string $x$, $R_T$ halts in the accepting state with exactly the same tape contents as when $T$ halts on input $x$, but with the tape head positioned at the rightmost nonblank symbol on the tape. (One reason this is useful is that we might want to use $T$ in a larger composite machine, but to erase the tape after $T$ has halted.)

   a. Show that there is no fixed TM $T_0$ so that $R_T = T T_0$ for every $T$. (In other words, there is no TM capable of executing the instruction "move the tape head to the rightmost nonblank tape symbol" in every possible situation.)

   b. Describe a general method for constructing $R_T$, given $T$.

**9.13.** Draw the *Insert*$(\sigma)$ TM, which changes the tape contents from $yz$ to $y\underline{\sigma}z$. Here $y \in (\Sigma \cup \{\Delta\})^*$, $\sigma \in \Sigma \cup \{\Delta\}$, and $z \in \Sigma^*$. You may assume that $\Sigma = \{a, b\}$.

**9.14.** Does every TM compute a partial function? Explain.

**9.15.** In each case, draw a TM that computes the indicated function. In the first five parts, the function is from $\mathcal{N}$ to $\mathcal{N}$. In each of these parts, assume that the TM uses unary notation—that is, the natural number $n$ is represented by the string $1^n$.

   a. $f(x) = x + 2$

   b. $f(x) = 2x$

   c. $f(x) = x^2$

   d. $f(x) = x/2$ ("/" means integer division.)

   e. $f(x) =$ the smallest integer greater than or equal to $\log_2(x + 1)$ (i.e., $f(0) = 0$, $f(1) = 1$, $f(2) = f(3) = 2$, $f(4) = \cdots = f(7) = 3$, and so on.)

   f. $f : \{a, b\}^* \times \{a, b\}^* \to \{0, 1\}$ defined by $f(x, y) = 1$ if $x = y$, $f(x, y) = 0$ otherwise.

   g. $f : \{a, b\}^* \times \{a, b\}^* \to \{0, 1\}$ defined by $f(x, y) = 1$ if $x < y$, $f(x, y) = 0$ otherwise. Here $<$ means with respect to "lexicographic," or alphabetical, order. For example, $a < aa$, $abab < abb$, etc.

   h. $f$ is the same as in the previous part, except that this time $<$ refers to canonical order. That is, a shorter string precedes a longer one, and the order of two strings of the same length is alphabetical.

   i. $f : \{a, b\}^* \to \{a, b\}^*$ defined by $f(x) = a^{n_a(x)} b^{n_b(x)}$ (i.e., $f(x)$ has the same symbols as $x$ but with all the $a$'s at the beginning).

**9.16.** The TM shown in Figure 9.23 computes a function from $\{a, b\}^*$ to $\{a, b\}^*$. For any string $x \in \{a, b\}^*$, describe the string $f(x)$.

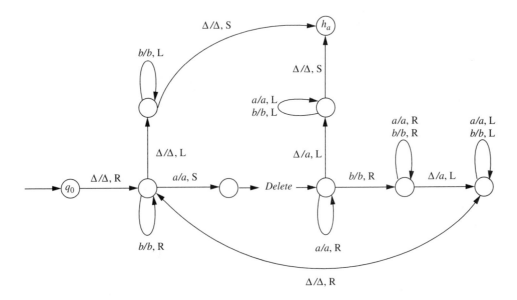

**Figure 9.23 |**

**9.17.** Suppose TMs $T_1$ and $T_2$ compute the functions $f_1$ and $f_2$ from $\mathcal{N}$ to $\mathcal{N}$, respectively. Describe how to construct a TM to compute each of these functions.

a. $f_1 + f_2$

b. the minimum of $f_1$ and $f_2$

c. $f_1 \circ f_2$

**9.18.** Draw a TM that takes as input a string of 0's and 1's, interprets it as the binary representation of a nonnegative integer, and leaves as output the unary representation of that integer (i.e., a string of that many 1's).

**9.19.** Draw a TM that does the reverse of the previous problem: accepts a string of $n$ 1's as input and leaves as output the binary representation of $n$.

**9.20.** In Figure 9.24 is a TM accepting the language $\{scs \mid s \in \{a, b\}^*\}$. Modify it so as to obtain a TM that computes the characteristic function of the same language.

**9.21.** In Example 9.3, a TM is given that accepts the language $\{ss \mid s \in \{a, b\}^*\}$. Draw a TM with tape alphabet $\{a, b\}$ that accepts this language.

**9.22.** In Section 9.5 we mentioned a variation of TMs in which the transition function $\delta$ takes values in $(Q \cup \{h_a, h_r\}) \times (\Gamma \cup \{\Delta\}) \times \{L,R\}$, so that the tape head must move either to the left or to the right on each move. It is not difficult to show that any ordinary TM can be simulated by one of these. Explain how the move $\delta(p, a) = (q, b, S)$ could be simulated by such a restricted TM.

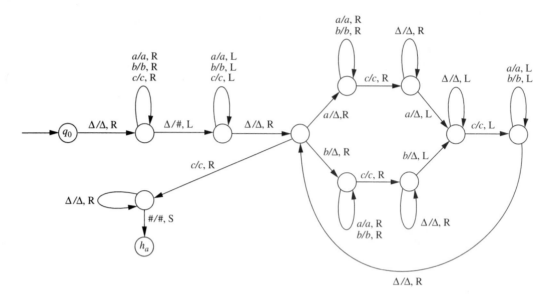

**Figure 9.24 |**

**9.23.** An ordinary TM can also be simulated by one in which $\delta$ takes values in $(Q \cup \{h_a, h_r\}) \times (\Gamma \cup \{\Delta\} \cup \{L,R\})$, so that writing a symbol and moving the tape head are not both allowed on the same move. Explain how the move $\delta(p, a) = (q, b, R)$ of an ordinary TM could be simulated by one of these restricted TMs.

    Exercises 9.24–9.25 involve a Turing machine with a doubly infinite tape. The tape squares on such a machine can be thought of as numbered left to right, as in an ordinary TM, but now the numbers include all negative integers as well as nonnegative. A configuration can still be described by a pair $(q, x\underline{a}y)$. There is no assumption about which square the string $x$ begins in; in other words, two configurations that are identical except for the square in which $x$ begins are considered the same. For this reason, we may adopt the same convention about the string $x$ as about $y$: when we specify a configuration as $(q, x\underline{a}y)$, we may assume that $x$ does not begin with a blank.

**9.24.** Construct a TM with a doubly-infinite tape that does the following: If it begins with the tape blank except for a single $a$ somewhere on it, it halts in the accepting state with the head scanning the square with the $a$.

**9.25.** Let $T = (Q, \Sigma, \Gamma, q_0, \delta)$ be a TM. Show that there is a TM $T_1 = (Q_1, \Sigma, \Gamma_1, q_1, \delta_1)$ with a doubly-infinite tape, with $\Gamma \subseteq \Gamma_1$, satisfying these two conditions:

    a. For any $x \in \Sigma^*$, $T_1$ accepts input $x$ if and only if $T$ does.

    b. For any $x \in \Sigma^*$, if $(q_0, \underline{\Delta}x) \vdash_T^* (h_a, y\underline{a}z)$, then $(q_1, \underline{\Delta}x) \vdash_{T_1}^* (h_a, y\underline{a}z)$.

**9.26.** In defining a multitape TM, another option is to specify a single tape head that scans the same position on all tapes simultaneously. Show that a machine of this type is equivalent to the multitape TM defined in Section 9.5.

**9.27.** Draw the portion of the transition diagram for the one-tape TM $M_2$ embodying the six steps shown in the proof of Theorem 9.1 corresponding to the move $\delta_1(p, a_1, a_2) = (q, b_1, b_2, R, L)$ of $M_1$.

**9.28.** Draw a transition diagram for a three-tape TM that works as follows: starting in the configuration $(q_0, \underline{\Delta}x, \underline{\Delta}y, \underline{\Delta})$, where $x$ and $y$ are strings of 0's and 1's of the same length, it halts in the configuration $(h_a, \underline{\Delta}x, \underline{\Delta}y, \underline{\Delta}z)$, where $z$ is the string obtained by interpreting $x$ and $y$ as binary representations and adding them.

**9.29.** What is the effect of the nondeterministic TM with input alphabet $\{0, 1\}$ whose transition table is shown below, assuming it starts with a blank tape? (Assuming that it halts, where is the tape head when it halts, and what strings might be on the tape?)

| $q$ | $\sigma$ | $\delta(q, \sigma)$ |
|---|---|---|
| $q_0$ | $\Delta$ | $\{(q_1, \Delta, R)\}$ |
| $q_1$ | $\Delta$ | $\{(q_1, 0, R), (q_1, 1, R), (q_2, \Delta, L)\}$ |
| $q_2$ | $0$ | $\{(q_2, 0, L)\}$ |
| $q_2$ | $1$ | $\{(q_2, 1, L)\}$ |
| $q_2$ | $\Delta$ | $\{(h_a, \Delta, S)\}$ |

**9.30.** Call the NTM in the previous exercise $G$. Let *Copy* be the TM in Example 9.4, which transforms $\underline{\Delta}x$ to $\underline{\Delta}x\Delta x$ for an arbitrary string $x \in \{0, 1\}^*$. Finally, let *Equal* be a TM that works as follows: starting with the tape $\underline{\Delta}x\Delta y$, it accepts if and only if $x = y$. Consider the NTM shown in Figure 9.25. (It is nondeterministic because $G$ is.) What language does it accept?

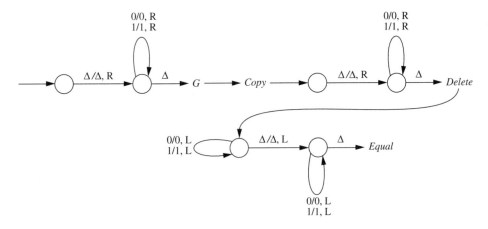

**Figure 9.25** |

**9.31.** Using the idea in the previous exercise, draw a transition diagram for an NTM that accepts the language $\{1^n \mid n = k^2 \text{ for some } k \geq 0\}$.

**9.32.** Using the same general technique, draw a transition diagram for an NTM that accepts the language $\{1^n \mid n \text{ is a composite integer } \geq 4\}$.

**9.33.** Suppose $L$ is accepted by a TM $T$. Describe how you could construct a nondeterministic TM to accept each of the following languages.

    a. The set of all prefixes of elements of $L$

    b. The set of all suffixes of elements of $L$

    c. The set of all substrings of elements of $L$

**9.34.** Figure 9.18$b$ shows the portion of the *Execute* TM corresponding to the portion of $M_1$ shown in Figure 9.18$a$. Consider the portion of $M_1$ shown in Figure 9.26. Assume as before that the maximum number of choices at any point in $M_1$ is 2, and that the moves shown are the only ones from state $r$. Draw the corresponding portion of *Execute*.

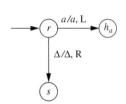

**Figure 9.26** |

**9.35.** Assuming the same encoding method discussed in Section 9.7, and assuming that $s(0) = 00$ and $s(1) = 000$, draw the TM that is encoded by the string

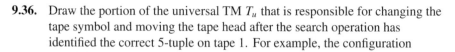

0001 000101000010100011 00001001000010100011 000010001000010000100011
00001010000010100011 00000100100000010100011 00000100010000000100010
00000010100000000100100011 000000010100000000100010011
00000000100100000000010010011 000000001000100000000100010011
000000001010101011

**9.36.** Draw the portion of the universal TM $T_u$ that is responsible for changing the tape symbol and moving the tape head after the search operation has identified the correct 5-tuple on tape 1. For example, the configuration

$\Delta 000101000010100011000010010000010000100110001\ldots$
$\Delta 010010010001\Delta\ldots$
$\Delta 0000\Delta\ldots$

would be transformed to

$\Delta 000101000010100011000010010000010000100110001\ldots$
$\Delta 0100100010001\Delta\ldots$
$\Delta 00000\Delta\ldots$

**9.37.** Table 7.2 describes a PDA accepting the language *pal*. Draw a TM that accepts this language by simulating the PDA. You can make the TM nondeterministic, and you can use a second tape to represent the stack.

**9.38.** Suppose we define the *canonical order* of strings in $\{0, 1\}^*$ to be the order in which a string precedes any longer string and the order of two equal-length strings is numerical. For example, the strings 1, 01, 10, 000, 011, 100 are listed here in canonical order. Describe informally how to construct a TM $T$ that enumerates the set of palindromes over $\{0, 1\}$ in canonical order. In other words, $T$ loops forever, and for every positive integer $n$, there is some point at which the initial portion of $T$'s tape contains the string

$$\Delta\Delta0\Delta1\Delta00\Delta11\Delta000\Delta\cdots\Delta x_n$$

where $x_n$ is the $n$th palindrome in canonical order, and this portion of the tape is never subsequently changed.

## MORE CHALLENGING PROBLEMS

**9.39.** Suppose you are watching a TM processing an input string, and that at each step you can see the configuration of the TM.

   a. Suppose that for some $n$, the tape head does not move past square $n$ while you are watching. If the pattern continues, will you be able to conclude at some point that the TM is in an infinite loop? If so, what is the longest you might need to watch in order to draw this conclusion?

   b. Suppose that in each move you observe, the tape head moves right. If the pattern continues, will you be able to conclude at some point that the TM is in an infinite loop? If so, what is the longest you might need to watch in order to draw this conclusion?

**9.40.** In each of the following cases, show that the language accepted by the TM $T$ is regular.

   a. There is an integer $n$ so that no matter what the input string is, $T$ never moves its tape head to the right of square $n$.

   b. For any $n \geq 0$ and any input of length $n$, $T$ begins by making $n + 1$ moves in which the tape head is moved right each time, and thereafter $T$ does not move the tape head to the left of square $n + 1$.

**9.41.** Suppose $T$ is a TM. For each integer $i \geq 0$, denote by $n_i(T)$ the number of the rightmost square to which $T$ has moved its tape head within the first $i$ moves. (For example, if $T$ moves its tape head right in the first five moves and left in the next three, then $n_i(T) = i$ for $i \leq 5$ and $n_i(T) = 5$ for $6 \leq i \leq 10$.) Suppose there is an integer $k$ so that no matter what the input string is, $n_i(T) \geq i - k$ for every $i \geq 0$. Does it follow that $L(T)$ is regular? Give reasons for your answer.

**9.42.** Let $T = (Q, \Sigma, \Gamma, q_0, \delta)$ be a TM with a doubly-infinite tape (see the comments preceding Exercise 9.24). Show that there is an ordinary TM $T_1 = (Q_1, \Sigma, \Gamma_1, q_1, \delta_1)$, with $\Gamma \subseteq \Gamma_1$, satisfying these two conditions:

   a. $L(T_1) = L(T)$.

   b. For any $x \in \Sigma^*$, if $(q_0, \underline{\Delta}x) \vdash_T^* (h_a, y\underline{a}z)$, then $(q_1, \underline{\Delta}x) \vdash_{T_1}^* (h_a, y\underline{a}z)$.

The proof requires constructing an ordinary TM that can simulate the action of a TM having a doubly-infinite tape. There are several ways you might do this. One is to allow an ordinary tape to "look like" a *folded* doubly-infinite tape, using a technique similar to that in the proof of Theorem 9.1. Another would use even-numbered squares to represent squares indexed by nonnegative numbers (i.e., the right half of the tape) and odd-numbered squares to represent the remaining squares.

**9.43.** In Figure 9.27 is a transition diagram for a TM $M$ with a doubly-infinite tape. First, trace the moves it makes on the input string $abb$. Then, for the ordinary TM $M_1$ that you constructed in the previous exercise to simulate $M$, trace the moves that $M_1$ makes in simulating $M$ on the same input.

**9.44.** Suppose $M_1$ is a two-tape TM, and $M_2$ is the ordinary TM constructed in Theorem 9.1 to simulate $M_1$. If $M_1$ requires $n$ moves to process an input string $x$, give an upper bound on the number of moves $M_2$ requires in order to simulate the processing of $x$. Note that the number of moves $M_1$ has made places a limit on the position of its tape head. Try to make your upper bound as sharp as possible.

**9.45.** Show that if there is a TM $T$ computing the function $f : \mathcal{N} \to \mathcal{N}$, then there is another one, $T'$, whose tape alphabet is $\{1\}$. Suggestion: suppose $T$ has tape alphabet $\Gamma = \{a_1, a_2, \ldots, a_n\}$. Encode $\Delta$ and each of the $a_i$'s by a string of 1's and $\Delta$'s of length $n + 1$ (for example, encode $\Delta$ by $n + 1$ blanks, and $a_i$ by $1^i \Delta^{n+1-i}$). Have $T'$ simulate $T$, but using blocks of $n + 1$ tape squares instead of single squares.

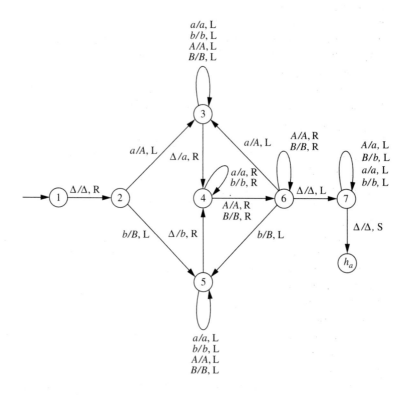

**Figure 9.27 |**

**9.46.** Describe how you could construct a TM $T_0$ that would accept input strings of 0's and 1's and would determine whether the input was a string of the form $e(T)$ for some TM $T$. ("Determine" means compute the characteristic function of the set of such encodings.)

**9.47.** Modify the construction in the proof of Theorem 9.2 so that if the NTM halts on every possible sequence of moves, the TM constructed to simulate it halts on every input.

**9.48.** Beginning with a nondeterministic Turing machine $T_1$, the proof of Theorem 9.2 shows how to construct an ordinary TM $T_2$ that accepts the same language. Suppose $|x| = n$, $T_1$ never has more than two choices of moves, and there is a sequence of $n_x$ moves by which $T_1$ accepts $x$. Estimate as precisely as possible the number of moves that might be required for $T_2$ to accept $x$.

**9.49.** Formulate a precise definition of a *two-stack automaton*, which is like a PDA, except that it is deterministic and a move takes into account the symbols on top of both stacks and can replace either or both of them. Describe informally how you might construct a machine of this type accepting $\{a^i b^i c^i \mid i \geq 0\}$. Do it in a way that could be generalized to $\{a^i b^i c^i d^i \mid i \geq 0\}$, $\{a^i b^i c^i d^i e^i \mid i \geq 0\}$, etc.

**9.50.** Describe how a Turing machine can simulate a two-stack automaton; specifically, show that any language that can be accepted by a two-stack machine can be accepted by a TM.

**9.51.** A *Post machine* is similar to a PDA, but with the following differences. It is deterministic; it has an auxiliary queue instead of a stack, and the input is assumed to have been previously loaded onto the queue. For example, if the input string is $abb$, then the symbol currently at the front of the queue is $a$. Items can be added only to the rear of the queue, and deleted only from the front. Assume that there is a marker $Z_0$ initially on the queue following the input string (so that in the case of null input $Z_0$ is at the front). The machine can be defined as a 7-tuple $M = (Q, \Sigma, \Gamma, q_0, Z_0, A, \delta)$, like a PDA. A single move depends on the state and the symbol currently at the front of the queue; and the move has three components: the resulting state, an indication of whether or not to remove the current symbol from the front of the queue, and what to add to the rear of the queue (a string, possibly null, of symbols from the queue alphabet).

Construct a Post machine to accept the language $\{a^n b^n c^n \mid n \geq 0\}$.

**9.52.** We can specify a configuration of a Post machine (see the previous exercise) by specifying the state and the contents of the queue. If the original marker $Z_0$ is currently in the queue, so that the string in the queue is of the form $\alpha Z_0 \beta$, then the queue can be thought of as representing the tape of a Turing machine, as follows. The marker $Z_0$ is thought of, not as an actual tape symbol, but as marking the right end of the string on the tape; the string $\beta$ is at the beginning of the tape, followed by the string $\alpha$; and the tape head is currently centered on the first symbol of $\alpha$—or, if $\alpha = \Lambda$, on the first blank square following the string $\beta$. In this way, the initial queue, which contains the string $\alpha Z_0$, represents the initial tape of the Turing machine with input string $\alpha$, except that the blank in square 0 is missing and the tape head scans the first symbol of the input.

Using this representation, it is not difficult to see how most of the moves of a Turing machine can be simulated by the Post machine. Here is an illustration. Suppose that the queue contains the string $abbZ_0ab$, which we take to represent the tape $ab\underline{a}bb$. To simulate the Turing machine move that replaces the $a$ by $c$ and moves to the right, we can do the following:

a.  remove $a$ from the front and add $c$ to the rear, producing $bbZ_0abc$

b.  add a marker, say \$, to the rear, producing $bbZ_0abc\$$

c.  begin a loop that simply removes items from the front and adds them to the rear, continuing until the marker \$ appears at the front. At this point, the queue contains $\$bbZ_0abc$.

d.  remove the marker, so that the final queue represents the tape $abc\underline{b}b$

The Turing machine move that is hardest to simulate is a move to the left. Devise a way to do it. Then give an informal proof, based on the simulation outlined in this discussion, that any language that can be accepted by a Turing machine can be accepted by a Post machine.

**9.53.** Show how a two-stack automaton can simulate a Post machine, using the first stack to represent the queue and using the second stack to help carry out the various Post machine operations. The first step in the simulation is to load the input string onto stack 1, using stack 2 first in order to get the symbols in the right order. Give an informal argument that any language that can be accepted by a Post machine can be accepted by a two-stack automaton. (The conclusion from this exercise and Exercises 50 and 52 is that the three types of machines—Turing machines, Post machines, and two-stack automata—are equivalent with regard to the languages they can accept.)

# Recursively Enumerable Languages

## 10.1 | RECURSIVELY ENUMERABLE AND RECURSIVE

In this chapter we study in more detail the languages that can be accepted by TMs, and consider other ways to characterize them. We begin by recalling the distinction mentioned in Section 9.2 between accepting a language $L$ and computing the characteristic function of $L$.

---

**Definition 10.1   Accepting a Language and Recognizing a Language**

Let $L \subseteq \Sigma^*$ be a language. A Turing machine $T$ with input alphabet $\Sigma$ is said to *accept* $L$ if $L(T) = L$. $T$ *recognizes*, or *decides*, $L$ if $T$ computes the characteristic function $\chi_L : \Sigma^* \to \{0, 1\}$. In other words, $T$ recognizes $L$ if $T$ halts in state $h_a$ for every string $x$ in $\Sigma^*$, producing output 1 if $x \in L$ and output 0 otherwise.

A language $L$ is *recursively enumerable* if there is a TM that accepts $L$, and *recursive* if there is a TM that recognizes $L$. (Sometimes these languages are called *Turing-acceptable* and *Turing-decidable*, respectively.)

---

**Theorem 10.1**

Every recursive language is recursively enumerable.

*Proof*

As we observed in Example 9.6, if $T$ is a Turing machine recognizing $L$, then we can get a TM accepting $L$ by modifying $T$ so that when it leaves output 0, it enters the reject state.

We have already identified the potential problem with the converse of Theorem 10.1. If $T$ is a Turing machine accepting $L$, there may be strings not in $L$ for which $T$ loops forever and therefore never produces an answer. Later we will see that this possibility cannot always be eliminated: There are recursively enumerable languages that are not recursive. For now, we record the partial result that is naturally suggested. It will be useful to generalize it slightly, to nondeterministic machines.

---

**Theorem 10.2**

If $L$ is accepted by a nondeterministic TM $T$, and every possible sequence of moves of $T$ causes it to halt, then $L$ is recursive.

*Proof*

We construct a three-tape TM $T'$ that is a modification of the TM $T_2$ in the proof of Theorem 9.2. In that case, $T_2$ simulated every possible finite sequence of moves of $T$, accepting if it found one that caused $T$ to accept and otherwise looping forever. The machine we want now is different in two respects. First, if $T'$ finds a sequence of moves of $T$ that accepts, it creates the output $\underline{\Delta}1$ on tape 1 before it halts. Second, if no sequence of moves would cause $T$ to accept, then eventually $T'$ determines this and halts normally with $\underline{\Delta}0$ on tape 1.

Recall that in the proof of Theorem 9.2, $T_2$ kept track of the sequence of moves it should try next by using a string of digits on tape 2, the $i$th digit specifying the choice $T_2$ should make at the $i$th step. If there is some integer $n$ so that $T$ rejects on or before its $n$th move, no matter what choices it makes, then the input string $x$ is not accepted. Furthermore, if $x$ is not accepted, there *must* be such an $n$. (In other words, if the input is not accepted and $T$ cannot loop forever, then there cannot be arbitrarily long sequences of moves before it halts. If this does not seem obvious, see Exercise 10.7.) This observation allows us to construct $T'$ as follows. Each time $T'$ simulates a sequence of moves of $T$ that ends in the reject state, it copies in the blank portion of tape 1 the sequence of digits currently on tape 2. In this way, tape 1 keeps a history of all sequences that are unsuccessful. (In the proof of Theorem 9.2, we assumed for the sake of simplicity that the digits were either 0 or 1; in general, they belong to the set $\{0, 1, \ldots, k - 1\}$, where $k$ is the maximum number of choices $T$ ever has from any configuration.) For each $n$, each time $T'$ finds that the last string of length $n$ (the one whose digits are all $k - 1$) represents an unsuccessful sequence, it searches the strings on tape 1 to see whether *all* possible sequences of that length appear, and therefore also represent unsuccessful sequences. If they do, it erases tape 1 and halts normally with output $\underline{\Delta}0$; otherwise it continues with the first string of digits of length $n + 1$.

---

Both the union and intersection operations preserve the property of recursive enumerability. The construction we use to prove this involves a TM capable of simulating two other TMs simultaneously.

**Theorem 10.3**

If $L_1$ and $L_2$ are recursively enumerable languages over $\Sigma$, then $L_1 \cup L_2$ and $L_1 \cap L_2$ are also recursively enumerable.

*Proof*

Suppose $T_1 = (Q_1, \Sigma, \Gamma_1, q_1, \delta_1)$ and $T_2 = (Q_2, \Sigma, \Gamma_2, q_2, \delta_2)$ are TMs accepting $L_1$ and $L_2$, respectively. We wish to construct TMs accepting $L_1 \cup L_2$ and $L_1 \cap L_2$. In both cases, it is useful to use a two-tape machine. We can model the construction after that of the FA in the proof of Theorem 3.4 and let the two tapes represent the tapes of $T_1$ and $T_2$, respectively.

We describe the solution for $L_1 \cup L_2$. The two-tape machine $T = (Q, \Sigma, \Gamma, q_0, \delta)$ begins by placing a copy of the input string, which is already on tape 1, onto tape 2. It inserts the marker # at the beginning of both tapes, in order to detect a crash resulting from $T_1$ or $T_2$ trying to move its tape head off the tape. From this point on, the simultaneous simulation of $T_1$ on tape 1 and $T_2$ on tape 2 is accomplished by allowing every possible move

$$\delta((p_1, p_2), (a_1, a_2)) = ((q_1, q_2), (b_1, b_2), (D_1, D_2))$$

where, for both values of $i$, $\delta_i(p_i, a_i) = (q_i, b_i, D_i)$. The possible outcomes of the simulation are

1. Neither $T_1$ nor $T_2$ ever stops, in which case $T$ never stops.
2. At least one of the two accepts, in which case $T$ accepts.
3. One of the two rejects before either has accepted. If they both reject simultaneously, $T$ rejects. If one rejects, $T$ abandons that simulation (i.e., ignores that tape) and continues with the other. If the other halts, either by accepting or by rejecting, then $T$ halts in the same way.

The construction causes $T$ to accept if and only if at least one of the two machines $T_1$ and $T_2$ accepts, and we conclude that $T$ accepts the language $L_1 \cup L_2$.

We can handle $L_1 \cap L_2$ the same way, except that this time $T$ can reject if either $T_1$ or $T_2$ rejects, and it can accept only when $T_1$ and $T_2$ have both accepted.

The set of recursive languages is also closed under unions and intersections; we leave the details to the exercises. For recursive languages, we can add the complement operation to the list as well.

**Theorem 10.4**

If $L$ is recursive, so is $L'$.

*Proof*

If $T$ is a Turing machine recognizing $L$, we can make it recognize $L'$ by interchanging the two outputs.

This simple proof cannot be adapted in any obvious way for recursively enumerable languages. It does not immediately follow that the corresponding statement for recursively enumerable languages is false (which it turns out to be); the next result suggests, however, that it is less likely to be true.

---

**Theorem 10.5**

If $L$ is a recursively enumerable language whose complement is recursively enumerable, then $L$ is recursive.

**Proof**

Let $T_1$ and $T_2$ be Turing machines accepting $L$ and $L'$, respectively. We construct a two-tape TM $T$ to recognize $L$, starting with the construction in the proof of Theorem 10.3 for the union of the two languages. The difference is that now we know in advance that on any input $x$, precisely one of the machines $T_1$ and $T_2$ will accept. Therefore, it is sufficient to modify $T$ as follows: when either $T_1$ or $T_2$ accepts, $T$ erases tape 1 (see Exercise 9.12) and leaves the appropriate output before halting—1 or 0, depending on whether the machine that accepts is the one accepting $L$ or the one accepting $L'$.

---

# 10.2 | ENUMERATING A LANGUAGE

To *enumerate* a set means to list the elements one at a time, and to say that a set is *enumerable* should perhaps mean that there is an algorithm for enumerating it. In fact this idea does lead to an equivalent characterization of recursively enumerable languages, and with an appropriate modification it can also be used to describe recursive languages.

We begin by saying precisely how a Turing machine enumerates a language $L$ (or, informally, "lists the elements of $L$"). It is convenient to allow a multitape machine with one tape that functions solely as the output tape.

---

**Definition 10.2     A TM Enumerating a Language**

Let $T$ be a $k$-tape TM ($k \geq 1$) and $L \subseteq \Sigma^*$. We say $T$ enumerates $L$ if it operates so that the following conditions are satisfied.

1. The tape head on the first tape never moves to the left, and no nonblank symbol printed on tape 1 is subsequently modified or erased.
2. For every $x \in L$, there is some point in the operation of $T$ when tape 1 has contents

$$x_1 \# x_2 \# \cdots \# x_n \# x \#$$

for some $n \geq 0$, where the strings $x_1, x_2, \ldots, x_n, x$ are distinct elements of $L$. If $L$ is finite, then nothing is printed after the # following the last element of $L$.

If $L$ is a finite language, the Turing machine in the definition can either halt normally when all the elements of $L$ appear on tape 1, or continue to make moves without printing any other strings on tape 1. If $L$ is infinite, $T$ continues to move forever.

Now we wish to show that a language is recursively enumerable (can be *accepted* by a TM) if and only if it can be enumerated by some TM. The idea of the proof is simple, although one direction turns out to be a little more subtle than it might first appear.

On the one hand, if we have a machine $T$ enumerating $L$, then given an input string $x$, we can test $x$ for membership in $L$ by just waiting to see whether $x$ ever appears on $T$'s output tape. A TM $T_1$ that carries out this strategy is guaranteed to *accept* $L$, because the strings for which the test is successful are precisely those in $L$; for all the others, $T_1$ loops forever, unless $L$ is finite.

On the other hand, if $T$ is a TM accepting $L$, then we consider all the strings in $\Sigma^*$, in some order such as the canonical order described in Section 9.5. In this ordering, shorter strings precede longer ones, and strings of the same length are ordered alphabetically (assuming some initial, arbitrary ordering on the symbols in $\Sigma$). For each string $x$, we try to decide whether to include $x$ in our enumeration by using $T$ to determine whether $x \in L$. Here is the place where the argument needs to be a little more sophisticated: If it should happen that $T$ loops forever on input $x$, and if we are not careful, we will never get around to considering any string beyond $x$. The construction in our official proof will be able to handle this problem.

**Theorem 10.6**

A language $L \subseteq \Sigma^*$ is recursively enumerable (i.e., can be accepted by some Turing machine) if and only if $L$ can be enumerated by some Turing machine.

**Proof**

Suppose $T$ is a TM enumerating $L$. A machine $T_1$ that accepts $L$ is constructed with one more tape than $T$, tape 1 being the extra tape that serves as the input tape. $T_1$ simulates $T$, except that every time # is written on tape 2, the simulation of $T$ pauses while $T_1$ compares its input string to the string listed just before the #. If the two strings match, $T_1$ accepts. It is clear that $T_1$ will accept precisely the strings that are generated on tape 2, which by assumption are the elements of $L$.

More precisely, $T_1$ can incorporate the transitions of $T$ intact, treating the tapes other than tape 1 as the tapes of $T$ and ignoring tape 1, with this change: Every transition that involves writing # on tape 2 is replaced by a sequence of transitions in which the tapes other than 1 and 2 are ignored, the input string is compared to the string just before the # on tape 2, and, if they do not match, $T_1$ is returned to the configuration that would have resulted from the original transition.

In the converse direction, suppose $T$ accepts $L$. We will construct a three-tape TM $T_1$ enumerating $L$. Tape 1 will be the output tape, tape 2 will be used by $T_1$ for generating strings in $\Sigma^*$, and tape 3 will be the tape $T_1$ uses for simulating the action of $T$ on each string generated. In order to avoid the difficulty discussed above, $T_1$ will simulate longer and longer finite sequences of moves of $T$, rather than trying to carry the processing of $T$ on a single string to completion. For this reason, tape 2 will save not only the strings that have been generated so far, but also the number of moves of $T$ that have been carried out on each one.

We adopt the canonical order on $\Sigma^*$. If $\Sigma = \{a, b\}$, for example, strings will be generated in the order

$$\Lambda, a, b, aa, ab, ba, bb, aaa, aab, \ldots, bbb, aaaa, aaab, \ldots$$

$T_1$ will make a series of passes. On the first pass, $T_1$ will generate the string $\Lambda$ and simulate one move of $T$ on that input. On the second pass, $T_1$ will simulate two moves of $T$ on input $\Lambda$, then generate $a$ and simulate one move on that input. On the third pass, $T_1$ will simulate three moves on $\Lambda$, two on $a$, and one on $b$. After the $i$th complete pass, the contents of tape 2 might be something like this:

$$\Delta\Delta \overbrace{11 \cdots 1}^{i} \Delta a \Delta \overbrace{11 \cdots 1}^{i-1} \Delta b \Delta \overbrace{11 \cdots 1}^{i-2} \Delta \cdots \Delta x \Delta 1$$

where $x$ is the $i$th string in canonical order. During the next pass, $T_1$ processes each of the $i$ strings already on tape 2 by adding an extra 1 after it, copying the string onto tape 3, simulating $T$ on that input string for the specified number of steps, and erasing tape 3. If the simulation results in $T$ accepting the input, $T_1$ copies that string onto tape 1 and follows it by #. The last step in this pass is to generate at the end of tape 2 the next element of $\Sigma^*$ (the one that comes after $x$), place a single 1 after it, and simulate one move of $T$ on that input.

Although we have not shown explicitly the bookkeeping devices that $T$ would need in order to carry out these steps, they are straightforward. It is clear that every string accepted by $T$ will eventually be listed on tape 1, and that no other string will.

In the second half of the proof of Theorem 10.6, you should notice that although the strings in $\Sigma^*$ are generated in canonical order on tape 2, the strings in $L$ will not in general be listed in that order on tape 1. (For example, if $T$ accepts $a$ after five moves and $b$ after two, $b$ would appear before $a$ on tape 1.) With the stronger assumption that $T$ is actually recursive, however, the simple construction outlined before the statement of the theorem can be carried out with no complications. On the other hand, it is also easy to show that if there is a TM enumerating $L$ in canonical order, then $L$ *must* be recursive. We state the result officially below, and leave the proof to the exercises.

> **Theorem 10.7**
>
> $L$ is recursive if and only if there is a Turing machine that enumerates $L$ in canonical order.
>
> **Proof**
> See Exercise 10.5.

We can summarize Theorems 10.6 and 10.7 informally by saying that a language is recursively enumerable if there is an algorithm for listing its elements, and a language is recursive if there is an algorithm for listing its elements in canonical order. Some characterizations of recursively enumerable languages in terms of Turing-computable functions will also be discussed in the exercises.

## 10.3 | MORE GENERAL GRAMMARS

We began our discussions of both regular languages and context-free languages by describing ways of generating strings: context-free grammars for CFLs, and regular expressions or regular grammars in the case of regular languages. We went on to find corresponding models of computation, or abstract machines, for recognizing strings in these languages.

We have discussed recursively enumerable languages so far in terms of machines capable of accepting them (Turing machines), because the TM has the distinction of being a *general* model of computation. We will see in this section, however, that a grammar of a type more general than a CFG is exactly what we need to generate the elements of a recursively enumerable language. We will also describe a slightly less general type of grammar, corresponding to languages that fall between context-free and recursively enumerable. The result will be a hierarchy of language types, ranging from very special (regular) to very general (recursively enumerable), each with its own type of grammar as well as its specific model of computation.

The "context-freeness" of a CFG lies in the fact that the left side of a production is a single variable and the production can be applied whenever that variable appears in the string, independent of the context. It is the context-freeness that allows us to prove the pumping lemma for CFLs, since any sufficiently long derivation must contain a "self-embedded" variable, a variable $A$ for which $S \Rightarrow^* vAz \Rightarrow^* vwAyz$.

We can relax the rules of CFGs by allowing the left side of a production to be more than a single variable. For example, we might use the production

$$\alpha A \beta \rightarrow \alpha \gamma \beta$$

if we wanted to allow the variable $A$ to be replaced by the string $\gamma$, but only when $A$ is immediately preceded in the string by $\alpha$ and immediately followed by $\beta$. Although productions of this type are general enough for our purposes, it is often more convenient to write them in the form

$$\alpha A \beta \rightarrow \gamma$$

or, even more simply,

$$\alpha \rightarrow \beta$$

In other words, a production is now thought of as simply a substitution of one string for another. The idea of strings replacing variables is retained in the sense that the left side of a production must contain at least one variable.

---

**Definition 10.3   Unrestricted Grammars**

An *unrestricted*, or *phrase-structure* grammar is a 4-tuple $G = (V, \Sigma, S, P)$, where $V$ and $\Sigma$ are disjoint sets of variables and terminals, respectively; $S$ is an element of $V$ called the start symbol; and $P$ is a set of productions of the form

$$\alpha \rightarrow \beta$$

where $\alpha, \beta \in (V \cup \Sigma)^*$ and $\alpha$ contains at least one variable.

---

Much of the notation developed for context-free grammars can be carried over intact. In particular,

$$\alpha \Rightarrow_G^* \beta$$

means that $\beta$ can be derived from $\alpha$ in zero or more steps, and

$$L(G) = \{x \in \Sigma^* \mid S \Rightarrow_G^* x\}$$

To illustrate the generality of these grammars, we consider the first two examples of non-context-free languages in Chapter 8.

---

**EXAMPLE 10.1**   An Unrestricted Grammar Generating $\{a^i b^i c^i \mid i \geq 1\}$

Let

$$L = \{a^i b^i c^i \mid i \geq 1\}$$

Our grammar will involve variables $A$, $B$, $C$, as well as two others to be explained shortly. There will be three types of productions: those that produce strings with equal numbers of $A$'s, $B$'s, and $C$'s, though not always in the order we want; those that allow the appropriate changes in the order of $A$'s, $B$'s, and $C$'s; and finally, those that change all the variables to the corresponding terminals, *if* the variables are in the right order.

Productions of the first two types are easy to find. The context-free productions

$$S \rightarrow ABCS \mid ABC$$

generate all strings of the form $(ABC)^n$, and the productions

$$BA \rightarrow AB \qquad CA \rightarrow AC \qquad CB \rightarrow BC$$

will allow the variables to realign themselves properly. For the third type, we cannot simply add productions like $A \rightarrow a$, because they might be used too soon, before the variables line themselves up correctly. Instead we say that $C$ can be replaced by $c$, but only if it is preceded by $c$ or $b$:

$$cC \to cc \qquad bC \to bc$$

$B$ can be replaced by $b$ if it is preceded by $b$ or $a$:

$$bB \to bb \qquad aB \to ab$$

and $A$ can be replaced by $a$ if it is preceded by $a$:

$$aA \to aa$$

Once we have an $a$ at the beginning to start things off, these productions allow the string to transform itself into lowercase, from left to right. But where does the first $a$ come from? It is still not correct to have $A \to a$, even with our restrictions on $b$'s and $c$'s. This would allow $ABC$ to transform itself into $abc$ wherever it occurs, and would therefore permit $ABCABC$ to become $abcabc$. One solution is to use an extra variable $F$ to stand for the left end of the string. Then we can say that $A$ can be replaced by $a$ only when it is preceded by $a$ or $F$:

$$aA \to aa \qquad FA \to a$$

We introduce the variable $F$ at the left end, using the production

$$S \to FS_1$$

and modify the earlier productions so that they involve $S_1$ instead of $S$. The final grammar is the one with productions

$$S \to FS_1 \qquad S_1 \to ABCS_1 \qquad S_1 \to ABC$$
$$BA \to AB \qquad CA \to AC \qquad CB \to BC$$
$$FA \to a \qquad aA \to aa \qquad aB \to ab$$
$$bB \to bb \qquad bC \to bc \qquad cC \to cc$$

The string $aabbcc$, for example, can be derived as follows. At each point, the underlined string is the one that is replaced in the subsequent step.

$$S \Rightarrow F\underline{S_1} \Rightarrow FABC\underline{S_1} \Rightarrow FAB\underline{CA}BC \Rightarrow FA\underline{BA}CBC$$
$$\Rightarrow FAAB\underline{CB}C \Rightarrow \underline{FA}ABBCC \Rightarrow \underline{aA}BBCC \Rightarrow aa\underline{B}BCC$$
$$\Rightarrow aab\underline{B}CC \Rightarrow aabb\underline{C}C \Rightarrow aabbc\underline{C} \Rightarrow aabbcc$$

It is easy to see that any string in $L$ can be derived from this grammar. In the other direction, any string of terminal symbols derived from $S$ has equal numbers of $a$'s, $b$'s, and $c$'s; the only question is whether illegal combinations such as $ba$ or $ca$ can occur. Notice first that if $S \Rightarrow^* \alpha$, then $\alpha$ cannot have a terminal symbol appearing after a variable, and so $\alpha \in \Sigma^* V^*$. Furthermore, any subsequent production leaves the string of terminals intact and either rearranges the variables or replaces one more by a terminal. Suppose $u \in L(G)$ and $u$ has an illegal combination of terminals, say $ba$. Then $u = vbaw$, and there is a derivation of $u$ that starts $S \Rightarrow^* vb\beta$ for some $\beta \in V^*$. This is impossible, however, because no matter what $\beta$ is, it is then impossible to produce $a$ as the next terminal.

In the derivation in this example, the movement of $A$'s to the left and $C$'s to the right and the "propagation" of terminal symbols to the right in the last phase might suggest the motion of a Turing machine's tape head and the moves the machine makes as it transforms its tape. This similarity is not a coincidence. The proof that these grammars can generate arbitrary recursively enumerable languages will use the ability of a grammar to mimic a TM and to carry out the same sorts of "computations." In any case, the idea of symbols migrating through the string is a useful technique and can be used again in our next example.

**EXAMPLE 10.2**   A Grammar Generating $\{ss \mid s \in \{a, b\}^*\}$

Let

$$L = \{ss \mid s \in \{a, b\}^*\}$$

A Turing machine might generate strings in $L$ nondeterministically by producing the first half arbitrarily and then making a copy immediately following. Our grammar will follow this approach, except that each symbol in the first half will be copied immediately after it is generated. Suppose we use a marker $M$ to denote the middle of the string and that at some point we have the string $sMs$. To produce a longer string of the same type, we may insert a symbol at the beginning, then move just past the $M$ to insert another copy of the same symbol. This will be accomplished by inserting the two symbols at the beginning, then letting the second migrate to the right until it passes the $M$. As in the first example we use a variable $F$ to designate the front of the string, and the first production in any derivation will be

$$S \rightarrow FM$$

Each time a new symbol $\sigma$ is added, the migrating duplicate symbol will be the variable that is the uppercase version of $\sigma$. The productions

$$F \rightarrow FaA \qquad F \rightarrow FbB$$

produce the symbols, and

$$Aa \rightarrow aA \qquad Ab \rightarrow bA \qquad Ba \rightarrow aB \qquad Bb \rightarrow bB$$

allow the variables to migrate past the terminals in the first half. Eventually the migrating variable hits $M$, at which point it deposits the corresponding terminal on the other side and disappears, using the productions

$$AM \rightarrow Ma \qquad BM \rightarrow Mb$$

To complete a derivation we need the productions

$$F \rightarrow \Lambda \qquad M \rightarrow \Lambda$$

The string $abbabb$ has the following derivation. As before, the underlined portion of each string is the left side of the production used next.

$$S \Rightarrow \underline{F}M \Rightarrow Fb\underline{BM} \Rightarrow \underline{F}bMb \Rightarrow Fb\underline{Bb}Mb$$

$$\Rightarrow Fbb\underline{BM}b \Rightarrow \underline{F}bbMbb \Rightarrow Fa\underline{Abb}Mbb \Rightarrow Fab\underline{Ab}Mbb$$

$$\Rightarrow Fabb\underline{AM}bb \Rightarrow \underline{F}abbMabb \Rightarrow abb\underline{M}abb \Rightarrow abbabb$$

It is reasonably clear that any string in $L$ can be generated by our grammar. We argue informally that no other strings are generated, as follows. First, every string in $L(G)$ has even length, because the only productions that change the ultimate length of the string increase it by 2. Second, when $M$ is finally eliminated in the derivation, all the terminal symbols in the final string are present, and half come before $M$. Those preceding $M$ are the terminals in the productions $F \rightarrow FaA$ and $F \rightarrow FbB$, because the only other productions that create terminals create them to the right of $M$. The farther to the left a terminal in the first half is, the more recently it appeared in the derivation, because the relative order of terminals in the first half never changes. Of any two variables created by these same two productions, however, the one appearing earliest reaches $M$ first because the two can never be transposed. Therefore, of two terminals in the second half, the one to the left came from the variable appearing more recently, and therefore the second half of the final string matches the first.

---

We are now ready to show that the languages generated by unrestricted grammars are precisely those accepted by Turing machines. In one direction we can simply construct a TM to simulate derivations in a grammar. In the other direction, we will take advantage of some of the features of unrestricted grammars that we have already observed, in order to construct grammars that can simulate Turing machine computations.

---

**Theorem 10.8**

For any unrestricted grammar $G = (V, \Sigma, S, P)$, there is a Turing machine $T = (Q, \Sigma, \Gamma, q_0, \delta)$ with $L(T) = L(G)$.

*Proof*

The TM we construct to accept $L(G)$ will be the nondeterministic composite machine

$$T = MovePastInput \rightarrow Simulate \rightarrow Equal$$

where the first component moves the tape head to the blank square following the input string, the second simulates a derivation in $G$ starting in this location and leaves the resulting string on the tape, and the third compares this result to the original input, accepting if and only if the two strings agree. If the input string $x$ is in $L(G)$, the nondeterministic simulation can choose the sequence of moves that simulates the derivation of $x$, and the result will be that $T$ accepts. The only way *Simulate* can leave a string of terminal symbols on the tape is as a result of carrying out the steps of a derivation; if $x \notin L(G)$, this component will either generate a string different from $x$ or fail to complete a derivation at all, and $T$ will fail to accept.

The *Simulate* TM simulates a derivation in much the same way that a nondeterministic top-down PDA simulates a derivation in a CFG (see Section 7.4). In the case of the PDA, however, terminal symbols at the left of the current string are removed from the stack, and the production used in each step involves the leftmost variable. In the case of the TM, the current string remains on the tape in its entirety, and the production used in a step can involve a substring appearing anywhere within the current string. The tape alphabet of *Simulate* will include all the symbols in $V \cup \Sigma$ and possibly others as well. The machine begins by moving one square to the right of where it starts and writing the start symbol $S$. Beginning at this point it enters a loop, which it may terminate after any number of iterations. At the beginning of each iteration, the portion of *Simulate*'s tape that it is using looks like $\Delta\gamma$, where $\gamma$ is the current string in the simulated derivation. The next iteration corresponds to a particular production $\alpha \rightarrow \beta$ of $G$, selected nondeterministically. The steps in the iteration are: attempting to find an occurrence of the string $\alpha$; if one is found, replacing it by $\beta$; and returning the tape head to the beginning of the resulting string. When *Simulate* chooses to exit the loop, it returns the tape head to the leftmost square of its tape and halts normally.

Nondeterminism is present in three places within *Simulate*: choosing a production to use in the next iteration of the loop, selecting an occurrence of the first symbol of $\alpha$ on the tape (which may or may not actually be the beginning of an occurrence of $\alpha$), and deciding when to exit the loop. Incorrect choices at any of these three points may lead to a crash, or to a string left on the tape that still contains variables, or to a string in $L(G)$ that does not match the original string input to $T$. It should be clear, however, that for any $x \in L(G)$, at least one choice of moves will cause *Simulate* to leave $x$ on the tape, and that no strings other than elements of $L(G)$ can be the final output of *Simulate*.

## EXAMPLE 10.3    The *Simulate* TM for a Simple Grammar

Consider the unrestricted grammar with productions

$$S \rightarrow aBS \mid \Lambda$$
$$aB \rightarrow Ba$$
$$Ba \rightarrow aB$$
$$B \rightarrow b$$

which generates the language of strings in $\{a, b\}^*$ with equal numbers of $a$'s and $b$'s. Figure 10.1 shows the *Simulate* TM discussed in the proof of Theorem 10.7. Note that in this example, the only productions in which the left and right sides are of unequal length are the $S$-productions, and $S$ appears only at the right end of the string. In a more general example, applying a production like $S \rightarrow aBS$ could be accomplished by using an *Insert* TM (Exercise 9.13) twice, and $S \rightarrow \Lambda$ would require a deletion.

You should trace the moves of *Simulate* as it simulates the derivation of a string in the language, say *abba*.

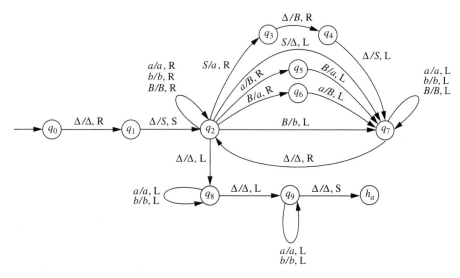

**Figure 10.1 |**
The *Simulate* TM for Example 10.3.

**Theorem 10.9**
For any recursively enumerable language $L \subseteq \Sigma^*$, there is an unrestricted grammar $G$ generating $L$.

*Proof*
Let $M = (Q, \Sigma, \Gamma, q_0, \delta)$ be a TM accepting $L$. The grammar $G$ that we construct will have three types of productions:

1. Productions that can generate two copies of an arbitrary string in $\Sigma^*$, along with some symbols that act as markers to keep the two copies separate.
2. Productions that can simulate a sequence of moves of $M$. During this portion of a derivation, one of the two copies of the original string is left unchanged; the other, representing the input tape to $M$, is modified accordingly. (Since this second copy will contain tape symbols from $T$, all the symbols in $\Gamma \cup \{\Delta\} - \Sigma$ will be included as variables in the grammar.)
3. Productions that can erase everything but the unmodified copy of the string, *provided* that the simulated moves of $M$ applied to the other copy cause $M$ to accept.

The two copies of the original string $a_1 a_2 \cdots a_k$ will take the form

$$(a_1 a_1)(a_2 a_2) \cdots (a_k a_k)$$

The symbols "(" and ")" are used here as variables. The first symbol $a$ of each pair $(a, a)$ will stay the same, while the second can be modified during the simulation.

When $M$ begins, there is a blank in square 0 of the tape. In addition, $M$ can use some of the blank portion of the tape to the right of the input string. This means that we actually need to begin with a string of the form

$$(\Delta\Delta)(a_1a_1)(a_2a_2)\cdots(a_ka_k)(\Delta\Delta)\cdots(\Delta\Delta)$$

If $M$ accepts $x$ by making moves that use $n$ blank squares to the right of the input, the corresponding derivation of $x$ in $G$ will begin by placing at least $n$ copies of $(\Delta\Delta)$ at the end of the string. (A derivation can begin by placing more than $n$ copies of this substring at the end; it will simply be longer than necessary. It may be, however, that no sequence of steps starting with fewer copies of this substring allows $x$ to be derived.)

It is now clear how $M$'s tape is represented in the simulation. In order to represent the complete TM configuration, we need a way of indicating both the state and the position of the tape head. We can do both by adding to our set of variables the states of $M$, and letting such a variable appear in the string just before the symbol-pair in the current position. Thus, the current string when the simulation is about to begin is

$$q_0(\Delta\Delta)(a_1a_1)(a_2a_2)\cdots(a_ka_k)(\Delta\Delta)\cdots(\Delta\Delta)$$

If at some point during the processing $M$ is in the configuration

$$(q, b_0b_1\cdots b_{i-1}\underline{b_i}b_{i+1}\cdots b_m)$$

the corresponding string in the derivation will be

$$(\Delta b_0)(a_1b_1)\cdots(a_{i-1}b_{i-1})q(a_ib_i)\cdots(a_kb_k)$$
$$(\Delta b_{k+1})\cdots(\Delta b_m)(\Delta\Delta)\cdots(\Delta\Delta)$$

(This assumes that $m$ is greater than $k$, the length of the original input string. In the other case the string will be slightly different.)

The productions that generate the starting string are these:

$$S \rightarrow S(\Delta\Delta) \mid T$$
$$T \rightarrow T(\sigma\sigma) \mid q_0(\Delta\Delta)$$

where there is a production $T \rightarrow T(\sigma\sigma)$ for every symbol $\sigma \in \Sigma$. Corresponding to each Turing machine move

$$\delta(p, a) = (q, b, \text{R})$$

where $a, b \in \Gamma \cup \{\Delta\}$, we have productions

$$p(\sigma a) \rightarrow (\sigma b)q$$

one for each $\sigma \in \Sigma \cup \{\Delta\}$. Note that the symbol $\sigma$ stays unchanged and the state variable has moved to the right of the symbol-pair. For each move

$$\delta(p, a) = (q, b, \text{S})$$

we have all the productions

$$p(\sigma a) \to q(\sigma b)$$

($\sigma \in \Sigma \cup \{\Delta\}$), and for each move

$$\delta(p, a) = (q, b, \mathrm{L})$$

we have the productions

$$(\sigma_1 \sigma_2) p(\sigma_3 a) \to q(\sigma_1 \sigma_2)(\sigma_3 b)$$

one for every possible combination of $\sigma_1, \sigma_3 \in \Sigma \cup \{\Delta\}$ and $\sigma_2 \in \Gamma \cup \{\Delta\}$. In all these cases, we may ignore Turing machine moves that halt in the reject state; the symbol $h_r$ is not required in any productions.

If the sequence of moves of $M$ leads to the accepting state $h_a$, and only in this case, the corresponding derivation produces a string with the symbol $h_a$ in it. The remaining productions allow us to erase from any string containing $h_a$ all the symbols in the second position of a pair, as well as all the auxiliary variables (that is, (, ), $\Delta$, and elements of $Q \cup \{h_a\}$), so as to leave only the terminal symbols of the input string accepted by $M$. Productions that accomplish this are

$$h_a(\sigma_1 \sigma_2) \to h_a(\sigma_1 \sigma_2)h_a \qquad (\sigma_1 \in \Sigma \cup \{\Delta\}, \sigma_2 \in \Gamma \cup \{\Delta\})$$
$$(\sigma_1 \sigma_2)h_a \to h_a(\sigma_1 \sigma_2)h_a \qquad (\sigma_1 \in \Sigma \cup \{\Delta\}, \sigma_2 \in \Gamma \cup \{\Delta\})$$
$$h_a(\sigma_1 \sigma_2) \to \sigma_1 \qquad (\sigma_1 \in \Sigma, \sigma_2 \in \Gamma \cup \{\Delta\})$$
$$h_a(\Delta \sigma) \to \Lambda \qquad (\sigma \in \Gamma \cup \{\Delta\})$$

The productions in the first two lines simply propagate copies of $h_a$ throughout the string, and those in the last two do the necessary erasing.

It is not hard to see that this grammar generates precisely the strings accepted by $M$, although we do not attempt a rigorous proof. In the example that follows, a sample derivation is included.

---

Obtaining a Grammar From a TM | **EXAMPLE 10.4**

This example refers to Example 9.2 and the TM pictured in Figure 9.4, which accepts the language of palindromes over $\{a, b\}$. Although there are 251 productions in the grammar, many are unnecessary since they involve combinations $(\sigma_1 \sigma_2)$ that never occur. Rather than listing them, we show a derivation of the string $aba$ in this grammar. The corresponding sequence of Turing machine moves simulated by the derivation is shown to the right. Since the TM moves its head to the blank square to the right of the input string and no farther, the derivation begins by producing a string with one copy of $(\Delta \Delta)$ on the right. At each step in the derivation, the underlined portion shows the left side of the production that will be used in the next step.

$$S \Rightarrow \underline{S}(\Delta\Delta)$$

$$\Rightarrow \underline{T}(\Delta\Delta)$$

$$\Rightarrow \underline{T}(aa)(\Delta\Delta)$$

$$\Rightarrow \underline{T}(bb)(aa)(\Delta\Delta)$$

$$\Rightarrow \underline{T}(aa)(bb)(aa)(\Delta\Delta)$$

$$\Rightarrow q_0(\underline{\Delta\Delta})(aa)(bb)(aa)(\Delta\Delta) \qquad\qquad (q_0, \underline{\Delta}aba)$$

$$\Rightarrow (\Delta\Delta)q_1(\underline{aa})(bb)(aa)(\Delta\Delta) \qquad\qquad \vdash \quad (q_1, \Delta\underline{a}ba)$$

$$\Rightarrow (\Delta\Delta)(a\Delta)q_2(\underline{bb})(aa)(\Delta\Delta) \qquad\qquad \vdash \quad (q_2, \Delta\Delta\underline{b}a)$$

$$\Rightarrow (\Delta\Delta)(a\Delta)(bb)q_2(\underline{aa})(\Delta\Delta) \qquad\qquad \vdash \quad (q_2, \Delta\Delta b\underline{a})$$

$$\Rightarrow (\Delta\Delta)(a\Delta)(bb)(aa)q_2(\underline{\Delta\Delta}) \qquad\qquad \vdash \quad (q_2, \Delta\Delta ba\underline{\Delta})$$

$$\Rightarrow (\Delta\Delta)(a\Delta)\underline{(bb)}q_3(aa)(\Delta\Delta) \qquad\qquad \vdash \quad (q_3, \Delta\Delta b\underline{a})$$

$$\Rightarrow (\Delta\Delta)(a\Delta)q_4\underline{(bb)}(a\Delta)(\Delta\Delta) \qquad\qquad \vdash \quad (q_4, \Delta\Delta\underline{b})$$

$$\Rightarrow (\Delta\Delta)q_4\underline{(a\Delta)}(bb)(a\Delta)(\Delta\Delta) \qquad\qquad \vdash \quad (q_4, \Delta\Delta b)$$

$$\Rightarrow (\Delta\Delta)(a\Delta)q_1\underline{(bb)}(a\Delta)(\Delta\Delta) \qquad\qquad \vdash \quad (q_1, \Delta\Delta\underline{b})$$

$$\Rightarrow (\Delta\Delta)(a\Delta)(b\Delta)q_5\underline{(a\Delta)}(\Delta\Delta) \qquad\qquad \vdash \quad (q_5, \Delta\Delta\Delta\underline{\Delta})$$

$$\Rightarrow (\Delta\Delta)(a\Delta)q_6\underline{(b\Delta)}(a\Delta)(\Delta\Delta) \qquad\qquad \vdash \quad (q_6, \Delta\Delta\underline{\Delta})$$

$$\Rightarrow (\Delta\Delta)(a\Delta)(b\Delta)h_a\underline{(a\Delta)}(\Delta\Delta) \qquad\qquad \vdash \quad (h_a, \Delta\Delta\Delta\underline{\Delta})$$

$$\Rightarrow (\Delta\Delta)(a\Delta)\underline{(b\Delta)}h_a(a\Delta)h_a(\Delta\Delta)$$

$$\Rightarrow (\Delta\Delta)\underline{(a\Delta)}h_a(b\Delta)h_a(a\Delta)h_a(\Delta\Delta)$$

$$\Rightarrow \underline{(\Delta\Delta)}h_a(a\Delta)h_a(b\Delta)h_a(a\Delta)h_a(\Delta\Delta)$$

$$\Rightarrow h_a\underline{(\Delta\Delta)}h_a(a\Delta)h_a(b\Delta)h_a(a\Delta)h_a(\Delta\Delta)$$

$$\Rightarrow h_a\underline{(a\Delta)}h_a(b\Delta)h_a(a\Delta)h_a(\Delta\Delta)$$

$$\Rightarrow ah_a\underline{(b\Delta)}h_a(a\Delta)h_a(\Delta\Delta)$$

$$\Rightarrow abh_a\underline{(a\Delta)}h_a(\Delta\Delta)$$

$$\Rightarrow abah_a\underline{(\Delta\Delta)}$$

$$\Rightarrow aba$$

## 10.4 | CONTEXT-SENSITIVE LANGUAGES AND THE CHOMSKY HIERARCHY

In this section we look briefly at *context-sensitive* grammars, which are more general than CFGs and less so than unrestricted grammars. The corresponding models of computation, called *linear-bounded automata*, lie between pushdown automata and Turing machines.

---

**Definition 10.4    Context-Sensitive Grammars**

A *context-sensitive* grammar (CSG) is an unrestricted grammar in which every production has the form

$$\alpha \to \beta \quad \text{with } |\beta| \geq |\alpha|$$

A context-sensitive language (CSL) is a language that can be generated by such a grammar.

---

A slightly different characterization of these languages makes it easier to understand the phrase *context-sensitive*. A language is context-sensitive if and only if it can be generated by a grammar in which every production has the form

$$\alpha A \beta \to \alpha X \beta$$

where $\alpha$, $\beta$, and $X$ are strings of variables and/or terminals, with $X$ not null, and $A$ is a variable (see Exercise 10.42). Such a production may allow $A$ to be replaced by $X$, depending on the context.

---

A CSG for $\{a^n b^n c^n \mid n \geq 1\}$    **EXAMPLE 10.5**

In Example 10.1 we presented a grammar for the language

$$L = \{a^n b^n c^n \mid n \geq 1\}$$

that was not context-sensitive. By modifying it slightly, however, we can see that $L$ is in fact a CSL. Instead of using a separate variable $F$ to indicate the front of the string, we can simply distinguish between the first $A$ in the string and the remaining $A$'s. You can check that the context-sensitive grammar with the productions below generates $L$.

$$S \to \mathcal{A}BCS_1 \mid \mathcal{A}BC$$

$$S_1 \to ABCS_1 \mid ABC$$

$$BA \to AB \quad CA \to AC \quad CB \to BC$$

$$\mathcal{A} \to a \quad aA \to aa \quad aB \to ab$$

$$bB \to bb \quad bC \to bc \quad cC \to cc$$

---

We obtained the class of context-sensitive grammars by imposing a restriction on the productions of an unrestricted grammar, and it seems natural to look for a corresponding restriction to place on a Turing machine. We can anticipate the sort of extra condition that might be appropriate by looking carefully at the Turing machine constructed in Theorem 10.7 to accept the language generated by a given unrestricted grammar $G$. The TM simulates a derivation in $G$, using the space on the tape to the right of the input string, and the tape head never needs to move farther right than one square past the right end of the current string in the derivation. If $G$ is actually context-sensitive, the string in a derivation is never longer than the string of terminals being derived. Therefore, for any input string of length $n$, the tape head never needs to move past square $2n$ (approximately) during the computation. In the definition below, the extra restriction that is adopted appears to be even a little stronger.

---

**Definition 10.5   Linear-Bounded Automata**

A *linear-bounded automaton* (LBA) is a 5-tuple $M = (Q, \Sigma, \Gamma, q_0, \delta)$ that is the same as a nondeterministic Turing machine except in the following respect. There are two extra tape symbols $\langle$ and $\rangle$, assumed not to be elements of $\Gamma$. $M$ begins in the configuration $(q_0, \langle x \rangle)$, with its tape head scanning the symbol $\langle$ on square 0 and the symbol $\rangle$ in the first square to the right of the input string $x$; in moving subsequently, $M$ is not permitted to replace the symbols $\langle$ or $\rangle$, or to move its head left from the square with $\langle$ or right from the square with $\rangle$.

---

**Theorem 10.10**

If $L \subseteq \Sigma^*$ is a context-sensitive language, there is a linear-bounded automaton accepting $L$.

*Proof*

Suppose $G = (V, \Sigma, S, P)$ is a CSG generating $L$. In the proof of Theorem 10.8, the Turing machine used the portion of the tape to the right of the input for the simulated derivation. That option is not available to us here, but a satisfactory alternative is to convert the portion of the tape between $\langle$ and $\rangle$ into two tracks, so that the second provides the necessary space. For this reason we let the tape alphabet of our machine $M$ contain pairs $(a, b)$, where $a, b \in \Sigma \cup V \cup \{\Delta\}$, in addition to elements of $\Sigma$. There may be other symbols needed as well.

The first action taken by $M$ will be to convert the tape configuration

$$\langle \underline{x_1} x_2 \cdots x_n \rangle$$

to

$$\langle \underline{(x_1, \Delta)} (x_2, \Delta) \cdots (x_n, \Delta) \rangle$$

This step corresponds to the *MovePastInput* component of the TM in the proof of Theorem 10.8. Next, $M$ places $S$ in the second track of square 1 and starts a loop exactly as before, except that the machine will reject if the string produced in the second track during any iteration has length greater than $n$. As before, $M$ may exit the loop at any time. When it does, it rejects if the second track does not match the input in the first track. Since $G$ is context-sensitive, a string appearing in the derivation of $x \in L$ cannot be longer than $x$, so that if the LBA begins with input $x$ there is a sequence of moves it can execute that will cause it to accept. If $x \notin L$, on the other hand, $M$ will either reject or loop forever, since no simulated derivation will be able to produce the string $x$.

As you can probably see from the proof of Theorem 10.10, the significant feature of an LBA is not that the tape head doesn't move past the input string at all, but that its motion is restricted to a portion of the tape bounded by some linear function of the input length (this explains the significance of the phrase *linear-bounded*). As long as this condition is satisfied, an argument using multiple tape tracks can be used to find an equivalent machine satisfying the stricter condition in Definition 10.5.

The strict converse of Theorem 10.10 does not hold, since the null string might be accepted by an LBA but cannot belong to any context-sensitive language. However, the obvious modification of the statement is true.

---

**Theorem 10.11**

If there is a linear-bounded automaton $M = (Q, \Sigma, \Gamma, q_0, \delta)$ accepting the language $L \subseteq \Sigma^*$, then there is a context-sensitive grammar generating $L - \{\Lambda\}$.

*Proof*

We give only a sketch of the proof, which is similar to that of Theorem 10.9. As before, the grammar is constructed so that a derivation generates two copies of a string, simulates the action of $M$ on one, and eliminates everything except the other from the string if and when the simulated moves of $M$ lead to acceptance.

The grammar differs from the previous one in that more variables are needed and they are more complicated. Previously the variables included only $S$, $T$, left and right parentheses, and one variable for each possible state of $M$. However, with these variables, productions such as $h_a(\sigma_1\sigma_2) \rightarrow \sigma_1$ would violate the context-sensitive condition. The way to salvage productions of this form is simply to interpret strings of the form $(\sigma_1\sigma_2)$ and $p(\sigma_1\sigma_2)$ as variables. This approach could have been used in the earlier proof as well, and many of the productions would have been context-sensitive as a result. The difference is that now we no longer need strings containing $(\Delta\Delta)$ and productions like $h_a(\Delta\sigma) \rightarrow \Lambda$, because initially there are no blanks between the tape markers of $M$.

In addition, we must pay attention to the tape markers $\langle$ and $\rangle$; thus we may also have variables such as $(\sigma_1\langle\sigma_2), (\sigma_1\sigma_2\rangle)$, and $(\sigma_1\langle\sigma_2\rangle)$ (as well as $p(\sigma_1\langle\sigma_2)$ and so forth), corresponding to points during the simulation when $\sigma_2$ is the leftmost, rightmost, and only symbol between the markers, respectively. In each case, $\sigma_1$ represents the terminal symbol originally in that position and is not modified during the simulation. Finally, since $M$'s tape head can move to the tape squares containing the symbols $\langle$ and $\rangle$, we will also have variables of the form $q(\sigma_1\langle\sigma_2)^L, q(\sigma_1\sigma_2\rangle)^R, q(\sigma_1\langle\sigma_2\rangle)^L$, and $q(\sigma_1\langle\sigma_2\rangle)^R$. The first one, for example, signifies that $M$ is in state $q$, its tape head is on the square containing $\langle$, and the next square contains $\sigma_2$ now but originally contained $\sigma_1$.

The first step in a derivation is to produce a string of the form

$$q_0(\sigma_1\langle\sigma_1\rangle)^L(\sigma_2\sigma_2)\cdots(\sigma_{n-1}\sigma_{n-1})(\sigma_n\sigma_n))$$

or

$$q_0(\sigma_1\langle\sigma_1\rangle)^L$$

Specifying productions that generate these strings is straightforward.

Because of the endmarkers, and because the states have been incorporated into the variables, there are more combinations to consider when describing the productions to be used in the LBA simulation. We give those corresponding to LBA moves in which the tape head moves right, and leave the other two cases as exercises.

Corresponding to the move

$$\delta(p, a) = (q, b, \mathrm{R})$$

we have these productions:

$$p(\sigma_1 a)(\sigma_2\sigma_3) \rightarrow (\sigma_1 b)q(\sigma_2\sigma_3)$$

$$p(\sigma_1\langle a)(\sigma_2\sigma_3) \rightarrow (\sigma_1\langle b)q(\sigma_2\sigma_3)$$

$$p(\sigma_1 a)(\sigma_2\sigma_3\rangle) \rightarrow (\sigma_1 b)q(\sigma_2\sigma_3\rangle)$$

$$p(\sigma_1\langle a)(\sigma_2\sigma_3\rangle) \rightarrow (\sigma_1\langle b)q(\sigma_2\sigma_3\rangle)$$

$$p(\sigma_1 a\rangle) \rightarrow q(\sigma_1 b\rangle)^R$$

$$p(\sigma_1\langle a\rangle) \rightarrow q(\sigma_1\langle b\rangle)^R$$

for every combination of $\sigma_1, \sigma_2 \in \Sigma$ and $\sigma_3 \in \Gamma \cup \{\Delta\}$. Notice that in the first four of these, both sides of the production consist of two variables, and in the last two, both sides consist of one variable. Corresponding to the move

$$\delta(p, \langle) = (q, \langle, \mathrm{R})$$

we have the productions

$$p(\sigma_1\langle\sigma_2)^L \rightarrow q(\sigma_1\langle\sigma_2)$$

$$p(\sigma_1\langle\sigma_2)\rangle)^L \rightarrow q(\sigma_1\langle\sigma_2))$$

for each $\sigma_1 \in \Sigma$ and $\sigma_2 \in \Gamma \cup \{\Delta\}$.

As in the previous proof, we need a way to eliminate everything but the original input once a variable of the form $h_a(\sigma_1\sigma_2)$ (or $h_a(\sigma_1\langle\sigma_2)$, etc.) shows up in a derivation. This time we can use productions such as

$$h_a(\sigma_1\sigma_2)(\sigma_3\sigma_4) \rightarrow h_a(\sigma_1\sigma_2)h_a(\sigma_3\sigma_4)$$

$$(\sigma_1\sigma_2)h_a(\sigma_3\sigma_4) \rightarrow h_a(\sigma_1\sigma_2)h_a(\sigma_3\sigma_4)$$

$$h_a(\sigma_1\sigma_2) \rightarrow \sigma_1$$

and other comparable ones that include the symbols $\langle$ and $\rangle$.

> It is reasonably clear from the way we have defined variables that the grammar we end up with will be context-sensitive. It is also possible to convince yourself that it generates precisely the nonnull strings accepted by $M$.

The four classes of languages that we have now studied—regular, context-free, context-sensitive, and recursively enumerable—are often referred to as the *Chomsky Hierarchy*. Chomsky himself designated the four types as type 3, type 2, type 1, and type 0, from most restrictive to most general. Each level of the hierarchy can be characterized by a class of grammars, as well as by a certain type of abstract machine, or model of computation. This hierarchy is summarized in Table 10.1.

**Table 10.1** | The Chomsky Hierarchy

| Type | Languages (grammars) | Form of productions in grammar | Accepting device |
|------|----------------------|-------------------------------|------------------|
| 3 | Regular | $A \to aB, A \to a$ <br> $(A, B \in V, a \in \Sigma)$ | Finite automaton |
| 2 | Context-free | $A \to \alpha$ <br> $(A \in V, \alpha \in (V \cup \Sigma)^*)$ | Pushdown automaton |
| 1 | Context-sensitive | $\alpha \to \beta$ <br> $(\alpha, \beta \in (V \cup \Sigma)^*, |\beta| \geq |\alpha|,$ <br> $\alpha$ contains a variable) | Linear-bounded automaton |
| 0 | Recursively enumerable (unrestricted or phrase-structure) | $\alpha \to \beta$ <br> $(\alpha, \beta \in (V \cup \Sigma)^*,$ <br> $\alpha$ contains a variable) | Turing machine |

The phrase *type 0 grammar* was actually applied to a grammar in which all productions are of the form $\alpha \to \beta$, where $\alpha$ is a string of one or more variables; it is easy to see, however, that any unrestricted grammar is equivalent to one of this type (Exercise 10.19).

The characterizations of all these types of languages in terms of grammars make it obvious that for $1 \leq i \leq 3$, every language of type $i$ is of type $i - 1$, except that a context-free language is context-sensitive only if it does not contain the null string. (For any context-free language, the set of nonnull strings in the language is a context-sensitive language.) Theorem 10.12 shows that we can make an even stronger statement about the case $i = 1$.

> **Theorem 10.12**
> Every context-sensitive language is recursive.
>
> *Proof*
> Suppose $L$ is generated by the context-sensitive grammar $G$. We have already seen in Theorem 10.10 that $L$ can be accepted by a linear-bounded automaton $M$, which is essentially a special type of nondeterministic Turing

machine. Now we show how to modify $M$ so that it still accepts $L$ but so that any sequence of moves will cause it to halt. It will then follow from Theorem 10.2 that $L$ is recursive.

Although the modified machine $M'$ will still use the markers $\langle$ and $\rangle$, and they will remain in place, $M'$ will no longer be prohibited from moving its tape head to the right of $\rangle$. The LBA $M$ simulates a derivation in $G$, using the second "track" of the tape between the two markers. At the end of each iteration of this simulation, $M'$ will perform two additional steps. The first is to copy the current string of the derivation onto the empty portion of the tape to the right. In effect, $M'$ will keep a history of the derivation; the string on the tape to the right of the $\rangle$ marker will look like

$$S \Delta \alpha_1 \Delta \alpha_2 \Delta \cdots \Delta \alpha_n$$

where $\alpha_i$ is the current string after the $i$th iteration of the simulation. The second step is to determine whether $\alpha_n$, the most recent string, is a duplicate of any of the previous $\alpha_i$'s, and to reject if it is.

With this modification, it is no longer possible for $M'$ to loop forever. Eventually one of three things will happen: Either the current string in the simulated derivation will match the original input $x$, in which case $M'$ accepts; or an iteration of the loop will result in a string longer than $x$, in which case $M'$ rejects; or one of the strings obtained will show up for the second time (since all these strings are length $|x|$ or shorter), which also causes $M'$ to reject. The strings $x$ for which some sequence of moves of $M'$ result in the first outcome are precisely those that can be generated by $G$, and we conclude that $L$ is accepted by a nondeterministic TM for which every sequence of moves eventually halts.

For each $i$ with $1 \leq i \leq 3$, the set of languages of type $i$ is a subset of the set of languages of type $i - 1$. For $i$ either 2 or 3, we know the inclusion is proper: There are context-sensitive languages that are not context-free (see Example 10.5) and context-free languages that are not regular. The last inclusion is also proper for a trivial reason, because $\{\Lambda\}$ is an example of a recursively enumerable, non-context-sensitive language. In order to show there are nontrivial examples, we recall from Theorems 10.1 and 10.12 that

$$CS \subseteq R \subseteq RE$$

(where the three sets contain context-sensitive, recursive, and recursively enumerable languages, respectively). It would therefore be sufficient to show either that $RE - R \neq \emptyset$ or that there is a recursive language $L$ for which $L - \{\Lambda\}$ is not context-sensitive. Both these statements are true. The proof of the first is postponed until Section 11.1, because it depends on a type of argument that will be introduced in the next section. The second statement is Exercise 11.33. The conclusion of either statement is that the class of recursive languages (which does not show up explicitly in Table 10.1, because there is no known characterization involving grammars) falls strictly between the two bottom levels of the hierarchy.

In spite of the results mentioned in the preceding paragraph, just about any language you can think of is context-sensitive. In particular, programming languages are. The non-context-free aspects of the C language mentioned in Example 8.4, such as variables having to be declared before they are used, can be accommodated by context-sensitive grammars.

The four levels of the Chomsky hierarchy satisfy somewhat different closure properties. The set of regular languages is closed under all the standard operations: union, intersection, complement, concatenation, Kleene*, and so forth. The set of context-free languages is not closed under intersection or complement. Once we show that there are recursively enumerable languages that are not recursive, it will follow from Theorem 10.5 that the set of recursively enumerable languages is not closed under complement. Although it is not difficult to show that the class of context-sensitive languages is closed under many of these operations (Exercise 10.44), the case of complements remained an open question for some time. Szelepcsényi and Immerman answered it independently in 1987 and 1988, by proving that if $L$ can be accepted by a linear-bounded automaton, then so can $L'$. Open questions concerning context-sensitive languages remain: It is unknown, for example, whether or not every CSL can be accepted by a deterministic LBA.

# 10.5 | NOT ALL LANGUAGES ARE RECURSIVELY ENUMERABLE

In Chapter 11 we will see an example of a language that cannot be accepted by any Turing machine. Rather than waiting for the example, however, we give a nonconstructive proof in this section that there must be such a language. There are several reasons for doing this. First the main idea of the proof is simple, and interesting in itself: The set of languages is much bigger than the set of Turing machines, and one machine can accept only one language; therefore, there must be a language with no machine to accept it. Second, we can draw an even stronger conclusion: Not only is there a language that is not recursively enumerable, but *most* languages are not recursively enumerable. (The set of languages that are not recursively enumerable is bigger than the set of languages that are.) Third, the proof introduces a type of "diagonal" argument that we will be able to use again when we actually look for an example.

The set of all languages is infinite, and the set of all Turing machines is infinite. Nevertheless, the first set is bigger than the second. Our first problem is to make sense of this idea, and to find a precise way to compare the sizes of two infinite sets.

Let us start with with finite sets. Most people would say that $A = \{a, b, c\}$ and $B = \{x, y, z\}$ are the same size because they both have three elements. This approach does not look promising for infinite sets, however—the whole point is that two sets with an "infinite number" of elements may not have the same size. We would like to be able to say that two sets have the same size without saying exactly what that size is.

In any case, "counting" the elements of a set $A$ can be interpreted as establishing a one-to-one correspondence between the elements of the set $\{1, 2, \ldots, n\}$ and the elements of $A$ (and in the process determining the number $n$): "one," "two," ... is short for "this is the element that will correspond to 1," "this is the element that will correspond to 2," and so forth. Rather than applying this process to $A$, then applying it to $B$, then comparing the results, we could simply try to match up the elements of $A$ and $B$ directly. In the case of $\{a, b, c\}$ and $\{x, y, z\}$ we can: There is a bijection (a one-to-one, onto function) from $A$ to $B$. An example is the function $f$ defined by $f(a) = x$, $f(b) = y$, and $f(c) = z$. Although $A$ and $B$ are different sets, we can view them as the same except for the labels we use to describe the elements: We can talk about $a$, $b$, and $c$, or about $f(a)$, $f(b)$, and $f(c)$. (This is exactly what it means to have a bijection from one to the other.) It seems appropriate, in particular, to say that whenever we have such a function, $A$ and $B$ are the same size.

This criterion can be applied to infinite sets as well as to finite; therefore, we adopt it as our definition.

> Two sets are the same size if there is a bijection from one to the other.

Note that the relation "is the same size as" is an equivalence relation. In particular, if $A$ and $B$ are the same size, then so are $B$ and $A$; and if $A$ and $B$ are the same size, and $B$ and $C$ are the same size, then so are $A$ and $C$.

Even though we are trying to avoid talking about the "size" of a set as a *quantity*, we want to be able to say informally that one set is bigger than another. For example, $\{p, q, r, s, t\}$ is bigger than $\{a, b, c\}$. This is because there is a *one-to-one* function from $\{a, b, c\}$ to $\{p, q, r, s, t\}$ (for example, the function $f$ for which $f(a) = p$, $f(b) = r$, and $f(c) = s$), but no bijection. In other words, there is a *subset* of $\{p, q, r, s, t\}$ that is the same size as $\{a, b, c\}$ (the subset $\{p, r, s\}$, for example), but the entire set is not. Again, this characterization of "bigger than" extends to infinite sets as well.

> A set $A$ is bigger than a set $B$ if there is a bijection from a subset of $A$ to $B$ but no bijection from $A$ to $B$.

(See Exercise 10.51 for another characterization in terms of one-to-one functions.) In the case of finite sets, of course, we are free to use our usual idea of size to compare two sets: $A$ is bigger than $B$ if it has more elements, and $A$ and $B$ are the same size if they have the same number of elements. For two infinite sets, however, we tend to proceed in the opposite direction. Rather than looking at how big the sets are in order to see whether there is a bijection from one to the other, we try to decide whether there is a bijection in order to compare the sizes.

One important difference between finite sets and infinite sets can be very confusing at first. If a finite set $A$ is the same size as a proper subset of $B$, then $B$ must be bigger than $A$. In other words, if there is a bijection of $A$ to a proper subset of $B$, then there cannot be a bijection from $A$ to $B$. In particular, if $B$ contains all the elements of $A$ and some more as well, then $B$ is bigger than $A$. As obvious as these statements seem, they are *not* true for infinite sets, as illustrated in Figure 10.2. For example, we cannot say that $B = \{0, 1, 2, 3, \ldots\}$ is bigger than $A = \{1, 2, 3, \ldots\}$, as we have defined "bigger," because the function $f : B \to A$ defined by $f(n) = n + 1$ is a bijection (Figure 10.2$a$). We cannot say that the set $B$ of all nonnegative integers is bigger than the set $A$ of nonnegative even integers (Figure 10.2$b$), because the func-

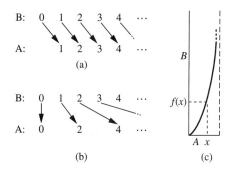

**Figure 10.2 |**

tion $f$ defined by $f(n) = 2n$ is a bijection from the first to the second. Finally, for an even more dramatic example, the set $B = \mathcal{R}^+$ of all nonnegative real numbers, is not bigger than the interval $A = [0, 1)$, because the formula $f(x) = \tan(\frac{\pi}{2}x)$ (whose graph is shown in Figure 10.2c) defines a bijection from $A$ to $B$. These results are counterintuitive. There is clearly a sense in which the set of natural numbers is twice as big as the set of nonnegative even integers, and $\mathcal{R}^+$ is infinitely many times as big as $[0, 1)$. However, it appears that according to our definition, "twice as big," or even "infinitely many times as big," does not imply "bigger" in the case of infinite sets.

The following observation may make these examples seem less surprising: Saying that there is a bijection from a set $S$ to a proper subset of itself is *equivalent* to saying that $S$ is infinite. One direction is easy, because there can be no bijection from a finite set $S$ to a set with fewer elements. For the other direction, see Exercise 10.25.

As you can see from the preceding paragraphs, it is necessary to think carefully about infinite sets, and it is dangerous to rely on intuitively obvious statements that you take for granted in the case of finite sets.

Not only are some infinite sets larger than others, but there are many different "sizes" of infinite sets (Exercises 10.47 and 10.49). For our purposes, however, it is enough to distinguish two kinds of infinite sets: those that are the same size as the set $\mathcal{N}$ of natural numbers, and those that are bigger, which account for all the rest.

---

**Definition 10.6    Countable and Uncountable Sets**

A set $S$ is *countably infinite* if there is a bijection from $\mathcal{N}$ to $S$, and *countable* if it is either countably infinite or finite. A set is *uncountably infinite*, or simply *uncountable*, if it is not countable.

---

Saying that $f : \mathcal{N} \to S$ is a bijection means that these three conditions hold:

1.  For every natural number $n$, $f(n) \in S$.
2.  For any two different numbers $m$ and $n$, $f(m) \neq f(n)$.
3.  Every element of $S$ is $f(n)$ for some natural number $n$.

Therefore, saying that $S$ is countably infinite (the same size as $\mathcal{N}$) means that the elements of $S$ can be listed (or "counted") as $f(0)$, $f(1)$, ..., so that every element of $S$ appears exactly once in the list. Saying that $S$ is countable means the same thing, except that the list may stop after a finite number of terms.

There are at least two ways in which one might misinterpret the phrase "can be listed." First, of course, it is never possible to *finish* counting or listing the elements of an infinite set. Saying that $S$ is countably infinite means that we can count elements of $S$ ("zero," "one," "two,"...) in such a way that for any $x \in S$, $x$ would be counted (included in the correspondence being established) if we continued the count long enough.

A second possible source of confusion is that when we say a set $S$ is countably infinite, we are saying only that "there exists" a bijection $f$. There may or may not be an algorithm allowing us to compute $f$, or an algorithm telling us how to list the elements of $S$. Whether or not a bijection exists has to do only with how many elements are in the set; whether or not there is a computable bijection also depends on what the elements are. In particular, every language $L$ over a finite alphabet is countable (Lemma 10.2 and Example 10.7); however, there is such an algorithm only if $L$ is recursively enumerable, and as we will see, not all languages are.

Figure 10.3 illustrates one way of thinking of a countable set. We may think of each underline as a space big enough for one element of a set. The set is countable if it can be made to "fit" into the indicated spaces.

If there is a bijection from $\mathcal{N}$ to $A$ and also one from $\mathcal{N}$ to $B$, then there is one from $A$ to $B$. Therefore, any two countably infinite sets are the same size. Similarly, as we noticed earlier, a set that is the same size as a countable set is also countable.

Not all uncountable sets are the same size, if there are in fact many different sizes of infinite sets. However, an immediate consequence of the following fact is that any uncountable set is bigger than any countable one.

**Lemma 10.1**   Every infinite set has a countably infinite subset.

***Proof***   We will show that if $S$ is infinite, there is a bijection $f$ from $\mathcal{N}$ to a subset of $S$. We will define $f$ one integer at a time, as follows. Since $S$ is infinite, there is at least one element; choose one, and call it $f(0)$. In general, suppose that for some $n \geq 0$, $f(0)$, $f(1)$, ..., $f(n)$ are distinct elements of $S$. Since $S$ is infinite, there is an element of $S$ that is not one of these; choose any such element, and call it $f(n + 1)$. Therefore, by the principle of mathematical induction, $f(n)$ can be defined for every $n \geq 0$ so that the elements $f(i)$ are all distinct. ∎

One other simple fact about countable sets will be useful, and we record it as Lemma 10.2.

$$\underline{\quad}\ \ \underline{\quad}\ \ \underline{\quad}\ \ \underline{\quad}\ \ \underline{\quad}\ \ \underline{\quad}\ \ \underline{\quad}\ \ \underline{\quad}\ \ \cdots$$

**Figure 10.3 |**
Spaces to put the elements of a countable set.

**Lemma 10.2**   Every subset of a countable set is countable.

**Proof**   See Exercise 10.24.  ∎

An immediate example of a countably infinite set is the set $\mathcal{N}$ itself, and we have already seen examples of countably infinite subsets of $\mathcal{N}$. It is not hard to find many more examples. The set

$$S = \{0, 1/2, 1, 3/2, 2, 5/2, \cdots\}$$

is countably infinite; the way we have defined it is to list its elements. The set $\mathcal{Z}$ of all integers, both nonnegative and negative, is countable, because we can list the elements this way:

$$\mathcal{Z} = \{0, -1, 1, -2, 2, \cdots\}$$

One way of thinking of $\mathcal{Z}$ is as the union of the two sets $\{0, 1, 2, \ldots\}$ and $\{-1, -2, -3, \ldots\}$. For any two countably infinite sets $A = \{a_0, a_1, a_2, \ldots\}$ and $B = \{b_0, b_1, b_2, \ldots\}$, we can list the elements of the union in the same way, $\{a_0, b_0, a_1, b_1, \ldots\}$, except that any $x \in A \cap B$ should be included only once in the list. The conclusion is that the union of two countably infinite sets is countably infinite. A more dramatic result, which provides a large class of examples, is the following, often expressed informally by saying that *a countable union of countable sets is countable*.

---

**Theorem 10.13**
Suppose that for each integer $i \geq 0$, $S_i$ is a countable set. Then the set

$$S = \bigcup_{i=0}^{\infty} S_i$$

is countable.

**Proof**
If all the $S_i$'s are empty, then $S$ is empty and therefore countable. Otherwise we assume, by relabeling the sets if necessary, that $S_0 \neq \emptyset$. We describe a way of listing the elements of the union. Consider the two-dimensional "array" in which the elements of $S_i$ are listed in the $i$th row. Since $S_i$ may be finite or infinite, these rows are likely to be of unequal length. Now consider the path shown in Figure 10.4.

It is easy to convince yourself that this path will eventually hit each element of $S$ at least once. It will hit an element more than once if that element belongs to $S_i$ for more than one $i$. Suppose we define the function $f$ by

$$f(n) = \begin{cases} a_{0,0} & \text{if } n = 0 \\ \text{the first element of } S - \{f(0), \ldots, f(n-1)\} \\ \quad \text{on the path} & \text{if } n > 0 \end{cases}$$

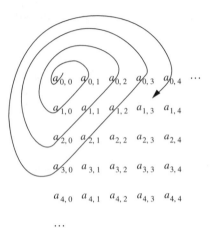

**Figure 10.4 |**
Listing the elements of $\cup_{n=0}^{\infty} S_n$.

Then $f$ is a bijection, either from $\{0, 1, \ldots, m\}$ to $S$ or from $\mathcal{N}$ to $S$, depending on whether the set $S$ is finite or infinite. Therefore, $S$ is a countable set.

Since each of the sets $\bigcup_{n=0}^{k} S_n$ is a subset of $S$, we can also conclude from Lemma 10.2 that a finite union of countable sets is countable.

Theorem 10.12 can be interpreted as saying that any uncountable set $A$ must be much, *much* bigger than any countable set $B$, because even the union of countably many sets the same size as $B$ is still countable (the same size as $B$) and therefore smaller than $A$.

**EXAMPLE 10.6**  $\mathcal{N} \times \mathcal{N}$ Is Countable

Let $S = \mathcal{N} \times \mathcal{N}$, the set of all ordered pairs of natural numbers. It follows easily from Theorem 10.13 that $S$ is countable, since

$$\mathcal{N} \times \mathcal{N} = \{(i, j) \mid i, j \geq 0\}$$
$$= \{(0, 0), (0, 1), (0, 2), \ldots\}$$
$$\cup \{(1, 0), (1, 1), (1, 2), \ldots\}$$
$$\cup \{(2, 0), (2, 1), (2, 2), \ldots\}$$
$$\cup \ldots$$

$$= \bigcup_{m=0}^{\infty} \{(m, j) \mid j \geq 0\}$$

$$= \bigcup_{m=0}^{\infty} (\{m\} \times \mathcal{N})$$

and each of the sets $\{m\} \times \mathcal{N}$ is countable because the function $f_m : \mathcal{N} \to \{m\} \times \mathcal{N}$ defined by $f_m(n) = (m, n)$ is a bijection. (Note that $\{m\} \times \mathcal{N}$ is the set of elements in the $m$th row of Figure 10.4.) However, we can be more explicit about the bijection $f$ from $\mathcal{N}$ to $\mathcal{N} \times \mathcal{N}$ illustrated in Figure 10.4 and described in the proof of Theorem 10.13. Let us consider the inverse of the bijection $f$, the function $f^{-1} : \mathcal{N} \times \mathcal{N} \to \mathcal{N}$, and give the formula for $f^{-1}(m, n)$—in other words, the formula that enumerates the pairs in $\mathcal{N} \times \mathcal{N}$.

We refer again to the path shown in Figure 10.4. Let $j \geq 0$; as the path loops through the array the $j$th time, it hits all the pairs $(m, n)$ for which $m + n = j$, and there are $j + 1$ such pairs. Furthermore, for a specific pair $(m, n)$ with $m + n = j$, there are $m$ other pairs $(p, q)$ with $p + q = j$ that get hit by the path before this one. Therefore, the total number of pairs preceding $(m, n)$ in the enumeration is

$$1 + 2 + \cdots + (m + n - 1) + (m + n) + m = (m + n)(m + n + 1)/2 + m$$

(see Example 2.7). This is just another way of saying that

$$f^{-1}(m, n) = (m + n)(m + n + 1)/2 + m$$

The function $f$ is often referred to as a *pairing* function and is useful in a number of counting arguments.

The argument used in this example can be modified easily to show that for any two countable sets $S$ and $T$, $S \times T$ is also countable.

---

## Languages Are Countable Sets    EXAMPLE 10.7

For any finite set $\Sigma$, the set $\Sigma^*$ of all strings over $\Sigma$ is countable. To see this, we write

$$\Sigma^* = \bigcup_{n=0}^{\infty} \Sigma^n$$

where $\Sigma^n$ is the set of strings over $\Sigma$ of length $n$. Since $\Sigma^n$ is finite and therefore countable, it follows from Theorem 10.13 that $\Sigma^*$ is also countable. In the simple case when $\Sigma = \{a, b\}$, one way of listing the elements of $\Sigma^*$ is to use the canonical order:

$$\{a, b\}^* = \{\Lambda, a, b, aa, ab, ba, bb, aaa, aab, \ldots\}$$

Finally, since a language $L$ over $\Sigma$ is a subset of $\Sigma^*$, Lemma 10.2 implies that $L$ is countable.

## The Set of Recursively Enumerable Languages Is Countable    EXAMPLE 10.8

Let $\mathcal{T}$ be the set of all Turing machines, and $RE$ the set of all recursively enumerable languages. Here we are following our convention that all the states of a Turing machine are elements of the fixed set $\mathcal{Q}$ and all the tape symbols elements of the set $\mathcal{S}$. In particular, the recursively enumerable languages all involve alphabets that are subsets of $\mathcal{S}$. It is possible to use Theorem 10.13 directly to show that $\mathcal{T}$ is countable; see Exercise 10.29. Instead, however, we use the encoding function $e : \mathcal{T} \rightarrow \{0, 1\}^*$ described in Section 9.6. The only property of $e$ that we need here is that it is one-to-one and therefore a bijection from $\mathcal{T}$ to some subset of $\{0, 1\}^*$. Since $\{0, 1\}^*$ is countable, any subset is, and therefore $\mathcal{T}$ is.

Now it is simple to show that $RE$ is countable as well. By definition, a recursively enumerable language $L$ can be accepted by some Turing machine. For each $L$, let $t(L)$ be such a TM. The result is a function $t$ from $RE$ to $\mathcal{T}$, and since a Turing machine accepts precisely one language, $t$ is one-to-one. Since $\mathcal{T}$ is countable, the same argument we used above shows that $RE$ is also.

---

Example 10.8 provides half of the result we are looking for. Now that we have shown the set of recursively enumerable languages to be countable, proving that there are uncountably many languages (i.e., that the set of languages is uncountable) will show that there must be non-recursively-enumerable languages.

As our first example of an uncountable set, however, we consider the set $\mathcal{R}$ of real numbers. (Theorem 10.14 actually says that a subset of $\mathcal{R}$ is uncountable, from which it follows that $\mathcal{R}$ itself is.) The proof is due to the nineteenth-century mathematician Georg Cantor. It is a famous example of a *diagonal* argument; although the logic is similar to the proof we will give for the set of languages, this proof may be a little easier to understand.

---

**Theorem 10.14**

The set $[0, 1) = \{x \in \mathcal{R} \mid 0 \leq x < 1\}$ is uncountable.

*Proof*

We use the fact that real numbers in $[0, 1)$ have infinite (possibly repeating) decimal expansions, with no digits before the decimal point. For example, $1/2 = .5000\ldots$, $1/3 = .333\ldots$, $\pi/4 = .7853981\ldots$, and so forth. It is not quite correct to say that every number in $[0, 1)$ has exactly one such expansion, because a nonzero number whose expansion terminates (or ends in an infinite string of 0's) also has an expansion ending with infinitely many 9's; for example, $1/2 = .4999\ldots$. If we agree to disallow expansions that end with strings of 9's, then every number in $[0, 1)$ has exactly one infinite decimal expansion, and every infinite decimal expansion represents a number in this interval.

We prove the theorem by contradiction. Suppose that $[0, 1)$ is countable, so that

$$[0, 1) = \{a_0, a_1, a_2, \ldots\}$$

For each $i \geq 0$, suppose the decimal expansion of $a_i$ is

$$a_i = .a_{i,0}a_{i,1}a_{i,2}\cdots$$

The contradiction is obtained by constructing a number $x \in [0, 1)$ that is not in the list. An easy way to guarantee that $x$ is different from $a_i$ for every $i$ is to make the decimal expansion of $x$ differ from that of $a_i$ in the $i$th position. Therefore, we define

$$x_i = \begin{cases} a_{i,i} + 1 & \text{if } a_{i,i} < 8 \\ 7 & \text{if } a_{i,i} \geq 8 \end{cases}$$

and let $x$ be the real number with decimal expansion $.x_0 x_1 x_2 \ldots$. The two cases in the definition are to make sure that the $x_i$'s are single digits and not eventually all 9's.

The *diagonal* aspect of the proof is that we have defined $x_i$ in terms of the $i$th diagonal term of the infinite two-dimensional matrix

$$\begin{array}{cccc} \underline{a_{0,0}} & a_{0,1} & a_{0,2} & a_{0,3} \quad \cdots \\ a_{1,0} & \underline{a_{1,1}} & a_{1,2} & a_{1,3} \quad \cdots \\ a_{2,0} & a_{2,1} & \underline{a_{2,2}} & a_{2,3} \quad \cdots \\ a_{3,0} & a_{3,1} & a_{3,2} & \underline{a_{3,3}} \quad \cdots \\ \cdots \end{array}$$

(the diagonal terms are underlined). It is clear that for every $i \geq 0$, $x_i \neq a_{i,i}$ and therefore that $x \neq a_i$. This is a contradiction, because $x \in [0, 1)$.

Note that in the proof, although finding *one* number not in the list is enough to obtain a contradiction, there are obviously many more. (The particular choice of $x_i$ is arbitrary, as long as it is neither $a_{i,i}$ nor 9.) Saying that a set is uncountable means that no matter *what* scheme you use to list elements, when you finish you will inevitably find that you have left most of the elements out.

---

**Theorem 10.15**

If $S$ is any countably infinite set, then the set $2^S$ of all subsets of $S$ is uncountably infinite. In particular, for any nonempty alphabet $\Sigma$, the set of languages over $\Sigma$ is uncountable.

***Proof***

We can simplify the proof slightly by noticing that since there is a bijection from $\mathcal{N}$ to $S$ (because $S$ is countably infinite), there is one from $2^{\mathcal{N}}$ to $2^S$. Therefore, it is enough to show that $2^{\mathcal{N}}$ is uncountable, for it will then follow that $2^S$ is also. (If $2^S$ were countable, $2^{\mathcal{N}}$, which is the same size, would be.)

Again the proof is by contradiction. Suppose $2^{\mathcal{N}}$ is countably infinite, and

$$2^{\mathcal{N}} = \{A_0, A_1, \ldots\}$$

The diagonal aspect of the previous proof was possible because we had on the one hand a list of numbers (one on each row), and on the other hand a list of the digits in each number (one in each column), and it was possible to consider the diagonal entries in the resulting matrix. We were looking for a number $x$, and we chose one so that $x$ differed from $a_i$ in the $i$th digit.

Now we have a list of subsets, and we may consider the integers that might or might not be elements of those subsets. We are looking for a subset $A$ of $\mathcal{N}$, and we can choose one so that $A$ differs from $A_i$ with respect to the natural number $i$. (The matrix involved here is the one shown in Figure 10.5, the matrix of Boolean formulas $i \notin A_j$, and the diagonal elements are the formulas $i \notin A_i$.) In other words, we can define $A$ by the formula

$$A = \{i \in \mathcal{N} \mid i \notin A_i\}$$

For any $i$, if $i \in A_i$, then $i \notin A$, and if $i \notin A_i$, then $i \in A$; therefore, $A \neq A_i$. This is a contradiction, because although $A$ is a subset of the natural numbers, it does not appear in the list.

The statement we have shown in this theorem is that $2^\mathcal{N}$ is uncountable, which is another way of saying that there is no bijection from $\mathcal{N}$ to $2^\mathcal{N}$. We should note that a more general statement is true: For *any* set $S$, the set $2^S$ is bigger than $S$ (Exercise 10.47). This statement is what allows us to say, as we noted earlier, that there are actually many different sizes of infinite sets.

**Corollary 10.1**  The set of languages over $\{0, 1\}$ that are not recursively enumerable is uncountable. In particular, there exists at least one such language.

***Proof***  The corollary follows from Theorem 10.15, from the countability of the set of recursively enumerable languages (Example 10.8), and from the fact that if $S$ is uncountable and $S_1 \subseteq S$ is countable, $S - S_1$ is uncountable (Exercise 10.27).  ∎

The proofs of Theorems 10.14 and 10.15 are nonconstructive, and the diagonal argument in these proofs appears to be closely associated with proof by contradiction. However, as we mentioned at the beginning of this section, we will construct an example of a non-recursively-enumerable language by using a diagonal argument that parallels these two very closely.

The results in Example 10.8 and Corollary 10.1 say that the set of languages that are not recursively enumerable is much bigger than the set of languages that are. Nevertheless, you might wonder how significant this conclusion is in the theory of computation. The nonconstructive proof does not shed any light on what aspects of a language might make it impossible for a TM to accept it. The same proof, in fact,

|   | 0 | 1 | 2 | 3 | ... |
|---|---|---|---|---|-----|
| 0 | $0 \notin A_0$ | $0 \notin A_1$ | $0 \notin A_2$ | $0 \notin A_3$ | ... |
| 1 | $1 \notin A_0$ | $1 \notin A_1$ | $1 \notin A_2$ | $1 \notin A_3$ | ... |
| 2 | $2 \notin A_0$ | $2 \notin A_1$ | $2 \notin A_2$ | $2 \notin A_3$ | ... |
| 3 | $3 \notin A_0$ | $3 \notin A_1$ | $3 \notin A_2$ | $3 \notin A_3$ | ... |
| ... | | | | | |

**Figure 10.5** |

shows that there must also be languages we cannot even *describe* precisely (because a precise description can be represented by a string, and the set of strings is countable). Maybe any language we might ever wish to study, or any language we *can* describe precisely, can be accepted by a TM; if this is true, then Corollary 10.1 is more of a curiosity than a negative result. At this stage in our discussion, such a possibility is conceivable. In the next chapter, however, we will see that things do not turn out this way.

# EXERCISES

**10.1.** Show that if $L_1$ and $L_2$ are recursive languages, then $L_1 \cup L_2$ and $L_1 \cap L_2$ are also recursive.

**10.2.** Consider the following alternative approach to the proof of Theorem 10.2. Given TMs $T_1$ and $T_2$ accepting $L_1$ and $L_2$, respectively, a one-tape machine is constructed to simulate these two machines sequentially. The tape $\Delta x$ is transformed to $\Delta x \# \Delta x$. $T_1$ is then simulated, using the second copy of $x$ as input and using the marker # to represent the end of the tape. If and when $T_1$ stops, either by accepting or crashing, the tape is erased except for the original input, and $T_2$ is simulated.

    a. Can this approach be made to work in order to show that the union of recursively enumerable languages is recursively enumerable? Why?

    b. Can this approach be made to work in order to show that the intersection of recursively enumerable languages is recursively enumerable? Why?

**10.3.** Is the following statement true or false? If $L_1, L_2, \ldots$ are any recursively enumerable subsets of $\Sigma^*$, then $\bigcup_{i=1}^{\infty} L_i$ is recursively enumerable. Give reasons for your answer.

**10.4.** Suppose $L_1, L_2, \ldots, L_k$ form a partition of $\Sigma^*$; in other words, their union is $\Sigma^*$ and any two are disjoint. Show that if each $L_i$ is recursively enumerable, then each $L_i$ is recursive.

**10.5.** Prove Theorem 10.7, which says that a language is recursive if and only if there is a Turing machine enumerating it in canonical order.

**10.6.** Suppose $L \subseteq \Sigma^*$. Show that $L$ is recursively enumerable if and only if there is a computable partial function from $\Sigma^*$ to $\Sigma^*$ that is defined precisely at the points of $L$.

**10.7.** The proof of Theorem 10.2 involves a result sometimes known as the "infinity lemma," which can be formulated in terms of trees. (See the discussion in the proof of Theorem 9.2 of the *computation tree* corresponding to a nondeterministic TM.) Show that if every node in a tree has at most a finite number of children, and there is no infinite path in the tree, then the tree is finite, which means that there must be a longest path from the root to a leaf node. (Here is the beginning of a proof. Suppose for the sake of contradiction that there is no longest path. Then for any $n$, there is a path from the root with more than $n$ nodes. This implies that the root node has infinitely many descendants. Since the root has only a finite number of children, at least one of its children must also have infinitely many descendants.)

**10.8.**   Describe algorithms to enumerate these sets. (You do not need to discuss the mechanics of constructing Turing machines to execute the algorithms.)

   a.   The set of all pairs $(n, m)$ for which $n$ and $m$ are relatively prime positive integers (relatively prime means having no common factor bigger than 1)

   b.   The set of all strings over $\{0, 1\}$ that contain a nonnull substring of the form $www$

   c.   $\{n \in \mathcal{N} \mid$ for some positive integers $x$, $y$, and $z$, $x^n + y^n = z^n\}$

**10.9.**   In Definition 10.2, the strings $x_i$ appearing on the output tape of $T$ are required to be distinct. Show that if $L$ can be enumerated in the weaker sense, in which this requirement is dropped, then $L$ is recursively enumerable.

**10.10.**   Show that if $f : \mathcal{N} \to \mathcal{N}$ is computable and strictly increasing, then the range of $f$ (or the set of strings representing elements of the range of $f$) is recursive.

**10.11.**   In each case, describe the language generated by the unrestricted grammar with the given productions. The symbols $a$, $b$, and $c$ are terminals, and all other symbols are variables.

   a.

$$S \to LaR \qquad L \to LD \mid \Lambda$$
$$Da \to aaD \qquad DR \to R \qquad R \to \Lambda$$

   b.

$$S \to LaR \qquad L \to LD \mid LT \mid \Lambda \qquad Da \to aaD \qquad Ta \to aaaT$$
$$DR \to R \qquad TR \to R \qquad R \to \Lambda$$

   c.

$$S \to ABCS \mid ABC$$
$$AB \to BA \qquad AC \to CA \qquad BC \to CB$$
$$BA \to AB \qquad CA \to AC \qquad CB \to BC$$
$$A \to a \qquad B \to b \qquad C \to c$$

   d.

$$S \to LA * R \qquad A \to a$$
$$L \to LI \qquad IA \to AI \qquad I* \to A * IJ \qquad IR \to A * R$$
$$JA \to AJ \qquad J* \to *J \qquad JR \to AR$$
$$LA \to EA \qquad EA \to AE \qquad E* \to E \qquad ER \to \Lambda$$

**10.12.** Consider the unrestricted grammar with the following productions.

$$S \rightarrow TD_1D_2 \qquad T \rightarrow ABCT \mid \Lambda$$

$$AB \rightarrow BA \qquad BA \rightarrow AB \qquad CA \rightarrow AC \qquad CB \rightarrow BC$$

$$CD_1 \rightarrow D_1C \qquad CD_2 \rightarrow D_2a \qquad BD_1 \rightarrow D_1b$$

$$A \rightarrow a \qquad D_1 \rightarrow \Lambda \qquad D_2 \rightarrow \Lambda$$

    a. Describe the language generated by this grammar.

    b. Find a single production that could be substituted for $BD_1 \rightarrow D_1b$ so that the resulting language would be

$$\{xa^n \mid n \geq 0, \ |x| = 2n, \ \text{and} \ n_a(x) = n_b(x) = n\}$$

**10.13.** Find unrestricted grammars to generate each of the following languages.

    a. $\{a^n b^n a^n b^n \mid n \geq 0\}$

    b. $\{a^n x b^n \mid n \geq 0, x \in \{a, b\}^*, |x| = n\}$

    c. $\{sss \mid s \in \{a, b\}^*\}$

    d. $\{ss^r s \mid s \in \{a, b\}^*\}$

**10.14.** In Example 10.3, trace the moves of *Simulate* as it simulates the derivation of the string *abba*. Show the state and tape contents at each step.

**10.15.** Suppose a nondeterministic TM is constructed as in the proof of Theorem 10.8 to accept $L(G)$, where $G$ is the grammar in Exercise 10.11(a). Draw the *Simulate* portion of the TM.

**10.16.** In the grammar in Example 10.4, give a derivation for the string *abba*.

**10.17.** Find a context-sensitive grammar generating the language $\{ss \mid s \in \{a, b\}^+\}$.

**10.18.** Find CSGs equivalent to each of the grammars in Exercise 10.11.

**10.19.** Show that if $L$ is any recursively enumerable language, then $L$ can be generated by a grammar in which the left side of every production is a string of one or more variables.

**10.20.** Show by examples that the constructions in the proof of Theorem 6.1 do not work to show that the class of recursively enumerable languages is closed under concatenation and Kleene*, or that the class of CSLs is closed under concatenation.

**10.21.** Show that if for some positive integer $k$, there is a nondeterministic TM accepting $L$ so that for any input $x$, the tape head never moves past square $k|x|$, then $L - \{\Lambda\}$ is a context-sensitive language.

**10.22.** Show that if $G$ is an unrestricted grammar generating $L$, and there is an integer $k$ so that for any $x \in L$, every string appearing in a derivation of $x$ has length $\leq k|x|$, then $L$ is recursive.

**10.23.** In the proof of Theorem 10.11, the CSG productions corresponding to an LBA move of the form $\delta(p, a) = (q, b, \text{R})$ are given. Give the productions corresponding to the move $\delta(p, a) = (q, b, \text{L})$ and those corresponding to the move $\delta(p, a) = (q, b, \text{S})$.

**10.24.** Show that any subset of a countable set is countable.

**10.25.** By definition, a set $S$ is finite if for some natural number $n$, there is a bijection from $S$ to $\{i \in \mathcal{N} \mid 1 \le i \le n\}$. An infinite set is one that is not finite. Show that a set $S$ is infinite if and only if there is a bijection from $S$ to some proper subset of $S$. (Lemma 10.1 might be helpful.)

**10.26.** Saying that a property is *preserved under bijection* means that if a set $S$ has the property and $f : S \to T$ is a bijection, then $T$ also has the property. Show that both countability and uncountability are preserved under bijection.

**10.27.** Show that if $S$ is uncountable and $T$ is countable, then $S - T$ is uncountable.

**10.28.** Let $Q$ be the set of all rational numbers, or fractions, negative as well as nonnegative. Show that $Q$ is countable by describing explicitly a bijection from $\mathcal{N}$ to $Q$.

**10.29.** In Example 10.8, the encoding function $e$ was used to show that the set of Turing machines is countable. Show the same thing without using $e$, by applying Theorem 10.13 directly.

**10.30.** Let $S$ be the set of all infinite sequences of 0's and 1's.
  a. Describe a bijection from $S$ to the set $2^{\mathcal{N}}$. It follows from Theorem 10.15, then, that $S$ is uncountable.
  b. Show directly, using a diagonal argument, that $S$ is uncountable. Begin by supposing that there is a list $s_0, s_1, \ldots$ of the elements of $S$, and find an $s \in S$ that is not in the list. Convince yourself, using your solution to part (a), that this proof is essentially the same as the proof given to Theorem 10.15.

**10.31.** In each case, determine whether the given set is countable or uncountable. Prove your answer.
  a. The set of all three-element subsets of $\mathcal{N}$
  b. The set of all finite subsets of $\mathcal{N}$
  c. The set of all finite partitions of $\mathcal{N}$ (A finite partition of $\mathcal{N}$ is a set of nonempty subsets $A_1, A_2, \ldots, A_k$, so that any two are disjoint and $\bigcup_{i=1}^{k} A_i = \mathcal{N}$.)
  d. The set of all functions from $\mathcal{N}$ to $\{0, 1\}$
  e. The set of all functions from $\{0, 1\}$ to $\mathcal{N}$
  f. The set of all functions from $\mathcal{N}$ to $\mathcal{N}$
  g. The set of all nonincreasing functions from $\mathcal{N}$ to $\mathcal{N}$
  h. The set of all regular languages over $\{0, 1\}$
  i. The set of all context-free languages over $\{0, 1\}$

**10.32.** We know that $2^{\mathcal{N}}$ is uncountable. Give an example of a set $S \subseteq 2^{\mathcal{N}}$ so that both $S$ and $2^{\mathcal{N}} - S$ are uncountable.

**10.33.** Show that the set of languages $L$ over $\{0, 1\}$ so that neither $L$ nor $L'$ is recursively enumerable is uncountable.

# MORE CHALLENGING PROBLEMS

**10.34.** Suppose $L$ is recursively enumerable but not recursive. Show that if $T$ is a TM accepting $L$, there must be infinitely many input strings for which $T$ loops forever.

**10.35.** Sketch a proof that the class of recursively enumerable languages is closed under the operations of concatenation and Kleene *. (Use nondeterminism.)

**10.36.** Canonical order is a specific way of ordering the strings in $\Sigma^*$, and its use in Theorem 10.7 is somewhat arbitrary. By an ordering of $\Sigma^*$, we mean simply a bijection from the set of natural numbers to $\Sigma^*$. For any such bijection $f$, and any language $L \subseteq \Sigma^*$, let us say that "$L$ can be enumerated in order $f$" means that the order of the enumeration is the same as the order induced on $L$ by $f$—in other words, there is a TM $T$ enumerating $L$, and if $x_i$ is the $i$th string appearing on the output tape of $T$, the sequence $f^{-1}(x_i)$ of natural numbers is increasing.

   For an arbitrary ordering $f$ of $\Sigma^*$, let $E(f)$ be the statement "For any $L \subseteq \Sigma^*$, $L$ is recursive if and only if it can be enumerated in order $f$." For exactly which types of orderings $f$ is $E(f)$ true? Prove your answer.

**10.37.** Let $f : \{0, 1\}^* \to \{0, 1\}^*$ be a partial function. Let $g(f)$, the *graph* of $f$, be the language $\{x\#f(x) \mid x \in \{0, 1\}^*\}$. Show that $f$ can be computed by a Turing machine if and only if the language $g(f)$ is recursively enumerable.

**10.38.** Suppose $L \subseteq \Sigma^*$. Show that $L$ is recursively enumerable if and only if there is a computable partial function from $\Sigma^*$ to $\Sigma^*$ whose *range* is $L$.

**10.39.** This exercise is taken from Dowling (1989). It has to do with an actual computer, which is assumed to use some fixed operating system under which all its programs run. A "program" can be thought of as a function from strings to strings: it takes one string as input and produces another string as output. On the other hand, a program written in a specific language can be thought of as a string itself.

   By definition, a program $P$ spreads a *virus* on input $x$ if running $P$ with input $x$ causes the operating system to be altered. It is safe on input $x$ if this doesn't happen, and it is safe if it is safe on every input string. A *virus tester* is a program IsSafe that when given the input $Px$, where $P$ is a program and $x$ is a string, produces the output "YES" if $P$ is safe on input $x$ and "NO" otherwise. (We make the assumption that in a string of the form $Px$, there is no ambiguity as to where the program $P$ stops.)

   Prove that if there is the actual possibility of a virus—that is, there is a program and an input that would cause the operating system to be altered—then there can be no virus tester that is both safe and correct. Hint: suppose there is such a virus tester IsSafe. Then it is possible to write a program $D$ (for *diagonal*) that operates as follows when given a program $P$ as input. It evaluates IsSafe(PP); if the result is "NO," it prints "XXX", and otherwise it alters the operating system. Now consider what $D$ does on input $D$.

**10.40.** Show that an infinite recursively enumerable set has an infinite recursive subset.

**10.41.** Find unrestricted grammars to generate each of the following languages.

a. $\{x \in \{a, b, c\}^* \mid n_a(x) < n_b(x) \text{ and } n_a(x) < n_c(x)\}$

b. $\{x \in \{a, b, c\}^* \mid n_a(x) < n_b(x) < 2n_c(x)\}$

c. $\{a^n \mid n = j(j+1)/2 \text{ for some } j \geq 1\}$ (Suggestion: if a string has $j$ groups of $a$'s, the $i$th group containing $i$ $a$'s, then you can create $j+1$ groups by adding an $a$ to each of the $j$ groups and adding a single extra $a$ at the beginning.)

**10.42.** Suppose $G$ is a context-sensitive grammar. In other words, for every production $\alpha \to \beta$ of $G$, $|\beta| \geq |\alpha|$. Show that there is a grammar $G'$, with $L(G') = L(G)$, in which every production is of the form

$$\alpha A \beta \to \alpha X \beta$$

where $A$ is a variable and $\alpha$, $\beta$, and $X$ are strings of variables and/or terminals, with $X$ not null.

**10.43.** A context-sensitive grammar is said to be in *Kuroda normal form* if each of its productions takes one of the four forms $A \to a$, $A \to B$, $A \to BC$, or $AB \to CD$, where $a$ is a terminal and the uppercase letters are variables. Show that every CSL can be generated by a grammar in Kuroda normal form.

**10.44.** Use the LBA characterization of context-sensitive languages to show that the class of CSLs is closed under union, intersection, and concatenation, and that if $L$ is a CSL so is $L^+$.

**10.45.** Suppose $G_1$ and $G_2$ are unrestricted grammars generating $L_1$ and $L_2$, respectively.

a. By modifying $G_1$ and $G_2$ if necessary, find an unrestricted grammar generating $L_1 L_2$.

b. By modifying the procedure described in the proof of Theorem 6.1, find an unrestricted grammar generating $L_1^*$.

c. Adapt your answer to part (b) to show that if $L_1$ is a CSL, then $L_1^+$ is also.

**10.46.** In the proof of Theorem 10.15, we assumed that the elements of $2^{\mathcal{N}}$ were $A_0, A_1, \ldots$, and constructed a set $A$ not in the list by letting $A = \{i \mid i \notin A_i\}$. Starting with the same list, find a different formula for a set $B$ not in the list.

**10.47.** The two parts of this exercise show that for any set $S$ (not necessarily countable), $2^S$ is larger than $S$. It follows that there are infinitely many "orders of infinity."

a. For any $S$, describe a simple bijection from $S$ to a subset of $2^S$.

b. Show that for any $S$, there is no bijection from $S$ to $2^S$. (You can copy the proof of Theorem 10.15, as long as you avoid trying to list the elements of $S$ or making any reference to the countability of $S$.)

**10.48.** In each case, determine whether the given set is countable or uncountable. Prove your answer.

a. The set of all real numbers that are roots of integer polynomials; in other words, the set of real numbers $x$ so that, for some nonnegative integer $n$ and some integers $a_0, a_1, \ldots, a_n$, $x$ is a solution to the equation

$$a_0 + a_1 x + a_2 x^2 + \cdots + a_n x^n = 0$$

b. The set of all nondecreasing functions from $\mathcal{N}$ to $\mathcal{N}$

c. The set of all functions from $\mathcal{N}$ to $\mathcal{N}$ whose range is finite

d. The set of all nondecreasing functions from $\mathcal{N}$ to $\mathcal{N}$ whose range is finite (i.e, all "step" functions)

e. The set of all periodic functions from $\mathcal{N}$ to $\mathcal{N}$ (A function $f : \mathcal{N} \to \mathcal{N}$ is periodic if, for some positive integer $P_f$, $f(x + P_f) = f(x)$ for every $x$.)

f. The set of all eventually periodic functions from $\mathcal{N}$ to $\mathcal{N}$ (A function $f : \mathcal{N} \to \mathcal{N}$ is eventually periodic if, for some positive $P_f$ and for some $N$, $f(x + P_f) = f(x)$ for every $x \geq N$.)

g. The set of all eventually constant functions from $\mathcal{N}$ to $\mathcal{N}$ (A function $f : \mathcal{N} \to \mathcal{N}$ is eventually constant if, for some $C$ and for some $N$, $f(x) = C$ for every $x \geq N$.)

**10.49.** We have said that a set $A$ is larger than a set $B$ if there is a bijection from $B$ to a subset of $A$, but no bijection from $B$ to $A$, and we have proceeded to use this terminology much as we use the $<$ relation on the set of numbers. What we have not done is to show that this relation satisfies the same essential properties that $<$ does.

a. The *Schröder-Bernstein Theorem* asserts that if $A$ and $B$ are sets and there are bijections $f$ from $A$ to a subset of $B$ and $g$ from $B$ to a subset of $A$, then there is a bijection from $A$ to $B$. Prove this statement. Here is a suggested approach. An *ancestor* of $a \in A$ is a point $b \in B$ so that $g(b) = a$, or a point $a_1 \in A$ so that $g(f(a_1)) = a$, or a point $b_1 \in B$ so that $g(f(g(b_1))) = a$, etc. In other words, an ancestor of $a \in A$ is a point $x$ in $A$ or $B$ so that by starting at $x$ and continuing to evaluate the two functions alternately, we arrive at $a$. If $g(f(g(b))) = a$ and $b$ has no ancestors, for example, we will say that $a$ has the three ancestors $f(g(b)), g(b)$, and $b$. Note that we describe the number of ancestors as three, even in the case that $f(g(b)) = b$ or $g(b) = a$. In this way, $A$ can be partitioned into three sets $A_0, A_1$, and $A_\infty$; $A_0$ is the set of elements of $A$ having an even (finite) number of ancestors, $A_1$ is the set of elements having an odd number, and $A_\infty$ is the set of points having an infinite number of ancestors. Ancestors of elements of $B$ are defined the same way, and we can partition $B$ similarly into $B_0, B_1$, and $B_\infty$. Show that there are bijections from $A_0$ to $B_1$, from $A_1$ to $B_0$, and from $A_\infty$ to $B_\infty$.

   b.  Show that the "larger-than" relation on sets is transitive. In other words, if there is a bijection from $A$ to a subset of $B$ but none from $A$ to $B$, and a bijection from $B$ to a subset of $C$ but none from $B$ to $C$, then there is a bijection from $A$ to a subset of $C$ but none from $A$ to $C$.

   c.  Show that the larger-than relation is asymmetric. In other words, if $A$ is larger than $B$, then $B$ cannot be larger than $A$.

   d.  Show that countable sets are the smallest infinite sets in both possible senses: Not only are uncountable sets larger than countable sets, but no infinite set can be smaller than a countable set.

**10.50.**  Let $I$ be the unit interval $[0, 1]$, the set of real numbers between 0 and 1. Let $S = I \times I$, the unit square. Use the Schröder-Bernstein theorem (see the previous exercise) to show that there is a bijection from $I$ to $S$. One way is to use infinite decimal expansions as in the proof of Theorem 10.14.

**10.51.**  Show that $A$ is bigger than $B$ if and only if there is a one-to-one function from $B$ to $A$ but none from $A$ to $B$. (One way is easy; for the other, Exercise 10.49 will be helpful.)

# 5

# Unsolvable Problems and Computable Functions

**A** ccording to the Church-Turing thesis, any algorithm can be programmed on a Turing machine. For this reason, any problem that cannot be solved by a Turing machine can legitimately be called *unsolvable*.

Having used a diagonal argument in Part IV to establish the existence of languages that no Turing machine can accept, we use a similar argument to produce an example, which begins our study of unsolvable problems. In Chapter 11, we consider a general method of reducing one language, or one decision problem, to another. The result is a large class of unsolvable problems, including problems having to do with TMs themselves, problems involving context-free languages, and others that can be stated in general combinatorial terms.

After looking at problems that cannot be solved, we return to those that can and try to characterize them independently of Turing machines. In Chapter 12, we prove that the functions computable by Turing machines are precisely those that can be obtained by beginning with certain initial functions and applying three operations: composition and two new operations, primitive recursion and unbounded minimalization. Finally, we mention a few other formulations of computability. We can see why they are equivalent to the Turing-machine formulation, and we can view this equivalence as further evidence that the Church-Turing thesis is correct. ■

# 11

# Unsolvable Problems

## 11.1 | A NONRECURSIVE LANGUAGE AND AN UNSOLVABLE PROBLEM

The set of recursively enumerable languages is countable and the set of non-recursively-enumerable languages is uncountable (Example 10.8 and Corollary 10.1). If we could somehow choose a language at random, it would almost certainly not be recursively enumerable. Although this observation does not make it obvious how to find a *specific* language $L$ no TM can accept, we can find one by using the same type of diagonal argument as in Chapter 10.

What will be the defining property of an element of $L$? In the diagonal argument in Theorem 10.15, starting with sets $A_i$, we obtained a set $A$ different from each $A_i$ in that

$$i \in A \quad \text{if and only if} \quad i \notin A_i$$

Here we want to show that for every Turing machine $T$, our language $L$ is different from $L(T)$, the language accepted by $T$. An analogous approach, therefore, is first to associate a string $x_T$ to each TM $T$ (in the same way that a natural number $i$ is associated with a set $A_i$), and then to let

$$x_T \in L \quad \text{if and only if} \quad x_T \notin L(T)$$

In other words, force $x_T$ to be accepted by any TM accepting $L$ precisely if it is not accepted by $T$.

One way to associate strings with TMs is simply to list all the strings in $\{0, 1\}^*$ $(x_0, x_1, \ldots)$, list all the TMs $(T_0, T_1, \ldots)$, and let the string associated with $T_i$ be $x_i$. In our previous example the assumption that it was possible to list all the subsets of $\mathcal{N}$ was made in order to obtain a contradiction. Here, we *can* list the TMs, because the set of all of them is countable. We might then consider the set $L$ of all strings $x_i$ for which $T_i$ does not accept $x_i$. Although this version of the diagonal argument works, there will be some advantage later on in associating a string with a TM $T$ in a less arbitrary way. A natural choice for $x_T$ is $e(T)$, the string that describes $T$ in our encoding scheme. This approach makes it unnecessary to use countability explicitly, since we do not need any particular ordering of either the set of TMs or the set of strings.

---

### Definition 11.1    The Languages *NSA* and *SA*

Let *NSA* (short for *non-self-accepting*) be the language

$$NSA = \{w \in \{0, 1\}^* \mid w = e(T) \quad \text{for some TM } T, \text{ and } w \notin L(T)\}$$

and *SA* (*self-accepting*) the language

$$SA = \{w \in \{0, 1\}^* \mid w = e(T) \quad \text{for some TM } T, \text{ and } w \in L(T)\}$$

---

### Theorem 11.1
The language *NSA* is not recursively enumerable.

***Proof***
For any $T$, the string $e(T)$ is an element of *NSA* if and only if it is *not* accepted by $T$. For $T$ to accept *NSA* it must be true that $e(T) \in NSA$ if and only if $e(T)$ *is* accepted by $T$. Therefore, no Turing machine $T$ can accept *NSA*.

---

The two languages *SA* and *NSA* are almost the complements of each other. More precisely, $\{0, 1\}^*$ is the union of the three disjoint sets *SA*, *NSA*, and $E'$, where $E = SA \cup NSA$, the set of all strings of the form $e(T)$ for some TM $T$. The following simple result will make it easy to draw the conclusions we want from this fact.

**Lemma 11.1**    The language $E = \{e(T) \mid T \text{ is a TM}\}$ is recursive.

***Proof***    The encoding function $e$ is described in Section 9.6. It is easy to check that a string $x$ of 0's and 1's is in $E$ if and only if it satisfies these conditions:

1. $x$ corresponds to the regular expression $0000^*1((0^+1)^5)^+$, so that the substring following the first 1 can be viewed as a sequence of 5-tuples.

2. For two distinct 5-tuples $y$ and $z$ in the string $x$, the first two of the five parts of $y$ cannot be the same as the first two of the five parts of $z$. (A deterministic TM cannot have two distinct moves for the same state-symbol combination.)

3. None of the 5-tuples in $x$ can have first part 0 or 00. (A TM cannot move from a halt state.)

4. The last part of each 5-tuple must be 0, 00, or 000 (representing one of the three directions).

Any string satisfying these conditions represents a TM, whether or not it carries out any meaningful computation. There is an algorithm to take an arbitrary element of $\{0, 1\}^*$ and determine the truth or falsity of each condition, and it is not difficult to implement such an algorithm on a Turing machine. ■

Of the three languages *NSA*, *SA*, and *E*, we now know that the first is not recursively enumerable and therefore not recursive, and the third is recursive. It follows from the formula $NSA = SA' \cap E$ that $SA$ cannot be recursive (Theorem 10.4 and Exercise 10.1). However, although the definitions of *SA* and *NSA* are obviously similar, the first language does turn out to be recursively enumerable.

---

**Theorem 11.2**

The language *SA* is recursively enumerable but not recursive.

*Proof*

It remains only to show that *SA* is recursively enumerable. The intuitive reason *NSA* is not recursively enumerable is that a TM $T$ for which $e(T) \in$ *NSA* might fail to accept this string by looping forever. In other words, the straightforward approach of testing $e(T)$ by simply executing $T$ on it does not work, because the strings for which we need the algorithm to halt (those in *NSA*) are precisely those for which it might not. In the case of *SA*, the difficulty disappears, since our straightforward algorithm *is* guaranteed to halt for the strings in the language.

Let us describe more systematically how to build a TM accepting *SA*. It operates by first testing the input string $x$ to see if $x = e(T)$ for some TM $T$ (i.e., to see if $x \in E$). If not, it rejects. Otherwise, it computes the encoded version $e(x) = e(e(T))$, concatenates $x$ with this to obtain $e(T)e(e(T))$, and executes a universal TM on this input. The result is that the TM accepts if and only if $T$ accepts $e(T)$, and thus the strings accepted are precisely those in *SA*.

---

The three languages *SA*, *NSA*, and $E'$ are closely related to the decision problem

**Self-accepting:** Given a TM $T$, does $T$ accept the string $e(T)$?

The three sets contain the strings representing yes-instances, no-instances, and non-instances, respectively, of the problem.

In order to solve a general decision problem $P$, we start the same way, by choosing an encoding function $e$ so that we can represent instances $I$ by strings $e(I)$ over some alphabet $\Sigma$. Let us give the names $Y(P)$ and $N(P)$ to the sets of strings representing yes-instances and no-instances of $P$. Then, if $E(P) = Y(P) \cup N(P)$, we have the third set $E'(P)$ of strings not representing instances, just as in our first example.

Any reasonable encoding function $e$ must be one-to-one, so that a string can represent at most one instance of $P$. It must be possible to *decode* a string $e(I)$ and recover the instance $I$. Finally, there should be an algorithm to decide whether a given string in $\Sigma^*$ represents an instance of $P$; in other words (since "algorithm" means TM), the language $E(P)$ should be recursive.

If we start with the decision problem $P$, solving it means answering the question of whether an arbitrary instance $I$ is a yes-instance of $P$, and the model of computation we use is the Turing machine. The question that a TM $T$ may be able to answer directly is whether a string $x$ *represents* a yes-instance (this is the *membership problem* for the language $Y(P)$). These two questions sound slightly different, and it sounds as though the second may be somewhat harder: Before we can even start thinking about whether an instance is a yes-instance, we must first decide whether a string represents an instance at all. However, we do not generally distinguish between the two problems. The extra work involved in the second simply reflects the fact that TMs require input strings encoded over the input alphabet. Because of the conditions we require our encoding function to satisfy, we will be able to answer the first question if and only if we can answer the second.

With this discussion, we are ready to define a *solvable*, or *decidable*, decision problem.

---

### Definition 11.2    Solvable, or Decidable, Decision Problems

If $e$ is a reasonable encoding of a decision problem $P$ over the alphabet $\Sigma$, we say $P$ is *solvable*, or *decidable*, if the associated language $Y(P) = \{e(I) \mid I$ is a yes-instance of $P\} \subseteq \Sigma^*$ is a recursive language.

---

### Theorem 11.3
The decision problem **Self-accepting** is unsolvable.

*Proof*
The theorem follows immediately from Definition 11.2 and Theorem 11.2.

---

As we have seen, the language *SA* happens to be recursively enumerable, whereas *NSA* is not. However, neither language is recursive, and the two can be thought of as representing essentially the same unsolvable problem. (For any problem $P$, just as in our example, if either $Y(P)$ or $N(P)$ fails to be recursively enumerable, then neither language can be recursive.) The strings in *NSA* represent no-instances of **Self-accepting**, or yes-instances of the complementary problem: Given a TM $T$, does $T$ fail to accept $e(T)$? An algorithmic procedure attempting to answer either question would eventually hit an instance (a yes-instance or a no-instance) it could not handle.

Finally, it is important to understand that a decision problem can be unsolvable and still have many instances for which answers are easy to find. There are obviously many TMs $T$ for which we can decide whether $T$ accepts $e(T)$. What makes **Self-**

**accepting** unsolvable is that there is no single algorithm guaranteed to produce the correct answer for every instance.

# 11.2 | REDUCING ONE PROBLEM TO ANOTHER: THE HALTING PROBLEM

Our first example of an unsolvable decision problem is the problem we have called **Self-accepting**. We used a diagonal argument to show it is unsolvable, and the characteristic circularity of this argument accounts for the convoluted nature of the problem itself. Once we have one unsolvable problem, however, others will be easier to find, including some that sound more natural and whose significance may be a little more obvious. For the time being, the unsolvable problems we obtain will continue to be problems about Turing machines; later in this chapter we will see some that are more diverse.

If we can establish that one decision problem, $P_1$, can be reduced to another, $P_2$, or that having a general solution to $P_2$ would guarantee a general solution to $P_1$, then it is reasonable to say informally that $P_1$ is no harder than $P_2$. It should then follow that if $P_2$ is solvable, $P_1$ is solvable (or equivalently, if $P_1$ is unsolvable, $P_2$ is unsolvable).

Let us start with two examples involving finite automata. First, let $P_1$ be the problem: Given a nondeterministic finite automaton $M$ and a string $x$, does $M$ accept $x$? The presence of nondeterminism means that a solution algorithm cannot be as straightforward as "run $M$ on $x$ and see what happens." However, the subset construction provides an algorithm (see the proof of Theorem 4.1) to take an NFA and produce an equivalent FA. We may therefore reduce $P_1$ to the problem $P_2$, for which the straightforward approach does work: Given an FA $M$ and a string $x$, does $M$ accept $x$? Let us look more carefully at the steps involved when we solve $P_1$ this way. We start with an arbitrary instance $I$ of $P_1$: a pair $(M, x)$, where $M$ is an NFA and $x$ is a string that might or might not be accepted by $M$. We answer the question by computing an instance $F(I)$ of $P_2$, consisting of a pair $(N, y)$, where $N$ is an FA and $y$ is a string. In this case, $N$ is the FA produced by the subset-construction algorithm, accepting the same language as $M$, and $y$ is simply $x$. Determining whether $y$ is accepted by $N$ tells us whether $x$ is accepted by $M$.

For the second example, let $P_1$ be the problem: Given two FAs $M_1$ and $M_2$, is $L(M_1) \subseteq L(M_2)$? As we described in Section 5.4, we can reduce this problem to $P_2$: Given an FA $M$, is $L(M) = \emptyset$? The reduction consists of starting with $I = (M_1, M_2)$, an instance of $P_1$, and computing an instance $F(I) = M$ of $P_2$ by letting $M$ be an FA accepting $L(M_1) - L(M_2)$ (see Theorem 3.4). Since $L(M_1) \subseteq L(M_2)$ if and only if $L(M_1) - L(M_2) = \emptyset$, $F(I)$ is a yes-instance of $P_2$ if and only if $I$ is a yes-instance of $P_1$; in other words, the answers for the two instances are the same.

In both these examples, the two crucial aspects of the reduction are: first, that we be able to carry out the computation of $F(I)$, given $I$; second, that the answer to the first question involving $I$ be the same as the answer to the second question involving $F(I)$.

---

**Definition 11.3    Reducing One Decision Problem to Another**

If $P_1$ and $P_2$ are decision problems, we say $P_1$ is reducible to $P_2$ (written $P_1 \leq P_2$) if there is an algorithmic procedure that allows us, given an arbitrary instance $I$ of $P_1$, to find an instance $F(I)$ of $P_2$ so that for every $I$, the answers for the two instances $I$ and $F(I)$ are the same.

---

The situation in which it is easiest to say precisely what the phrase *algorithmic procedure* means is that in which $P_1$ and $P_2$ are the membership problems for two languages $L_1 \subseteq \Sigma_1^*$ and $L_2 \subseteq \Sigma_2^*$, respectively. In this case an instance of $P_1$ is a string $x \in \Sigma_1^*$ and an instance of $P_2$ is a string $y \in \Sigma_2^*$. Finding a $y$ for each $x$ means computing a function from $\Sigma_1^*$ to $\Sigma_2^*$, and this can be done directly by a TM. It makes sense in this case to talk about reducing the first language to the second.

---

**Definition 11.3a    Reducing One Language to Another**

If $L_1$ and $L_2$ are languages, over alphabets $\Sigma_1$ and $\Sigma_2$, respectively, we say that $L_1$ is reducible to $L_2$, denoted $L_1 \leq L_2$, if there is a Turing-computable function $f : \Sigma_1^* \to \Sigma_2^*$ so that for any $x \in \Sigma_1^*$,

$$x \in L_1 \quad \text{if and only if} \quad f(x) \in L_2$$

(This type of reducibility is sometimes called *many-one* reducibility.)

---

If $L_1 \leq L_2$, being able to solve the membership problem for $L_2$ allows us to solve the problem for $L_1$, as follows. If we have a string $x \in \Sigma_1^*$ and we want to decide whether $x \in L_1$, we can answer the question indirectly by computing $f(x)$ and deciding whether that string is in $L_2$. The answers to the two questions are the same, because $x \in L_1$ if and only if $f(x) \in L_2$.

In a more general situation, as we discussed in the previous section, we can normally identify the decision problems $P_1$ and $P_2$ with the membership problems for the corresponding languages $Y(P_1)$ and $Y(P_2)$, assuming that we have appropriate encoding functions. This means in particular that the statement $P_1 \leq P_2$ is equivalent to the statement $Y(P_1) \leq Y(P_2)$ (see Exercises 11.23–11.25). In the proof of Theorem 11.5, we discuss the reduction used in the proof, both at the level of problem instances, which is normally a little easier to think about, and at the level of languages, which allows us to be a little more precise. After that we will normally stick to the one most directly applicable.

The most obvious reason for thinking about reductions is that we might be able to solve a problem $P$ by reducing it to another problem $Q$ that we already know how to solve. However, it is important to separate the idea of reducing one problem to another from the question of whether either of the problems can be solved. The specific reason for discussing reductions in this chapter is to obtain more examples of *un*solvable problems.

> **Theorem 11.4**
>
> For any languages $L_1 \subseteq \Sigma_1^*$ and $L_2 \subseteq \Sigma_2^*$ with $L_1 \leq L_2$, if $L_2$ is recursive then $L_1$ is recursive (or equivalently, if $L_1$ is not recursive, neither is $L_2$). For any decision problems $P_1$ and $P_2$ with $P_1 \leq P_2$, if $P_2$ is solvable then $P_1$ is solvable (or, if $P_1$ is unsolvable, $P_2$ is unsolvable).
>
> *Proof*
>
> Suppose $T_2$ is a language recognizing, or deciding, $L_2$, and suppose $T_f$ is a TM computing the function $f : \Sigma_1^* \to \Sigma_2^*$ involved in the reduction. Let $T_1$ be the composite TM $T_1 = T_f T_2$. On input $x \in \Sigma_1^*$, $T_1$ first computes $f(x)$, then halts with output 1 or 0, depending on whether $f(x)$ is in $L_2$ or not. The assumption that $f$ is a reduction of $L_1$ to $L_2$ means that the output is 1 if $x \in L_1$ and 0 otherwise, and it follows that $T_1$ recognizes $L_1$.
>
> The second statement of the theorem follows from our previous discussion of the relationship between decision problems and the corresponding languages.

If the problem of whether a TM $T$ accepts the string $e(T)$ is unsolvable, we should not expect to be able to solve the more general membership problem for recursively enumerable languages, which we abbreviate **Accepts**.

**Accepts:** Given a TM $T$ and a string $w$, is $w \in L(T)$?

It is worth mentioning once more why the obvious approach to the problem (give the input string $w$ to the TM $T$, and see what happens) is not a solution: This approach will produce an answer only if $T$ halts, not if it loops forever.

An instance of **Accepts** consists of a pair $(T, w)$, where $T$ is a Turing machine and $w$ a string. With our encoding function $e$, we can represent such a pair by the string $e(T)e(w)$, and so we consider the language

$$Acc = \{e(T)e(w) \mid w \in L(T)\}$$

> **Theorem 11.5**
>
> **Accepts** is unsolvable.
>
> *Proof*
>
> The intuitive idea of the proof is the observation we have already made: If we could decide, for an arbitrary TM $T$ and an arbitrary string $w$, whether $T$ accepted $w$, then we could decide whether an arbitrary TM $T$ accepted $e(T)$, and we know that this is impossible. To make this precise, we will reduce **Self-accepting** to **Accepts** and use the last statement in Theorem 11.4. In order to show that **Self-accepting** can be reduced to **Accepts**, we must describe an algorithm for producing an instance $F(I)$ of **Accepts** from a given instance $I$ of **Self-accepting**. $I$ is a Turing machine $T$, and $F(I)$ is

to be a pair $(T_1, w)$, where $T_1$ is a TM and $w$ is a string. We want $T_1$ to accept $w$ if and only if $T$ accepts the string $e(T)$. The natural choice, therefore, is to let $T_1 = T$ and $w = e(T)$.

At the level of strings, we can show **Accepts** is unsolvable by showing the language $Acc$ is not recursive, using the language $SA$. According to the first part of Theorem 11.4, it is sufficient to show $SA \le Acc$, because we know from Theorem 11.2 that $SA$ is not recursive.

Since elements of both languages are strings of 0's and 1's, what we need is a computable function $f : \{0, 1\}^* \to \{0, 1\}^*$ such that for any $x \in \{0, 1\}^*$,

$$x \in SA \quad \text{if and only if} \quad f(x) \in Acc$$

The first part of the proof already suggests how to define $f(x)$ in the case when $x = e(T)$ for some $T$; we want $f(x)$ to represent the pair $(T, e(T))$, and so we define $f(x) = f(e(T)) = e(T)e(e(T)) = xe(x)$. For a string $x$ that is not of the form $e(T)$, $f(x)$ must not be an element of $Acc$, and an easy way to guarantee this is to define $f(x) = \Lambda$.

If the string $x$ is in $SA$, then $x = e(T)$ for some TM $T$ accepting $x$. In this case, the string $f(x) = xe(x) = e(T)e(x)$ is an element of $Acc$. Conversely, if $x \notin SA$, then either $x$ is not of the form $e(T)$ at all, in which case $f(x) = \Lambda$, or $x$ is $e(T)$ for some $T$ not accepting $x$, in which case $f(x) = xe(x)$. In either case, $f(x) \notin Acc$.

To finish the proof it is sufficient to show that our function $f$ can be computed by a TM. We can proceed in two steps. First, we make a second copy of the input string $x$ and test the copy (using Lemma 11.1) to determine whether it is $e(T)$ for some $T$. If it is not, we simply erase the tape and leave the tape head in square 0, so as to produce output $\Lambda$. If it is, we erase all but the original copy of $x$, write the encoded string $e(x)$ on the tape after $x$, and halt with the tape head on square 0.

In this proof, the argument involving instances $T$ and $(T_1, x)$ of the two problems seems simpler and more straightforward than the one involving languages. However, if you compare them carefully, you can see that the key steps are almost exactly the same. The definition $f(x) = xe(x)$ in the second argument is simply the string version of the definition $F(T) = (T, e(T))$ in the first. The details that make the second proof more complicated have to do first with deciding whether the input string is an instance of the problem, and then with the necessary decoding and encoding of strings.

The most well-known unsolvable problem, the *halting problem*, is closely related to the membership problem for recursively enumerable languages. For a given TM $T$ and a given string $w$, instead of asking whether $T$ accepts $w$, it asks whether $T$ halts (by accepting or rejecting) on input $w$. We abbreviate the problem **Halts**.

**Halts:** Given a TM $T$ and a string $w$, does $T$ halt on input $w$?

Just as before, we can consider the corresponding language

$$H = \{e(T)e(w) \mid T \text{ halts on input } w\}$$

**Theorem 11.6**
The halting problem **Halts** is unsolvable.

*Proof*
We will show that **Accepts** can be reduced to **Halts**, and it will follow from Theorems 11.4 and 11.5 that **Halts** is unsolvable.

For both problems, an instance is a pair consisting of a TM and a string. Given a pair $(T, w)$, an instance of **Accepts**, we must construct another pair $(T_1, w_1)$, an instance of **Halts**, so that the answers are the same in both cases. This means that $T_1$ and $w_1$ must be constructed so that $T_1$ halts on input $w_1$ if and only if $T$ accepts $w$. In other words, if $T$ accepts $w$, $T_1$ must halt on $w_1$, and if $T$ either rejects $w$ or loops forever on $w$, $T_1$ must not halt on $w_1$. Let us choose $w_1 = w$ (why not?), and try to obtain $T_1$ by modifying $T$. In two of the three cases, $T_1$ can process $w$ the same way $T$ does, because if $T$ either accepts $w$ or loops forever on $w$, our constraints allow $T_1$ to do the same thing. If $T$ rejects $w$, however, $T_1$ must not halt on $w$.

In order to accomplish this, it is almost sufficient to obtain $T_1$ from $T$ by changing any move of the form $\delta(p, a) = (h_r, b, D)$ to $\delta(p, a) = (p, a, S)$. This change means that if $T$ ever arrives in state $p$ with $a$ on the current square, $T_1$ is stuck in this state and on this square forever. The reason this change is not quite sufficient is that $T$ might enter the reject state by trying to move its tape head left, off the tape. Let us therefore incorporate one other modification in our machine $T_1$. $T_1$ will begin by inserting a new symbol, say #, in square 0, moving everything else over one square, and then move to $q_0$ with the tape head in square 1. Aside from the moves required to do that, $T_1$ has the same moves as $T$ (except for the modification already described), as well as the additional moves $\delta(q, \#) = (q, \#, S)$ for all possible states $q$. The effect is that if $T$ ever tries to move its tape head off the tape, $T_1$ will enter an infinite loop with its tape head on square 0.

This algorithm for obtaining $T_1$ from $T$ gives us the reduction we need, and we conclude that **Halts** is unsolvable.

The fact that the decision problem **Self-accepting** is unsolvable is interesting because it shows that easy-to-state problems *can* be unsolvable; the problem itself is sufficiently contrived that the answer for any particular instance may not be especially significant. The membership problem for recursively enumerable languages is more general but may still sound a little esoteric. However, the chances are that you have thought about something very similar to the halting problem yourself.

Almost anyone who has written a computer program involving **for**-loops or **while**-loops has encountered the problem of *infinite* loops. Infinite loops written by novice programmers often involve errors that are easy to spot (failure to increment a variable inside a loop, missing or improper initializations, and so on). As you become a more sophisticated programmer, you learn not only to avoid these basic errors but also to recognize potential trouble spots inside loops that may cause them not to terminate. It might seem as though, with a careful enough analysis, any infinite loop can be detected.

Even without knowing anything about the halting problem, we can see that this is unrealistic by considering an example from mathematics. Many famous, long-standing open problems have to do with the existence or nonexistence of an integer satisfying some specific property. *Goldbach's Conjecture*, made in 1742, is that every even integer 4 or greater can be expressed at least one way as the sum of two primes. (For example, $18 = 5 + 13$ and $100 = 41 + 59$.) Although the statement has been confirmed for values of $n$ up to about $4 \times 10^{14}$, and most mathematicians assume the conjecture is true, no one has proved it. (In 2000 the publishing company Faber and Faber offered a prize of $1 million to anyone who could furnish a proof by March 15, 2002.) However, testing whether a specific integer is the sum of two primes is a very simple calculation. Therefore, it is easy to write a computer program, or construct a Turing machine, to execute the following algorithm:

```
n = 4
conjecture = true
while (conjecture)
{   if (n is not the sum of two primes)
       conjecture = false
    else
       n = n + 2
}
```

The program terminates if and only if there is an even integer greater than 4 that is not the sum of two primes. Thus, in order to find out whether Goldbach's conjecture is true, all we would have to do is decide whether our program runs forever.

In any case, whether we consider programs like this or programs you might write in your computer science classes, the fact that the halting problem is unsolvable says that there cannot be any general method to test a program and decide whether it will terminate. This could be frustrating to mathematicians who are trying to prove Goldbach's conjecture. On the one hand, if they are unable to find a proof, they cannot take much comfort from the unsolvability of the halting problem, because there *may* be a simpler alternative method of deciding the conjecture (presumably a way that uses facts about integers and primes, rather than simply facts about programs); on the other hand, there may not!

Some problems related to the halting problem are discussed in the exercises. For example, another question to which an answer would be useful is: Given a computer program (or a Turing machine), are there any input values for which it would loop forever? See Exercise 11.12.

## 11.3 | OTHER UNSOLVABLE PROBLEMS INVOLVING TMS

We began this chapter with the problem of whether a TM $T$ accepts the input string $e(T)$, which is a special case of **Accepts**. We begin this section by considering two other useful special cases.

First, rather than considering only the string $e(T)$, we might try to restrict the problem the other way, by fixing a Turing machine $T$ and allowing a solution algorithm to depend on $T$. For *some* machines $T$ there is such an algorithm, but for at least one there is not. Consider the universal Turing machine $T_u$ introduced in Section 9.6, and the decision problem $P_u$: Given $w$, does $T_u$ accept $w$? If we had a general solution to this problem, then we could solve **Accepts**, by taking an arbitrary pair $(T, x)$ and deciding whether $T_u$ accepted the string $e(T)e(x)$. (In other words, we can reduce **Accepts** to the problem $P_u$ by assigning to an instance $(T, x)$ of **Accepts** the instance $e(T)e(x)$ of $P_u$.) Therefore, $P_u$ is unsolvable.

Let us consider another special case of Accepts obtained by restricting the string, this time to the null string. We define **Accepts-$\Lambda$** to be the decision problem

$$\text{Given a Turing machine } T, \text{ is } \Lambda \in L(T)?$$

(i.e., does $T$ eventually reach the accepting state, if it begins with a blank tape?)

---

**Theorem 11.7**
The problem **Accepts-$\Lambda$** is unsolvable.

*Proof*
We show that our decision problem is unsolvable by showing that **Accepts** can be reduced to it:

$$\textbf{Accepts} \leq \textbf{Accepts-}\Lambda$$

This time, starting with a pair $(T, x)$, we must find a Turing machine $T_1$ so that $(T, x)$ is a yes-instance of **Accepts** (i.e., $T$ accepts $x$) if and only if $T_1$ is a yes-instance of **Accepts-$\Lambda$** (i.e., $T_1$ accepts $\Lambda$). This seems difficult at first: What does accepting input $\Lambda$ have to do with accepting input $x$? However, we are allowed to use $x$ in the construction of $T_1$. $T_1$ can *start* with an empty tape (so that if it ever accepts, it will be $\Lambda$ that is accepted), but create a tape with $x$ on it by simply writing $x$. The computation it performs at that point will be exactly the same as the computation performed by $T$ on input $x$. In other words, we choose $T_1$ to be the composite TM

$$T_1 = Write(x)T$$

where $Write(x)$ is the TM that halts with tape contents $\underline{\Delta}x$ when started with a blank tape. It is clear that $T_1$ accepts input $\Lambda$ if and only if $T$ accepts input $x$. (Note that $Write(x)$ assumes the tape is initially blank, and thus $T_1$ is likely to crash on any input other than $\Lambda$. This is not a problem, because the only aspect of $T_1$ that concerns us is what it does on input $\Lambda$.)

The construction of $T_1$ in terms of $(T, x)$ can be carried out algorithmically, and it follows that **Accepts-$\Lambda$** is unsolvable.

---

In general, we show that a problem is unsolvable by finding another unsolvable problem $P$ to reduce to it. The more candidates we have for $P$, the easier this process is likely to be. We present several more examples of unsolvable problems involving TMs.

---

**Theorem 11.8**
The following decision problems are all unsolvable.

> **AcceptsSomething:** Given a TM $T$, is $L(T)$ nonempty?
>
> **AcceptsEverything:** Given a TM $T$, with input alphabet $\Sigma$, is $L(T) = \Sigma^*$?
>
> **Subset:** Given two TMs $T_1$ and $T_2$, is $L(T_1) \subseteq L(T_2)$?
>
> **WritesSymbol:** Given a TM $T$, and a symbol $a$ in its tape alphabet, does $T$ ever write $a$ if it is started with a blank tape?

*Proof*
We show that **AcceptsSomething** is unsolvable by showing that **Accepts-$\Lambda$** can be reduced to it. For both problems, an instance is a Turing machine. We will describe how to start with a TM $T$ and construct a TM $T_1$ so that $T$ accepts $\Lambda$ if and only if $T_1$ accepts at least one string. We construct $T_1$ so that no matter what its input is, the computation it performs is the one performed by $T$ on $\Lambda$. $T_1$ simply erases its input first and then executes $T$; it is the composite machine

$$T_1 = EraseTape \to T$$

where *EraseTape* erases its input string and leaves the tape head on square 0. If $T$ accepts $\Lambda$, then $T_1$ will eventually accept, no matter what its original input is, and otherwise $T_1$ will never accept. Since the function that takes $T$ to $T_1$ is computable, this is the reduction we want.

The function we have just constructed is also a reduction of **Accepts-$\Lambda$** to **AcceptsEverything**, because the machine $T_1$ accepts either everything (if $T$ accepts $\Lambda$) or nothing. Therefore, **AcceptsEverything** is also unsolvable.

An instance of **Subset** is a pair $(T_1, T_2)$ of Turing machines, and it is a yes-instance if $L(T_1) \subseteq L(T_2)$. Let us give two different proofs of unsolvability, using the two problems we have just shown are unsolvable. First, we will show that **AcceptsEverything** can be reduced to **Subset**. This means that, starting with a TM $T$, we want to construct a pair $(T_1, T_2)$ so that $T$ accepts every string over its input alphabet if and only if $L(T_1) \subseteq L(T_2)$. The way to proceed here is to ignore everything but the *set* $A = L(T)$, and to find two other sets $B$ and $C$ so that $A = \Sigma^*$ if and only if $B \subseteq C$. An appropriate choice is to let $B = \Sigma^*$ and $C = A$. (A subset of $\Sigma^*$ *is* $\Sigma^*$ if and only if it *contains* $\Sigma^*$.) Therefore, we may let $T_1$ be the trivial TM with input alphabet $\Sigma$ that immediately accepts, no matter what the input, so that $L(T_1) = \Sigma^*$, and let $T_2 = T$. This way of constructing $(T_1, T_2)$ from $T$ gives us the reduction from **AcceptsEverything** to **Subset**.

Second, let us show that the problem **AcceptsNothing**: Given a TM $T$, is $L(T) = \emptyset$? can be reduced to **Subset**. **AcceptsNothing** is the complementary problem to **AcceptsSomething**, and its unsolvability follows from that of **AcceptsSomething**; this will therefore provide another proof that **Subset** is unsolvable. This time, starting with $T$, we want $(T_1, T_2)$ so that $L(T) = \emptyset$ if and only if $L(T_1) \subseteq L(T_2)$. Since a set is empty if and only if it is a subset of the empty set, we may let $T_1$ be $T$ and $T_2$ be the trivial TM that immediately rejects every input. Then $L(T_1) = L(T)$, $L(T_2) = \emptyset$, and the condition we want is true.

Finally, we show that **Accepts-$\Lambda$** can be reduced to **WritesSymbol**, which will prove the unsolvability of **WritesSymbol**. Starting with a TM $T$, an instance of **Accepts-$\Lambda$**, we want to construct a pair $(T_1, a)$ (where $T_1$ is a TM and $a$ is a symbol in its tape alphabet), in such a way that $T$ accepts $\Lambda$ if and only if $T_1$ eventually writes $a$ when started with a blank tape. "Starting with a blank tape" means processing $\Lambda$; so the trick here is to fix it so that $T$ and $T_1$ perform essentially the same computation, except that if $T$ halts, $T_1$ writes $a$, and $T_1$ never writes $a$ in any other situation. This is not difficult: Let $T_1$ be a TM with the same input and tape alphabets as $T$ except for one new tape symbol $a$, and the same transitions as $T$ except that any accepting move

$$\delta(p, \sigma) = (h_a, \tau, D)$$

of $T$ becomes

$$\delta(p, \sigma) = (h_a, a, D)$$

instead. Starting with input $\Lambda$, the two machines perform exactly the same computation until they accept, and $T_1$ writes an $a$ if and only if this happens. Therefore, we have the reduction we need.

# 11.4 | RICE'S THEOREM AND MORE UNSOLVABLE PROBLEMS

An important class of decision problems contains those of the form: Given a language, does it have a certain property? Because a Turing machine is a basic way of specifying a language, we will be interested in formulating the problem this way:

Given a Turing machine $T$, does $L(T)$ have property $R$?

Several of the decision problems in the previous section are of this type. In the case of **Accepts-$\Lambda$**, having property $R$ means containing the null string. In the first two problems listed in Theorem 11.8, the language has property $R$ if it is nonempty, or if it is all of $\Sigma^*$, respectively.

There is a good reason for concentrating on this class of decision problems: For just about any property $R$ we choose, the resulting problem is unsolvable! "Just about any" property means any *nontrivial* property of recursively enumerable languages—in other words, any property satisfied by some, but not all, such languages. The only cases in which the problem is solvable are those in which the solution is either "Answer yes for every instance" or "Answer no for every instance." This result, known as Rice's theorem, will provide us at one stroke with many more examples of unsolvable problems.

---

**Theorem 11.9  Rice's theorem**

If $R$ is a property of languages that is satisfied by some but not all recursively enumerable languages, then the decision problem

$$\mathbf{P}_R: \text{Given a TM } T, \text{ does } L(T) \text{ have property } R?$$

is unsolvable.

*Proof*

Suppose $R$ is a nontrivial language property in the sense of the theorem. The idea of the proof, as usual, is to reduce some other unsolvable problem to $\mathbf{P}_R$. We may take the other unsolvable problem to be **Accepts-**$\Lambda$. Starting with $T$, an arbitrary instance of **Accepts-**$\Lambda$, we want to find an instance $T'$ of $\mathbf{P}_R$ so that the answers for $T$ and $T'$ are the same.

A rough description of $T'$ is that it accepts either one language $L_1$ or another language $L_2$. It decides which by temporarily ignoring its input and executing $T$ on the string $\Lambda$. If $T$ accepts $\Lambda$, $T'$ returns to its original input and accepts the language $L_1$; otherwise it accepts $L_2$. The way $T'$ accomplishes this is to start by moving its tape head past the input string and simulating the execution of $T$ on a blank tape (taking appropriate precautions so that the original input is not disturbed and so that if this step terminates then $T'$ can erase the tape and return to its original initial configuration).

In order for things to come out right, we should choose $L_1$ to be a language satisfying $R$ and $L_2$ a language not satisfying $R$; this would guarantee that $T'$ is a yes-instance of $\mathbf{P}_R$ if and only if $T$ is a yes-instance of **Accepts-**$\Lambda$. There is no difficulty executing the first part of this strategy. There is at least one language satisfying $R$, because $R$ is nontrivial, and we may select any one as $L_1$. There is a potential problem, however, with the second part: If $T$ fails to accept $\Lambda$ by looping forever, then $T'$ cannot accept anything, so that $L(T_2) = \emptyset$. Since we cannot eliminate this possibility, this choice for $L_2$ is forced on us (and we can make sure that it is carried out by letting $T'$ reject if $T$ rejects $\Lambda$).

Where does this leave us? If $\emptyset$ happens to be a language not satisfying property $R$, then we have exactly what we want—$T'$ accepts a language satisfying property $R$ if and only if $T$ accepts $\Lambda$. For the other case, we use a trick. So far we have shown that if $R$ is any nontrivial property not satisfied

by the empty language, **Accepts-**$\Lambda$ can be reduced to $\mathbf{P}_R$. If $R$ is satisfied by the empty set, then we use an indirect argument to show that $\mathbf{P}_R$ is unsolvable.
We reduce **Accepts-**$\Lambda$ to $\mathbf{P}_{R'}$, where $R'$ is the complementary property *not R* (this is possible because $R'$ is a nontrivial property not satisfied by $\emptyset$), and conclude that $\mathbf{P}_R$ is unsolvable because $\mathbf{P}_{R'}$ is.

Here is a list, somewhat arbitrary and certainly not complete, of decision problems whose unsolvability follows immediately from Rice's theorem. Some of them we have already shown to be unsolvable, by directly reducing other unsolvable problems to them.

1. **AcceptsSomething:** Given a TM $T$, is $L(T)$ nonempty?
2. **AcceptsTwo:** Given a TM $T$, does $T$ accept at least two strings?
3. **AcceptsFinite:** Given a TM $T$, is the language accepted by $T$ finite?
4. **AcceptsEverything:** Given a TM $T$ with input alphabet $\Sigma$, is $L(T) = \Sigma^*$?
5. **AcceptsRegular:** Given a TM $T$, is the language accepted by $T$ regular?
6. **AcceptsRecursive:** Given a TM $T$, is the language accepted by $T$ recursive?

Many decision problems involving Turing machines do not fit the format required for applying Rice's theorem directly. The problems **Accepts** and **Halts** do not, because in both cases an instance is not a TM but a pair $(T, x)$. The problem **Subset** in Theorem 11.8 involves more than one Turing machine, as does the problem

**Equivalent**: Given TMs $T_1$ and $T_2$, is $L(T_1) = L(T_2)$?

To convince ourselves that **Equivalent** is unsolvable, we might argue as follows. For any specific recursively enumerable language $L_2$, such as $L_2 = \{\Lambda\}$, the problem

**Accepts-**$L_2$: Given a TM $T$, is $L(T) = L_2$?

is unsolvable because of Rice's theorem (the property of being $L_2$ is a nontrivial language property). However, the problem **Accepts-**$L_2$ is reducible to **Equivalent**, because if $T_2$ is a TM accepting $L_2$, then for any instance $T$ of **Accepts**$(L_2)$, the pair $(T, T_2)$ is an instance of **Equivalent** having the same answer. Therefore, **Equivalent** is unsolvable.

Rice's theorem also does not apply directly to decision problems involving the *operation* of a Turing machine, as opposed to the language accepted by the machine. Some such problems are solvable, and some are not. The problem

Given a TM $T$, does $T$ make more than 100 moves on input $\Lambda$?

can obviously be solved: Being "given" a TM means in particular being given enough information to trace the processing of a fixed string for a certain fixed number of moves. An example of an unsolvable problem that involves the operation of a TM and therefore cannot be immediately proved unsolvable using Rice's theorem is **WritesSymbol**, in Theorem 11.8. In view of that problem, it may seem surprising that the following problem is solvable:

Given a TM $T$, does $T$ ever write a nonblank symbol when started with input $\Lambda$?

See Exercise 11.15.

Finally, even for a problem of the right form (Given $T$, does $L(T)$ satisfy property $R$?), Rice's theorem cannot be applied if the property $R$ is trivial. Remember that "trivial" is used here to describe a property that is possessed either by all the recursively enumerable languages or by none of them. Deciding whether the property is trivial may not be trivial. If the *property* is trivial, however, then the *decision problem* is trivial in the sense that the answer is either yes for every instance or no for every instance. An example of the first case is the problem: Given a TM $T$, can $L(T)$ be accepted by a TM that never halts after an odd number of moves? Here the answer is always yes. We can modify any TM if necessary so that instead of halting after an odd-numbered move, it makes an extra (unnecessary) move before halting. An example of the second case is the problem: Given a TM $T$, is $L(T)$ the language *NSA*? (See definition 11.1.) Here the answer is always no: No matter what $T$ is, $L(T)$ cannot be *NSA*, because *NSA* is not recursively enumerable.

## 11.5 | POST'S CORRESPONDENCE PROBLEM

In this section we show that a combinatorial problem known as Post's Correspondence problem (**PCP**) is unsolvable. Although the details of the proof are rather involved, the problem itself can be understood easily even by someone who knows nothing about Turing machines, and using its unsolvability is one way of showing that a number of decision problems involving context-free grammars are also unsolvable.

The problem was first formulated by Emil Post in the 1940s. An instance of **PCP** is called a *correspondence system* and consists of a set of pairs $(\alpha_1, \beta_1)$, $(\alpha_2, \beta_2), \ldots, (\alpha_n, \beta_n)$, where the $\alpha_i$'s and $\beta_i$'s are nonnull strings over an alphabet $\Sigma$. The question we are interested in for an instance like this is whether there is a sequence of one or more integers $i_1, i_2, \ldots, i_k$, each $i_j$ satisfying $1 \leq i_j \leq n$ and the $i_j$'s not necessarily distinct, so that

$$\alpha_{i_1}\alpha_{i_2}\cdots\alpha_{i_k} = \beta_{i_1}\beta_{i_2}\cdots\beta_{i_k}$$

The instance is a yes-instance if there is such a sequence, and we call the sequence a solution sequence for the instance.

It is helpful in visualizing the problem to think of $n$ distinct groups of *dominoes*, each domino from the $i$th group having the string $\alpha_i$ on the top half and the string $\beta_i$ on the bottom half (see Figure 11.1$a$), and to imagine that there are an unlimited number of identical dominoes in each group. Finding a solution sequence for this instance means lining up one or more dominoes in a horizontal row, each one positioned vertically, so that the string formed by their top halves matches the string formed by their bottom halves (see Figure 11.1$b$). Duplicate dominoes can be used, and it is not necessary to use all the distinct domino types.

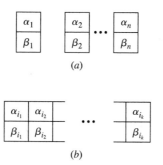

(a)

(b)

**Figure 11.1 |**

A Simple Correspondence System   **EXAMPLE 11.1**

Consider the correspondence system described by this picture:

| 10 | 01 | 0 | 100 | 1 |
|---|---|---|---|---|
| 101 | 100 | 10 | 0 | 010 |

In any solution sequence for this instance of **PCP**, domino 1 must be used first, since it is the only one in which the two strings begin with the same symbol. One solution sequence is the following:

| 10 | 1 | 01 | 0 | 100 | 100 | 0 | 100 |
|---|---|---|---|---|---|---|---|
| 101 | 010 | 100 | 10 | 0 | 0 | 10 | 0 |

and you can verify for yourself that there is also a solution sequence beginning

| 10 | 100 |
|---|---|
| 101 | 0 |

**PCP** has a feature shared by many of the unsolvable problems we have considered. There is a trivial way to arrive at the correct answer for any instance, *if* the answer is yes: Just try all ways of lining up one domino, then all ways of lining up two, and so forth. Of course, a mindless application of this approach is doomed to failure in the case of a no-instance. Saying that **PCP** is unsolvable says on the one hand that reasoning about this approach will not help (for any $n$, you can try all sequences of $n$ dominoes and still not be sure there is no sequence of $n + 1$ that works), and on the other hand that no other approach is guaranteed to do better.

We show that **PCP** is unsolvable by introducing a slightly different problem, showing that it can be reduced to **PCP**, and then showing that it is unsolvable by showing that the membership problem **Accepts** can be reduced to it. An instance of the *Modified* Post's correspondence problem (**MPCP**) is exactly the same as an instance of **PCP**, except that a solution sequence for the instance is required to begin with domino 1. In other words, a solution sequence consists of a sequence of zero or more integers $i_2, i_3, \ldots, i_k$ so that

$$\alpha_1 \alpha_{i_2} \cdots \alpha_{i_k} = \beta_1 \beta_{i_2} \cdots \beta_{i_k}$$

---

**Theorem 11.10**
**MPCP** can be reduced to **PCP**. (Therefore, if **MPCP** is unsolvable, so is **PCP**.)

*Proof*
Let $I$ be an arbitrary instance of **MPCP**, represented by the $n$ pairs $(\alpha_1, \beta_1)$, $(\alpha_2, \beta_2), \ldots, (\alpha_n, \beta_n)$. We construct an instance $J$ of **PCP** having the $n + 1$ pairs

$$(\alpha_1', \beta_1'), (\alpha_2', \beta_2'), \ldots, (\alpha_n', \beta_n'), (\alpha_{n+1}', \beta_{n+1}')$$

The symbols involved will be those in the instance $I$, plus two additional symbols # and \$, and the pairs will be constructed as follows: For each pair

$$(\alpha_i, \beta_i) = (a_1 a_2 \cdots a_r, b_1 b_2 \cdots b_s)$$

of $I$, define the pair $(\alpha_i', \beta_i')$ by the formula

$$(\alpha_i', \beta_i') = (a_1 \# a_2 \# \cdots a_r \#, \# b_1 \# b_2 \cdots \# b_s)$$

*except* that the string $\alpha_1'$ has an extra # at the beginning. The last pair in the instance $J$ is

$$(\alpha_{n+1}', \beta_{n+1}') = (\$, \#\$)$$

The idea behind this construction is that the pairs of $J$ correspond, generally speaking, to the pairs of $I$, except that although $J$ is an instance of **PCP** (rather than **MPCP**), the distribution of #'s will guarantee that the only pair that can possibly begin a solution sequence for $J$ is pair 1.

On the one hand, if $i_2, i_3, \ldots, i_k$ is a solution sequence for the instance $I$ of **MPCP**, which means that

$$\alpha_1 \alpha_{i_2} \cdots \alpha_{i_k} = \beta_1 \beta_{i_2} \cdots \beta_{i_k}$$

then it is easy to see that

$$\alpha_1' \alpha_{i_2}' \cdots \alpha_{i_k}' \alpha_{n+1}' = \beta_1' \beta_{i_2}' \cdots \beta_{i_k}' \beta_{n+1}'$$

so that the sequence $1, i_2, \ldots, i_k, i_{n+1}$ is a solution sequence for the instance $J$ of **PCP**. Therefore, if $I$ is a yes-instance of **MPCP**, then $J$ is a yes-instance of **PCP**.

On the other hand, if $i_1, i_2, \ldots, i_k$ is any solution sequence for the instance $J$, which means

$$\alpha_{i_1}' \alpha_{i_2}' \cdots \alpha_{i_k}' = \beta_{i_1}' \beta_{i_2}' \cdots \beta_{i_k}'$$

then we must have $i_1 = 1$ and $i_k = n + 1$, because the strings of the first pair must begin with the same symbol and those of the last pair must end with the same symbol. It is conceivable that some of the other $i_j$'s are also $n+1$, but if $i_m$ is the last $i_j$ to equal $n+1$, then $1, i_2, \ldots, i_m$ is also a solution sequence for the instance $J$. It is then easy to check that $i_2, \ldots, i_{m-1}$ is a solution sequence for the instance $I$ of **MPCP**.

We have shown that $I$ is a yes-instance of **MPCP** if and only if $J$ is a yes-instance of **PCP**, which implies that

$$\textbf{MPCP} \leq \textbf{PCP}$$

---

**Theorem 11.11**
**MPCP** is unsolvable.

*Proof*
We want to show that **Accepts** is reducible to **MPCP**. Let $(T, w)$ be an arbitrary instance of **Accepts**, so that $T = (Q, \Sigma, \Gamma, q_0, \delta)$ is a Turing machine and $w$ is a string over the input alphabet $\Sigma$. We wish to construct an instance $(\alpha_1, \beta_1), (\alpha_2, \beta_2), \ldots, (\alpha_n, \beta_n)$ of **MPCP** (a *modified correspondence system*) that has a solution sequence if and only if $T$ accepts $w$.

It will be convenient to assume that $T$ never halts in the reject state $h_r$. Since there is an algorithm to convert any TM into an equivalent one that enters an infinite loop whenever the original one would reject (see the proof of Theorem 11.6), we may make this assumption without loss of generality. Some additional notation and terminology will be helpful. For an instance $(\alpha_1, \beta_1), (\alpha_2, \beta_2), \ldots, (\alpha_n, \beta_n)$ of **MPCP**, we will say that a *partial solution* is a sequence $i_2, i_3, \ldots, i_j$ so that $\alpha = \alpha_1 \alpha_{i_2} \cdots \alpha_{i_j}$ is a prefix of $\beta = \beta_1 \beta_{i_2} \cdots \beta_{i_j}$. A little less precisely, we might say that the string $\alpha$ obtained this way is a partial solution, or that the two strings $\alpha$ and $\beta$ represent a partial solution. Secondly, we introduce temporarily a new notation for representing TM configurations. For $x, y \in (\Gamma \cup \{\Delta\})^*$ with $y$ not ending in $\Delta$, and $q \in Q$, we will write $xqy$ to represent the configuration that we normally denote by $(q, xy)$, or by $(q, x\underline{\Delta})$ in the case where $y = \Lambda$. In other words, the symbols in $x$ are those preceding the tape head, which is centered on the first symbol of $y$ if $y \neq \Lambda$ and on $\Delta$ otherwise.

In order to simplify the notation, we assume from here on that $w \neq \Lambda$. This assumption will not play an essential part in the proof, and we will indicate later how to take care of the case when $w = \Lambda$.

Here is a rough outline of the proof. The symbols involved in our pairs will be those that appear in the configurations of $T$, together with an additional symbol #. We want to specify pairs $(\alpha_i, \beta_i)$ in our modified correspondence system so that for any $j$, if

$$q_0 \Delta w, \ x_1 q_1 y_1, \ldots, x_j q_j y_j$$

are successive configurations through which $T$ moves in processing the input string $w$, starting with the initial configuration $q_0 \Delta w$, a partial solution can be obtained that looks like

$$\alpha = \#q_0 \Delta w \# x_1 q_1 y_1 \# x_2 q_2 y_2 \# \cdots \# x_j q_j y_j$$

Moreover, we want any partial solution to be a prefix of one like this—or at least, to start deviating from this form only after an occurrence of an accepting configuration $x h_a y$ in the string. Next, if we have a partial solution

$$\alpha = \#q_0 \Delta w \# x_1 q_1 y_1 \# \cdots \# x_j h_a y_j$$

which will imply in particular, given our earlier remarks, that $T$ accepts $w$, we want additional pairs $(\alpha_i, \beta_i)$ that will allow the prefix $\alpha$ to "catch up with" $\beta$, so that there will actually be a solution sequence for the instance of **MPCP**. Finally, we want to guarantee that *only* in that case do we have a solution sequence. If we can specify the modified correspondence system in a way that accomplishes these things, it will follow fairly easily that the system has a solution sequence if and only if $T$ accepts $w$.

Here is a more detailed outline of how the pairs in our instance of **MPCP** are constructed. We choose the pair $(\alpha_1, \beta_1)$, with which a solution sequence is constrained to start, as follows:

$$\alpha_1 = \#$$

$$\beta_1 = \#q_0 \Delta w \#$$

The portion of $\beta_1$ between the #'s represents the initial configuration of $T$. Now suppose, for example, that $\delta(q_0, \Delta) = (q_1, a, \text{R})$. Corresponding to that move of $T$, we will have a pair

$$(q_0 \Delta, a q_1)$$

and we make sure that this is the only possible choice for the next pair $(\alpha_{i_2}, \beta_{i_2})$ in a partial solution. Using this pair next produces the partial solution

$$\alpha = \alpha_1 \alpha_{i_2} = \#q_0 \Delta$$

$$\beta = \beta_1 \beta_{i_2} = \#q_0 \Delta w \# a q_1$$

At this point, the only correct way to add to $\alpha$ is to add the symbols of $w$. Moreover, it is appropriate to add the same symbols to $\beta$, because they appear in the configuration that follows $q_0 \Delta w$. Therefore, we include in our modified correspondence system pairs $(\sigma, \sigma)$ for every $\sigma \in \Gamma \cup \{\Delta\}$, as well as the pair (#, #). Using these, we can obtain the partial solution

$$\alpha = \#q_0 \Delta w \#$$

$$\beta = \#q_0 \Delta w \# a q_1 w \#$$

Now $\alpha$ has caught up to the *original* string $\beta$, and the new $\beta$ has a second portion representing the configuration of $T$ after the first move. The process of extending the partial solution continues in the same way. At each step, as long as the accepting state $h_a$ has not appeared, the string $\beta$ in the partial solution is one step ahead of $\alpha$. Thus, the next portion to be added to $\alpha$ is determined, and the pairs $(\alpha_i, \beta_i)$ are such that every time $\alpha_i$'s are used to complete the required configuration of $T$ in the string $\alpha$, the corresponding $\beta_i$'s, which are added to $\beta$, specify the configuration of $T$ one move later. In this way, we guarantee that any partial solution is of the desired form. Roughly speaking, it remains only to include pairs $(\alpha_i, \beta_i)$ that allow $\alpha$ to catch up to $\beta$ once the configuration includes the accepting state $h_a$.

This discussion should make it easier to understand the following definition of the pairs $(\alpha_i, \beta_i)$ making up the instance of **MPCP**. The pairs are grouped into several types; the order is not significant, and therefore no subscripts are specified except for the first pair.

$$(\alpha_1, \beta_1) = (\#, \#q_0\Delta w\#)$$

**Pairs of Type 1:** For all choices of $a \in \Gamma \cup \{\Delta\}$, the pairs

$$(a, a)$$

$$(\#, \#)$$

**Pairs of Type 2:** For all choices of $q \in Q$, $p \in Q \cup \{h_a\}$, and $a, b, c \in \Gamma \cup \{\Delta\}$, the pairs

$$(qa, pb) \qquad \text{if } \delta(q, a) = (p, b, \text{S})$$

$$(qa, bp) \qquad \text{if } \delta(q, a) = (p, b, \text{R})$$

$$(cqa, pcb) \qquad \text{if } \delta(q, a) = (p, b, \text{L})$$

$$(q\#, pa\#) \qquad \text{if } \delta(q, \Delta) = (p, a, \text{S})$$

$$(q\#, ap\#) \qquad \text{if } \delta(q, \Delta) = (p, a, \text{R})$$

$$(cq\#, pca\#) \qquad \text{if } \delta(q, \Delta) = (p, a, \text{L})$$

**Pairs of Type 3:** For all choices of $a, b \in \Gamma \cup \{\Delta\}$, the pairs

$$(h_a a, h_a)$$

$$(a h_a, h_a)$$

$$(a h_a b, h_a)$$

**Pairs (actually only one) of Type 4:**

$$(h_a \#\#, \#)$$

The proof of the theorem now follows the intuitive argument above. First we make the following claim.

*Claim:* If we have any partial solution

$$\alpha = \gamma\#$$

$$\beta = \gamma\#z\#$$

to the modified correspondence system, where $z$ represents a nonhalting configuration of $T$, we may extend it to a partial solution

$$\alpha' = \gamma\#z\#$$

$$\beta' = \gamma\#z\#z'\#$$

where $z'$ represents the configuration of $T$ one move later. Moreover, the string $\beta'$ shown is the only one that can correspond to this $\alpha'$ in a partial solution.

We establish the claim in the case when

$$\alpha = \gamma\#$$
$$\beta = \gamma\#a_1 \cdots a_k q a_{k+1} \cdots a_{k+m}\#$$

and $m > 0$ and $\delta(q, a_{k+1}) = (p, b, \mathrm{R})$. The other cases are similar. The pairs that allow us to extend the partial solution are these: first, the pairs $(a_1, a_1), \ldots, (a_k, a_k)$ of type 1; then, the pair $(q a_{k+1}, bp)$ of type 2; next, any remaining pairs $(a_{k+2}, a_{k+2}), \ldots, (a_{k+m}, a_{k+m})$; and finally, the pair $(\#, \#)$. The partial solution produced is

$$\alpha' = \gamma\#a_1 \cdots a_k q a_{k+1} \cdots a_{k+m}\#$$
$$\beta' = \gamma\#a_1 \cdots a_k q a_{k+1} \cdots a_{k+m}\#a_1 \cdots a_k b p a_{k+2} \cdots a_{k+m}\#$$

Sure enough, the substring of $\beta'$ between the last two #'s is the machine configuration resulting from the move indicated. Furthermore, it is easy to see that at no point in this process is there any choice as to which pair to use, and so the claim is established in this case.

Suppose, on the one hand, that $T$ accepts input $w$. This means that there is a sequence of consecutive configurations of $T$, beginning with $(q_0, \underline{\Delta}w)$ and ending with an accepting configuration. If these configurations are represented by the strings $z_0, \ldots, z_j$, an easy induction argument using the claim above shows that there is a partial solution

$$\alpha = \#z_0\# \cdots \#z_{j-1}\#$$
$$\beta = \#z_0\# \cdots \#z_{j-1}\#z_j\#$$

to the modified correspondence system. The string $z_j$ representing the accepting configuration is of the form

$$u h_a v$$

where the strings $u$ and/or $v$ may be null. If at least one is nonnull, we may extend the partial solution, using one pair of type 3 and others of type 1, to obtain

$$\alpha' = \alpha z_j\#$$
$$\beta' = \alpha z_j\#z_j'\#$$

where $z_j'$ still contains $h_a$ but has at least one fewer symbol than $z_j$. In a similar way, we can continue to extend the partial solution, so that the strings between consecutive #'s decrease in length by either one or two symbols at each step, until we have a partial solution of the form

$$\alpha''\#$$
$$\alpha''\#h_a\#$$

Applying the pair of type 4 now yields a solution sequence for the modified correspondence system.

Conversely, suppose $T$ does not accept $w$; our assumption is that in this case it loops forever. Then for any partial solution of the modified correspondence system of the form

$$\alpha = \#z_0\#z_1\#\cdots\#z_k\#$$

$$\beta = \#z_0\#z_1\#\cdots\#z_k\#z_{k+1}\#$$

where no $z_i$ contains #, the strings $z_i$ represent consecutive configurations of $T$. Again this is an induction proof, this time on the number of #'s in the partial solution, and the induction step is furnished by the last part of the claim above. It follows that $h_a$ never appears in any partial solution; in particular, the pair of type 4 is never used. Since $\alpha_1$ and $\beta_1$ have different numbers of #'s, and since the pair of type 4 is the only other pair with this property, we may conclude that there is no solution sequence for the modified correspondence system.

We have shown that the modified correspondence system has a solution sequence if and only if $T$ accepts input $w$, and the proof is complete.

The only modification of the proof that is necessary in the case $w = \Lambda$ is that the initial pair is (#, #$q_0$#) instead of (#, #$q_0\Delta w$#).

---

A Correspondence System for a Simple TM    **EXAMPLE 11.2**

Let $T$ be the TM pictured in Figure 11.2, which accepts all strings in $\{a, b\}^*$ ending with $b$. Let us examine the modified correspondence system constructed as in the proof of Theorem 11.11, for two strings $w$ that are not accepted by $T$ and one that is. The only difference is in the initial pair.

The pairs of type 2 are these:

$(q_0\Delta, \Delta q_1)$ $\qquad$ $(q_1a, aq_1)$ $\qquad$ $(q_2a, aq_1)$

$(q_0\#, \Delta q_1\#)$ $\qquad$ $(q_1b, bq_1)$ $\qquad$ $(q_2b, h_a\Delta)$

$(aq_1\#, q_2a\Delta\#)$ $\qquad$ $(aq_1\Delta, q_2a\Delta)$

$(bq_1\#, q_2b\Delta\#)$ $\qquad$ $(bq_1\Delta, q_2b\Delta)$

$(\Delta q_1\#, q_2\Delta\Delta\#)$ $\qquad$ $(\Delta q_1\Delta, q_2\Delta\Delta)$

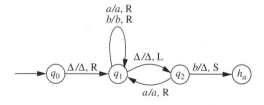

**Figure 11.2**

For the input string $\Lambda$, pair 1 is $(\#, \#q_0\#)$. The following partial solution is the longest possible, and the only one (except for smaller portions of it) ending in #:

| # | $q_0\#$ | $\Delta q_1\#$ |
|---|---|---|
| $\#q_0\#$ | $\Delta q_1\#$ | $q_2\Delta\Delta\#$ |

Clearly no solution sequence exists.

The input string $a$ causes $T$ to loop forever. In this case, pair 1 is $(\#, \#q_0\Delta a\#)$. In the partial solution shown below, the last domino appears for the second time, and it is not hard to see that longer partial solutions would simply involve repetitions of the portion following the first occurrence.

| # | $q_0\Delta$ | $a$ | # | $\Delta$ | $q_1a$ | # | $\Delta$ | $aq_1\#$ | $\Delta$ | $q_2a$ | $\Delta$ | # |
|---|---|---|---|---|---|---|---|---|---|---|---|---|
| $\#q_0\Delta a\#$ | $\Delta q_1$ | $a$ | # | $\Delta$ | $aq_1$ | # | $\Delta$ | $q_2a\Delta\#$ | $\Delta$ | $aq_1$ | $\Delta$ | # |

| $\Delta$ | $aq_1\Delta$ | # | $\Delta$ | $q_2a$ |
|---|---|---|---|---|
| $\Delta$ | $q_2a\Delta$ | # | $\Delta$ | $aq_1$ |

Finally, for the input string $b$, which is accepted by $T$, pair 1 is $(\#, \#q_0\Delta b\#)$, and the solution sequence is shown below.

| # | $q_0\Delta$ | $b$ | # | $\Delta$ | $q_1b$ | # | $\Delta$ | $bq_1\#$ | $\Delta$ | $q_2b$ | $\Delta$ | # |
|---|---|---|---|---|---|---|---|---|---|---|---|---|
| $\#q_0\Delta b\#$ | $\Delta q_1$ | $b$ | # | $\Delta$ | $bq_1$ | # | $\Delta$ | $q_2b\Delta\#$ | $\Delta$ | $h_a\Delta$ | $\Delta$ | # |

| $\Delta h_a\Delta$ | $\Delta$ | # | $h_a\Delta$ | # | $h_a\#\#$ |
|---|---|---|---|---|---|
| $h_a$ | $\Delta$ | # | $h_a$ | # | # |

# 11.6 | UNSOLVABLE PROBLEMS INVOLVING CONTEXT-FREE LANGUAGES

For some decision problems involving context-free grammars and languages, there are solution algorithms. The membership problem for CFLs (Given a context-free grammar $G$ and a string $x$, is $x \in L(G)$?) is solvable, and in Section 8.3 we were also able to solve such problems as whether a given CFL is finite or infinite. In this section, however, we will consider two techniques for obtaining unsolvability results involving CFGs.

The first approach uses Post's correspondence problem, discussed in the previous section. We begin by describing a useful construction in which two CFGs are obtained from an instance of **PCP**.

Suppose $I$ is the correspondence system

$$(\alpha_1, \beta_1), (\alpha_2, \beta_2), \ldots, (\alpha_n, \beta_n)$$

where the $\alpha_i$'s and $\beta_i$'s are strings over $\Sigma$. Let

$$C = \{c_1, c_2, \ldots, c_n\}$$

where the $c_i$'s are symbols not contained in $\Sigma$. The terminal symbols of both our grammars will be the symbols of $\Sigma \cup C$. Let $G_\alpha$ be the CFG with start symbol $S_\alpha$ and the $2n$ productions

$$S_\alpha \rightarrow \alpha_i S_\alpha c_i \mid \alpha_i c_i \quad (1 \le i \le n)$$

and let $G_\beta$ be the one with start symbol $S_\beta$ and productions

$$S_\beta \rightarrow \beta_i S_\beta c_i \mid \beta_i c_i \quad (1 \le i \le n)$$

Then $L(G_\alpha)$ is the language of all strings of the form

$$\alpha_{i_1} \alpha_{i_2} \cdots \alpha_{i_k} c_{i_k} c_{i_{k-1}} \cdots c_{i_1} \quad (k \ge 1)$$

and $L(G_\beta)$ is the same except that each $\alpha_{i_j}$ is replaced by $\beta_{i_j}$.

There are a number of examples, two of which we describe below, of decision problems involving CFGs to which **PCP** can be reduced using this construction.

---

**Theorem 11.12**

The problem **CFGNonemptyIntersection**: Given two CFGs $G_1$ and $G_2$, is $L(G_1) \cap L(G_2)$ nonempty? is unsolvable.

*Proof*

We can reduce **PCP** to **CFGNonemptyIntersection** as follows. For an arbitrary instance $I$ of **PCP**, consisting of the pairs $(\alpha_i, \beta_i)$ with $1 \le i \le n$, construct the instance $(G_\alpha, G_\beta)$ of **CFGNonemptyIntersection**, where $(G_\alpha$ and $G_\beta)$ are as described above. Then strings in the intersection $L(G_\alpha) \cap L(G_\beta)$ are precisely the strings $x$ for which, on the one hand,

$$x = \alpha_{i_1} \alpha_{i_2} \cdots \alpha_{i_k} c_{i_k} c_{i_{k-1}} \cdots c_{i_1}$$

and, on the other hand,

$$x = \beta_{j_1} \beta_{j_2} \cdots \beta_{j_m} c_{j_m} c_{j_{m-1}} \cdots c_{j_1}$$

The symbols $c_i$ act here as a control. There is a string $x$ satisfying both these equations if and only if $k = m$, $i_p = j_p$ for $1 \le p \le k$, and $I$ is a yes-instance of **PCP**. Therefore, $I$ is a yes-instance of **PCP** if and only if $(G_\alpha, G_\beta)$ is a yes-instance of **CFGNonemptyIntersection**. Since **PCP** is unsolvable, so is **CFGNonemptyIntersection**.

---

**Theorem 11.13**

The problem **IsAmbiguous**: Given a CFG, is it ambiguous? is unsolvable.

*Proof*

Again we start with an arbitrary instance $I$ of **PCP**, with pairs $(\alpha_i, \beta_i)$ for $1 \le i \le n$, and construct the CFGs $G_\alpha$ and $G_\beta$ as above. We obtain an instance $G$ of **IsAmbiguous** by letting the variables be $S$, $S_\alpha$, and $S_\beta$ and the productions those of $G_\alpha$ and $G_\beta$ along with the two additional productions

$$S \to S_\alpha \mid S_\beta$$

The language generated by $G$, therefore, is precisely $L(G_\alpha) \cup L(G_\beta)$.

If the correspondence system $I$ has a solution sequence $i_1, i_2, \ldots, i_k$, then

$$\alpha_{i_1} \alpha_{i_2} \cdots \alpha_{i_k} = \beta_{i_1} \beta_{i_2} \cdots \beta_{i_k}$$

and the string

$$\alpha_{i_1} \alpha_{i_2} \cdots \alpha_{i_k} c_{i_k} c_{i_{k-1}} \cdots c_{i_1}$$

which is in $L(G_\alpha) \cap L(G_\beta)$, has two leftmost derivations in $G$, beginning with the productions $S \to S_\alpha$ and $S \to S_\beta$, respectively. Conversely, if $G$ is ambiguous, then since both $G_\alpha$ and $G_\beta$ are clearly unambiguous, there must be some string derivable from both $S_\alpha$ and $S_\beta$. This string is therefore in $L(G_\alpha) \cap L(G_\beta)$, and it follows as in the previous proof that there is a solution sequence for the instance $I$.

We conclude that **PCP** $\leq$ **IsAmbiguous** and that the second problem is unsolvable.

Another somewhat more direct approach to decision problems involving context-free languages is to develop a set of strings representing Turing machine computations and to show that they can be described in terms of context-free grammars.

It will be helpful in this discussion to use the same notation for describing TM configurations that we used in the previous section, in which the configuration $(q, x\underline{a}y)$ is written $xqay$. A complete *computation* of a TM can be described by a sequence of successive configurations, starting with the initial configuration corresponding to some input string and ending with an accepting configuration. For reasons that will be apparent shortly, we represent alternate configurations in such a sequence by the reverse of the string.

---

### Definition 11.4    Valid Computations of a TM

Let $T = (Q, \Sigma, \Gamma, q_0, \delta)$ be a Turing machine. A *valid computation* of $T$ will mean a string

$$z_0 \# z_1^r \# z_2 \# z_3^r \cdots \# z_{n-1}^r \# z_n \#$$

if $n$ is even, or

$$z_0 \# z_1^r \# z_2 \# z_3^r \cdots \# z_{n-1} \# z_n^r \#$$

if $n$ is odd, where in either case $\#$ is a symbol not in $\Gamma$; each $z_i$ describes a configuration of $T$; $z_0$ describes the initial configuration corresponding to some input string $x \in \Sigma^*$; $z_n$ describes an accepting configuration; and for each $i < n$, $z_i \vdash_T z_{i+1}$.

Note that the sequences of moves represented by these "valid computations" cause the TM to accept. The intuitive explanation for reversing every other entry in a sequence like this is that strings of the form $z\#z'\#$, where $z$ and $z'$ are successive configurations, look too much like strings of the form $ww$ to be obtainable from a CFG. The string $z\#(z')^r\#$ looks more like $ww^r$, which is simply a palindrome.

**Lemma 11.2**  For a Turing machine $T$, the sets

$$L_1 = \{z\#(z')^r\# \mid z \text{ and } z' \text{ represent configurations of } T \text{ for which } z \vdash_T z'\}$$

and

$$L_2 = \{z^r\#z'\# \mid z \text{ and } z' \text{ represent configurations of } T \text{ for which } z \vdash_T z'\}$$

are both context-free languages.

***Proof***  We prove the result for $L_1$, and the proof for $L_2$ is similar. We can show that $L_1$ is a CFL by describing how to construct a PDA $M$ accepting it. $M$ will have in its alphabet both states and tape symbols of $T$ (including $\Delta$), and these two sets are assumed not to overlap. A finite automaton is able to check that the input string is of the form $z\#z'\#$, where $z$ and $z'$ are in the set $\Gamma^*Q\Gamma^*$, and this is part of what $M$ does, rejecting if the input string is illegal.

For the rest of the proof, we need to show that $M$ can operate so that if the first portion $z$ of the input is a configuration of $T$, then the stack contents when $z$ has been processed are $(z')^r Z_0$, where $z \vdash_T z'$. (This allows $M$ to process the input remaining after the first # by simply matching input symbols against stack symbols.)

We consider the case in which

$$z = xpay$$

where $p$ is a state and $a$ is a tape symbol of $T$, and the move of $T$ in state $p$ with tape symbol $a$ is

$$\delta(p, a) = (q, b, \mathrm{L})$$

The other cases can be handled similarly.

In this case, if $x = x_1 c$ for some string $x_1$ and some tape symbol $c$, then $T$ moves from the configuration $xpay = x_1cpay$ to the configuration $x_1qcby$. If $x$ is null, $T$ rejects by trying to move its tape head left from square 0.

$M$ can operate by pushing input symbols onto its stack until it sees a state of $T$; at this point, the stack contains the string $x^r Z_0$. We may specify that $M$ rejects if the top stack symbol is $Z_0$ (that is, if $x$ is null). Otherwise, the stack contains

$$cx_1^r Z_0$$

$M$ has now read the state $p$, and the next input symbol is $a$. It pops the $c$, replaces it by $bcq$, and continues to read symbols and push them onto the stack until it encounters the first #. This means $z$ has been processed completely. The stack contents are then

$$y^r bcq x_1^r Z_0 = (x_1 qcby)^r Z_0$$

and the string $x_1qcby$ is the configuration we want.  ∎

**Theorem 11.14**

For any TM $T$, the set $C_T$ of valid computations of $T$ can be expressed as $L(G_1) \cap L(G_2)$ for two context-free grammars $G_1$ and $G_2$.

*Proof*

Let *Init* and *Accept* be the sets of strings representing initial and accepting configurations, respectively. In other words, *Init* contains strings of the form $q_0$ or $q_0 \Delta x$, where $q_0$ is the initial state of $T$ and $x$ is a nonnull string over the input alphabet of $T$; and *Accept* is the set of strings of the form $y h_a z$, where $y$ and $z$ can contain tape symbols and/or blanks but $z$ does not end with a blank. These two languages are actually regular, and therefore certainly context-free. Now we define the two languages

$$L_3 = Init\{\#\}L_2^*(\{\Lambda\} \cup Accept^r\{\#\})$$

and

$$L_4 = L_1^*(\{\Lambda\} \cup Accept\{\#\})$$

Here $L_1$ and $L_2$ are the languages defined in Lemma 11.2, and $Accept^r = \{x^r \mid x \in Accept\}$. It follows from Lemma 11.2 that both $L_3$ and $L_4$ can be obtained from CFLs using union, concatenation, and Kleene $*$ and are therefore context-free.

Strings in either $L_3$ or $L_4$ have the general form

$$z_0 \# z_1^r \# z_2 \# z_3^r \# \cdots z_{k-1}^r \# z_k \#$$

if $k$ is even, or

$$z_0 \# z_1^r \# z_2 \# z_3^r \# \cdots z_{k-1} \# z_k^r \#$$

if $k$ is odd, where each $z_i$ represents a configuration of $T$ and $z_0$ is an initial configuration. The relationship between consecutive pieces of such a string $z$ depends on whether $z \in L_3$ or $z \in L_4$. In the first case,

$$z = z_0 \#(z_1^r \# z_2 \#)(z_3^r \# z_4 \#) \cdots$$

where each of the parenthesized substrings is in $L_2$, and $z_i \vdash z_{i+1}$ for odd values of $i$. In the other case,

$$z = (z_0 \# z_1^r \#)(z_2 \# z_3^r \#) \cdots$$

where each parenthesized string is in $L_1$ and $z_i \vdash z_{i+1}$ for every even $i$. If $z$ is an element of both $L_3$ and $L_4$, it follows that $z_i \vdash z_{i+1}$ for every $i$. In this case, it also follows from the definitions of $L_3$ and $L_4$ that the last substring $z_k$ must represent an accepting configuration, since $z_k \#$ is what remains either after the factors in $L_2$ (if $k$ is odd) or after the factors in $L_1$ (if $k$ is even). The conclusion is that the set $C_T$ of valid computations of $T$ is precisely the intersection $L_3 \cap L_4$, and thus the proof of the theorem is complete.

The set $C_T$ of valid computations of $T$ is viewed here as a subset of $(\Gamma \cup \{\Delta\} \cup Q \cup \{h_a\})^*$, where $\Gamma$ and $Q$ are the tape alphabet and state set, respectively, of $T$. For some of the unsolvability results we are developing, it is helpful also to look at the complement of this set, which is simpler in one respect than $C_T$ itself.

**Lemma 11.3**  The set $C_T'$ is a context-free language.

**Proof**  A string $x$ over this alphabet fails to be in $C_T$ if $x$ does not end in #; otherwise, if

$$x = z_0\#z_1\#z_2\# \cdots \#z_k\#$$

and no $z_i$ contains #, $x$ fails to be in $C_T$ if and only if one or more of the following conditions holds.

1.  For some even $i$, $z_i$ does not represent a TM configuration.
2.  For some odd $i$, $z_i^r$ does not represent a TM configuration.
3.  $z_0$ does not represent an initial configuration.
4.  Neither $z_k$ nor $z_k^r$ represents an accepting configuration.
5.  For some even $i$, $z_i$ and $z_{i+1}^r$ represent configurations of $T$ but the condition $z_i \vdash_T z_{i+1}^r$ fails.
6.  For some odd $i$, $z_i^r$ and $z_{i+1}$ are configurations but the condition $z_i^r \vdash_T z_{i+1}$ fails.

It is easy to see that each condition individually can be tested by a PDA; in some cases an FA would suffice, and in the others we can use arguments similar to those in the proof of Lemma 11.2 (for the last two conditions in particular, nondeterminism can be used to select a particular value of $i$, and testing that the condition fails for that $i$ is no harder than testing that it holds). Therefore, $C_T'$ is the union of CFLs, and so it is a CFL itself.  ∎

The underlying fact that allows us to apply these results is that the problem of determining whether there *are* any valid computations for a given TM is unsolvable. This is just another way of expressing the unsolvability of **AcceptsSomething**, which is a corollary of Rice's theorem. We list two immediate applications, and there is further discussion in the exercises.

***Second proof of Theorem 11.12.***  This time we prove that **CFGNonemptyIntersection** is unsolvable by showing that **AcceptsSomething** is reducible to it. Given a Turing machine $T$, an instance of **AcceptsSomething**, it follows from Theorem 11.14 that there are context-free grammars $G_1$ and $G_2$ so that $L(G_1) \cap L(G_2)$ is the set $C_T$ of valid computations of $T$. Moreover, you can easily convince yourself that there is an algorithm to construct the grammars $G_1$ and $G_2$ from $T$. (This is necessary, of course, in order to obtain the desired reduction.) Since $T$ is a yes-instance of **AcceptsSomething** if and only if the pair $(G_1, G_2)$ is a yes-instance of **CFGNonemptyIntersection**, the first problem is reducible to the second, and the second is therefore unsolvable.  ∎

> **Theorem 11.15**
>
> The decision problem **CFGGeneratesAll**: Given a CFG $G$ with terminal alphabet $\Sigma$, is $L(G) = \Sigma^*$? is unsolvable.
>
> *Proof*
> We show that **AcceptsNothing** (Given $T$, is $L(T) = \emptyset$?) is reducible to **CFGGeneratesAll**. Starting with a TM $T$, there is an algorithm to construct a context-free grammar $G$ with terminal alphabet $\Sigma_1$ so that $L(G)$ is the complement $C_T'$ of the set of valid computations of $T$. Saying that $T$ accepts no strings is equivalent to saying that there are no valid computations of $T$, or that $C_T'$ contains every string over $\Sigma_1$. Therefore, $T$ is a yes-instance of **AcceptsNothing** if and only if $G$ is a yes-instance of **CFGGeneratesAll**.

# EXERCISES

**11.1.** Show that the relation $\leq$ on the set of languages (or on the set of decision problems) is reflexive and transitive. Give an example to show that it is not symmetric.

**11.2.** Let $P_2$ be the decision problem: Given a natural number $n$, is $n$ evenly divisible by 2? Consider the numerical function $f$ defined by the formula $f(n) = 5n$.

   a. To what other decision problem $P$ does $f$ reduce $P_2$?

   b. Find a numerical function $g$ that reduces $P$ to $P_2$. It should have the same property that $f$ does; namely, computing the function does not explicitly require solving the problem that the function is supposed to reduce.

**11.3.** Show that if $L_1$ and $L_2$ are languages over $\Sigma$ and $L_2$ is recursively enumerable and $L_1 \leq L_2$, then $L_1$ is recursively enumerable.

**11.4.** Show that if $L \subseteq \Sigma^*$ is neither empty nor all of $\Sigma^*$, then any recursive language over $\Sigma$ can be reduced to $L$.

**11.5.** *Fermat's last theorem*, until recently one of the most famous unproved statements in mathematics, asserts that there are no integer solutions $(x, y, z, n)$ to the equation $x^n + y^n = z^n$ satisfying $x, y > 0$ and $n > 2$. Show how a solution to the halting problem would allow you to determine the truth or falsity of the statement.

**11.6.** Show that every recursively enumerable language can be reduced to the language $Acc = \{e(T)e(w) \mid T \text{ is a TM and } T \text{ accepts input } w\}$.

**11.7.** As discussed at the beginning of Section 11.3, there is at least one TM $T$ so that the decision problem Given $w$, does $T$ accept $w$? is unsolvable. Show that any TM accepting a nonrecursive language has this property.

**11.8.** Show that for any $x \in \Sigma^*$, the problem **Accepts** can be reduced to the problem: Given a TM $T$, does $T$ accept $x$? (This shows that, just as **Accepts**-$\Lambda$ is unsolvable, so is **Accepts**-$x$, for any $x$.)

**11.9.** Construct a reduction from **Accepts**-$\Lambda$ to the problem **Accepts**-$\{\Lambda\}$: Given a TM $T$, is $L(T) = \{\Lambda\}$?

**11.10.** a. Given two sets $A$ and $B$, find two sets $C$ and $D$, defined in terms of $A$ and $B$, so that $A = B$ if and only if $C \subseteq D$.

  b. Show that the problem **Equivalent** can be reduced to the problem **Subset**.

**11.11.** a. Given two sets $A$ and $B$, find two sets $C$ and $D$, defined in terms of $A$ and $B$, so that $A \subseteq B$ if and only if $C = D$.

  b. Show that the problem **Subset** can be reduced to the problem **Equivalent**.

**11.12.** For each decision problem given, determine whether it is solvable or unsolvable, and prove your answer.

  a. Given a TM $T$, does it ever reach a state other than its initial state if it starts with a blank tape?

  b. Given a TM $T$ and a nonhalting state $q$ of $T$, does $T$ ever enter state $q$ when it begins with a blank tape?

  c. Given a TM $T$ and a nonhalting state $q$ of $T$, is there an input string $x$ that would cause $T$ eventually to enter state $q$?

  d. Given a TM $T$, does it accept the string $\Lambda$ in an even number of moves?

  e. Given a TM $T$, is there a string it accepts in an even number of moves?

  f. Given a TM $T$ and a string $w$, does $T$ loop forever on input $w$?

  g. Given a TM $T$, are there any input strings on which $T$ loops forever?

  h. Given a TM $T$ and a string $w$, does $T$ reject input $w$?

  i. Given a TM $T$, are there any input strings rejected by $T$?

  j. Given a TM $T$, does $T$ halt within ten moves on every string?

  k. Given a TM $T$, is there a string on which $T$ halts within ten moves?

  l. Given TMs $T_1$ and $T_2$, is $L(T_1) \subseteq L(T_2)$ or $L(T_2) \subseteq L(T_1)$?

**11.13.** Let us make the informal assumption that Turing machines and computer programs written in the C language are equally powerful, in the sense that anything that can be programmed on one can be programmed on the other. Give a convincing argument that both these decision problems are unsolvable:

  a. Given a C program and a statement $s$ in the program and a specific set $I$ of input data, is $s$ ever executed when the program is run on input $I$?

  b. Given a C program and a statement $s$ in the program, is there a set $I$ of input data so that $s$ is executed when the program runs on input $I$?

**11.14.** Show that the following decision problems involving unrestricted grammars are unsolvable.

    a. Given a grammar $G$ and a string $w$, does $G$ generate $w$?

    b. Given a grammar $G$, does it generate any strings?

    c. Given a grammar $G$ with terminal alphabet $\Sigma$, does it generate every string in $\Sigma^*$?

    d. Given grammars $G_1$ and $G_2$, do they generate the same language?

**11.15.** Show that the decision problem **WritesNonblank**: Given a Turing machine $T$, does it ever write a nonblank symbol on its tape when started with a blank tape? is solvable, by providing a decision algorithm.

**11.16.** Here is a "proof" that the decision problem in the previous exercise is unsolvable.

> Given a TM $T$, construct a TM $T_1$ as follows: $T_1$ has the same tape alphabet as $T$ except that it has one additional symbol #. The states of $T_1$ are the same as those of $T$. The transitions of $T_1$ are the same, except that for any transition of $T$ in which a nonblank symbol is written, the corresponding transition of $T_1$ writes # and halts. Therefore, starting with an empty tape, $T$ writes a nonblank symbol if and only if $T_1$ writes the symbol #. Since the problem Given $T_1$, does it write the symbol # when started with an empty tape? is unsolvable (because **WritesSymbol** is), **WritesNonBlank** is unsolvable.

The conclusion reached here is false; explain precisely what is wrong with the argument.

**11.17.** Refer to the correspondence system in Example 11.2, in the case where the input string is $ab$. Find the solution sequence.

**11.18.** In each case below, either give a solution to the correspondence system or show that none exists.

a.
| 100 | 101 | 110 |
|-----|-----|------|
| 10  | 01  | 1010 |

b.
| 1  | 01  | 0   | 001 |
|----|-----|-----|-----|
| 10 | 101 | 101 | 0   |

**11.19.** Show that the special case of **PCP** in which the alphabet has only two symbols is still unsolvable.

**11.20.** Show that the special case of **PCP** in which the alphabet has only one symbol is solvable.

**11.21.** Show that each of these decision problems for CFGs is unsolvable.

    a. Given two CFGs $G_1$ and $G_2$, is $L(G_1) = L(G_2)$?

    b. Given two CFGs $G_1$ and $G_2$, is $L(G_1) \subseteq L(G_2)$?

    c. Given a CFG $G$ and a regular language $R$, is $L(G) = R$?

**11.22.** In the second proof of Theorem 11.12, given at the end of Section 11.6, describe in reasonable detail the steps of the algorithm which, starting with a TM $T$, constructs CFGs $G_1$ and $G_2$ so that $L(G_1) \cap L(G_2)$ is the set of valid computations of $T$.

# MORE CHALLENGING PROBLEMS

**11.23.** Suppose $P_1$ and $P_2$ are decision problems, and $Y(P_1) \subseteq \Sigma_1^*$ and $Y(P_2) \subseteq \Sigma_2^*$ are the corresponding languages (that is, the languages of strings representing yes-instances of $P_1$ and $P_2$, respectively, with respect to some reasonable encoding functions $e_1$ and $e_2$). Suppose the function $f$ defines a reduction from $P_1$ to $P_2$; in other words, for any instance $I$ of $P_1$, $f(I)$ is an instance of $P_2$ having the same answer. Show that $Y(P_1) \leq Y(P_2)$. Describe a function from $\Sigma_1^*$ to $\Sigma_2^*$ that gives a reduction.

**11.24.** Suppose $P_1$, $P_2$, $Y(P_1)$, and $Y(P_2)$ are as in the previous exercise. Suppose also that there is at least one no-instance of $P_2$. Show that if there is a function $t : \Sigma^* \to \Sigma^*$ reducing $Y(P_1)$ to $Y(P_2)$, then there is another (computable) function $t'$ reducing $Y(P_1)$ to $Y(P_2)$ and having the property that for every $x \in \Sigma^*$ that corresponds to an instance of $P_1$, $t'(x)$ corresponds to an instance of $P_2$.

**11.25.** Let $P_1$, $P_2$, $Y(P_1)$, and $Y(P_2)$ be as in Exercise 11.23. Suppose $t : \Sigma_1^* \to \Sigma_2^*$ is a reduction of $Y(P_1)$ to $Y(P_2)$. According to Exercise 11.24, we may assume that for every string $x$ in $\Sigma_1^*$ representing an instance of $P_1$, $t(x)$ represents an instance of $P_2$. Show that $P_1 \leq P_2$. Describe a function $f$ that gives a reduction. (In other words, for an instance $I$ of $P_1$, say how to calculate an instance $f(I)$ of $P_2$.)

**11.26.** This exercise presents an example of a language $L$ so that neither $L$ nor $L'$ is recursively enumerable. Let $Acc$ and $AE$ be the languages over $\{0, 1\}$ defined as follows.

$$Acc = \{e(T)e(w) \mid T \text{ is a TM that accepts the input string } w\}$$

$$AE = \{e(T) \mid T \text{ is a TM accepting every string in its input alphabet}\}$$

($H$ and $AE$ are the sets of strings representing yes-instances of the problems **Accepts** and **AcceptsEverything**, respectively.) $Acc'$ and $AE'$ denote the complements of these two languages.

   a.  Show that $Acc \leq AE$.

   b.  Show that $Acc' \leq AE'$.

   c.  Show that $AE'$ is not recursively enumerable.

   d.  Show that $Acc' \leq AE$. (If $x = e(T)e(z)$, let $f(x) = e(S_{T,z})$, where $S_{T,z}$ is a TM that works as follows. On input $w$, $S_{T,z}$ simulates the computation performed by $T$ on input $z$ for up to $|w|$ moves. If this computation would cause $T$ to accept within $|w|$ moves, $S_{T,z}$ enters an infinite loop; otherwise $S_{T,z}$ accepts. Show that if $f(x)$ is defined appropriately for strings $x$ not of the form $e(T)e(z)$, then $f$ defines a reduction from $Acc'$ to $AE$.)

e.  Show that $AE$ is not recursively enumerable.

**11.27.**  If $AE$ is the language defined in the previous exercise, show that if $L$ is any language whose complement is not recursively enumerable, then $L \le AE$.

**11.28.**  Find two unsolvable decision problems, neither of which can be reduced to the other, and prove it.

**11.29.**  In this problem TMs are assumed to have input alphabet $\{0, 1\}$. For a finite set $S \subseteq \{0, 1\}^*$, $P_S$ denotes the decision problem: Given a TM $T$, is $S \subseteq L(T)$?

a.  Show that if $x, y \in \{0, 1\}^*$, then $P_{\{x\}} \le P_{\{y\}}$.

b.  Show that if $x, y, z \in \{0, 1\}^*$, then $P_{\{x\}} \le P_{\{y,z\}}$.

c.  Show that if $x, y, z \in \{0, 1\}^*$, then $P_{\{x,y\}} \le P_{\{z\}}$.

d.  Show that for any two finite subsets $S$ and $U$ of $\{0, 1\}^*$, $P_S \le P_U$.

**11.30.**  Repeat the previous problem, but this time letting $P_S$ denote the problem: Given a TM $T$, is $L(T) = S$?

**11.31.**  For each decision problem given, determine whether it is solvable or unsolvable, and prove your answer.

a.  Given a TM $T$, does $T$ eventually enter every one of its nonhalting states if it begins with a blank tape?

b.  Given a TM $T$, is there an input string that causes $T$ to enter every one of its nonhalting states?

**11.32.**  Show that the problem **CSLIsEmpty:** given a linear-bounded automaton, is the language it accepts empty? is unsolvable. Suggestion: use the fact that Post's correspondence problem is unsolvable, by starting with an arbitrary correspondence system and constructing an LBA that accepts precisely the strings $\alpha$ representing solutions to the correspondence system.

**11.33.**  This exercise establishes the fact that there is a recursive language over $\{a, b\}$ that is not context-sensitive. (Note that the argument outlined below uses a diagonal argument. At this point, a diagonal argument or something comparable is the only technique known for constructing languages that are not context-sensitive.)

a.  Describe a way to enumerate explicitly the set of context-sensitive grammars generating languages over $\{a, b\}$. You may make the assumption that for some set $A = \{A_1, A_2, \ldots\}$, every such grammar has start symbol $A_1$ and only variables that are elements of $A$.

b.  If $G_1, G_2, \ldots$ is the enumeration in part (a), and $x_1, x_2, \ldots$ are the nonnull elements of $\{a, b\}^*$ listed in canonical order, let $L = \{x_i \mid x_i \notin L(G_i)\}$. Show that $L$ is recursive and not context-sensitive.

**11.34.**  Is the decision problem: Given a CFG $G$, and a string $x$, is $L(G) = \{x\}$? solvable or unsolvable? Give reasons for your answer.

**11.35.** Is the decision problem: Given a CFG $G$ and a regular language $R$, is $L(G) \subseteq R$? solvable or unsolvable? Give reasons for your answer.

**11.36.** Is the decision problem: Given a CFG $G$, with terminal alphabet $\Sigma$, is $\Sigma^* - L(G)$ finite? solvable or unsolvable? Give reasons for your answer.

**11.37.** Show that the problem: Given a CFG $G$ with terminal alphabet $\Sigma$, is $L(G) \neq \Sigma^*$? is unsolvable by directly reducing **PCP** to it. Suggestion: if $G_\alpha$ and $G_\beta$ are the CFGs constructed from an instance of **PCP** as in Section 11.5, show that there is an algorithm to construct a CFG generating $(L(G_\alpha) \cap L(G_\beta))'$.

# CHAPTER

# 12

# Computable Functions

## 12.1 | PRIMITIVE RECURSIVE FUNCTIONS

Not all functions, even those with precise definitions, can be computed by TMs. The uncomputable functions we have seen so far are the characteristic functions of nonrecursive languages. In this chapter we will concentrate on numerical functions— functions of zero or more nonnegative integer variables, whose values are nonnegative integers—and try to find a way to characterize the ones that can actually be computed. The focus on numerical functions is not as restrictive as it might sound, because we will soon develop a way to describe any function from strings to strings by encoding both arguments and function values as numbers.

Recall that a partial function $f$ from $\mathcal{N}$ to $\mathcal{N}$ is Turing-computable if there is a Turing machine $T$ so that, starting with input $1^n$, $T$ halts in the state $h_a$ with output $1^{f(n)}$ if $f$ is defined at $n$ and fails to accept otherwise. We can easily adapt the non-constructive argument from Section 10.5 to show that there are many uncomputable functions. The set of Turing machines is countable; the set of partial functions from $\mathcal{N}$ to $\mathcal{N}$ is uncountable; and a TM can compute at most one partial function from $\mathcal{N}$ to $\mathcal{N}$. Therefore, the set of uncomputable functions must be uncountable.

We can also provide explicit examples of uncomputable functions from $\mathcal{N}$ to $\mathcal{N}$, just as we provided examples of nonrecursive languages. Our first example, as you might expect, involves Turing machines and a diagonal-like argument.

**EXAMPLE 12.1**  The Busy Beaver Function

Let us define $b : \mathcal{N} \to \mathcal{N}$ as follows. $b(0)$ is 0. For $n > 0$, $b(n)$ is obtained by considering TMs having $n$ nonhalting states and tape alphabet $\{0, 1\}$. We can assume, by relabeling the states if necessary, that the set of nonhalting states in all these machines is $\{q_0, q_1, \ldots, q_{n-1}\}$, and for each $n$ there are therefore only a finite number of TMs of this type. We restrict our attention to those that halt on input $1^n$, and we let $b(n)$ be the largest number of 1's that any of these machines leaves on the tape when it halts. (The number $b(n)$ is therefore a measure of how *busy* a TM of this type can be before it halts. It has also been suggested that the term "busy beaver" might refer to the resemblance between 1's on the tape and twigs arranged by a beaver.)

Suppose, for the sake of contradiction, that $b$ is computable. Then it is possible to find a TM $T_b$ having tape alphabet $\{0, 1\}$ that computes it (Exercise 9.45). Let $T = T_b T_1$, where $T_1$ is a TM also having tape alphabet $\{0, 1\}$ that moves its tape head to the first square to the right of its starting position in which there is either a 0 or a blank, writes a 1 there, and halts. Let $m$ be the number of states of $T$. By definition of the function $b$, no TM with $m$ states and tape alphabet $\{0, 1\}$ can end up with more than $b(m)$ 1's on the tape if it halts on input $1^m$. However, $T$ is a machine of this type that halts with output $1^{b(m)+1}$. This contradiction shows that $b$ is not computable.

---

The function $b$ has been precisely defined but is not computable. A formula like

$$f(n) = |2^{n+5} - (3n + 1)^8|$$

on the other hand, defines a function that *is* obviously computable. The difference between these two functions is not so much that one is defined by words and the other by a mathematical formula. Consider the function $b_2$, where $b_2(n)$ is the largest number of 1's that can be left on the tape of a TM with tape alphabet $\{0, 1\}$ and two nonhalting states, if it starts with input $1^n$ and eventually halts. This is also a definition in words, superficially almost identical to that of $b$, and you can convince yourself that $b_2$ is computable. The property $b_2$ and $f$ have in common is that the definition either is, or can be replaced by, a constructive one. The proof in the example above is subtle but shows that $b$ lacks this property.

Trying to decide whether a definition in words can be replaced by a constructive one can be difficult. What we can do, however, is to formulate an appropriate notion of "constructive," so that the functions definable in this way will be precisely the computable functions. The definition of the function $f$ in the algebraic formula is constructive in the sense that $f$ is obtained by applying various arithmetic operations to simpler elementary functions (the identity function and various constant functions). We will take the same approach, except that the operations we use will be more general than arithmetic operations like addition and multiplication.

First we give a precise definition of the elementary functions we are allowed to start with. Notice that all the initial functions in the definition are total functions. In this definition and the ones that follow, we adopt the convention of using lowercase letters for integers and uppercase for vectors, or $m$-tuples.

---

**Definition 12.1    Initial Functions**

The initial functions are the following:

1. *Constant* functions: For each $k \geq 0$ and each $a \geq 0$, the constant function $C_a^k : \mathcal{N}^k \to \mathcal{N}$ is defined by the formula

$$C_a^k(X) = a \qquad \text{for every } X \in \mathcal{N}^k$$

In the case $k = 0$ we may identify the function $C_a^k$ with the number $a$.

2. The *successor* function $s : \mathcal{N} \to \mathcal{N}$ is defined by the formula

$$s(x) = x + 1$$

3. *Projection* functions: For each $k \geq 1$ and each $i$ with $1 \leq i \leq k$, the projection function $p_i^k : \mathcal{N}^k \to \mathcal{N}$ is defined by the formula

$$p_i^k(x_1, x_2, \ldots, x_i, \ldots, x_k) = x_i$$

Now we are ready to consider ways of combining functions to obtain new ones. We start with composition, essentially as defined in Chapter 1, and another operation involving a type of recursive definition.

---

**Definition 12.2    Composition**

Suppose $f$ is a partial function from $\mathcal{N}^k$ to $\mathcal{N}$, and for each $i$ with $1 \leq i \leq k$, $g_i$ is a partial function from $\mathcal{N}^m$ to $\mathcal{N}$. The partial function obtained from $f$ and $g_1, g_2, \ldots, g_k$ by composition is the partial function $h$ from $\mathcal{N}^m$ to $\mathcal{N}$ defined by the formula

$$h(X) = f(g_1(X), g_2(X), \ldots, g_k(X)) \qquad (X \in \mathcal{N}^m)$$

---

We have chosen here to restrict ourselves to functions whose values are single integers, rather than $k$-tuples; otherwise, we could write $h = f \circ g$, where $g$ is the function from $\mathcal{N}^m$ to $\mathcal{N}^k$ defined by $g(X) = (g_1(X), \ldots, g_k(X))$.

Notice that in this definition, in order for $h(X)$ to be defined, it is necessary and sufficient that each $g_i(X)$ be defined and that $f$ be defined at the point $(g_1(X), \ldots, g_k(X))$. If all the functions $f, g_1, \ldots, g_k$ are total, then $h$ is total.

For a familiar example, let *Add*: $\mathcal{N} \times \mathcal{N} \to \mathcal{N}$ be the usual addition function ($Add(x, y) = x + y$), and let $f$ and $g$ be partial functions from $\mathcal{N}^k$ to $\mathcal{N}$. Then the function $Add(f, g)$ obtained from *Add*, $f$, and $g$ by composition is normally written $f + g$.

The simplest way to define a function $f$ from $\mathcal{N}$ to $\mathcal{N}$ recursively is to define $f(0)$ first, and then for any $k \geq 0$ to define $f(k + 1)$ in terms of $f(k)$. A standard example is the factorial function:

$$0! = 1 \qquad (k + 1)! = (k + 1) * k!$$

In the recursive step, the expression for $f(k + 1)$ involves both $k$ and $f(k)$. We can generalize this by substituting any expression of the form $h(k, f(k))$, where $h$ is a function of two variables. In order to use this approach for a function $f$ of more than one variable, we simply restrict the recursion to the last coordinate. In other words, we start by saying what $f(x_1, x_2, \ldots, x_n, 0)$ is, for any choice of $(x_1, \ldots, x_n)$. This means specifying a constant when $n = 0$ and a function of $n$ variables in general.

Then in the recursive step, we say what $f(x_1, x_2, \ldots, x_n, k + 1)$ is, in terms of $f(x_1, \ldots, x_n, k)$. Let the $n$-tuple $(x_1, \ldots, x_n)$ be denoted by $X$. In the most general case, $f(X, k + 1)$ may depend on $X$ and $k$ directly, in addition to $f(X, k)$, just as $(k + 1)!$ depended on $k$ as well as on $k!$. Thus a reasonable way to formulate the recursive step is to say that

$$f(X, k + 1) = h(X, k, f(X, k))$$

for some function $h$ of $n + 2$ variables.

---

**Definition 12.3    The Primitive Recursion Operation**

Suppose $n \geq 0$, and $g$ and $h$ are functions of $n$ and $n + 2$ variables, respectively. The function obtained from $g$ and $h$ by the operation of *primitive recursion* is the function $f : \mathcal{N}^{n+1} \to \mathcal{N}$ defined by the formulas

$$f(X, 0) = g(X)$$
$$f(X, k + 1) = h(X, k, f(X, k))$$

for every $X \in \mathcal{N}^n$ and every $k \geq 0$.

---

In the factorial example, $n = 0$, $g$ is the number (or the function of zero variables) $C_1^0 = 1$, and $h(x, y) = (x + 1) * y$.

Here again, if the functions $g$ and $h$ are total functions, $f$ is total. If either $g$ or $h$ is not total, the situation is a little more complicated. If $g(X)$ is undefined for some $X \in \mathcal{N}^n$, then $f(X, 0)$ is undefined, $f(X, 1) = h(X, 0, f(X, 0))$ is undefined, and in general $f(X, k)$ is undefined for each $k$. For exactly the same reason, if $f(X, k)$ is undefined for *some* $k$, say $k = k_0$, then $f(X, k)$ is undefined for every $k \geq k_0$; equivalently, if $f(X, k_1)$ is defined, then $f(X, k)$ is defined for every $k \leq k_1$. These observations will be useful a little later in showing that a function obtained by primitive recursion from computable functions is also computable.

At this point we have a class of initial functions, and we have two operations with which to obtain new functions. Although other operations are necessary in order to obtain all computable functions, it will be useful to formalize the set of functions we can obtain with the tools we have developed.

---

**Definition 12.4    Primitive Recursive Functions**

The set *PR* of *primitive recursive* functions is defined as follows.

1. All initial functions are elements of *PR*.
2. For any $k \geq 0$ and $m \geq 0$, if $f : \mathcal{N}^k \to \mathcal{N}$ and $g_1, g_2, \ldots, g_k : \mathcal{N}^m \to \mathcal{N}$ are elements of *PR*, then the function $f(g_1, g_2, \ldots, g_k)$ obtained from $f$ and $g_1, g_2, \ldots, g_k$ by composition is an element of *PR*.

> 3. For any $n \geq 0$, any function $g : \mathcal{N}^{n+1} \to \mathcal{N}$ in *PR*, and any function $h : \mathcal{N}^{n+2} \to \mathcal{N}$ in *PR*, the function $f : \mathcal{N}^{n+1} \to \mathcal{N}$ obtained from $g$ and $h$ by primitive recursion is in *PR*.
>
> 4. No other functions are in the set *PR*.

Just as in Chapter 2, we might characterize these functions a little more explicitly (see the discussion after Example 2.18) by saying that primitive recursive functions are those having *primitive recursive derivations*. A function $f$ has a primitive recursive derivation if there is a finite sequence of functions $f_0, f_1, \ldots, f_j$ so that $f_j = f$ and each function $f_i$ in the sequence is an initial function, or can be obtained from earlier functions in the sequence by composition, or can be obtained from earlier functions in the sequence by primitive recursion.

**EXAMPLE 12.2** Addition and Multiplication

Let us show that the functions *Add* and *Mult* from $\mathcal{N} \times \mathcal{N}$ to $\mathcal{N}$, defined by the formulas

$$Add(x, y) = x + y \qquad Mult(x, y) = x * y$$

are both primitive recursive. We start by finding a primitive recursive derivation for *Add*. Since *Add* is not an initial function, and there is no obvious way to obtain it by composition, we try to obtain it from simpler functions using primitive recursion. If *Add* is obtained from $g$ and $h$ by primitive recursion, $g$ and $h$ must be functions of one and three variables, respectively. The equations are

$$Add(x, 0) = g(x)$$

$$Add(x, k + 1) = h(x, k, Add(x, k))$$

$Add(x, 0)$ should be $x$, and thus we may take $g$ to be the initial function $p_1^1$. In order to get $x + k + 1$ (i.e., $Add(x, k + 1)$) from the three quantities $x$, $k$, and $x + k$, we can simply take the successor of $x + k$. In other words, $h(x, k, Add(x, k))$ should be $s(Add(x, k))$. This means that $h(x_1, x_2, x_3)$ should be $s(x_3)$, or $s(p_3^3(x_1, x_2, x_3))$. Therefore, a derivation for *Add* can be obtained as follows:

$$
\begin{aligned}
f_0 &= p_1^1 & \text{(an initial function)} \\
f_1 &= s & \text{(an initial function)} \\
f_2 &= p_3^3 & \text{(an initial function)} \\
f_3 &= s(p_3^3) & \text{(obtained from } f_1 \text{ and } f_2 \text{ by composition)} \\
f_4 &= Add & \text{(obtained from } f_0 \text{ and } f_3 \text{ by primitive recursion)}
\end{aligned}
$$

This way of ordering the five functions is not the only correct one. Any ordering in which *Add* is last and $s$ and $p_3^3$ both precede $s(p_3^3)$ would work just as well.

To obtain *Mult*, we try primitive recursion again. We have

$$Mult(x, 0) = 0$$

$$Mult(x, k + 1) = x * (k + 1)$$

$$= Add(x * k, x)$$

$$= Add(x, Mult(x, k))$$

Remember that we are attempting to write this in the form $h(x, k, Mult(x, k))$. Since $x$ and $Mult(x, k)$ are the first and third coordinates of the 3-tuple $(x, k, Mult(x, k))$, we use the function $f = Add(p_1^3, p_3^3)$, obtained from $Add$, $p_1^3$, and $p_3^3$ by composition. The function $Mult$ is obtained from 0 (i.e., the initial function $C_0^1$) and $f$ using the operation of primitive recursion. Therefore, $Mult$ is also primitive recursive.

---

This derivation of $Mult$, and many arguments involving primitive recursive functions, can be simplified somewhat by using the following general result.

**Theorem 12.1**
Let $f$ be a primitive recursive function of $n$ variables. Then

1. For any $k \geq 1$, any function $g$ of $n + k$ variables obtained from $f$ by introducing "dummy" variables (e.g., if $n = 2$ and $k = 1$, $g(x_1, x_2, x_3) = f(x_1, x_3)$) is also primitive recursive.
2. Any function $g$ of $n$ variables obtained from $f$ by *permuting* variables (e.g., if $n = 2$, $g(x_1, x_2) = f(x_2, x_1)$) is primitive recursive.
3. For any $k$ with $1 \leq k \leq n$, any function $g$ of $n - k$ variables obtained from $f$ by *substituting constants* for $k$ of the variables of $f$ (e.g., if $n = 2$ and $k = 1$, $g(x) = f(5, x)$) is primitive recursive.
4. For any $k$ with $1 \leq k \leq n$, any function $g$ of $n - k$ variables obtained from $f$ by *repeating a variable* $k$ times (e.g., if $n = 3$ and $k = 1$, $g(x_1, x_2) = f(x_1, x_2, x_1)$) is primitive recursive.

*Proof*
These are all variants of the same general situation:

$$g(x_1, x_2, \ldots, x_r) = f(z_1, z_2, \ldots, z_n)$$

where for each $i$, $z_i$ is either $x_j = p_j^r(x_1, \ldots, x_r)$ for some $j$, or $a = C_a^r(x_1, \ldots, x_r)$ for some $a$. For example, the function $g$ shown in part 1 could be written

$$g(x_1, x_2, x_3) = f(p_1^3(x_1, x_2, x_3), p_3^3(x_1, x_2, x_3))$$

In all four cases, the result is true because all the functions $p_j^r$ and $C_a^r$ are primitive recursive, and $g$ is obtained from $f$ and some of these functions by composition.

An Application of Theorem 12.1  **EXAMPLE 12.3**

Let $f$ be the function of two variables defined by

$$f(x, y) = y^x + x^x + x^7$$

where we define $0^0 = 1$ in order to make the function total. To show that $f$ is primitive recursive, we look first at the function $g$ defined by $f_1(x, y) = x^y$. We can write

$$f_1(x, 0) = 1$$
$$f_1(x, k+1) = Mult(x, x^k)$$
$$= Mult(x, f_1(x, k))$$

By considering the formula $h(x, y, z) = Mult(x, z)$ and using part 1 of the theorem, we can see that $f_1$ is primitive recursive. Since $y^x = f_1(y, x)$, it follows from part 2 that the first term in the formula for $f$ is primitive recursive. The second and third terms are primitive recursive functions of $x$ because of parts 4 and 3 of the theorem, respectively, and therefore primitive recursive functions of $x$ and $y$ as a result of part 1. Finally, since $f(x, y) = Add(Add(y^x, x^x), x^7)$, we can use the fact that composition preserves primitive recursiveness to conclude that $f$ is primitive recursive.

## EXAMPLE 12.4   The Predecessor Function and Proper Subtraction

The subtraction function, with the modification necessary to guarantee that its values are always nonnegative, is primitive recursive. To show this, we begin with the function *Pred* (short for *predecessor*), defined by

$$Pred(x) = \begin{cases} 0 & \text{if } x = 0 \\ x - 1 & \text{if } x \geq 1 \end{cases}$$

The formulas

$$Pred(0) = 0$$
$$Pred(k + 1) = k$$

together with part 1 of Theorem 12.1 show that *Pred* can be derived from primitive recursive functions using primitive recursion. If we define *Sub* by

$$Sub(x, y) = \begin{cases} x - y & \text{if } x \geq y \\ 0 & \text{otherwise} \end{cases}$$

then you can easily check the equations

$$Sub(x, 0) = x$$
$$Sub(x, k + 1) = Pred(Sub(x, k))$$

from which it follows that *Sub* is primitive recursive. This operation is often written $\dot{-}$ and is referred to as *proper subtraction*, or the *monus* operation.

Although we have not actually finished producing examples of primitive recursive functions, we close this section by proving two results, which together show that the set of primitive recursive functions is a proper subset of the set of computable functions.

**Theorem 12.2**
Every primitive recursive function is a computable total function.

*Proof*
The way we have defined the set of primitive recursive functions makes structural induction appropriate for proving things about them. We show the following three statements: Every initial function is a total computable function; any function obtained from total computable functions by composition is also a total computable function; and any function obtained from total computable functions by primitive recursion is also a total computable function.

We have previously observed, in fact, that initial functions are total functions and that functions obtained from total functions by composition or primitive recursion are total; thus we may concentrate on the conclusions involving computability. It is almost obvious that all the initial functions are computable, and we omit the details. For the sake of simplicity, we show that if $h : \mathcal{N}^m \to \mathcal{N}$ is obtained from $f : \mathcal{N}^2 \to \mathcal{N}$ and $g_1$ and $g_2$, both functions from $\mathcal{N}^m$ to $\mathcal{N}$, by composition, and if these three functions are computable, then $h$ is. The argument is valid even if all the functions are partial functions, and it extends in an obvious way to the more general case in which $f$ is a function of $k$ variables.

Let $T_f$, $T_1$, and $T_2$ be TMs computing $f$, $g_1$, and $g_2$, respectively. We will construct a TM $T_h$ to compute $h$. To simplify notation, we denote by $X$ the $m$-tuple $(x_1, x_2, \ldots, x_m)$ and by $1^X$ the string $1^{x_1} \Delta 1^{x_2} \Delta \cdots \Delta 1^{x_m}$.

The TM $T_h$ begins with tape contents $\underline{\Delta} 1^X$, and it must use this input twice, once to compute each of the $g_i$'s. It does this by copying the input to produce the tape

$$\Delta 1^X \underline{\Delta} 1^X$$

executing $T_1$ to produce $\Delta 1^X \underline{\Delta} 1^{g_1(X)}$, and then making another copy of the input and executing $T_2$, to obtain

$$\Delta 1^X \Delta 1^{g_1(X)} \underline{\Delta} 1^{g_2(X)}$$

At this point it deletes the original input and executes $T_f$ on the input $1^{g_1(X)} \Delta 1^{g_2(X)}$, which produces the desired output.

For any choice of $X$, $T_h$ fails to accept during the execution of $T_i$ if $g_i(X)$ is undefined, and fails to accept during the execution of $T_f$ if both $g_i(X)$'s are defined but $f(g_1(X), g_2(X))$ is undefined. Therefore, $T_h$ computes $h$.

For the final step of the proof, suppose that $g : \mathcal{N}^n \to \mathcal{N}$ and $h : \mathcal{N}^{n+2} \to \mathcal{N}$ are computable and that $f$ is obtained from $g$ and $h$ by primitive recursion. We let $T_g$ and $T_h$ be TMs computing $g$ and $h$, respectively, and we construct a TM $T_f$ to compute $f$.

The original tape of $T_f$ looks like this:

$$\underline{\Delta} 1^{x_1} \Delta 1^{x_2} \Delta \cdots \Delta 1^{x_n} \Delta 1^{x_{n+1}}$$

which we abbreviate $\underline{\Delta}1^X\Delta1^{x_{n+1}}$. As before, $X$ denotes $(x_1,\ldots,x_n)$. In the case in which $f(X, x_{n+1})$ is defined, $T_f$ works as follows. First, it determines whether $x_{n+1}$ is 0, and if it is, $T_f$ returns the tape head to square 0, executes $T_g$, and halts normally. If $x_{n+1}$ is not 0, the tape contents are $\Delta1^X\Delta1^{k+1}$ for some $k$, and in this case $T_f$ computes $f(X, 0)$, uses it to compute $f(X, 1)$, uses that to compute $f(X, 2), \ldots$, and ultimately uses $f(X, k)$ to compute $f(X, k+1)$. It prepares to do this by creating the tape

$$\#1^X\Delta1^k\Delta1^X\Delta1^{k-1}\Delta1^X\Delta\cdots\Delta1^2\Delta1^X\Delta1^1\Delta1^X\Delta1^0\underline{\Delta}1^X$$

It executes $T_g$ and moves the tape head, obtaining

$$\#1^X\Delta1^k\Delta1^X\Delta\cdots\Delta1^1\underline{\Delta}1^X\Delta1^0\Delta1^{f(X,0)}$$

Here we use the fact that $f(X, 0) = g(X)$. At this point $T_f$ begins a loop, during each iteration of which it executes $T_h$ and moves the tape head. After the first iteration, since $f(X, 1) = h(X, 0, f(X, 0))$, the tape looks like this:

$$\#1^X\Delta1^k\Delta1^X\Delta\cdots\underline{\Delta}1^X\Delta1^1\Delta1^{f(X,1)}$$

and $T_f$ is ready to execute $T_h$ again to compute $f(X, 2)$. Continued iterations finally produce

$$\underline{\#}1^X\Delta1^k\Delta1^{f(X,k)}$$

at which point changing # to $\Delta$ and executing $T_h$ once more produces the desired result.

From the remarks after Definition 12.3 we know that if $f(X, k+1)$ is defined, each of the steps in this computation can be carried out successfully. If $f(X, k+1)$ is undefined, then either the execution of $T_g$ on the input $1^X$ fails to accept, or, for some $i$ with $0 \le i \le k$, the execution of $T_h$ on the input $1^X\Delta1^i\Delta1^{f(X,i)}$ fails to accept. We may therefore conclude that $T_f$ accepts the input $1^X\Delta1^{k+1}$ if and only if $f(X, k+1)$ is defined.

**Theorem 12.3**
There is a computable total function from $\mathcal{N}$ to $\mathcal{N}$ that is not primitive recursive.

*Proof*
The proof is informal. We describe a function that cannot be primitive recursive, and present an argument based on the Church-Turing thesis that it is computable.

We begin by fixing an alphabet $\Sigma$ containing all the symbols we might need to describe numerical functions. Any primitive recursive function is specified by a primitive recursive derivation that, in turn, can be specified by a string over $\Sigma$. The remainder of the proof depends on the following statement: There is an algorithm to determine, given some string in $\Sigma^*$, whether it represents a primitive recursive derivation of a function of one variable. This is intuitively plausible, although a detailed description of the algorithm would be very messy.

The proof uses a diagonal argument. First, place an ordering on $\Sigma$, so that we may consider the canonical order on the set $\Sigma^*$ (strings ordered by length, and strings of the same length ordered alphabetically). Now define the function $f : \mathcal{N} \to \mathcal{N}$ as follows. For each $i$, examine the strings of $\Sigma^*$ in order, discarding those that do not represent primitive recursive derivations of functions from $\mathcal{N}$ to $\mathcal{N}$, until the $i$th string is found that does represent such a derivation; let the function being derived be $f_i$, and let

$$f(i) = f_i(i) + 1$$

The function $f$ is total. On the one hand, $f$ is computable, since we have described an algorithm for finding the derivation of $f_i$ and the derivation constitutes an algorithm for computing $f(i)$. On the other hand, $f$ cannot be primitive recursive. Every primitive recursive function of one variable is $f_i$ for some $i$, and for any $i$, $f$ is different from $f_i$ because $f(i) \neq f_i(i)$.

There are functions defined in more conventional ways that can be shown to be total, computable, and not primitive recursive. One of the most well known is called Ackermann's function; its definition involves a sort of recursion, so that it is clearly computable, but it can be shown to grow more rapidly than any primitive recursive function. A readable discussion of this function can be found in the text by Hennie (1977).

# 12.2 | PRIMITIVE RECURSIVE PREDICATES AND SOME BOUNDED OPERATIONS

Several of the functions considered in the last section, such as *Pred* and *Sub*, have been defined by *cases*. Those two functions are simple enough that a direct primitive recursive derivation is feasible. However, for an arbitrary function $f$ defined by

$$f(X) = \begin{cases} f_1(X) & \text{if } P_1(X) \text{ is true} \\ f_2(X) & \text{if } P_2(X) \text{ is true} \\ \cdots \\ f_k(X) & \text{if } P_k(X) \text{ is true} \end{cases}$$

it would be more convenient to have a general principle allowing us to draw conclusions about $f$ from properties of the functions $f_i$ and the conditions $P_i(X)$.

A "condition" $P$ depending on the variable $X \in \mathcal{N}^n$, so that $P(X)$ is either true or false, is called a *predicate*. More precisely, it is an *n-place* predicate, which is a partial function from $\mathcal{N}^n$ to {true, false}. Closely associated with a predicate $P$ is its *characteristic function* $\chi_P : \mathcal{N}^n \to \{0, 1\}$, defined by

$$\chi_P(X) = \begin{cases} 1 & \text{if } P(X) \text{ is true} \\ 0 & \text{otherwise} \end{cases}$$

Since $\chi_P$ is a numerical function, all the properties of functions that we have discussed in Section 12.1 are applicable to it and, by association, to $P$. In particular, $P$ is computable if $\chi_P$ is, and $P$ is primitive recursive if $\chi_P$ is. If the characteristic function $\chi_L$ of a language $L$ is computable, we can decide whether a given input is in $L$. When we say that $\chi_P$ is computable, we are saying something similar: There is an algorithm to determine whether a given $X$ satisfies $P$ or makes $P(X)$ true.

Predicates take the values true and false, and therefore it makes sense to apply the logical operators $\wedge$ (AND), $\vee$ (OR), and $\neg$ (NOT) to them. For example, $(P_1 \wedge P_2)(X)$ is true if and only if both $P_1(X)$ and $P_2(X)$ are true. Not surprisingly, these operations preserve the primitive recursive property.

---

**Theorem 12.4**

If $P_1$ and $P_2$ are primitive recursive $n$-place predicates, then so are the predicates $P_1 \wedge P_2$, $P_1 \vee P_2$, and $\neg P_1$.

*Proof*

The result follows from these three equations, which you can verify easily:

$$\chi_{P_1 \wedge P_2} = \chi_{P_1} * \chi_{P_2}$$

$$\chi_{P_1 \vee P_2} = \chi_{P_1} + \chi_{P_2} \dotminus \chi_{P_1 \wedge P_2}$$

$$\chi_{(\neg P_1)} = 1 \dotminus \chi_{P_1}$$

(Recall that $\dotminus$ denotes proper subtraction, introduced in Example 12.4.)

---

**EXAMPLE 12.5**   Relational Predicates

Among the simplest predicates are the relational predicates *LT*, *EQ*, *GT*, *LE*, *GE*, and *NE*. The expression $LT(x, y)$ is true if $x < y$ and false otherwise, and the definitions of the other five are similarly suggested by their names. These predicates are all primitive recursive. In order to show this, we first introduce the function *Sg* of one variable defined by

$$Sg(0) = 0 \qquad Sg(k+1) = 1$$

This function takes the value 0 if $x = 0$ and the value 1 otherwise, and its definition makes it clear that it is primitive recursive. Now we may write

$$\chi_{LT}(x, y) = Sg(y \dotminus x)$$

since $x < y$ if and only if $y \dotminus x > 0$. This equation shows that $\chi_{LT}$ is obtained from primitive recursive functions by composition and is therefore primitive recursive. The result for the equality predicate follows from the formula

$$\chi_{EQ}(x, y) = 1 \dotminus (Sg(x \dotminus y) + Sg(y \dotminus x))$$

(Note that if $x < y$ or $x > y$, then one of the terms $x \dotminus y$ and $y \dotminus x$ is nonzero, and the expression in parentheses is nonzero, causing the final result to be 0. If $x = y$, both terms in the parenthesized expression are 0, and the final result is 1.)

Although the other four relational predicates can be handled in the same way, it is easier to use the formulas

$$LE = LT \vee EQ$$

$$GT = \neg LE$$

$$GE = \neg LT$$

$$NE = \neg EQ$$

which together with Theorem 12.4 imply that all these predicates are primitive recursive.

---

If $P$ is an $n$-place predicate and $f_1, f_2, \ldots, f_n : \mathcal{N}^k \to \mathcal{N}$, we may form the $k$-place predicate $Q = P(f_1, \ldots, f_n)$, and it is clear that the characteristic function $\chi_Q$ is obtained from $\chi_P$ and $f_1, \ldots, f_n$ by composition. Therefore, if $P$ is a primitive recursive predicate and all the functions $f_i$ are primitive recursive, then $Q$ is primitive recursive. Combining this general fact with Theorem 12.4, we see that arbitrarily complicated predicates constructed using relational and logical operators, such as

$$(f_1 = (3f_2)^2 \wedge (f_3 < f_4 + f_5)) \vee \neg(P \vee Q)$$

are primitive recursive as long as the basic constituents (in this case, the functions $f_1, \ldots, f_5$ and the predicates $P$ and $Q$) are primitive recursive.

Now we are in a better position to return to the idea of a function defined by cases and to establish a sufficient condition for such a function to be primitive recursive.

---

**Theorem 12.5**
Suppose $f_1, f_2, \ldots, f_k$ are primitive recursive functions from $\mathcal{N}^m$ to $\mathcal{N}$, $P_1, P_2, \ldots, P_k$ are primitive recursive $n$-place predicates, and for every $X \in \mathcal{N}^n$, exactly one of the conditions $P_1(X), \ldots, P_k(X)$ is true. Then the function $f : \mathcal{N}^n \to \mathcal{N}$ defined by

$$f(X) = \begin{cases} f_1(X) & \text{if } P_1(X) \text{ is true} \\ f_2(X) & \text{if } P_2(X) \text{ is true} \\ \ldots \\ f_k(X) & \text{if } P_k(X) \text{ is true} \end{cases}$$

is primitive recursive.

**Proof**
The last of the three assumptions guarantees that the definition of $f$ is unambiguous. It implies that for every $X$, exactly one of the values $\chi_{P(X)}$ is 1 and the others are all 0. Therefore,

$$f = f_1 * \chi_{P_1} + f_2 * \chi_{P_2} + \cdots + f_k * \chi_{P_k}$$

and the result follows from the fact that all the functions appearing on the right side of this formula are primitive recursive.

**EXAMPLE 12.6** ## The *Mod* and *Div* Functions

For natural numbers $x$ and $y$ with $y > 0$, we denote by $Div(x, y)$ and $Mod(x, y)$ the integer quotient and remainder, respectively, when $x$ is divided by $y$. For example, $Div(8, 5) = 1$, $Mod(8, 5) = 3$, and $Mod(12, 4) = 0$. As it stands, these are not total functions on $\mathcal{N} \times \mathcal{N}$, because we do not allow division by 0; however, it will be useful to extend the definition and to show that the results are actually primitive recursive. Let us say that for any $x$, $Div(x, 0) = 0$ and $Mod(x, 0) = x$. Then the usual formula

$$x = y * Div(x, y) + Mod(x, y)$$

still holds for every $x$ and $y$, and

$$0 \le Mod(x, y) < y$$

is true as long as $y > 0$.

We begin by showing that *Mod* is primitive recursive. The derivation involves recursion in the *first* variable, and for this reason we let

$$R(x, y) = Mod(y, x)$$

According to part 2 of Theorem 12.1, the primitive recursiveness of *Mod* follows from that of $R$. The following formulas can be verified easily.

$$R(x, 0) = Mod(0, x) \ = \ 0$$

$$R(x, k + 1) = Mod(k + 1, x)$$
$$= \begin{cases} R(x, k) + 1 & \text{if } x \ne 0 \text{ and } R(x, k) + 1 < x \\ 0 & \text{if } x \ne 0 \text{ and } R(x, k) + 1 = x \\ k + 1 & \text{if } x = 0 \end{cases}$$

For example,

$$R(5, 6 + 1) = Mod(7, 5) = Mod(6, 5) + 1$$

since $5 \ne 0$ and $Mod(6, 5) + 1 = 1 + 1 < 5$, and

$$R(5, 9 + 1) = Mod(10, 5) = 0$$

since $5 \ne 0$ and $Mod(9, 5) + 1 = 4 + 1 = 5$. The function $h$ defined by

$$h(x_1, x_2, x_3) = \begin{cases} x_3 + 1 & \text{if } x_1 \ne 0 \text{ and } x_3 + 1 < x_1 \\ 0 & \text{if } x_1 \ne 0 \text{ and } x_3 + 1 = x_1 \\ x_2 + 1 & \text{if } x_1 = 0 \end{cases}$$

is not a total function, since it is undefined if $x_1 \ne 0$ and $x_3 + 1 > x_1$. However, the modification

$$h(x_1, x_2, x_3) = \begin{cases} x_3 + 1 & \text{if } x_1 \ne 0 \text{ and } x_3 + 1 < x_1 \\ 0 & \text{if } x_1 \ne 0 \text{ and } x_3 + 1 \ge x_1 \\ x_2 + 1 & \text{if } x_1 = 0 \end{cases}$$

works just as well. The function $R$ is obtained by primitive recursion from $C_0^1$ and this modified $h$, and Theorem 12.5 implies that $h$ is primitive recursive. Therefore, so are $R$ and *Mod*.

The function $Div$ can now be handled in a similar way. If we define $Q(x, y)$ to be $Div(y, x)$, then it is not hard to check that $Q$ is obtained by primitive recursion from $C_0^1$ and the primitive recursive function $h_1$ defined by

$$h_1(x_1, x_2, x_3) = \begin{cases} x_3 & \text{if } x_1 \neq 0 \text{ and } Mod(x_2, x_1) + 1 < x_1 \\ x_3 + 1 & \text{if } x_1 \neq 0 \text{ and } Mod(x_2, x_1) + 1 = x_1 \\ 0 & \text{if } x_1 = 0 \end{cases}$$

(Note that for any choice of $(x_1, x_2, x_3)$, precisely one of the predicates appearing in this definition is true.)

---

The operations that can be applied to predicates to produce new ones include not only logical operations such as AND, but also universal and existential quantifiers. For example, if $Sq$ is the 2-place predicate defined by

$$Sq(x, y) = (y^2 = x)$$

then it is reasonable to apply the existential quantifier ("there exists") to the second variable in order to obtain the 1-place predicate $PerfectSquare$, defined by

$$PerfectSquare(x) = (\text{there exists } y \text{ with } y^2 = x)$$

The predicate $Sq$ is primitive recursive. Does it follow that $PerfectSquare$ is? The answer is: No, it does not follow, but yes, this predicate is primitive recursive. Placing a quantifier in front of a primitive recursive predicate does not always produce a primitive recursive predicate, and placing a quantifier in front of a computable predicate does not always produce something computable.

We can easily find an example to illustrate the second statement, by considering an unsolvable problem from Chapter 11 that can be obtained this way. Given an alphabet $\Sigma$, we can impose an ordering on it, which makes it possible to consider the canonical order on $\Sigma^*$. For a natural number $x$, denote by $s_x$ the $x$th string with respect to that ordering. Let $T_u$ be the universal Turing machine of Section 9.6, and let $H$ be the 2-place predicate defined by

$$H(x, y) = (T_u \text{ halts after exactly } y \text{ moves on input } s_x)$$

$H$ is clearly computable and is in fact primitive recursive. However, the 1-place predicate

$$Halts(x) = (\text{there exists } y \text{ so that } T_u \text{ halts after } y \text{ moves on input } s_x)$$

is not computable, because to compute it would mean solving the halting problem.

One difference between these two examples, which is enough to guarantee that $PerfectSquare$ is computable even though $Halts$ is not, is that for a given $x$ there is a *bound* on the values of $y$ that need to be tested in order to determine whether the predicate "there exists $y$ such that $y^2 = x$" is true. Since $y^2 \geq y$, for example, any $y$ for which $y^2 = x$ must satisfy $y \leq x$. In particular, there is an algorithm to determine whether $PerfectSquare(x)$ is true: Try values of $y$ in increasing order until a value is found satisfying either $y^2 = x$ or $y > x$. The predicate $Halts$ illustrates the fact that if the simple trial-and-error algorithm that comes with such a bound is not available, there may be no algorithm at all.

This discussion suggests that if we start with any $(n + 1)$-place predicate $P$, we may consider the new predicate $E_P$ that results from applying the existential quantifier to the last variable in a restricted way, by specifying a bounded range for this variable. We can do the same thing with the universal quantifier ("for every"), and in both cases this *bounded* quantification preserves the primitive recursive property.

---

**Definition 12.5    Bounded Quantifications**

Let $P$ be an $(n + 1)$-place predicate. The *bounded existential quantification* of $P$ is the $(n + 1)$-place predicate $E_P$ defined by

$E_P(X, k) = $ (there exists $y$ with $0 \leq y \leq k$ such that $P(X, y)$ is true)

The *bounded universal quantification* of $P$ is the $(n+1)$-place predicate $A_P$ defined by

$A_P(X, k) = $ (for every $y$ satisfying $0 \leq y \leq k$, $P(X, y)$ is true)

---

**Theorem 12.6**
If $P$ is a primitive recursive $(n + 1)$-place predicate, both the predicates $E_P$ and $A_P$ are also primitive recursive.

---

In order to simplify the proof of Theorem 12.6, it is useful to introduce two other "bounded operations." We start by considering a simple special case in which the resulting function is a familiar one.

The factorial function is defined recursively in Chapter 2. Here we use the definition

$$x! = \prod_{i=1}^{x} i$$

where, in general, $\prod_{i=j}^{k} p_i$ stands for the product $p_j * p_{j+1} * \cdots * p_k$ if $k \geq j$, and 1 if $k < j$. (In the second case, we think of it as the *empty* product; 1 is the appropriate value, since we want the empty product multiplied by any other product to be that other product.) We can generalize this definition by allowing the factors to be more general than $i$—in particular, to involve other variables—and by allowing sums as well as products.

**Lemma 12.1**   Let $n \geq 0$, and suppose that $g : \mathcal{N}^{n+1} \to \mathcal{N}$ is primitive recursive. Then the functions $f_1, f_2 : \mathcal{N}^{n+1} \to \mathcal{N}$ defined below are also primitive recursive:

$$f_1(X, k) = \sum_{i=0}^{k} g(X, i)$$

$$f_2(X, k) = \prod_{i=0}^{k} g(X, i)$$

for any $X \in \mathcal{N}^n$ and $k \geq 0$. (The functions $f_1$ and $f_2$ are said to be obtained from $g$ by *bounded sums* and *bounded products*, respectively.)

***Proof*** We give the proof for $f_1$, and the other is almost identical. We may write

$$f_1(X, 0) = g(X, 0)$$
$$f_1(X, k + 1) = f_1(X, k) + g(X, k + 1)$$

Therefore, $f_1$ is obtained by primitive recursion from the two primitive recursive functions $g_1$ and $h$, where $g_1(X) = g(X, 0)$ and $h(X, y, z) = z + g(X, y + 1)$. ∎

Note the slight discrepancy between the definition of bounded product, in which the product starts with $i = 0$, and the previous definition of $x!$. It is not difficult to generalize the theorem slightly so as to allow the sum or product to begin with the $i = i_0$ term, for any fixed $i_0$ (Exercise 12.33).

---

**Proof of Theorem 12.6**

By definition of bounded universal quantification, $A_P(X, k)$ is true if and only if $P(X, i)$ is true for every $i$ with $0 \leq i \leq k$. Therefore, $\chi_{A_P}(X, k) = 1$ if and only if all the terms $\chi_P(X, i)$ are also 1. This equivalence implies that

$$\chi_{A_P}(X, k) = \prod_{i=0}^{k} \chi_P(X, i)$$

The primitive recursiveness of $A_P$ follows immediately from Lemma 12.1.

Saying that there is an $i$ so that $0 \leq i \leq k$ and $P(X, i)$ is true is the same as saying that $P(X, i)$ is not always false for these $i$'s. In other words,

$$E_P(X, k) = \neg A_{\neg P}(X, k)$$

It follows from this formula that $E_P$ is also primitive recursive.

---

So far, the bounded versions of the operations in this section preserve the primitive recursive property, whereas the unbounded versions do not even preserve computability. In order to characterize the computable functions as those obtained by starting with initial functions and applying certain operations, we need at least one operation that preserves computability but not primitive recursiveness. This is because the initial functions are primitive recursive, and not all computable functions are. The operation of *minimalization* turns out to have this feature. We introduce its bounded version here and examine the general operation in the next section.

For an $(n + 1)$-place predicate $P$, and a given $X \in \mathcal{N}^n$, we may consider the smallest value of $y$ for which $P(X, y)$ is true. To turn this operation into a bounded one, we specify a value of $k$ and ask for the smallest value of $y$ that is less than or equal to $k$ and satisfies $P(X, y)$. There may be *no* such $y$ (whether or not we bound the possible choices by $k$); therefore, because we want the bounded version of our function to be total, we introduce an appropriate default value for the function in this case.

### Definition 12.6     Bounded Minimalization

For an $(n + 1)$-place predicate $P$, the *bounded minimalization* of $P$ is the function $m_P : \mathcal{N}^{n+1} \to \mathcal{N}$ defined by

$$m_P(X, k) = \begin{cases} \min\{y \mid 0 \leq y \leq k \text{ and } P(X, y)\} & \text{if this set is not empty} \\ k + 1 & \text{otherwise} \end{cases}$$

The symbol $\mu$ is often used for the minimalization operator, and we sometimes write

$$m_P(X, k) = \overset{k}{\mu} y [P(X, y)]$$

An important special case is that in which $P(X, y)$ is $(f(X, y) = 0)$, for some $f : \mathcal{N}^{n+1} \to \mathcal{N}$. In this case $m_P$ is written $m_f$ and referred to as the bounded minimalization of $f$.

### Theorem 12.7

If $P$ is a primitive recursive $(n + 1)$-place predicate, its bounded minimalization $m_P$ is a primitive recursive function.

*Proof*

We show that $m_P$ can be obtained from primitive recursive functions by the operation of primitive recursion. For $X \in \mathcal{N}^n$, $m_P(X, 0)$ is 0 if $P(X, 0)$ is true and 1 otherwise. In order to evaluate $m_P(X, k + 1)$, we consider three cases. First, if there exists $y \leq k$ for which $P(X, y)$ is true, then $m_P(X, k + 1) = m_P(X, k)$. Second, if there is no such $y$ but $P(X, k + 1)$ is true, then $m_P(X, k + 1) = k + 1$. Third, if neither of these conditions holds, then $m_P(X, k + 1) = k + 2$. It follows that the function $m_P$ can be obtained by primitive recursion from the functions $g$ and $h$, where

$$g(X) = \begin{cases} 0 & \text{if } P(X, 0) \text{ is true} \\ 1 & \text{otherwise} \end{cases}$$

$$h(X, y, z) = \begin{cases} z & \text{if } E_P(X, y) \text{ is true} \\ y + 1 & \text{if } \neg E_P(X, y) \wedge P(X, y + 1) \text{ is true} \\ y + 2 & \text{if } \neg E_P(X, y) \wedge \neg P(X, y + 1) \text{ is true} \end{cases}$$

Since $P$ and $E_P$ are primitive recursive predicates, the functions $g$ and $h$ are both primitive recursive.

---

**EXAMPLE 12.7**     The *n*th Prime Number

For $n \geq 0$, let $PrNo(n)$ be the $n$th prime number: $PrNo(0) = 2$, $PrNo(1) = 3$, $PrNo(2) = 5$, and so on. Let us show that the function $PrNo$ is primitive recursive.

First we observe that the 1-place predicate *Prime*, defined by

$$Prime(n) = (n \geq 2) \wedge \neg(\text{there exists } y \text{ such that } y \geq 2 \wedge y \leq n - 1 \wedge Mod(n, y) = 0)$$

is primitive recursive, and *Prime*(n) is true if and only if $n$ is a prime.

For any $k$, $PrNo(k + 1)$ is the smallest prime greater than $PrNo(k)$. Therefore, if we can just place a bound on the set of integers greater than $PrNo(k)$ that may have to be tested in order to find a prime, then we can use the bounded minimalization operator to obtain $PrNo$ by primitive recursion. The number-theoretic fact that makes this possible was proved in Example 2.5: For any positive integer $m$, there is a prime greater than $m$ and no larger than $m! + 1$.

With this in mind, let

$$P(x, y) = (y > x \ \wedge \ Prime(y))$$

Then

$$PrNo(0) = 2$$
$$PrNo(k + 1) = m_P(PrNo(k), PrNo(k)! + 1)$$

We have shown that *PrNo* can be obtained by primitive recursion from the two functions $C_2^0$ and $h$, where

$$h(x, y) = m_P(y, y! + 1)$$

Therefore, *PrNo* is primitive recursive.

# 12.3 | UNBOUNDED MINIMALIZATION AND $\mu$-RECURSIVE FUNCTIONS

For a predicate $P$ we have defined $m_P(X, k)$, or $\overset{k}{\mu}y[P(X, y)]$, to be the smallest $y$ in the range $0 \leq y \leq k$ for which $P(X, y)$ is true, if there is one, and $k + 1$ if there is not. The default value was specified in order to make the function $m_P$ a total function. Now we want to remove the constraints on the values of $y$ in the definition of the function. If there is at least one value of $y$ for which $P(X, y)$ holds, then we can find the smallest one by examining the values of $y$ in increasing order. If there is not, we may not be able to determine there is not. Because we want the unbounded version of the minimalization operation to preserve computability, it follows that we should *not* specify a default value for the function—because in the case in which the function should have this value, we might not be able to determine that it should! For this reason, the operation will no longer be guaranteed to produce a total function, even when applied to primitive recursive predicates. Therefore, we do not expect the operation to preserve the primitive recursive property.

---

**Definition 12.7    Unbounded Minimalization**

If $P$ is an $(n + 1)$-place predicate, the *unbounded minimalization* of $P$ is the partial function $M_P : \mathcal{N}^n \to \mathcal{N}$ defined by

$$M_P(X) = min\ \{y \mid P(X, y)\ \text{is true}\}$$

$M_P(X)$ is undefined at any $X \in \mathcal{N}^n$ for which there is no $y$ satisfying $P(X, y)$.

The notation $\mu y[P(X, y)]$ is also used for $M_P(X)$. In the special case in which $P(X, y) = (f(X, y) = 0)$, we write $M_P = M_f$ and refer to this function as the unbounded minimalization of $f$.

---

The fact that we want $M_P$ to be a computable partial function for any computable predicate $P$ also has another consequence. Suppose, again, that the algorithm we are relying on for computing $M_P(X)$ is the simple-minded one of evaluating $P(X, y)$ for increasing values of $y$. Suppose also that for a particular $y_0$, $P(X, y_0)$ is undefined. Although there might be a value $y_1 > y_0$ for which $P(X, y_1)$ is true, we will never get around to considering $P(X, y_1)$ if we get stuck in an infinite loop while trying to evaluate $P(X, y_0)$. We can avoid this problem by stipulating that unbounded minimalization be applied only to total predicates or total functions.

Unbounded minimalization is the last of the operations we need in order to characterize the computable functions. Notice that in the definition below, this operator is applied only to predicates defined by some numeric function being zero.

---

**Definition 12.8    $\mu$-Recursive Functions**

The set $\mathcal{M}$ of $\mu$-recursive, or simply *recursive*, partial functions is defined as follows.

1. Every initial function is an element of $\mathcal{M}$.
2. Every function obtained from elements of $\mathcal{M}$ by composition or primitive recursion is an element of $\mathcal{M}$.
3. For every $n \geq 0$ and every total function $f : \mathcal{N}^{n+1} \to \mathcal{N}$ in $\mathcal{M}$, the function $M_f : \mathcal{N}^n \to \mathcal{N}$ defined by

$$M_f(X) = \mu y[f(X, y) = 0]$$

   is an element of $\mathcal{M}$.
4. No other functions are in the set $\mathcal{M}$.

---

Just as in the case of primitive recursive functions, a function is in the set $\mathcal{M}$ if and only if it has a finite, step-by-step derivation, where at each step either a new initial function is introduced or one of the three operations is applied to initial functions, to functions obtained earlier in the derivation, or to both. As long as unbounded minimalization is not used, the function obtained at each step in such a sequence is primitive recursive. Once unbounded minimalization appears in the sequence, the functions may cease to be primitive recursive or even total. Note that if $f$ is obtained by composition or primitive recursion, it is possible for $f$ to be total even when not all the functions from which it is obtained are total. Thus it is conceivable that in the derivation of a $\mu$-recursive function, unbounded minimalization could be used more than once, even if its first use produces a nontotal function. However, in the proof of Theorem 12.10 we show that any $\mu$-recursive function actually has a derivation in which unbounded minimalization is used only once.

---

**Theorem 12.8**
All $\mu$-recursive partial functions are computable.

*Proof*
The proof is by structural induction. We have already observed in the proof of Theorem 12.2 that the initial functions are computable. That proof also shows that partial functions obtained from computable functions by either composition or primitive recursion are computable. Therefore, to complete the proof it is sufficient to show that if $f : \mathcal{N}^{n+1} \to \mathcal{N}$ is a computable total function, then its unbounded minimalization $M_f$ is a computable partial function.

If $T_f$ is a Turing machine computing $f$, we have already mentioned the intuitive idea behind the construction of a TM $T$ to compute $M_f$. For any input value $X$, $T$ simply computes $f(X, 0)$, $f(X, 1)$, ..., until it discovers an $i$ for which $f(X, i) = 0$, and halts in $h_a$ with $i$ as its output. If there is no such $i$, the computation continues forever, which is acceptable because $M_f(X)$ is undefined in that case. The details of constructing such a $T$ are straightforward.

---

## 12.4 | GÖDEL NUMBERING

It is easy to formulate statements *in* the English language *about* the English language. In Section 9.6 we have done something comparable in a formal language: We have constructed strings of 0's and 1's that describe languages of strings of 0's and 1's, in the sense that they specify Turing machines accepting languages. This seemingly innocuous technique makes possible the diagonal argument, with its characteristic circularity (Turing machines accepting or not accepting their own encodings), and the diagonal argument leads to profound results about the limits of computation.

The logician Kurt Gödel used a similar idea in the 1930s (around the time of the initial papers by Turing, Church, Post, *et al.*), developing an encoding scheme to assign numbers to statements and formulas in an axiomatic system. As a result, Gödel was able to describe logical relations between objects in the system by numerical formulas expressing relations between numbers. His ingenious use of these techniques allowed him to establish unexpected results concerning logical systems. Gödel's *incompleteness theorem* says, roughly speaking, that any formal system comprehensive enough to include the laws of arithmetic must, if it is consistent, contain true statements that cannot be proved within the system.

Although we will not be discussing Gödel's results directly, the idea of "Gödel numbering" will be useful. The first step is simply to encode sequences of several numbers as single numbers. One application will be to show that a more general type of recursive definition than we have considered so far gives rise to primitive recursive functions. A little later we will extend our "arithmetization" to objects such as TMs. This will allow us to represent a sequence of calculations involving numbers by a sequence of numbers, and it will be the principal ingredient in the proof that all computable functions are $\mu$-recursive.

There are a variety of Gödel-numbering schemes. Most depend on a familiar fact about numbers: Every positive integer can be factored into primes, and this factorization is unique except for differences in the order of the factors.

---

**Definition 12.9     Gödel Number of a Sequence of Natural Numbers**

For any finite sequence $x_0, x_1, \ldots, x_n$ of natural numbers, the *Gödel number* of the sequence is the number

$$gn(x_0, x_1, \ldots, x_n) = 2^{x_0} 3^{x_1} 5^{x_2} \cdots (PrNo(n))^{x_n}$$

where $PrNo(n)$ is the $n$th prime (see Example 12.7).

---

The Gödel number of any sequence is greater than or equal to 1, and every integer greater than or equal to 1 is the Gödel number of a sequence. The function *gn* is not one-to-one; for example,

$$gn(0, 1, 2) = gn(0, 1, 2, 0, 0) = 2^0 3^1 5^2$$

However, if $gn(x_0, x_1, \ldots, x_m) = gn(y_0, y_1, \ldots, y_m, y_{m+1} \cdots y_{m+k})$, then

$$\prod_{i=0}^{m} PrNo(i)^{x_i} = \prod_{i=0}^{m} PrNo(i)^{y_i} \prod_{i=m+1}^{m+k} PrNo(i)^{y_i}$$

and because a number can have only one prime factorization, we must have $x_i = y_i$ for $0 \le i \le m$ and $y_{m+1} = \cdots = y_{m+k} = 0$. Therefore, two sequences having the same Gödel number are identical, except that they may end with a different number of 0's. In particular, for any $n \ge 1$, every positive integer is the Gödel number of at most one sequence of $n$ integers.

For any $n$, the Gödel numbering we have defined for sequences of length $n$ determines a function from $\mathcal{N}^n$ to $\mathcal{N}$. We will be imprecise and use the name *gn* for any of these functions. All of them are primitive recursive.

If we start with a positive integer $g$ and wish to *decode* $g$ to find a sequence $x_0$, $x_1, \ldots, x_n$ whose Gödel number is $g$, we may proceed by factoring $g$ into primes. For each $i$, $x_i$ is the number of times $PrNo(i)$ appears as a factor of $g$. For example, the number 59895 has the factorization

$$59895 = 3^2 5^1 11^3 = 2^0 3^2 5^1 7^0 11^3$$

and is therefore the Gödel number of the sequence 0,2,1,0,3 (or any other sequence obtained from this by adding extra 0's). The prime number 31 is the Gödel number of the sequence 0,0,0,0,0,0,0,0,0,0,1, since $31 = PrNo(10)$. This type of calculation will be needed often enough that we introduce a function just for this purpose.

## The Power to Which a Prime is Raised in the Factorization of $x$    EXAMPLE 12.8

The function *Exponent*: $\mathcal{N}^2 \to \mathcal{N}$ is defined by letting $Exponent(i, x)$ be the exponent of $PrNo(i)$ in the prime factorization of $x$, if $x > 0$, and 0 if $x = 0$. For example, $Exponent(4, 59895) = 3$, as we have seen, since the fourth prime, 11, appears three times as a factor of 59895. (Remember, 2 is the *zeroth* prime.)

*Exponent* is primitive recursive. For $x > 0$ and $i \geq 0$, $PrNo(i)^y$ divides $x$ evenly if and only if $y \leq Exponent(i, x)$. In other words, $Exponent(i, x) + 1$ is the smallest $y$ for which $(PrNo(i))^y$ does not divide $x$ evenly. This expression ("the smallest $y$ for which ...") involves a minimalization, and since we can easily find a specific $k$ depending on $x$ for which $(PrNo(i))^k$ is guaranteed not to divide $x$ evenly (e.g., $k = x$), we can make it a bounded minimalization. For $x > 0$,

$$Exponent(i, x) = \overset{x}{\mu}y[Mod(x, (PrNo(i))^y) > 0] \mathbin{\dot{-}} 1$$

The primitive recursiveness of *Exponent* now follows.

Many common recursive definitions do not obviously fit the strict pattern required by the operation of primitive recursion. The standard definition of the Fibonacci function, for example, involves the formula

$$f(n + 1) = f(n) + f(n - 1)$$

The right side apparently is not of the form $h(n, f(n))$ because it also depends on $f(n - 1)$. In a more general situation, $f(n + 1)$ might depend on even more, conceivably all, of the terms $f(0), f(1), \ldots, f(n)$. This type of recursion is known as *course-of-values* recursion, and it bears the same relation to ordinary primitive recursion that the strong principle of mathematical induction does to the ordinary principle (see Section 2.3).

One simple way to use Gödel numbers is to recast such recursive definitions to fit the required form. Suppose $f$ is defined recursively, so that $f(n+1)$ depends on some or all of the numbers $f(0), \ldots, f(n)$ (and possibly also directly on $n$). Intuitively, what we need in order to describe $f$ in terms of primitive recursion is another function $f_1$ for which

**1.** Knowing $f_1(n)$ would allow us to calculate $f(n)$.

**2.** $f_1(n + 1)$ depends only on $n$ and $f_1(n)$.

If we temporarily relax the requirement that $f_1(n)$ be a *number*, we might consider the entire sequence $f_1(n) = (f(0), f(1), \ldots, f(n))$. Then condition 1 is satisfied, since $f(n)$ is simply the last term of the sequence $f_1(n)$. In addition, since $f(n + 1)$ can be expressed in terms of $n$ and $f(0), \ldots, f(n)$, the entire sequence $(f(0), \ldots, f(n), f(n + 1))$ can be said to depend only on $n$ and the sequence $(f(0), \ldots, f(n))$, so that $f_1$ also satisfies condition 2. To make this intuitive idea work, all we need to do is to use the Gödel numbers of the sequences, instead of the sequences themselves: Instead of saying that $f(n + 1)$ depends directly on $f(0), \ldots, f(n)$, we say that $f(n+1)$ depends on the single value $gn(f(0), \ldots, f(n))$. The two versions are intuitively equivalent, since each of the numbers $f(i)$ can be derived from the single value $gn(f(0), \ldots, f(n))$.

---

**Theorem 12.9**

Suppose $g : \mathcal{N}^n \to \mathcal{N}$ and $h : \mathcal{N}^{n+2} \to \mathcal{N}$ are primitive recursive functions, and $f : \mathcal{N}^{n+1} \to \mathcal{N}$ is obtained from $g$ and $h$ by course-of-values recursion; that is,

$$f(X, 0) = g(X)$$
$$f(X, k + 1) = h(X, k, gn(f(X, 0), \ldots, f(X, k)))$$

Then $f$ is primitive recursive.

**Proof**

First we define $f_1 : \mathcal{N}^{n+1} \to \mathcal{N}$ by the formula

$$f_1(X, k) = gn(f(X, 0), f(X, 1), \ldots, f(X, k))$$

Then $f$ can be obtained from $f_1$ by the formula

$$f(X, k) = Exponent(k, f_1(X, k))$$

Therefore, it will be sufficient to show that $f_1$ is primitive recursive.
We have

$$f_1(X, 0) = gn(f(X, 0)) = 2^{f(X,0)} = 2^{g(X)}$$

$$f_1(X, k + 1) = \prod_{i=0}^{k+1} PrNo(i)^{f(X,i)}$$

$$= \prod_{i=0}^{k} PrNo(i)^{f(X,i)} * PrNo(k + 1)^{f(X,k+1)}$$

$$= f_1(X, k) * PrNo(k + 1)^{h(X,k,f_1(X,k))}$$

$$= h_1(X, k, f_1(X, k))$$

where the function $h_1$ is defined by

$$h_1(X, y, z) = z * PrNo(y + 1)^{h(X,y,z)}$$

Because $2^g$ and $h_1$ are primitive recursive and $f_1$ is obtained from these two by primitive recursion, it follows that $f_1$ is also primitive recursive.

Now we are ready to apply our Gödel numbering techniques to Turing machines. A computable function $f$ is computed by a sequence of steps. If we can manage to represent these steps as operations on numbers, then we will have a way of building the function $f$ from more rudimentary functions. Because a TM move can be thought of as a transformation of the machine from one configuration to another, all we need do to describe the move numerically is represent the TM configuration by a number.

We begin by assigning a number to each state. The halt states $h_a$ and $h_r$ are assigned the numbers 0 and 1, respectively. If $Q$ is the set of nonhalting states, then we let the elements of $Q$ be $q_2, q_3, \ldots, q_s$, where $q_2$ is always assumed to be the initial state.

The natural number to use in describing the tape head position is the number of the tape square the head is scanning. Finally, we assign the number 0 to the blank symbol $\Delta$ (we will sometimes write 0 instead of $\Delta$), and we assume that the nonblank tape symbols are $1, 2, \ldots, t$. This allows us to define the *tape number* of the TM at any point to be the Gödel number of the sequence of symbols currently on the tape. Note that because we are identifying $\Delta$ with 0, the tape number is the same no matter how many trailing blanks we include in the sequence. The tape number of a blank tape is 1.

Since the configuration of the TM is determined by the state, the tape head position, and the current contents of the tape, we define the *configuration number* to be the number

$$gn(q, P, tn)$$

where $q$ is the number of the current state, $P$ is the current head position, and $tn$ is the current tape number. The most important feature of the configuration number is that from it we can reconstruct all the details of the configuration; we will be more explicit about this in the next section.

# 12.5 | ALL COMPUTABLE FUNCTIONS ARE $\mu$-RECURSIVE

> **Theorem 12.10**
> Every computable partial function $f : \mathcal{N}^n \to \mathcal{N}$ is $\mu$-recursive.

The main outline of the proof has been provided for us by the Gödel numbering scheme presented in the last section and the resulting arithmetization of Turing machines. If $f$ is computed by the Turing machine $T$, we will complete the proof by defining the functions appearing in the formula

$$f = Result_T \circ f_T \circ InitConfig^{(n)}$$

and showing that they are $\mu$-recursive and that the formula holds.

For any $n$-tuple $X$, $InitConfig^{(n)}(X)$ will be the number of the initial TM configuration corresponding to input $X$. This number does not depend on the TM we use, because we have agreed to label the initial state of any TM as $q_2$. The numeric function $f_T$ corresponds to the processing done by $T$. For an input $X$ in the domain of $f$, if $n$ is the number representing the initial configuration of $T$ corresponding to input $X$, then $f_T(n)$ represents the accepting configuration ultimately reached by $T$; for integers $n$ corresponding to other inputs $X$, $f_T(n)$ is undefined. The function $Result_T$ has the property that if $n$ is the number of an accepting configuration in which the string representing output $f(X)$ is on the tape, then $Result_T(n) = f(X)$.

The function $Result_T$ is one of several whose value at a number $m$ depends on whether $m$ is the number of a configuration of $T$. The first step is therefore to examine the 1-place predicate $IsConfig_T$ defined by

$$IsConfig_T(n) = (n \text{ is a configuration number for } T)$$

**Lemma 12.2**   $IsConfig_T$ is a primitive recursive predicate.

**Proof**   Let $s_T$ be one more than the number of nonhalting states of $T$ (recall that they are numbered beginning with 2), and let $ts_T$ be the number of nonblank tape symbols of $T$. A number $m$ is a configuration number for $T$ if and only if

$$m = 2^q 3^p 5^{tn}$$

where $q \le s_T$, $p$ is arbitrary, and $tn$ is the Gödel number of a sequence of natural numbers, each one between 0 and $ts_T$.

The statement that $m$ is of the general form $2^a 3^b 5^c$ can be expressed by saying that $m \ge 1$ and for every $i > 2$, $Exponent(i, m) = 0$. An equivalent formulation is

$$(m \ge 1) \wedge (\text{for every } i, i \le 2 \vee Exponent(i, m) = 0)$$

For numbers $m$ of this form, the conditions on $q$ and $tn$ are equivalent to the statement

$$(Exponent(0, m) \le s_T) \wedge (Exponent(2, m) \ge 1) \wedge (\text{for every } i, Exponent(i, tn) \le ts_T)$$

In order to show that the conjunction of these two predicates is primitive recursive, it is sufficient to show that both of the universal quantifications can be replaced by *bounded* universal quantifications. This is true because $Exponent(i, n) = 0$ when $i > n$; the first occurrence of "for every $i$" can be replaced by "for every $i \le m$" and the second by "for every $i \le tn$."   ■

**Lemma 12.3**   The function $InitConfig^{(n)} : \mathcal{N}^n \to \mathcal{N}$ is primitive recursive.

**Proof**   Because the initial state of any TM is designated $q_2$, and the tape head is initially on square 0, we may write

$$InitConfig^{(n)}(x_1, x_2, \ldots, x_n) = gn(1, 0, t^{(n)}(x_1, \ldots, x_n))$$

where $t^{(n)}(x_1, \ldots, x_n)$ is the tape number of the tape containing the input string $\Delta 1^{x_1} \Delta 1^{x_2} \Delta \cdots \Delta 1^{x_n}$. It is therefore sufficient to show that the function $t^{(n)}$ is primitive recursive. The proof is by mathematical induction on $n$. The basis step, $n = 0$, is clear, since $t^{(n)}$ is constant in that case. Suppose that $k \ge 0$ and that $t^{(k)}$ is primitive recursive. The number $t^{(k+1)}(x_1, \ldots, x_k, x_{k+1}) = t^{(k+1)}(X, x_{k+1})$ is the tape number for the tape containing

$$\Delta 1^{x_1} \Delta \cdots \Delta 1^{x_k} \Delta 1^{x_{k+1}}$$

Counting the symbols in the string $\Delta 1^{x_1} \Delta \cdots \Delta 1^{x_k}$, we find that the string $1^{x_{k+1}}$ occupies tape squares $k + \sum_{i=1}^{k} x_i + 1$ through $k + \sum_{i=1}^{k} x_i + x_{k+1}$. This means that the additional factors in the tape number resulting from the 1's in this last block are those of the form

$$PrNo\left(k + \sum_{i=1}^{k} x_i + j\right) \quad (1 \le j \le x_{k+1})$$

In other words, we may write

$$tn^{(k+1)}(X, x_{k+1}) = tn^{(k)}(X) * \prod_{j=1}^{x_{k+1}} PrNo\left(k + \sum_{i=1}^{k} x_i + j\right)$$

The first factor, viewed as a function of $X$, is primitive recursive according to the induction hypothesis. Therefore, by Theorem 12.1, it is still primitive recursive when viewed as a function of $k + 1$ variables. The second is of the form

$$\prod_{j=1}^{x_{k+1}} g(X, j)$$

for a primitive recursive function $g$, and is therefore primitive recursive by Lemma 12.1. The result follows because the set of primitive recursive functions is closed under multiplication. ∎

As we discussed earlier, we want $Result_T(n)$ to be $f(X)$ if $n$ represents the accepting configuration with output $f(X)$. This will be the case if, for any $n$ representing a configuration, we simply define $Result_T(n)$ to be the number of the tape square containing the last nonblank symbol on the tape in this configuration, or 0 if there are no nonblank symbols. We may also let $Result_T(n)$ be 0 if $n$ does not represent a configuration.

**Lemma 12.4** The function $Result_T : \mathcal{N} \to \mathcal{N}$ is primitive recursive.

**Proof** Because the tape number for the configuration represented by $n$ is $Exponent(2, n)$ and the prime factors of the tape number correspond to the squares with nonblank symbols, we may write

$$Result_T(n) = \begin{cases} HighestPrime(Exponent(2, n)) & \text{if } IsConfig(n) \\ 0 & \text{otherwise} \end{cases}$$

where for any positive $k$, $HighestPrime(k)$ is the number of the largest prime factor of $k$, and $HighestPrime(0) = 0$ (e.g., $HighestPrime(2^3 5^5 19^2) = 7$, because 19 is $PrNo(7)$). It is not hard to see that the function $HighestPrime$ is primitive recursive, and it follows that $Result_T$ is also. ∎

The only remaining piece is $f_T$, the numerical function corresponding to the processing done by $T$ itself. At this point we make the simplifying assumption that $T$ never attempts to move its tape head left from square 0. This involves no loss of generality because any TM is equivalent to one with this property. It will be helpful next to introduce explicitly the functions that produce the current state, tape head position, tape number, and tape symbol from the configuration number. The respective formulas are

$$State(m) = Exponent(0, m)$$

$$Posn(m) = Exponent(1, m)$$

$$TapeNum(m) = Exponent(2, m)$$

$$Symbol(m) = Exponent(PrNo(Posn(m)), TapeNum(m))$$

for any $m$ that is a configuration number for $T$, and 0 otherwise. Because $IsConfig_T$ is a primitive recursive predicate, all four functions are primitive recursive.

The main ingredient in the description of $f_T$ is another function

$$Move_T : \mathcal{N} \rightarrow \mathcal{N}$$

Roughly speaking, $Move_T$ calculates the effect on the configuration number of a single move of $T$. More precisely, if $m$ is the number for a configuration of $T$ in which $T$ can move, then $Move_T(m)$ is the configuration number after the move, and if $m$ is the number of a halting configuration or any other configuration in which $T$ cannot move, $Move_T(m) = 0$.

**Lemma 12.5** The function $Move_T : \mathcal{N} \rightarrow \mathcal{N}$ is primitive recursive.

***Proof*** We may write

$$Move_T(m) = \begin{cases} gn(NewState(m), NewPosn(m), NewTapeNum(m)) \\ \quad \text{if } m \text{ is a configuration number} \\ 0 \quad \text{otherwise} \end{cases}$$

The three functions *NewState*, *NewPosn*, and *NewTapeNum* all have the value 0 at any point $m$ that is not a configuration number. For a configuration number $m$, *NewState*($m$) is the resulting state if $T$ can move from configuration $m$, and *State*($m$) otherwise; the other two functions are defined similarly. Thus, in order to show that $Move_T$ is primitive recursive, it is sufficient to show that these three *New* functions are. In the argument it will help to have one more function, *NewSymbol*, defined analogously.

So far, our description of *NewState*($m$) has involved three cases. One case corresponds to the primitive recursive predicate $\neg IsConfig_T$. The other two cases may be divided into subcases, corresponding to the possible combinations of *State*($m$) and *Symbol*($m$). Because these two functions are primitive recursive, so are the predicates defining the subcases. In each subcase, the value of *NewState*($m$) is either $m$ or the value specified by the transition table for $T$. Therefore, since *NewState* is defined by cases that involve only primitive recursive functions and predicates, it must also be primitive recursive. The argument to show that *NewSymbol* is primitive recursive is exactly the same.

The proof for *NewPosn* is almost the same. This function may also be defined by cases, the same ones involved in the definition of *NewState*. In each case, *NewPosn*($m$) is either 0, if $m$ is not a configuration number; *Posn*($m$), if $T$ cannot move from configuration $m$, or if the move does not change the position of the tape head; $Posn(m) + 1$, if the move shifts the head to the right; or $Posn(m) \dot{-} 1$, if the move shifts the head to the left. Therefore *NewPosn* is primitive recursive.

The definition of *NewTapeNum* can also be made using the same cases, with slightly more complicated formulas. Suppose that $Posn(m) = i, Symbol(m) = j$, and $NewSymbol(m) = j'$. The difference between $TapeNum(m)$ and $NewTapeNum(m)$ is that the first number involves the factor $PrNo(i)^j$ and the second has $PrNo(i)^{j'}$ instead; the exponents differ by $j - j' = NewSymbol(m) - Symbol(m)$. Thus in this subcase, $NewTapeNum(m)$ can be expressed as

$$TapeNum(m) * PrNo(Posn(m))^{NewSymbol(m) \dot{-} Symbol(m)}$$

if $NewSymbol(m) \geq Symbol(m)$, and

$$Div(TapeNum(m), PrNo(Posn(m))^{Symbol(m) \dot{-} NewSymbol(m)})$$

otherwise. Since both formulas define primitive recursive functions, the function *NewTapeNum* is primitive recursive. ∎

Now that we have described the effect of one move of $T$ on the configuration number, we can generalize to a sequence of $k$ moves. Consider the function $Trace_T : \mathcal{N}^2 \to \mathcal{N}$ defined as follows:

$$Trace_T(m, 0) = \begin{cases} m & \text{if } IsConfig_T(m) \\ 0 & \text{otherwise} \end{cases}$$

$$Trace_T(m, k + 1) = \begin{cases} Move_T(Trace(m, k)) & \text{if } IsConfig_T(m) \\ 0 & \text{otherwise} \end{cases}$$

It is clear from Lemma 12.5 that $Trace_T$ can be obtained by primitive recursion from two primitive recursive functions and is therefore primitive recursive itself. Assuming that $m$ is a configuration number, we may describe $Trace_T(m, k)$ as the number of the configuration after $k$ moves, if $T$ starts in configuration $m$—or, if $T$ is unable to make as many as $k$ moves from configuration $m$, as the number of the last configuration $T$ reaches starting from configuration $m$.

We need just one more auxiliary function before we can complete the proof of Theorem 12.10. Let $Accepting_T : \mathcal{N} \to \mathcal{N}$ be defined by

$$Accepting_T(m) = \begin{cases} 0 & \text{if } IsConfig_T(m) \wedge Exponent(0, m) = 0 \\ 1 & \text{otherwise} \end{cases}$$

$Accepting_T(m)$ is 0 if and only if $m$ is the number of an accepting configuration for $T$, and $Accepting_T$ is clearly primitive recursive.

---

**Proof of Theorem 12.10**

The proof is largely a matter of putting together the completed pieces. Let $T$ be a TM computing $f$ as discussed above. Then for any $m$ and $k$, $Accepting_T(Trace_T(m, k))$ is 0 if and only if $m$ is a configuration number for $T$ and, beginning in configuration $m$, $T$ accepts within $k$ moves. Let *MovesToAccept* : $\mathcal{N} \to \mathcal{N}$ be defined by

$$MovesToAccept(m) = \mu k[Accepting_T(Trace_T(m, k)) = 0]$$

and define $f_T : \mathcal{N} \to \mathcal{N}$ by

$$f_T(m) = Trace_T(m, MovesToAccept(m))$$

We may describe the functions *MovesToAccept* and $f_T$ as follows. If $m$ is a configuration number for $T$ and $T$ eventually accepts when starting from configuration $m$, then *MovesToAccept(m)* is the number of moves from that point before $T$ accepts, and $f_T(m)$ is the number of the accepting configuration that is eventually reached. For any other $m$, both functions are undefined. Because *MovesToAccept* is obtained from a primitive recursive (total) function by unbounded minimalization, *MovesToAccept* is $\mu$-recursive, and because $f_T$ is obtained by composition from $\mu$-recursive functions, $f_T$ is also $\mu$-recursive.

We claim that

$$f = Result_T(f_T(InitConfig^{(n)}))$$

which means that for any $X$, $f(X)$ is defined if and only if $Result_T(f_T(InitConfig^{(n)}(X)))$ is defined, and that if these numbers are defined, then they are equal. To see this, on the one hand, suppose that $f(X)$ is defined. In this case, if $T$ begins in the configuration $InitConfig^{(n)}(X)$, it eventually accepts. Therefore, $f_T(InitConfig^{(n)}(X))$ is the configuration number of the accepting configuration $(h_a, \underline{\Delta}1^{f(X)})$, and when $Result_T$ is applied to this configuration number it produces $f(X)$. On the other hand, suppose that $f(X)$ is undefined. Then $T$ fails to accept input $X$, and this means that $f_T(InitConfig^{(n)}(X))$ is undefined. The proof is complete.

## 12.6 | NONNUMERIC FUNCTIONS AND OTHER APPROACHES TO COMPUTABILITY

The technique of Gödel numbering allows us to extend the definitions of primitive recursive and $\mu$-recursive to functions involving strings, and to obtain the corresponding generalization of Theorems 12.8 and 12.10. The idea is that if $f$ takes the string $x$ to the string $f(x)$, we can describe $f$ in terms of the related numerical function $\rho_f$ which takes the Gödel number of $x$ to that of $f(x)$. Although we discuss only functions of one variable in this section, the extension to functions of several variables is straightforward (Exercise 12.36).

---

**Definition 12.10     Gödel Numbering of Strings**

Let $\Sigma$ be an alphabet with elements

$$a_1, a_2, \ldots, a_s$$

The Gödel number $gn(x)$ of the string $x = a_{i_0}a_{i_1} \cdots a_{i_m} \in \Sigma^*$ is defined by

$$gn(x) = gn(i_0, i_1, \ldots, i_m) = 2^{i_0} \ldots (PrNo(m))^{i_m}$$

The Gödel number of $\Lambda$ is defined to be 1.

The fact that none of the exponents in the formula for $gn(x)$ can be 0 has two consequences. First, since the factorization of a positive integer into primes is unique, the function $gn: \Sigma^* \to \mathcal{N}$ is one-to-one. Second, numbers such as $3 = 2^0 3^1$ or $10 = 2^1 2^0 5^1$ cannot be the Gödel number of any string. Note also that for any $x \in \Sigma^*$, the highest power to which any prime can appear in the factorization of $gn(x)$ is the number of symbols in $\Sigma$.

Because $gn: \Sigma^* \to \mathcal{N}$ is not a bijection, it is not correct to speak of $gn^{-1}$. It is convenient, however, to define a function from $\mathcal{N}$ to $\Sigma^*$ that is a *left* inverse of $gn$, as follows:

$$gn'(n) = \begin{cases} x & \text{if } n = gn(x) \\ \Lambda & \text{if } n \text{ is not } gn(x) \text{ for any string } x \end{cases}$$

The default value $\Lambda$ is chosen arbitrarily. Saying that $gn'$ is a left inverse of $gn$ means that for any $x \in \Sigma^*$,

$$gn'(gn(x)) = x$$

Now suppose that $f : \Sigma_1^* \to \Sigma_2^*$ is a partial function, where $\Sigma_1$ and $\Sigma_2$ are alphabets. We define the corresponding numerical function $\rho_f : \mathcal{N} \to \mathcal{N}$ by saying that if $n$ is the Gödel number of $x$, then $\rho_f(n)$ is the Gödel number of $f(x)$. Note that the one-to-one property of $gn$ is necessary for this definition to make sense. We can also express $\rho_f$ concisely in terms of the left inverses of the two Gödel-numbering functions. If $g_1 : \Sigma_1^* \to \mathcal{N}$ and $g_2 : \Sigma_2^* \to \mathcal{N}$ are the functions that assign Gödel numbers, and $g_1'$ and $g_2'$ are their respective left inverses, then the formula for $\rho_f$ is

$$\rho_f(n) = g_2(f(g_1'(n)))$$

To understand this formula better, trace the right side of the formula using Figure 12.1. The formula says that beginning at the lower left of the diagram, $\rho_f$ is computed by following the arrows up, over, and down.

Since $g_1'$ is a left inverse for $g_1$, the formula

$$\rho_f(g_1(x)) = g_2(f(g_1'(g_1(x))))$$
$$= g_2(f(x))$$

holds for any string $x$ in $\Sigma_1^*$. This formula says that in the figure, both ways of getting from the upper left to the lower right produce the same result, and this is just another

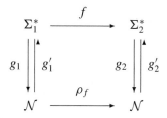

**Figure 12.1** |

way of saying that the numerical function $\rho_f$ mirrors the action of the string function $f$: If $f$ takes the string $x$ to the string $y$, $\rho_f$ takes the number $gn(x)$ to the number $gn(y)$.

---

**Definition 12.11     Primitive Recursive String Functions**

Let $f : \Sigma_1^* \to \Sigma_2^*$ and $\rho_f : \mathcal{N} \to \mathcal{N}$ be defined as above. The function $f$ is said to be primitive recursive if and only if $\rho_f$ is. Similarly, $f$ is $\mu$-recursive if and only if $\rho_f$ is.

---

**Theorem 12.11**

Let $f : \Sigma_1^* \to \Sigma_2^*$. Then $f$ is computable if and only if $f$ is $\mu$-recursive.

*Proof*

As above, we denote by $g_1$ and $g_2$ the Gödel-numbering functions for the two alphabets, and by $g_1'$ and $g_2'$ their respective left inverses.

Suppose on the one hand that $f$ is computable, and let $T_f$ be a TM (whose tape alphabet contains the symbols of $\Sigma_1$ and $\Sigma_2$) computing $f$. We want to show that $\rho_f : \mathcal{N} \to \mathcal{N}$ is $\mu$-recursive, and according to Theorem 12.10 it is sufficient to show that $\rho_f$ is computable. Although we will not show all the details, it is easy to see from the definition of $\rho_f$ that a composite Turing machine can be constructed from three simpler ones: one that takes the initial tape $\Delta 1^n$ and halts with tape $\Delta g_1'(n)$; the TM $T_f$, which then halts with tape $\Delta f(g_1'(n))$; and a third that calculates the Gödel number of this string to yield the result, $g_2(f(g_1'(n))) = \rho_f(n)$.

On the other hand, suppose that $f$ is $\mu$-recursive. Then by definition, $\rho_f$ is $\mu$-recursive. Therefore, by Theorem 12.8, $\rho_f$ is computable. Let $T$ be a TM computing it. From the formula for $\rho_f$ we have

$$g_2'(\rho_f(n)) = g_2'(g_2(f(g_1'(n))))$$
$$= f(g_1'(n))$$

for any $n$. (In Figure 12.1, this formula can be interpreted as saying that both paths from the lower left to the upper right produce the same result.) Applying this formula when $n = g_1(x)$, we obtain

$$f(x) = f(g_1'(g_1(x))) = g_2'(\rho_f(g_1(x)))$$

Just as before, we can now construct a composite TM $T_f$ to perform this computation, and it follows that $f$ is computable.

---

The theory of computability and recursive functions is a large and well-developed subject, and this chapter is no more than a brief introduction. We close by mentioning briefly a few other approaches.

Just as unrestricted grammars provide a way of generating languages, they can be used to characterize computable functions. If $G = (V, \Sigma, S, P)$ is a grammar, and $f$ is a partial function from $\Sigma^*$ to $\Sigma^*$, $G$ is said to compute $f$ if there are variables $A, B, C$, and $D$ in the set $V$ so that for any $x$ and $y$ in $\Sigma^*$,

$$f(x) = y \quad \text{if and only if} \quad AxB \Rightarrow^*_G CyD$$

It can be shown, using arguments not unlike those in Theorems 10.8 and 10.9, that the functions computable in this way are precisely those that can be computed by Turing machines.

Computer programs written in high-level programming languages can be viewed as computing functions from strings to strings. It is natural to consider the set of functions that can be computed by such programs, say those written in C. If we remove the physical limitations imposed by any particular implementation, so that there is an unlimited amount of memory, no limit to the size of integers, and so on, then "C-computable" and Turing-computable are the same.

Although high-level languages such as C have many features that facilitate writing programs, these features make no difference as far as which functions can be computed. We might consider a drastically pared-down programming language, which has variables whose values are natural numbers; statements of the form

$$X \leftarrow X + 1$$

and

$$X \leftarrow X \overset{.}{-} 1$$

which cause variables to be incremented and decremented; "conditional go-to" statements of the form

$$\text{if } X \neq 0 \text{ go to } L$$

where $L$ is an integer label in the program; statements of the form

$$\text{read}(X)$$

$$\text{write}(X)$$

and nothing else. Even with a language such as this, it is possible to compute all Turing-computable functions. One approach to proving this would be to write a program in this language to simulate an arbitrary TM. Doing so would involve some sort of arithmetization of TMs similar to Gödel numbering: One integer variable would represent the state, another the head position, a third the tape contents, and so on. Another approach would be via Theorem 12.10: to show that the set of functions computable using this language contains the initial functions and is closed under all the operations permitted for $\mu$-recursive functions.

Finally, this language, or even a less restricted programming language, can compute only Turing-computable functions. This might be shown directly, by simulating on a TM each feature of the language, and in this way building a TM to execute a program in the language. It can also be shown with the help of Theorem 12.8. Just as a TM configuration can be described by specifying a state, a tape head position, and a string, a program configuration can be described by specifying a statement (the next statement to be executed) and the current values of all variables. These parameters can be assigned Gödel numbers, configuration numbers can be defined, and each step in the execution of the program can be viewed as a transformation of the Gödel number, just as in the proof of Theorem 12.10. As a result, any function computed by such a program can be shown to be $\mu$-recursive.

Other formalisms have been introduced to describe computable functions, and other abstract machines can be shown to be equivalent to Turing machines in computing power. Up to this point, every attempt to formulate precisely the idea of "effective computability" has produced the same set of functions, those that can be computed by TMs. One reasonable conclusion to be drawn is that we are justified in treating "effectively computable" as synonymous with "Turing-computable."

## EXERCISES

**12.1.**  Let $f : \mathcal{N} \to \mathcal{N}$ be the function defined as follows: $f(n)$ is the maximum number of moves an $n$-state TM with tape alphabet $\{0, 1\}$ can make if it starts with input $1^n$ and eventually halts. Show that $f$ is not computable.

**12.2.**  Define $f : \mathcal{N} \to \mathcal{N}$ by letting $f(n)$ be the maximum number of 1's that an $n$-state TM with no more than $n$ tape symbols can leave on the tape, assuming that it starts with input $1^n$ and always halts. Show that $f$ is not computable.

**12.3.**  Show that the uncomputability of the busy-beaver function (Example 12.1) implies the unsolvability of the halting problem.

**12.4.**  Suppose we define $bb(n)$ to be the maximum number of 1's that can be printed by an $n$-state Turing machine with tape alphabet $\{0, 1\}$, assuming it starts with a blank tape and eventually halts. Show that $bb$ is not computable.

**12.5.**  Show that if $f : \mathcal{N} \to \mathcal{N}$ is a total function, then $f$ is computable if and only if the decision problem: Given natural numbers $n$ and $C$, is $f(n) > C$? is solvable.

**12.6.**  Suppose that instead of including all constant functions in the set of initial functions, $C_0^0$ were the only constant function included. Describe what the set $PR$ obtained by Definition 12.4 would be.

**12.7.**  Suppose that in Definition 12.4, the operation of composition is allowed but that of primitive recursion is not. What functions are obtained?

**12.8.**  If $g(x) = x$ and $h(x, y, z) = z + 2$, what function is obtained from $g$ and $h$ by primitive recursion?

**12.9.**  Here is a primitive recursive derivation. $f_0 = C_1^0$; $f_1 = C_0^2$; $f_2$ is obtained from $f_0$ and $f_1$ by primitive recursion; $f_3 = p_2^2$; $f_4$ is obtained from $f_2$ and $f_3$ by composition; $f_5 = C_0^0$; $f_6$ is obtained from $f_5$ and $f_4$ by primitive recursion; $f_7 = p_1^1$; $f_8 = p_3^3$; $f_9 = s$; $f_{10}$ is obtained from $f_9$ and $f_8$ by composition; $f_{11}$ is obtained from $f_7$ and $f_{10}$ by primitive recursion; $f_{12} = p_1^2$; $f_{12}$ is obtained from $f_6$ and $f_{12}$ by composition; $f_{14}$ is obtained from $f_{11}$, $f_{12}$, and $f_3$ by composition; and $f_{15}$ is obtained from $f_5$ and $f_{14}$ by primitive recursion. Give simple formulas for $f_2$, $f_6$, $f_{14}$, and $f_{15}$.

**12.10.** Find two functions $g$ and $h$ so that the function $f$ defined by $f(x) = x^2$ is obtained from $g$ and $h$ by primitive recursion.

**12.11.** Give complete primitive recursive derivations for each of the following functions.

    a. $f : \mathcal{N}^2 \to \mathcal{N}$ defined by $f(x, y) = 2x + 3y$

    b. $f : \mathcal{N} \to \mathcal{N}$ defined by $f(n) = n!$

    c. $f : \mathcal{N} \to \mathcal{N}$ defined by $f(n) = 2^n$

    d. $f : \mathcal{N} \to \mathcal{N}$ defined by $f(n) = n^2 \dotminus 1$

    e. $f : \mathcal{N}^2 \to \mathcal{N}$ defined by $f(x, y) = |x - y|$

**12.12.** Show that for any $n \geq 1$, the functions $Add_n$ and $Mult_n$ from $\mathcal{N}^n$ to $\mathcal{N}$, defined by

$$Add_n(x_1, \ldots, x_n) = x_1 + x_2 + \cdots + x_n$$

$$Mult_n(x_1, \ldots, x_n) = x_1 * x_2 * \cdots * x_n$$

respectively, are both primitive recursive.

**12.13.** Show that if $f : \mathcal{N} \to \mathcal{N}$ is primitive recursive, $A \subseteq \mathcal{N}$ is a finite set, and $g$ is a total function agreeing with $f$ at every point not in $A$, then $g$ is primitive recursive.

**12.14.** Show that if $f : \mathcal{N} \to \mathcal{N}$ is an *eventually periodic* total function, then $f$ is primitive recursive. *Eventually periodic* means that for some $n_0$ and some $p > 0$, $f(x + p) = f(x)$ for every $x \geq n_0$.

**12.15.** Show that each of the following functions is primitive recursive.

    a. $f : \mathcal{N}^2 \to \mathcal{N}$ defined by $f(x, y) = max\{x, y\}$

    b. $f : \mathcal{N}^2 \to \mathcal{N}$ defined by $f(x, y) = min\{x, y\}$

    c. $f : \mathcal{N} \to \mathcal{N}$ defined by $f(x) = \lfloor \sqrt{x} \rfloor$ (the largest natural number less than or equal to $\sqrt{x}$)

    d. $f : \mathcal{N} \to \mathcal{N}$ defined by $f(x) = \lfloor \log_2(x + 1) \rfloor$

**12.16.** Suppose $P$ is a primitive recursive $(k + 1)$-place predicate, and $f$ and $g$ are primitive recursive functions of one variable. Show that the predicates $A_{f,g}P$ and $E_{f,g}P$ defined by

$$A_{f,g}P(X, k) = (\text{for every } i \text{ with } f(k) \leq i \leq g(k), \ P(X, i))$$

$$E_{f,g}P(X, k) = (\text{there exists } i \text{ with } f(k) \leq i \leq g(k) \text{ so that } P(X, i))$$

are both primitive recursive.

**12.17.** Show that if $g : \mathcal{N}^2 \to \mathcal{N}$ is primitive recursive, then $f : \mathcal{N} \to \mathcal{N}$ defined by

$$f(x) = \sum_{i=0}^{x} g(x, i)$$

is primitive recursive.

**12.18.** Show that the function *HighestPrime*, introduced in the proof of Lemma 12.4, is primitive recursive.

**12.19.** In addition to the bounded minimalization of a predicate, we might define the bounded maximalization of a predicate $P$ to be the function $m^P$ defined by

$$m^P(X, k) = \begin{cases} \max\{y \le k \mid P(X, y) \text{ is true}\} & \text{if this set is not empty} \\ 0 & \text{otherwise} \end{cases}$$

    a. Show $m^P$ is primitive recursive by finding two primitive recursive functions from which it can be obtained by primitive recursion.

    b. Show $m^P$ is primitive recursive by using bounded minimalization.

**12.20.** Give an example to show that the unbounded universal quantification of a computable predicate need not be computable.

**12.21.** Show that the unbounded minimalization of any predicate can be written in the form $\mu y[f(X, y) = 0]$, for some function $f$.

**12.22.** True or false: if unbounded minimalization applied to a primitive recursive predicate yields a total function, the function is primitive recursive. Explain your answer.

**12.23.** The set of $\mu$-recursive functions was defined to be the smallest set that contains the initial functions and is closed under the operations of composition, primitive recursion, and unbounded minimalization (applied to total functions). In the definition, no explicit mention is made of the bounded operators (universal and existential quantification, bounded minimalization). Do bounded quantifications applied to $\mu$-recursive predicates always produce $\mu$-recursive predicates? Does bounded minimalization applied to $\mu$-recursive predicates or functions always produce $\mu$-recursive functions? Explain.

**12.24.** Is the problem: Given a Turing machine $T$ computing some partial function $f$, is $f$ a total function? solvable? Explain.

**12.25.** Consider the function $f$ defined recursively as follows:

$$f(0) = f(1) = 1; \quad \text{for } x > 0, \ f(x) = 1 + f(\lfloor \sqrt{x} \rfloor)$$

Show that $f$ is primitive recursive.

**12.26.** Suppose that $f : \mathcal{N} \to \mathcal{N}$ is a $\mu$-recursive total function that is a bijection from $\mathcal{N}$ to $\mathcal{N}$. Show that its inverse $f^{-1}$ is also $\mu$-recursive.

**12.27.** Let $\Sigma$ be an alphabet. Show that the 1-place predicate *Isgn* defined by

$$Isgn(x) = (x = gn(s) \text{ for some string } s \in \Sigma^*)$$

is primitive recursive.

**12.28.** a. Give reasonable definitions of primitive recursive and recursive for a function $f : \Sigma^* \to \mathcal{N}$, where $\Sigma$ is an alphabet.

    b. Using your definition, show that $f : \{a, b\}^* \to \mathcal{N}$ defined by $f(x) = |x|$ is primitive recursive.

# MORE CHALLENGING PROBLEMS

**12.29.** Let $b : \mathcal{N} \to \mathcal{N}$ be the busy-beaver function discussed in Example 12.1. Show that $f$ is eventually larger than any computable function; in other words, for any computable total function $g : \mathcal{N} \to \mathcal{N}$, there is an integer $k$ so that $f(n) > g(n)$ for every $n \geq k$.

**12.30.** In the discussion after Example 12.1 we defined $b_2(n)$ to be the largest number of 1's that can be left on the tape of a 2-state TM with tape alphabet $\{0, 1\}$, if it starts with input $1^n$ and eventually halts.

  a. Give a convincing argument that $b_2$ is computable.

  b. Is the function $b_k$ (identical to $b_2$ except that "2-state" is replaced by "$k$-state") computable for every $k \geq 2$? Why or why not?

**12.31.**  a. Show that the function $f : \mathcal{N}^2 \to \mathcal{N}$ defined by $f(x, y) = $ (the number of integer divisors of $x$ less than or equal to $y$) is primitive recursive. Use this to show that the 1-place predicate *Prime* (see Example 12.7) is primitive recursive.

  b. Show that the function $f : \mathcal{N}^3 \to \mathcal{N}$ defined by $f(x, y, z) = $ (the number of integers less than or equal to $z$ that are divisors of both $x$ and $y$) is primitive recursive. Use this to show that the 2-place predicate $P$ defined by $P(x, y) = $ ($x$ and $y$ are relatively prime) is primitive recursive.

**12.32.** Show that both these functions from $\mathcal{N}$ to $\mathcal{N}$ are primitive recursive.

  a. $f(n) = $ the leftmost digit in the decimal representation of $2^x$

  b. $f(n) = $ the $n$th digit of the infinite decimal expansion of $\sqrt{2} = 1.414213\ldots$ (i.e., $f(0) = 1$, $f(1) = 4$, and so on)

**12.33.** Show that if $g : \mathcal{N}^{n+1} \to \mathcal{N}$ is primitive recursive, and $l, m : \mathcal{N} \to \mathcal{N}$ are both primitive recursive, then the functions $f_1$ and $f_2$ from $\mathcal{N}^{n+1}$ to $\mathcal{N}$ defined by

$$f_1(X, k) = \prod_{i=l(k)}^{m(k)} g(X, i) \qquad f_2(X, k) = \sum_{i=l(k)}^{m(k)} g(X, i)$$

are primitive recursive.

**12.34.** Suppose we copy the proof of Theorem 12.3, but using recursive derivations instead, as follows. Consider the strings in $\Sigma^*$ in canonical order; for each $i$, find the $i$th string representing a "$\mu$-recursive derivation" of a function of one variable, and let the function be called $f_i$; define $f$ by the formula $f(i) = f_i(i) + 1$. Then (apparently) we have exhibited an algorithm for computing $f$, but $f$ cannot be $\mu$-recursive. Explain the seeming contradiction.

**12.35.** In each case below, show that the function from $\{a, b\}^*$ to $\{a, b\}^*$ is primitive recursive.

  a. $f$ is defined by $f(x) = xa$

     b.   $f$ is defined by $f(x) = ax$

     c.   $f$ is defined by $f(x) = x^r$

**12.36.**   a.   Give definitions of primitive recursive and recursive for a function $f : (\Sigma^*)^n \rightarrow \Sigma^*$ of $n$ string variables.

     b.   Using your definition, show that the concatenation function from $(\Sigma^*)^2$ to $\Sigma^*$ is primitive recursive.

# Introduction to Computational Complexity

So far in our discussion of decision problems, we have considered only the qualitative question of whether the problem is solvable. In real life, the computational resources available for solving problems are limited: There is only so much time and space available. As a result, there are problems solvable in principle for which even medium-sized instances are too hard in practice. In Part VI, we consider the idea of trying to identify these *intractable* problems, by describing in some way the amounts of computer time and memory needed in order to answer instances of a certain size.

In Chapter 13, we first introduce notation and terminology involving growth rates that allow us to discuss in a meaningful way questions such as "How much time?" In the rest of the chapter, we relate these quantitative issues to our specific model of computation and then discuss some of the basic *complexity classes*: ways of categorizing decision problems and languages according to their inherent complexity.

In trying to distinguish between tractable and intractable problems, a criterion commonly used is polynomial-time solvability on a Turing machine. Many problems are tractable according to this criterion, and some can be shown not to be; we can adapt the reduction technique of Chapter 11 in order to obtain examples of both types. Perhaps even more interesting are problems whose status with respect to this criterion is still up in the air—problems for which no one has found either a polynomial-time solution or a proof that none exists. The notion of *NP*-completeness is a way of approaching this topic. In the last two sections, we give Cook's proof of the *NP*-completeness of the satisfiability problem and several examples of combinatorial problems that can be shown to be *NP*-complete by using polynomial-time reductions.

∎

# CHAPTER

# 13

# Measuring and Classifying Complexity

## 13.1 | GROWTH RATES OF FUNCTIONS

The complexity of computational problems can be discussed by choosing a specific abstract machine as a model of computation and considering how much time and/or space machines of that type require for the solutions. In order to compare two problems it is necessary to look at instances of different sizes. Using the criterion of runtime, for example, the most common approach is to compare the *growth rates* of the two runtimes, each viewed as a function of the instance size. Before we introduce definitions and notation for discussing growth rates of quantities such as runtime, we consider an example in which four simple functions are contrasted.

| The Growth Rates of Polynomial and Exponential Functions | **EXAMPLE 13.1** |
|---|---|

We consider the functions $p_1(n) = 2n^2$, $p_2(n) = n^2 + 3n + 7$, $p_3(n) = n^3$, and $q(n) = 2^n$. Table 13.1 shows the values of these four functions for some selected values of $n$, and these few values are enough to make certain trends apparent. For small values of $n$, $p_2(n)$ is significantly larger than $p_1(n)$. By the time we reach $n = 1000$, however, the lower order terms $3n + 7$ in $p_2$ are relatively negligible, and the extra factor of 2 in the leading term of $p_1$ accounts almost entirely for the difference between the two. The polynomial $p_3$ is of higher degree, and even without the extra terms this value grows more rapidly than either of the first two.

A more striking trend is the growth of the exponential function $q$. Once $n$ is larger than about 10, there is no contest: If the function values represent nanoseconds of runtime (one nanosecond is one billionth of a second), $p_3(1000)$ is one second, and $q(1000)$ is more than $3 * 10^{282}$ centuries.

The table illustrates the effect of different growth rates. The two functions $p_1$ and $p_2$ have different sizes, primarily because of the factor of 2, but the same (quadratic) growth rate. The growth rate of the cubic polynomial is larger, and all three are eventually dwarfed by the

**Table 13.1** | Selected values of polynomial and exponential functions

| $n$ | $p_1(n) = 2n^2$ | $p_2(n) = n^2 + 3n + 7$ | $p_3(n) = n^3$ | $q(n) = 2^n$ |
|---|---|---|---|---|
| 1 | 2 | 11 | 1 | 2 |
| 2 | 8 | 17 | 8 | 4 |
| 3 | 18 | 25 | 27 | 8 |
| 5 | 50 | 47 | 125 | 32 |
| 10 | 200 | 137 | 1000 | 1024 |
| 20 | 800 | 467 | 8000 | 1048576 |
| 50 | 5000 | 2567 | 125000 | $1.13 * 10^{15}$ |
| 100 | 20000 | 10307 | 1000000 | $1.27 * 10^{30}$ |
| 1000 | 2000000 | 1003007 | 1000000000 | $1.07 * 10^{301}$ |

exponential function. Once we say how to talk precisely about growth rates, one of the most useful distinctions will be that between polynomial growth rates and exponential growth rates. Many of the features evident in this example will persist in general.

The simplest situation in which two functions $f$ and $g$ will be said to have the same growth rate is when $f$ is exactly proportional to $g$, or $f = Cg$ for some constant $C$. (The size of $C$ is irrelevant, as long as it is independent of $n$.) Because it is unusual for two runtimes to be exactly proportional, we generalize by allowing one function to be *approximately* proportional to the other, which means that $f < Cg$ for some constant $C$ and $f > Dg$ for some other (positive) constant $D$. Again, the sizes of $C$ and $D$ are not relevant. The first part of Definition 13.1 involves a single inequality, so that we can talk about one growth rate being no greater than another; in order to consider functions with equal growth rates we can simply use the statement twice, the second time with the two functions reversed. The other way in which the definition generalizes the simplest case is that it allows the inequality to fail at a finite set of values of $n$, to take care of the case when functions are undefined or have unrepresentative values at a few points.

---

**Definition 13.1    Notation for Comparing Growth Rates**

Suppose $f, g : \mathcal{N} \to \mathcal{N}$ are partial functions, and each is defined at all but a finite number of points. We write

$$f(n) = O(g(n))$$

or simply $f = O(g)$, if there are constants $C$ and $n_0$ so that for every $n \geq n_0$, $f(n)$ and $g(n)$ are defined and $f(n) \leq Cg(n)$. We write

$$f = \Theta(g)$$

to mean that $f = O(g)$ and $g = O(f)$. Finally,

$$f(n) = o(g(n))$$

or $f = o(g)$ means that for *every* positive constant $C$, there is a constant $n_0$ so that for every $n \geq n_0$, $f(n) \leq Cg(n)$.

The statements $f = O(g)$, $f = \Theta(g)$, and $f = o(g)$ are read "$f$ is big-oh of $g$," "$f$ is big-theta of $g$," and "$f$ is little-oh of $g$," respectively. All these statements can be rephrased in terms of the ratio $f(n)/g(n)$, provided that $g(n)$ is eventually greater than 0. Saying that $f = o(g)$ means that the limit of this ratio as $n$ approaches infinity is 0; the statement $f = O(g)$ means only that the ratio is *bounded*. If $f = \Theta(g)$, and both functions are eventually nonzero, then both the ratios $f/g$ and $g/f$ are bounded, which is the same as saying that the ratio $f/g$ must stay between two fixed positive values (or is "approximately constant"). If the statement $f = O(g)$ fails, we write $f \neq O(g)$, and similarly for the other two. Saying that $f \neq O(g)$ means that it is impossible to find a constant $C$ so that $f(n) \leq Cg(n)$ for all sufficiently large $n$; in other words, the ratio $f(n)/g(n)$ is unbounded. This means that although the ratio $f(n)/g(n)$ may not be large for all large values of $n$, it is large for infinitely many values of $n$.

A statement like $f = O(g)$ describes a relationship between two functions. It is not an equation, and it makes no sense, for example, to write $O(f) = g$. The notation is fairly well-established, although a variation that is a little more precise is to define a *set* $O(g)$ and to write $f \in O(g)$ instead of $f = O(g)$.

The statement $f = O(g)$ conveys no information about the values of $f(n)$ and $g(n)$ for any particular $n$. It says that in the long run (that is, for *sufficiently large* values of $n$), $f(n)$ is no larger than a function proportional to $g$. The constant of proportionality may be very large, so that the actual value of $f(n)$ may be much larger than $g(n)$. Nevertheless, we say in this case that the *growth rate* of $f$ is no larger than that of $g$. The terminology is most appropriate when the two functions $f$ and $g$ are both nondecreasing, or at least eventually nondecreasing, and most of the functions we are interested in will have this property. If $f = \Theta(g)$, we say $f$ and $g$ have the same growth rate; as we have seen, this is a way of saying that the two values are approximately proportional, or that the ratio is approximately constant, for large values of $n$. If $f = o(g)$, it is appropriate to say that the growth rate of $f$ is smaller than that of $g$, because according to the definition, no positive constant is small enough to remain a constant of proportionality as $n$ gets large. In this case, although $f(n)$ *will* eventually be smaller than $g(n)$, in fact much smaller, the statement says nothing about how large $n$ must be before this happens.

We have introduced the idea of two functions having the same growth rate, or of one having a smaller growth rate than another. This terminology is not misleading, in the sense that these two relations (on the set of partial functions from $\mathcal{N}$ to $\mathcal{N}$ defined for all sufficiently large $n$) satisfy at least most of the crucial properties we associate with the corresponding relations on numbers. It is clear from the definitions that if $f = o(g)$, then $f = O(g)$, so that "smaller than" implies "no larger than" in reference to growth rates. We would also expect that if $f = o(g)$, then $g \neq O(f)$) (if the growth rate of $f$ is smaller than that of $g$, then it cannot be true that the growth rate of $g$ is no larger than that of $f$), and this is easy to check. Theorem 13.1 contains several other straightforward properties of these relations.

---

**Theorem 13.1**

The relation $R_1$ defined by

$$f R_1 g \quad \text{if and only if} \quad f = O(g)$$

interpreted informally to mean the growth rate of $f$ is no larger than that of $g$, is reflexive and transitive.

The relation $R_2$ defined by

$$f R_2 g \quad \text{if and only if} \quad f = o(g)$$

interpreted to mean the growth rate of $f$ is less than that of $g$, is transitive and asymmetric (i.e., if $f R_2 g$, then $\neg g R_2 f$).

The relation $R_3$ defined by

$$f R_3 g \quad \text{if and only if} \quad f = \Theta(g)$$

($f$ and $g$ have the same growth rate) is an equivalence relation.

**Proof**

We verify the statements involving $R_1$ and leave the others as exercises. The relation $R_1$ is reflexive, because in the definition we can take the constants $C$ and $n_0$ to be 1 and 0, respectively. Suppose that $f = O(g)$ and $g = O(h)$. Then for some constants $C_1, n_1, C_2,$ and $n_2$,

$$f(n) \leq C_1 g(n) \quad \text{for all } n \geq n_1$$
$$g(n) \leq C_2 h(n) \quad \text{for all } n \geq n_2$$

Let $n_0$ be the larger of $n_1$ and $n_2$. Then for $n \geq n_0$, both inequalities hold, and thus

$$f(n) \leq C_1 g(n) \leq C_1 C_2 h(n)$$

We conclude that $f = O(h)$, because in the definition we can take $C$ to be $C_1 C_2$.

---

A polynomial function is either identically 0 or of the form

$$p(n) = a_k n^k + a_{k-1} n^{k-1} + \cdots + a_1 n + a_0$$

where $a_k \neq 0$. In the latter case, $k$ is the degree of the polynomial. It is easy to check that if the leading coefficient $a_k$ is positive, then $p(n) > 0$ for all sufficiently large $n$. Usually we will be interested only in polynomials having this property, and we may simply regard $p(n)$ as undefined if it is negative. An exponential function is one of the form

$$q(n) = a^n$$

for some fixed number $a > 1$. If the coefficients $a_i$ of a polynomial or the base $a$ of an exponential function are not integers, we may obtain an integer function by ignoring the fractional part; in both cases, the growth rate is not affected.

On the basis of Example 13.1, we would probably conjecture that any quadratic polynomial has a smaller growth rate than any cubic, and that either one has a smaller growth rate than an exponential function. The next theorem generalizes both these statements.

---

**Theorem 13.2**

Let $p$ be the polynomial

$$p(n) = a_k n^k + a_{k-1} n^{k-1} + \cdots + a_1 n + a_0$$

where $k \geq 0$ and $a_k > 0$, and let $q$ be the exponential function $q(n) = a^n$, where $a > 1$. Then $p(n) = \Theta(n^k)$ and $p = o(q)$.

**Proof**

First we show that $p(n) = O(n^k)$. We can write

$$\frac{p(n)}{n^k} = a_k + \frac{a_{k-1}}{n} + \cdots + \frac{a_1}{n^{k-1}} + \frac{a_0}{n^k}$$

and we can choose $n_0$ so that for any $n \geq n_0$, each of the $k$ terms

$$\left|\frac{a_{k-1}}{n}\right|, \left|\frac{a_{k-2}}{n^2}\right|, \ldots, \left|\frac{a_1}{n^{k-1}}\right|, \left|\frac{a_0}{n^k}\right|$$

is less than $1/k$. It follows in the first place that for $n \geq n_0$, $p(n)$ is defined (i.e., nonnegative), because even if all the coefficients $a_{k-1}, \ldots, a_0$ were negative, the quantity

$$\frac{a_{k-1}}{n} + \cdots + \frac{a_1}{n^{k-1}} + \frac{a_0}{n^k}$$

would still be less than 1 in absolute value, so that

$$\frac{p(n)}{n^k} > a_k - 1 \geq 0$$

In the second place, for $n \geq n_0$,

$$\frac{p(n)}{n^k} \leq a_k + 1$$

and therefore the inequality in the definition of $O$ is satisfied with $C = a_k + 1$.

The proof that $n^k = O(p(n))$ is similar. Choosing $n_0$ even slightly larger if necessary, so that each of the terms $|a_{k-1}/n|, \ldots, |a_0/n^k|$ is less than or equal to $1/(2k)$ for all $n \geq n_0$, we have

$$\frac{p(n)}{n^k} \geq a_k - \frac{1}{2}$$

which can be rewritten

$$n^k \leq \left(\frac{1}{a_k - 1/2}\right) * p(n)$$

To show that $p = o(q)$, it will now be sufficient to show that $n^k = o(q(n))$, because we have already observed that $p(n) \leq (a_k + 1)n^k$ for all sufficiently large $n$. Our proof uses the fact that the ratio $\log n / n$ approaches 0 as $n$ increases, where log is the natural logarithm to the base $e$. For another, slightly more direct proof, see Exercise 13.7.

We can write

$$n^{k+1} = (z(n))^n$$

where $z(n)$ is the real number

$$z(n) = e^{(k+1)(\log n / n)}$$

(From the second formula, it follows that $\log(z(n)) = (k+1) \log n / n$. Using this, you can verify that both sides of the first formula have the same logarithm.) Since the exponent in this expression approaches 0 as $n$ increases, and since $e^0 = 1 < a$, we can choose $n_0$ so that $z(n) \leq a$ for all $n \geq n_0$. It follows that for $n \geq n_0$,

$$n^{k+1} = z(n)^n \leq a^n$$

and therefore

$$n^k \leq \frac{a^n}{n}$$

which implies that $n^k = o(a^n)$.

A tabulation such as the one in Example 13.1 would obviously look different for polynomials of different degrees and for exponential functions with a different base. At $n = 1000$, for example, $(1.01)^n$ is still only about 20959. However, the "exponential growth" is still there, as the second part of the theorem confirms; it just takes a little longer for its effects to become obvious. When $n = 10000$, $(1.01)^n$ is greater than $10^{43}$, whereas $(10000)^3 = 10^{12}$, or one trillion.

## 13.2 | TIME AND SPACE COMPLEXITY OF A TURING MACHINE

The model of computation we have chosen is the Turing machine. When a TM answers a specific instance of a decision problem, we can measure the time (the number of moves) and the space (the number of tape squares) required by the computation. The most obvious measure of the size of an instance is the length of the input string that encodes it, and the most common approach is to consider the worst case: the maximum time or space that might be required by any input string of that length. With this in mind, we can now define the time and space complexity of an ordinary, deterministic TM.

---

> **Definition 13.2** **The Time and Space Complexity of a Turing Machine**
>
> Let $T$ be a Turing machine. The time complexity of $T$ is the function $\tau_T$ defined on the natural numbers as follows. For a natural number $n$, $\tau_T(n)$ is the maximum number of moves $T$ can make on any input string of length $n$. If there is an input string $x$ with $|x| = n$ so that $T$ loops forever on input $x$, $\tau_T(n)$ is undefined.
>
> The space complexity function $s_T$ of $T$ is defined as follows. If no input string of length $n$ causes $T$ to use an infinite number of tape squares, $s_T(n)$ is the maximum number of tape squares used by $T$ for any input string of length $n$. (If $T$ is a multitape TM, the "number of tape squares" means the maximum of the numbers for the individual tapes.) Otherwise (if some input of length $n$ causes $T$ to loop forever, and this infinite loop causes an infinite number of tape squares to be used), $s_T(n)$ is undefined.

---

The Time Complexity of a Simple TM | **EXAMPLE 13.2**

We consider the Turing machine $T$ of Example 9.3, shown in Figure 13.1, which accepts the language $\{ss \mid s \in \{a, b\}^*\}$. We derive the formula for $\tau_T(n)$ for an even integer $n$ and leave the other case as an exercise.

An input string of length $2k$ is processed in three phases: First, find the middle, changing all the symbols to uppercase along the way; second, change the first half back to lower case, while moving the tape head to the beginning; third, compare the two halves. In the first phase, one move positions the tape head at the first input symbol, $2k + 1$ moves are required to change the first symbol and find the rightmost symbol, and $2k$ more moves are needed to change the symbol and return the tape head to the leftmost lowercase symbol. Each subsequent pass deals with two fewer lowercase symbols and therefore requires four fewer moves. The total number of moves in the first phase is

$$1 + (4k + 1) + (4(k - 1) + 1) + \cdots + (4(0) + 1) = 1 + 4 \sum_{i=0}^{k} i + (k + 1) = 2k^2 + 3k + 2$$

(The result in Example 2.7 is used here.) Phase two requires $k + 1$ moves. For even-length inputs, the total time for the first two phases depends only on the input length. In the third phase, the input strings requiring the most moves are those in the language. This phase consists of $k$ passes, one for each symbol in the first half. In each pass, there are $k$ moves to the right, $k$ to the left, and one more to the right, for a total of $2k + 1$ moves. The third phase therefore contains at most $2k^2 + k$ moves. Adding these three numbers and including the final move to the accepting state, we obtain

$$4k^2 + 5k + 4 = n^2 + 5n/2 + 4$$

moves. Because odd-length input strings require fewer moves, we may conclude that

$$\tau_T(n) = O(n^2)$$

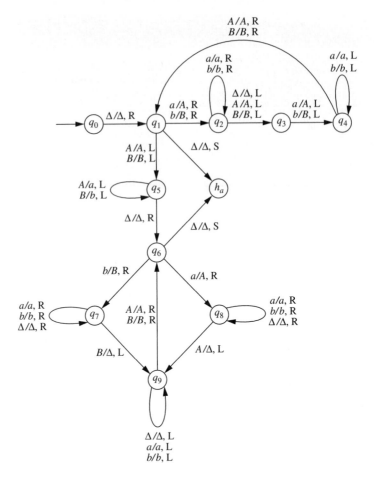

**Figure 13.1 |**
A Turning machine to accept $\{ss \mid s \in \{a, b\}^*\}$.

We might ask whether there is a TM accepting this language with a significantly smaller time complexity. A complete answer to this question is a little complicated. It looks at first as though the number of actual comparisons a TM must make in order to recognize a string in the language should be simply proportional to the string's length. The quadratic behavior of the machine in Figure 13.1 is the result of the repeated back-and-forth motions of the tape head, which seem to be necessary in phases one and three. There are ways to reduce the number of these motions without changing the overall approach. For example, in the first phase we could make the TM convert *two* symbols at the left end to uppercase, then two at the right, and so forth, and in the final matching phase we could ask the TM to remember two symbols from the first half before it sends its tape head to the second half to try to match them. These improvements ought to cut the back-and-forth motion almost in half, at the expense of an increase in the number of states. Furthermore, if going from one to two is good, going from one to a number bigger than two ought to be even better. (If there were some way to get the TM to remember the entire first half of the input in the third phase, we could eliminate the extraneous motions in that phase altogether. There is no way to do this, unfortunately, because the number of states is finite.)

Any Turing machine that looks at all $n$ input symbols must make at least $n$ moves. For this language, any TM following an approach similar to that in Figure 13.1 will probably need at least twice that many. Our tentative conclusion from the preceding paragraph is that we may be able to reduce the runtime beyond that bare minimum by an arbitrarily large factor. This conclusion turns out to be correct, not only for this example but in general. By increasing the number of states and/or tape symbols, one can produce a comparable "linear speed-up" of any Turing machine, and there are similar results for space complexity. We may conclude that the number of moves a TM makes or the number of tape squares it uses on a particular input string is not by itself very meaningful; a more significant indicator is the growth rate of the function. Reducing the runtime by a large constant factor still leaves us with a quadratic growth rate, and it can be shown that the time complexity of any one-tape TM accepting this language is quadratic or higher.

Another way to reduce the runtime would be to increase the number of tapes. In this example, using a two-tape TM makes it possible to recognize the language in linear runtime by avoiding back-and-forth motions altogether (Exercise 13.22). In more general examples, this is too much to expect, and the growth rate of the runtime can be reduced in this way only to about the square root of the original (Exercise 13.25).

---

As Example 13.2 has suggested, looking at the growth rate of a TM's time complexity tells us something about the efficiency of the algorithm embodied by the machine. Of two TMs recognizing the same language (with the same number of tapes), the one for which the growth rate of the time complexity is smaller will be preferable, at least for sufficiently long input strings. We can now turn this statement around in order to compare the complexity, or difficulty, of two languages. If recognizing $L_1$ can be accomplished by a $k$-tape TM with time complexity $f_1$, and the time complexity of any $k$-tape TM recognizing $L_2$ grows faster than $f_1$, it is reasonable to say that $L_2$ is more complex, or difficult to recognize, than $L_1$.

You might not expect that the time or space complexity of a *nondeterministic* Turing machine would be a useful concept; after all, such a machine is allowed to take shortcuts by making guesses. However, many of the most interesting decision problems have solutions that can be described easily by using nondeterminism, and we will see that adding this ingredient will be helpful in categorizing languages, or decision problems, according to their complexity.

> **Definition 13.3　The Time and Space Complexity of a Nondeterministic Turing Machine**
>
> Let $T$ be a nondeterministic TM accepting a language $L \subseteq \Sigma^*$. For an input string $x$, we define the computation time $\tau_x$ as follows. First, $\tau_x$ is undefined if it is possible for $T$ to loop forever on input $x$; otherwise, if $x \in L$, $\tau_x$

is the minimum number of moves required for $T$ to accept input $x$, and if $x \notin L$, $\tau_x$ is the minimum number of moves required for $T$ to reject $x$. The *nondeterministic time complexity* of $T$ is the function $\tau_T$, where $\tau_T(n)$ is the maximum value of $\tau_x$ over strings $x$ with $|x| = n$. Thus $\tau_T(n)$ is defined unless there is a string of length $n$ on which $T$ might loop forever.

Similarly, $s_x$ is undefined if $T$ might loop forever on input $x$; otherwise it is the minimum number of tape squares that might be used in accepting $x$, if $x \in L$, and the minimum number of tape squares that might be used before rejecting input $x$, if all choices of moves cause $T$ to reject $x$. As in the deterministic case, for a multitape TM, "number of tape squares" means the maximum over all the tapes. The *nondeterministic space complexity* of $T$ is the function $s_T$, where $s_T(n)$ is undefined if $T$ can loop forever on some input of length $n$, and otherwise $s_T(n)$ is the maximum of the numbers $s_x$ for $|x| = n$.

This definition is not as difficult to interpret as it might appear at first. Fortunately, the complication caused by $\tau_T$ or $s_T$ being undefined at some points will not usually arise. For the languages we will be interested in (or for the decision problems we will be trying to solve), Turing machines are available that cannot loop forever. In particular, we will usually be considering TMs $T$ for which $\tau_T \leq f$ for some total function $f$ on the natural numbers, and this is understood to imply that $\tau_T$ is also a total function.

The number $\tau_T(n)$ is supposed to measure the time that might be required for $T$ to determine whether a string $x$ of length $n$ is in the language $L$ accepted by $T$. If $x \in L$ and $T$ makes the right choice of moves on input $x$, then it reaches the accepting state within $\tau_T(n)$ moves. If $|x| = n$ and $x \notin L$, then there is a sequence of no more than $\tau_T(n)$ moves causing $T$ to reject input $x$. Another way to say this is that for any input $x$, if we trace all possible sequences of $\tau_T(|x|)$ or fewer moves, then we have the answer for the string $x$.

Another way to visualize the situation is to use the idea of *parallel* computation. One might imagine several "parallel processors" carrying out simultaneously all the possible computations $T$ can execute on input $x$. We could answer the question for $x$ if we could monitor these independent computations for the first $\tau_T(|x|)$ moves. In practice this might not be feasible, because the number of processors required may continue to grow with the number of steps in the computation.

**EXAMPLE 13.3**     The Time Complexity of a Simple NTM

Consider the Turing machine pictured in Figure 13.2, which accepts the language

$$L = \{x \in \{a, b\}^* \mid \text{ for some } k \geq 2 \text{ and some } w \text{ with } |w| \geq 1, x = w^k\}$$

A straightforward deterministic approach to recognizing this language would be to determine whether the input string $x$ is of the form $w^k$ for a string $w$ with $|w| = 1$, or for a string $w$ with

$|w| = 2, \ldots,$ or for a string $w$ with length $|x|/2$. The machine in Figure 13.2 uses nondeterminism instead. Let us temporarily ignore the first component, $Place(\$)$, and concentrate on the remaining parts, which also begin with the tape head on square 0. The machine moves past the input string, generates an arbitrary string $w$ on the tape, makes an identical copy of $w$, makes an arbitrary number of additional copies, deletes all the blanks that separate the copies, and compares the resulting string to the original input. The nondeterminism appears both in the construction of $w$ and in the choice of the number of copies made. If the input string is of the form $w^k$, where $|w| \geq 1$ and $k \geq 2$, then the sequence of moves in which that string is generated on the tape causes the TM to accept; because the string generated *is* of this form, any input that is not causes the final comparison to fail and the TM to reject.

The purpose of $Place(\$)$ is to prevent the possibility of infinite loops, which would otherwise be possible in two places: in the generation of $w$ or in the production of additional copies of $w$. $Place(\$)$ places the special marker in square $3n + 2$, where $n$ is the length of the input. Thereafter, since no moves are specified for the tape symbol $\$$, the machine crashes if the tape head ever moves that far right on the tape. The number $3n + 2$ is chosen to allow for the extreme case in which $|w| = 1$ and $n$ copies of $w$ are generated, so that the copies and the blanks separating them require a total of $2n$ tape squares.

Although calculating the exact nondeterministic time complexity of this machine is complicated, finding a big-oh answer is not so hard. If the string $w$ that is generated has length $m$, and $k$ copies are made, then in order for the input string of length $n$ to be accepted, $km$ must be $n$. From this point on we can argue as follows. Moving past the input and generating $w$ takes time roughly proportional to $n + m$. Creating each additional copy of $w$ requires time proportional to $m^2$, and this occurs $k - 1$ times, so that this total is proportional to $km^2 = mn$. The first deletion of a blank takes time proportional to $m$, the second requires time proportional to $2m, \ldots,$ and the last requires time proportional to $(k - 1)m$; the total of these is therefore proportional to $k^2m = kn$. Finally, still assuming that the input and the string created nondeterministically have the same length $n$, comparing them takes time proportional to $n^2$. It is now clear that the overall time complexity is $O(n^2)$.

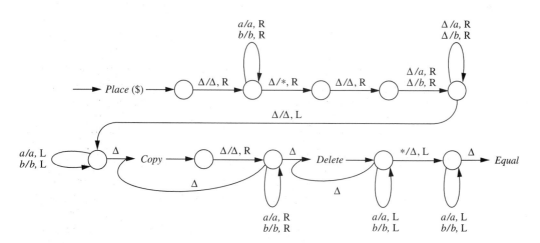

**Figure 13.2 |**

The space complexity of our nondeterministic Turing machine is easy to calculate. The rightmost tape square visited is the one just to the right of the last copy of $w$ that is created. Again, we are only interested in the case when the input string is accepted, so that the total amount of space used (including the space required for the input) is $n + 2 + k(m + 1) = 2n + k + 2$, where as before, $k$ is the number of copies of $w$ that are created. Because $k$ is no larger than $n$, we conclude that the TM has linear space complexity.

---

Example 13.3 illustrates in a simple way something that we will often see later. To decide whether $x$ is in this language, we must answer the question: Do there exist a string $w$ and an integer $k$ so that $x = w^k$? A deterministic algorithm to answer the question consists of testing every possible choice of $w$ and $k$ to see if any choice works. Although nondeterminism can eliminate the "every possible choice" aspect of the algorithm by guessing, the TM must still test deterministically the choice it guesses. Many interesting decision problems have the same general form: Is there some number (or some choice of numbers, or some path, ...) that works? The obvious nondeterministic approach to such a problem is to choose values by guessing and then test them to see if they work. If $T$ is a nondeterministic TM answering the question in this way, we can interpret the time complexity $\tau_T$ informally by thinking of $\tau_T(n)$ as measuring the time required to *test* a possible solution. The assumption is that the time required for guessing a solution to test is relatively small.

## 13.3 | COMPLEXITY CLASSES

Now that we have defined the time and space complexity of a Turing machine, we can begin to discuss the inherent complexity of a computational problem. Just as in Chapter 11, we are interested in decision problems. An instance of such a problem can be encoded as a string; we may then consider the language of encoded yes-instances; and we can describe the complexity of the problem by considering the complexity functions of machines that solve it.

The complexity classes in Definition 13.4 are classes of *languages*. In Chapter 11 we could avoid distinguishing between the decision problem and the language corresponding to it, because the only issue was whether or not the problem was solvable. Any encoding was all right, as long as it was possible, in principle, to decode a string representing an instance. Now that we are concerned with how much time or space is required to solve a problem, we must be a little more careful about the encoding we use. On the one hand, we do not want the difficulty of solving a problem to be dramatically increased because of the difficulty of encoding an instance or decoding a string; on the other hand, we do not want the description of an algorithm's runtime in terms of the instance size to be distorted because the encoding results in instance strings that are longer than necessary. (For example, suppose a problem involves integer input. An algorithm that has linear runtime when the integers are encoded in unary notation may turn out to be exponential when binary notation is used instead.) For the most part, it will be sufficient to keep in mind that the encoding we adopt should be "reasonable" in this sense.

> **Definition 13.4    Basic Complexity Classes**
>
> For a function $f : \mathcal{N} \to \mathcal{N}$, we define the following complexity classes.
>
> 1. $Time(f)$ is the set of languages that can be recognized by a Turing machine $T$ with $\tau_T \leq f$.
> 2. $Space(f)$ is the set of languages that can be recognized by a Turing machine $T$ with $s_T \leq f$.
> 3. $NTime(f)$ is the set of languages that can be accepted by an NTM $T$ with nondeterministic time complexity function $\tau_T \leq f$.
> 4. $NSpace(f)$ is the set of languages that can be accepted by an NTM $T$ with nondeterministic space complexity function $s_T \leq f$.
>
> In all four cases, the machines are allowed to be multitape TMs.

At this point we introduce a convention that occasionally will be useful in the remainder of this chapter and the next. It is possible for a Turing machine to halt before it has finished reading all its input, so that its time complexity function might be less than $n$. More commonly, however, a TM reads all its input. In any case, the rules we are following for having a TM recognize a language require that the machine erase all its input and leave the answer, 0 or 1, in square 1 of the tape. Because it is impossible to do this for an input string of length $n$ in fewer than $2n + 2$ moves, we interpret $Time(f)$ to mean $Time(g)$, where $g(n) = max(f(n), 2n+2)$. For the sake of consistency, we also follow this convention for $Space(f)$ and for the corresponding nondeterministic complexity classes. (In the case of space, a more common approach is to consider a slightly different TM model, in which there is a read-only input tape and one or more work tapes. If "space" is taken to mean the number of tape squares used on the work tapes, it is possible to consider $Space(f)$ for functions $f$ satisfying $f(n) < n$. We consider this briefly in the exercises.)

Apart from this convention, the classes in Definition 13.4 make sense for arbitrary functions $f$. It is often useful to impose some additional restrictions, however, without which the complexity classes sometimes exhibit surprising and unintuitive behavior. Adopting the extra restrictions will not change things in any significant way when it comes to discussing practical, real-world problems.

> **Definition 13.5    Step-counting Functions**
>
> A function $f : \mathcal{N} \to \mathcal{N}$ is a *step-counting* function if there is a TM $T$ so that for any $n$ and any input string of length $n$, $T$ halts in exactly $f(n)$ moves.

It is easy to see how such functions might be useful. If $f$ is a step-counting function, $T$ is a TM halting in $f(n)$ moves as in the definition, and $T'$ is any Turing machine, then a composite TM $T_1$ can be constructed that executes $T'$, except that it halts when $T$ halts if that happens first. In other words, $T$ can be used as a *clock* in conjunction with other machines. In a similar way, if we want to constrain the space resources of a TM $T$ during its computation, we can use a step-counting function $f$ in order to mark a space of exactly $f(n)$ squares to be used by $T$.

It is obvious from the definition that if $f$ is a step-counting function, then $f$ can be computed by a TM in such a way that the number of steps in the computation of $f(n)$ is essentially $f(n)$. It is also true, though much less obvious, that a relaxed form of this condition is still sufficient for a function to be a step-counting function.

**Lemma 13.1**  If $f : \mathcal{N} \rightarrow \mathcal{N}$ is a positive function, and if there is a constant $C > 1$ so that $f(n) > Cn$ for all but a finite number of integers $n$, then $f$ is a step-counting function if and only if $f$ can be computed in time $O(f)$ (i.e., there is a Turing machine $T$ computing $f$, and a constant $K$, so that for every $n$, $T$ computes $f(n)$ in no more than $Kf(n)$ steps).

The proof is omitted.  ∎

It is not hard to show using Lemma 13.1 that most familiar functions are, in fact, step-counting functions. (See also Exercises 13.12 and 13.13.)

Having defined the basic complexity classes, we should remind ourselves that there are "infinitely complex" languages—that is, languages not in *Time*($f$) or *Space*($f$) for *any* $f$ because they cannot be recognized by any TM. However, solvable problems can still be arbitrarily complex. Theorem 13.3 deals with time complexity, and its proof uses a diagonal argument.

---

**Theorem 13.3**

Let $f : \mathcal{N} \rightarrow \mathcal{N}$ be any step-counting function. Then for some constant $C$, *Time*($f$) is a proper subset of *Time*($Cn^2 f^2$).

*Proof*
It is sufficient to construct a language $L$ that is in the second class but not the first. We begin with the encoding function function $e$ from Section 9.6, which can be modified in a straightforward way to encode multitape TMs as well as ordinary TMs. Let

$$L = \{w \in \{0, 1\}^* \mid w = e(T) \text{ for some (possibly multitape) TM } T,$$
$$\text{which rejects input } w \text{ in } f(|w|) \text{ or fewer moves}\}$$

To show that $L$ is not in *Time*($f$), suppose for the sake of contradiction that $L$ is recognized by some TM $T_1$ satisfying $\tau_{T_1} \leq f$. We can modify $T_1$ without changing $\tau_{T_1}$ so that $T_1$ *accepts* $L$. Now consider $T_1$ operating on the input $w = e(T_1)$. $T_1$ halts on $w$ within $f(|w|)$ moves. If it accepts, then $w \notin L$, by the definition of $L$; then, however, $T_1$ should not accept $w$, because $T_1$ accepts $L$. If it rejects, then $w \in L$; however, then $T$ *should* accept $w$. Therefore, there is no such machine $T_1$.

Now we wish to show that $L$ is in *Time*($Cn^2 f^2$) for some constant $C$. To see that $L$ is recursive, we need only the assumption that $f$ is computable. A Turing machine can check whether $w \in L$ by determining whether $w$ is of the form $e(T)$, and if it is, computing $f(n) = f(|w|)$ and simulating $T$ on input $w$ for $f(n)$ moves. Testing that the input string is $e(T)$ for some $T$ can be done in time proportional to $n^2$; see the proof of Lemma 11.1 for the steps required in the one-tape case. The additional assumption on $f$ implies that computing $f(n)$ can be done in time proportional to $f(n)$. Finally, if the input is $e(T)$, simulating a single move of $T$ can be completed in time proportional to $nf(n)$; the factor of $n$ takes care of searching the input string (the specifications of $T$) for the move corresponding to the current state and tape symbols, and the factor of $f(n)$ may be necessary if $T$ is a multitape TM, because of the back-and-forth movement in the current string (whose length is at most proportional to $f(n)$) to locate the head positions on the various tapes of $T$. Simulating $f(n)$ moves can therefore be done in time proportional to $n(f(n))^2$. Combining these terms and estimating conservatively, we can say that the total number of moves required is $O(n^2(f(n))^2)$.

It is possible to show that if the function $f$ is a step-counting function, then the function $Cn^2(f(n))^2$, or a function that differs from this one at only a finite number of points, is also. This means that by applying the theorem repeatedly, we obtain a sequence of more and more complex languages. This is a simple case of more general "hierarchy" results, which specify conditions on functions $f$ and $g$ that are sufficient to obtain languages in $Time(g) - Time(f)$. There are similar "space hierarchy" theorems, which show in particular that there are decision problems whose solutions require Turing machines of arbitrarily great space complexity.

In the remainder of this section, we note some of the simple relationships among the complexity classes in Definition 13.4, and mention several others with little or no proof.

**Theorem 13.4**

For any function $f$, $Time(f) \subseteq NTime(f)$ and $Space(f) \subseteq NSpace(f)$.

*Proof*

Any deterministic Turing machine can be considered to be a nondeterministic TM, and the two definitions of time complexity coincide. The proof is similar for space complexity.

**Theorem 13.5**

For any function $f$, $Time(f) \subseteq Space(f)$ and $NTime(f) \subseteq NSpace(f)$.

*Proof*

If $T$ makes at least one and no more than $f(n)$ moves and is required to leave the tape head on square 0, the tape head can visit no more than $f(n)$ squares of the tape.

---

**Theorem 13.6**
Suppose $f$ is a step-counting function. Then

1. $NTime(f) \subseteq Space(f)$.
2. If $L \in NSpace(f)$, then for some constant $C$, $L \in Time(C^f)$.
3. $NSpace(f) \subseteq Space(Cf^2)$ for some constant $C$ (Savitch's Theorem).

***Sketch of Proof***
The first statement can be shown easily by revisiting the proof of Theorem 9.2, in which a TM is constructed to simulate a given NTM. If the NTM has time complexity $f$ and $f$ is a step-counting function, then the simulation can be carried out in such a way that each finite sequence of moves on an input of length $n$ can be tried without using more than $f(n)$ tape squares.

For the second statement, we begin with an NTM that accepts $L$ and has space complexity bounded by $f$. This assumption puts a limit on the number of distinct configurations the machine can enter, as a function of the input length, during its computation. The idea of the proof is to consider these configurations as the vertices of a *directed graph*; there is an arc from one vertex to another if the second configuration can be reached from the first in one TM move. We choose the starting vertex to be the one corresponding to the initial configuration for a given input. Then asking whether the input string is accepted is the same as asking whether any of the vertices representing halting configurations can be reached from the starting vertex; this question can be answered by adapting one of the standard graph-searching algorithms. The fact that the runtime of the graph algorithm is polynomial in the number of vertices makes it possible to show that it can be implemented on a Turing machine within time $C^f$ for some constant $C$.

The idea of interpreting the configurations of a nondeterministic TM as the vertices of a graph is also useful in the proof of the third statement, Savitch's theorem. This time, we are not concerned about runtime, but space is at a premium. One approach is to have the TM implement a recursive function $Test(c_1, c_2, j)$, which is to test whether configuration $c_2$ can be reached from $c_1$ within $2^j$ moves. By using the TM tape as a stack of "activation records," and carefully reusing space for the recursive calls, we are able to carry out the computation within the specified space constraints.

---

By combining Theorems 13.5 and 13.6, we see in particular that for a step-counting function $f$, $NTime(f) \subseteq Time(C^f)$ for some constant $C$. In fact, this result does not require the assumption that $f$ be step-counting, and it can easily be obtained directly from the proof of Theorem 9.2. In that proof, we constructed a Turing machine to try all possible finite sequences of moves of a given NTM. The number of sequences of $k$ or fewer moves is simply the number of nodes in the first $k$ levels of the "computation tree." Because there is an upper bound on the number of moves possible at each step, this number is bounded by $c^k$ for some constant $c$, and the result follows without difficulty.

This observation tells us that if we have a nondeterministic TM accepting $L$ with nondeterministic time complexity $f$, we can eliminate the nondeterminism at the cost of an exponential growth in the time complexity. If this is really the *best* we can do, then the presence of nondeterminism can make a dramatic difference in the time required for a solution, and it is reasonable to expect that for many problems, making a lucky guess is the only way of obtaining an answer within a reasonable time. Whether this is actually the case will be discussed further in Chapter 14.

# EXERCISES

**13.1.** Suppose $f, g, h, k : \mathcal{N} \to \mathcal{N}$.

a. Show that if $f = O(h)$ and $g = O(k)$, then $f + g = O(h + k)$ and $fg = O(hk)$.

b. Show that if $f = o(h)$ and $g = o(k)$ then $f + g = o(h + k)$ and $fg = o(hk)$.

c. Show that $f + g = \Theta(max(f, g))$.

**13.2.** Let $f_1(n) = 2n^2$, $f_2(n) = n^2 + 3n^{3/2}$, $f_3(n) = n^3 / \log n$, and

$$f_4(n) = \begin{cases} 2n^2 & \text{if } n \text{ is even} \\ n^2 \log n & \text{if } n \text{ is odd} \end{cases}$$

For each of the twelve combinations of $i$ and $j$, determine whether $f_i = O(f_j)$, and whether $f_i = o(f_j)$, and give reasons.

**13.3.** Suppose $f$ is a total function from $\mathcal{N}$ to $\mathcal{N}$ and that $f = O(p)$ for some polynomial function $p$. Show that there are constants $C$ and $D$ so that $f(n) \leq Cp(n) + D$ for every $n$.

**13.4.** a. Show that each of the functions $n!$, $n^n$, and $2^{2^n}$ has a growth rate greater than that of any exponential function.

b. Of these three functions, which has the largest growth rate and which the smallest?

**13.5.** a. Show that each of the functions $2^{\sqrt{n}}$ and $n^{\log n}$ has a growth rate greater than that of any polynomial and less than that of any exponential function.

b. Which of these two functions has the larger growth rate?

**13.6.** Classify the function $(\log n)^{\log n}$ with respect to its growth rate (polynomial, exponential, in-between, etc.)

**13.7.** Give a proof of the second statement in Theorem 13.2 that does not use logarithms. One way to do it is to write $n = n_0 + m$, and to consider the formula

$$n^k = n_0^k \left(\frac{n_0 + 1}{n_0}\right)^k \left(\frac{n_0 + 2}{n_0 + 1}\right)^k \cdots \left(\frac{n_0 + m}{n_0 + m - 1}\right)^k$$

**13.8.** In Example 13.2, find a formula for $\tau_T(n)$ when $n$ is odd.

**13.9.**  Find the time complexity function for each of these TMs:

    a.  The TM in Example 9.2 accepting the language of palindromes over $\{0, 1\}$.

    b.  The *Copy* TM shown in Figure 9.12.

**13.10.**  Show that if $L$ can be recognized by a TM $T$ with a doubly infinite tape, and $\tau_T = f$, then $L$ can be recognized by an ordinary TM with time complexity $O(f)$.

**13.11.**  Show that for any solvable decision problem, there is a way to encode instances of the problem so that the corresponding language can be recognized by a TM with linear time complexity.

**13.12.**  Show that if $f$ and $g$ are step-counting functions, then so are $f + g$, $f * g$, $f \circ g$, and $2^f$.

**13.13.**  Show that any polynomial with positive integer coefficients and a nonzero constant term is a step-counting function.

**13.14.**  Show that the following decision problem is unsolvable: Given a Turing machine $T$ and a step-counting function $f$, is the language accepted by $T$ in $Time(f)$?

**13.15.**  Is the problem, Given a Turing machine $T$, is $\tau_T \leq 2n$? solvable or unsolvable? Give reasons.

**13.16.**  Suppose $s$ is a step-counting function satisfying $s(n) \geq n$. Let $L$ be a language accepted by a (multitape) TM $T$, and suppose that the tape heads of $T$ do not move past square $s(n)$ on any of the tapes for an input string of length $n$. Show that $T \in Space(s)$. (Note: the reason it is not completely obvious is that $T$ may have infinite loops. Use the fact that if during a computation of $T$ some configuration repeats, then $T$ is in an infinite loop.)

**13.17.**  If $T$ is a TM recognizing $L$, and $T$ reads every symbol in the input string, then $\tau_T(n) \geq 2n + 2$. Show that any language that can be accepted by a TM $T$ with $\tau_T(n) = 2n + 2$ is regular.

**13.18.**  Suppose $L_1, L_2 \subseteq \Sigma^*$, $L_1 \in Time(f_1)$, and $L_2 \in Time(f_2)$. Find functions $g$ and $h$ so that $L_1 \cup L_2 \in Time(g)$ and $L_1 \cap L_2 \in Time(h)$.

**13.19.**  As we mentioned in Section 13.3, we might consider an alternate Turing machine model, in which there is an input tape on which the tape head can move in both directions but cannot write, and one or more work tapes, one of which serves as an output tape. For a function $f$, denote by $DSpace(f)$ the set of languages that can be recognized by a Turing machine of this type which uses no more than $f(n)$ squares on any work tape for any input string of length $n$. The only restriction we need to make on $f$ is that $f(n) > 0$ for every $n$. Show that both the language of palindromes over $\{0, 1\}$ and the language of balanced strings of parentheses are in $DSpace(1 + \lceil \log_2(n + 1) \rceil)$. ($\lceil x \rceil$ means the smallest integer greater than or equal to $x$.)

# MORE CHALLENGING PROBLEMS

**13.20.** If $f$ and $g$ are total, increasing functions from $\mathcal{N}$ to $\mathcal{N}$, and $f = O(g)$ and $g \neq O(f)$, does it follow that $f = o(g)$? Either give a proof or find functions that provide a counterexample.

**13.21.** If $f$ and $g$ are total, increasing functions from $\mathcal{N}$ to $\mathcal{N}$, does it follow that one of the two statements $f = O(g)$, $g = O(f)$ must hold? Either give a proof or find functions that provide a counterexample.

**13.22.** Describe in at least some detail a two-tape TM accepting the language of Example 13.2 and having linear time complexity.

**13.23.** Let $f : \mathcal{N} \to \mathcal{N}$. Show that if $L$ can be recognized by a TM $T$ so that $\tau_T(n) \leq f(n)$ for all but finitely many $n$, then $L \in Time(f)$. (Recall our convention that $Time(f)$ means $Time(\max(f, 2n + 2))$.)

**13.24.** Suppose that $f$ is a function satisfying $n = o(f)$, and $L \in Time(f)$. Show that for any constant $c > 0$, $L \in Time(cf)$.

**13.25.** Show that if $L$ can be recognized by a multitape TM with time complexity $f$, then $L$ can be recognized by a one-tape machine with time complexity $O(f^2)$.

**13.26.** According to Theorem 13.3, for any step-counting function $f$, there is a recursive language $L$ so that the time complexity of any TM recognizing $L$ must be greater than $f$ for at least one $n$. Generalize this by showing that for any such $f$, there is a recursive language $L$ so that for any TM $T$ recognizing $L$, $\tau_T(n) > f(n)$ for infinitely many values of $n$.

**13.27.** Show that for any total computable function $f : \mathcal{N} \to \mathcal{N}$, there is a step-counting function $g$ so that $g(n) > f(n)$ for every $n$.

# 14

# Tractable and Intractable Problems

## 14.1 | TRACTABLE AND POSSIBLY INTRACTABLE PROBLEMS: *P* AND *NP*

We may use the classification of languages described in the last chapter to compare the complexity of two languages. For example, if $L_1 \in Time(f)$ and $L_2 \notin Time(f)$, then it is reasonable to say that $L_2$ is, at least in some ways, more complex than $L_1$. Now we would like to identify those languages that are *tractable*, those we can recognize within reasonable time and space constraints. In other words, we would like to know which decision problems we can actually solve.

Although there is no clear line separating the hard problems from the easy ones, one normally expects a tractable problem to be solvable in *polynomial* time. The most common problems for which no polynomial-time algorithms are known seem to require exponential runtimes. As we have seen in Section 13.1, even moderately sized worst-case instances of such problems are likely not to be feasible. With this in mind, we define complexity classes containing the languages recognizable in polynomial time and polynomial space, respectively, as well as corresponding nondeterministic complexity classes.

---

**Definition 14.1    The Sets *P*, *NP*, *PSpace*, and *NPSpace***

$$P = \bigcup_{C>0,k\geq0} Time(Cn^k)$$

$$PSpace = \bigcup_{C>0,k\geq0} Space(Cn^k)$$

$$NP = \bigcup_{C>0,k\geq0} NTime(Cn^k)$$

$$NPSpace = \bigcup_{C>0,k\geq0} NSpace(Cn^k)$$

---

The sets $P$ and $PSpace$ include any language that can be recognized by a TM with time complexity or space complexity, respectively, bounded by some polynomial.

We may speak informally of decision problems being in $P$ or $PSpace$, provided we keep in mind our earlier comments about reasonable encoding methods. Saying that the tractable problems are precisely those in $P$ cannot be completely correct. For example, if two TMs solving the same problem had time complexities $(1.000001)^n$ and $n^{1000}$, respectively, one might prefer to use the first machine on a typical problem instance, in spite of Theorem 13.2. However, in real life, "polynomial" is more likely to mean $n^2$ or $n^3$ than $n^{1000}$, and "exponential" normally turns out to be $2^n$ rather than $(1.000001)^n$.

Another point in favor of the polynomial criterion is that it seems to be invariant among the various models of computation. Changing the model can change the time complexity, but by no more than a polynomial factor; roughly speaking, if a problem can be solved in polynomial time on *some* computer, then it is in $P$.

It is obvious from Theorem 13.5 that $P \subseteq PSpace$ and $NP \subseteq NPSpace$. The following result, which follows easily from the theorems in Section 13.3, describes some other simple relationships among these four sets. In particular, having defined $NPSpace$, we can now forget about it.

---

**Theorem 14.1**

$P \subseteq NP \subseteq PSpace = NPSpace$.

**Proof**

We have already noted the first inclusion. The second inclusion follows from the first part of Theorem 13.6. The equality follows from the third part of Theorem 13.6, because for any $k$, $NSpace(Cn^k) \subseteq Space(Dn^{2k})$ for some constant $D$. The last two statements also use the fact that with minor restrictions, polynomials are step-counting functions.

---

One would assume that allowing nondeterminism should allow dramatic improvements in the time complexity required to solve some problems. An NTM, as we have seen in Section 13.2, has an apparently significant advantage over an ordinary TM, because of its ability to guess. The quadratic time complexity of the NTM in Example 13.3 reflected the fact that we can test a proposed solution in quadratic time; it does not obviously follow that we can test *all* solutions within quadratic time. As we observed in Section 13.3, replacing a nondeterministic TM by a deterministic one as in the proof of Theorem 9.2 can cause the time complexity to increase exponentially; in fact, this is true of all the general methods known for eliminating nondeterminism from a TM. It is therefore not surprising that there are many languages, or decision problems, in $NP$ for which no deterministic polynomial-time algorithms are known. In other words, there are languages in $NP$ that are not known to be in $P$.

What *is* surprising is that there are no languages in $NP$ that are known *not* to be in $P$. Although the most reasonable guess is that $P$ is a proper subset of $NP$, no one has managed to prove this statement. It is not for lack of trying; the problems known to be in $NP$ include a great many interesting problems that have been studied intensively for many years, for which researchers have tried without success to find either a polynomial-time algorithm or a proof that none exists. A general rule of thumb is that finding good lower bounds is harder than finding upper bounds. In principle, it is easier to exhibit a solution to a problem than to show that the problem has no efficient solutions. In any case, the $P \stackrel{?}{=} NP$ question is one of the outstanding open problems in theoretical computer science.

Whether the second inclusion in Theorem 14.1 is a strict inclusion is also an open question. We can summarize both these questions by saying that the role of nondeterminism in the description of complexity is not thoroughly understood.

In the last part of this section, we will study two problems in $NP$ that are interesting for different reasons. The first can easily be shown to be in $NP$; however, we will see in the next section that it is, in a precise sense, a *hardest* problem in $NP$. The second also turns out to be in $NP$, though not obviously so, since it does not seem to fit the "guess a solution and test it in polynomial time" pattern.

**EXAMPLE 14.1**    ## The CNF-Satisfiability Problem

An instance of this problem is a logical expression, which contains variables $x_i$ and the logical connectives $\wedge$, $\vee$, and $\neg$ (AND, OR, and NOT, respectively). We use the notation $\overline{x}_i$ to denote the negation $\neg x_i$, and the term *literal* to mean either an $x_i$ or an $\overline{x}_i$. The expression is assumed to be in *conjunctive normal form* (CNF), which means that it is a conjunction

$$C_1 \wedge C_2 \wedge \cdots \wedge C_c$$

of subexpressions $C_i$, each of which is a disjunction (i.e., formed with $\vee$'s) of literals. For example,

$$(x_1 \vee x_3 \vee x_4) \wedge (\overline{x}_1 \vee x_3) \wedge (\overline{x}_1 \vee x_4 \vee \overline{x}_2) \wedge \overline{x}_3 \wedge (x_2 \vee \overline{x}_4)$$

is a CNF expression with five *conjuncts*. In general, one variable might appear more than once within a conjunct, and a conjunct itself might be duplicated. We do, however, impose the extra requirement that for some $v \geq 1$, the distinct variables be precisely $x_1, x_2, \ldots, x_v$, with none left out.

You can verify easily that the expression above is *satisfied*—made true—by the truth assignment

$$x_2 = x_4 = true \qquad x_1 = x_3 = false$$

The CNF-satisfiability problem (**CNF-Sat** for short) is this: Given an expression in conjunctive normal form, is there a truth assignment that satisfies it?

We can encode instances of the CNF-satisfiability problem in a straightforward way, omitting parentheses and $\vee$'s and using unary notation for variable subscripts. For example, the expression

$$(x_1 \vee \overline{x}_2) \wedge (x_2 \vee x_3 \vee \overline{x}_1) \wedge (\overline{x}_4 \vee x_2)$$

will be represented by the string

$$\wedge x1\overline{x}11 \wedge x11x111\overline{x}1 \wedge \overline{x}1111x11$$

We define *CNF-Satisfiable* to be the language over $\Sigma = \{\wedge, x, \overline{x}, 1\}$ containing the encodings of all yes-instances of **CNF-Sat**.

Is our encoding scheme a reasonable one? We might try to answer this by considering an instance with $k$ literals (not necessarily distinct), $c$ conjuncts, and $v$ distinct variables. If $n$ is the length of the string encoding this instance, then

$$n \leq k(v + 1) + c \leq k^2 + 2k$$

The first inequality depends on the fact that all the strings $x1^i$ and $\overline{x}1^i$ all have length $\leq v + 1$, and the second is true because $v$ and $c$ are both no larger than $k$. This relationship between $n$ and $k$ implies that any polynomial in $n$ is bounded by a polynomial in $k$, and $k$ seems like a reasonable measure of the size of the problem instance. Therefore, if *CNF-Satisfiable* $\in NP$, it makes sense to say that the decision problem **CNF-Sat** is in *NP*.

We can easily describe in general terms the steps a one-tape Turing machine $T$ needs to follow in order to accept *CNF-Satisfiable*. The first step is to verify that the input string represents a valid CNF expression in which the variables are precisely $x_1, x_2, \ldots, x_v$ for some $v$. Assuming the string is valid, $T$ attempts to satisfy the expression, keeping track as it proceeds which conjuncts have been satisfied so far and which variables within the unsatisfied conjuncts have been assigned values. The iterative step consists of finding the first conjunct not yet satisfied; choosing a literal within that conjunct that has not been assigned a value (this is the only place where nondeterminism is used); giving the variable in that literal the value that satisfies the conjunct; marking the conjunct as satisfied; and giving the same value to all subsequent occurrences of that variable in unsatisfied conjuncts, marking any conjuncts that are satisfied as a result. The loop terminates in one of two ways. Either all conjuncts are eventually satisfied, or the literals in the first unsatisfied conjunct are all found to have been falsified. In the first case $T$ accepts, and in the second it rejects. If the expression is satisfiable, and only in this case, the correct choice of moves causes $T$ to guess a truth assignment that works.

The TM $T$ can be constructed so that, except for a few steps that take time proportional to $n$, all its actions are minor variations of the following operation: Begin with a string of 1's in the input, delimited at both ends by some symbol other than 1, and locate some or all of the other occurrences of this string that are similarly delimited. We leave it to you to convince yourself that a single operation of this type can be done in polynomial time, and that the number of such operations that must be performed is also no more than a polynomial. (The nondeterministic time complexity of $T$ is $O(n^3)$; see Exercise 14.2.) Our conclusion is that *CNF-Satisfiable*, and therefore **CNF-Sat**, is in *NP*.

The number of distinct truth assignments to an expression with $j$ distinct variables is $2^j$. Although this fact does not by itself imply that the decision problem is not in $P$, it tells us that the brute-force approach of trying all solutions will not be helpful in attempting to find a polynomial-time algorithm. We will return to **CNF-Sat** in the next section.

## The Primality Problem  ░ EXAMPLE 14.2

This is the familiar decision problem, Given a positive integer $n$, is $n$ prime? Here the observations in the second paragraph in Section 13.3 are relevant. A solution that is polynomial, even linear, when unary notation is used for the integer $n$ is exponential if binary notation is used instead, because the number of binary digits needed to encode $n$ is only about $\log n$. Let us agree that for this problem "polynomial-time solution" means polynomial, not in $n$, but in $\log n$, the length of the input string. In particular, therefore, the algorithm in which we actually test all possible divisors up to $\sqrt{n}$ is not helpful. Even if we could test each divisor in constant time, the required time would be proportional to $\sqrt{n}$, which is not bounded by any polynomial function of $\log n$.

This problem also seems to illustrate the importance of whether a problem is posed *positively* or *negatively*. The *composite decision problem*: Given an integer $n > 1$, is it composite (i.e., nonprime)? has a simple nondeterministic solution—namely, guess a possible factorization $n = p * q$ and test by multiplying that it is correct—and therefore is in *NP*. The primality problem is not *obviously* in *NP*, since there is no obvious way to "guess a solution." At the language level, the fact that a language is in *NP* does not immediately imply that its complement is (Exercises 14.3 and 14.4).

To see that the primality problem *is* in *NP*, we need some facts from number theory. First recall from Chapter 1 the congruence-mod-$n$ relation $\equiv_n$, defined by $a \equiv_n b$ if and only if $a - b$ is divisible by $n$. Of the two facts that follow, the first is due to Fermat, and we state it without proof.

1. A positive integer $n$ is prime if and only if there is a number $x$, with $1 < x < n - 1$, satisfying

$$x^{n-1} \equiv_n 1, \text{ and for every } m \text{ with } 1 < m < n - 1, \ x^m \not\equiv_n 1$$

2. If $n$ is not prime, then for any $x$ with $0 < x < n - 1$ satisfying $x^{n-1} \equiv_n 1$, we must also have $x^{(n-1)/p} \equiv_n 1$ for some $p$ that is a prime factor of $n - 1$.

We can check the second statement without too much trouble. If $x^{n-1} \equiv_n 1$ and $n$ is not prime, then by statement 1, $x^m \equiv_n 1$ for some $m < n - 1$. We observe that the smallest such $m$ must be a divisor of $n - 1$. The reason is that when we divide $n - 1$ by $m$, we get a quotient $q$ and a remainder $r$, so that

$$n - 1 = q * m + r \quad \text{and} \quad 0 \le r < m$$

This means that $x^{n-1} = x^{qm+r} = (x^m)^q * x^r$, and because $x^{n-1}$ and $x^m$ are both congruent to 1 mod $n$, we must have $(x^m)^q \equiv_n 1$ and therefore $x^r \equiv_n 1$. It follows that the remainder $r$ must be 0, because $r < m$ and by definition $m$ is the smallest *positive* integer with $x^m \equiv_n 1$. Therefore, $n - 1$ is divisible by $m$.

Now, any proper divisor $m$ of $n - 1$ is of the form $(n - 1)/j$, for some $j > 1$ that is a product of (one or more) prime factors of $n - 1$. Therefore, some multiple of $m$, say $a * m$, is $(n - 1)/p$ for a single prime $p$. Because $x^{a*m} = (x^m)^a \equiv_n 1$, statement 2 follows.

The significance of the first statement is that it gives us a way of expressing the primeness of $n$ that starts, "*there is* a number $x$ so that . . . ," and thus we have a potential nondeterministic solution: Guess an $x$ and test it. At first, testing $x$ seems to require that we test *all* the numbers $m$ with $1 < m < n - 1$ to make sure that $x^m \not\equiv_n 1$. If this is really necessary, the nondeterminism is no help—we might as well go back to the usual test for primeness, trying divisors of $n$. The significance of statement 2 is that in order to test $x$, we do *not* have to try all the $m$'s, but only those of the form $(n - 1)/p$ for some prime factor $p$ of $n - 1$. (According to statement 2, if $n$ is not a prime, some $m$ of this form will satisfy $x^m \equiv_n 1$.) How do we find the prime factors of $n - 1$? We guess!

With this introduction, it should now be possible to see that the following recursive nondeterministic procedure accepts the set of primes.

Is_Prime($n$)

if $n = 2$ return *true*
else if $n > 2$ and $n$ is even return *false*
else
{　guess $x$ with $1 < x < n$
　if $x^{n-1} \not\equiv_n 1$ return *false*
　guess a factorization $p_1, p_2, \ldots, p_k$ of $n - 1$
　for $i = 1$ to $k$
　　if not Is_Prime($p_i$) return *false*
　if $p_1 * p_2 * \cdots p_k \neq n - 1$ return *false*
　for $i = 1$ to $k$
　　if $x^{(n-1)/p_i} \equiv_n 1$ return *false*
　return *true*
}

A TM can simulate this recursion by using its tape to keep a stack of "activation records," as mentioned once before in the sketch of the proof of Theorem 13.6. In order to execute the "return *false*" statement, however, it can simply halt in the reject state.

It is still necessary to show that this nondeterministic algorithm can be executed in polynomial (nondeterministic) time. We present only the general idea, and leave most of the details to the exercises. It is helpful to separate the time required to execute Is_Prime($n$) into two parts: the time required for the $k$ recursive calls Is_Prime($p_i$), and all the rest. It is not hard to see that for some constant $c$ and some integer $d$, the nondeterministic time for everything but the recursive calls is bounded by $c(\log n)^d$ (remember that $\log n$ is the length of the input string). If $T(n)$ is the total nondeterministic time, then

$$T(n) \leq c(\log n)^d + \sum_{i=1}^{k} T(p_i)$$

This inequality can be used in an induction proof that $T(n) \leq C(\log n)^{d+1}$, where $C$ is some sufficiently large constant. In the induction step, if we know from our hypothesis that $T(p_i) \leq C(\log p_i)^{d+1}$ for each $i$, then we only need to show that

$$c(\log n)^d + \sum_{i=1}^{k} C(\log p_i)^{d+1} \leq C(\log n)^{d+1}$$

This follows from the inequality

$$c(\log n)^d + \sum_{i=1}^{k} C(\log p_i)^{d+1} \leq C\left(\sum_{i=1}^{k} \log p_i\right)^{d+1}$$

which is true if the constant $C$ is chosen sufficiently large, because the sum on the right side is simply $\log(p_1 * \cdots * p_k) = \log(n - 1)$.

## 14.2 | POLYNOMIAL-TIME REDUCTIONS AND *NP*-COMPLETENESS

As we have seen, the classes *Time*($f$) and *Space*($f$) allow us to compare the complexity, or difficulty, of two problems or two languages. Just as in Chapter 11, however, it is useful to introduce a way of describing the *relative* complexity of $L_1$ and $L_2$, without having to pin down the absolute complexity of either language.

For the type of reducibility introduced in that chapter, $L_1$ is reducible to $L_2$ if there is a *computable* function $f$ so that deciding whether $x \in L_1$ is equivalent to deciding whether $f(x) \in L_2$. $L_1$ is "no harder than" $L_2$, in the sense that testing membership in $L_1$ can be done in two steps, computing $f$ and testing membership in $L_2$. The phrase "no harder than" is reasonable because we distinguish only two degrees of hardness, possible and impossible; if testing membership of a string in $L_2$ is possible, then testing a string that must first be obtained by computing $f$ is still possible, because $f$ is computable.

Now, however, we are using a finer classification system, and we want our comparison to be quantitative as well as qualitative. An appropriate way to modify the definition is to specify that the reducing function $f$ should be computable in a reasonable amount of time, where "reasonable" is taken to mean polynomial.

---

**Definition 14.2    Polynomial-time Reducibility**

If $L_1$ and $L_2$ are languages, over alphabets $\Sigma_1$ and $\Sigma_2$, respectively, we say $L_1$ is *polynomial-time reducible* to $L_2$, written $L_1 \leq_p L_2$, if there is a function $f : \Sigma_1^* \to \Sigma^*$ so that for any $x \in \Sigma^*$, $x \in L_1$ if and only if $f(x) \in L_2$, and $f$ can be computed in polynomial time—that is, there is a TM with polynomial time complexity that computes $f$.

---

The following properties of the relation $\leq_p$ are not surprising and are consistent with our understanding of what "no harder than" should mean in this context.

---

**Theorem 14.2**

1. $\leq_p$ is transitive: if $L_1 \leq_p L_2$ and $L_2 \leq_p L_3$, then $L_1 \leq_p L_3$.
2. If $L_2 \in P$ and $L_1 \leq_p L_2$, then $L_1 \in P$.
3. If $L_2 \in NP$ and $L_1 \leq_p L_2$, then $L_1 \in NP$.

**Proof**

(1) Suppose that the three languages are over the alphabets $\Sigma_1$, $\Sigma_2$, and $\Sigma_3$, respectively, and $f : \Sigma_1^* \to \Sigma_2^*$ and $g : \Sigma_2^* \to \Sigma_3^*$ are the two functions involved in the reductions. Then $g \circ f : \Sigma_1^* \to \Sigma_3^*$, and for every $x \in \Sigma_1^*$, $x \in L_1$ if and only if $g \circ f(x) \in L_3$. Therefore, it is sufficient to show that $g \circ f$ is polynomial-time computable. We can find Turing machines $T_f$ and $T_g$ computing $f$ and $g$ so that for every $n$,

$$\tau_{T_f}(n) \leq Cn^j + D \quad \text{and} \quad \tau_{T_g}(n) \leq Cn^k + D$$

for some integers $j$ and $k$ and some constants $C$ and $D$. The composition $T = T_f T_g$ of the two TMs computes the function $g \circ f$. The proof that $T$ has polynomial time complexity is a consequence of the fact that the composition of polynomials is a polynomial. Consider the number $\tau_x$ of moves made by $T_f$ in computing $f(x)$. If $\tau_x \leq |x|$, then $T_f$ cannot change the rightmost symbol in the input string $x$ or write any symbols to the right of it, and thus $|f(x)| = |x|$. Otherwise, we can say that $|f(x)| \leq \tau_x$, since a TM needs to make at least $|f(x)|$ moves to create an output string of length $f(x)$. In either case, we have

$$|f(x)| \leq \tau_x + |x| \leq \tau_{T_f}(|x|) + |x|$$

We may conclude that for any $x \in \Sigma_1^*$,

$$\tau_T(|x|) \leq \tau_{T_f}(|x|) + \tau_{T_g}(|f(x)|)$$
$$\leq C|x|^j + D + C|f(x)|^k + D$$
$$\leq C|x|^j + D + C(\tau_{T_f}(|x|) + |x|)^k + D$$
$$\leq C|x|^j + D + C(C|x|^j + D + |x|)^k + D$$

The first line here is obtained by considering the two phases of the computation performed by $T$. The second and fourth lines both use the previous inequalities involving $\tau_{T_f}$ and $\tau_{T_g}$, and the third line uses the previous inequality involving $|f(x)|$. The only feature of the last expression that we need is that it is a polynomial in $|x|$. It follows that $\tau_T$ is bounded by a polynomial.

(2) The assumption is that there is a TM $T_2$ with polynomial time complexity recognizing $L_2$, and there is a function $f : \Sigma_1^* \to \Sigma_2^*$, computed by a TM $T_f$ with polynomial time complexity, so that for any $x \in \Sigma_1^*$, $x \in L_1$ if and only if $f(x) \in L_2$. Let $T$ be the composite TM $T_f T_2$. Then it is clear that $T$ recognizes the language $L_1$, and the argument in part (1) shows that $T$ has polynomial time complexity. Therefore, $L_1 \in P$.

(3) The argument here is essentially the same as in part (2), except that now $T_2$ is an NTM *accepting* $L_2$ in polynomial time. The composite machine $T = T_f T_2$ accepts $L_1$, and the calculation in part (1) is still correct when $\tau_T$ and $\tau_{T_g}$ are interpreted as nondeterministic time-complexity functions.

If we continue to require "reasonable" encodings of problem instances, we can extend Definition 14.1 and Theorem 14.2 to decision problems. We can therefore talk about one decision problem being polynomial-time reducible to another, and we can use these techniques to show that decision problems are in $P$ or $NP$.

In our first example of a polynomial-time reduction, we show that the problem **CNF-Sat** discussed in Example 14.1 can be reduced to a decision problem involving undirected graphs. The point of the reduction is not to show that a language is in $P$ or $NP$ (we know already that **CNF-Sat** is in $NP$, and there is no immediate prospect of showing that the graph problem is in $P$). Rather, we interpret the result to say that even though **CNF-Sat** appears to be a difficult problem in *NP*, the other problem is no easier.

**EXAMPLE 14.3** A Polynomial-time Reduction Involving **CNF-Sat**

We begin with some terminology. A graph is a pair $G = (V, E)$, where $V$ is a finite nonempty set of *vertices* and $E$ is a finite set of *edges*, or unordered pairs of vertices. (The term *unordered* means that the pair $(v_1, v_2)$ is considered to be the same as the pair $(v_2, v_1)$.) The edge $(v_1, v_2)$ is said to join the vertices $v_1$ and $v_2$, or to have end points $v_1$ and $v_2$, and two vertices joined by an edge are *adjacent*. A *subgraph* of $G$ is a graph whose vertex set and edge set are subsets of the respective sets of $G$. A *complete* graph, sometimes called a *clique*, is a graph in which any two vertices are adjacent.

A schematic diagram of a graph $G$ with seven vertices and ten edges is shown in Figure 14.1. $G$ has a complete subgraph with four vertices (3, 5, 6, and 7), and obviously, therefore, several complete subgraphs with fewer than four vertices. The *complete subgraph problem* is this: Given a graph $G$ and an integer $k$, does $G$ have a complete subgraph with $k$ vertices? It is easy to see that the problem is in *NP*: a nondeterministic TM can take a string encoding an instance $(G, k)$, nondeterministically select $k$ of the vertices, and then examine the edges to see whether every pair is adjacent.

We let *CompleteSub* be the language corresponding to the complete subgraph problem; we may assume that vertices are represented in unary notation, and that a graph is described by a string of vertices, followed by a string of vertex-pairs, each pair representing an edge. So that strings can be decoded uniquely, 0's are inserted appropriately. We will show that **CNF-Sat** is polynomial-time reducible to the complete subgraph problem, or that *CNF-Satisfiable* $\leq_p$ *CompleteSub*.

When we discussed reductions in Chapter 11, in the context of solvability, we gave two definitions: Definition 11.3a, involving languages, and Definition 11.3, involving actual problem instances. The reduction here is easier to understand using the second approach. It will then be straightforward to confirm the polynomial-time aspect of the reduction by considering the corresponding string function.

We must construct for each CNF expression $x$ an instance $f(x)$ of the complete subgraph problem (that is, a graph $G_x$ and an integer $k_x$), so that for any $x$, $x$ is satisfiable if and only if $G_x$ has a complete subgraph with $k_x$ vertices.

Let $x$ be the expression

$$x = \bigwedge_{i=1}^{c} \bigvee_{j=1}^{d_i} a_{i,j}$$

where each $a_{i,j}$ is a literal. We want the vertices of $G_x$ to correspond precisely to the occurrences of the terms $a_{i,j}$ in $x$; we let

$$V_x = \{(i, j) \mid 1 \leq i \leq c \quad \text{and} \quad 1 \leq j \leq d_i\}$$

The edges of $G_x$ are now specified so that the vertex $(i, j)$ is adjacent to $(l, m)$ if and only if the corresponding literals are in different conjuncts of $x$ and there is a truth assignment to $x$

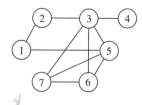

**Figure 14.1 |**

that makes them both true. The way to do this is to let

$$E_x = \{((i, j), (l, m)) \mid i \neq l \quad \text{and} \quad a_{i,j} \neq \neg a_{l,m}\}$$

Finally, we take the integer $k_x$ to be $c$, the number of conjuncts in the expression $x$.

If $x$ is satisfiable, then there is a truth assignment $\Theta$ so that for each $i$ there is a literal $a_{i,j_i}$ that is given the value *true* by $\Theta$. The vertices

$$(1, j_1), (2, j_2), \ldots, (k, j_k)$$

then determine a complete subgraph of $G_x$, because we have specified the edges of $G_x$ so that any two of these vertices are adjacent.

On the other hand, suppose there is a complete subgraph of $G_x$ with $k_x$ vertices. Because none of the corresponding literals is the negation of another, there is a truth assignment that makes them all true; and because these literals must be in distinct conjuncts, this assignment makes at least one literal in each conjunct true. Therefore, $x$ is satisfiable.

Now let us consider how long it takes, beginning with the string $w$ representing $x$, to construct the string representing $(G_x, k_x)$. The vertices of the graph can be constructed in a single scan of $w$. For a particular literal in a particular conjunct of $x$, a new edge is obtained for each literal in another conjunct that is not the negation of the first one. Finding another conjunct, identifying another literal within that conjunct, and comparing that literal to the original one can each be done within polynomial time, and it follows that the overall time is still polynomial.

---

The polynomial-time reducibility relation $\leq_p$ is used, as in Example 14.3, to measure the relative complexity of two languages. However, it also allows us to describe a kind of absolute complexity: We can consider the idea of a *hardest* language in *NP*. (Not *the* hardest because it will turn out that many languages share this distinction.)

**Definition 14.3     *NP*-hard and *NP*-complete Languages**

A language $L$ is said to be *NP*-hard if $L_1 \leq_p L$ for every $L_1 \in NP$. (In other words, every decision problem in *NP* is polynomial-time reducible to the one represented by $L$.) The language $L$ is *NP*-complete if $L \in NP$ and $L$ is *NP*-hard.

> **Theorem 14.3**
> 1. If $L$ and $L_1$ are languages for which $L$ is *NP*-hard and $L \leq_p L_1$, then $L_1$ is also *NP*-hard.
> 2. If $L$ is any *NP*-complete language, then $L \in P$ if and only if $P = NP$.
>
> ***Proof***
> Both parts of the theorem follow immediately from Theorem 14.2.

Just as before, Definition 14.3 and Theorem 14.3 can also be extended to decision problems. An *NP*-complete problem is one for which the corresponding language is *NP*-complete, and Theorem 14.3 provides a way of obtaining more *NP*-complete problems—provided that we can find one to start with. It is not at all obvious that we can. The set *NP* contains problems that are diverse and seemingly unrelated: problems involving graphs, networks, sets and partitions, scheduling, number theory, logic, and more. It is reasonable to expect that some of these problems will be more complex than others, and perhaps even that some will be "hardest." An *NP*-complete problem, however, is not only hard but archetypal: Finding a good algorithm to solve it guarantees that there will be comparable algorithms for every other problem in *NP*!

Exercise 14.14 describes a way to obtain an "artificial" *NP*-complete language. In the next section we will see a remarkable result of Stephen Cook: The language *CNF-Satisfiable* (or the decision problem **CNF-Sat**) is *NP*-complete. This fact, together with the technique of polynomial-time reduction and Theorem 14.3, will allow us to show that many interesting and widely studied problems are *NP*-complete.

Theorem 14.3 indicates both ways in which the idea of *NP*-completeness is significant in complexity theory. On the one hand, if someone were ever to demonstrate that some *NP*-complete problem could be solved by a polynomial-time algorithm, then the $P \overset{?}{=} NP$ question would be resolved; *NP* would disappear as a separate entity, and researchers would redouble their efforts to find polynomial-time algorithms for problems now known to be in *NP*, confident that they were not on a wild-goose chase. On the other hand, as long as the question remains open (or if someone actually succeeds in proving that $P \neq NP$), the difficulty of a problem $P$ can be established convincingly by showing that some other problem already known to be *NP*-hard can be polynomial-time reduced to $P$.

## 14.3 | COOK'S THEOREM

The idea of *NP*-completeness was introduced by Stephen Cook in 1971, and our first example of an *NP*-complete problem is the CNF-satisfiability problem (Example 14.1), which he proved is *NP*-complete. The details of the proof are complicated, and that is perhaps to be expected. Rather than using specific features of a decision problem to construct a reduction, as we were able to do in Example 14.3, we must now show there is a "generic" polynomial-time reduction from *any* problem in *NP* to this one. Fortunately, once we have one *NP*-complete problem, obtaining others will be considerably easier.

In the proof, as in Example 14.3, we will use the notation

$$\bigwedge_{i=1}^{n} A_i$$

to denote the conjunction

$$A_1 \wedge A_2 \wedge \cdots \wedge A_n$$

and the same sort of shorthand with disjunction. As in Example 14.1, $\overline{a}$ stands for the negation of $a$.

In one section of the proof, the following result about Boolean formulas is useful.

**Lemma 14.1**   Let $F$ be any Boolean expression involving the variables $a_1, a_2, \ldots, a_t$. Then $F$ is logically equivalent to an expression in conjunctive normal form: one of the form

$$\bigwedge_{i=1}^{k} \bigvee_{j=1}^{l_i} b_{i,j}$$

where each $b_{i,j}$ is either an $a_r$ or an $\overline{a}_r$.

***Proof***   It will be easiest to show first that any such $F$ is equivalent to an expression in *disjunctive normal form*—that is, one of the form

$$\bigvee_{i=1}^{k} \bigwedge_{j=1}^{l_i} b_{i,j}$$

To do this, we introduce the following notation. For any assignment $\Theta$ of truth values to the variables, and for any $j$ from 1 to $t$, we let

$$\alpha_{\Theta,j} = \begin{cases} a_j & \text{if the assignment } \Theta \text{ makes } a_j \text{ true} \\ \overline{a}_j & \text{otherwise} \end{cases}$$

Then the assignment $\Theta$ makes each of the $\alpha_{\Theta,j}$'s true; and if the assignment $\Phi$ assigns a different truth value to $a_j$, $\alpha_{\Theta,j}$ is false for the assignment $\Phi$. In other words, the conjunction $\wedge_{j=1}^{t} \alpha_{\Theta,j}$ is satisfied by the assignment $\Theta$ and not by any other assignment. It follows that if $S$ is the set of all assignments satisfying the expression $F$, then the assignments that satisfy one of the disjuncts of the expression

$$F_1 = \bigvee_{\Theta \in S} \bigwedge_{j=1}^{t} \alpha_{\Theta,j}$$

are precisely those that satisfy $F$. Since $F$ and $F_1$ are satisfied by exactly the same assignments, they must be logically equivalent.

We can finish the proof by applying our preliminary result to the expression $\neg F$. If $\neg F$ is equivalent to

$$\bigvee_{i} \bigwedge_{j} b_{i,j}$$

then De Morgan's law implies that $F$ is equivalent to

$$\bigwedge_i \bigvee_j \neg b_{i,j}$$

Recall from Example 14.1 that *CNF-Satisfiable* is the language of encoded yes-instances of the CNF-satisfiability problem. It is a language over $\Sigma = \{\wedge, x, \overline{x}, 1\}$.

---

**Theorem 14.4    Cook's Theorem**
The language *CNF-Satisfiable*, or the problem **CNF-Sat**, is *NP*-complete.

*Proof*
We saw in Example 14.1 that *CNF-Satisfiable* $\in NP$, and now we must show it is *NP*-hard. To a large extent we will be able to work directly with the problem instances themselves; with this in mind, let *CNF* be the set of all CNF expressions (with arbitrarily many variables, whose names are arbitrary). Because languages in *NP* can be specified by specifying a nondeterministic TM with polynomial-time complexity, we can formulate the statement of the theorem as follows. For any polynomial $p$, and any NTM $T = (Q, \Sigma_1, \Gamma, q_0, \delta)$ satisfying $\tau_T \le p$, there is a function

$$g : \Sigma_1^* \to CNF$$

so that

1.  For any $x \in \Sigma_1^*$, $x$ is accepted by $T$ if and only if $g(x)$ is satisfiable.
2.  The corresponding function $f : \Sigma_1^* \to \Sigma^*$ that reduces $L(T)$ to *CNF-Satisfiable*, obtained by relabeling variables in CNF expressions and encoding the expressions over $\Sigma$, is computable in polynomial time.

Constructing $g$ so that it satisfies statement 1 is the hard part of the proof; verifying that the resulting function $f$ is polynomial-time computable will be straightforward.

We make the simplifying assumption that $T$ never attempts to move its tape head left from square 0; modifying the TM this way, if necessary, can be done without destroying the polynomial time complexity. We may also assume, without any loss of generality, that $p(n) \ge n$ for each $n$. Let us call two configurations $C$ and $C'$ of $T$ *consecutive* in either of these two cases: Either $C \vdash_T C'$, or $C = C'$ and $T$ cannot move from configuration $C$. We can then describe the strings in $L$ as precisely those strings $x$ for which there is a sequence $C_0, C_1, \ldots, C_{p(|x|)}$ of consecutive configurations of $T$ so that $C_0$ is the initial configuration with input $x$ and $C_{p(|x|)}$ is an accepting configuration. Starting with $x \in \Sigma_1^*$, therefore, our goal is to find a CNF expression $g(x)$ that is satisfiable if and only if there is such a sequence of configurations.

In order to do this, we introduce three groups of Boolean variables, and we *associate* with variables in the three groups statements about the current state, tape contents, and tape head position of $T$, respectively, after a certain number of moves. A CNF formula constructed from these variables therefore corresponds to, and has the same logical structure as, a statement about configurations of $T$. An assignment of truth values to all the variables corresponds to specifying the state, tape head position, and contents of each tape square position at each step; if we define the function $g$ correctly, $g(x)$ is satisfied if and only if the corresponding choices for states, tape symbols, and so on, constitute a computation of $T$ that results in the string $x$ being accepted.

We begin by enumerating all the states and tape symbols of $T$. Let

$$Q = \{q_0, q_1, \ldots, q_{t-2}\}, \; q_{t-1} = h_r, \quad \text{and} \quad q_t = h_a$$
$$q_0 = \Delta \quad \text{and} \quad \Sigma_1 = \{\sigma_1, \sigma_2, \ldots, \sigma_s\}$$
$$\Gamma = \{\sigma_0, \ldots, \sigma_s, \sigma_{s+1}, \ldots, \sigma_{s'}\}$$

Let us fix the string $x = \sigma_{i_1} \sigma_{i_2} \cdots \sigma_{i_n} \in \Sigma_1^*$, and let $N = p(|x|) = p(n)$. Since $\tau_T \le p$, the statement we are trying to construct needs to involve only the first $N + 1$ configurations of $T$. Therefore, we may consider only the tape squares $0, 1, \ldots, N$, because in $N$ moves $T$ cannot move its tape head farther right than square $N$.

We are now ready to describe the three classes of Boolean variables that are used in our expression, and for each variable, the statement to be associated with it, which specifies one detail of a Turing machine configuration.

$Q_{i,j}$ : after $i$ moves, $T$ is in state $q_j$

$H_{i,k}$ : after $i$ moves, the tape head is on square $k$

$S_{i,k,l}$ : after $i$ moves, the symbol in square $k$ is $\sigma_l$

Here the subscripts $i$ and $k$ vary from 0 to $N$, $j$ varies from 0 to $t$, and $l$ varies from 0 to $s'$.

Our CNF formula $g(x)$ is the conjunction of seven clauses:

$$g(x) = \bigwedge_{i=1}^{7} g_i(x)$$

In each case, we give the statement associated with $g_i(x)$. One of the seven expressions is extremely simple; of the remaining six, we show explicitly how to construct three representative ones, and leave the other three as exercises.

1. The expression $g_1(x)$ is associated with the statement that the configuration of $T$ at time 0 (i.e., after 0 moves) is the initial configuration $(q_0, \underline{\Delta}x)$ corresponding to input string $x$, and $g_1(x)$ is

$$Q_{0,0} \wedge H_{0,0} \wedge S_{0,0,0} \wedge \bigwedge_{k=1}^{n} S_{0,k,i_k} \wedge \bigwedge_{k=n+1}^{N} S_{0,k,0}$$

It is the only portion of $g(x)$ that depends directly on $x$.

2. The expression $g_2(x)$ is associated with the statement that after $N$ steps $T$ is in the accepting state. We let $g_2(x)$ be the expression $Q_{N,t}$.

3. The statement corresponding to $g_3(x)$ is the primary one involving the transition function of $T$, and it is the most complicated. It says that whenever $T$ is in a configuration from which it can move, the state and current symbol one step later are those that result from one of the legal moves of $T$. Suppose we denote by $CM$ (for "can move") the set of pairs $(j, l)$ for which $\delta(q_j, \sigma_l) \neq \emptyset$. We want our statement to say the following: For every $i$ from 0 to $N - 1$, for every tape square $k$ between 0 and $N$, and for every pair $(j, l) \in CM$, if at time $i$ the tape head is at square $k$ and the current state-symbol combination is $(j, l)$, there is one of the moves in $\delta(q_j, \sigma_l)$ so that at time $i + 1$, the state, the symbol at square $k$, and the new tape head position are precisely those specified by that move. If there is only one move in the set $\delta(q_j, \sigma_l)$, say $(q_{j'}, \sigma_{l'}, D)$, the appropriate expression for that choice of $i$, $j$, $k$, and $l$ can be written

$$(Q_{i,j} \wedge H_{i,k} \wedge S_{i,k,l}) \rightarrow (Q_{i+1,j'} \wedge H_{i+1,k'} \wedge S_{i+1,k,l'})$$

where

$$k' = \begin{cases} k+1 & \text{if } D = \text{R} \\ k & \text{if } D = \text{S} \\ k-1 & \text{if } D = \text{L} \end{cases}$$

Because, in general, $\delta(q_j, \sigma_l)$ may have several elements, we need

$$(Q_{i,j} \wedge H_{i,k} \wedge S_{i,k,l}) \rightarrow \bigvee_m (Q_{i+1,j_m} \wedge H_{i+1,k_m} \wedge S_{i+1,k,l_m})$$

where $m$ ranges over all moves in $\delta(q_j, \sigma_l)$ and, for a given $m$, $(j_m, l_m, k_m)$ is the corresponding triple $(j', l', k')$ for that move. Thus the complete expression we want (except that it is not in conjunctive normal form) looks like this:

$$\bigwedge_{i,j,k,l} ((Q_{i,j} \wedge H_{i,k} \wedge S_{i,k,l}) \rightarrow \bigvee_m (Q_{i+1,j_m} \wedge H_{i+1,k_m} \wedge S_{i+1,k,l_m}))$$

where $i$ ranges from 0 to $N - 1$, $k$ ranges from 0 to $N$, and $(j, l)$ varies over all pairs in $CM$. To obtain $g_3(x)$, we apply Lemma 14.1 to each of the conjuncts of this formula; the result is

$$\bigwedge_{i,j,k,l} F_{i,j,k,l}$$

where $F_{i,j,k,l}$ is in conjunctive normal form and the number of literals in the expression is bounded independently of $n$.

4. The expression $g_4(x)$ is associated with the statement that for any $i$, if $T$ cannot move at time $i$, then the configuration at time $i + 1$ is unchanged.

Although it might seem as if satisfying the conjunction $g_1(x) \wedge g_2(x) \wedge g_3(x) \wedge g_4(x)$ that we have constructed so far places enough constraints on the values of the variables for the associated statement to imply the acceptance of $x$ by $T$, this is not quite correct. There are truth assignments satisfying the expression but violating basic rules of TMs. For example, an assignment could specify that $Q_{0,0}$ and $Q_{0,1}$ were both true, or that $S_{1,2,l}$ was false for every $l$. The three remaining conjuncts are designed to correct these problems.

5. The statement corresponding to $g_5(x)$ says that $T$ is in exactly one state at each step.

6. The expression $g_6(x)$ represents the statement that at each step, there is exactly one symbol in each square of the tape. "Exactly one" means at least one and never as many as two, and the expression will be the conjunction of two subexpressions. The first ("at least one") is

$$\bigwedge_{i,k} (S_{i,k,0} \vee S_{i,k,1} \vee \cdots \vee S_{i,k,s'})$$

and according to De Morgan's law, the second ("never two") can be written

$$\bigwedge_{i,k,l_1,l_2} (\overline{S}_{i,k,l_1} \vee \overline{S}_{i,k,l_2})$$

Here $i$ and $k$ range from 0 to $N$, and $(l_1, l_2)$ ranges over all pairs with $l_1 \neq l_2$.

7. The last subexpression $g_7(x)$, is associated with the statement that the only changes in the tape are those associated with legal moves of $T$. In other words, for each $i$ and each $k$, if the tape head is not on square $k$ at time $i$, then the symbol in that square is unchanged at time $i + 1$.

The expression $g(x)$ that we have constructed has exactly the same logical structure as the associated statement, which says that there is a sequence of consecutive configurations of $T$, beginning with input $x$ and ending with an accepting configuration. On the one hand, if $T$ accepts $x$, this statement is *true*—it is made true by a particular way of specifying the state, tape head position, and tape contents at each time from 0 to $N$. Therefore, the expression $g(x)$ is *satisfied* by the corresponding assignment of truth values to the Boolean variables in our three classes. Conversely, if a certain assignment of values to the variables causes $g(x)$ to be satisfied, then because the logical structure of the associated statement mirrors that of $g(x)$ exactly, that particular way of specifying the state, tape head position, and tape contents at each time causes the associated statement to be *true*. That statement says that $T$ begins with input $x$ and processes it in a way that is consistent with all the rules of TMs in general, is consistent with the specific rules in its transition table, and leads to acceptance of $x$ within $p(|x|)$ moves. Therefore, if $g(x)$ is satisfiable, $x$ is accepted by $T$.

Now we must estimate the time required to compute the function $f$ : $\Sigma_1^* \to \Sigma^*$. First we consider a TM $T_g$ that writes the expression $g(x)$—using the same notation as for $f$, except that the variable names may not be correct. $T_g$ uses a number of ingredients to construct $g(x)$, among them the input string $x$, the integers $n = |x|$ and $N = p(n)$, the integers $t, s$, and $s'$, and the transition table for $T$, which consists of a set of 5-tuples $(u, v, u', v', D)$ representing moves $(q_{u'}, \sigma_{v'}, D)$ in the set $\delta(q_u, \sigma_v)$. The TM $T_g$ starts by entering all this information at the beginning of its tape, in a "reference" section that will not be disturbed until $T_g$ has finished writing $g(x)$ and is ready to erase everything but that string. Following this reference section is also enough room for all active integer variables $i$, $j$, $k$, and so on, used in the expression. The computation of $p(n)$ can be done in polynomial time, and $T_g$ can create this reference area in polynomial time.

The argument pertaining to the construction of $g(x)$ can be summarized as follows. The total number of literals in the expression $g(x)$ is bounded by a polynomial function of $|x|$, and the time required to compute and write each one is no worse than polynomial; therefore, $T_g$ has polynomial time complexity. We will not attempt a complete, detailed proof; looking at one or two representative cases should be enough to convince you that the conclusion is correct.

Consider the second of the two portions of $g_6(x)$, which we can rewrite in the form

$$\bigwedge_{i=0}^{N} \bigwedge_{k=0}^{N} \bigwedge_{l_1=0}^{s'} \bigwedge_{l_2 \neq l_1} (\overline{S}_{i,k,l_1} \vee \overline{S}_{i,k,l_2})$$

Since $s'$ is constant, the number of literals in this formula is $O(N^2) = O(p(|x|)^2)$. Suppose, for example, that for some specific values of $i$, $k$, $l_1$, and $l_2$, $T_g$ has just written the conjunct $\overline{S}_{i,k,l_1} \vee \overline{S}_{i,k,l_2}$. Let us go through the steps it must take to write the next literal. It begins by incrementing $l_2$, if possible, until another value not equal to $l_1$ is found. (If this is not possible, it increments $l_1$ if possible and sets $l_2$ to 0; if $l_1$ is already $s'$, it increments $k$ if possible; and so on.) Assuming that $T_g$ is able to find a new 4-tuple $(i, k, l_1, l_2)$ in the appropriate range, it then writes $\overline{S}$, followed by the strings representing $i$, $k$, and $l_1$. How long does all this take? In order to test whether $l_2$ can be incremented, $l_2$ must be compared with $s'$. The number of moves required depends on the sizes of $l_2$ and $s'$ and on the distance between them on the tape. $l_2$ and $s'$ are bounded independently of $|x|$, and the two portions of the tape being compared are no farther apart than the length of the reference section plus the length of the portion of $g(x)$ already written. If all these quantities are bounded by polynomials in $|x|$, the resulting number of moves is also. A similar argument applies if further comparisons ($l_1$ to $s'$, or $k$ to $N$, etc.) are necessary. Once the new values of $i$, $k$, $l_1$, $l_2$ are set, then writing the literal involves copying the strings $1^i$, $1^k$, and $1^{l_1}$. In each case, since the three integers are bounded by polynomials, and the total distance the head must travel in order to write each new symbol is likewise bounded, the total time for writing $\overline{S}_{i,k,l_1}$ is at worst polynomial.

In the case of a subexpression like $g_3(x)$, things may be a little less obvious. The formula looks like

$$\bigwedge_{i=0}^{N-1} \bigwedge_{k=0}^{N} \bigwedge_{j=0}^{t} \bigwedge_{(j,l)\in CM} F_{i,k,j,l}$$

where the fourth conjunction is over the indicated values of $l$. Each $F_{i,k,j,l}$ is itself in CNF and involves certain variables that depend on $\delta(q_j, \sigma_l)$, as well as $Q_{i,j}$, $H_{i,k}$, and $S_{i,k,l}$. The important point is that there is a fixed number, independent of $n$, that bounds the number of literals in $F_{i,k,j,l}$, so that the number of literals in $g_3(x)$ is also no more than a polynomial function of $n$. Once $T_g$ has finished writing one of these literals, it uses rules in its program (i.e., its transition table) to determine which type of literal to write next and how to compute the correct subscripts. The number of steps required to write it is no worse than polynomial, for the same reasons as in the case of $g_6(x)$.

In order to obtain $f(x)$ from $g(x)$, the only remaining step is to relabel the variables so that they are $x_1, x_2, \ldots, x_\nu$ for some $\nu$. At each step, the first of the literals that have not yet been relabeled is located and given the next available number, then all other occurrences of it are found and relabeled. We leave it to you to check that a Turing machine can accomplish this job within time bounded by a polynomial function of $|g(x)|$, and thus by a polynomial function of $|x|$. The proof is now complete.

# 14.4 | SOME OTHER *NP*-COMPLETE PROBLEMS

Now that we know **CNF-Sat** is an *NP*-hard problem, we can find others by following the model in Chapter 11. We show that a problem is unsolvable by reducing another unsolvable problem to it; we show that a problem is *NP*-hard by showing that another *NP*-hard problem is polynomial-time reducible to it (Theorem 14.3). We have already done this once, in Example 14.3, and the following Theorem records the conclusion.

---

**Theorem 14.5**
The complete subgraph problem is *NP*-complete.

---

Soon we will look at two other decision problems involving undirected graphs. Our next example is one of several possible variations on the CNF-satisfiability problem; see the book *Computational Complexity* (Addison-Wesley, Reading, MA, 1994) by Papadimitriou for a discussion of some of the others. We denote by **3-Sat** the following decision problem: Given an expression in CNF in which every conjunct is the disjunction of three or fewer literals, is there a truth assignment satisfying the expression? The language *3-Satisfiable* will be the corresponding language of encoded yes-instances, using the encoding method discussed in Example 13.1. There is an obvious sense in which **3-Sat** is no harder than **CNF-Sat**. On the other hand, it is not significantly easier.

---

**Theorem 14.6**
**3-Sat** is *NP*-complete.

*Proof*
The fact that *3-Satisfiable* is in *NP* follows from the fact that *CNF-Satisfiable* is in *NP*. We will prove that *3-Satisfiable* is *NP*-hard by showing that *CNF-Satisfiable* is polynomial-time reducible to it.

Let $\Sigma = \{x, \overline{x}, \wedge, 1\}$, let $C \subseteq \Sigma^*$ be the set of strings representing expressions in CNF, and let 3-$C$ be the subset of $C$ corresponding to those expressions in which each conjunct contains no more than three literals. (Then $C$ contains the strings in $\Sigma^*$ that represent instances of **CNF-Sat**, and 3-$C$ those that represent instances of **3-Sat**.) Because a TM can easily determine in polynomial time whether an element of $\Sigma^*$ is in $C$, we will construct a function

$$f : C \to 3\text{-}C$$

so that for any $x \in C$, $x$ represents a satisfiable expression if and only if $f(x)$ does. To simplify the discussion, we ignore the encoding and write elements of $C$ and 3-$C$ in ordinary CNF notation.

Let

$$x = \bigwedge_{i=1}^{n} A_i$$

where each $A_i$ is a disjunction of literals. We define $f(x)$ by the formula

$$f(x) = \bigwedge_{i=1}^{n} B_i$$

where $B_i = A_i$ whenever $A_i$ contains three or fewer literals, and if $A_i = \bigvee_{j=1}^{k} a_j$ with $k > 3$,

$$B_i = (a_1 \vee a_2 \vee \alpha_1) \wedge (a_3 \vee \overline{\alpha}_1 \vee \alpha_2) \wedge (a_4 \vee \overline{\alpha}_2 \vee \alpha_3) \wedge \cdots$$
$$\wedge (a_{k-3} \vee \overline{\alpha}_{k-5} \vee \alpha_{k-4}) \wedge (a_{k-2} \vee \overline{\alpha}_{k-4} \vee \alpha_{k-3}) \wedge (a_{k-1} \vee a_k \vee \overline{\alpha}_{k-3})$$

Here we want each $\alpha_j$ to be a new variable not occurring in $x$, and we also require that no $\alpha_j$ occur in more than one $B_i$.

Suppose $\Theta$ is a truth assignment satisfying $x$, which means that it satisfies each of the $A_i$'s, and consider any fixed $i$. We want to show that with the same assignment $\Theta$, some choice of values for the extra variables $\alpha_j$ in $B_i$ makes $B_i$ true. Since $\Theta$ satisfies $A_i$, it must make one of the $a_j$'s true. We now consider three cases.

1. If $\Theta$ makes $a_1$ or $a_2$ true, then assigning the value *false* to every $\alpha_l$ makes $B_i$ true, since every conjunct after the first involves an $\overline{\alpha}_l$.

2. If $\Theta$ makes $a_{k-1}$ or $a_k$ true, then assigning the value *true* to every $\alpha_l$ makes $B_i$ true, since every conjunct except the last involves an $\alpha_l$.

3. For any $m$ with $2 < m < k - 1$, all the conjuncts before the one containing $a_m$ contain an $\alpha_l$ for some $l$ with $1 \le l \le m - 2$; and all the conjuncts after this one contain an $\overline{\alpha}_l$ for some $l$ with $m - 1 \le l \le k - 3$. Therefore, if $\Theta$ makes $a_m$ true, then letting $\alpha_l$ be *true* for $1 \le l \le m - 2$ and *false* for the remaining $l$'s causes the expression to be satisfied.

It follows that for any assignment satisfying $x$, that assignment together with some choice for the auxiliary variables satisfies $f(x)$.

Conversely, if $\Theta$ does not satisfy $x$, then $\Theta$ fails to satisfy some $A_i$ and therefore makes all the $a_j$'s in $A_i$ false. It is not hard to see that with that assignment $\Theta$, no assignment of values to the extra variables can make $B_i$ true. For the first conjunct of $B_i$ to be true, $\alpha_1$ must be true; for the second to be true, $\alpha_2$ must be true; $\ldots$; for the next-to-last to be true, $\alpha_{k-3}$ must be true; and now the last conjunct is forced to be false. Therefore, if $x$ is unsatisfiable, so is $f(x)$.

Now that we have the function $f$, we can easily obtain a function $f_1 :$ $\Sigma^* \to \Sigma^*$ so that for any $x$, $x \in$ *Satisfiable* if and only if $f(x) \in 3$-*Satisfiable*. To complete the proof it is enough to show that $f_1$ is computable in polynomial time, and this follows almost immediately from the fact that the length of $f(x)$ is bounded by a polynomial function of $|x|$.

In addition to the complete subgraph problem, studied in Example 14.3, many other important combinatorial problems can be formulated in terms of graphs. A little more terminology will be helpful. A *vertex cover* for a graph $G$ is a set $C$ of vertices so that any edge of $G$ has an endpoint in $C$. For a positive integer $k$, we may think of the integers $1, 2, \ldots, k$ as distinct "colors," and use them to color the vertices of a graph. A *k-coloring* of $G$ is an assignment to each vertex of one of the $k$ colors so that no two adjacent vertices are colored the same. In the graph $G$ shown in Figure 14.1, the set $\{1, 3, 5, 7\}$ is a vertex cover for $G$, and it is easy to see that there is no vertex cover having fewer than four vertices. Clearly, since there is a complete subgraph with four vertices, $G$ cannot be $k$-colored for any $k < 4$. Although the absence of a complete subgraph with $k + 1$ vertices does not automatically imply that the graph has a $k$-coloring, you can easily check that in this case there is a 4-coloring of $G$.

The *vertex cover problem* is this: Given a graph $G$ and an integer $k$, is there a vertex cover for $G$ with $k$ vertices? The *k-colorability problem* is the problem: Given $G$ and $k$, is there a $k$-coloring of $G$? Both problems are in *NP*. In the second case, for example, colors between 1 and $k$ can be assigned nondeterministically to all the vertices, and then the edges can be examined to determine whether each one has different-colored endpoints. In order to show that both problems are *NP*-complete, therefore, it is sufficient to show that they are both *NP*-hard.

**Theorem 14.7**

The vertex cover problem is *NP*-complete.

*Proof*

We show that the problem is *NP*-hard by reducing the complete subgraph problem to it. That is, we show that an instance $I = (G, k)$ of the complete subgraph problem can be transformed in polynomial time to an instance $f(I) = (G_1, k_1)$ of the vertex cover problem in such a way that $G$ has a complete subgraph with $k$ vertices if and only if $G_1$ has a vertex cover with $k_1$ vertices.

If $G = (V, E)$, let $G_1$ be the *complement* of $G$: $G_1 = (V, E_1)$, where

$$E_1 = \{(i, j) \mid i, j \in V \quad \text{and} \quad (i, j) \notin E\}$$

and let $k_1 = |V| - k$.

On the one hand, if vertices $v_1, v_2, \ldots, v_k$ determine a complete subgraph of $G$, then since no edge of $G_1$ joins two of the $v_i$'s, every edge in $G_1$ must have as an endpoint an element of $V - \{v_1, \ldots, v_k\}$, so that this set of $k_1$ vertices is a vertex cover for $G_1$.

Conversely, suppose $U = \{u_1, \ldots, u_{|V|-k}\}$ is a vertex cover for $G_1$. Then the set $V - U$ has $k$ vertices; we will show that it determines a complete subgraph of $G$. By the definition of complement, any two vertices are joined either by an edge in $G$ or by one in $G_1$. However, two vertices in $V - U$ cannot be joined by an edge in $G_1$, because by definition of vertex cover, an edge in $G_1$ must contain a vertex in $U$. Therefore, two vertices in $V - U$ must be joined by an edge in $G$.

Because the transformation from $G$ to $G_1$ can be carried out in polynomial time, the proof is complete.

**Theorem 14.8**

The $k$-colorability problem is *NP*-complete.

*Proof*

We show that **3-Sat** is polynomial-time reducible to the $k$-colorability problem. This means we must show how to construct, for each CNF expression $x$ in which all conjuncts have three or fewer literals, a graph $G_x$ and an integer $k_x$ so that $x$ is satisfiable if and only if there is a $k_x$-coloring of $G_x$.

The construction is very simple for the $x$'s with fewer than four distinct variables and more complicated for the others. In the first case, we let $I_1$ be a fixed yes-instance of the $k$-colorability problem and $I_0$ a fixed no-instance. We simply *answer* the instance $x$, and let the assigned value be $I_1$ if $x$ is a yes-instance and $I_0$ otherwise. This clearly works, provided that answering these instances of **3-Sat** is possible in polynomial time; you can convince yourself that there is a polynomial $p$ so that all possible truth assignments (no more than eight) can be tested for any one of these simple instances $x$ within time $p(|x|)$.

For the remaining cases, let $x = A_1 \wedge A_2 \wedge \cdots \wedge A_c$ be an instance of **3-Sat** with the $n$ variables $x_1, x_2, \ldots, x_n$, where $n \geq 4$. We construct the instance $(G_x, k_x)$ by letting $k_x = n + 1$ and defining the graph $G_x = (V_x, E_x)$ as follows. There are $3n + c$ vertices:

$$V_x = \{x_1, x_2, \ldots, x_n, \quad \overline{x}_1, \overline{x}_2, \ldots, \overline{x}_n,$$
$$y_1, y_2, \ldots, y_n, \quad A_1, A_2, \ldots, A_c\}$$

There are six types of edges:

$$E_x = \{(x_i, \overline{x}_i) \mid 1 \leq i \leq n\} \cup \{(y_i, y_j) \mid i \neq j\} \cup \{(y_i, x_j) \mid i \neq j\}$$
$$\cup \{(y_i, \overline{x}_j) \mid i \neq j\} \cup \{(x_i, A_j) \mid x_i \notin A_j\} \cup \{(\overline{x}_i, A_j) \mid \overline{x}_i \notin A_j\}$$

(The notation $x_i \notin A_j$ means that the literal $x_i$ does not occur in the conjunct $A_j$.)

Suppose, on the one hand, that this graph is $(n + 1)$-colorable. No two of the $y_i$'s can be colored the same, because any two are adjacent; therefore, $n$ distinct colors are required for those vertices. Let us assume that the $y_i$'s are colored with the colors $1, 2, \ldots, n$. For any fixed $i$, consider the vertices $x_i$ and $\overline{x}_i$. Neither can be colored the same as $y_j$ for any $j \neq i$, because they are both adjacent to every such $y_j$; and they cannot be colored the same, because they are adjacent to each other; the only possibility is that color $i$ is used for one and color $n + 1$ for the other.

We have now accounted for the first $3n$ vertices, and we consider the remaining $c$. For each $j$ with $1 \leq j \leq c$, there must be some variable $x_i$ so that neither $x_i$ nor $\overline{x}_i$ appears in $A_j$, because $A_j$ has no more than three literals and there are at least four distinct variables. Since $A_j$ is adjacent to both $x_i$ and $\overline{x}_i$, and one of them is colored $n + 1$, $A_j$ cannot be. The vertex $A_j$ must be colored with color $i$ for some $i$ with $1 \leq i \leq n$. One of the two vertices $x_i$ and $\overline{x}_i$ is colored $i$; the one that is must appear in the conjunct $A_j$, because otherwise it would be adjacent to the vertex $A_j$. Let $z_j$ be a literal (either $x_i$ or $\overline{x}_i$) appearing in $A_j$ that is colored the same as $A_j$. Then no $z_j$ is the negation of any other $z_l$, because if it were, one of the two would be colored $n + 1$. This means that there is a way of assigning truth values to the variables that makes every $z_j$ true. The effect of this assignment is to satisfy each $A_j$, and it follows that $x$ is satisfiable.

This argument is essentially reversible. We begin by coloring each $y_i$ with color $i$. If $x$ is satisfied by the assignment $\Theta$, then each conjunct $A_j$ contains a literal $z_j$ that is made true by $\Theta$. If $z_j$ is either $x_i$ or $\overline{x}_i$, we color it with color $i$ and its negation with color $n + 1$. Once we have done this, if $x_l$ is a literal remaining uncolored, so is $\overline{x}_l$; we use color $l$ to color whichever one is made true by $\Theta$, and $n + 1$ to color the other. To see that this is permissible, suppose for example that $x_l$ is colored with $l$. If $x_l \notin A_j$, then $A_j$ cannot be colored $l$ because of $x_l$ (because $x_l \notin A_j$), and $A_j$ cannot be colored $l$ because of $\overline{x}_l$, because $\overline{x}_l$ is not true for the assignment $\Theta$. We conclude that if $x$ is satisfiable, then $G_x$ is $(n + 1)$-colorable.

> As in the previous theorem, it is easy to see that this construction can be carried out in polynomial time, and thus **3-Sat** is polynomial-time reducible to the $k$-colorability problem.

Although we now have five examples of *NP*-complete problems, the problems now known to be *NP*-complete number in the thousands, and the list is growing constantly. The book by Garey and Johnson remains a very good reference for a general discussion of the topic and contains a varied list of problems, grouped according to category (graphs, sets, and so on).

*NP*-completeness is still a somewhat mysterious property. Some decision problems are in $P$, and others that seem similar turn out to be *NP*-complete (Exercises 14.15 and 14.22). In the absence of either an answer to the $P \overset{?}{=} NP$ question or a definitive characterization of tractability, people generally take a pragmatic approach. Many real-life decision problems require some kind of solution. If a polynomial-time algorithm does not present itself, maybe the problem can be shown to be *NP*-complete by choosing a problem that is, from the large group available, and constructing a reduction. In this case, it is probably not worthwhile spending a lot more time looking for a polynomial-time solution. The next-best thing might be to look for an algorithm that produces an approximate solution, or one that provides a solution for a restricted set of instances. Both approaches represent active areas of research.

## EXERCISES

**14.1.** In studying the CNF-satisfiability problem, what is the reason for imposing the restriction that an instance must contain precisely the variables $x_1, \ldots, x_v$, with none left out?

**14.2.** The nondeterministic Turing machine we described that accepts *CNF-Satisfiable* repeats the following operation or minor variations of it: starting with a string of 1's in the input string, delimited at both ends by a symbol other than 1, and locating some or all of the other occurrences of this string that are similarly delimited. How long does an operation of this type take on a one-tape TM? Use your answer to argue that the TM accepting *CNF-Satisfiable* has time complexity $O(n^3)$.

**14.3.** a. Show that if $L \in Time(f)$, then $L' \in Time(f)$.

b. Show that if $L \in P$, then $L' \in P$, and if $L \in PSpace$, then $L' \in PSpace$.

c. Explain carefully why the fact that $L \in NP$ does not obviously imply that $L' \in NP$.

**14.4.** a. Let $L_1$ and $L_2$ be languages over $\Sigma_1$ and $\Sigma_2$, respectively. Show that if $L_1 \leq_p L_2$, then $L' \leq_p L_2'$.

b. Show that if there is an *NP*-complete language $L$ whose complement is in *NP*, then the complement of any language in *NP* is in *NP*.

**14.5.** Show that if $L_1, L_2 \subseteq \Sigma^*$, $L_1 \in P$, and $L_2$ is neither $\emptyset$ nor $\Sigma^*$, then $L_1 \leq_p L_2$.

**14.6.** a. If every instance of problem $P_1$ is an instance of problem $P_2$, and if $P_2$ is hard, then $P_1$ is hard. True or false?

b. Show that **3-Sat** $\leq_p$ **CNF-Sat**, or, at the language level, *3-Satisfiable* $\leq_p$ *CNF-Satisfiable*.

c. Generalize the result in part (b) in some appropriate way.

**14.7.** In each case, find an equivalent expression that is in conjunctive normal form.

a. $a \rightarrow (b \wedge (c \rightarrow (d \vee e)))$

b. $\vee_{i=1}^{n}(a_i \wedge b_i)$

**14.8.** In the proof of Cook's theorem (Theorem 14.4), given a nondeterministic TM $T$ with input alphabet $\Sigma_1$, we constructed a function $g_1 : \Sigma_1^* \rightarrow CNF$ so that for any $x \in \Sigma_1^*$, $x$ is accepted by $T$ if and only if $g_1(x)$ is satisfiable. The idea is that the expression $g_1(x)$ "says" that $x$ is accepted by $T$, in the sense that $g(x)$ is constructed from a number of atoms, each of which is associated with a statement about some detail of $T$'s configuration after a certain number of steps. Consider the following much simpler function $g_2 : \Sigma_1^* \rightarrow CNF$. For any $x \in \Sigma_1^*$, $g_2(x)$ is a single atom, labeled $a_x$. For each $x$, we associate the atom $a_x$ with the statement "$T$ accepts $x$." There is an obvious similarity between the expressions $g_1(x)$ and $g_2(x)$; both depend on $x$, and both are associated with statements that say $x$ is accepted by $T$. Explain the essential difference, which is the reason Cook's theorem doesn't have a trivial one- or two-line proof.

**14.9.** Show that if $k \geq 4$, the $k$-satisfiability problem is *NP*-complete.

**14.10.** Find an unsatisfiable CNF expression involving three variables in which each conjunct has exactly three literals and involves all three variables, so that the number of conjuncts is as small as possible.

**14.11.** Show that both these decision problems are in $P$.

a. *DNF-Satisfiability*: Given a Boolean expression in disjunctive normal form (the disjunction of clauses, each of which is a conjunction of literals), is it satisfiable?

b. *CNF-Tautology*: Given a Boolean expression in CNF, is it a tautology (i.e., satisfied by every possible truth assignment)?

**14.12.** Show that the general satisfiability problem, Given an arbitrary Boolean expression, not necessarily in conjunctive normal form, involving the variables $x_1, x_2, \ldots, x_v$, is it satisfiable? is *NP*-complete.

**14.13.** Explain why it is appropriate to insist on binary notation when encoding instances of the primality problem, but not necessary to do this when encoding subscripts in instances of the satisfiability problem.

**14.14.** Consider the language $L$ of all strings $e(T)e(x)1^n$, where $T$ is a nondeterministic Turing machine, $n \geq 1$, and $T$ accepts $x$ by some sequence of no more than $n$ moves. Show that the language $L$ is *NP*-complete.

**14.15.** Show that the 2-colorability problem (Given a graph, is there a 2-coloring of the vertices?) is in $P$.

**14.16.** Consider the following algorithm to solve the vertex cover problem. First, we generate all subsets of the vertices containing exactly $k$ vertices. There are $O(n^k)$ such subsets. Then we check whether any of the resulting subgraphs is complete. Why is this not a polynomial-time algorithm (and thus a proof that $P = NP$)?

**14.17.** Let $f$ be a function in $PF$, the set of functions from $\Sigma^*$ to $\Sigma^*$ computable in polynomial time. Let $A$ (a language in $\Sigma^*$) be in $P$. Show that $f^{-1}(A)$ is in $P$, where by definition, $f^{-1}(A) = \{z \in \Sigma^* \mid f(z) \in A\}$.

**14.18.** In an undirected graph $G$, with vertex set $V$ and edge set $E$, an *independent set* of vertices is a set $V_1 \subseteq V$ so that no two elements of $V'$ are joined by an edge in $E$. Let **IS** be the decision problem: Given a graph $G$ and an integer $k$, is there an independent set of vertices with at least $k$ elements? Denote by **VC** and **CSG** the vertex cover problem and the complete subgraph problem, respectively. Construct a polynomial-time reduction from each of the three problems **IS**, **VC**, and **CSG** to each of the others. (Part of this problem has already been done, in the proof of Theorem 14.7. In the remaining parts, you are not to use the $NP$-completeness of any of these problems.)

## MORE CHALLENGING PROBLEMS

**14.19.** In Example 14.2, the claim was made that the time required for carrying out the steps other than the recursive calls in the algorithm Is_Prime($n$) is $O((\log n)^d)$ for some integer $d$. Show that this is true, and find the smallest $d$ that works.

**14.20.** Complete the argument in Example 14.2, by showing the following: if $T(n)$ satisfies the inequality

$$T(n) \leq c(\log n)^d + \sum_{i=1}^{k} T(p_i)$$

where $n - 1 = p_1 \cdots p_k$ is the prime factorization of $n - 1$, and $c$ and $d$ are positive constants, then $T(n) = O((\log n)^{d+1})$.

**14.21.** For languages $L_1, L_2 \subseteq \{0, 1\}^*$, let

$$L_1 \oplus L_2 = L_1\{0\} \cup L_2\{1\}$$

a.  Show that $L_1 \leq_p L_1 \oplus L_2$ and $L_2 \leq_p L_1 \oplus L_2$.

b.  Show that for any languages $L$, $L_1$, and $L_2$ over $\{0, 1\}$, with $L \neq \{0, 1\}^*$, if $L_1 \leq_p L$ and $L_2 \leq_p L$, then $L_1 \oplus L_2 \leq_p L$.

**14.22.** Show that the 2-Satisfiability problem is in $P$.

**14.23.** Show that both $P$ and $NP$ are closed under the operations of union, intersection, concatenation, and Kleene $*$.

**14.24.** A *subexponential* function from $\mathcal{N}$ to $\mathcal{N}$ is one that is $O(2^{n^c})$ for every positive real number $c$. Show that if there is an *NP*-complete language in *Time*$(f)$ for some subexponential function $f$, then $NP \subseteq Subexp$, where

$$Subexp = \bigcup \{Time(f) \mid f \text{ is subexponential}\}$$

**14.25.** Show that the following decision problem is *NP*-complete: Given a graph $G$ in which every vertex has even degree, and an integer $k$, does $G$ have a vertex cover with $k$ vertices? (The degree of a vertex is the number of edges containing it.) Hint: given an arbitrary graph $G$, find an way to modify it by adding three vertices so that all the vertices of the new graph have even degree.

**14.26.** Give an alternate proof of the *NP*-completeness of the vertex cover problem, by directly reducing **CNF-Sat** to it. Below is a suggested way to proceed; show that it works.

Starting with a CNF expression $x = \bigwedge_{i=1}^{m} A_i$, where $A_i = \bigvee_{j=1}^{n_i} a_{i,j}$ and $x$ involves the $n$ variables $v_1, \ldots, v_n$, construct an instance $(G, k)$ of the vertex cover problem as follows: first, there are vertices $v_l^t$ and $v_l^f$ for each variable $v_l$, and these two are connected by an edge; next, for each conjunct $A_i$ there is a complete subgraph $G_i$ with $n_i$ vertices, one for each literal in $A_i$; finally, for a variable $v_l$ and a conjunct $A_i$, there is an edge from the vertex in $G_i$ corresponding to $v_l$, either to $v_l^t$ (if $v_l$ appears in $A_i$) or to $v_l^f$ (if $v_l$ doesn't appear in $A_i$). Finally, let $k$ be the integer $n + (n_1 - 1) + \cdots + (n_m - 1)$.

**14.27.** Show that the following decision problem is *NP*-complete. Given a finite set $A$, a collection $C$ of subsets of $A$, and an integer $k$, is there a subset $A_1$ of $A$ having $k$ or fewer elements so that $A_1 \cap S \neq \emptyset$ for each $S$ in the collection $C$?

**14.28.** The *exact cover* problem is the following: given finite subsets $S_1, \ldots, S_k$ of a set, with $\bigcup_{i=1}^{k} S_i = A$, is there a subset $J$ of $\{1, 2, \ldots, k\}$ so that for any two distinct elements $i$ and $j$ of $J$, $S_i \cap S_j = \emptyset$ and $\bigcup_{i \in J} S_i = A$?

Show that this problem is *NP*-complete by constructing a reduction from the $k$-colorability problem.

**14.29.** The *sum-of-subsets* problem is the following: Given a sequence $a_1, a_2, \ldots, a_n$ of integers, and an integer $M$, is there a subset $J$ of $\{1, 2, \ldots, n\}$ so that $\sum_{i \in J} a_i = M$?

Show that this problem is *NP*-complete by constructing a reduction from the exact cover problem.

**14.30.** The *partition* problem is the following: Given a sequence $a_1, a_2, \ldots, a_n$ of integers, is there a subset $J$ of $\{1, 2, \ldots, n\}$ so that $\sum_{i \in J} a_i = \sum_{i \notin J} a_i$?

Show that this problem is *NP*-complete by constructing a reduction from the sum-of-subsets problem.

**14.31.** The *0-1 knapsack* problem is the following: Given two sequences $w_1, \ldots, w_n$ and $p_1, \ldots, p_n$ of nonnegative numbers, and two numbers $W$ and $P$, is there a subset $J$ of $\{1, 2, \ldots, n\}$ so that $\sum_{i \in J} w_i \leq W$ and

$\sum_{i \in J} p_i \geq P$? (The significance of the name is that $w_i$ and $p_i$ are viewed as the *weight* and the *profit* of the $i$th item, respectively; we have a "knapsack" that can hold no more than $W$ pounds, and the problem is asking whether it is possible to choose items to put into the knapsack subject to that constraint, so that the total profit is at least $P$.)

Show that the 0-1 knapsack problem is *NP*-complete by constructing a reduction from the partition problem.

# REFERENCES

There are a number of texts that discuss the topics in this book. Hopcroft, Motwani, and Ullman (2001) and Lewis and Papadimitriou (1998) are both recent editions of books that previously established themselves as standard references. Others that might serve as useful complements to this book include Sipser (1997), Sudkamp (1996), and Linz (2001), and more comprehensive books for further reading include Davis, Sigal, and Weyuker (1994) and Floyd and Beigel (1994).

The idea of a finite automaton appears in McCulloch and Pitts (1943) as a way of modeling neural nets. Kleene (1956) introduces regular expressions and proves their equivalence to FAs, and NFAs are investigated in Rabin and Scott (1959). Theorem 5.1 and Corollary 5.1 are due to Nerode (1958) and Myhill (1957). Algorithm 5.1 appears in Huffman (1954) and in Moore (1956). The Pumping Lemmas (Theorem 5.2a and Theorem 8.1a) were proved in Bar-Hillel, Perles, and Shamir (1961).

Context-free grammars were introduced in Chomsky (1956) and pushdown automata in Oettinger (1961); their equivalence is shown in Chomsky (1962), Evey (1963), and Schützenberger (1963). LL(1) grammars are introduced in Lewis and Stearns (1968) and LL($k$) grammars in Rosenkrantz and Stearns (1970). Knuth (1965) characterizes the grammars corresponding to DCFLs.

Turing's 1936 paper introduces Turing machines and universal Turing machines and proves the unsolvability of the halting problem. Church (1936) contains the first explicit statement of the Church-Turing thesis. Hennie (1977) contains a good general introduction to Turing machines.

Chomsky's papers of 1956 and 1959 contain the proofs of Theorems 11.1 and 11.2, as well as the definition of the Chomsky hierarchy. The equivalence of context-sensitive grammars and linear-bounded automata is shown in Kuroda (1964).

Post's correspondence problem was discussed in Post (1946). A number of the original papers by Turing, Post, Kleene, Church, and Gödel having to do with computability and solvability are reprinted in Davis (1965). Kleene (1952), Davis (1958), and Rogers (1967) are further references on computability, recursive function theory, and related topics.

Rabin (1963) and Hartmanis and Stearns (1965) are two early papers dealing with computational complexity. The class $P$ was introduced in Cobham (1964), and Cook (1971) contains the definition of $NP$-completeness and the proof that the satisfiability problem is $NP$-complete. Karp's 1972 paper exhibited a number of $NP$-complete problems and helped to establish the idea as a fundamental one in complexity theory. Garey and Johnson (1978) is the standard introductory reference on $NP$-completeness and contains a catalogue of the problems then known to be $NP$-complete. Recent references on computational complexity include Balcazar (1988 and 1990), Bovet and Crescenzi (1994), Papadimitriou (1994), and many of the chapters of van Leeuwen (1990).

# BIBLIOGRAPHY

Balcazar JL, Diaz J, Gabarro J: *Structural Complexity I.* New York: Springer-Verlag, 1988.

Balcazar JL, Diaz J, Gabarro J: *Structural Complexity II.* New York: Springer-Verlag, 1990.

Bar-Hillel Y, Perles M, Shamir E: On Formal Properties of Simple Phrase Structure Grammars, *Zeitschrift für Phonetik Sprachwissenschaft und Kommunikations-forschung* 14: 143–172, 1961.

Boas RP: Can We Make Mathematics Intelligible? *American Mathematical Monthly* 88: 727–731, 1981.

Bovet DP, Crescenzi P: *Introduction to the Theory of Complexity.* Englewood Cliffs, NJ: Prentice Hall, 1994.

Carroll J, Long D: *Theory of Finite Automata with an Introduction to Formal Languages.* Englewood Cliffs, NJ: Prentice Hall, 1989.

Chomsky N: Three Models for the Description of Language, *IRE Transactions on Information Theory* 2: 113–124, 1956.

Chomsky N: On Certain Formal Properties of Grammars, *Information and Control* 2: 137–167, 1959.

Chomsky N: Context-free Grammars and Pushdown Storage, Quarterly Progress Report No. 65, Cambridge, MA: Massachusetts Institute of Technology Research Laboratory of Electronics, 1962, pp. 187–194.

Church A: An Unsolvable Problem of Elementary Number Theory, *American Journal of Mathematics* 58: 345–363, 1936.

Cobham A: The Intrinsic Computational Difficulty of Functions, *Proceedings of the 1964 Congress for Logic, Mathematics, and Philosophy of Science,* New York: North Holland, 1964, pp. 24–30.

Cook SA: The Complexity of Theorem Proving Procedures, *Proceedings of the Third Annual ACM Symposium on the Theory of Computing*, New York: Association for Computing Machinery, 1971, pp. 151–158.

Davis MD: *Computability and Unsolvability.* New York: McGraw-Hill, 1958.

Davis, MD: *The Undecidable.* Hewlett, NY: Raven Press, 1965.

Davis, MD, Sigal R, Weyuker EJ: *Computability, Complexity, and Languages: Fundamentals of Theoretical Computer Science*, 2nd ed. New York: Academic Press, 1994.

Dowling WF: There Are No Safe Virus Tests, *American Mathematical Monthly* 96: 835–836, 1989.

Earley J: An Efficient Context-free Parsing Algorithm, *Communications of the ACM* 13(2): 94–102, 1970.

Evey J: Application of Pushdown Store Machines, *Proceedings, 1963 Fall Joint Computer Conference*, Montvale, NJ: AFIPS Press, 1963, pp. 215–227.

Floyd RW, Beigel R: *The Language of Machines: An Introduction to Computability and Formal Languages.* New York: Freeman, 1994.

Garey MR, Johnson DS: *Computers and Intractability: A Guide to the Theory of NP-Completeness.* New York: Freeman, 1979.

Hartmanis J, Stearns RE: On the Computational Complexity of Algorithms, *Transactions of the American Mathematical Society* 117: 285–306, 1965.

Hennie FC: *Introduction to Computability.* Reading, MA: Addison-Wesley, 1977.

Hopcroft JE., Motwani R, Ullman J: *Introduction to Automata Theory, Languages, and Computation*, 2nd ed. Reading, MA: Addison-Wesley, 1979.

Huffman DA: The Synthesis of Sequential Switching Circuits, *Journal of the Franklin Institute* 257: 161–190, 275–303, 1954.

Immerman N: Nondeterministic Space is Closed under Complementation, *SIAM Journal of Computing* 17: 935–938, 1988.

Karp RM: Reducibility Among Combinatorial Problems. In *Complexity of Computer Computations.* New York: Plenum Press, 1972, pp. 85–104.

Kleene SC: *Introduction to Metamathematics*. New York: Van Nostrand, 1952.

Kleene SC: Representation of Events in Nerve Nets and Finite Automata. In Shannon CE, McCarthy J (eds), *Automata Studies*. Princeton, NJ: Princeton University Press, 1956, pp. 3–42.

Knuth, DE: On the Translation of Languages from Left to Right, *Information and Control* 8: 607–639, 1965.

Kuroda SY: Classes of Languages and Linear-Bounded Automata, *Information and Control* 7: 207–223, 1964.

Levine JR, Mason T, Brown D: *lex & yacc*, 2nd ed. Sebastopol, CA: O'Reilly & Associates, 1992.

Lewis HR, Papadimitriou C: *Elements of the Theory of Computation*, 2nd ed. Englewood Cliffs, NJ: Prentice Hall, 1998.

Lewis PM II, Stearns RE: Syntax-directed Transduction, *Journal of the ACM* 15: 465–488, 1968.

Linz P: *An Introduction to Formal Languages and Automata*, 3rd ed. Sudbury, MA: Jones and Bartlett, 2001.

McCulloch WS, Pitts W: A Logical Calculus of the Ideas Immanent in Nervous Activity, *Bulletin of Mathematical Biophysics* 5: 115–133, 1943.

Moore EF: Gedanken Experiments on Sequential Machines. In Shannon CE, and McCarthy J (eds), *Automata Studies*. Princeton, NJ: Princeton University Press, 1956, pp. 129–153.

Myhill J: Finite Automata and the Representation of Events, WADD TR-57-624, Wright Patterson Air Force Base, OH, 1957, pp. 112–137.

Nerode A: Linear Automaton Transformations, *Proceedings of the American Mathematical Society* 9: 541–544, 1958.

Oettinger AG: Automatic Syntactic Analysis and the Pushdown Store, *Proceedings of the Symposia in Applied Mathematics* 12, Providence, RI: American Mathematical Society 9, 1961 pp. 104–109.

Ogden O: A Helpful Result for Proving Inherent Ambiguity, *Mathematical Systems Theory* 2: 191–194, 1968.

Papadimitriou CH: *Computational Complexity*. Reading, MA: Addison-Wesley, 1994.

Paulos JA: *Once upon a Number: The Hidden Logic of Stories*. New York: Basic Books, 1999.

Post EL: A Variant of a Recursively Unsolvable Problem, *Bulletin of the American Mathematical Society* 52: 246–268, 1946.

Rabin MO: Real-Time Computation, *Israel Journal of Mathematics* 1: 203–211, 1963.

Rabin MO, Scott D: Finite Automata and their Decision Problems, *IBM Journal of Research and Development* 3: 115–125, 1959.

Rogers H, Jr: *Theory of Recursive Functions and Effective Computability*. New York: McGraw-Hill, 1967.

Rosenkrantz DJ, Stearns RE: Properties of Deterministic Top-down Grammars, *Information and Control* 17: 226–256, 1970.

Salomaa A: *Jewels of Formal Language Theory*. Rockville, MD: Computer Science Press, 1981.

Savitch WJ: Relationships between Nondeterministic and Deterministic Tape Complexities, *Journal of Computer and System Sciences* 4: 2, 177–192, 1970.

Schützenberger MP: On Context-free Languages and Pushdown Automata, *Information and Control* 6: 246–264, 1963.

Sudkamp TA: *Languages and Machines: An Introduction to the Theory of Computer Science*, 2nd ed. Reading, MA: Addison-Wesley, 1996.

Sipser M: *Introduction to the Theory of Computation*. Boston, MA: PWS, 1997.

Szelepcsény R: The Method of Forcing for Nondeterministic Automata, *Bulletin of the EATCS* 33: 96–100, 1987.

Turing AM: On Computable Numbers with an Application to the Entscheidungsproblem, *Proceedings of the London Mathematical Society* 2: 230–265, 1936.

van Leeuwen J (ed): *Handbook of Theoretical Computer Science (Volume A, Algorithms and Complexity)*. Amsterdam: MIT Press/Elsevier, 1990.

Younger DH: Recognition and Parsing of Context-free Languages in Time $n^3$, *Information and Control* 10(2): 189–208, 1967.

# INDEX OF NOTATION

# INDEX